P9-CKB-251

ROAD MAP

Writing A COLLEGE HANDBOOK

FIFTH EDITION

INSTRUCTOR'S EDITION

FIFTH EDITION

Writing

A COLLEGE HANDBOOK
INSTRUCTOR'S EDITION

James A. W. Heffernan

DARTMOUTH COLLEGE

John E. Lincoln

Janet Atwill

UNIVERSITY OF TENNESSEE

W. W. Norton & Company

NEW YORK   LONDON

The text of this book is composed in Stone Serif with the display set in Frutiger.
Composition by TSI Graphics.
Manufacturing by R. R. Donnelley & Sons.

ISBN 0-393-97657-2

Editor: Jennifer Bartlett
Developmental Editor: Kurt Wildermuth
Permissions Manager: Kristin Sheerin
Editorial Assistant: Isobel Evans
Production Manager: Diane O'Connor
Associate Managing Editor: Marian Johnson
Text & Cover Design: Joan Greenfield

W. W. Norton & Company, Inc., 500 Fifth Avenue, New York, N.Y. 10110
www.wwnorton.com

W. W. Norton & Company Ltd., 10 Coptic Street, London WC1A 1PU

1 2 3 4 5 6 7 8 9 0

Contents

Contents

Contents

8   *Style: Using a Community's Language*   *127*

Contents

12 Document Design   209

Contents

PART 2   CRAFTING SENTENCES

13 *The Simple Sentence*   247

14 *Modifiers*   262

Contents

Contents

Contents

PART 4   RESEARCH AND WRITING

36 *The Research Process*   **519**

PART 5   WRITING IN ACADEMIC CONTEXTS

Contents

Preface to the Fifth Edition

WELCOME

With this fifth edition, James Heffernan and John Lincoln welcome a new coauthor, Janet Atwill, of the University of Tennessee, Knoxville. A well-established specialist in rhetoric, Janet is thoroughly conversant with current scholarship in the field. She has brought new perspectives, new expertise, and new energy to this edition. Janet has sharpened our focus on the roles of race, class, and gender in writing; she has strengthened our treatment of the rhetorical contexts in which writers and readers operate; she has offered special guidance on writing as a form of public service moving well beyond the walls of the classroom or the boundaries of the college campus; and she has brought us fully up-to-date on the new forms of reading, research, writing, and document design in the age of computers and the Internet. The result is a book that melds the best of our previous editions with the most innovative new approaches in rhetoric and the technology of communication.

Welcome, Janet.

THE BOOK ITSELF

For the first time, *Writing: A College Handbook* comes to you in full color. In fact, this elegant new design employs color *rhetorically,* emphasizing and differentiating points as it gives our pages visual clarity.

Previous editions of this book set out to show that good writing is not simply the absence of grammatical error but the presence of rhetorical power. This remains our leading aim. With new guidance on topics ranging from the writer's audience to use of the Internet, our basic approach is unchanged. While identifying the mistakes commonly made in student writing and showing how to correct them, we emphasize what student writers can do rather than what they can't or shouldn't do. Above all, we try to show them how to generate the kind of writing that informs, excites, delights, and persuades the readers for whom it is written. While we have maintained the positive, empowering approach to the writing process that has always distinguished *Writing: A College Handbook,* we have incorporated several new emphases.

Since many instructors like to start by introducing students to the writing process as a whole, Part 1, "The Process of Writing," begins with a five-chapter overview of that process. Users of the fourth edition will see that we continue to illustrate the writing process with various examples of student writing-in-progress and with successive versions of one student essay as it evolves from early drafts to final draft. But we have made a number of needed changes. We now emphasize that the process of writing has powerful civic and social dimensions. And we start with considerations of audience and purpose, because even prior to setting pen to paper, student writers must consider their readers, the context in which they are writing, and their purpose or goals for the assignment.

In chapter 1, we explain that writing is a process of participation, of making ideas public and making a difference in the world. We also ask student writers to examine the ways in which effective writing makes a difference—both within the academy and in the many communities in which they participate, such as clubs and organizations, citizen groups, places of work, and new communities in cyberspace.

Many writing courses recognize the importance of collaboration by making use of peer review groups and similar activities. So chapter 2 now treats collaboration (in section 2.6), and talks about the benefits of working with other reader-writers and receiving feedback. This chapter also offers planning strategies for various writing situations, and illustrates that effective writing often means balancing multiple purposes and, in some instances, multiple contexts and audiences.

Chapter 3, on active writing and reading, has been expanded to treat reading as a rhetorical act, acknowledging that we read—just as we write—for many purposes. We continue to treat writing and reading as a form of inquiry, but in this edition we place special emphasis on investigating cultural assumptions about race, class, and gender. We focus on these assumptions so that students understand the literacy skills and practices that they bring to their writing and reading, and where these practices come from. And such cultural assumptions are important when thinking about audience and context. A new section (3.5) presents the basics of field research: constructing research questions and collecting data through observing, notetaking, interviewing, and surveys. And chapter 3 also includes new sections on analyzing advertising and cultural codes (3.8 and 3.9), with strategies and assignments for helping students examine visual as well as written rhetoric.

In addition, we have strengthened and expanded the rest of Part 1. Because a writer's language and style choices depend upon his or her audience, chapter 8 focuses on style in the context of community and discusses language and language expectations in various communities. The new chapter 11, on argument, includes a section on treating the opposition with respect. The new chapter 12, on document design, demonstrates the use of visual information in texts designed for diverse audiences. Computer-graphics programs offer many choices for producing finished documents, and so this chapter features full-color annotated model documents from standard and online media.

Part 2 retains its positive approach by repeatedly stressing the rhetorical impact of a particular construction when it is correctly and effectively used. Presenting lively examples from student and professional writing, we show students how they can exploit the rich, vital, and inexhaustible resources of the English language. Our chief aim in the whole of Part 2, in fact, is summed up by the title of chapter 27: "Invigorating Your Style."

The emphasis on rhetorical effect in Part 2 is reinforced by the exercises. Instead of merely calling for the correction of errors, many of them ask for short sentences to be combined in more than one way so that students can see what rhetorical effects they can achieve with various constructions. Also, nearly all of the exercises consist of consecutive sentences that work together to tell a story, build a description, or develop a point.

The newly revised chapter 28, "Academic English for Nonnative Speakers," helps international students learn the kinds of skills that native speakers acquire without conscious effort, such as when and how to use *the*, *a*, and *an*, and how to choose between gerunds and infinitives.

We have expanded and strengthened Part 4, "The Research Paper," to account for changes in composition theory and in research processes. We now include extensive treatment of electronic research sources, including online databases and Web sites. We give students detailed strategies for both conducting Internet research and evaluating Web sites, and we provide a new research paper that uses Internet sources. The section on MLA documentation has been thoroughly updated and now includes guidelines for citing electronic sources such as Web sites, emails, listservs, and CD-ROMs. We also include, in chapter 37, detailed information on conducting interviews.

In Part 5, "Writing in Academic Contexts," chapter 41 discusses writing about literature and offers two sample essays, one on a short story and one on a poem. Chapter 42 treats writing and research in different disciplines and includes citation information for APA, CBE, and *CMS* styles. It also discusses how to present tables and figures in research papers; how to write examinations, applications, and letters; and how to write personal statements when applying for admission to a school of business, law, medicine, or graduate study.

In Part 6, "Writing in Nonacademic Contexts," chapter 43 discusses writing in occupational settings. The entirely new chapter 44 presents public service as a form of collaborative inquiry, and provides strategies for oral as well as written communication in public-service contexts—from holding productive meetings to creating brochures and writing press releases. Chapter 45, also new, discusses grant writing for nonprofit groups and offers guidance on locating funding sources and creating successful applications.

SUPPLEMENTARY MATERIALS

Writing: A College Handbook, Fifth Edition, is supported by a complete instructional package.

For the student: *Writing: A College Workbook*, Fifth Edition, is a basic textbook on the writing of sentences and the handling of punctuation and mechanics. It parallels and supplements Parts 2 and 3 of the handbook and includes basic instruction on sentence structure as well as over one hundred exercises—ranging from recognition and error correction to sentence-combining to revising and editing complete paragraphs and essays—printed on tear-out pages that can be assigned as classwork or homework. An electronic answer pamphlet for the workbook is available to instructors upon request.

The Instructor's Edition of *Writing: A College Handbook* offers chapter overviews, teaching tips, notes on nonnative speakers, selected bibliographies, suggestions for peer work, backgrounds, quotations, and answers to the exercises.

New to the Fifth Edition is the *Writing: A College Handbook* Web site, which offers an array of resources for students and instructors. Highlights of the site include six hundred mail-to exercises and quizzes that correspond to sections of the handbook; Parts 2, 3, and 4 of the handbook online, fully hyperlinked and annotated; a databank of downloadable document models in MLA, *CMS*, APA, and CBE styles; an electronic library of scholarly articles in rhetoric and composition; and links to useful sites for writing and research across the disciplines.

Acknowledgments

We have incurred many debts in the preparation of this book, and we are happy to acknowledge them here. It began as *The Dartmouth Guide to Writing*, by John E. Lincoln—a book of lessons and exercises issued by Dartmouth College for its students under a grant from the Lilly Foundation.

For help with the fifth edition, we are grateful, first of all, to the teachers who acted as reviewers and consultants on the manuscript: Stuart Blythe, Indiana University, Purdue University, South Bend; Lisa Langstraat, University of Southern Mississippi; Renee Shea, Bowie State University; Ann Larabee, Michigan State University; Alan Bickford, Macon State College; Rachel Smith, Emporia State University; Rebecca Moore Howard, Syracuse University; and Libby Miles, University of Rhode Island.

We are grateful as well to the specialist consultants who reviewed the manuscript with an eye toward our treatment of particular topics: Stuart Blythe consulted on electronic-discourse issues, and he coauthored, with Janet Atwill, the chapter on document design. Leslie LaChance, University of Tennessee, Knoxville, offered good counsel on our revisions of the chapter on academic English for nonnative speakers.

We are indebted to many others for various kinds of help. At the University of Tennessee, Janet Atwill would like to thank the students who contributed their writing: Ramona Coleman, Jill Holland, David May, and Carmen North. Brandon Scott Sweeten deserves special thanks for contributing both his paper and his research assistance. Rachel Patton deserves special thanks for her research assistance, as does Lenika Swoope, who helped with research and whose careful editorial work was invaluable to the project. Thanks also to Wayne Montgomery, Reference Librarian, California Polytechnic State University.

We must record here, too, our indebtedness to the many students from other academic institutions who have contributed examples of their writing—Rick Kurihara, Adam Usadi, Cirri Washington, Julie Cusick, Arturo Garcia, Neil Okun.

Acknowledgments

Special thanks are also due to the authors of all the supplementary materials that accompany the book. Matthew Henry, Richland College, Dallas County Community College, and Susan Miller, Santa Fe Community College, provided able and timely revisions of supplementary TASP and CLAST pamphlets, respectively. Leslie LaChance revised and updated the Instructor's Edition. Cindy Moore, Indiana University, Purdue University, Fort Wayne, delivered a careful and thorough revision of the workbook. Finally, we thank Stanley Kranc and Keith Gibson, Penn State University, for the enthusiasm and creativity they have brought to their work on the *Writing: A College Handbook* Web site.

In addition, we wish to thank present and former members of our publisher's staff for their contributions: Ethelbert Nevin II and John E. Neill each played a part in persuading John Lincoln and Jim Heffernan to write the first edition of the book. John W. N. Francis and the late John Benedict gave superb editorial guidance for the first two editions, and Julia Reidhead, Marian Johnson, Carol Hollar-Zwick, and Peter Simon did outstanding editorial and marketing work on the third and fourth editions.

For help with the fifth edition, we owe special thanks to Kurt Wildermuth, who contributed astute editing, wise judgment, and, most importantly, good humor to this project. Kurt's many fine suggestions went far above and beyond his duties as a manuscript editor. We thank Isobel Evans, who coordinated and edited the ancillaries, managed the permissions, patiently answered all of our questions, and somehow kept track of the infinite details that attend such a project. And we thank our editor, Jennifer Bartlett, who, among other things, helped us to maintain our faith in the integrity of textbook publishing. We also acknowledge here Joan Greenfield, our designer, and Diane O'Connor, who supervised the production of the book.

Lastly, we wish to thank our spouses and our children: Nancy Heffernan; Mary Lincoln; Donald Lazare; Andrew and Virginia Heffernan; Chris, Peter, and Brian Lincoln; and Peter Nathan Foltz.

Introduction

TALKING AND WRITING

Talking is something most of us seem to do naturally. We learn to talk almost automatically, first imitating the words we hear and then imitating the ways in which people around us put them together. Well before we learn how to put words on paper, we unconsciously learn how to use them in speech.

But no one learns to write automatically. You cannot write even a single letter of the alphabet without a conscious effort of mind and hand, and to get beyond the single letter, you must be shown how to form words, how to put words together into sentences, and how to punctuate those sentences.

Writing, then, is a means of communication you must consciously learn. And part of what makes it hard to learn is that written words usually have to express your meaning in your absence, have to "speak" all by themselves. When you speak face to face with a listener, you can communicate in many different ways. You can raise or lower the pitch or volume of your voice to emphasize a point; you can grin, frown, wink, or shrug; you can use your hands to shape a meaning when you don't quite have the words to do it; you can even make your silence mean something. But in writing you have to communicate without facial expressions, gestures, or body English of any kind. You have to speak with words and punctuation alone.

Punctuation does have an impact

Furthermore, writing is a solitary act. When you talk, you normally talk to someone who talks back, who raises questions, who lets you know whether or not you are making yourself clear. But when you write, you work alone. Even if you are writing a letter to a friend, he or she will not suddenly materialize to prod or prompt you into speech, to help you fill in the gaps that often occur when you try to tell a story or give an explanation off the top of your head. To write well, you have to anticipate the reactions of a reader you cannot see or hear.

But writing does have one big advantage over speaking. It gives you time to think, to try out your ideas on paper, to choose your words, to read what you have written, to rethink, revise, and rearrange it, and most important, to consider its effect on a reader. Writing gives you time to find the best possible way of stating what you mean. And the more you study the craft of writing, the better you will use your writing time.

ACADEMIC ENGLISH, OTHER DIALECTS, AND DISCOURSE COMMUNITIES

This book aims to help you write effectively in English. But since there are many kinds of English, you should know which kind this book teaches—and why.

The language called "English" is used in many parts of the world. It is spoken not only in England but also in the British West Indies and in countries that were once British colonies—such as Canada, the United States, Australia, India, and Nigeria. These are all "English-speaking" countries, but they have different ways of using English. Sometimes, for instance, they have different words for the same thing:

truck (U.S.) = lorry (Great Britain)

pond (U.S.) = billabong (Australia)

Sometimes they have different ways of spelling or pronouncing the same word:

check (U.S.) = cheque (Great Britain and Canada)

labor (U.S.) = labour (Great Britain and Canada)

recognize (U.S.) = recognise (Great Britain and Canada)

laugh: pronounced "laff" in the U.S., "lahff" in Great Britain

paint: pronounced "paynt" in the U.S., "pint" in Australia

Sometimes they use different grammatical forms:

The jury has reached a verdict. (U.S.)

The jury have reached a verdict. (all other English-speaking countries)

You may have already noticed differences such as these. Even if you have never traveled abroad, you have probably heard British or Australian speech. When you did, you could undoubtedly tell after just a few words that what you were hearing was different from any kind of English commonly spoken in North America. The reason for the difference is that a living language never stands still. Like the people who speak it and the world they speak it in, it changes. And if English-speaking peoples live far enough apart, the English they use will change in divergent ways. That is why English sounds different in different parts of the world.

Just as English varies from one country to another, it also varies from one region of a country to another, and from one cultural or ethnic group to another. Consider these statements:

She says I be crazy.

She says I am crazy.

They ain't got no ponies; they got big horses. I rode one, real big uns.

They don't have any ponies; they have big horses. I rode one, a really big one.

I have three brother and two sister.

I have three brothers and two sisters.

These statements illustrate four dialects—four kinds of English used in North America. The first statement in each pair illustrates a regional or ethnic dialect; the second illustrates standard, or academic, English. Each of these dialects has its own distinctive character and rules. But of them all, academic English is the only one normally taught in schools and colleges, the only one normally required in business and the professions, and the only one widely used in writing—especially in print. Why does academic English enjoy this privilege? Is it always better than any other kind? And if you were raised to speak an ethnic or regional dialect, must you stop speaking that dialect in order to learn the academic one?

There is no easy answer to the first of these three questions. But the answer to the second one is no. Academic English is not always better than any other kind. In a spoken exchange, it can sometimes be less expressive—and therefore less effective—than a regional or ethnic dialect. Compare for instance, the original version of a regional proverb with the academic version:

Them as has, gets; them as ain't, gets took.

Those who have, get; those who do not have, get taken.

These two statements strike the ear in different ways. While the first has the expressive vitality of regional speech, the second—the academic version—sounds comparatively stiff.

Part of what makes the original version so effective is the tradition that stands behind it. Because of that tradition, the answer to the third question we raised is also no. A regional or ethnic dialect is not just a way of speaking; it is the living record of a shared heritage and shared concerns.

For this reason, no one who speaks such a dialect should be forced to give it up.

The same is true for anyone who speaks a kind of English peculiar to a discourse community: a group that defines itself largely by the way it speaks or writes a language used by others in different ways. The magazine *The Source,* for instance, is written largely in hip-hop, the speech of urban rappers: a kind of English in which *ripping it* is used for *performing, drops* for *arrives,* and *breaks it down* for *speaks.*

But just as many people can learn how to read both *The Source* and *The New York Times,* most people can learn how to speak and write more than one dialect. Academic English is what you will normally be expected to use in your writing. During college, it is what teachers will expect you to use in essays, exams, reports, and research papers. After college, it is what others will expect you to use in anything you write for business or professional purposes. For all of these reasons, academic English is what this book aims to help you learn.

GRAMMAR AND RHETORIC

The grammar of a language is the set of rules by which its sentences are made. You started learning the rules of English grammar as soon as you started to talk. Well before you learned how to write, you could have said which of these two statements made sense:

> *Eggs breakfast fried I two for had.

> I had two fried eggs for breakfast.

The words in each statement are the same, but you can readily see that only the second arrangement makes sense. What you know about the English language tells you that some ways of arranging the seven words are acceptable and others are not. You may not be able to say just why the word order in the first arrangement is wrong, but you know that it is.

Good writing requires a working knowledge of grammar, a basic command of the rules that govern the forming of a sentence. But good writing is more than the act of obeying grammatical rules. It is also the art of using rhetoric—of arranging words, phrases, sentences, and paragraphs in such a way as to engage and sustain the reader's attention.

The power of rhetoric can sometimes be felt in a single sentence: Virginia Woolf wrote, "Women have burnt like beacons in all the works of all the poets from the beginning of time." General George S. Patton said to his

*From this point on, nonstandard constructions in this book generally are marked with a star. We also use asterisks to mark misspelled words and other errors in student drafts.

troops after a battle, "You have been baptized in fire and blood and have come out steel." Martin Luther King Jr. said to a crowd of civil-rights demonstrators, "I have a dream." Good sentences like these not only take their place in a paragraph but also make a place for themselves, striking the reader with their own special clarity and force. One aim of this book, therefore, is to help you maximize the rhetorical impact of every sentence you write.

Yet you do not normally write single sentences in isolation. You write them in sequence, and rhetoric is the art of making that sequence effective— of moving from one sentence to another in a paragraph, and from one paragraph to another in an essay. It is the art of sustaining a continuity while continually moving ahead, of developing a description, a narrative, an explanation, or an argument in such a way as to take the reader with you from beginning to end. The ultimate aim of this book, therefore, is to explain the rhetoric of the writing process as a whole.

Objectives of this book
1. teach rhetoric writing
2. correct use of grammar.

USING THIS BOOK: TO STUDENTS

Your teacher may assign certain chapters to your class or, after seeing your work, may refer you individually to the sections you need. Either way, it will help you to know what the book offers.

The book has six main parts. Part 1, "The Process of Writing," surveys the whole writing process from early draft to final draft. It treats different kinds of writing such as exposition and persuasion, and specific parts of the writing process such as paragraphing and choosing words. Part 2, "Crafting Sentences," shows you how to make sentence structure work for you. We explain things you should not do, such as misplacing modifiers and misusing the passive voice. But we stress the things you can and should do, such as highlighting the main point of each sentence and varying your sentence patterns to invigorate your style. Part 3, "Punctuation and Mechanics," treats punctuation, spelling, and the use of mechanical conventions such as capitals and italics. Part 4, "Research and Writing," directs you through the research process from start to finish, and treats everything from asking the right questions to using the Internet. Part 5, "Writing in Academic Contexts," focuses on the kind of writing you will most likely do in college across the disciplines. It offers a thorough treatment of documentation styles in the humanities, social sciences, and physical sciences. (We have made these documentation sections easy to find by using color-coded bands: green for MLA, gold for *CMS*, plum for APA, and gray for CBE.) Part 6, "Writing in Nonacademic Contexts," illustrates how to draw upon academic writing skills to become proficient and effective writers beyond college. When you can communicate effectively, in the workplace and elsewhere, you have the power to change the world.

The Process of Writing

1

Building Rhetorical Power 1

1.1 WHAT IS RHETORICAL POWER?

This book aims to help you develop **rhetorical power**, which is the power to persuade and to communicate: to express what you feel, what you believe, what you know, and what you have discovered about yourself and the world around you.

Many such discoveries spring from reading. Reading generates writing just as eating and breathing keep us alive. From reading you can learn about a particular topic or about the feelings of those you hope to persuade or inform. You can read good writing to study its construction and to see how writers capture and hold a reader's attention. Reading different types of writing—from editorials and essays to lab reports and business letters—can help you understand various ways of organizing and presenting ideas. Reading helps you exercise the powers of interpretation that make you a better writer.

Consider the role reading and writing played in one student's course project. Susan's assignment in her education course was to write a conflict-resolution study unit for a fifth-grade class in a local school. To get started, Susan reread and took notes on theories of conflict resolution in her college textbooks. She researched the topic of conflict resolution for children in the library and on the Internet, and she wrote a list of conflict-resolution principles she thought young children could understand. Next, she studied fifth-grade textbooks to get a sense of the kind of writing elementary school students were used to reading. She wrote a draft of the unit, which she gave to her education professor for feedback. After studying her professor's comments, she wrote her final draft, which she presented to the fifth-grade class. Susan's project required her to read and write in several different ways. She read to learn about her subject and to understand the kind of writing fifth-graders could comprehend; she read her own drafts and the comments provided by her professor. She wrote to take notes before she created her first draft; then she wrote several additional drafts before arriving at a final version.

1.2 WHY READ AND WRITE?

Reading and writing are ways you can express and understand yourself. They are among the most important ways you join and participate in the many communities in your life: your school community, clubs and organizations, citizen groups, workplaces, and new communities in cyberspace.

READING AND WRITING TO EXPRESS AND UNDERSTAND YOURSELF

When you write about your ideas, feelings, and experiences, you are creating a kind of mirror. That mirror can show you what you value, fear, and desire; it can help you understand where you've been and where you're going. Together with reading, writing can also help you to organize yourself. Reading the experiences of others can help you think about your own experiences. Through writing you can turn a painful event in your life into a story with a beginning, a middle, and an end. Putting together language is a way of putting yourself together; it is a way of preparing yourself to participate in all the communities you live in—and those you hope to enter.

READING AND WRITING TO PARTICIPATE IN COMMUNITIES

ACADEMIC COMMUNITIES   When you listen to people you have known for a long time, you normally find them easy to understand because you know what they are talking about. For the same reason you find them easy to talk to.

In many ways, entering the academic communities you find in college is like talking with people you've just met. By listening to new people and asking them questions, you begin to understand what they are talking about. Likewise, by reading about a particular discipline, which is a field of knowledge explored by members of a distinct academic community, you begin to understand that discipline and to raise the kinds of questions that the discipline is equipped to pursue. In an economics class, for instance, you begin to ask about the relation between inflation and the rate of unemployment. As you learn more, you may begin to write about this relation.

CLUBS, ORGANIZATIONS, AND CITIZEN GROUPS   Reading and writing play important roles in clubs (such as a campus hiking or rowing club), formal

4

organizations (fraternities, sororities, and professional organizations), and citizen groups (such as Habitat for Humanity, Students for Environmental Action). While such groups conduct many of their activities using speech, they still depend on reading and writing to define themselves and to record group business and history. Groups define their identities in many ways: they prepare mission statements, print brochures, and post Web sites; they circulate information in email and newsletters.

Reading and writing play special roles in a democracy. In the earliest Greek democracy, citizens participated in their government by taking turns serving as representatives. Obviously, our democracy is very different; most people consider voting the primary way we participate in government. One distinctive feature of our democracy, however, is that citizens have the freedom to voice their concerns, to discuss and negotiate, and to make public arguments. Reading and writing are the tools that give us voice and bring about change. We must read to become informed about issues we want to debate or influence. Even in public meetings, writing frequently serves as a guide for speaking, and the results of important public meetings are almost always preserved in written records. Whatever the medium—Internet, magazines, or newspapers—reading and writing remain powerful means of creating awareness and influencing public opinion. They are tools that build and repair democracies.

WORK COMMUNITIES   Reading and writing are among the most important tools you will ever use. Like groups, work communities use reading and writing to define their objectives, circulate information, and accomplish goals. If you have a job now, reading and writing probably played a role in your getting that job, even if you're working as a cook in a fast-food restaurant or as a cashier at the campus bookstore. Someone had to write the job description, which you had to read in order to decide if the job was right for you. You may have had to take a reading, writing, or other kind of skills test. When you were hired, someone had to record information to put you on the payroll; and you probably had to read and fill out more forms before you started working. Your job training probably involved reading descriptions of the business's policies and your responsibilities.

Reading and writing are part of the simplest jobs. Just think how important they are in the following work communities:

▶ In a civil-engineering firm, a team of engineers designs a containment facility for waste from a nuclear-energy plant. The engineering firm must write a proposal that will be read and approved by officials at the energy plant. Government agencies expect reports on the facility's design, safety, and environmental impact. A community environmental action group expects a written response to a list of concerns it has raised about the facility.

5

▶ In a hospital, a nurse in a neurointensive care unit must write a report on a patient's condition to be used by a doctor in prescribing treatment and by an insurance company for approving payment.

▶ In a midsize company, a personnel manager must write an employee handbook that outlines the company's policy on sick leave, family leave, and vacations.

▶ In a high school, a first-year history teacher must write out course objectives, lesson plans, study units, and exams.

COMMUNITIES IN CYBERSPACE Computer technology and the Internet have changed each of the communities discussed above. Schools use the Internet for research and for communication among instructors and students. Clubs and organizations communicate with members via email. Citizen groups around the world work together on issues of common concern. Work communities rapidly transmit and access information and collaborate with other communities. The Internet also offers you, as an individual, the opportunity to connect with people around the world who share your interests and concerns—from collecting baseball cards to tracking meteors. Using the new technology requires sophisticated reading and writing skills. Any Web site, for example, no matter how fancy its graphics, relies on your ability to interpret text. What you write in an online discussion group may be read and judged by hundreds or thousands of people. Even if you want to experience "real-time" conversations with friends on the Internet or to hold a video conference, you have to know where to find programs, how to download and install them, and how to use them—information for which you might have to read reference materials or instruction manuals. Reading and writing are keys to the doors of electronic communities.

EXERCISE   **Reading and Writing**

1. List all the kinds of writing you do in an average week. In group discussion or in writing, describe how those kinds of writing are related to different communities.

2. Describe the kinds of writing you do to record your experiences or feelings.

3. Discuss the information sources that help you decide whom to vote for in campus, local, state, and federal elections.

4. List your hobbies and interests. Pick one item on your list and use at least two Internet search engines or directories to find communities with active discussion groups on the subject.

Preparing to Write 2

You might compare the process of writing to taking a trip. Some trips you take without planning in advance. Other trips you plan carefully. Suppose you are taking your first trip to Alaska. This is a trip you might want to plan carefully. You may already know some things about the state without ever having been there. You may know, for example, that the Alaska Range, southeast of Fairbanks, offers some of the most dramatic mountain scenes in the world. You may also know that in the Kenai Fjord National Park you can find marine wildlife ranging from sea otters to humpback whales. Knowing that these things are there doesn't mean that you won't learn much more from your actual visit. Indeed, you may have many questions about this place you plan to visit. How are the mountain ranges there different from those in the Rockies? Why are some forms of wildlife and vegetation more common than others? If part of the purpose of the trip is to take photographs for a professional portfolio, you will probably do research to make sure you take advantage of the extraordinary scenery in the state. The knowledge you begin with, the questions you want to answer, the plans you make, and the research you do all contribute to making your trip successful.

What you will find in this chapter and throughout part 1 are strategies to make your writing process as effective as possible. A strategy is a tool for helping you develop and shape a particular piece of writing. Sometimes these strategies are simply terms to help you make decisions as you write; in chapter 2, ways of defining purpose and reader/writer roles are examples of this kind of strategy. Other strategies take the form of questions to answer; in chapter 3, triple-viewing is an example of this kind of strategy. Both kinds of strategies will help you achieve your goals in writing and learn about yourself and your world.

2.2 CRAFTING EXPLORATORY QUESTIONS

One of the most productive ways to begin the writing process is to craft questions. An exploratory question helps provide focus for inquiry. A good exploratory question may also express *dissonance* in the writer's values, knowledge, or experience. Literally, dissonance means discord or conflict, but dissonance can also signify a gap in the writer's knowledge or understanding. Dissonance is an important feature of a good exploratory question because it suggests that the writer does indeed have something new to learn in the writing process.

A good exploratory question has several characteristics:

▶ It is a question you don't already know how to answer.

EXAMPLE: What has happened to punk music?

▶ It is open-ended, something that cannot be answered with a *yes* or a *no*.

EXAMPLE: Why is hip-hop so popular?

▶ It expresses dissonance in the writer's knowledge, values, or understanding.

EXAMPLES: Why is voter turnout so low in my hometown?
Why am I uncomfortable with genetic theories of intelligence?

Sandy's English teacher gave her class the assignment of exploring values in their everyday culture. Students discussed different ways they talked about values. Sandy began with the question "What does it mean to 'sell out'?" Her teacher encouraged her to craft a question that expressed some dissonance in her understanding of the idea. Sandy was curious about the idea of "selling out" because while she heard other people use the term to express a negative judgment about a person, group, or celebrity, the term didn't mean very much to her. She decided to explore two questions:

▶ What kind of judgment are people making when they accuse someone of "selling out"?

▶ Why does it never occur to me to accuse someone of "selling out"?

Writing Exploratory Questions

1. Write three exploratory questions about values in your everyday culture.

2. If your teacher has assigned a subject, write three or more exploratory questions on that subject. How would you describe the dissonance in your questions? In other words, are values or experiences in conflict or is there a gap in knowledge or understanding?

A Good Exploratory Question:

▶ asks a question you can't already answer

▶ is open-ended (can't be answered with a *yes* or a *no*)

▶ expresses dissonance

2.3 UNDERSTANDING RHETORICAL CONTEXTS

A rhetorical context is a framework for communication. What you say in a classroom will usually differ from what you say at a party with friends because the people, places, and things you discuss are different. What you write in a personal letter will differ from what you write in a college lab report because you are writing for readers with different expectations and using different forms of writing. In order to understand the rhetorical context in which you write, you must understand *purpose, forms of writing* (or *genres*) typically used in the context, *writer and reader roles,* and *tone.*

PURPOSE

As you prepare to write, you will want to clarify the purpose of your text. Most writing seeks to achieve one or more of the following purposes: *self-expression, exposition,* and *persuasion.*

SELF-EXPRESSION

Self-expressive writing conveys the author's *experiences, attitudes,* and *feelings.* Diaries, memoirs, and personal letters are largely self-expressive. When you are asked to write an essay on a personal subject, you are commonly urged to be self-expressive—as in the paragraph below:

9

I can recall a childhood filled with music. I believe my mom and dad had every album of every rhythm and blues artist. Mom and Dad, sisters, brothers, and I would gather in the living room to listen to music. I would snap my fingers, throw my little nine-year-old hips from side to side as the Spinners soulfully vibrated through the speakers—"I'll be working my way back to you, girl." Then Dad would flip a switch, the turntable would do its magic, and a new sound, "Dancing in the Street" by Martha Reeves and the Vandellas, found me twirling in my own unrehearsed choreography— enjoying the music, my dancing, and my family.

—college student

EXPOSITION   When you focus on a particular subject, especially to *describe or explain* it, your purpose is exposition. Much of the writing you do in college has exposition as at least part of its purpose. For example, when your political-science teacher asks you on an essay exam to discuss *liberal pluralism,* she is asking you to explain the concept in order to demonstrate that you understand it. Exposition is not restricted to academic writing; it plays an important role in many different rhetorical contexts. The explanation below is from a karate organization's newsletter:

Isshinryu karate is based on the teachings of the late Master Tatsuo Shimabuku. He believed that karate was a philosophy based on the principle of inner power and outward peace; consequently, he promoted peace when possible, power when necessary. Shimabuku maintained that one resorted to karate only when the life of one's family or oneself was in danger. For Shimabuku, mastering the art of karate was a kind of self-mastery. Shimabuku believed that self-discipline created a kind of harmony that was the first step to harmony with others. So, in many ways, the ultimate goal of Isshinryu karate is to promote situations where using the art is unnecessary.

—college student

PERSUASION   When you write in order to *prompt your readers to change* in some way, your purpose is persuasion. This kind of writing can be found in many different contexts. The most obvious place is the editorial page of your school or local newspaper. However, persuasion is also the purpose of many personal and business letters as well as job applications. Persuasion does not mean that you are simply trying to provoke your readers to "do" something. You might think of persuasion on a continuum, with creating awareness at one end and provoking an action at the other end.

creating awareness   changing an attitude   provoking an action

Often the purpose of a persuasive text is simply to create awareness of an issue. Suppose you want your fraternity to hold a fund-raiser to help buy computers for a nearby elementary school. First, you may have to help some fraternity members see that the school needs help and that the fraternity should give something back to the community it belongs to. Once you've created this awareness, you may still need to change the attitudes of members who think the school already has more money than it needs. When you've persuaded a majority that the school really does need help and that the members should furnish it, you may have to convince them to take a specific action—like holding a car wash or a fund-raising dance.

In the following letter to the editor of a local newspaper, the writer aims to change the attitude of those who think that visitors to national parks should pay entrance fees:

> Charging entrance fees to national parks undermines the very principle on which these parks were developed. The lands secured for these parks were deemed to be national treasures that should be shared by all. The national parks system was designed to allow equal access. People understood that their tax dollars paid for and preserved these parks, and, in turn, they felt a sense of responsibility for protecting these national treasures. Charging people for entering the park undermines not only the concept of equal access but also this sense of public responsibility. Those who pay to enter may decide that they want more for their money, which will lead only to more commercial development. Only a generation ago, many national parks were surrounded by relatively undeveloped properties. Today, these parks are surrounded by water rides, outlet malls, and motels with huge signs flashing their lowest rates. The parks themselves have admitted more concessionaires with kiddie rides and cheap souvenirs. Charging entrance fees further blurs the boundary between national parks and amusement parks.
>
> —college student

BALANCING MULTIPLE PURPOSES   Much of the writing you do has more than one purpose. Consequently, having rhetorical power often means knowing how to balance multiple purposes. For example, in order to change the minds of fraternity brothers who believe local schools have plenty of money, your text may have to combine persuasion with exposition. It may be necessary to explain the local tax system to convince fraternity members that the school's need is real. Similarly, Sandy's assignment to explore her own everyday culture combines self-expression with exposition. Sandy will answer her exploratory questions by examining her experiences and feelings, as well as those of her peers, and by questioning some of the media messages aimed at young adults. She will share her final text with her classmates and her teacher. All of her readers will expect her to explain her definition of "selling out," but they will also expect her to share her attitudes toward it and, if necessary, the personal experiences that led to her understanding of the term.

The key to balancing multiple purposes is knowing the right proportion for each purpose. If you write a two-thousand-word essay for your fraternity brothers that merely explains how local taxes work to fund public school, you probably won't be very successful in motivating them to hold a fund-raiser next month for an elementary school down the street. In this case, explaining the tax system is only a means to the end of persuading fraternity members that the school is in need.

FORMS OF WRITING: GENRES

Genre is a word commonly used to describe a specific form of writing. Some common genres are *academic essays, research papers, formal letters, personal letters, letters to the editor, email, and formal reports.* You already know that different situations call for different kinds of writing: a birthday present may call for a personal letter of thanks; a lab experiment requires a formal report. The better you know the genre that suits your rhetorical context, the more effectively you will write.

WRITER AND READER ROLES

You might think of a rhetorical context as a play in which you and your reader take distinctive roles. For example, when you write an assigned essay on the Keynesian theory of employment, you play a student trying to show that you can explain the theory while your teacher judges how well you do. On the other hand, when you write a letter to a close friend, you don't expect to be judged at all. You play yourself, and you expect your reader to be sympathetic to you as well as familiar with your life. Understanding your role as a writer enables you to reach the reader you are writing for, to *address* that reader in terms that make you believable and worthy of respect.

Writer and reader roles may assume any one of the following forms:

WRITER AND READER AS PEERS Both parties have equal knowledge or shared experiences; neither has more power or authority than the other. It is common for the writer to express personal feelings. In this kind of writing, typified by a personal letter or email, the language is usually informal and may include slang and contractions.

WRITER AS NOVICE AND READER AS EXPERT Most of the writing students do as undergraduates falls into this category. A student writes as a "novice," a learner, a person acquiring the knowledge and experience that will someday make him or her an expert. Unless the assignment is to write a personal essay, novices who are writing for experts generally focus on a particular subject rather than on personal feelings. Novices demonstrate respect for their audiences by following the guidelines of the assignment, carefully revising and proofreading their texts, and handing in clean, readable final papers.

WRITER AS EXPERT AND READER AS NOVICE   In this case, writers have special knowledge or experience to convey to readers, such as explaining how to create a Web page or begin an exercise program. In this kind of writing, specialized terms should be explained. When a teacher asks you to write an essay that explains a process, you are being asked to teach the reader what you know.

OTHER WRITER AND READER RELATIONSHIPS   Sometimes writer and reader roles do not fit neatly into any one category, especially when writers and readers have different levels of power and authority. For example, when you write to a legislator, religious leader, or business executive, you are writing to someone with special power or authority. In these cases, you can show respect for the reader's role by avoiding slang and contractions and keeping the focus of your text on the subject rather than your personal feelings. Also, though you may know more than a legislator or business executive does about a particular subject, such as recycling, you should aim to sound helpfully informative rather than over-confident.

TONE

The human voice always carries a tone. Imagine, for instance, how these questions would sound if spoken aloud.

> Would you please turn down that music?
>
> Would you *please* turn down that music.

The words of both questions are exactly the same. Only the tone is different. The first question is polite; the second, insistent.

Though it is harder to hear the tone of a written word than the tone of a spoken one, the tone of a text largely depends on the writer's attitude toward the reader and the topic. The tone of your writing may be earnest or playful, calm or impassioned, authoritative or tentative. You can also choose to sound *personal* or *impersonal* and to come across as *straightforward* or *ironic*.

PERSONAL OR IMPERSONAL   The tone of a text is personal when the author as *I* treats the reader as *you* and writes from an explicitly subjective viewpoint—as in the student's description of her family's love of music (see p. 9, "Self-Expression").

The tone of a text is impersonal when the author avoids using *I* and *you* and keeps the focus on the subject matter objectively viewed—as in the student's account of Isshinryu karate ("Exposition").

STRAIGHTFORWARD OR IRONIC   Tone also depends on the way you guide readers to "take" or interpret what you write. Suppose, for instance, your college newspaper reviews a new piece of student sculpture made from a concrete slab and the rusted box springs of an old bed. The review might begin with this sentence:

> The new sculpture outside the student union is an important artistic contribution to the campus.

Depending on what follows, this statement may be either straightforward or ironic. It would be straightforward if the writer went on to say exactly why she sincerely believes the sculpture *is* a work of art:

> The new sculpture outside the student union is an important artistic contribution to the campus. In the past, the college has been very unreceptive toward nontraditional art. The sculpture of the Greek god Hermes, together with the landscape paintings in Memorial Hall, seemed to be all the "art" we needed on campus. These traditional artistic forms reflect a very limited definition of art. As Professor Larson, Head of the Art Department, has suggested, many artists believe that art should make us uncomfortable and prompt us to look at the world in new ways. According to Dr. Larson, "modern art often challenges our expectations rather than satisfies them."

On the other hand, the whole review would be ironic if the writer went on to claim that all trash—or anything unexpected—makes "important" art:

> The new sculpture outside the student union is an important artistic contribution to the campus. As the Head of the Art Department has suggested, the sculpture challenges our expectations rather than satisfies them. Indeed, I have not talked to one student who came to school expecting to find a rusted bed on the campus lawn. Since we do not want our college to be known for its limited conception of art, I propose that we commission more sculptures to complement this new addition to the campus—perhaps a rusted pickup truck or a discarded washing machine.

CONTROLLING TONE · Tone is an important writer's tool, but one that must be handled carefully. An ironic tone can sometimes deteriorate into unimaginative sarcasm. Moreover, if you try to switch back and forth between ironic and straightforward tones in the same document, you must do it very carefully or readers will simply conclude that you are confused.

WRITING IN UNFAMILIAR RHETORICAL CONTEXTS

Suppose your hiking club has asked you to write a report on the group's plans for next year. One of the most helpful things you can do is to find a sample report to use as a model for the text you need to write. You can find many models in this textbook. You can also look for models in the context in which you're writing. In the case of your hiking club, that would mean looking for reports that have been written in the past. Once you have found a sample, see how it serves its purpose, what role the writer plays in relation to the reader, and what the tone is. If possible, have someone who knows the context well read a draft of your report.

Writing in Unfamiliar Rhetorical Contexts   IN BRIEF

1. Find a good sample of the kind of writing you're expected to do.

2. Analyze the sample text for:

   ▶ purpose

   ▶ writer and reader roles

   ▶ tone

3. Have someone with more experience in the context read a draft of your writing.

2.4 WRITING IN RESPONSE TO CLASSROOM ASSIGNMENTS

Understanding classroom assignments is an important part of being a successful student. Knowing the subject material of a discipline isn't enough; you must know how to present what you know. Effectively presenting material requires that you understand exactly what your instructor expects, and this means understanding the assignment's form and purpose.

Certain key words can help you determine purpose. For example, if your assignment contains words like *describe, explain, discuss* or *compare and contrast,* your teacher is probably expecting *exposition.* If the assignment contains words like *argue* or *make a case for,* your teacher is probably expecting *persuasion.* Your teacher will be reading to see whether or not you know and understand course material and to see if you are learning how specialists in a discipline ask questions, do research, and explain and defend their ideas. In most cases, when your teacher asks you to write persuasively, she is expecting you to support your argument with material you have learned in the course.

IN BRIEF   **Writing in Response to Classroom Assignments**

1. Look for key words that define the purpose of the assignment:
   - ▶ **exposition:** describe, explain, discuss, compare and contrast
   - ▶ **persuasion:** argue, make a case for
2. Look for words that specify the assignment's form: **essay, report, research paper, research report**
3. Find out the expected length.
4. Find out whether any or all of the following are expected:
   - ▶ discussion of assigned reading
   - ▶ additional research
   - ▶ your opinion or reaction
5. Ask your teacher to explain any aspect of the assignment you find unclear.

2.5 CYBERSPACE AS A RHETORICAL SITUATION

Writing email, entering online discussion groups, and posting texts on Web sites present special challenges, especially as you consider writer/reader relationships and forms of writing.

WRITER/READER RELATIONSHIPS IN CYBERSPACE

Writer/reader relationships in cyberspace are unique because you have very little control over who reads your writing. Writing an email message to someone is different from writing a letter because your reader can instantly forward your message to anyone he or she chooses. The situation is even more extreme in online discussion groups and Web sites, where you may have no idea who is following the discussion or looking through your Web site. Consequently, when you write in cyberspace you must exercise caution to protect both your privacy and your safety. Remember that anything you write about controversial subjects or people you know can be forwarded to others without your knowledge or permission. If you have your own Web page or post texts on another Web site, you must also bear in mind that people look through Web sites for many different reasons. In the interest of safety, you might think twice before posting your address or phone number on any Web site, including your own.

FORMS OF WRITING IN CYBERSPACE

The form and appearance of your writing in cyberspace are also difficult to control. While your email program (like Pine, Netscape Communicator, or Netscape WebMail) may allow you to format paragraphs and characters, the way your text appears to your reader will depend on your reader's email program. Consequently, line length, line breaks, paragraph and character formatting may be lost or transformed into other characters or symbols. Italics and underlining are character formats that are often lost or transformed. Underlining, for example, may go from Moby-Dick to _Moby-Dick_. One way of reducing confusion in online discussions is for participants to agree to use the same program.

The appearance of your Web site can also change depending on your reader's Internet browser, computer monitor, and modem speed. The browser LYNX, for example, cannot display images; the word IMAGE appears instead. Colors on Web sites can vary dramatically from one monitor to another. The ease with which a reader can download a page on your Web site depends on both the file size of your images and the speed of your reader's modem. Downloading images can be very frustrating if your file size is large and your reader's modem is relatively slow. (For a full discussion of document design, see chapter 12.)

2.6 COLLABORATIVE WRITING

In school, organizations, and the world of work, many projects require collaboration. Working with others on a project has many advantages. It allows you to use the special talents of each individual in a group. Working with others also has a way of fostering more creativity and sharper problem-solving skills. Though collaborative projects vary greatly, a few general principles can make group work more productive and enjoyable:

> ▶ GET TO KNOW THE PEOPLE YOU ARE WORKING WITH. Learn each other's names and take time to learn the special talents and skills that each person brings to the project.

▶ SET GUIDELINES FOR CONDUCTING MEETINGS.   Some groups work more effectively if they appoint one person as a chair who helps keep the group on task and on schedule.

▶ CREATE A PROJECT PLAN AND SCHEDULE.   A plan should break the work down into stages and assign due dates for each stage.

▶ DIVIDE RESPONSIBILITIES.   Collaboration can work in one of two ways. Either all members work on each stage of the entire project or the project is divided into parts, with each group member responsible for a specific part of the project.

▶ FINISH THE PROJECT BEFORE THE DEADLINE.   Give yourself at least two or three extra days to account for problems you didn't anticipate and to give you time to put the finishing touches on your project.

EXERCISE 2	Analyzing Purpose and Form

1. If your teacher has given you a writing assignment, analyze its purpose and form.
2. If you are on an active listserv, find a posting that you think communicates effectively. Describe the purpose and form of the posting.

Strategies for Active Writing and Reading

3

3.1 WHY USE STRATEGIES FOR ACTIVE WRITING AND READING?

Strategies for active writing and reading can help you reinforce your strengths as a writer and develop your skills wherever they fall short of what you think they should be. For example, you may be able to read factual material quickly and easily and do well on multiple-choice tests about assigned reading. However, you may have trouble taking essay exams that require discussion of the ideas you have read about. If so, you can use reading strategies to help you understand how and why a writer has made a specific argument; and you can use writing strategies that help you consider the causes, effects, and implications of the topic under discussion.

3.2 CHOOSING STRATEGIES FOR WRITING AND READING

This chapter offers a number of strategies with different emphases and aims. Some strategies are designed to help you explore your experiences and values or to point you in the direction of useful research. Other strategies are designed to help you investigate your culture, critically analyze texts and media, or use the Internet.

The following guidelines will help you make good choices among the strategies in this chapter.

1. CONSIDER YOUR PURPOSE FOR WRITING. For example, if you are writing an expressive essay, use strategies that help you recall and reevaluate your experience. See "Brainstorming," "Branching and Looping," and "Triple-viewing" (3.4).

2. CONSIDER YOUR WRITING HABITS. If you have anxiety and inhibitions about writing, use strategies that encourage you to express rather than criticize yourself—strategies like brainstorming or branching and looping. If you find it easier to express yourself than to evaluate and understand your experiences, use strategies that encourage critical analysis—like triple-viewing.

3. CONSIDER YOUR PURPOSE FOR READING. Are you reading for a class meeting, for an exam, or for a term paper? Your purpose should determine how you read and the kind of notes you take. For example, if you are reading in preparation for writing a term paper, you can use the strategies explained in 3.6.

4. USE STRATEGIES THAT HELP EXPAND YOUR WRITING, RESEARCH, AND THINKING SKILLS. Try something new. For example, if you usually read to get started writing, consider using the field research strategies (3.5) for a change.

3.3 WRITING ON A TOPIC

CHOOSING A TOPIC

If your assignment is to write an essay on a topic you choose yourself, here are five ways to find a good topic:

1. USE YOUR EXPERTISE. Use your expertise to explain your interest, hobby, or activity to someone unfamiliar with it or to help someone acquire or improve a skill—like taking nature photographs.

2. EXPLORE SOMETHING IN YOUR CULTURE. You may find interesting topics to explore in activities that are important to you and your friends, such as reading science fiction. Think about trends in clothing, music, or Web page design.

3. REMEMBER A MOMENT THAT POWERFULLY MOVED YOU. Think about things you have done, like giving a speech for the first time or backpacking in the mountains. Have you traveled someplace or visited a cultural landmark that impressed you, such as Martin Luther King Jr.'s grave, the Wall commemorating soldiers who died in the Vietnam War, or the Holocaust Museum?

4. CHOOSE A TOPIC YOU WANT TO KNOW MORE ABOUT. Explore something you'd like to learn about. What is Java Script? What kinds of computer operating systems besides Windows are available? What is the history of the National Collegiate Athletic Association? What different careers could you pursue with your major? What happened to women's professional baseball?

5. SURF THE NET. Use Internet search directories to explore interests you already have or things you'd like to learn more about. Use several directories that have the categories for hobbies, celebrities, entertainment, politics, international cultures, and lifestyles. Look around your room for books, magazines, CDs, souvenirs, even T-shirts, and use their specific names as terms for search engines. Remember the "I love San Francisco" T-shirt your parents bought for you when you were eight years old? Look up some of the landmarks on the shirt, such as the Golden Gate Bridge or even Alcatraz!

MAKING AN ASSIGNED TOPIC YOUR OWN

If you have been given a general topic to write about, try to connect that topic to your own interests and experience. Suppose you are asked to write about free enterprise for a course in economics. If you've ever sold anything of your own, whether goods or services (such as lawn mowing or baby-sitting), you know what it means to run a business of your own. If at different times you've worked for someone else and for yourself, you have firsthand experience of the difference between the predictability of a set wage and the unpredictability of profit, between security and risk. So personal experience can help you find your way into a topic that may at first seem large and abstract.

NARROWING A TOPIC

You will be able to explore a topic more effectively if it is not too broad. Connecting a topic to your personal experience, as described above, is one way of narrowing a topic. You can also narrow a topic by considering its subcategories and thinking about specific examples. Suppose you have been given the assignment of writing an essay on values in education. Think of subcategories related to the general topic; next think of examples of those subcategories; then try to think of even more specific examples.

General Topic: Values in Education

Subcategories	Examples	More Specific Examples
types of values	honesty	honor codes
value controversies	random drug testing	civil liberties versus reducing drugs in school
	sex education	making condoms available at school

3.4 STRATEGIES FOR EXPLORING THROUGH WRITING

Once you have narrowed a topic to a manageable size, the following strategies can help you recall what you already know about the topic, to view that knowledge in new ways, and to discover its implications. Often these strategies will help you see where you need to learn more about your topic through research and writing.

BRAINSTORMING

Brainstorming can break the hammerlock of your inhibitions and anxieties by releasing ideas and feelings that may be hidden inside you. At its simplest, brainstorming means beginning with a topic or an idea, putting pen to paper or fingers to keyboard, and setting down whatever comes to mind. When brainstorming, you needn't worry about paragraphing, spelling, or punctuation, and if you're using a computer, you can dim the lights of your monitor so that you can't even see what you're writing. To give brainstorming a try, start writing this way for at least five minutes.

BRANCHING AND LOOPING

Branching and looping help you explore a subject by creating a picture of related ideas and a pattern of connections. Branching starts with a single word or phrase and grows from there by a process of association—but not free association. Since all main branches radiate from one key term, branching is a process of exploring the implications of that term, of seeing the range and variety of thoughts it can evoke, of moving from the general to the specific.

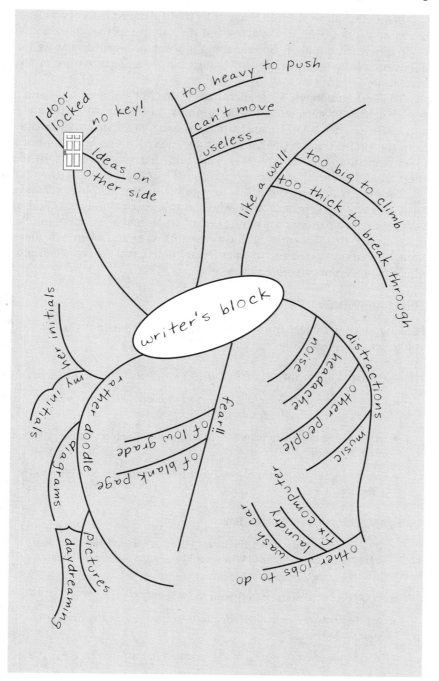

Branching allows the mind to wander to the detailed ends of an idea—the most slender twigs of the tree—and then return to the source to develop a new main branch. So branching is a way of organizing as well as discovering your ideas—a way of brainstorming and patterning at the same time.

The best equipment for branching is a sheet of unlined paper and a pen or pencil. To start, write a word or phrase in the middle of the sheet and circle it. Then add a main branch for each idea that grows directly from the circled term, a smaller branch for each idea that sprouts from a main branch, and so on. You may soon find that you have to turn the sheet around to continue writing.

Looping is the periodic return to your main idea. Looping prefigures what an essay does, for example, which is to create from a collection of various points a pattern of meaning organized around a central point. So, in returning to the center of the branching diagram when you have thought your way to the end of a particular branch, you are actually beginning the process of organizing an essay.

TRIPLE-VIEWING

Looking at your subject from these three different perspectives can lead you to see new possibilities.

THINK ABOUT YOUR SUBJECT IN ITS CONTEXT

▶ How would you describe this subject to someone unfamiliar with it? What are its distinctive features?

▶ Who are the important people associated with the subject? What roles do they play?

▶ Where are the important places associated with the subject? Why are they significant?

THINK ABOUT YOUR SUBJECT IN TIME

▶ What do you know about the history of your subject? How has your subject changed over time? Where could you go to learn more about its history?

▶ What is your personal history with the subject?

▶ Are there any causes (reasons) or effects (consequences) associated with your subject?

▶ What changes in your subject do you expect in the future?

THINK ABOUT YOUR SUBJECT IN RELATION TO OTHER SUBJECTS

▶ In what different classifications can you place your subject? (For example, if you are exploring punk music, would you say there are different types of punk?)

▶ Using your answers above, how does your subject compare to and contrast with members of the same classification? (For example, how is one type of punk different from another?) How does it compare and contrast with different classifications? (For example, how is punk similar to and different from, say, techno music?)

▶ Can you make a creative comparison (or analogy) for your subject? (For example, listening to punk music is like. . . .)

DRAMATIZING THE TOPIC WITH QUESTIONS

Another way of generating ideas about a topic is to dramatize it with six basic questions:

▶ What happened? (the action)

▶ Who was involved? (agents, spectators, and anyone else affected by it)

▶ When and where did it happen? (the setting)

▶ How did it happen? (the method)

▶ Why did it happen? (the cause or motive)

▶ What effect did it have? (the consequence)

To see how this dramatizing method works in practice, suppose your topic is the effect of acid rain on trees. You can investigate it with questions like these:

What does acid rain do to trees? What happens to their leaves? What do their roots do? What happens to the bark and branches?

Who is responsible for acid rain? If it comes from the burning of high-sulfur industrial fuels, which industries are burning them? Who runs those industries? And who is affected by the damage that acid rain does to trees?

When and where does acid rain affect trees? What parts of the world or the country are most affected? How does a forest appear after an acid rainfall? How often does acid rain fall?

How does acid rain develop? How does the acid get to the clouds? How do the clouds carry the acid to the forests?

Why does acid rain occur? Is it because we are burning too much fuel? Is it because we are using the wrong kind of fuel? Is it because we care more about promoting industry than protecting the environment?

What effect does the damage to trees have? How does it affect the timber supply? What does it do to birds and other wildlife? How does it affect people living near forests or elsewhere? Does acid rain reduce the capacity of trees to absorb carbon dioxide? If so, how much more global warming will result?

To answer all of these questions, you would need to do some reading and research (3.5 and 3.6). But when you dramatize your topic with questions, you are decisively beginning to investigate it.

EXERCISE 1   **Asking Questions to Dramatize Your Topic**

Using each of the six categories illustrated by the example given above, ask at least twelve questions about your topic.

QUESTIONING ASSUMPTIONS ABOUT GENDER, RACE, AND CLASS

Any piece of writing may be driven by unstated assumptions about gender, race, class, or all three. To see how much these assumptions drive your own writing, use the questions below.

QUESTIONS ABOUT GENDER

▶ Are women or men classified by negative terms?

▶ Are members of either gender reduced to categorical terms, such as *dependent* for women and *independent* for men?

▶ Is either gender treated as essentially superior to the other?

▶ Is heterosexuality treated as normal and homosexuality as abnormal?

QUESTIONS ABOUT RACE

▶ Are negative terms used to describe racial and ethnic identities?

▶ Are racial stereotypes at work?

QUESTIONS ABOUT CLASS

▶ Are economic issues being addressed or ignored?

▶ Are there assumptions that money does not play a role in power and influence?

▶ Are class stereotypes at work?

3.5 EXPLORING THROUGH TALKING AND OBSERVING

SHARING IDEAS WITH OTHERS

One of the simplest ways to explore a subject is to share your ideas with others. Try first to explain your subject to a friend, then try to explain why the subject is important to you. Invite your friend to ask you questions. Often someone else can detect dissonances that are not obvious to you. Taking notes on your friend's questions and observations may make the discussion more useful for your writing project.

DOING FIELD RESEARCH

Field research is a way of learning based on careful observation. Field researchers often supplement observation with interviews and surveys. This kind of research can be especially important when you explore your own culture because it allows you to build on your own knowledge and experience.

Field research, together with small-scale surveys and individual interviews, is called qualitative research. When you conduct qualitative research, the conclusions you reach can be applied only to the group you study, not other groups like it. For example, when Terri's teacher assigned to students the task of exploring something in their own culture, Terri decided to focus on her friends who attend their university's football games. The conclusions Terri reached after doing field research offered some very interesting insights about this group of students; however, Terri couldn't apply those conclusions to students in general. Only specialized statistical research can lead to conclusions about groups in general.

Basic field observation research can be divided into three stages:

1. Constructing research questions

2. Observing and notetaking

3. Interpreting notes (or data)

The process of conducting surveys and interviews can be divided into three stages as well:

1. Creating interview or survey questions

2. Conducting the interview or administering the survey

3. Interpreting interview responses or survey results

CONSTRUCTING RESEARCH QUESTIONS AND HYPOTHESES   Because there is no limit to the different things you can observe, especially in an activity that is important to you, your research should be guided by questions or hypotheses that you believe are important to investigate. Usually that means exploring a hunch or a contradiction—or perhaps what you think is a misunderstanding about the group and its activities.

Research Questions   Research questions should be designed to help you focus on important dimensions of the subject. They should not be yes/no questions. For example, Steve wanted to explore the interactions of people in his favorite chatroom. One question he wanted to explore was "Why do people participate in chatrooms?"

Hypotheses   Another way of guiding field research is to state judgments about the activity that your observation will either confirm or contradict. For example, Steve had been participating in several Internet chatrooms. He was a rather shy person, and he had thought many times about the reasons people joined chatrooms. He chose one hypothesis that he wanted to explore using field observation and a survey. His hypothesis: People who are active participants in Internet chatrooms are uncomfortable in ordinary social situations.

OBSERVING AND NOTETAKING   Doing field research places you in a complex situation because you must balance your role as a participant and as an observer. Your role as researcher requires you to step back from your ordinary engagement with the group or activity—to try to pretend you are an outsider—though, of course, you are not.

Taking the Role of Observer   In most cases, you will need to explain your project to the group and get their approval. Advanced field research involves observing an activity more than once—the more the better. In beginning field research, two times may be enough; and it is important that your observations take place in the same conditions—the same hour and place, for example. Usually you have to do something concrete to clarify your role as observer—setting your chair apart from the group, for example. If you are observing a chatroom, you might want to indicate when you logged on, but you could *not* participate in the discussion.

Taking Notes   Your notetaking should aim to capture the details of the experience. You want to be sure to note:

people	activities
places	conversations

If you are doing advanced field research, you may want to tape or video record the experience. In some cases, you may want to have a written transcript of conversations in order to study them in more detail.

INTERPRETING YOUR NOTES Your notes should be used either to answer your research question or to confirm or contradict your research hypothesis. Field researchers do this in a number of ways. Two common ways are analysis and coding.

Analysis When you analyze your notes, you observe significant patterns in the experience and the behavior of the participants. For example, Steve focused on the different types of interactions people had in the chatroom. He divided their interactions into four categories: questions, detailed answers, short reactions, and explanations.

Coding Coding means putting notes in the patterns or categories you derive from your analysis. This process should further help you in answering your question or exploring your hypothesis because it helps you understand which types of behavior seem to be most important. Steve studied transcripts of his chatroom and classified participants' interactions using his four categories.

CONDUCTING AN INTERVIEW

Interviews can give you information that is hard to find simply through observation. Interview responses are not hard scientific data, but they can help provide insights into more dimensions of the group or activity you are exploring. One of the reasons you must be careful in interpreting interview responses is that people who are interviewed sometimes try to "help out" the interviewer by giving responses they think the interviewer wants. Of course, this isn't any help if you're really trying to find out what others are thinking. You can avoid problems like this by carefully constructing your interview questions in advance and testing them out on friends or a few willing participants from the group you are studying.

For the interview itself, you must have a setting that will be free of interruptions, and you will need to have a dependable means of recording responses. If you conduct more than one interview and you want to compare responses, make sure you give the same questions to each person in the same or comparable conditions. (For an in-depth discussion of conducting an interview, see 37.6.)

Interview Question Guidelines

1. Edit your interview questions for clarity.

2. Avoid asking yes/no questions.

3. Avoid asking questions designed to elicit a particular response. For example: "Isn't it true that . . . ?"

4. Ask questions related to your research question or hypothesis.

CREATING A SURVEY

A survey for basic field research can take two forms: multiple-choice and open-ended. For example, a multiple-choice question for Steve's survey of chatroom participants might be:

How often do you visit this chatroom?

> a. less than once a month
> b. once a month
> c. once a week
> d. once a day
> e. more than once a day

You could make this an open-ended question by leaving blank space where you now have a range of answers. Or you could ask an open-ended question tailored to elicit more about participants' attitudes:

How would you describe the role this chatroom plays in your social life?

In what kinds of social situations are you the most comfortable?

Obviously, it is much easier to compare the results of a multiple-choice survey. For example, you can analyze responses and determine that 10 percent of the participants visit the chatroom more than once a day, 20 percent visit once a week, etc.

EXERCISE 2   **Creating a Survey**

1. Create a survey Steve could use online to investigate his hypothesis that avid chatroom participants are uncomfortable in traditional social situations. What challenges does such a survey present?

2. Create a survey you could use to explore something in your culture.

Conducting Field Research

1. Your conclusions apply only to the group you study.

2. Balance your role as participant with your role as observer.

3. Have a dependable means for recording your observations.

4. Use your research questions or your hypotheses to guide your analysis of what you observe.

5. Carefully construct your interview and survey questions and test your questions before using them.

3.6 EXPLORING THROUGH READING: GUIDELINES FOR ACTIVE READING

Reading is one of the main ways you expand the limits of your knowledge and experience. Reading can help you get started on a writing project; it can provide you with the information and understanding you need to write well. **Active reading** involves understanding the context in which something was written—its author, source and date of publication, audience, scope, and purpose. Active reading also involves knowing how to explore a text, the way a miner might hunt for gold. To show you how to read a text actively, this section raises a series of questions about the following excerpt from Lani Guinier's *The Tyranny of the Majority* (1994):

> I have always wanted to be a civil rights lawyer. This lifelong ambition is based on a deep-seated commitment to democratic fair play—to playing by the rules as long as the rules are fair. When the rules seem unfair, I have worked to change them, not subvert them. When I was eight years old, I was a Brownie. I was especially proud of my uniform, which represented a commitment to good citizenship and good deeds. But one day, when my Brownie group staged a hatmaking contest, I realized that uniforms are only as honorable as the people who wear them. The contest was rigged. The winner was assisted by her milliner mother, who actually made the winning entry in full view of all the participants. At the time, I was too young to be able to change the rules, but I was old enough to resign, which I promptly did.
>
> To me, fair play means that the rules encourage everyone to play. They should reward those who win, but they must be acceptable to those who lose. The central theme of my academic writing is that not all rules lead to elemental fair play. Some even commonplace rules work against it.

The professional milliner competing with amateur Brownies stands as an example of rules that are patently rigged or patently subverted. Yet, sometimes, even when rules are perfectly fair in form, they serve in practice to exclude particular groups from meaningful participation. When they do not encourage everyone to play, or when, over the long haul, they do not make the losers feel as good about the outcomes as the winners, they can seem as unfair as the milliner who makes the winning hat for her daughter.

Sometimes, too, we construct rules that force us to be divided into winners and losers when we might have otherwise joined together. This idea was cogently expressed by my son, Nikolas, when he was four years old, far exceeding the thoughtfulness of his mother when she was an eight-year-old Brownie. While I was writing one of my law journal articles, Nikolas and I had a conversation about voting prompted by a *Sesame Street Magazine* exercise. The magazine pictured six children: four children had raised their hands because they wanted to play tag; two had their hands down because they wanted to play hide-and-seek. The magazine asked its readers to count the number of children whose hands were raised and then decide what game the children would play.

Nikolas quite realistically replied, "They will play both. First they will play tag. Then they will play hide-and-seek." Despite the magazine's "rules," he was right. To children, it is natural to take turns. The winner may get to play first or more often, but even the "loser" gets something. His was a positive-sum solution that many adult rule-makers ignore.

The traditional answer to the magazine's problem would have been a zero-sum solution: "The children—all the children—will play tag, and only tag." As a zero-sum solution, everything is seen in terms of "I win; you lose." The conventional answer relies on winner-take-all majority rule, in which the tag players, as the majority, win the right to decide for all the children what game to play. The hide-and-seek preference becomes irrelevant. The numerically more powerful majority choice simply subsumes minority preferences.

In the conventional case, the majority that rules gains all the power and the minority that loses gets none. For example, two years ago Brother Rice High School in Chicago held two senior proms. It was not planned that way. The prom committee at Brother Rice, a boys' Catholic high school, expected just one prom when it hired a disc jockey, picked a rock band, and selected music for the prom by consulting student preferences. Each senior was asked to list his three favorite songs, and the band would play the songs that appeared most frequently on the lists.

Seems attractively democratic. But Brother Rice is predominantly white, and the prom committee was all white. That's how they got two proms. The black seniors at Brother Rice felt so shut out by the "democratic process" that they organized their own prom. As one black student put it: "For every vote we had, there were eight votes for what they wanted. . . . [W]ith us being in the minority we're always outvoted. It's as if we don't count."

Some embittered white seniors saw things differently. They complained that the black students should have gone along with the majority: "The majority makes a decision. That's the way it works."

In a way, both groups were right. From the white students' perspective, this was ordinary decisionmaking. To the black students, majority rule sent the message: "we don't count" is the "way it works" for minorities. In a racially divided society, majority rule may be perceived as majority tyranny.

That is a large claim, and I do not rest my case for it solely on the actions of the prom committee in one Chicago high school. To expand the range of the argument, I first consider the ideal of majority rule itself, particularly as reflected in the writings of James Madison and other founding members of our Republic. These early democrats explored the relationship between majority rule and democracy. James Madison warned, "If a majority be united by a common interest, the rights of the minority will be insecure." The tyranny of the majority, according to Madison, requires safeguards to protect "one part of the society against the injustice of the other part."

For Madison, majority tyranny represented the great danger to our early constitutional democracy. Although the American revolution was fought against the tyranny of the British monarch, it soon became clear that there was another tyranny to be avoided. The accumulations of all powers in the same hands, Madison warned, "whether of one, a few, or many, and whether hereditary, self-appointed, or elective, may justly be pronounced the very definition of tyranny."

As another colonist suggested in papers published in Philadelphia, "We have been so long habituated to a jealousy of tyranny from monarchy and aristocracy, that we have yet to learn the dangers of it from democracy." Despotism had to be opposed "whether it came from Kings, Lords or the people."

The debate about majority tyranny reflected Madison's concern that the majority may not represent the whole. In a homogeneous society, the interest of the majority would likely be that of the minority also. But in a heterogeneous community, the majority may not represent all competing interests. The majority is likely to be self-interested and ignorant or indifferent to the concerns of the minority. In such case, Madison observed, the assumption that the majority represents the minority is "altogether fictitious."

Yet even a self-interested majority can govern fairly if it cooperates with the minority. One reason for such cooperation is that the self-interested majority values the principle of reciprocity. The self-interested majority worries that the minority may attract defectors from the majority and become the next governing majority. The Golden Rule principle of reciprocity functions to check the tendency of a self-interested majority to act tyrannically.

So the argument for the majority principle connects it with the value of reciprocity: You cooperate when you lose in part because members of the current majority will cooperate when they lose. The conventional case for the fairness of majority rule is that it is not really the rule of a fixed group—The Majority—on all issues; instead it is the rule of shifting majorities, as the losers at one time or on one issue join with others and become part of the governing coalition at another time or on another issue. The result will be a fair system of mutually beneficial cooperation. I call a majority that rules but does not dominate a Madisonian Majority.

The problem of majority tyranny arises, however, when the self-interested majority does not need to worry about defectors. When the majority is fixed and permanent, there are no checks on its ability to be overbearing. A majority that does not worry about defectors is a majority with total power.

In such a case, Madison's concern about majority tyranny arises. In a heterogeneous community, any faction with total power might subject "the minority to the caprice and arbitrary decisions of the majority, who instead of consulting the interest of the whole community collectively, attend sometimes to partial and local advantages."

"What remedy can be found in a republican Government, where the majority must ultimately decide," argued Madison, but to ensure "that no one common interest or passion will be likely to unite a majority of the whole number in an unjust pursuit." The answer was to disaggregate the majority to ensure checks and balances or fluid, rotating interests. The minority needed protection against an overbearing majority, so that "a common sentiment is less likely to be felt, and the requisite concert less likely to be formed, by a majority of the whole."

Political struggles would not be simply a contest between rulers and people; the political struggles would be among the people themselves. The work of government was not to transcend different interests but to reconcile them. In an ideal democracy, the people would rule, but the minorities would also be protected against the power of majorities. Again, where the rules of decisionmaking protect the minority, the Madisonian Majority rules without dominating.

CONSIDERING THE CONTEXT

Consider the context in which the book or article was written. In order to understand *what* you are reading, you have to have some idea of *who* wrote it and *why*. Use the following checklist:

▶ Learn something about the author. Biographical information often appears at the beginning or end of an article or book and often on a book jacket (for biographical-research resources, see 36.4). This information will help you understand the author's purpose, and this will help you interpret what he or she has written. For example, if you had the book jacket to *The Tyranny of the Majority*, you would find a few sentences on the back cover explaining that Guinier graduated from Yale Law School, that she was a Special Assistant to Assistant Attorney General Drew S. Days III, that she had been a lawyer for the NAACP Legal Defense and Educational Fund, and that she is currently a professor of law at the University of Pennsylvania. This information can help you interpret what you read in several ways. You know that she has been thoroughly trained in the law, having graduated from one of the most prestigious law schools in the country; you know that she has had political experience, having worked in an attorney general's office. You also know that she has a history of dealing with civil rights issues, because she once worked with the NAACP. Finally, you know that her career has not been exclusively political, because she is a law professor at another prestigious university.

▶ Consider the date of publication and the press (if you're reading a book) or journal or magazine (if you're reading an article). Does the publication date affect the reliability of what you're reading? For example, an article about AIDS written ten years ago would not give an accurate picture of the disease, because the last decade has produced new and effective treatments. You should also know that some magazines and book presses support specific special interests. For example, as a magazine published by the Republican National Party, *The Rising Tide* expresses the values and perspectives of that party. Likewise, as a magazine published by the Labor Resource Center at Queens College, City University of New York, *New Labor Forum* supports the interests of labor unions. *The Rising Tide* can reliably tell you what strategists for the Republican Party think, and *New Labor Forum* can reliably tell you what labor unions want. But neither can be wholly objective on the topics of government and labor-management relations.

▶ Consider the full title and a book's table of contents. What do they tell you about the subject and the author's purpose? For example, the full title of Guinier's book is *The Tyranny of the Majority: Fundamental Fairness in a Representative Democracy*. That title almost tells you the thesis of Guinier's argument. She is writing about representative democracy, which is the kind of democracy practiced in the United States. You know that we vote to elect representatives and that the candidate winning the *majority* of the votes wins the election. You know that *tyranny* is a word with negative connotations. You might even look it up in the dictionary, where you would find definitions like "a government in which a single rule is vested with absolute power" and "absolute power, esp. when exercised unjustly or cruelly" (*The American Heritage Dictionary* 1350). Guinier is clearly suggesting that majority rule can have negative, even *tyrannical* consequences, and you can probably fairly guess that the book will discuss ways to create more *fairness* in our democracy.

▶ If you're reading a book, examine the foreword, preface, or introduction to learn how the author defines its purpose, audience, and scope. The foreword to Guinier's book, written by Stephen L. Carter, professor of law at Yale University, provides a summary of Guinier's argument.

LOOKING UP WORDS AND REFERENCES

Look up words and references to people and places that are unfamiliar to you. Keep a good dictionary nearby to look up unfamiliar words. Often dictionaries will identify people and places as well, sometimes in separate sections at the end of the dictionary. Desk encyclopedias can also be helpful, as are online and CD-ROM encyclopedias. For example, in the first paragraph of the excerpt from Guinier's book, you will find the word *milliner* and references to James Madison. You may guess the meaning of *milliner* and you may know a little bit about James Madison; however, taking a moment to confirm the meaning of the word or to find some background information on Madison can make a world of difference in accurately reading and fully understanding Guinier's discussion.

READING WITH QUESTIONS

Read with questions in mind. Write and revise your questions as you read. Reading with questions in mind helps you read more actively by forcing you to dig deeper—to *find* things as you read, instead of just letting your eyes move across the page. For example, you might begin reading Guinier's chapter with a question based on the title: "What is unfair about representative democracy?" As you read further, you may ask, "What does Guinier mean by a 'Madisonian Majority'"?

READING TO TAKE NOTES

Read prepared to take notes. Taking notes as you read helps you remember important points and understand how they are related. If you are reading a text you own, you may make notes in the margins and underline or highlight important points. However, writing out your notes is usually more effective in improving your comprehension of material.

READING WITH YOUR PURPOSE IN MIND

Reading a chapter in your physics textbook is obviously very different from reading the sports page to find out how the polls are ranking your college football team. Because reading literature (along with writing about it) is discussed in chapter 41, we focus here on the kind of reading you do in other courses and when you want to learn or understand something on your own.

Though you often read for more than one purpose, try to define the most important purpose as you prepare to read.

1. **READING FOR FACTUAL DETAILS** When you scan the newspaper for sports scores, stock quotes, and election results, you are usually reading for factual details. In your college assignments, you read for factual details when you need to memorize important dates or formulae. Reading for factual details assumes you already understand the concepts behind the details. For example, knowing that last week the Standard and Poor's 500 reached 1,275.47 and the Russell 2000 was up 5.86 won't mean much to you unless you understand the concepts behind these indexes of the stock market.

2. **READING TO LEARN ABOUT A SUBJECT** When you read a chapter in a college textbook, you are reading to learn about a subject. This kind of reading often includes factual details, but those details occur in the context of a more general discussion of a subject. Consequently, you need to understand how the book treats the subject.

For example, you may read a chapter in your economics textbook on the world economy. There are many ways of talking about the world economy. Your chapter, however, subdivides the subject into three parts: exchange rates, balance of payments, and trade deficits. As you read the chapter, you must first understand how these terms are being defined and then examine how they are related. Factual details will make sense only after you understand the general concepts.

3. **READING TO UNDERSTAND AN ARGUMENT** In your coursework and your daily life, you encounter many arguments designed to influence your attitudes and, in some cases, provoke you to take an action. Sometimes people make arguments simply to express their judgments on issues. To understand an argument, you must be able to determine four things: its *thesis, supporting points, evidence,* and *values and assumptions.*

The **thesis** of an argument is the overall attitude or judgment the author wants you to adopt or the action the author wants you to take.

The **supporting points** of an argument are the reasons the author provides to convince you of the argument's thesis.

Evidence consists of specific examples or facts the author uses to explain or defend the argument's supporting points.

Values and assumptions are the moral bases, principles, and attitudes—stated or unstated—that underlie the argument.

A good training of critical reading & thus critical thinking

37

EXAMPLE: A student has written a letter to the editor of the campus newspaper on the subject of the student activity fee. Here is an outline of her argument and her underlying point of view.

[handwritten note in margin: This statement is a normative statement.]

▶ thesis: "The student activity fee should be cut back to the level it was at in 1995."

▶ first supporting point: "Our university's activity fee is higher than that of any other college in our conference."

▶ evidence: She lists the activity fees for every Big Ten school.

▶ second supporting point: "The fee increase has not provided more support for any student organization."

▶ evidence: She lists the amount six student organizations received last year; her statistics show that their budgets were cut, not increased.

▶ values and assumptions: students should get their money's worth from increases in the activity fee.

IN BRIEF   **Guidelines for Active Reading**

1. Consider the context in which the book or article was written.
   ▶ Who wrote it and why? Where and when was it published?
   ▶ What do the title and table of contents tell you about what you're reading?
   ▶ How does the author describe the purpose, audience, and scope of the book in the foreword, preface, or introduction?
2. Look up unfamiliar words and references to people and places.
3. Read with questions in mind; revise your questions as you read, and write new ones as they occur to you.
4. Read with your purpose in mind.

3.7 WRITING IN RESPONSE TO READING

Throughout your college career and your life, you will probably be called on to write in response to reading. We focus here on two types of response: *subjective responses* and *analytical responses*.

SUBJECTIVE RESPONSES

One way to begin writing about anything you read is to write about the way it feels to *you*. Do you like or dislike it? Why? Is it easy to understand or difficult? Does it answer a question you've wondered about or tell you something you've never thought about before? Does it leave you with further questions? How do you feel about the author?

Usually you write a subjective response only for yourself—to help get your mind and heart into the subject. Unless your instructor has asked you to turn in your subjective response as an assignment, don't worry about paragraphing and punctuation as you write. The point of most subjective responses is to help you actively engage what you are reading.

The paragraphs below were written by a student in response to the excerpt from Guinier's *The Tyranny of the Majority*.

> Well, Guinier begins with what it was like for her to be treated unfairly when she was a kid. All kids have some experiences with this. Can I think of some times when I felt like a minority who never got a turn?
>
> My example is like the one Guinier gives about kids taking turns playing games. I am afraid I remember being one of the kids who was unfair to another kid. I was really young, like 7, but I still remember it; and it still feels awful to think about it. A kid in our neighborhood had a kidney disease—he died before he got to junior high. We used to vote on what games we would play—kickball or hide and seek. Because of his illness, he couldn't run very fast. I don't remember why playing hide and seek involved more running than kickball, but I guess it did. When we'd start to play hide and seek, he'd say that he wanted to play something else. We didn't ignore him. We said, ok, let's take a vote; but, of course, he never won; he was always outvoted. It seemed like voting was "playing fair." But it also sort of seems like the "election" was rigged.
>
> Guinier quotes Madison writing, "If a majority be united by a common interest, the rights of the minority will be insecure." I know she's going to focus on race; it's interesting that she doesn't just dive right into it. But she does get you thinking about basic experiences of unfairness and then relating them to really complicated political, governmental stuff. . . . How do the interests of majorities and minorities get pulled so far apart?
>
> The "principle of reciprocity"—accepting defeat. The minority is supposed to accept defeat because. . . . Because why? Basically, she says the minority has "to trust" that the majority will "be fair." That either people will be minorities in some situations but parts of a majority in others—like being one of only 3 girls in my physics class of 50 students, but being one of 13 girls in my English class of 20. But Guinier's point is: What happens if you never change minority or majority roles—if you're always either one or the other. And the minority has to trust the majority to be fair. Well, that kid in my neighborhood wasn't stupid. We voted but he knew we weren't fair to him.

As you can see from this student's writing, subjective responses don't ignore the subject matter of the reading. Instead, they relate elements of the reading to your experiences, ideas, and feelings.

ANALYTICAL RESPONSES

To analyze a piece of writing is to take it apart in order to show how the writer explains a subject or makes an argument (2.3, "Purpose"). Once you identify the components of a piece, you can explain their relation to each other and to the chief point the writer is trying to make. (To be sure that you understand a writer's main point, you must know whether he or she is being straightforward or ironic; see 2.3, "Tone.")

FINDING THE WRITER'S MAIN POINT   To find the writer's main point, you can do one or more of the following:

1.   USE THE TITLE AS A GUIDE.   "Where College Fails Us," the title of an essay by Caroline Bird (see pp. 75–76), clearly forecasts her main point and enables readers to recognize this point when it appears in the first sentence of her second paragraph: "But college has never been able to work its magic for everyone."

2.   LOOK FOR THE MAIN POINT IN THE FIRST SENTENCE OF THE OPENING PARAGRAPH.

> People feel safer behind some kind of physical barrier. If a social situation is in any way threatening, then there is an immediate urge to set up such a barricade. For a tiny child faced with a stranger, the problem is usually solved by hiding behind its mother's body and peeping out at the intruder to see what he or she will do next. If the mother's body is not available, then a chair or some other piece of solid furniture will do. If the stranger insists on coming closer, then the peeping face must be hidden too. If the insensitive intruder continues to approach despite these obvious signals of fear, then there is nothing for it but to scream or flee.
> —Desmond Morris, *Manwatching: A Field Guide to Human Behavior*

3.   LOOK FOR THE MAIN POINT IN THE LAST SENTENCE OF THE OPENING PARAGRAPH.

> In her stunning memoir of bicultural girlhood, *The Woman Warrior*, Maxine Hong Kingston writes, "There is a Chinese word for the female *I*—which is 'slave.' Break the women with their own tongues!" English contains no such dramatic instance of the ways in which language shapes women's reality. We can, after all, use the same "I" as men do. We can, but we're not supposed to, at least not often. In myriad ways the rules of polite

discourse in this country serve, among other purposes, not to enslave but certainly to silence women and thus to prevent them from uttering the truth about their lives.

—Nancy Mairs, "Who Are You?"

4. WATCH FOR THE MAIN POINT TO BE IMPLIED.

I once choked a chicken to death. It was my only barefaced, not to say barehanded, confrontation with death and the killer in me and it happened on my grandparents' farm. I couldn't have been more than nine or ten and no firearms were included or necessary. I was on my knees and the chicken fluttered its outstretched wings with the last of the outraged protest. I gripped, beyond release, above its swollen crop, its beak gaping, translucent eyelids sliding up and down. . . . My grandfather, who was widely traveled and world-wise, in his eighties then, and had just started using a cane from earlier times, came tapping at that moment around the corner of the chicken coop and saw what I was doing and started gagging at the hideousness of it, did a quick assisted spin away and never again, hours later nor for the rest of his life, for that matter, ever mentioned the homicidal incident to me. Keeping his silence, he seemed to understand; and yet whenever I'm invaded by the incident, the point of it seems to be his turning away from me.

—Larry Woiwode, "Guns"

The last sentence states the would-be point of the incident but merely implies the main point of the paragraph: the grandfather's turning away made the writer recognize himself as a killer.

5. WATCH FOR THE MAIN POINT TO EMERGE.   In Caroline Bird's "Where College Fails Us," the main point emerges in the second paragraph.

Identifying the Main Point   EXERCISE 3

In each of the following passages, one sentence expresses the main point. Identify that sentence.

1. The history of Florida is measured in freezes. Severe ones, for example, occurred in 1747, 1766, and 1774. The freeze of February, 1835, was probably the worst one in the state's history. But, because more growers were affected, the Great Freeze of 1895 seems to enjoy the same sort of status in Florida that the Blizzard of '88 once held in the North. Temperatures on the Ridge on February 8, 1895, went into the teens for much of the night. It is said that some orange growers, on being told what was happening out in the groves, got

up from their dinner tables and left the state. In the morning, it was apparent that the Florida citrus industry had been virtually wiped out.

—John McPhee, "Oranges"

2. In early human history a Stone Age, a Bronze Age, or an Iron Age came into unhurried gestation and endured for centuries or even millennia; and as one technology gradually displaced or merged with another, the changes wrought in any single lifetime were easily absorbed, if noticed at all. But a transformation has come about in our own time. A centenarian born in 1879 has seen, in the years of his own life, scientific and technological advances more sweeping and radical than those that took place in all the accumulated past. He has witnessed—and felt the personal impact of—the Age of Electricity, the Automobile Age, the Aviation Age, the Electronic Age, the Atomic Age, the Space Age, and the Computer Age, to name but a few of the "ages" that have been crowding in upon us at such an unprecedented rate, sometimes arriving virtually side by side. Let us use the shortcut designation the "Age of Science" to encompass them all.

—Albert Rosenfeld, "How Anxious Should Science Make Us?"

JUDGING THE SUPPORTING POINTS IN AN ESSAY   To summarize an essay, you must be able to identify its main point and its chief supporting points. To analyze an essay, you must also be able to judge the relevance and strength of each supporting point. You should therefore try to answer these questions:

1.   ARE THE SUPPORTING POINTS STATEMENTS OF FACT OR OPINIONS?   A statement of fact can be indisputably verified. An opinion is a statement that may be impossible to verify but can be supported by facts—and usually needs such support to make an impression on the reader.

Since an opinion cannot stand on its own feet, you should take a hard look at what is said to support it. Sometimes there is no supporting statement at all, and sometimes the supporting statement turns out to be nothing but another opinion. When a writer says that "young people no longer work seriously" to persuade us that the nation is declining, the supporting statement is mere opinion. It cannot be verified until we know who the "young people" are, what their "work" is, and how to measure their seriousness.

Between a statement of fact and an opinion stands another kind of statement: the assertion made with a number. Suppose you read that there are eight million rats in New York City. This looks like a statement that can be checked and verified—a fact. But who can actually count the number of rats in New York? Contrary to popular belief, numbers have no special authority over words. The figures a writer cites are only as reliable as the methods used to get them or the source from which they come.

In general, therefore, you should read with a question mark between you and the page. Be on the watch for deceptive exaggeration, "figures" that come out of thin air, and editorial opinion masquerading as reportorial fact. Life is too short for you to check out every unsupported claim or surprising new "fact" for yourself; usually you must trust the writer. But you can reasonably ask that a writer earn your trust—by respecting the difference between statements of fact and opinions.

2. ARE THERE ENOUGH SUPPORTING POINTS?   In the paragraph on barriers (p. 40), Desmond Morris's main point is that "people feel safer behind some kind of physical barrier," and he supports this point by describing what a child does when confronted by a stranger. But Morris's paragraph on the child is merely the opening of a chapter in which he describes the barrier signals that grown-ups use, the subtle movements and postures with which adults continue to shield themselves in unfamiliar company. By citing specific examples of adult as well as child behavior, Morris convincingly supports his point in the chapter as a whole.

3. ARE THE SUPPORTING POINTS RELEVANT TO THE MAIN POINT?   A main point "supported" by irrelevant points is like a house trying to rest on a foundation that is laid beside it. If, for instance, a writer wants to show that women should not be allowed to engage in combat, the fact that many women do not want to serve in the armed forces at all is irrelevant. The question is whether the women who *do* want to fight should be allowed to do so.

4. HAS THE WRITER CONSIDERED OPPOSING POINTS?   To be wholly convincing, an argument must recognize the major points that can be set against it (11.6). When you read a completely one-sided essay on a subject you know has at least two sides, you may be sure that the argument is slanted.

5. ARE THERE ANY FALLACIES IN THE WRITER'S ARGUMENT?   Fallacies are mistakes in reasoning (11.5).

Analyzing a Paragraph

Read the following paragraph and answer these questions: (1) What is the main point? (2) What are the supporting points? (3) Are any of the supporting points not strictly relevant to the main point? (4) Which sentences are statements of fact and which are opinions?

[1] No wild animal has been a greater incitement to the discovery of new worlds than the beaver. [2] North America was largely explored by men seeking to profit from an insatiable European market for felt hats made from shorn and pressed beaver fur. [3] The Hudson's Bay Company, established in 1669 to trade with the Indians for beaver pelts, was the effective government of most of Canada from the French and Indian War until the mid-nineteenth century. [4] American beaver traders such as Jedediah Smith preceded gold miners and settlers to the West Coast by several decades. [5] During the height of the beaver trade, after the steel trap began to be produced industrially and before new felt-making processes depressed the price of a beaver pelt by some 80 percent, a beaver trapper could average a daily income estimated at thirty-two times that of a farm laborer. [6] It's no wonder that mountain men explored every watershed from Santa Fe to Vancouver in the 1820s. [7] Even after beaver prices fell in the 1840s, an estimated 500,000 beavers were being killed every year, primarily for their fur, which was (and is) used to make coats and collars.

—David Rains Wallace, "The Mind of the Beaver"

Reading Analytically

Tone

What is the writer's attitude toward the subject?
Can the writing be taken at face value, or is it ironic?

Main Point

What is the writer's main point?
Where is it stated or how is it implied?

Supporting Points

What are the supporting points?
Are the supporting points facts or opinions?
Are there enough supporting points?
Are they relevant to the main point?
Has the writer considered opposing points of view?
Are there any fallacies in the writer's argument?

SUMMARIZING

Summarizing a piece of writing is a good way to test and demonstrate your understanding of it. The summary of an essay should begin by stating its main point and then proceed to the chief supporting points.

> The gist of Guinier's argument is that majority rule is not necessarily fair rule because the majority does not always reflect the whole. First, the majority may not have the same interests—or concerns—as the minority. As an example, Guinier describes the conflict over prom music at a predominantly white Chicago high school. African American students decided to have their own prom because every time the school voted on the type of music that would be played at the prom, they were outvoted by white students. Second, majority rule is not fair when the majority always contains the same members. According to Guinier, majority rule is fair only when there is "reciprocity." In other words, people are willing to "lose" on some issues when they know they have a chance to "win" on others. A majority will try harder to be fair if its members know they will someday be in the minority. When groups in a democracy don't take turns winning, there is no reciprocity; and Guinier argues that without reciprocity majority rule will eventually be unfair.

Summarizing

EXERCISE 5

Summarize the essay "Insiders and Outsiders in Japanese Society" (in 6.8).

PARAPHRASING

Paraphrasing is restating a short passage in your own words. Besides demonstrating your understanding of what you read, paraphrasing enables you to discuss texts without quoting every word of them. If you plan to analyze a particular passage in detail, you should quote it in full. But if you simply want to convey the essential point of the passage, you can paraphrase all or part of it.

> QUOTATION: According to Thoreau, the legendary Kouroo artist spent hundreds of years making a perfect staff because, "having considered that in an imperfect work time is an ingredient, but into a perfect work time does not enter, he said to himself, 'It shall be perfect in all respects, though I should do nothing else in my life.'"

> PARAPHRASE: According to Thoreau, the legendary Kouroo artist spent hundreds of years making a perfect staff because he believed that time had nothing to do with perfection, and he was willing to spend his whole life pursuing it.

While the quotation makes an awkward bulge in the writer's sentence, the paraphrase fits nicely. Slightly compressing the original, it clearly expresses Thoreau's essential point. (When paraphrasing, be sure to acknowledge your source. If you don't, you will be guilty of plagiarism [37.8].)

EXERCISE 6   **Paraphrasing**

Restate each of the following passages in one sentence, using your own words.

1. Most people who bother with the matter at all would admit that the English language is in a bad way, but it is generally assumed that we cannot by conscious action do anything about it.
   —George Orwell

2. A good city street neighborhood achieves a marvel of balance between its people's determination to have essential privacy and their simultaneous wishes for differing degrees of contract, enjoyment, or help from people around.
   —Jane Jacobs

WRITING AN INTERPRETIVE ESSAY

To interpret a piece of writing is to explain what it means. Though interpretation calls for many of the analytical skills discussed above, it commonly aims not so much to judge as to elucidate: to show what the writer has to teach us. Essentially, an interpretive essay constructs an argument *about* the writer's meaning. Here is an example:

THOREAU'S TREATMENT OF TIME IN *WALDEN*

Henry David Thoreau's *Walden* is an account of the author's attempt to remove himself from society and live a life of self-sufficiency at Walden Pond. Yet strangely enough, Thoreau seems highly preoccupied with one of the very things that dominate the society he has left behind: time. If he is truly independent of society, if he has really forsaken the world of clock-watching business managers and wage-earners, why is he so concerned with measuring time? Why does he have so much to say about it? The answer, I think, is that Thoreau measures his life at Walden not by clock time but by nature's time: not in hours and minutes but in mornings, evenings, seasons, deaths, and births.

Thoreau is sufficiently free from conventional notions of time that he can imagine a life without any time at all. He illustrates such a life with the story of the Kouroo artist who set out to make the perfect staff, and who devoted hundreds of years to the project because he believed that

Introduction: topic leads to question; question leads to statement of thesis.

time had nothing to do with perfection, and he was willing to spend his whole life pursuing it. "As he made no compromise with Time," says Thoreau, "Time kept out of his way, and only sighed at a distance because he [Time] could not overcome him" (218). This story represents the ideal state that Thoreau would like to achieve. For him, the ultimate achievement would be to make time stand still.

Supporting point #1: story of Kouroo artist shows the ideal of freedom from time.

But Thoreau knows that time cannot be stopped. At Walden, therefore, he decides to regulate his life not by the clock time that mechanically runs society but by the natural cycles that govern every living thing on earth, and even the earth itself. The morning of each new day at Walden marks the beginning of a new life, just as spring marks the awakening of the pond from its long winter's death. Thoreau measures his life at Walden by these natural patterns of cyclic renewal. Though he actually spent two years at Walden Pond, he compresses the story of his sojourn into just one complete cycle that begins with the building of his house in the spring and ends—after summer and fall and the chill of winter—with the glorious return of spring. "As every season seems best to us in its turn," he writes, "so the coming in of spring is like the creation of Cosmos out of Chaos and the realization of the Golden Age" (209). The calendar might say that he was one or two years older, but Thoreau feels reborn when spring returns.

Supporting point #2: Thoreau was reborn each morning and in the spring.

In Thoreau's concept of time, hours and minutes give way to the immeasurable rhythms of nature and life itself. He ends *Walden* with the story of the bug that suddenly emerged from the wood of a table. Many years before, its egg had been deposited in the tree from which the table was made; one day it gnawed its way out, "hatched perchance by the heat of an urn" (222). With no knowledge of how many years it had been buried and no desire to find out, it simply appeared because it had reached at last the peak of its life-cycle.

Supporting point #3: story of bug illustrates triumph over time.

In *Walden,* then, Thoreau urges us to disregard the years in which we have imprisoned ourselves and to stop measuring our existence by the clock and calendar. Instead, he shows us how to measure existence by the number of times we experience a renewal of our lives.

Conclusion

WORKS CITED

Thoreau, Henry D. *Walden.* Ed. William Rossi. 2nd ed. New York: Norton, 1992.

This analysis of *Walden* illustrates a good way of organizing an interpretive essay. The author (a first-year college student) begins with a specific topic (Thoreau's concept of time), defines a problem (the conflict between a desire for freedom and a preoccupation with time), and then proposes a solution in the form of a thesis (Thoreau measures life at Walden not by clock time but by nature's time). To develop the thesis, he writes three paragraphs on three specific things from the text: the story of the Kouroo artist, the passage on spring, and the story of the bug. In each of these paragraphs he quotes from *Walden,* but only enough to make his points.

He uses paraphrase to keep down the amount of material quoted and thus to keep the reader's eye on the line of interpretation he develops.

(For further advice on writing about works of literature and for guidance on writing research papers about literary topics, see chapter 41 and sections 42.4 and 42.5.)

EXERCISE 7   **Introducing an Interpretive Essay**

Following the model shown above, write the introductory paragraph for an interpretive essay on any work chosen by you or your teacher. Your paragraph should (1) identify a topic, (2) define a problem, and (3) propose a solution in the form of a thesis to be developed.

EXERCISE 8   **Writing an Interpretive Essay**

Using the thesis generated for the previous exercise, write an interpretive essay in which you specifically refer to at least three passages from the work you have chosen. Include at least three quotations from the work, but be careful to limit the length of each one.

3.8 ANALYZING ADVERTISING

Every day you are surrounded by messages and images from media such as television, the Internet, newspapers, and radio. Many of these messages and images are advertisements for products and services. Analyzing an ad can show you how it tries to manipulate your assumptions, desires, and insecurities. Analyzing ads can also help you understand how values in your culture are created and reinforced. For example, despite the record of women's achievements in the last century, many ads still suggest that a woman's most important achievement is finding the right man.

Advertisers create messages that appeal to the needs of specific audiences, called *target audiences*. When you analyze advertising, look for three things:

1. the ad's target audience

2. appeals to the needs of the target audience

3. product claims

TARGET AUDIENCES

Stereotypes based on gender identification are almost always used in advertising. To help determine the target audience for an ad, try to see how it classifies the genders. For example, is the ad appealing to a young adult man's desire to be strong and independent or a young adult woman's desire to be attractive? Or are both genders included in the target audience?

Sample target audiences

- elementary and junior high girls and/or boys
- high school girls and/or boys
- young single women and/or men
- young married women and/or men

APPEALS TO NEEDS

Advertisers appeal to many types of needs. The following categories are based on Hugh Rank's *The Pitch* (1982) and include specific words advertisers use to appeal to these needs.

basic needs

food ("tasty")

activity ("exciting")

surroundings ("comfort")

sex ("alluring")

health ("healthy")

security ("protect")

economy ("save")

"territory" needs

neighborhood ("hometown")

nation ("country")

nature ("earth")

love and belonging needs

intimacy ("lover")

family ("Mom," "Dad," "Kids")

groups ("team")

"certitude" needs*	growth needs
religion ("right")	esteem ("respected")
science ("research")	play ("fun")
best people ("elite")	generosity ("gift")
most people ("popular")	creativity ("creative")
average people ("typical")	

*"Certitude" needs involve security, stability, trust, and identity.

PRODUCT CLAIMS

Advertisers use the following strategies to make claims and to evade responsibility for those claims. These strategies are based on Carl P. Wrighter's *I Can Sell You Anything* (1972).

STRATEGIES FOR MAKING CLAIMS

The "We're Different and Unique" Claim

Stating simply that there is nothing else quite like the product advertised.

EXAMPLE: Calvin Klein jeans—"The Return of the Original Calvin."

The Endorsement or Testimonial

Using experts or celebrities to gain credibility for the ad's claim and/or to give the product the "star power" associated with famous people.

EXAMPLE: Omega watches—"Cindy Crawford's Choice."

STRATEGIES TO EVADE RESPONSIBILITY FOR CLAIMS

The Weasel Word

Modifiers negate or qualify a claim: helps, like, virtually, can be, up to, tackles, fights, resists, the feel of, the look of, looks like, fortified, enriched.

EXAMPLES: The Chevy Cavalier—"It can go **up to** 100,000 miles before its first scheduled tuneup"; L'Oreal lipstick—"Now colour so pure, so weightless, it's **virtually** irresistible."

The Unfinished Claim

Ad claims that the product is "better" or has "more" of something, but does not finish the comparison.

EXAMPLE: The Hyundai Sonata—"It looks different, and it is different."

"Water Is Wet" Claim

Ad claims something about the product that is true for any brand in that product category.

EXAMPLE: Revlon ColorStay Haircolor—"Color penetrates deep into every strand."

Compliment the Consumer

Ad flatters the potential consumer.

EXAMPLE: Toyota RAV4—"Nothing says more about you than what you drive, especially if it's an RAV4. Just the simple act of driving the RAV4 says it loud and clear: you are you and no one else is."

The Vague Claim

Claim is unclear. This category often uses weasel words and may overlap with other categories. The key to the vague claim is the use of words that defy exact verification.

EXAMPLE: Salem cigarettes—"It's Not What You Expect."

The "So What" Claim

Claim may be true, but it does not mean the product has any real advantage over any comparable product.

EXAMPLE: Sauder Furniture—"The new Pacifica Computer Desk by Sauder is the ideal station from which to usher in the millennium."

The Scientific or Statistical Claim

Claim uses scientific language and/or statistics for credibility—when no real scientific evidence or statistical proof has been presented.

EXAMPLE: Clinique skincare—"In fact, our 3-Step System is so good at creating great skin, millions of women swear by it. . . . Clinique. Allergy Tested. 100% Fragrance Free."

3.9 ANALYZING CULTURAL CODES

All cultures have assumptions about desirable and undesirable lifestyles. Advertisers often shape their messages to appeal to the cultural assumptions of target audiences. Sometimes, instead of making claims about their products, advertisers focus on identifying their products with lifestyles. These ads may suggest that a target audience will achieve a desired lifestyle by purchasing the product, or they may be aimed at making a target audience feel better about their present lifestyle. These ads often appeal to gender stereotypes and anxieties about social relationships. Often an ad will present a scene as part of a story, suggesting what has gone before and what will happen later. For example, the Alizé Red Passion ad is aimed at a target audience of young women; the ad suggests that women who drink Alizé have a glamorous, sophisticated lifestyle.

When you look for cultural codes, use the following questions:

1. What kind of lifestyle does the ad present?

   ▶ social or economic status

   ▶ personality characteristics

   ▶ marital or relationship status

   ▶ gender stereotypes

2. Does the ad suggest a story about relationships, personal fulfillment, or economic gain?

3. Does the ad appeal to the anxieties of a particular target audience?

Seasons Greetings

BLADES
BOARD AND SKATE

EXERCISE 9   **Analyzing Ads**

Analyze the target audience, appeals to needs, product claims, and cultural codes in the ads for the PR*Bar and Blades.

Exploratory Drafting and Thesis Statements

4

4.1 EXPLORATORY DRAFTING

Exploratory drafting can help you pursue an important question and lead you to an insight that can be the basis of your thesis statement. Exploratory writing can be guided by a general aim—to express yourself, to explain something, or to persuade (2.3). In exploratory writing, you try to answer your exploratory question without worrying about an introduction or conclusion, paragraphing, spelling, or completing all your sentences.

For example, Carmen's English teacher gave the class the following assignment:

> Write an essay that explores and questions values in your everyday culture—values expressed by the music you listen to, the clothes you wear, the TV programs and movies you watch, the issues you discuss with friends, and the hobbies and activities in which you participate. The following questions should help you get started:
>
> • What is distinctive about your culture—what separates it from the culture in which your parents or teachers grew up?
>
> • What do people misunderstand about your culture?
>
> Your readers will be your teacher, your classmates, and anyone else you want to reach who stands outside your culture. In an essay of 700–800 words, or $2\frac{1}{2}$ double-spaced pages, try to explain to the specified audience some defining element of your culture.

Carmen decided to explore punk feminism—a part of her culture she knew her mother's generation didn't understand and a part she thought she could learn about from exploring. She began with the exploratory question "What do people not understand about women and punk culture?"

She first used triple-viewing (3.4). Using this strategy helped her recall her knowledge of and experiences with punk feminist music; it also helped her think about the personal and cultural values punk feminist music affirms and challenges. She listened to some of her favorite CDs and then reread her responses to the triple-viewing. She began to answer her question with the exploratory draft below:

> I think about people my parents' age saying my generation is apathetic—that the feminist movement is dead. And then I think about my mother telling me to turn down my Huggy Bear CD—or Hole, or Bikini Kill—or Sleater-Kinney—even Propagandhi—which my former hippy mother should love.
>
> When my mother was my age, the mainstream culture was things like the Brady Bunch, June Cleaver and spray starch. Well—I know it was more complicated than that—I know it was also about Vietnam and civil rights, but my childhood was still very different from hers. My childhood was metal detectors in my high school, lectures on AIDS that started when I was in 4th grade, cyberspace, cybermalls, cybersex. No one I know had a stay at home mom, and of my closest friends I'm the only one with parents who haven't divorced. You can only find a new way of looking at the world—of looking at being a *women—from your own point in time. Why shouldn't the feminism of my generation look different from my mother's?
>
> Lots of women my age want to be feminists and still want to fall in love with a guy. We want to feel sexy without being treated like sex objects—we want to define what it means to be a strong woman and not read someone else's prescription in a book.
>
> That's why I like punk feminism—Riot Grrrls like Bikini Kill, Huggy Bear, and Sleater-Kinney. These women deal with the pressures of my generation, like commercialization.
>
> Punk feminists write about commercialization turning people, feelings, and relationships into products (Bikini Kill's "Jet Ski," "Reject All American").
>
> They sing about dehumanizing technology that confuses manufactured images with reality and people with numbers. Through their music punk feminists try to speak out against the forces that threaten to wipe out human feeling, instinct, and impulse (Bikini Kill's "Distinct Complicity" and "Tony Randall"; Sleater-Kinney's "God Is a Number").
>
> These women want to be feminists without rejecting men. Many of them search for new ways of looking at male/female relationships—Huggy Bear's "new renegade girl/boy hyper-nation." They write songs about oppression, but they also write love songs ("S-K—"Burn, Don't Freeze"). They are very open about sex—but that is part of the feminist message: Men don't call all the shots. And if women are sexy, don't mistake that for

*Misspelled words and other errors in writing samples are marked with asterisks.

weakness. If they are "bad" women, it is because they are calling themselves "bad"—not taking on someone else's judgment (B-K's "Finale"). The one stereotype of women they seem most determined to overturn is that of being a victim—especially Bikini Kill ("Bloody Ice Cream," "No Backrub").

Punk feminists don't believe in putting a lid on things. They believe women's power resides in following their impulses and expressing themselves in as many different ways as they can imagine. If they scream, it's because they have to be heard. If they shock you, it's because they think they need to shock you into feeling something—into being aware of life— with all its pleasures and suffering. Being radical for punk feminists is about living radically: "People who talk about revolution and class struggle without referring explicitly to everyday life, without understanding what is subversive about love and what is positive in the refusal of constraints, such people have a corpse in their mouth" (Raoul Vaneigem. Quotation from the liner notes to Huggy Bear's "Taking the Rough with the Smooch").

Women my age aren't apathetic. We just live in a different world from the one that gave birth to the feminist movement of the '60s. Feminist punk music is about the pressures on women of my generation.

Carmen's exploratory draft helped her express her feelings about her mother's attitudes toward young feminists and helped her define the main characteristics of punk feminism. By the end of her draft, Carmen had a general statement that could be the basis of her thesis statement: "Feminist punk music is about the pressures on women of my generation."

For one more example of what you can do with exploratory drafting, read the student's draft below:

Looking back, I guess it was pretty stupid. No climbing experience and nothing to climb with but a thin clothesline rope, and yet there we were in the middle of the old abandoned copper mine crawling and sliding our way down to the bottom which Eddie had heard somewhere was over a hundred feet down. For a while a great adventure, a colossal marvelous cave. Outcroppings like gargoyles all over the walls. But after about three hours, we were dirty and cut up from a few minor falls, and the muscles in our fingers and hands and arms all ached from climbing, so we decided to go back up. Then it hit us. On the way down we'd sort of slid rather than climbed our way down a fifteen-foot almost sheer *precepice and nobody thought to leave a rope hanging there so we could climb back up. Now we tried again and again to scramble up the *precepice but *niether of us could do it. It was scary. We looked up to the top of the mine where the light was but it seemed so far away—not much bigger than a single star in a coal-black sky. We felt trapped. But we weren't giving up. Not yet. We tried to find a way around the *precepice and couldn't. Then we tried throwing the rope up to catch it somehow on the top of the *precepice but that didn't work either. Finally on the bottom of the mine I found two old rusty pipes. They were only about seven feet long, but Eddie noticed that the ends of each pipe were threaded, so we screwed the pipes together to make a long pole. Bracing the pole on the ground beside the *precepice, we helped each other climb the pole and get out of the cave.

As I think back on this whole thing I'm not sure why we both felt so proud. We hadn't really done anything spectacular, and when we got home, nobody was surprised to see us. There was no celebration and no story in the paper. But maybe it was just that by working together, we figured our own way out of that place. We rescued each other. We had a problem that might have gotten really serious and we found a solution. Working together, depending on each other—there was nobody else—we found out what it means to be independent.

Once again, exploratory drafting leads the writer to his main point. As Andrew tells his story and tries to discover its significance, the memory of fear gives way to the memory of pride, and this memory in turn prompts him to ask why he felt proud. The answer is a point already implied by the story, but not made explicit until the end: in finding their way out of the cave, Andrew and his friend discovered what it means to be dependent and independent at the same time.

EXERCISE 1   **Exploratory Drafting**

Use one of the strategies in 3.4 to pursue an exploratory question (2.2). After a break, read what you have written to see if you can sharpen your question or if a new, more important question comes to mind. Then write an exploratory draft to help you answer the question.

4.2 USING AN EXPLORATORY DRAFT

An exploratory draft can lead you to your thesis statement. It can also contain the key points that will make your thesis more specific—points that can be the basis of your final text.

You will probably find your exploratory draft most useful if you take a good break after writing it. Then read what you have written, underline parts of the text that seem to answer your exploratory question, then make a list of major points. If possible, place supporting points and examples under your major points.

Carmen made the following list of major points, supporting points, and examples:

—each generation has to define feminism for itself

—punk feminists speak out about resisting commercialization—turning people, feelings, relationships into products

> ▶ Bikini Kill's "Jet Ski," "Reject All American"; Huggy Bear's "Teen Tighterns"

—punk feminists write about dehumanizing technology

—punk feminists believe that being strong doesn't have to mean rejecting men

> ▶ Sleater-Kinney, "Burn, Don't Freeze"

> ▶ but don't mistake a sexy woman for a weak one or a sex object

> ▶ overturn the victim stereotype

—punk feminists believe that self expression is an important part of women's power

> ▶ "Distinct Complicity"

> ▶ liner notes to Huggy Bear's "Taking the Rough with the Smooch"

Using Your Exploratory Draft   **EXERCISE 2**

Read your exploratory draft to see if you have a statement that answers your question. Next, underline the points in your draft that are relevant to your question and make a list of major points, placing examples and supporting points under each.

4.3 ANSWERING AN EXPLORATORY QUESTION WITH A THESIS STATEMENT

A statement of thesis answers your exploratory question and expresses the main point of your essay by making a precise, specific assertion *about* the topic. A thesis statement expresses your unique insight or way of explaining a subject and often forecasts how you will develop and organize your text.

Sometimes a thesis is discovered *in the writing process*—not just neatly formulated before the writing begins. Also, not every essay makes its thesis explicit; sometimes the thesis is merely implied. But whether or not the final version of your essay includes an explicit statement of your thesis, you should write it out for your own guidance. Your exploratory question and the list of main points from your exploratory draft can help you do so.

Carmen returned to her exploratory question and looked over the main points from her exploratory draft before she drafted her thesis statement.

EXPLORATORY QUESTION: Why does my generation need punk feminism?

Feminist punk confronts the pressures on my generation of women and offers new visions of male/female relationships and women's power.

The second part of Carmen's thesis statement is specific, but her statement about the "pressures on my generation" is still too general. What pressures does she mean? Is there any relationship between these pressures and feminist punk's "new visions"? Carmen tried to answer those questions in a new version of her thesis statement:

Feminist punk music challenges consumer culture and traditional male/female relationships, leading to new ways of looking at women's power.

Asking questions about generalizations in your thesis statement can help you make it more pointed, specific, and provocative.

The following examples show how you can use a question to turn a vague generalization into an effective thesis:

TOPIC: Soap operas

VAGUE GENERALIZATION: I believe soap operas have had a negative influence in my life. (Why?)

EFFECTIVE THESIS: Soap operas have encouraged me to believe that romance is equal to sex, that women must be beautiful to be loved, and that good people are always rewarded by wealth.

TOPIC: *Seinfeld*

VAGUE GENERALIZATION: *Seinfeld* was not a show about "nothing." (What was it about?)

EFFECTIVE THESIS: *Seinfeld* depicted the friendships, resentments, and commitments that develop in a mobile, urban society.

TOPIC: Baseball players' salaries

VAGUE GENERALIZATION: Baseball players' salaries are too high. (What should be done about them?)

EFFECTIVE THESIS: To keep baseball players' salaries from overburdening teams, team owners should recalculate the value of each player every year.

Formulating a Thesis

Reread your exploratory question and use your list of points to write several versions of your thesis statement. When your thesis statement contains generalizations, use questions to make your thesis more specific. Explain which thesis statement you think is best—and why.

5 Planning and Organizing Your Text

5.1 WHY MAKE A PLAN?

If you have formulated a statement of thesis that satisfies you, you have already started to **organize your text**. You have given yourself a sense of direction by identifying your most important point. With this point firmly in mind, you can draw other points from the material generated by your exploratory strategies (chapter 3) and your exploratory draft (chapter 4). **Planning your text** means choosing the material that best suits your purpose, audience, and thesis and then arranging that material in the most effective way.

Planning and organizing doesn't mean stopping the flow of new material. Even now you may turn back to rethink your original idea, and for this reason writing is sometimes called a **recursive process**—a process of periodically recurring (literally, running back) to your starting point. In thus returning, you may discover and add new ideas at any point, right up to the production of the final draft. To make your text effective, you must know how to shape, reshape, and refine your ideas so that your readers can grasp them.

If your text is an essay, it is usually a series of answers to the most basic questions a reader might ask:

What are you talking about?	Introduction
What point are you trying to make?	Statement of thesis
Can you explain that?	Development
What's it all add up to?	Conclusion

In this chapter we explain how to organize an essay that answers these questions. But to answer them effectively, you first need to know something about your readers.

5.2 PLANNING WITH YOUR READERS IN MIND

Who are your readers? In college they are often your teachers or *the* teacher of the course in which you are writing the paper. But, in a writing course, your readers may include your fellow students, who are commonly asked to read and discuss each other's work. Also, because learning to write well means learning how to write for different audiences, teachers of writing courses sometimes assign not only a topic but a particular set of readers—a specified audience. As a challenge, you may be asked to explain a lab experiment to readers who know nothing about science, to tell a group of senior citizens what they can do with the Internet, to persuade a software company to give you a job or a banker to give you a loan so that you can start a business. In assignments of this kind, the teacher is not so much your reader as your coach, helping you to reach the specified audience.

You can learn how to reach a specified audience by considering the following questions:

1. HOW MUCH DO YOUR READERS KNOW ABOUT THE TOPIC?   Try to tell your readers only as much as they need to know in order to understand. If you underestimate their knowledge, you will bore them by telling them things they already know; if you overestimate their knowledge, you may confuse them with unfamiliar terms or incomplete explanations. How much do your readers need to know? This depends on both your topic and your audience. If you are writing a lab report for your chemistry professor, you can assume that he or she already knows the meaning of technical terms such as *fractionation*. But for readers unfamiliar with chemistry, you would have to explain such terms. (For more on this point, see 42.2.) The same is true for any specialized terms you cannot reasonably expect your readers to know.

2. HOW DO YOUR READERS FEEL ABOUT THE TOPIC?   If you're writing about inline skating for readers who may never have tried it, you can't assume much interest. You will have to create interest either by explaining what makes inline skating so much fun or by relating it to a sport you know your readers enjoy. If you *can* assume your readers are interested in your topic, do they all feel the same way about it? And how strongly do they hold their views? If you want to write about smoking restrictions for an audience of fellow students, you have to realize that their attitudes toward smoking probably range from strong aversion to strong attachment.

3. **WHAT IS YOUR READERS' RELATION TO YOU?**   Are you a student writing for other students? Are you a job hunter writing to a prospective employer? Are you an expert (in any particular sport or hobby) writing for a novice? The better you know your relation to your readers, the better you will communicate (2.3, "Writer and Reader Roles").

4. **DO YOUR READERS DIFFER FROM YOU IN RACE, CLASS, GENDER, OR CULTURAL BACKGROUND?**   If so, you can hardly assume that their experience and points of view will match yours. Whenever you generalize from your own experience, you must think carefully about the experience of your readers. (For advice on using language that respects differences, see 8.2 and 8.3.)

5. **DO YOUR READERS DIFFER FROM YOU IN RELIGIOUS BELIEFS OR POLITICAL ATTITUDES?**   If so, their view of your topic may differ drastically from your own. If, for instance, you intend to argue that all U.S. healthcare services should be federally regulated, you need to recognize that many Americans regard federal regulation as federal interference with their lives. Likewise, if you wish to argue in favor of physician-assisted suicide, you need to know that some religious groups believe it wrong under any circumstances.

6. **HOW DO YOUR READERS EXPECT YOU TO TREAT THE TOPIC?**   Sometimes this question is answered by the terms of an assignment. Professional writers—especially journalists—often work under instructions from editors who tell them not only what to write but also how to treat it. When you get a writing assignment, therefore, you should learn as much as you can about the approach you are expected to take. (See 2.4. For further guidance on what is expected in essays written for specialized fields in the humanities, social sciences, and natural sciences, see chapter 42.)

7. **HOW LONG IS THE FINISHED ESSAY SUPPOSED TO BE?**   You already know that teachers often specify a minimum or maximum number of words for the essays they require in their courses. Outside the classroom, length requirements are regularly imposed on contestants in writing contests and on everyone who writes for newspapers, magazines, and other publications. Whatever you write for such a publication—an essay, a story, or a letter to the editor—you should know what sort of length is expected if you hope to see your words in print. But don't be afraid of writing too much or too little on your first draft. Aim to get all your thoughts about the topic down on paper. If you end up with too many words, you can tighten your sentences and cut out redundant points when you revise. If you end up with too few words, you can identify points that need further development.

Planning with Your Readers in Mind

▶ How much do your readers know about the topic?

▶ How do they feel about the topic?

▶ What is their relation to you?

▶ Do they differ from you in race, class, gender, or cultural background?

▶ Do they differ from you in religious beliefs or political attitudes?

▶ How do they expect you to treat the topic?

▶ How long is the finished text supposed to be?

Planning with Your Readers in Mind

Suppose you are explaining why a particular sport, hobby, or subject fascinates you. Write two sample paragraphs of explanation: one for readers who share your interest and knowledge and one for those who don't. Also, make a list of any specialized terms that you should define for the reader.

5.3 PLANNING THE ORGANIZATION OF MAJOR POINTS

Once you have considered the readers you will be writing for, you can select and arrange your major points. To do so, you should first make a list of all the points you have identified up to now. Carmen made the following list and then underlined the points she thought were most important:

—feminist punk music challenges commercial culture

—feminist punkers sing about dehumanizing technology

—feminist punkers believe women can be strong without rejecting men— they affirm women's sexuality

—feminist punkers believe that self expression is an important part of women's power

Your next task is to decide on the order or arrangement of your major points. To decide that, you must know what arrangements are possible and which are better than others for your particular topic, aim, and audience. In other words, the choice of order depends on your *rhetorical strategy*, on what you plan to do in your essay. Following are some of the arrangements you might use—alone or in combination:

1.   CHRONOLOGICAL ORDER   Because this arrangement follows the order of events in time, it works well in essays written to explain a procedure, such as pitching a tent, or a natural process, such as the migration of birds. (On explaining procedures and processes, see 6.9.) It is also commonly used in narrative (6.2), as well as in essays that use narrative.

2.   SPATIAL ORDER   Spatial arrangement follows the order of objects in space and therefore works well in descriptive writing (6.1). Spatial order typically follows the movements of an imaginary eye surveying a scene— moving around a room, or across a landscape from left to right, or from foreground to background. It can also shift in scale, as when it moves from a comprehensive view to a close-up.

3.   CAUSE AND EFFECT ORDER   Cause and effect order allows you to explain one point as the reason for or as the result of another. In an essay on why women long to be thin (p. 101), René Cardle starts with the fact that many American women are obsessed with losing weight. Then she explains the reasons for this development. Similarly, in the first part of his freewriting exercise on the cave (p. 59), Andrew briefly presents his and Eddie's predicament as a result of the way they came down (sliding and leaving no rope). In the final version of his essay, Andrew emphasizes causal order by starting with himself and Eddie at the bottom of the cave (p. 74), and then moving back up to explain how they got there. Thus he modifies chronological order with causal order.

4.   CLIMACTIC ORDER   When you order your writing climactically, you arrange points in order of ascending importance, rising from least important to most important. Climactic order sometimes corresponds to chronological order. In other cases, the most important point or event comes first; then the rest of the text explains what led up to it.

5.   OPPOSITIONAL ORDER   This arrangement opposes one point to another. It often works well at the start of a persuasive essay written for readers who are likely to resist the thesis. You can also use oppositional order to compare and contrast two things (6.6) or just to highlight their differences.

6.   CATEGORICAL ORDER   This order helps you explain one large group as a collection of two or more subgroups. The student author of an essay on Brooklyn teenagers, for instance, divided them into two groups: a minority of drug-free "ducks," who go to school every day, and a majority of drug-taking "hard rocks," who regularly skip school and beat up the ducks. He put the ducks first because he was writing for a group of students who

would be called ducks if they lived in Brooklyn. Then he turned to the hard rocks, who live by a code that most of his readers would find strange. Thus he presented the two groups in an order that suited his topic and his audience. (For more on this method of arrangement, see 6.8.)

To see how you might use some of these arrangements, consider what Carmen did. Since she was writing for both students and adults who might not understand feminist punk music, she decided to use climactic order to organize her text. She began with the point that seemed easiest for others to understand about feminist punkers—their desire to resist commercial culture—and ended with the point others might find hardest to understand—their belief that women's power depends in part on self-expression.

Arranging Your Major Points

EXERCISE 2

Read your exploratory draft and any other notes from the planning process. Randomly list all the points you have so far accumulated. Then underline the most important points, arrange them as well as you can, and identify the order(s) you have used.

5.4 PLANNING WITH AN OUTLINE

After deciding how to arrange your major points, you must decide how to connect your minor points to the major ones. The best way to plan your connections is to **make an outline**, which may be either a *tree diagram* or a *vertical list*. But whichever you choose, you should think of an outline as a *tentative* plan for your essay, not a rigid scheme. If new ideas or new questions come to mind while you are writing, feel free to revise your outline or even to scrap it altogether and make a new one.

OUTLINING WITH A TREE DIAGRAM

A **tree diagram** is a regulated version of a branching diagram (3.4, "Branching and Looping"). Its branches are arranged to be read from left to right, and they spread out in one direction only, down from the thesis like the branches of a tree reflected in water. Because the tree is open-ended, it leaves space for you to visualize more branches. So once you have drawn the tree to organize your major and minor points, you can make it grow by adding more points as they come to mind. Carmen's tree diagram illustrates this kind of growth.

The items marked with an asterisk (*) were not among the points Carmen originally took from her freewritten material; these items came to her as she was laying out the branches of the tree. The tree diagram served not just as a record of her thoughts, but as a means of discovering new ones.

OUTLINING WITH A VERTICAL LIST

After you have produced some freewritten material, making a vertical outline of it is a good way to check the organization of your material—to see where the sequence and development are good, and also to spot any gaps where more information is needed. To outline your material vertically, write your thesis at the head of the page and then use headings and indented subheadings:

THESIS: Feminist punk music challenges consumer culture and traditional male/female relationships, leading to new ways of looking at women's power.

    I. Punk feminists challenge commercialization.
       A. Challenge turning people, feelings, relationships into products in B-K's "Jet Ski"
       B. Challenge determination by consumer culture
          1. B-K's "Distinct Complicity"
          2. B-K's "No Backrub"
       C. Punk bands' mail-order services are an alternative economic network.

    II. Punk feminists believe women can be strong without rejecting men, and they affirm women's sexuality.
       A. Men shouldn't determine women's self-images—S-K's "Burn, Don't Freeze"
       B. Women can be sexy without being sex objects.

    III. Punk feminists believe that self expression is an important part of women's power.
       A. Refusing constraints
          1. Huggy Bear's liner notes
          2. B-K's "Distinct Complicity"
       B. Refusing to give up

USING AN OUTLINE

The best way to use an outline is to follow it as a guide, not as a dictator. Just because you've made an outline doesn't mean that you can't ever remake it or depart from it as you write. As we've said before, writing is a recursive process; at any stage you may turn back or run back (recur) to its first stage: back to prewriting techniques, back to searching for new ideas.

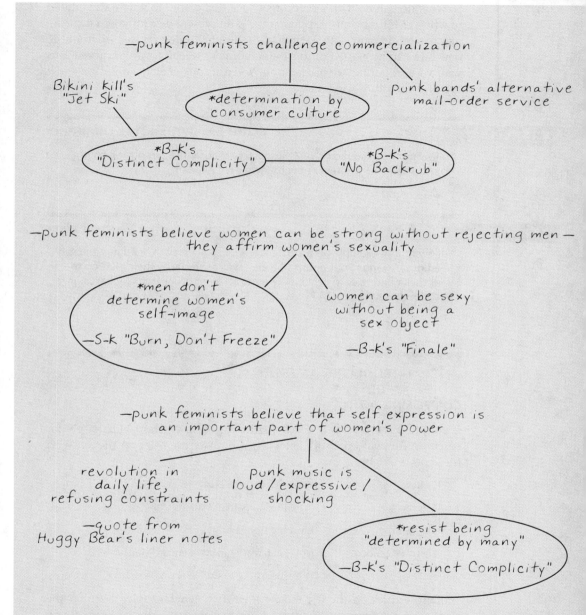

—punk feminists challenge commercialization

Bikini kill's "Jet Ski"

*determination by consumer culture

punk bands' alternative mail-order service

*B-k's "Distinct Complicity"

*B-k's "No Backrub"

—punk feminists believe women can be strong without rejecting men — they affirm women's sexuality

*men don't determine women's self-image

—S-k "Burn, Don't Freeze"

women can be sexy without being a sex object

—B-k's "Finale"

—punk feminists believe that self expression is an important part of women's power

revolution in daily life, refusing constraints

—quote from Huggy Bear's liner notes

punk music is loud / expressive / shocking

*resist being "determined by many"

—B-k's "Distinct Complicity"

THESIS: Feminist punk music challenges consumer culture and traditional male/female relationships, leading to new ways of looking at women's power.

So what do you do with a brand-new idea that comes to you in the middle of writing? If it obviously supports the point you're developing in a particular paragraph, you can take it up right away. If it doesn't, see whether the new idea can be grafted onto a branch of your tree diagram or tucked into your vertical outline for use later on. You can thus make your outline grow even as you follow its guidance.

EXERCISE 3   **Outlining with a Tree Diagram**

Following the example on p. 71, use a tree diagram to arrange all your points. Then add whatever new branches are needed.

EXERCISE 4   **Outlining with a Vertical List**

Following the example on p. 70, create a vertical list with headings and subheadings. Arrange your points in such a way as to clarify their relation to your thesis and to each other, putting them in an order that will best support the thesis.

5.5   INTRODUCING AN ESSAY

COMPOSING A TITLE

If your text is an essay, it needs a title. It should be short but sharply focused on the main point of the essay. Compare the titles on the left with those on the right:

College	Where College Fails Us
Lawyers	When Lawyers Help Villains
The Mine	Escaping from a Mine
First-Year Students	How First-Year Students Manage Money
College	Why Returning to College Beats Arriving

While the titles on the left merely identify a general topic, those on the right make the topic specific and tell the reader what to expect. Also, if you can think of a good working title as you outline your essay, it can guide you through the writing of the essay itself. When you finish writing, you can reword the title if necessary to make it more precise.

WRITING THE INTRODUCTION

The introduction comes first for the reader but not necessarily first for the writer. Since you can't write a good introduction until you know what you're introducing, you may want to plunge immediately into the middle of your draft, write your way to a conclusion, and only then write your introduction. But whenever you write it, this section may help you to make it effective. To see the difference between a weak introduction and a strong one, compare the draft version of Carmen's introduction with her revised version:

DRAFT

DIFFERENT WORLDS, DIFFERENT STRUGGLES

People my age have grown up hearing that my generation is apathetic and that feminism is dead. I think of this almost every time my parents tell me to turn down my CD player. Maybe if they listened, they wouldn't have these attitudes about my generation. People can define a new vision of the world only from where they stand. Feminist punk music attacks consumer culture and offers new ways of looking at male/female relationships and women's power.

REVISION

DIFFERENT WORLDS, DIFFERENT STRUGGLES

It's like a yearly rerun, though I don't know if it is a sit-com or a soap opera. In December we will visit my mother's parents. My grandmother will fix a huge meal. Then my parents, my aunt, my uncle and his wife will sit around the living room talking about the 60s. They will open a couple of bottles of wine, and with every sip their roles in student protests will grow more important. By the time they go to bed, you'd think my uncle had started Earth Day and my mother had started the feminist movement. Sometimes they try to be careful about what they say, knowing I might be listening. But I've heard it all before. "Young people today are apathetic." "The feminist movement is dead." I just re-adjust my headphones, turn up "Her Jazz" by Huggy Bear: " mental . . . men-torn . . . you had your way, baby, you had your say and had your way with that girl now come on outta yr world . . . this is happening without yr permission . . . the arrival of a new renegade girl/boy hyper-nation." Of course, if I were playing Huggy Bear on their CD player they'd tell me to turn it down—or off; and when they do that, they don't hear the voice of my generation. We aren't apathetic, and I consider myself a feminist—even if I occasionally *wear* a Wonderbra instead of burning it on the steps of the campus administration building. The feminist movement isn't dead; it's just taken new forms, and one place it can be found is in feminist punk music.

By telling the family story, Carmen creates interest and helps the reader understand her attitudes toward her mother's generation of feminists.

You don't always need to end your opening paragraph with a perfect preview of your essay, a complete statement of what it will show. To excite curiosity, you may end with a question or with a point that stops well short of the major one you will eventually make. The only thing a good introduction must do is to forecast what will follow, and it can do this in a virtually endless number of ways. Here are some of them:

1. **LEAD UP TO AN EXPLICIT STATEMENT OF YOUR THESIS.**

THE TOWN DUMP

The town dump of Whitemud, Saskatchewan, could only have been a few years old when I knew it, for the village was born in 1913 and I left there in 1919. But I remember the dump better than I remember most things in that town, better than I remember most of the people. I spent more time with it, for one thing; it had more poetry and excitement in it than people did.

—Wallace Stegner

2. **DEFINE A CONFLICT, PROBLEM, OR QUESTION YOU AIM TO RESOLVE.**

ESCAPING FROM A MINE

A slow, forbidding breeze chilled me as I watched Eddie struggling to get a grip on a rock wall that must have been at least fifteen feet high. He cursed. The breeze passed, but the chill on my face remained as I looked around again at where we were. The four rudely cut walls that had held so much mystery and excitement for us a few hours ago now loomed threateningly over our heads. One hundred feet up was our salvation—the opening to the copper mine, looking not much bigger than a single star in a coal-black sky. The sharp overhangings and gargoylelike outcroppings jutted harshly from the sides of the massive cave, ominously reminding us that we had climbed in, and now we had to climb out. But we couldn't. For at least an hour we tried to scale that one section of the mine wall, and couldn't see how to do it.

—Andrew Lyle

3. **TELL A STORY THAT ILLUSTRATES THE MAIN POINT YOU WILL GO ON TO MAKE.**

DOUBLE VISION

When I was a little girl, my mother told me to wait for the light to turn green before I crossed the street and to cross always at the corner. This I did. Indeed, I was positive as a very young child that I would get mashed like a potato if I even so much as stepped a foot off the sidewalk while the light burned red. I followed my mother's advice until I realized that she herself jaywalked constantly, dodging in and out of moving traffic—and pulling me with her. So after a while I followed her example and not her advice.

—Lynn Minton

Minton tells a personal story to introduce the main point of her essay, which is that adults are hypocritical.

4. MOVE FROM A GENERALIZATION TO A SPECIFIC CASE.

COLLEGE: DEPAUW

American families differ greatly in their expectations about what going to college will mean in their children's lives. In the intellectual community to which my parents belonged, college was as necessary as learning to read. It was an intellectual experience and the gateway to the rest of life. All my life I expected to go to college, and I was prepared to enjoy it.

—Margaret Mead

5. INDICATE THE METHOD OF YOUR ESSAY.

HOW FAMILIES CREATE CULTURE IN EAST AND WEST

Sociologists study the family because it is the basic unit of society. As a Chinese student who lived with an American family for six months, I could compare it with my own family in China. In so doing, I learned that the main differences between the two countries originate within the family. Though I was raised to tell my parents everything and to depend on others, each member of the American family had a private life, and the children were trained to be independent, to refuse help even when they needed it. The differences between my family and the American one help to explain why Eastern and Western cultures have such different attitudes toward privacy, dependence, and independence.

—college student

6. CHALLENGE A WIDESPREAD ASSUMPTION OR STEREOTYPE.

WHERE COLLEGE FAILS US

The case *for* college has been accepted without question for more than a generation. All high school graduates ought to go, says Conventional Wisdom and statistical evidence, because college will help them earn more money, become "better" people, and learn to be more responsible citizens than those who don't go. But college has never been able to work its magic for everyone. And now that close to half our high school graduates are attending, those who don't fit the pattern are becoming more numerous, and more obvious. College graduates are selling shoes and driving taxis; college students sabotage each other's experiments and forge letters of recommendation in the intense competition for admission to graduate school. Others find no stimulation in their studies, and drop out—often encouraged by college administrators.

—Caroline Bird

7.   ESTABLISH A HISTORICAL CONTEXT FOR YOUR TOPIC.

TAKING BACK THE PEOPLE'S AIR

Broadcasters who complain that they shouldn't be burdened with any more public service obligations can trace the source of their troubles back to Herbert Hoover. It was clear to Hoover, as it was to the broadcasters of his day, that those making money from public airwaves owed the public something in return.

—Janine Jaquet

8.   TO ACCOMMODATE READERS WHO MAY NOT AGREE WITH YOU, EXPLAIN THE POSITION YOU AIM TO OPPOSE.

FREE SPEECH PROTECTIONS AND CONSTRAINTS

Since the Oklahoma City bombing, incidents of domestic terrorism and hate crimes raise the issue of censorship on the Internet. Few people dispute that the Internet has played a large role in the growth of hate groups. The Internet not only helps these groups recruit new members, but also provides information that may enable terrorist acts—like instructions for bomb making. But while the Internet is currently protected by the First Amendment, it is also subject to laws against threats that lead to violence. In other words, though material on the Internet is not now subject to censorship, it is subject to the same legal constraints that govern other forms of speech—spoken and printed. Since it is already regulated in this way, Internet "speech" needs no more restriction than any other forms of speech.

—college student

EXERCISE 5   **Composing a Title and
                                              Writing an Introduction**

After reviewing 5.5, "Composing a Title," think of a title for your essay. Then, using any one of the methods explained above, write an introduction.

Introducing an Essay

▶ Lead up to an explicit statement of your thesis.

▶ Define a conflict, problem, or question you aim to resolve.

▶ Tell a story that illustrates the main point you will go on to make.

▶ Move from a generalization to a specific case.

▶ Indicate the method of your essay.

▶ Challenge a widespread assumption or stereotype.

▶ Establish a historical context for your topic.

▶ Explain the position you aim to oppose.

5.6 SHAPING THE MIDDLE PARAGRAPHS

If you have made an outline or drawn a tree diagram, you have already clustered certain points under each of several headings. You have seen how the mere act of arranging points can lead to your thinking of new points. Now is a good time to review the organization of major points (5.3).

Each heading in your outline can serve as the topic of a paragraph. For instance, the branch labeled "punk feminists believe that self expression is an important part of women's power" led Carmen to write the following paragraph:

> Feminist punkers don't believe in putting a lid on things. They believe women's power comes from following their impulses and expressing themselves in as many different ways as they can imagine. If they scream, it's because they have to scream in order to be heard. If they shock you, it's because they think they need to shock you into feeling something—into being aware of life—with all its pleasures and suffering. This is one reason feminist punk (like all punk) is loud, repetitive, and sometimes disturbing. As Bikini Kill puts it in "Distinct Complicity," life is the struggle against being "determined by many" by "those who refuse to conquer hesitation." Sometimes their messages aren't very optimistic. This song doesn't end by saying it is possible to escape being determined. But by crying out, feminists punkers are at least saying that they aren't giving up.

Using your outline or tree diagram as a guide, write one paragraph for each of its headings. If you find that a particular heading generates more or less than one paragraph, feel free to modify the outline or tree diagram. Remember that this is only a first draft.

5.7 CONCLUDING AN ESSAY

To end an essay effectively, ask yourself what final impression you want to make on your reader. You can leave a strong impression by any one of the following means:

1. MAKE THE IMPLICATIONS OF YOUR THESIS EXPLICIT.

    We have found that violence on prime-time network TV cultivates exaggerated assumptions about the threat of danger in the real world. Fear is a universal emotion, and easy to exploit. The exaggerated sense of risk and insecurity may lead to increasing demands for protection, and to increasing pressure for the use of force by established authority. Instead of threatening the social order, television may have become our chief instrument of social control.

    —George Gerbner and Larry Gross,
    "The Scary World of TV's Heavy Viewer"

2. ECHO YOUR INTRODUCTION IN TERMS THAT WIDEN ITS SIGNIFICANCE.

    Poetry is seldom useful, but always memorable. I think I learned more from the town dump than I learned from school: more about people, more about how life is lived, not elsewhere but here, not in other times but now. If I were a sociologist anxious to study in detail the life of any community, I would go very early to its refuse piles. For a community may be as well judged by what it throws away—what it has to throw away and what it chooses to—as by any other evidence. For whole civilizations we have sometimes no more of the poetry and little more of the history than this.
    —Wallace Stegner, "The Town Dump"

3. RECOMMEND A SPECIFIC COURSE OF ACTION.

    The physically handicapped have the liabilities of a minority group. Shouldn't they be given the rights of a minority group? The answer is affirmative. It is time the action was also.
    —Nancy Weinberg, "Disability Isn't Beautiful"

4. **ANSWER A QUESTION POSED BY THE INTRODUCTION.**

> What, then, can we conclude about mathematics and sex? If math anxiety is in part the result of math avoidance, why not require girls to take as much math as they can possibly master? If being the only girl in "trig" is the reason so many women drop math at the end of high school, why not provide psychological counseling and support for those young women who wish to go on? Since ability in mathematics is considered by many to be unfeminine, perhaps fear of success, more than any bodily or mental dysfunction, may interfere with girls' ability to learn math.
>
> —Sheila Tobias, "Who's Afraid of Math, and Why?"

5. **REFLECT ON THE EXPERIENCE THAT THE ESSAY RECORDS.**

> We hadn't done anything spectacular, and when we got home, no one was surprised to see us. There was no celebration and no story in the paper. Yet looking back on our escape from the mine, I realize now why we both felt something more than relief. We felt proud that we had not panicked or simply given up and waited for help. We had faced a problem together, and we had finally found a solution. Paradoxically, by depending on each other—there was no one else—we discovered what it means to be independent. In a sense, we rescued each other.
>
> —Andrew Lyle, "Escaping from a Mine"

6. **REAFFIRM YOUR THESIS WITH A FINAL TELLING EXAMPLE.** To end an essay on the amount of garbage produced by New York City, Katie Kelley tells what she saw and heard at Fresh Kills, a Staten Island dumping site:

> "It sure has changed out here," one worker, who has been at Fresh Kills for years, told me. "Why, there used to be fresh natural springs over there." He gestured out over the hundreds of acres of garbage. Natural crab beds once flourished in the area. Now they, too, are gone, buried under tons of garbage.

Options for Concluding an Essay

IN BRIEF

▶ Make the implications of your thesis explicit.

▶ Echo your introduction in terms that widen its significance.

▶ Recommend a specific course of action.

▶ Answer a question posed by the introduction.

▶ Reflect on the experience that the essay records.

▶ Reaffirm your thesis with a telling example.

Concluding an Essay

Turn to René Cardle's essay "Why Do Women Long to Be Thin?" (p. 101).
Place a slip of paper over the last paragraph. Then read the essay and write
your own concluding paragraph.

Comparing Endings

After you complete exercise 7, read Cardle's concluding paragraph and
compare it with the one you wrote. Explain what each ending does and
how well it works.

Ending an Essay

Write a paragraph to end the essay you have been writing in this chapter.

Developing Your Text

A **method of development** is a way of achieving your writing aim: a way of expressing your feelings, of explaining something in the world outside yourself, or of persuading the reader to accept your opinion. A method of development can also guide the organization of your writing. For example, when you use chronological narration you organize events in time. The order of those events can help you organize sentences in a paragraph. Chronological narration can also help you organize several paragraphs of an essay if you use one paragraph for each event you describe.

Some methods of development—such as *description* and *narration*—may become ends in themselves. You may simply aim to describe a particular object or to tell a particular story. But a method of development commonly serves as a means to a further end. To explain how to create a Web page, for instance, you would need to describe how a file transfer program sends a Web page to a server, where others can have access to it; to help persuade readers that a corporation-sponsored daycare center is a good investment, you might tell a story of how such a center has changed the life of one working parent.

This chapter presents various methods of development and shows how they can help you achieve your purpose in writing and organizing your text.

6.1 USING DESCRIPTION

Description is writing about the way things appear, the way they are constructed, or the way they act. Like every other method of development, description calls for some choices. You must decide which details to identify, how to arrange them, and how to use the description in a particular text. But as you make your choices, you may find it helpful to know that description usually takes one of three forms: *external, analytical or technical,* or *evocative*.

EXTERNAL DESCRIPTION

An external description enables the reader to visualize and recognize the person, object, or scene described. In the passage below, the writer surveys the scene in a park, recording sights and sounds:

> On a warm spring day, people in Washington, La., are sitting on their front stoops listening to zydeco or gospel and eating ham sandwiches and drinking bottles of Turbo Dog. It's spring, and it's so green you can't believe it: there are tendrils of lacy light green Spanish moss, thick patches of overgrown grass, rubbery leaves, shiny dark green magnolias the color of English club leather, vines growing around vines growing around thick lichen-covered trunks.
>
> —Jennifer Moses, *New York Times*, May 9, 1999

EXERCISE 1   **External Description**

Briefly describe the appearance of a place on campus and see if other students recognize that place from your description.

ANALYTICAL OR TECHNICAL DESCRIPTION

Analytical or technical description enables the reader to understand the structure of an object:

> The panda's "thumb" is not, anatomically, a finger at all. It is constructed from a bone called the radial sesamoid, normally a small component of the wrist. In pandas, the radial sesamoid is greatly enlarged and elongated until it almost equals the metapoidal bones of the true digits in length. The radial sesamoid underlies a pad on the panda's forepaw; the five digits form the framework of another pad, the palmar. A shallow furrow separates the two pads and serves as a channel-way for bamboo stalks.
>
> —Stephen Jay Gould, "The Panda's Thumb"

Gould's language is precise, objective, technical ("radial sesamoid," "metapoidal bones"), and above all analytical. He focuses not on the furry surface of the panda's paw but on the framework of "thumb" and finger bones that underlie it. This analytical description serves an argumentative aim. Gould wants to show that the panda—which long ago had nothing but five fingers in its paw—gradually developed its radial sesamoid to do the work of an opposable thumb, to operate like a human thumb in grasping the bamboo stalks that pandas love to eat. Analytically described, the panda's paw helps Gould to substantiate the theory of evolution.

Analytical or Technical Description

EXERCISE 2

Describe in a paragraph any one of the following in such a way that a reader can understand its structure, design, or function:

a skateboard	a motorcycle
a hair dryer	a tulip
a book bag	a portable CD player
an oak tree	a human hand
a Siamese cat	a chocolate éclair
a tennis racket	a coffeemaker

EVOCATIVE DESCRIPTION

Evocative description re-creates the impression made by an object or a scene. Such a description can appeal not just to the eye but also to other senses:

> The church I attended as a child still stands. It is small, almost tiny, and made of very old, silver-gray lumber, painted white a couple of decades ago, when an indoor toilet was also added. It is simple, serene, sweet. It used to nestle amid vivid green foliage at a curve in a sandy dirt road; inside, its rough-hewn benches smelled warmly of pine. Its yard was shaded by a huge red oak tree, from which people took bits of bark to brew a tonic for their chickens. I remember my mother boiling the bark she'd cut from the tree and feeding the reddish brown "tea" to her pullets, who, without it, were likely to cannibalize each other. The county, years later, and without warning, cut down the tree and straightened and paved the road. In an attempt to create a tourist industry where none had existed before, they flooded the surrounding countryside. The fisher people from far away who whiz by in their pickup trucks today know nothing about what they see. To us, they are so unconnected to the land they appear to hover above it, like ghosts.
>
> —Alice Walker, *Anything We Love Can Be Saved*

Explaining Evocative Description

Compare the following two descriptions and explain what makes the second more evocative than the first:

1. I couldn't stand Palatka. It was poor, seedy, smelly, and ugly, and the weather was always bad. I couldn't relate to the people either. My stay there was a nightmare.

2. Situated on the banks of the St. Johns River, Palatka was surrounded by dense tropical foliage in limitless swamps. It was always hot, and it rained daily. The town's main street, made of bricks, was called Lemon Street. Weeds grew out of the spaces between the bricks and out of the cracks in the sidewalks and at the bottom of the concrete buildings, so that to a stranger the vegetation appeared to be strangling the town. There was a paper mill in town. It supplied most of the blacks and poorer whites with employment. Each morning at six they were summoned to work by a whistle that woke the entire area. Shortly thereafter Palatka was blanketed by a lavender haze and filled with a terrible stench.
   —Pat Jordan, *A False Spring*

Writing Evocative Description

Using Alice Walker's paragraph on p. 83 as a model, write an evocative description of a place you lived in or visited as a child. Assume that your reader has never seen this place, and describe as many sights, sounds, and smells as possible.

6.2 USING NARRATION

Narration is telling or writing about a sequence of events. Like description, narration calls for authorial choice at every stage. Stories do not tell themselves; events become a story only when a writer has chosen, arranged, and linked them in a series. Also, besides deciding how to begin and end the sequence, the author is free to follow or not follow *chronological order*. Here we treat both of these alternatives.

CHRONOLOGICAL NARRATION

The simplest kind of narration follows chronological order, the order in which the narrated events actually occurred or could have occurred:

> American feminism has a long history in a country with a short history. From the official birth of organized feminism in 1848 at a village chapel in Seneca Falls, New York, American feminists undertook a protracted struggle in defense of women's rights to education, work, and political power, culminating in the conquest of their right to vote in 1920. Then, afterwards, for almost half a century, feminism was kept in the backstage of the American scene. Not that women ceased to fight. In one of the most noted expressions of women's struggles, the 1955 bus boycott in Montgomery, Alabama, that arguably ushered in the civil rights movement in the South, and changed American history for ever, was enacted predominantly by African-American women organizing their communities.
>
> —Manuel Castells, *The Power of Identity*

A short chronological narrative, or anecdote, can readily serve an explanatory aim. The following anecdote helps to explain how Harry Houdini used the police to publicize his prowess:

> When he arrived in London in 1900 the twenty-six-year-old magician did not have a single booking. His news clippings eventually inspired an English agent, who had Houdini manacled to a pillar in Scotland Yard. Seeing that Houdini was securely fastened, Superintendent Melville of the Criminal Investigation Department said he would return in a couple of hours, when the escapist had worn himself out. By the time Melville got to the door, the magician was free to open it for him.
>
> The publicity surrounding his escape from the most prestigious police force in the world opened up many another door for him.
>
> —Daniel Mark Epstein, "The Case of Harry Houdini"

Narrating to Explain Personality
EXERCISE 5

Write a short chronological narrative, or anecdote, that helps to explain the personality of anyone you know, including yourself.

Narrating a Conflict
EXERCISE 6

Using chronological order, write a brief narration of a conflict or misunderstanding you have seen or experienced.

NONCHRONOLOGICAL NARRATION

Although short narrative can follow chronological order with good results, strict adherence to chronological order in an extended narrative can lead to a boring succession of "and then"s. To keep the story lively and to clarify its meaning, you may need to depart from chronological order, moving backward to explain the cause of a particular event or jumping forward to identify its ultimate effect:

Writer begins story of what happened in 1964.

> In June 1964 . . . two Italian fishing boats, working in tandem with a crew of 18, were dragging their nets along the bottom of the Adriatic. Toward dawn, as they pulled up the nets after a long trawl, the fishermen realized their catch was unusually heavy. . . . When they finally swung the nets inboard they saw an ungainly, prehistoric-looking figure missing both feet. It was, in fact, a 500-pound Greek statue covered with nearly 2,000 years of sea encrustations.

Writer flashes forward to 1977.

> In November 1977, this life-size bronze fetched the highest known price ever paid for a statue—$3.9 million. The work is attributed to the fourth century B.C. Greek artist Lysippus. . . . Professor Paolo Moreno of Rome University, author of two books on Lysippus, identifies the statue as the portrait of a young athlete after victory and suggests that it may have been plundered by ancient Romans from Mount Olympus. The ship bearing the statue was probably sunk in a storm and there may well have been other treasures on board. Pliny the Elder tells us Lysippus made more than 1,500 works, all of them bronze, but it was doubted that any of the originals had survived—until this one surfaced.

Writer flashes back to ancient times.

Writer resumes story of what happened in 1964.

> The fishermen stealthily unloaded the barnacle-covered masterpiece in Fano, near Rimini, and took it to the captain's house, where it was put on a kitchen table and propped up against a wall.
>
> —Bryan Rosten, "Smuggled!"

EXERCISE 7   **Using Flashbacks and Flash-forwards**

Using at least one flashback and one flash-forward, tell the story of one of the following:

▶ your first day in college

▶ your first meeting with someone who later became important in your life

▶ the first time you felt that you were doing something wrong

▶ your first date

6.3 COMBINING DESCRIPTION AND NARRATION

Description and narration usually go hand in hand. In the narrative below, Rosa Parks tells of her refusal to comply with the Alabama law that in 1955 required African Americans to give up their bus seats to whites.

> Having to take a certain section [on a bus] because of your race was humiliating, but having to stand up because a particular driver wanted to keep a white person from having to stand was, to my mind, most inhumane. . . .
>
> Over the years, I had had my own problems with the bus drivers. In fact, some did tell me not to ride their buses if I felt that I was too important to go to the back door to get on. One had evicted me from the bus in 1943, which did not cause anything more than just a passing glance.
>
> On December 1, 1955, I had finished my day's work as a tailor's assistant in the Montgomery Fair department store and I was on my way home. There was one vacant seat on the Cleveland Avenue bus, which I took, alongside a man and two women across the aisle. There were still a few vacant seats in the white section in the front, of course. We went to the next stop without being disturbed. On the third, the front seats were occupied and this one man, a white man, was standing. The driver asked us to stand up and let him have those seats, and when none of us moved at his first words, he said, "You all make it light on yourselves and let me have those seats." And the man who was sitting next to the window stood up, and I made room for him to pass by me. The two women across the aisle stood up and moved out.
>
> When the driver saw me still sitting, he asked if I was going to stand up and I said, "No, I'm not."
>
> And he said, "Well, if you don't stand up, I'm going to call the police and have you arrested."
>
> I said, "You may do that."
>
> He did get off the bus, and I still stayed where I was. Two policemen came on the bus. One of the policemen asked me if the bus driver had asked me to stand and I said yes.
>
> He said, "Why don't you stand up?"
>
> And I asked him, "Why do you push us around?"
>
> He said, "I do not know, but the law is the law and you're under arrest."
>
> —Rosa Parks, "The Montgomery Bus Boycott, 1955–56," from *Voices of Freedom: An Oral History of the Civil Rights Movement*

By carefully describing how passengers were seated on the bus and how one event led to another, Parks helps the reader understand the injustices that brought about the civil rights movement.

EXERCISE 8

Narrating Events in and out of Chronological Order

This exercise has two parts. First, tell in strict chronological order the story of the most memorable trip you have taken. Then retell the story in nonchronological order, starting not with the beginning but with the part of the trip you remember best. Then work backward and forward from that point.

EXERCISE 9

Using Description in Narration

Use as much description as possible to expand the narrative you wrote for exercise 5.

EXERCISE 10

Using a Story to Make a Point

Tell a story about anyone you know that could be used to illustrate a general point about the experience of growing up. Or tell a story about your experience of a conflict—a story that could be used to illustrate a general point about relationships between people. Whichever story you tell, state its point at the end.

6.4 USING EXAMPLES

You can develop almost any point by using examples. The author of the following paragraphs uses a series of examples to show how law-abiding Canadians are:

> When the great cattle drives of the American Midwest flowed north to railheads in Canada, cowboys adjusted to the shock of being asked to surrender their guns to the single policeman who met them at the border. One Mountie rode into Sitting Bull's camp a few days after the Battle at Little Big Horn, noted fresh American scalps and horses with U.S. cavalry brands, and advised Sitting Bull to obey Canadian laws or he, the Mountie, would deport the whole tribe. And Sitting Bull nodded.

During the Klondike gold rush of the nineties, the American town of Skagway in the Alaskan panhandle was run by a ruthless American gangster and gunfights in the streets were common. Across the border in Canada, Yukon mining towns were so law-abiding that a miner safely could leave his poke of gold in an unlocked cabin.

—June Callwood, "Portrait of Canada"

Stating the Point Made by Examples

Each of the following passages offers at least one example to explain or illustrate a point. State the point in a single short sentence and briefly explain how the examples support it.

1. A hockey player rushing up ice travels at more than twenty-five miles an hour; a slap shot hurls a frozen rubber disc toward a goalie at one hundred miles an hour. Everything that happens in hockey—passing, stickhandling, checking, shooting—happens fast.
   —Jeff Greenfield, "The Iceman Arriveth"

2. Hold an apple in your hand. Is it an apple? Yes. The object in your hand belongs to the clumps of space-time we call the set of apples— all apples anywhere ever. Now take a bit, chew it, swallow it. Let your digestive tract take apart the apple's molecules. Is the object in your hand still an apple? Yes or no? Take another bite. Is the new object still an apple? Take another bite, and so on down to void. The apple changes from thing to nonthing, to nothing. But where does it cross the line from apple to nonapple? When you hold half an apple in your hand, the apple is as much there as not. The half apple foils all-or-none descriptions. The half apple is a *fuzzy* apple, the gray between the black and the white. *Fuzziness is grayness*.
   —Bart Kosko, *Fuzzy Thinking: The New Science of Fuzzy Logic*

Using Examples

Develop the following point by adding a series of short examples: Some of the most important things we need to know have to be learned outside a classroom.

6.5 USING ANALOGY

An **analogy** is a statement linking two things that we normally put in different categories. Here are three examples:

1. The surface of the Earth is like the skin of an orange, which cannot be spread out flat unless it is torn into strips. That is why flat maps of the whole Earth always distort its appearance.

2. Starting college was like being a child in the middle of a candy store. Everywhere I turned I found an exotic treat, something I wanted to taste. But I couldn't taste everything, much less consume it all. A child who eats too much candy develops a stomachache. A college student who joins too many clubs has too little time for course work, and must eventually suffer the pain of low grades. So I had to learn how to resist the sweet temptations of college life.

3. Since the lattice-work molecular structure of metal normally vibrates, sending electrons through a copper wire by ordinary conduction is like shooting a bunch of pellets through a chain-link fence in the middle of an earthquake. Because the fence is shaking, some of the pellets hit the links or bounce off each other instead of passing through. But superconduction occurs when supercooling stops the vibration of the conductor. Superconduction, therefore, is like firing pellets through the fence when the earthquake is over. Because the fence stands still, all the pellets get through.

You can use analogy not just to explain, but to make arguments:

> Defenders of so-called "passive" euthanasia distinguish between killing a patient and letting one die. But whether euthanasia is morally right or wrong under any circumstances, allowing a preventable death to occur is morally no better than causing it. The practitioner of "passive" euthanasia is like a lifeguard allowing a man to drown. Suppose that the man is depressed or even suffering from an incurable disease, that he has asked the lifeguard to hold him under, and that the lifeguard has refused. If the lifeguard's duty is to save the lives of swimmers, letting the man sink to his death in deep water is not morally different from drowning him. Likewise, if a doctor's duty is to prolong the lives of patients, letting any one of them die is not morally different from giving a fatal injection.

Arguing by analogy takes special care. If the two things being compared don't correspond in essential ways, the argument will be misleading, unconvincing, or both. (For more on this point, see 11.5, "False Analogy.")

Using Analogy

The federal government estimates that more than twenty-six million American adults are functionally illiterate, unable to read such things as recipes, warning labels, and want ads. Construct an analogy that begins, "To be functionally illiterate in our society is like . . ."

Arguing by Analogy

In a presidential campaign, one candidate proposed that no one should be granted a driver's license unless he or she had been tested for drugs. Construct an analogy that could be used to argue for or against this proposal.

6.6 USING COMPARISON AND CONTRAST

While analogy links two things that we normally put in different categories, such as an orange and the Earth, comparison and contrast operates on two things that we normally put in the same category. Typically, writers compare and contrast two things in order to show how they differ, and often to show that one of them is better than the other.

> You see things vacationing on a motorcycle in a way that is completely different from any other. In a car you're always in a compartment, and because you're used to it you don't realize that through that car window everything you see is just more TV. You're a passive observer and it is all moving by you boringly in a frame.
>
> On a cycle the frame is gone. You're completely in contact with it all. You're *in* the scene, not just watching it anymore, and the sense of presence is overwhelming. That concrete whizzing by five inches below your foot is the real thing, the same stuff you walk on, it's right there, so blurred you can't focus on it, yet you can put your foot down and touch it anytime, and the whole thing, the whole experience, is never removed from immediate consciousness.
>
> —Robert Pirsig, *Zen and the Art of Motorcycle Maintenance*

BLOCK STRUCTURE AND ALTERNATING STRUCTURE

You can organize a comparison and contrast in either of two ways: in blocks or in regular alternation. In a block-structured comparison and contrast, each of the two things considered gets a block of sentences or an entire paragraph to itself. In the example above, for instance, Pirsig devotes most of his first paragraph to traveling by car and all of his second to traveling by motorcycle. But you can also compare and contrast two things by alternating back and forth between them:

> For much of recorded history, China has been more advanced than the West. Chinese philosophy, poetry, science, and government were for long periods more sophisticated than those of Europe, and China's standard of living may have been higher. China, after all, invented paper, gunpowder, the magnetic compass, the clock, the wheelbarrow, and nautical and ship-building innovations such as the rear rudder. Chinese technicians were casting molten iron seventeen centuries before Europeans figured out how to do it. Chinese peasants used seed drills 2,000 years ago to plant several rows of grain at a time; Europeans did not use seed drills until the seventeenth century. Chinese mathematicians calculated pi to five decimal places in the third century B.C. and used coordinate geometry more than a millennium before Europeans became skilled at it. In other words, the world as we know it—in which the West is modern and China is backward—is a relatively recent phenomenon. For much of history, it's been the other way around. It's just that China never exploited its innovations.
> —Nicholas Kristof and Sheryl Wudunn, *China Wakes*

Here the writer moves back and forth between China and Europe while also moving down a list of corresponding features.

WRITING AN ESSAY OF COMPARISON AND CONTRAST

Because alternating structure continually reminds the reader that two things are being compared and contrasted, it can work well for one or two paragraphs. But steady alternation can become monotonous. For this reason, an essay that makes extensive use of comparison and contrast should combine alternation with block structure. The passage below uses block structure for the first two paragraphs and alternating structure for the third one:

> The first time I ever really thought about the difference between American and Russian graffiti was last year, on San Francisco's famous Haight Street. The walls of the houses and even the sidewalks were crowded with fresh appeals to remember the "Summer of Love," addressed to something called the "Poe-lice"—spelled like that, with a hyphen. Superimposed here and there on brightly painted murals of people and flowers were sprawling names and mysterious inscriptions.

Graffiti started to appear all over Moscow only quite recently. Before perestroika,[†] you couldn't buy felt-tip pens or spray paint, because the state couldn't see any point to them; they weren't included in the production plans. Yet even today Russian inscriptions are depressingly unoriginal—most of them varying little from the words Holden Caulfield[††] tried to erase from the wall at his sister's school. The rest consist of the words rap and techno and the names of U.S. rock bands. It is hard to drive through some neighborhoods without absorbing a scrawled update from American show business.

The explanation for the variety of American wall painting and the monotony of ours seems to be quite simple. The Russian teen-ager is likely to transfer to the nearest wall a trademark that has mysteriously lodged in his memory, and then examine it curiously in an attempt to understand how it found its way inside his head. The American teen-ager, on the other hand, in tracing his esoteric, indecipherable signature, is an image-maker adding his own logo to the cluttered symbols around him. When he traces a mysterious zigzag on the concrete support of a bridge, he is already beginning to carve his niche in life.

—Victor Pelevin, *The New York Times Magazine*, June 8, 1997

(trans. Andrew Bromfield)

[†]Refers to the expansion of freedom of speech and expression in the Soviet Union during the mid-1980s.

[††]The narrator and protagonist in J. D. Salinger's *Catcher in the Rye*.

Comparing and Contrasting with Block Structure

Taking as a model the two paragraphs by Pirsig on p. 91, use block structure to compare and contrast the two items in any one of the following pairs:

men's basketball/women's basketball

Internet search engine/Internet search directory

Republicans/Democrats

East Coast/West Coast

cable TV/satellite TV

crime/terrorism

high school/college

Web site/chatroom

Comparing and Contrasting with Alternating Structure

Taking as a model the paragraph by Kristof and Wudunn on p. 92, use alternating structure to compare and contrast the two items in any one of the following pairs:

> hardware/software
>
> conservatives/liberals
>
> TV/movies
>
> print news (newspapers)/TV news
>
> email/letters
>
> videotapes/DVD
>
> astronomy/astrology
>
> spamming/computer virus

Using Comparison and Contrast to Explain a Point

Using comparison and contrast, write an essay that explains any one of the following:

1. Why shopping online is better than shopping in stores or vice versa

2. Why a laptop computer is better than a desktop computer

3. Why living on one's own is better than living with one's family or vice versa

4. Why email is better than letters or vice versa

5. Why running one's own business is better than working for someone else or vice versa

6. Why custom is sometimes more powerful than law

6.7 USING DEFINITIONS

Definition enhances the clarity of your writing. Whatever you aim to do in your text, you cannot reach your readers unless they can readily understand your words. Whenever you use a term that your readers are unlikely to know, or whenever you use a common word in a specialized sense, you can help your reader by defining it.

The most common and also least effective way to define a word or phrase is to quote the dictionary. In addition to or instead of quoting the dictionary, use one or more of these methods:

1. DEFINING BY SYNONYM

    Apathetic means "indifferent."

    Prevaricate means "lie."

    Clandestinely means "secretly."

The form of the synonym should correspond to the form of the word being defined. *Apathetic* (adjective) means not "indifference" (noun) but "indifferent" (adjective).

2. DEFINING BY COMPARISON, CONTRAST, OR ANALOGY

    The *plover* is a bird that lives on the shore, like the sandpiper. But the plover is usually fatter, and unlike the sandpiper, it has a short, hard-tipped bill.

    While burglary is the stealing of property from a place, *robbery* is the stealing of property from a person.

    A *lien* on a piece of property is like a leash on a dog. It's a way of legally attaching the property to someone who has a claim against the property owner.

3. DEFINING BY FUNCTION

    An *orthopedist* treats bone diseases.

    An *ombudsman* defends an individual in a conflict with an institution.

4. DEFINING BY CLASSIFICATION   You can define a word by naming the class of the person or thing it denotes and then giving one or more distinctive features:

	CLASS	FEATURE
An *orthopedist*	is a doctor	who specializes in bones.
A *skylight*	is a window	set in the roof of a building.

5. DEFINING BY EXAMPLE   You can define a word by giving examples after classifying the person or thing it denotes:

A *crustacean* is a shelled creature such as a lobster, a shrimp, or a crab.

A *planet* is a heavenly sphere such as Jupiter, Mercury, Mars, or Earth.

6.   DEFINING BY ETYMOLOGY   Etymology is the study of the roots of words. You can sometimes define a word by giving its root meaning and thus showing where it came from:

Intuition comes from the Latin words *in* (meaning "in" or "into") and *tueri* (meaning "look" or "gaze"). Literally, therefore, it means a "looking inward."

COMBINING METHODS OF DEFINITION

A single definition may combine two or more methods. In the passage below, the writer defines *bioneer* by using synonyms, describing functions, and providing examples:

A bioneer is a biological pioneer, an ecological inventor who's got an elegant and often simple set of solutions for environmental conundrums. The term comes from the pen of Kenny Ausubel, cofounder of Seeds of Change, a company that conserves and sells seeds for native plants that have been overshadowed by mega-agriculture's mighty, and unsustainable, hybrids. . . . Who are the bioneers? John Todd creates "living machines" that use various plants to carry out simple miracles of waste treatment. Vinnie McKinney's Elixir Farms gathers and preserves neglected and rare strains of medicinal herbs, particularly herbs used in Chinese medicine. John Roulac researches worthwhile uses for that infamous "weed," hemp. The list goes on, but what unites [bioneers] is the belief that in paying attention to how nature works, we can find the best ways to heal nature.

—Jon Spayde, *Utne Reader,* March–April 1999

EXERCISE 18   **Defining**

Using at least two of the methods described above, define one of the following words:

hypocrite	poverty
ecology	cyberspace
feminist	racism
celebrity	cell phone
spamming	computer virus

6.8 EXPLAINING BY ANALYZING: CLASSIFICATION AND DIVISION

Analyzing means looking closely at the parts of an object or group. To analyze a *single* object, such as the human body, you divide it into its parts, such as the heart, the brain, the stomach, and the liver. To analyze a *group* of objects or persons, you divide and classify them, cutting one group into two or more smaller groups. To analyze the American people, for instance, you could divide and classify them in political categories (such as voters and nonvoters), in ethnic groups (such as Italian, Hispanic, and African American), or in regional groups (such as Northerners and Southerners). In so doing, you would be using *classification* and *division*.

Classification is a way of ordering the world around us. It's the arrangement of objects, people, or ideas into classes or groups. Whenever you speak of professors, sophomores, women, men, jocks, or nerds, you are grouping individuals together as a class because of one or more things they have in common. You can do the same with individual objects or ideas. You can classify motorcycles, cars, and trucks as "motor vehicles"; apples, pears, and oranges as "fruits"; monarchy, democracy, and plutocracy as "political systems."

Classification usually goes hand in hand with division. If, for instance, you divide "fruit juices" into fresh, frozen, canned, and powdered, you have identified four different forms of juice. But instead of dividing the juices according to their forms, you could divide them according to their flavors: apple, orange, grapefruit, lemon, and so on. How you divide and classify depends on your purpose. When you bring home groceries, you commonly divide and classify them at first into just two groups: those that need refrigeration and those that don't. In everyday living, then, everyone has to classify and divide in order to cope with a world of individual objects and people. And what is true in everyday living is also true in writing. Whenever you write about a group of people, objects, or ideas, you need a system of classifying and dividing them. Consider how the student author of this essay uses classification and division to explain Japanese society.

Insiders and Outsiders in Japanese Society

[1] Many things about Japanese society puzzle Americans. But hardest of all for Americans to understand is the Japanese devotion to groups. Unlike Americans, the Japanese do not usually think of themselves as independent individuals. They act as members of a community, of a company, or at the very least of a family, which is the minimum social unit. Whatever the group, its very existence depends on the basic difference between

insiders and outsiders. Understanding that difference is the key to understanding Japanese society as a whole, and the Japanese family in particular.

[2] The first thing to be understood about *insiders* and *outsiders* is that these are relative terms. Japanese society cannot be imagined as a tight little circle of insiders surrounded by a great big ring of outsiders. It is rather a world of bubbles. In each bubble is a group of people who think of each other as insiders and who look upon all the other people in all the other bubbles as outsiders. No one can be absolutely classified as either an insider or an outsider. To be inside one bubble is, inevitably, to be outside all the others.

[3] The system is complicated because one big bubble may sometimes contain many small ones. A big company, for instance, may include many departments or sections, and each of those sections is a bubble of insiders who work together closely, see each other often, and think of all other company workers as outsiders. Yet as soon as the insiders of a particular section think of their whole company in relation to a competitor, everyone who works for the company becomes an insider, and the outsiders are those who work for the competition.

[4] The opposition between insiders and outsiders becomes still more evident when we turn from Japanese companies to Japanese families. The Japanese family does not merge with other families, or with society at large. While American families often entertain large numbers of casual acquaintances, Japanese families seldom open their doors to anyone but insiders: family members or relatives. On the rare occasions when a close friend of the family is invited, he or she thereby becomes an insider—in effect, one of the family. Everyone else remains an outsider, and is literally kept outside the family home.

[5] The opposition between insiders and outsiders also explains why the actual structure of the Japanese family differs so much from the way it appears to the outside world, especially to Americans. Most Americans think the typical Japanese family is totally ruled by the husband, with the wife no more than a servant. In fact, the modern Japanese family is ruled by the wife. It is she who takes all of her husband's salary, oversees all household repairs and expenditures, and supervises the education of the children. Inside the family, she has absolute authority.

[6] Yet as soon as the family confronts an outsider, the husband plays the ruler. A perfect example of this switch is what happens when a Japanese family goes out to eat. Before the family leaves the house, the wife gives the husband enough cash to pay the bill. When the family members sit down in the restaurant, the wife decides what the children will eat and often what her husband will eat as well, overruling him if she finds his choices too expensive. But as soon as the waiter arrives, the husband orders for the entire family as if he had made all the choices himself. In so doing, he represents the family for the eyes of an outsider, and so long as those eyes are watching, he is in charge. When he finishes paying the check with the money that his wife has allowed him, she and the children bow to him and say, "Thank you for a good meal, Father."

[7] To understand Japanese society, then, one must understand both the power of the group and the distinction between insiders and outsiders. Since all members of a group are insiders, they can act as individuals among themselves, arguing with each other until they agree or until one of them—the wife in the case of a family group—decides for all. But to outsiders they present a united front. Once they turn from confronting each other to confronting the outside world, insiders cease to be individuals and become part of a group which determines what their public roles will be.

—Rick Kurihara

Using the basic distinction between insiders and outsiders, Rick divides and classifies all individuals in relation to groups, and thus explains how group mentality in Japan governs individual action. This essay also shows how different means of exposition can work together. (For more on this topic, see 6.11.)

Using Classification and Division to Explain Yourself   **EXERCISE 19**

Write an essay in which you (1) name any group to which you belong; (2) explain what the members of the group have in common; (3) divide the group into two or more subgroups; (4) explain each of the subgroups; and (5) explain which subgroup you belong to.

6.9   EXPLAINING A PROCESS

A process is a sequence of actions that lead or should lead to a predictable result. The way you explain a process depends on your purpose—on whether you want to teach the process or simply help your reader understand it.

TEACHING A PROCESS

To teach a process so that your readers can carry it out, you must explain every thing and every step it requires, as in this explanation of how to re-place spark plugs:

To replace worn plugs, you need three tools that you can buy at any auto-motive parts store: a ratchet wrench with a short extension handle, a spark plug socket, and a spark plug gauge. The most important thing to know about spark plugs is that you have to remove and replace them *one at a time*. If you take them all out at once, you will have to disconnect all of their wires at the same time, and you will probably not remember which plugs they came from. Since each plug has its own wire and since the car will not run if the wires are mixed up, you should never have more than one wire disconnected at any one time. The owner's manual for your car will tell you where the spark plugs are. Once you have located them, you must do five things with each plug in turn. First, disconnect the wire attached to it. Second, with the spark plug socket placed over the plug and the ratchet wrench in the socket, remove the plug by turning the wrench counterclockwise. Third, use the spark plug gauge to measure the size of the little gap in the electrode—the small open square of metal that sticks up out of the threaded tube at one end of the spark plug. If the gap is too big, the electrode is worn, and the plug must be replaced. Fourth, insert the old plug or a new one by turning it clockwise with your fingers until it sticks, and then using the wrench to turn it a quarter of a circle more. Fifth, reconnect the wire that belongs to that particular plug.

—Jim Robb

REPORTING A PROCESS

If you aim to help your readers understand a process rather than teaching them to carry it out, just report its chief stages:

In contact with the proper food on leaving the egg, the caterpillar begins to eat immediately and continues until it has increased its weight hundreds of times. On each of the first three segments of the body is a pair of short legs ending in a sharp claw. These legs correspond to the six legs of the adult insect. In addition, the caterpillar has up to ten short, fleshy feet called prolegs, which are shed before it changes form. The insect passes its pupal stage incased in comparatively rigid integuments—layers—that form a chrysalis. Most butterfly chrysalides remain naked, unlike those of the moth, which have a protective cocoon. Breathing goes on through an air opening while the complete adult, or imago, develops. Wings, legs, proboscis, even the pigment in the scales, form in the tight prison of the crysalis. At maturity, the chrysalis splits its covering and wriggles out as an imago, or perfect insect. Hanging from a leaf or rock, it forces blood, or haemolymph, into the veins of its wet wings, straightening them to their normal span. Soon the wings are dry, and the insect flies into a life of nectar drinking and courtship.

—"Butterfly," *Funk & Wagnalls New Encyclopedia*

In this reporting explanation, the writer describes the stages through which the insect passes, but does not explain everything about its transformation. The writer is trying to help readers understand the overall process—not teach them how to become butterflies themselves.

Teaching a Process

Write a teaching explanation of any simple process that you know well and that can be taught in writing, such as subscribing to a listserv, changing the batteries in a watch, or setting the clock on a VCR. When you have finished, see if a reader can actually perform the process by following your instructions.

Reporting a Process

Write a reporting explanation of any process you know well, such as climbing a cliff, painting a picture, making a clay pot, taking or developing a good photograph. If you use any specialized terms, be sure to define them as you go.

6.10 EXPLAINING CAUSE AND EFFECT

Since any situation or event can provoke questions about its causes, its effects, or both, one good way of explaining anything is to raise such questions. Why do Americans charge so much on credit cards? How do Americans' credit-card debts affect the economy? Why have there been so many recent incidents of gun violence in American high schools? How has gun violence in schools changed the daily lives of high school students? For a particular situation or event there may be several causes, several effects, or both. Consider the following essay:

WHY DO WOMEN LONG TO BE THIN?

[1] "I've just *got* to lose ten pounds by the end of the month," said Karen. Sitting opposite me at a little square white table in the North Campus cafeteria, she was doggedly crunching her way through a salad of iceberg lettuce and sliced cucumbers, trying hard not to look at the mountain of chocolate sauce, vanilla ice cream, whipped cream, and chopped walnuts that had just been served to some junk food addict at the next table. Karen is not fat, but she'll never be thin enough to eat anything she wants without feeling guilty. As I looked at her while dutifully sipping my own Diet Coke, I asked myself why nearly all young women in America yearn to lose weight.

Situation to be explained

First cause:
magazine ads and
articles

[2] Part of the reason can be found in magazines like *Seventeen* and *Glamour*, which are cunningly designed to reach teenage girls in their most impressionable years. The articles and ads in these magazines all preach the gospel of thinness. The typical ad shows a skinny model along with some gorgeous guy who is gazing at her with enraptured eyes. The typical article reveals a new diet, a new kind of exercise, or just some new piece of evidence for the argument that thinner is better.

[3] An article about the lead singer in the group called Wilson Phillips, for instance, reported that she was always put in the back when pictures were taken for their albums. When she asked why, she was told that the image of her fat body might scare album buyers away. So she determined to lose weight and did. As a result, she now stands in the front of the album pictures, and her story exemplifies what young women are endlessly told: while fatness pushes you out of the picture, thinness brings you popularity and self-confidence.

Second cause: TV
commercials and
programs

[4] Television tells us much the same. Fat women seldom appear in TV commercials except to show what they looked like before the sponsor's product slimmed them down. In TV programs, fat women are just as scarce. With a few exceptions such as Roseanne Barr and Oprah Winfrey, the women we see in TV programs are thin. Any actress who gets fat may suffer the fate of Delta Burke. After years of work in the series called *Designing Women*, she was fired after gaining weight. Though the show's producers claimed she was fired for not doing a good job, I suspect the real reason is that she dared to be fat.

Third cause:
books on fitness
and dieting by
slim female
celebrities

[5] Besides the messages about fat that we get from magazines and television, books feed us a steady diet of advice on how to lose weight, be fit, and stay fit. Often these books are gobbled up because they are written or promoted by famous women with beautifully slim figures. Jane Fonda is no authority on nutrition, but some years back, when the diving board scene of *On Golden Pond* showed how thin she could be even in her forties, her book on fitness became a best-seller.

[6] In a variety of ways, then, magazines, television, and books relentlessly preach the message that women must be thin. While fatness, we are told, leads to neglect, unemployment, and loneliness, thinness makes a woman desirable, successful, and perhaps even glamorous, like Jane Fonda or Cher. But we hear far too much about the bad effects of being fat and the good effects of being thin. We hear far too little about the bad effects of the yearning to be thin. This yearning turns some women into anorexics, who starve themselves to death, and others into bulimics, who ravage their stomachs by gorging and disgorging food. Even those who try to lose weight by ordinary dieting—like my friend Karen—too often allow the quest for thinness to become an obsession that rules their lives.

Effects of thinness
and fatness,
effects of
yearning for
thinness

[7] What would happen, I wonder, if American women decided to shuck this obsession? Well, for one thing, the people who make billions of dollars every year by selling diet pills and fitness plans would find themselves out of business. At the same time, instead of letting magazines and TV shows tell them how to look, instead of basing their self-esteem on the size or shape of their bodies, women could restart the business of running their own lives.

Effects of breaking the obsession with thinness

—René Cardle

Explaining Cause and Effect

EXERCISE 22

1. Despite all the messages telling women they should be thin, Americans as a whole are increasingly overweight. Identify what you believe are the causes of Americans' weight problems.
2. Discuss the effects of unemployment on any community you know about.
3. Explain the causes or effects of any event or condition you know about.
4. Discuss the potential effects of the kind of biased search engines described below:

One of the most troubling developments in cyberspace is a form of "insidious" subterfuge being perpetrated by some search engines, says Tim Berners-Lee, 44, inventor of the Web and director of the World Wide Web Consortium (W3C). He's concerned about some search services' practice of secretly letting their "platinum partners" buy top positions in search results, making them appear to be the best site to find what's being searched for. People expect unbiased results when they search the Web, he says. In other media, "a line is drawn between editorial content and advertising." He'd like to see search engines that deliver unbiased searches label themselves as such and to see others spell out their policies. But "on the Web we don't have that yet."   —*USA Today*, April 12, 1999

6.11 COMBINING METHODS OF DEVELOPMENT

Good essays often combine two or more methods of development. Rick Kurihara's essay on insiders and outsiders (pp. 97–99), for instance, not only classifies and divides Japanese society; it also compares and contrasts Japanese society with American society (paragraphs 1 and 4), constructs the analogy of bubbles (paragraphs 2 and 3), and uses an example to illustrate Japanese family life (paragraph 6).

EXERCISE 23   **Combining Methods of Development**

Using at least three methods of development discussed in this chapter, write an essay in which you explain to a high school senior the operation of any team, club, or organization at your college.

Writing Paragraphs

A **paragraph** is usually a block of sentences set off by spacing or indentation at the beginning. Though commonly part of an essay, it can and sometimes does serve as an essay in its own right, and the writing of one-paragraph essays will give you small-scale practice in organization. For that reason, much of this chapter deals with the single paragraph as a self-contained unit.

7.1 WHY USE PARAGRAPHS?

Part of the answer to this question is that a text is like a long stairway. Unless it is interrupted now and then as if by a landing, a place to stop before continuing, the reader may simply get tired or bored. Have you ever turned the page of a book or an article to find nothing but a solid block of print? Did you heave a little sigh, or a big one? That's because you expect to *see* paragraph breaks at regular intervals, especially where the writer's thought turns. Compare these two ways of presenting the same passage:

> It's a never-ending task being a Nielsen family. Want to watch TV? First you turn the set on, then you punch a button telling Nielsen Media Research that it's you, a 27-year-old college-educated male making $59,000 a year, sitting there in front of the tube. Then you can choose your channel. Walk into the room where your 25-year-old wife is already engrossed in *Friends*? Push the button to tell Nielsen you're there. Run to the bathroom during a commercial? Yep, that button should be pushed again, as it should be yet again when you return. And if you have a baby, once she hits two, she too will have to learn to push her own special Nielsen button. The whole family will do this for two years, all for a token reward. Television's power lies in its ability to reach tens of millions of viewers at a time. But whether the second night of *60 Minutes* or the fledgling Animal

Planet cable channel survives depends on just a handful of people—not television executives, but the anonymous button-pushing families whose viewing gets translated into the ubiquitous Nielsen ratings. The numbers aren't just fodder for TV columnists and *Entertainment Tonight*. They determine how some $48 billion is spent annually on television advertising. And as the number of channels multiplies and the Internet threatens to nibble away at time spent in front of the tube, each and every viewer has become precious in a fiercely competitive business. From network shows to cable networks to local newscasts, one tenth of a rating point up or down can determine life or death. That makes Nielsen, the sole provider of those numbers in the United States, a key player in determining what viewers see. And with its numbers drawing increasing scrutiny, Nielsen is causing the TV industry a lot of angst.

Topic
established.

It's a never-ending task being a Nielsen family. Want to watch TV? First you turn the set on, then you punch a button telling Nielsen Media Research that it's you, a 27-year-old college-educated male making $59,000 a year, sitting there in front of the tube. Then you can choose your channel. Walk into the room where your 25-year-old wife is already engrossed in *Friends*? Push the button to tell Nielsen you're there. Run to the bathroom during a commercial? Yep, that button should be pushed again, as it should be yet again when you return. And if you have a baby, once she hits two, she too will have to learn to push her own special Nielsen button. The whole family will do this for two years, all for a token reward.

New paragraph
marks first point
made about the
topic.

Television's power lies in its ability to reach tens of millions of viewers at a time. But whether the second night of *60 Minutes* or the fledgling Animal Planet cable channel survives depends on just a handful of people—not television executives, but the anonymous button-pushing families whose viewing gets translated into the ubiquitous Nielsen ratings.

New paragraph
marks second
point made
about the topic.

The numbers aren't just fodder for TV columnists and *Entertainment Tonight*. They determine how some $48 billion is spent annually on television advertising. And as the number of channels multiplies and the Internet threatens to nibble away at time spent in front of the tube, each and every viewer has become precious in a fiercely competitive business. From network shows to cable networks to local newscasts, one tenth of a rating point up or down can determine life or death. That makes Nielsen, the sole provider of those numbers in the United States, a key player in determining what viewers see. And with its numbers drawing increasing scrutiny, Nielsen is causing the TV industry a lot of angst.

—Elizabeth Jensen, "Meet the Nielsens,"
Brill's Content, March 1999

Dividing a Passage into Paragraphs   EXERCISE 1

In the following passage, we have deliberately run the author's original three paragraphs into one. Divide the passage into what you think were the original three paragraphs and state the main point of each.

There are days when I find myself unduly pessimistic about the future of man. Indeed, I will confess that there have been occasions when I swore I would never again make the study of time a profession. My walls are lined with books expounding its mysteries; my hands have been split and rubbed raw with grubbing into the quicklime of its waste bins and hidden crevices. I have stared so much at death that I can recognize the lingering personalities in the faces of skulls and feel accompanying affinities and repulsions. One such skull lies in the lockers of a great metropolitan museum. It is labeled simply: Strand-looper, South Africa. I have never looked longer into any human face than I have upon the features of that skull. I come there often, drawn in spite of myself. It is a face that would lend reality to the fantastic tales of our childhood. There is a hint of Wells' *Time Machine* folk in it—those pathetic, childlike people whom Wells pictures as haunting earth's autumnal cities in the far future of the dying planet. Yet this skull has not been spirited back to us through future eras by a time machine. It is a thing, instead, of the millennial past. It is a caricature of modern man, not by reason of its primitiveness but, startlingly, be-cause of a modernity outreaching his own. It constitutes, in fact, a mysterious prophecy and warning. For at the very moment in which students of humanity have been sketching their concept of the man of the future, that being has already come, and lived, and passed away.

—Loren Eiseley, "Man of the Future"

Building Paragraphs   EXERCISE 2

The paragraphs below and on p. 108 each consist of just one or two sentences. Combine some of these paragraphs so that each new paragraph develops a new point rather than simply extending an old one.

The weekend rolls around, and most of us want to spend time with those dear to us. Our wallets tell us that we have ten bucks for an outing with the family.

No problem—we can pack a lunch and head for the Smoky Mountain National Park. The ten dollars goes in the gas tank, and away we go for hiking, fishing, biking, or just sightseeing.

> Unfortunately, this type of family recreation may become a fond but distant memory as our government considers passing a bill requiring entrance fees for admittance to the park.
>
> If this bill is passed, one of our greatest natural resources will be in danger. Families who frequent the park now may no longer be able to afford it.
>
> Those who can pay to enter may decide that they want more for their money. This, in turn, could cause more commercial development of the land inside the park.
>
> How long will it be before we can't tell the difference between a national park and an amusement park?

7.2 COMMUNICATING YOUR MAIN POINT

PLACING YOUR MAIN POINT

You can emphasize a point by putting it at the beginning or the end of a paragraph, or in both places—provided you don't simply repeat it. The last sentence of this paragraph, for instance, not only recalls the meaning of the first one but adds something new:

> It seems to me that the safest and most prudent of bets to lay money on is surprise. There is a very high probability that whatever astonishes us in biology today will turn out to be usable, and useful, tomorrow. This, I think, is the established record of science itself, over the past two hundred years, and we ought to have more confidence in the process. It worked this way for the beginnings of chemistry; we obtained electricity in this manner; using surprise as a guide, we progressed from Newtonian physics to electro-magnetism, to quantum mechanics and contemporary geophysics and cosmology. In biology, evolution and genetics were the earliest big astonishments, but what has been going on in the past quarter century is simply flabbergasting. For medicine, the greatest surprises lie still ahead of us, but they are there, waiting to be discovered or stumbled over, sooner or later.
>
> —Lewis Thomas, "Medical Lessons from History"

FORECASTING YOUR MAIN POINT

To forecast the main point of a paragraph, start with a lead sentence—a sentence that tells the reader where you are headed. The lead sentence is sometimes the topic sentence of the paragraph, the sentence that states its main point. But not every good paragraph begins with a topic sentence, and in some paragraphs the main point is merely implied. So a lead sentence can do its forecasting in any one of the following ways:

1. STATING THE MAIN POINT

Eddie and I had come to the mine earlier that day for adventure. When we got there, the sun was shining on the remote dunes, stained red with copper sediment. An old, chillingly frank sign warned us "Danger: Keep Out!" Undaunted, I peered into the mine. The walls bulged as if they were going to fall down, blocking my view of the bottom. Eddie, who had been to the mine several times before, said he thought it was over a hundred feet deep. Carefully we worked our way down into the chasm, lowering ourselves inch by inch until we finally reached the bottom. We spent hours scaling the walls, exploring the caves, and marveling at the vastness of the mine.

—Andrew Lyle

2. STATING THE TOPIC

I have grown fond of semicolons in recent years. The semicolon tells you that there is still some question about the preceding full sentence; something needs to be added; it reminds you sometimes of Greek usage. It is almost always a greater pleasure to come across a semicolon than a period. The period tells you that that is that; if you didn't get all the meaning you wanted or expected, anyway you got all the writer intended to parcel out and now you have to move along. But with a semicolon there you get a pleasant little feeling of expectancy; there is more to come; read on; it will get clearer.

—Lewis Thomas, "Notes on Punctuation"

The lead sentence announces the topic (semicolons) and thus leads up to the main point, which comes at the end.

3. ASKING A QUESTION

Can you remember tying on your shoes this morning? Could you give the rules for when it is proper to call another person by his first name? Could you describe the gestures you make in conversation? These examples illustrate how much of our behavior is "out of awareness," and how easy it is to get into trouble in another culture.

—Edward T. Hall, "The Anthropology of Manners"

The opening question initiates a series of questions that lead to the main point, which (once again) appears at the end.

4. **SETTING A NEW DIRECTION**

> . . . When my father sent love letters to my mother, my grandmother would open and hide them, and when my mother told her parents she was going to marry this man, my grandmother said if that happened, it would kill her.
>
> *Not likely, of course.* My grandmother is a woman who used to crack Brazil nuts open with her teeth, a woman who once lifted a car off the ground, when there was an accident and it had to be moved. She has been representing her death as imminent ever since I've known her—twenty-five years—and has discussed, at length, the distribution of her possessions and her lamb coat. Every time we said goodbye, after our annual visit to Winnipeg, she'd weep and say she'd never see us again. But in the meantime, while every relative of her generation, and a good many of the younger ones, has died (usually nursed by her), she has kept making knishes, shopping for bargains, tending the healthiest plants I've ever seen.
>
> —Joyce Maynard, "Four Generations"

Here the lead sentence forecasts the main point of the paragraph simply by setting a new direction. The main point of the paragraph is nowhere stated in a topic sentence but is nonetheless clearly implied: my grandmother knows how to survive.

EXERCISE 3   **Forecasting Your Main Point**

In the following passage by a first-year college student, we have deleted the opening sentence of paragraph 3. Write a sentence that forecasts its main point.

[1] Going to college for most people means the onset of new freedoms and many responsibilities. In my first semester of college, new responsibilities helped me to develop values and maturity. This opportunity to mature is what drew me to college in the first place, and I especially felt the change in myself when the semester ended. Upon returning home for the Christmas holidays, I experienced new freedoms and respect from my parents.

[2] Before I went to college, I lived under their watchful eyes. My father pried me from the TV set whenever he knew I had homework to do, and my mother made sure I ate something besides hamburgers and pizza at least once a day. They also took turns reminding me to wear whatever I needed to keep me warm and dry whenever it was wet or cold. Most important of all, they never let me out of the

house at night without asking where I was bound and setting a time for my return.

[3] Since no one checked me in or out, I could stay up all night if I chose. I could eat pizza till I looked like one, and I could watch TV till my eyes glazed over. Starting college, in fact, was like being a child in the middle of a candy store. Everywhere I turned I found an exotic treat, something I wanted to taste. But I couldn't taste everything, much less consume it all. To get any work done, I had to learn how to say no to myself.

EMPHASIZING YOUR MAIN POINT

You can emphasize the main point of a paragraph by repeating key words or by placing the main point at the beginning or end.

REPEATING KEY WORDS OR PHRASES You may have been told that you should never repeat a word or phrase when you write, that you should scour your brain or your thesaurus for synonyms to avoid using a word or phrase again. That is nonsense. If repetition gets out of control, it will soon become monotonous and boring. But selective repetition keeps the eye of the reader on your main point. Compare these two paragraphs:

As a student begins her last year of high school, she may start to wonder what college or university is right for her. She will usually apply to several schools for *admission.* At ____ College, the student actually *exchanges* information on herself through her *application* and other forms and interviews for information about the school. It is through a *fair admissions process* that ____ College and its candidates for entrance learn a lot about each other. This *fair exchange* of ideas and insight in the *admissions process* can be seen through the college's *application* for *admission,* the guidance counselor forms, and the alumni *interview.*

—college student

Uncontrolled repetition

To me the *interview* comes as close as possible to being the quintessence of proper admissions procedure. It is a well-known secret (to use a paradox) that one can study for the achievement tests and the S.A.T. From personal experience I also know that schools "pad" grades and that students can receive marvelous grades without one iota of knowledge in a subject. One cannot, however, "fudge" an *interview.* One can buy a new suit and put on false airs, but 999 times out of 1,000 the *interviewer* can easily unmask the fraud and can thus reveal the true person.

—college student

Selective repetition

7.3 PARAGRAPH DEVELOPMENT

Using *list structure, chain structure,* or *a combination of the two,* you can develop your paragraphs to ensure their coherence, so that the reader sees a continuous line of thought passing from one sentence to the next.

USING LIST STRUCTURE

List structure uses a sequence of sentences with the same basic pattern to develop a general point, which is usually stated in the first sentence. Each sentence is a new item in a list of examples:

> They were a diverse group. *There were* priests *who* had brooded over the problem of a world in eternity and made the startling discovery that a holy mission summoned them away. *There were* noblemen in the great courts *who* stared out beyond the formal lines of the garden and saw the vision of new empires to be won. *There were* young men without places *who* depended on daring and their swords and were willing to soldier for their fortunes. *There were* clerks in the countinghouses, impatient of the endless rows of digits, *who* thought why should they not reach out for the wealth that set their masters high? *There were* journeymen without employment and servants without situations and peasants without land and many others whom war or pestilence displaced *who* dreamed in desperation of an alternative to home. Through the eighteenth century their numbers grew and, even more, through the nineteenth.
>
> —Oscar Handlin, *Race and Nationality in American Life*

EXERCISE 4   **Using List Structure**

Develop the following paragraph by adding to it at least three more examples in sentences that repeat the italicized words:

> As I jogged along the highway early this morning, *I thought* of all the different roads my friends from high school were starting on. *I thought* of Ruth, *who* was headed for Syracuse to major in broadcast journalism.

USING CHAIN STRUCTURE

Another way of ensuring coherence in your paragraphs is to make your sentences form a chain. As long as each sentence is linked in meaning to the sentence before it, the reader can follow your line of thought:

The process of learning is essential to our lives. All higher animals seek it deliberately. They are inquisitive and they experiment. An experiment is a sort of harmless trial run of some action which we shall have to make in the real world; and this, whether it is made in the laboratory by scientists or by fox-cubs outside their earth. The scientist experiments and the cub plays; both are learning to correct their errors of judgment in a setting in which errors are not fatal. Perhaps this is what gives them both their air of happiness and freedom in these activities.

—Jacob Bronowski, *The Common Sense of Science*

The sentences in this paragraph are connected like the links in a chain:

LEAD SENTENCE: The process of learning is essential to our lives.

A. All higher animals seek it deliberately.

B. They are inquisitive and they experiment.

C. An experiment is a sort of harmless trial run of some action which we shall have to make in the real world; and this, whether it is made in the laboratory by scientists or by fox-cubs outside their earth.

D. The scientist experiments and the cub plays; both are learning to correct their errors of judgment in a setting in which errors are not fatal.

E. Perhaps this is what gives them both their air of happiness and freedom in these activities.

Only the second sentence is directly linked to the lead sentence; each of the others is linked in meaning to the sentence just before it.

For the writer, the advantage of chain structure is that each sentence tends to suggest or generate the next sentence. The idea of the process of learning leads to the idea of learners (*All higher animals*); *animals* leads to a comment on what they do (*experiment*); *experiment* leads to a definition of that term (*An experiment is a sort . . .*), and so on. When you use chain structure, you are not free to forget about the topic sentence entirely, but you are free to experiment, to pursue the trail opened up by your own sentences, and even to discover something you did not foresee when you wrote the topic sentence. When Jacob Bronowski started this paragraph with a sentence about the process of learning, did he expect to end the paragraph with a sentence about happiness and freedom?

Using chain structure, develop one of the following paragraphs by adding at least three more sentences to it. Be sure that each new sentence is linked to the one before it.

1. LEAD SENTENCE: In recent years, letter writing has been dramatically changed by the fax machine.

A. A fax machine can send a letter to its destination in a tiny fraction of the time required for delivery by mail.

2. LEAD SENTENCE: The federal government estimates that approximately 28 million American adults are functionally illiterate.

A. A person who is functionally illiterate cannot understand such ordinary pieces of writing as recipes, labels on medicine bottles, instructions for the use of an appliance, and applications.

COMBINING LIST STRUCTURE AND CHAIN STRUCTURE

The following paragraph by a first-year college student shows how list structure and chain structure can work together:

> Going home for the Christmas vacation gave me the chance to see my life at college in a new light. At home, relatives and friends asked me how I liked the school and my classmates. I answered most of their questions with one-word responses, but I also questioned myself. Had I made any real friends? Did I like the campus atmosphere? Did I enjoy my courses as well as learn from them? As I thought about these questions, I realized that every one of them had a two-sided answer. I had picked up many acquaintances, but I could not yet call anyone my friend. I liked the general atmosphere of the campus, but disliked its conservative air. I enjoyed my courses, but felt many self-doubts. I had to admit to myself that I had no settled opinion about anything at college. I was still finding my way.
>
> —Adam Usadi

Basically, this paragraph uses a chain structure with two lists attached to it—a list of questions and a list of answers:

LEAD SENTENCE: Going home for the Christmas vacation gave me the chance to see my life at college in a new light.

A. At home, relatives and friends asked me how I liked the school and my classmates.

B. I answered most of their questions with one-word responses, but I also questioned myself.

   1. Had I made any real friends?

   2. Did I like the campus atmosphere?

   3. Did I enjoy my courses as well as learn from them?

   C. As I thought about these questions, I realized that every one of them had a two-sided answer.

      1. I had picked up many acquaintances, but I could not yet call anyone my friend.

      2. I liked the general atmosphere of the campus, but disliked its conservative air.

      3. I enjoyed my courses, but I felt many self-doubts.

         D. I had to admit to myself that I had no settled opinion about anything at college.

            E. I was still finding my way.

Using List and Chain Structure Together

EXERCISE 6

Expand the following paragraph by using a combination of list and chain structure to add supporting points. (Doing this exercise may require some reading.)

LEAD SENTENCE: The strongest weapon we can use in the war against AIDS is knowledge of the way it spreads.

A. For one thing, it can spread from a mother to her unborn child.

   1. If a woman is infected, her child has a 50 percent chance of inheriting the virus.

   2. So any woman who thinks that she could be infected should be tested for the virus before she considers having a child.

B. Second, it can spread from a drug needle.

7.4 TRANSITIONS WITHIN PARAGRAPHS

SIGNALING TURNS

Transitional words and phrases guide readers through a paragraph by signaling turns in thought, shifts in viewpoint, or movement from one point to another. Use transitional words and phrases for any one of the following purposes:

1. MARKING TIME

   I had begun to teach in *1964* in Boston in a segregated school so crowded and so poor that it could not provide my fourth grade children with a classroom. We shared an auditorium with another fourth grade and the choir and a group that was rehearsing, *starting in October*, for a Christmas play that, somehow, never was produced. *In the spring* I was shifted to another fourth grade that had had a string of substitutes all year. The 35 children in the class hadn't had a permanent teacher since they entered kindergarten. *That year*, I was their thirteenth teacher.

   —Jonathan Kozol, *Savage Inequalities*

2. MARKING ADDITION

   Lauryn Hill has demonstrated how rap music and hiphop culture can be positive social forces. Like male rappers, Hill addresses issues like police brutality and the criminal "injustice" system, but she *also* writes about single motherhood and access to education and opportunity. Hill has started two non-profit organizations for urban youth. *Furthermore*, she has resisted letting commercial success dilute her message, turning down movie offers that she believed would shift attention away from her social and political agenda.

   —college student

3. MARKING CONFLICT OR CONTRAST

   Computers may rival but they can never replace human intelligence. Computers and humans both solve problems through pattern matching. *However*, computers can only improve their problem-solving abilities by searching patterns more exhaustively, while humans improve by searching more efficiently.

   —college student

4. **MARKING THE SHIFT FROM CAUSE TO EFFECT**

   The world of religion and philosophy was shocked recently when Henry P. Van Dusen and his wife ended their lives by their own hands. Dr. Van Dusen had been president of Union Theological Seminary; for more than a quarter-century he had been one of the luminous names in Protestant theology. He enjoyed world status as a spiritual leader. News of the self-inflicted deaths of the Van Dusens, *therefore,* was profoundly disturbing to all those who attach a morel stigma to suicide and regard it as a violation of God's laws.

   —Norman Cousins, "The Right to Die"

5. **MARKING LIKENESS (COMPARING)**

   Geniuses have an uncanny power to defy physical handicaps and create masterpieces in the face of obstacles that might overwhelm the rest of us. John Milton was blind when he wrote the greatest of English epics, *Paradise Lost. Likewise,* Beethoven was deaf when he composed some of his greatest symphonies.

   —college student

6. **MARKING NUMERICAL ORDER**

   A local minimum wage has the potential to benefit the city as a whole. *First,* an adequate increase will raise many families out of poverty, taking them off public assistance rolls. *Second,* higher wages mean more tax revenues for the city, money that can be used to improve our schools, roads, and parks. *Finally,* by raising the standard of living for some, we increase the quality of life for all by reducing the human suffering that leads to division, resentment, and crime.

   —college student

7. **MARKING SPATIAL ORDER**

   The crowded subway car was like a microcosm of the city. *To my right,* two college students argued over a Beckett play. *Across* the aisle, a young couple tried to quiet a fussy baby. *To my left,* a woman—probably in her 70s—studied stock quotes in the *Wall Street Journal.*

   —college student

Transitional Words and Phrases: A Selective List

To Mark a Shift in Time

a few weeks ago

two years ago

previously

earlier

in the past

before

at present

now

nowadays

meanwhile

in the future

later

eventually

To Mark Spatial Order

nearby

in the distance

below

above

in front

in back

to the right

to the left

To Mark Numerical Order

first, second, etc.

in the first place

secondly, thirdly, etc.

to begin with, next, finally

To Signal Conflict or Contrast

but

nevertheless

however

conversely

on the other hand

still

otherwise

in contrast

unfortunately

instead

To Mark a Shift from Cause to Effect

therefore

hence

as a result

consequently

accordingly

To Mark Addition

besides

moreover

in addition

furthermore

To Compare

likewise

similarly

Signaling Turns within the Paragraph

At one or more points in each of the following passages a transitional word or phrase is missing. Find the points and insert suitable transitions.

1. Opponents of a bill granting marriage rights to gays in Vermont argued that homosexuality is immoral and that it will lead to the breakdown of society. Homosexuality has existed throughout history. Some of the world's greatest geniuses have been gay or lesbian. Whether one approves the gay/lesbian lifestyle or not, one has to respect the contributions of such people as Michelangelo and Tchaikovsky.

2. Higher education in America has hit a new low. In liberal-arts colleges, the abolition of many or even all specific requirements for graduation has left students to find their own way, which is often a closed alley. Allowed to take any courses they want, many students concentrate on just one subject or specialized skill. They graduate with narrow minds.

3. Revolution and moderation seldom go hand in hand. In the early years of the French Revolution, the moderate Girondists were outmaneuvered by the bloodthirsty Jacobins, who launched a reign of terror. Within months after the moderate Mensheviks launched the Russian Revolution of 1917, the radical Bolsheviks seized power and established a government of ruthless repression.

4. In the seventeenth century, a voyage across the Atlantic took more than two months. Jet service takes less than three hours.

PARAGRAPHING IN ACTION

Now that you have seen how good paragraphs are put together, consider a passage that badly needs paragraph structure:

[1] My life has been a very satisfying one so far. [2] I've faced many challenges and attained some of the goals I've set. [3] I am one of five children. [4] I have two older sisters and two younger brothers. [5] My father was a successful chef. [6] He had a college degree in electrical engineering, but chose to study cooking instead. [7] He traveled in Europe and worked with many different chefs. [8] He had a great influence on all of our lives. [9] He showed me what determination and hard work could do for a person. [10] My mother was a good mother. [11] She guided me in a very

practical way. [12] I was able to learn and grow under their supervision. [13] At times, it's hard to attain confidence in some situations, but I think of my parents and continue on. [14] I enjoy knitting and making things for others and I also love to cook. [15] Preparing economical meals is a constant challenge. [16] I like to read a lot. [17] I also enjoy watching my son grow up. [18] Children are a tremendous challenge. [19] I read to him and try to let him be as creative as possible. [20] I have also helped my husband go through his last year of college. [21] It was a proud moment for me to watch him walk up and get his degree. [22] I enjoyed working with him and learning as he did. [23] You really get a good feeling when you've helped someone. [24] Your rewards are twofold. [25] Helping others is my main goal in life. [26] I enjoy people. [27] So far, my life has been satisfactory to me. [28] I've got future goals set to attain. [29] I've got lots of hard work ahead of me. [30] I just look forward to going day by day and getting further toward my one goal of a college education with a challenging job.

The only thing that makes this set of sentences a "paragraph" is the indentation at the beginning. Every sentence here makes sense in itself, but reading these sentences one after the other is like trying to keep up with a kangaroo. The writer moves in short, sudden leaps, and the reader never knows where she will land next. She goes from challenges and goals to sisters and brothers, from parents to knitting and cooking, from helping others to helping herself. What point is she trying to make? She herself seems unsure. To reorganize a jumble like this, she must think about the connections and the differences between her sentences, and she must decide what her main point is. Only then can she write a paragraph that makes sense.

Rereading these sentences in the light of what you know about paragraph structure, you may see that there is matter here for at least two paragraphs: one on the writer's childhood and the influence of her parents, the other on her life and goals as a wife, mother, and college student. This division in the material becomes obvious if you examine the links between the sentences. The first sentence looks like a lead sentence, and the second is connected to it, but the third sentence has nothing to do with *challenges* and *goals,* and not until sentence 15 does either of those words appear again. Sentences 3–13 are really a detour from the road that the first two sentences open up, and therefore need to be taken out and reorganized under a topic sentence of their own.

Sentences 3–13 can be used to make a paragraph because they all concern the same topic—the writer's childhood and her parents. But to develop a paragraph from these sentences, the writer will first have to identify one of them as a lead sentence, a sentence that can state or forecast the main point of the whole group. A likely candidate is sentence 12: *I was able to learn and grow under their supervision.* To make this sentence work at the beginning of the paragraph, the writer will have to change *their* to *my parents'*. She will then have the start of a paragraph:

> I was able to learn and grow under my parents' supervision.

Now see how this lead sentence can help the writer organize the other sentences in the 3–13 group:

LEAD SENTENCE: I was able to learn and grow under my parents' supervision.

3. I am one of five children.

4. I have two older sisters and two younger brothers.

5. My father was a successful chef.

6. He had a college degree in electrical engineering, but chose to study cooking instead.

7. He traveled in Europe and worked with many different chefs.

8. He had a great influence on all of our lives.

9. He showed me what determination and hard work could do for a person.

10. My mother was a good mother.

11. She guided me in a very practical way.

13. At times, it's hard to attain confidence in some situations, but I think of my parents and continue on.

There are still some problems here. The lead sentence forecasts a discussion of the writer's parents, but sentences 3 and 4 concern her brothers and sisters. Though the brothers and sisters are obviously related to the writer's parents, they are not connected with her parents' supervision of her, or—except in the phrase *our lives* (sentence 8)—with their influence on her. When sentences 3 and 4 are cut out, you actually begin to see a paragraph taking shape:

> I was able to learn and grow under ⃞my parents'⃞ supervision.
>
> 5. My ⃝father⃝ was a successful chef.

The writer now has a definite link between the topic sentence and the one that follows it. In fact, she has the beginnings of a paragraph combining list structure and chain structure:

LEAD SENTENCE: I was able to learn and grow under my parents' supervision. [formerly sentence 12]

1. A. My father had a great influence on my life. [8, with *all of our lives* changed to *my life*]

    B. He showed me what determination and hard work could do for a person. [9]

    C. He had a college degree in electrical engineering, but chose to study cooking instead. [6]

    D. He traveled in Europe and worked with many different chefs. [7]

    E. He was a successful chef. [5]

2. A. My mother was a good mother. [10]

    B. She guided me in a very practical way. [11]

CONCLUDING SENTENCE: At times, it's hard to attain confidence in some situations, but I think of my parents and continue on. [13]

With the basic structure of the paragraph established, the writer can improve it further by adding transitional words and combining some of the sentences:

LEAD SENTENCE: I was able to learn and grow under my parents' supervision.

1. A. My father had a great influence on me *because* he showed me what determination and hard work could do for a person.

    B. He had a college degree in electrical engineering, but chose to study cooking instead, traveling in Europe and working with many different chefs.

    C. He *thus became* a successful chef *himself.*

2. A. My mother was a good mother *who* guided me in a very practical way.

CONCLUDING SENTENCE: At times, it's hard to attain confidence in some situations, but I think of my parents and continue on.

There is still room for development in this paragraph. To balance the chain of sentences about the father, the writer should say more about the mother, explaining how she gave guidance and what she taught. Specific statements here would enrich the paragraph and clarify the meaning of the topic sentence.

Shaping the rest of the original passage into paragraph form is harder. For one thing, there is no obvious lead sentence. Nearly all of the other sentences concern the writer's challenges and goals, but no one sentence on this subject forecasts the rest in the way that sentence 12 forecasts sentences 5–13. The writer speaks of past goals in sentences 1–2, 20–24, and 27, of present challenges and satisfactions in sentences 14–19 and 26, and of future goals in sentences 28–30. Most revealingly, she does not seem to know whether her main goal is helping others (sentence 25) or helping herself (sentence 30), or what the relation between these goals might be. Before she can write a coherent paragraph on her goals, she will have to do some more thinking and decide just what they are.

Expanding a Paragraph   EXERCISE 8

Expand the final version of the paragraph given on p. 122 by inserting at least two sentences about the mother after sentence 2.A.

Forming a Paragraph   EXERCISE 9

Choose a lead sentence from the following list and rearrange the remaining sentences to complete a paragraph, combining them and adding words where necessary:

1. The announcement of this principle led scientists in the United States and Great Britain to test and prove it by various devices.

2. The zoetrope was a cylinder covered with images.

3. According to this principle, the human eye retains an image for a fraction of a second longer than the image is present.

4. The principle was announced in 1824 by a British scholar named Peter Mark Roget.

5. One of these was a toy known as a zoetrope.

6. These simple applications of Roget's principle eventually led to the development of the motion picture.

7. Motion pictures originated from the discovery of the principle known as the persistence of vision.

8. Another device was a small book of drawings that seemed to move when flipped by the thumb.

9. The motion picture is actually a rapid succession of still pictures put together by the persistence of vision in the eye.

10. The images merged into a single picture when the cylinder was spun.

7.5 TRANSITIONS BETWEEN PARAGRAPHS

A good essay is more than a collection of separate paragraphs. It is made up of paragraphs linked to each other not only by the substance of what they say but also by the transitions between them. We have already explained how to signal turns and transitions within the paragraph (7.4). Likewise, there are various ways to link one paragraph with another, or to signal a turn as you begin the new one. Here are four ways to do so:

1. USE A TRANSITIONAL WORD OR PHRASE.

> As a young girl I could say anything to my two male friends, and they would know exactly what I meant. My words were never misunderstood. If I asked Shawn to go skating with me, we both knew that it was only a friendly gesture. When I asked Mark to spend the night at our house, there was nothing romantic implied. We slept quietly in the same room with nothing but occasional snoring to wake one of us up.
>
> Now, *however,* I have to be very careful of what I say to male friends.
>
> —college student

For a selective list of transitional words and phrases, see p. 118.

2. START A NEW PARAGRAPH BY ANSWERING ONE OR MORE QUESTIONS RAISED IN THE ONE BEFORE.

> . . . What should we talk about in order to make the right impression, or not to make the wrong one?
>
> The *answer* has to be something more important than the weather, something that allows us to learn what serious interests we share.
>
> —college student

3. START A NEW PARAGRAPH BY ASKING A QUESTION ABOUT A POINT YOU HAVE JUST MADE.

> . . . One has not only a legal but a moral responsibility to obey just laws. Conversely, one has a moral responsibility to disobey unjust laws. I would agree with St. Augustine that "an unjust law is no law at all."
>
> Now, what is the difference between the two? How does one determine whether a law is just or unjust?
>
> —Martin Luther King Jr., "Letter from Birmingham Jail"

4. START A NEW PARAGRAPH BY ECHOING A KEY WORD OR RECALLING A KEY IDEA
FROM THE ONE BEFORE.

. . . My peers look at my rattletrap and think I am a cursed child, with no hope of ever being popular. They are quite wrong, though. Once you get to know him, Harry is the American dream car.

He's far from a dream at first glance. He is ugly. . . .

Harry also complicates my life because of his faulty fuel gauge. Thirty miles after I fill him with gas, the needle falls directly from full to empty, so I have to depend on the odometer to tell me how much gas I've got left. Unfortunately, Harry's mileage per gallon drops drastically from summer to winter, as I discovered one night last December. While I was driving to a jumping meet in fifteen-degree weather, Harry sucked the last drop of unleaded gasoline from his tank and stopped. I had to decide whether to hunt for gas and miss the jumping meet or abandon Harry for two hours. I chose the latter.

This sort of thing would never happen to the driver of a late-model car.

—college student

Writing Paragraphs

To Direct Each Paragraph

Forecast your main point with a lead sentence that tells the reader where you are headed.

Signal each turn of your thought with an apt word or phrase.

To Ensure Coherence

Use a sequence of sentences with the same basic pattern (list structure);
or link each new sentence to the sentence before it (chain structure);
or use a combination of list and chain structures.

To Emphasize the Main Point

Repeat key words or phrases;
or place the main point at the beginning or end.

To Link Each New Paragraph to the One Before

Start with a transitional word or phrase;
or start by answering questions raised in the previous paragraph;
or start by echoing a key word or recalling a key idea from the previous paragraph.

1. In the following passage, one or more words at the beginning of the second paragraph have been deleted. Use a transitional word or phrase to clarify the shift between the two paragraphs.

> As children growing up in a small town, my brother and I were the only ones whose father was "different." He couldn't sing the national anthem or remember the words of the Pledge of Allegiance and found it difficult to comprehend the intricacies of football and baseball.
>
> . . . he was a very special parent. On rainy days he was always waiting for us at the school door, rubbers in hand; if we were ill he was there to take us home. He worked in town and was available to take us to music and dancing lessons or on little drives. When I was a small child he planted beside my window a beautiful oak tree that grew to be taller than our home.
>
> —Janet Heller, "About Morris Heller"

2. In the following passage, we have deleted the first sentence of the second paragraph and the first two sentences of the third. For each of those paragraphs write one or two opening sentences to clarify the transition from one paragraph to the next.

> Outside, in our childhood summers—the war. The summers of 1939 to '45. I was six and finally twelve; and the war was three thousand miles to the right where London, Warsaw, Cologne crouched huge, immortal under nights of bombs or, farther, to the left where our men (among them three cousins of mine) crawled over dead friends from foxhole to foxhole towards Tokyo or, terribly, where there were children (our age, our size) starving, fleeing, trapped, stripped, abandoned.
>
> . . . A shot would ring in the midst of our play, freezing us in the knowledge that here at last were the first Storm Troopers till we thought and looked—Mrs. Hightower's Ford. And any plane passing overhead after dark seemed pregnant with black chutes ready to blossom. There were hints that war was nearer than it seemed— swastikaed subs off Hatteras or the German sailor's tattered corpse washed up at Virginia Beach with a Norfolk movie ticket in his pocket.
>
> . . . Our deadly threats were polio, being hit by a car, drowning in pure chlorine if we swam after eating. No shot was fired for a hundred miles. (Fort Bragg—a hundred miles.) We had excess food to shame us at every meal, excess clothes to fling about us in the heat of play.
>
> —Reynolds Price, *Permanent Errors*

Style: Using a Community's Language

8

8.1 LANGUAGE AND GROUP IDENTITY

Groups of every kind communicate in distinctive ways. They use specialized terms or give common words a special twist. Compare these two music reviews:

> DJ Riz ups the ante on *Live From Brooklyn,* out now on the same LOUD-affiliated label that brought you Casual's "V.I.P." . . . Combining the tried and true formula of the digging tape with studio-quality production and smooth turntable trickery, *Live* is a two-part extravaganza of rare grooves. Rizzo scratches, blends, and juggles his way through virtually all of the hot beats of the last few years.
>
> —DJ Ayres, *Loop Hole Magazine*
> <www.loopholemag.com>, January 1999

> Astor Piazzolla's 1968 "tango operita" is an organic work, not at all like the dance revues *Tango Argentino* and the more recent *Forever Tango*, both of which played on Broadway. Although tangos dominate, *Maria* is really more a dramatic cantata or oratorio, and the vivid porteño poetry of Horacio Ferrer's Spanish libretto about the Buenos Aires streets ultimately calls the shots.
>
> —Richard Traubner, *Opera News*, February 1999

If you like rap music and identify with hip-hop culture, the first excerpt probably made perfect sense. The second review uses specialized terms ("cantata" and "oratorio"); the first uses common words ("digging" and "grooves") in specialized senses. To write about a specialized subject or communicate with those who know about that subject, you need to know its specialized terms.

127

EXERCISE 1   **Using Specialized Terms**

> List your hobbies and the activities and organizations in which you par-
> ticipate. Pick two and then list several specialized terms related to each.

LANGUAGE EXPECTATIONS IN AN ACADEMIC COMMUNITY

Academic communities also have their own languages. The specialized
language of an academic community helps its members speak in the most
precise terms about its subject of study. For example, as a young child you
knew some basic economic theory. You quickly learned that if you tried to
spend more money than you had, you either had to ask your parents for a
loan or wait and save for your purchase. Now, however, if you have taken a
college-level economics class, you have specialized terms, like "deficit
spending" and GDP (gross domestic product), to describe more complex
economic activities. These specialized terms allow you to speak more precisely about economics. In fact, you can't learn economic theory without
learning these specialized terms.

Since you show that you understand a field of study by correctly
using its specialized terms, you must be certain that you understand these
terms and are able to use them when you write papers or take tests. Keep
track of terms that are defined in your textbooks or in course lectures. If
you hear a word that you don't understand, look it up in your textbook or
dictionary.

EXERCISE 2   **Using Academically Specialized Terms**

> In a textbook on any academic subject find four or five specialized terms.
> Then use each term in a sentence of your own.

8.2 USING GENDER-INCLUSIVE LANGUAGE

Sexist language is language demeaning to either sex, particularly words
and phrases that mark women as inferior to men or restrict them because
of their gender. To make your writing fair to both genders, use language
that includes both of them unless you have good reason for excluding one.

1.   Use gender-inclusive terms to designate any job or position that can be held by a member of either sex:

> Beverly Pepper is an American ~~sculptress.~~ *sculptor.*

> The ~~stewardess~~ checked her list of passengers. *flight attendant*

> U.S. ~~Congressmen~~ are elected for two-year terms. *representatives*

In using words like those just above, you can change the *-man* ending to *-person,* as in *Congresspersons* and *chairperson.* But since the *-person* ending can be awkward, use alternatives whenever possible: *letter carriers* (for mailmen), *business executives* or *business owners* (for businessmen), *meteorologists* (for weathermen), *fire fighter* (for fireman), and so on.

2.   Whenever *man* or a *man*-word refers to both sexes, replace it with a genderless alternative such as *person, human,* or *people:*

> Modern ~~man~~ takes electricity for granted. *people*

> ~~Mankind~~ as we know it first appeared about forty thousand years ago. *Humankind*

> Voters seldom get the chance to choose the best ~~man~~ available. *person*

3.   When a pronoun refers to a word of unspecified gender, try to do one of the following:

a. Make the word and the pronoun plural:

> ~~A doctor~~ needs years of training before ~~he is~~ ready to operate. *Doctors* *or* *they are*

> ~~Any student~~ who thinks ~~he~~ can easily pass organic chemistry ~~is~~ deceiving ~~himself.~~ *Students* *or they* *are* *themselves.*

b. Use a feminine pronoun to balance the use of a masculine one:

> What a doctor expects from his patients is not quite the same as what a

lawyer expects from ~~his~~ clients. *her*

EXERCISE 3   **Using Gender-inclusive Language**

Following is the opening paragraph of a book first published in 1953. Revise any words or phrases that unjustifiably fail to include women. If you make any singular pronouns plural, be sure to make their antecedents (20.1) plural also.

> Since he came down from the trees, man has faced the problem of survival, not as an individual but as a member of a social group. His continued existence is testimony to the fact that he has succeeded in solving the problem; but the continued existence of want and misery, even in the richest of nations, is evidence that his solution has been, at best, a partial one.
> —Robert Heilbroner, *The Worldly Philosophers*

8.3 RESPECTING OTHERS

To reach the widest possible audience, to attract and persuade readers of different ethnic backgrounds, religious affiliations, physical conditions, or sexual orientation, and to show consideration for people in general, you should use terms respectful of any group you write about. Generally, these are the terms that members of groups use to describe themselves.

Groups deserving of respect include not just races, religious organizations, and ethnic minorities but also other minorities such as those commonly called "elderly" or "handicapped."

Since the terms that groups apply to themselves are so difficult to fix, and since members of particular groups do not always agree on what they wish to be called, we cannot offer here any list of preferred terms. All we can offer is a single piece of advice: before writing about any group—whether singled out by race, ethnic identity, religion, sexual orientation, or age—try to learn what its members wish to be called. Consulting an up-to-date dictionary may be helpful.

EXERCISE 4   **Respecting Others**

Name the ethnic, racial, or religious group(s) to which you belong, and for each group named give the term you prefer to be called.

8.4 MAKING LANGUAGE CHOICES

Diction consists of the words you choose. The choices you make establish your level of diction—that is, your level of formality. This may be high, low, in the middle, or mixed.

MIDDLE LEVEL

To see how the middle level of diction is set and maintained, consider the following passage from an essay written for a college course:

> Fears based on ignorance can sometimes be conquered by scientific fact. In 1938 a radio program called *War of the Worlds* actually terrified large numbers of Americans by pretending to report that the Earth was being invaded by people from Mars. But as we now know from instrumental exploration of Mars itself, the idea that "Martians" could invade the Earth is _____.

As is right for a piece on a serious subject aimed at an intelligent and some-what critical audience (the instructor), this passage is neither casual nor highly formal in tone. Words such as *conquered, invaded,* and *exploration* establish a level of diction that is clearly above the colloquial. But the diction is not highly formal. It is written at the middle level of diction, the normal level for most college and professional writing, the level consistent with academic English.

What, then, should the last word be? Here are some words that would fit the meaning of the passage. Choose one:

insupportable	silly
preposterous	false
incredible	crazy
ludicrous	loony
groundless	bull
absurd	

A quick glance down the list should make you see that these eleven words descend through several levels of diction, from the high formality of *insupportable* through the informality of *crazy* to the outright slanginess of *bull*. If you chose a word from the middle of the list—*ludicrous, groundless, absurd, silly,* or *false*—you chose sensibly, for these words are all at the middle level of diction, and can fit into most contexts without seeming either coarse or pretentious, too low or too high. Slang words like *loony* and *bull* may be all right in conversation, but they do not suit a formal discussion of human fears, and the odds are they will not suit the audience either. So why not *insupportable,* from the top of the list? This word is impressively long, but its very length makes it carry more weight than most sentences can bear, and seasoned writers do not use long words just to impress their readers. In this case, the meaning of *insupportable* can readily be conveyed by a shorter word such as *groundless.*

Whether you actually choose *groundless* or another word from the middle group depends on the shade of meaning you want (see 8.5).

HIGHLY FORMAL LEVEL

Some occasions call for highly formal diction:

> I feel that this award was not made to me as a man but to my work—a life's work in the agony and sweat of the human spirit, not for glory and least of all for profit, but to create out of the materials of the human spirit something which did not exist before. So this award is only mine in trust. It will not be difficult to find a dedication for the money part of it commensurate with the purpose and significance of its origin. But I would like to do the same with the acclaim too, by using this moment as a pinnacle from which I might be listened to by the young men and women already dedicated to the same anguish and travail, among whom is already that one who will some day stand here where I am standing.
>
> —William Faulkner, Nobel Prize acceptance speech

Faulkner is delivering a speech of acknowledgment on a ceremonial occasion. Such a speech requires language of high formality—stately words like *dedication, commensurate, pinnacle,* and *travail.*

INFORMAL OR LOW LEVEL: COLLOQUIALISMS AND SLANG

Colloquialisms and slang are words commonly used in conversation and sometimes in writing. They often appear, for instance, in sports reporting:

> Baker led off the ninth with a scorcher into the rightfield corner, and took second when Bailey bobbled the ball. Muzio caught Lehmann looking at a slider on the outside corner, but Tetrazzini clouted the next delivery into the upper deck. In the bottom of the inning Tom Stewart retired the Sox to ice the win.

Strictly speaking, slang is one step lower than colloquial diction. While "led off" is colloquial, "ice the win" has the racy flavor of slang. (Dictionaries use the word *informal* to designate colloquialisms alone, and put slang in a separate category; see 8.14.)

MIXED LEVELS: PRO AND CON

Even when you are choosing most of your words from the middle level of diction, you may occasionally need a highly formal word, or—on the other hand—a piece of slang:

> In Moulmein, in Lower Burma, I was hated by large numbers of people—the only time in my life that I have been important enough for this to happen to me. I was sub-divisional police officer of the town, and in an aimless, petty kind of way anti-European feeling was very bitter. No one had the guts to raise a riot, but if a European woman went through the bazaars alone somebody would probably spit betel juice over her dress.
> —George Orwell, "Shooting an Elephant"

Since Orwell is writing about violent feelings, the slang word *guts* belongs here. Together with *spit,* it illustrates and vivifies the abstract phrase *anti-European feeling.*

Orwell's slang is effective because he uses it sparingly and purposefully. When overused, slang loses its bite:

> When I got out of high school, I figured I wouldn't start college right off because books were messing me up at the time and I wanted to get my head together before I hit the books again.

Just as bad is a sentence that suddenly lurches into slang with no good reason for doing so:

> When I finished high school, I decided not to enter college immediately because academic work was freaking me out.

In formal writing, therefore, use slang sparingly, or not at all:

> When I finished high school, I decided not to enter college immediately because I just couldn't stomach any more academic work.

The verb *stomach* has plenty of force; you could also use *swallow* or simply *take.* The more you write, the more you will find variety and power within the middle range of diction. You will know when to use formal words or slang.

Making Diction Consistent   EXERCISE 5

Revise the following passage to eliminate any unjustified slang or excessive formality in its diction:

> While I'm complaining, let me mention another gripe about New York. It's impossible to get a haircut here! When I inhabited a house

in the town of Rye, I had a terrific barber, a person who, every month
or so, would give me a straightforward trim for $8.50, a price which
was reasonable in my opinion. He always cut my tresses exactly as I   5
wanted him to, and he never suggested that a different style would
be more beneficial. I like simple haircuts but have yet to get one in
the five months I've been attending Columbia University, which is
right here in New York City. It is my considered opinion that all of the
barbers left town years ago, to be replaced by hair stylists, as they   10
label themselves, men who use scissors on a man's locks in the way
bad sculptors use their mitts to put soft clay into some kind of shape.
If I present a request for a simple trim, these bums spray my head
with water, comb my hair in every direction but the right one, grab
tufts, and start hacking. They try to layer it in ways only a high-priced 15
fashion model could ever want; and they leave the sideburns raw,
claiming that's how men of taste want them. Then they plug in their
damned hair dryers and blow up the mess they've made. In conclusion, they have the effrontery to submit a bill for a monetary sum in
excess of $15. You can't win.   20

8.5 CHOOSING WORDS FOR THEIR DENOTATION

The denotation of a word is its explicit meaning. To write precisely is to
choose the word that means exactly what you want to say. Consider again
this uncompleted sentence:

> But as we now know from instrumental exploration of Mars itself, the idea
> that "Martians" could invade the Earth is _____.

To fill in the blank, you might first consult a thesaurus, a book that gives
you a cluster of synonyms for each of the words it alphabetically lists.
Some computer programs now include an online thesaurus that will give
you a list of synonyms on your screen.

Suppose you're looking for a word that means something like *crazy* but
is somewhat more formal, to suit the context. A thesaurus might give you
as synonyms *ludicrous, groundless, absurd, silly,* and *false.* Any one of these
words would make sense in the blank, and all of them come from the middle level of diction. But to choose the word that best fits your meaning,
you need to know exactly what each one means. A good dictionary will tell
the following:

Ludicrous means "worthy of scornful laughter."

Groundless means "unsupported by evidence." A *groundless* belief is not necessarily *silly, absurd,* or *ludicrous,* or even *false.* It simply has no basis in what is known.

Absurd means "irrational" or "nonsensical" but not "frivolous"; deadly serious people can sometimes have completely absurd ideas.

Silly means "frivolous," "foolish," or "thoughtless."

False means "not true." A statement may be *false* without being either *silly, ludicrous,* or *absurd.* It would be *absurd* to say that the first president of the United States was King George III, but merely *false* to say that the first president was Thomas Jefferson.

Learning what every word denotes is not easy. But if you read extensively and use your dictionary often, you will come to know the shades of difference between words with similar meanings. This knowledge, in turn, will help you express more precisely your *own* opinion of an idea—such as the idea that Martians could invade the Earth. No one else can fill in the blank for you.

Choosing Words for Their Denotation

EXERCISE 6

Using a good dictionary where necessary, answer each of the following questions.

   EXAMPLE: Should you use *fatal* or *deadly* to describe a weapon that can kill?

   ANSWER: deadly

1. If your meaning is "annoy continually," should you use *bother* or *harass?*

2. If your meaning is "defy," should you use *flaunt* or *flout?*

3. Should you use *toady* or *flatterer* to mean "someone who lavishly praises another for material gain"?

4. Is an impartial judge *uninterested* or *disinterested* in the case brought before her?

5. If your meaning is "express strong disapproval of," should you use *criticize* or *denounce?*

8.6 CHOOSING WORDS FOR THEIR CONNOTATION

The connotation of a word is its implicit meaning: the feeling, attitude, or set of associations it implies.

Take *house* and *home*. Both denote a dwelling place or residence. But their connotations differ sharply. *House* connotes little more than it denotes—a place where people can live—while *home* normally connotes family affection, memories of childhood, and a reassuring sense of welcome.

Precisely because they involve feelings, the connotations of a word are sometimes too personal and variable to be defined. The connotations of *steak*, for instance, will be different for a vegetarian and for a Texas cattle rancher. Yet many words do have widely accepted connotations, and these determine the electrical charge of a word—positive or negative, favorable or unfavorable, generous or harsh.

Compare the adjectives in each of the following sentences:

Ray is ambitious; Ralph is pushy.

Ray is tough-minded; Ralph is ruthless.

Ray is foresighted; Ralph is calculating.

Ray is firm; Ralph is stubborn.

Each pair of adjectives in these sentences is joined by denotation but split by connotation. While the words describing Ray are generous, the words applied to Ralph are loaded with negative connotations. Loaded language appeals only to readers who themselves are already loaded with the prejudices of the writer. If you want to persuade readers who have various views, you should try to choose words with connotations that are fair to your subject. This does not mean that you must never describe anyone in terms like *pushy, stubborn, calculating,* or *ruthless;* it means only that before you use such words, you must be sure that you mean them.

Recognizing Connotations

Following are groups of three words alike in denotation but unlike in connotations. Arrange the words so that the one with the most favorable connotation is first and the one with the least favorable connotation is last. If you have trouble arranging them, your dictionary may help you.

EXAMPLE:

pushy   ambitious   aggressive
ambitious, aggressive, pushy

1. frugal	stingy	thrifty
2. scent	stench	odor
3. call	scream	yell
4. firmly	harshly	sternly
5. prejudiced	partial	bigoted
6. slender	emaciated	skinny
7. retreat	flee	depart
8. mistake	blunder	error
9. dull	stupid	unintelligent
10. question	interrogate	ask

Choosing Words by Connotation

Replace the italicized word in each sentence with a word of similar denotation but more favorable connotation.

EXAMPLE: After I showed him my receipt, the store owner admitted
                      mistake.
his *blunder.*
     ^

1. Ramona's skydiving reflects her *foolhardy* nature.

2. Felipe thinks she should be more *timid*.

3. In return, she *ridicules* him.

4. They make an *eccentric* couple.

5. Whenever they go out together, he wears a coat and tie, and she dresses *sloppily.*

8.7 CHOOSING GENERAL AND SPECIFIC WORDS

Words range in meaning from the most general to the most specific. If you want to identify something named Fido that runs, barks, and wags its tail, you can call it a *creature*, an *animal*, a *dog*, a *hound*, or a *basset*. Each of the words in this series is more specific than the one before, and each of them has its use:

Fido is the most lovable *creature* I know.

Fido is the first *animal* I ever liked.

Fido is one of our three *dogs.*

Fido is the fastest *hound* I've ever seen.

We have three hounds: a dachshund named Willy, a greyhound named Mick, and a *basset* named Fido.

Almost everything can be classified in several different ways, with words ranging from the very general to the very specific. If someone moves, for instance, you can write that she *moves,* or more specifically that she *walks,* or still more specifically that she *struts.*

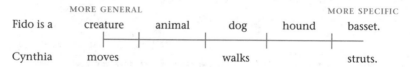

A concrete or specific word names something you can see, touch, taste, smell, or hear. Examples are *fingernail, strawberry, sandpaper, smoke, whisper,* or *scream.* An abstract or general word names a feeling *(love)*, a state of being *(misery)*, an idea *(democracy)*, a theory *(evolution)*, a field of study *(biology)*, or a class of things too broad to be visualized *(creature, plant, organism)*. Abstract words can be used to categorize or contain a collection of items, as in "She went to Mexico and returned with a vanload of *souvenirs."*

But too many abstract words turn writing into fog. Good writing combines the abstract and the concrete, the general and the specific:

The cartilage in my ankle ripped painfully when I hit the icy sidewalk. As I lay on my back, cursing myself for jogging in subzero weather, the chill of the morning wind made me shiver. I tried to raise my body, but my ankle would not move, and all I could do was fall back on my concrete bed. I felt nothing but pain, cold, and dismay.   —college student

Dismay is an abstract word, but it perfectly sums up all the concrete details that come before it.

Recognizing General and Specific Words

Following are groups of three words. Arrange the words in order, from the most abstract or general to the most specific or concrete.

EXAMPLE: walk　go　strut
go, walk, strut

1. sofa　　　　property　　furniture
2. poodle　　　animal　　　dog
3. whale　　　 creature　　 mammal
4. dwelling　　shelter　　　cottage
5. pitcher　　　athlete　　　ballplayer
6. automobile　Chevrolet　　vehicle
7. run　　　　move　　　　spring
8. meat　　　　pork　　　　food
9. literature　　novel　　　　book
10. pain　　　　problem　　 toothache
11. maple　　　plant　　　　tree

Using Abstract Words

Use one abstract noun to sum up each of the following sets of three specific words.

EXAMPLE: kiss, smile, hug
affection

1. snarl, spit, scream
2. wheezing, stumbling, aching
3. pale, rigid, breathless
4. diamonds, marble, gold
5. laughter, singing, dancing

| EXERCISE 11 | **Using Specific and Concrete Words** |

Replace the italicized words with words or phrases that are more specific or concrete.

EXAMPLE: Janet ~~spoke~~ *whispered* to Tom.

1. During the road race there were three *accidents*.

2. *Defects* in the pavement made driving hazardous.

3. Also, the *weather* made visibility poor.

4. One car *went* off the road and *made contact with an object*.

5. A second *moved* into a *cavity* by the side of the road.

6. A third *got* out of control when its right front tire *malfunctioned*.

7. The driver of one car suffered an *injury*.

8.8 USING WORDS FIGURATIVELY: SIMILE AND METAPHOR

Figurative language helps to make the writer's meaning vividly clear. While ordinary comparisons bring together two things of the same kind, figurative words and phrases bring together two things of a different kind, comparing something abstract or unfamiliar with something concrete, familiar, or both:

ORDINARY COMPARISON:
Boston is like Philadelphia; it lives on its past.

FIGURATIVE COMPARISON:
Sending one police officer to stop a riot is like shooting a squirt gun at a forest fire.

A figurative word or phrase can be a *simile* or a *metaphor.*

1. In a **simile**, the writer says or implies that one thing is *like* another:

After the mole devoured its prey, it sank into the earth *as a submarine sinks into the water.*
                                                    —Konrad Z. Lorenz, adapted

Her eyes were *like two hard, cold pebbles from the ocean.*
                                                    —college student

The guide shooed his charges back along the gravel path *as if they were chickens,* which was what they sounded like.

—Margaret Atwood

He stumbled out into the hall *as if his legs were tied together with rope.*

—college student

2. In a metaphor, which is a compressed or intensified version of the simile, the writer says or implies that one thing *is* another:

An angry man *is a raging bull.*

What does education often do? It makes a straight-cut ditch of a free, meandering brook.

—Henry David Thoreau

Every muscle in my body ached and cried for mercy.

—college student

Using Figurative Language

EXERCISE 12

In each of the following sentences, an abstract word or phrase is italicized. Make it concrete or specific by changing it to a simile or metaphor.

EXAMPLE: Life is *something to be organized.*

REVISED: Life is like a lump of clay; it is our task to mold it.

1. Travel books are *descriptions* of far-off places.
2. Entering a roomful of strange people is *frightening.*
3. The first week of college is *confusing.*
4. The fat man *moved awkwardly* across the street.
5. The child accepted the story *trustingly.*

8.9 AVOIDING MIXED METAPHOR

A **mixed metaphor** is a set of two or more metaphors that do not mesh:

> When the proposal was made, he smelled a rat, and he set out to nip it in the bud.

> If we cannot get the deficit under control, the ship of state may soon come to the end of the road.

In the first example, a rat turns into a bud; in the second, a ship travels a road. To correct a mixed metaphor, make your metaphors consistent:

> EDITED: When the proposal was made, he smelled a rat, and he set out to trap it.

> EDITED: If we cannot get the deficit under control, the ship of state may soon capsize.

8.10 CONTROLLING CLICHÉS

Clichés are the old coins of language: phrases that once made a striking impression but have since been rubbed smooth by repeated handling. (The mixed metaphors above, for instance, are all clichés.) We use clichés because they come readily to mind, because they can quickly fill up or fill out a sentence, and because many of them are figures of speech and therefore seem colorful or catchy. But overuse of clichés leads to passages like this:

> *At this point in time,* we should *let bygones be bygones, bury the hatchet,* and *put our shoulders to the wheel.* We cannot *stand idly by;* we must *make hay while the sun shines. In the final analysis,* if we fail, we will have *only ourselves to blame.*

When you spot a cliché in your writing, you can sometimes give it a new twist, as in *Halfway up the ladder of success, she found several rungs missing.* But if you can't give it a new twist, replace the cliché with a carefully chosen word or phrase. Compare the original version of each sentence given below with the edited version:

▶ ~~At this point in time, we~~ cannot get a loan.   [We]   [now]

▶ In rural areas doctors are ~~few and far between.~~   [scarce.]

The industrious
▸ ~~Busy as a bee, the~~ cobbler worked from dawn to sundown.

solved the problem.
▸ Jerry's proposal ~~hit the nail on the head.~~

Replacing Clichés

Replace every cliché in the following sentences with a well-chosen word or phrase.

talked   *early*
EXAMPLE: We ~~chewed the fat~~ until the ~~wee~~ hours of the morning.

1. The Dean's recent report sent shock waves through the entire college.
2. It revealed that only half the students were putting their shoulders to the wheel.
3. The rest were just having a ball and painting the town red every night.
4. The president of the college said that all these students should be made to straighten up and fly right.
5. But she and the faculty couldn't see eye to eye on how to get this proposal off the ground.

Replacing Your Own Clichés

Using as many clichés as possible, write a paragraph arguing that all thin persons in the United States should immediately go on a junk-food binge. Then rewrite the paragraph and see if you can squeeze every one of those clichés out of it.

8.11 USING IDIOMS

An idiom is a combination of words that is peculiar to a specific language but follows no known rule. No rule, for instance, explains why speakers of British English say "Let's have *a* coffee," while speakers of American English say "Let's have coffee." In American English, some idioms combine an adjective or participle with a preposition (dependent *on*, bored *with*, superior *to*); others combine a verb with one or more *particles*—prepositions serving as adverbs (look *into*, look *down on*). Here is a partial list of such idioms:

according *to*

abide *by* (a rule, regulation, or agreement)

able *to*

agree *with* (a person)

bored *with*

capable *of*

compare *to* or *with* (see Glossary of Usage)

complain *to* (a person)

complain *about* (a thing)

comply *with*

conform *to*

cooperate *with*

dependent *on*

desirous *of*

differ *with* (meaning *disagree with*)

differ *from* (meaning *is different from,* as in "Body building differs from weight lifting.")

different *from*

disgust / disgusted *with*

independent *of*

inferior *to*

preferable *to*

prior *to*

responsible / responsibility *for*

superior *to*

sure *to*

waiting *for* (expecting)

waiting *on* (serving)

For an extended list of phrasal verbs (verb-particle combinations), with sample sentences and brief definitions, see 28.2.

Choosing Prepositions

Fill each blank with an appropriate preposition.

> EXAMPLE: Some people always complain ____ the weather ____ any-
> one who will listen.

> ANSWER: about, to

1. Crane's disgust ____ her country's special racial policies and her hatred ____ its rulers drove her ____ self-imposed exile.

2. She had no confidence ____ the government's promises ____ gradual reform.

3. She could no longer silently cooperate ____ its demeaning laws.

4. Only ____ exile could she speak and write freely ____ them.

5. But she longed ____ the day when she could return ____ a country that would at last be free ____ oppression.

8.12 AVOIDING JARGON, PRETENTIOUS WORDS, AND EUPHEMISMS

Jargon, pretentious words, and euphemisms can muffle the impact of a sentence or choke the flow of its meaning. For this reason, you should generally avoid all three.

JARGON

Jargon is technical terminology. Technical terms belong in writing on a specialized subject, but they seldom suit essays on subjects of general interest, especially when ordinary words can be used in their place:

> ▶ When I asked my parents if I could use the car, the ~~feedback~~ was ^answer ~~negative.~~ ^no.

> ▶ [or] When I asked my parents if I could use the car, ~~the feedback~~ ^they ~~was negative.~~ ^said no.

> ▶ ~~Upwardly mobile~~ ^Ambitious lawyers often work seventy hours a week.

145

If you are writing on a specialized subject for general readers, make sure you explain any technical terms as you go along. You can often do so with a parenthesized word or phrase:

▶ She fractured her tibia (shinbone) in three places.

PRETENTIOUS WORDS

Pretentious words and phrases are too long and high-flown for the meaning they actually deliver. Substitute simpler words wherever possible:

▶ Were it not for the ~~lucrative financial rewards~~, she would have *money,*
~~tendered her resignation.~~ *quit.*

▶ ~~Large size passenger vehicles utilize excessive quantities of fuel.~~ *Big cars use too much gas.*

▶ Years of research have ~~impacted positively on~~ our understanding *improved*

of cancer.

EUPHEMISMS

A euphemism is a word or expression that takes the sting out of an unpleasant reality. A euphemism for *dead* is *departed;* euphemisms for *kill* include *eliminate* and *harvest.* Since euphemisms veil the truth instead of stating it openly, you should use them only when plainer words would needlessly hurt the feelings of those you are writing for or about.

But euphemisms should never be used to hide the truth or spare the feelings of those who have done wrong. George Orwell gives a chilling example:

Defenseless villagers are bombarded from the air, the inhabitants driven out into the countryside, the cattle machine-gunned, the huts set on fire with incendiary bullets: this is called *pacification.*

EXERCISE 16   **Changing Jargon, Pretentious Words, and Euphemisms into Plain English**

The following sentences are disfigured by jargon, euphemisms, or pretentious words. Using your dictionary if necessary, rewrite each sentence in plain English.

EXAMPLE: The very thought of flying ~~made her paranoid.~~ *frightened her.*

1. Young children need positive feedback from their parents and teachers regularly.

2. Nonsupportive articulations impact negatively on their development.

3. While interacting with them, therefore, grownups should utilize encouraging words as much as possible.

4. Also, children should be urged to verbalize their feelings, especially when they are experiencing sadness.

5. A child whose mother or father has passed on, for instance, needs a sympathetic listener.

8.13 AVOIDING WORDINESS

Wordiness is an excess of words: more words than you need for the meaning you aim to deliver. To help you eliminate wordiness, here is one general technique and several specific ones:

IDENTIFYING THE MOST IMPORTANT WORDS

If you can't figure out how to improve a sentence that sounds wordy, underline the most important words and make a sentence out of them, using a minimum of linking words:

EXAMPLE: It is a matter of the gravest possible importance to the health of anyone with a history of a problem with disease of the heart that he or she should avoid the sort of foods with a high percentage of saturated fats.

REVISED: Anyone with a history of heart disease should avoid saturated fats.

AVOIDING SPECIFIC SOURCES OF WORDINESS

1. AVOID REPEATING A WORD UNLESS YOU NEED IT AGAIN FOR CLARITY OR EMPHASIS:

  ▶ Of all the different topics of controversy, from politics to religion to the environment, environmental questions, nothing appears to get people so inflamed as the topic of those questions dealing with sex.

For clarity, *topic* is repeated just once, at the end of the sentence. See also p. 111, "Emphasizing Your Main Point."

2. AVOID REDUNDANCY—USING TWO OR MORE WORDS THAT MEAN ESSENTIALLY
THE SAME THING:

> ► The defendant was accused of six ~~illegal~~ crimes.

> ► This ~~particular~~ problem has been ignored.

3. IN GENERAL, AVOID STARTING SENTENCES WITH PHRASES SUCH AS *THERE IS* AND
IT IS:

> ► ~~There are many~~ Many women ~~who~~ have to work.

> ► ~~It is this that~~ This makes cities flourish.

Occasionally, however, *There is, There are,* or *There were* can be used with
good effect to open a paragraph ("There are two reasons for acting now"),
to line up the sentences in a list-structure paragraph (7.3, "Using List Structure"), or to serve as a placeholder when the subject is too long to go easily
before the verb ("There were two reasons for the breakdown in essential
services").

4. WHEREVER POSSIBLE, TURN NOUNS INTO VERBS:

> ► The crew ~~had an encounter with~~ encountered an emergency.

> ► ~~The reason for his decision~~ He decided to visit Spain ~~was his desire~~ because he wanted to see a
bullfight.

> ► [or] ~~The reason for his decision to visit~~ He went to Spain ~~was his desire~~ to see a
bullfight.

5. WHEREVER POSSIBLE, GET RID OF ADJECTIVE CLAUSES LIKE *WHO ARE, WHICH
WAS,* AND *THAT HAD BEEN:*

> ► Students ~~who are~~ in the band have to practice twice a week.

6. WHEREVER POSSIBLE, REPLACE PREPOSITIONAL PHRASES WITH SINGLE WORDS:

> ► She spoke ~~in regard to~~ about water pollution.

> ► We ~~are in~~ need ~~of~~ intelligent players ~~with intelligence.~~

> ► They were ~~in a state of~~ noticeably confused ~~confusion.~~

7. AVOID THE VERB *TO BE* IN SENTENCES LIKE THE FOLLOWING:

   ▶ Shakespeare is considered ~~to be~~ the greatest of all English playwrights.

   ▶ Loss of memory may ~~be indicative of~~ *indicate* Alzheimer's disease.

8. WHEN POSSIBLE, AVOID *THE FACT THAT:*

   ▶ ~~The fact that Jennifer Lopez appeared~~ *Jennifer Lopez's appearance* nearly caused a riot.

   ▶ ~~Due to the fact that~~ *Because* my paper was wordy, I had to rewrite it.

For more on *due to,* see the Glossary of Usage.

9. AVOID VERBAL DETOURS:

   ▶ When we try to understand what God is, our first problem is that ~~of nonencounter at the level of vision.~~ *we cannot see him.*

Making Sentences Concise

The following sentences are wordy. Without dropping anything essential to their meaning, make each of them more concise.

   EXAMPLE: The chipmunk ~~who was~~ hiding in the stone wall put its head out ~~in a wary fashion.~~ *warily.*

1. Photographers who worked in the nineteenth century faced many hardships and perils.

2. In their quest for pictures that would be perfect, some fell off mountains or buildings.

3. While engaged in photographing wildlife, they were attacked by elephants, rhinoceroses, lions, tigers, and, in addition, wild dogs.

4. But they were just as likely to die in the darkroom as they were to die in a jungle.

5. Darkrooms were dangerous due to the fact that the chemicals that were required for film processing in the nineteenth century were highly poisonous.

6. It is a fact that photographers had to breathe for several hours each day an atmosphere that was filled with noxious fumes.

(Continued on p. 150.)

7. In 1852 one photographer nearly experienced death from inhalation of mercury fumes.

8. Furthermore, there were some poisonous substances which penetrated the skin.

9. Worst of all were the hazards of consuming anything of a liquid nature in the darkroom.

10. In 1891, a Baltimore photographer who was well known mistook a solution of pyrogallic acid for a glass of whiskey and water.

11. As a resulting consequence, he died in three days' time.

12. For all these reasons, photography in the nineteenth century was considered to be an unhealthy occupation.

EXERCISE 18

Editing a Draft

The following passage illustrates weaknesses of wording common in many drafts. Improve the wording as best you can.

A LIFE OF RESISTANCE

Black Boy is an autobiographical account of the childhood of Richard Wright. In the autobiography Wright describes how all the odds were stacked against him from his birth until the day many years later when he headed north to Chicago. The book portrays his struggle for success against these seemingly insurmountable odds, and the story 5 illustrates in particular how his strong sense of justice allowed him to succeed. This sense of justice is shown partly in the way he responded when others tried to control his actions and behavior. Whenever someone tried to control him, his response depended on how he assessed the fairness of what they wanted him to do. 10

Richard would not agree to submit to a punishment he felt he did not deserve. Richard had encounters with this kind of punishment while he was living with his grandmother and one of his aunts. Her name was Aunt Addie, and she was mean to Richard, and she was a teacher at a church school. His aunt was continually trying to 15 prove to the other students that she didn't favor Richard, who was her nephew. She tried to prove this by constantly punishing Richard for things he had not done. Finally she pushed him to the limit when she started attempting to punish him at home for things he had not even done at school. Richard assured her that he had not done the 20 things she was accusing him of doing. This assurance only made her furious, angry. She threatened him and warned him she would beat him physically. Then Richard grabbed a kitchen knife to defend himself. He told Aunt Addie that he was not guilty of doing the things she said he had done. He said he would not accept her abusiveness just because she wanted to prove something to the other kids at school. 25

When Aunt Addie saw the knife, she became even more angry, and she told Richard he was crazy. However, from that point in time onward, she stopped accusing Richard of every little thing, and, in fact, she started ignoring him totally. She said he was a lost cause. Richard found that being on his aunt's lost cause list was quite enjoyable, and he was glad that he had defied her by not accepting the punishment that he felt, with his sense of justice, he did not deserve. 30

8.14 USING THE DICTIONARY

A good dictionary is the indispensable tool of a good writer. This sample entry from *The American Heritage Dictionary* shows you what a dictionary can tell you about a single word—even a word you use often:

Spelling — **cool** (kōol) *adj.* **cooler, coolest.** **1.** Moderately cold; neither warm nor very cold. **2.** Reducing discomfort in hot weather; allowing a feeling of coolness: *a cool blouse.* **3.** Not excited; calm; controlled. **4.** Showing dislike, disdain, or indifference; unenthusiastic; not cordial: *a cool greeting.* **5.** Calmly audacious or bold; impudent. **6.** Designating or characteristic of colors, such as blue and green, that produce the impression of coolness. **7.** *Slang.* Having a quiet, indifferent, and aloof attitude. **8.** *Slang.* Excellent; first-rate; superior. **9.** *Informal.* Without exaggeration; entire; full: *He lost a cool million.* —*v.* **cooled, cooling, cools.** —*tr.* **1.** To make less warm. **2.** To make less ardent, intense, or zealous. —*intr.* **1.** To become less warm. **2.** To become calm. —**cool it.** *Slang.* To calm down, slow down, or relax. —**cool one's heels.** *Informal.* To be kept waiting for a long time. —*n.* **1.** Anything that is cool or moderately cold: *the cool of early morning.* **2.** The state or quality of being cool. **3.** *Slang.* Composure: *recover one's cool.* [Middle English *col,* Old English *cōl.* See **gel-³** in Appendix.*] —**cool'ly** *adv.* —**cool'ness** *n.*

Synonyms: cool, composed, collected, unruffled, nonchalant, imperturbable, detached. These adjectives apply to persons to indicate calmness, especially in time of stress. *Cool* has the widest application. Usually it implies merely a high degree of self-control, though it may also indicate aloofness. *Composed* and *collected* more strongly imply conscious display of self-discipline and absence of agitation. *Composed* also often suggests serenity or sedateness, and *collected,* mental concentration. *Unruffled* emphasizes calmness in the face of severe provocation that may have produced agitation in others present. *Nonchalant* describes a casual exterior manner that suggests, sometimes misleadingly, a lack of interest or concern. *Imperturbable* stresses unshakable calmness considered usually as an inherent trait rather than as a product of self-discipline. *Detached* implies aloofness and either lack of active concern or resistance to emotional involvement.

Labels (left margin): Spelling · Pronunciation · Definition as adjective · General usage · Slang usage · Verb forms · Definition as noun · History of the word · Related forms

Labels (right margin): Comparative and superlative forms · Definition as verb · Definition as intransitive verb · Informal or colloquial usage · Distinctions in meaning between the word and others like it

1. **SPELLING, SYLLABLE DIVISION, PRONUNCIATION**   You already know how to spell and pronounce a one-syllable word like *cool,* but what about a longer word, such as *government?* The definition of this word begins "govern-ment (gŭv'ərn-mənt)." With the word broken into three syllables, you can tell where to divide it when you need to hyphenate it at the end of a line. The phonetic spelling in parentheses tells you to pronounce it with the accent on the first syllable (gŭv'). The pronunciation key at the beginning of the dictionary (and at the bottom of each page) explains that *ŭ* sounds like the *u* in *cut* and ə sounds like the *e* in *item.*

2. **PARTS OF SPEECH**   Like many other words, *cool* can be used in various ways. The abbreviation *adj.* tells you it is being defined first as an adjective; the entry then goes on to explain what it means when used as a verb (—*v.*) and as a noun (—*n.*).

3. **FORMS**   For certain parts of speech several forms of the word are given. For example, *adj.* is followed by *cooler* and *coolest.*

4. **DEFINITIONS**   When a word can function in various ways (as adjective or verb, for instance), a separate set of numbered definitions is given for each. Some dictionaries begin with the earliest meaning of the word and then proceed in order to the latest ones, but most dictionaries—like the *American Heritage*—simply begin with the central, commonest meaning.

5. **USAGE LABELS**   These identify words or uses of words that are not part of current academic English.

WORD	LABEL	MEANING
cool	Informal *or* Colloquial	entire, full
cool	Slang	composure
yclept	Archaic *or* Obsolete	named, called
calculate	Regional *or* Dialect	think, suppose
nowheres	Nonstandard	nowhere

The level of diction is often set by the sense in which a word is used. *Cool* is informal when used to mean "full" ("a cool million") but slang when used to mean "composure" ("Don't blow your cool").

You will also find labels indicating words that are specialized and will therefore have to be explained for most readers:

WORD	LABEL	MEANING
ganef	Yiddish	thief, rascal
gamophylous	Botany	having united leaves

6.   TRANSITIVE AND INTRANSITIVE USE OF THE VERB   A verb may be transitive *(tr.)*, intransitive *(intr.)*, or both. After —*tr.* in the sample entry are definitions for *cool* as a transitive verb, one that acts on a direct object (as in "The icy stream cooled the beer"). Under —*intr.* are definitions of *cool* as an intransitive verb, a verb without a direct object (as in "The beer cooled slowly"). Sometimes the abbreviations *v.t.* and *v.i.* are used instead.

7.   ETYMOLOGY   The etymology of the word being defined—its history or derivation—is given in brackets: [   ]. Some dictionaries put it at the beginning of the entry. In our sample it comes near the end of the first part; there we learn that *cool* can be traced to the Old English word *cōl.* "See **gel-**[3] in Appendix" means that under the heading **gel-**[3] in the Appendix you can find still older roots for the word *cool* in a prehistoric group of languages known as Indo-European. You can also find other words that come from the same roots (including *chill, cold, congeal, jelly,* and *glacier*). Sometimes you can find definitions of word roots. If you look up *calculate,* for instance, you will find that it comes from the Latin word *calculus,* which means "a small stone." (The ancient Romans used small stones for reckoning.)

8.   RELATED FORMS   A related form is a variation on the form of the word being defined. For *cool,* the related forms include the adverb *coolly* (note the spelling) and the noun *coolness.* Sometimes these related forms have separate entries of their own.

9.   SYNONYMS   In a standard dictionary, entries for some words include definitions of synonyms. These can help you choose the exact word for your meaning. (A thesaurus provides lists of synonyms, but does not usually define them.)

EXERCISE 19

This is a five-part exercise.

1. From any piece or pieces of writing you have read recently, choose five words that you don't recognize or that you aren't sure you understand.

2. Write out the sentence in which each word appears, citing its author in parentheses.

3. Using the sentences to guide you, define each word as well as you can.

4. Look up each word in your dictionary and write out the definition you find there. Give the name of the dictionary in parentheses.

5. Use each word in a sentence of your own.

EXAMPLE:

1. perfunctory

2. Some beavers, especially young or solitary old ones, are sloppy and per-functory builders. (David Rains Wallace)

3. sort of careless, I think

4. "done or acting routinely and with little interest or care"

5. Not even looking at me, she mumbled a perfunctory "thanks" and walked away.

Choosing the Right Words

IN BRIEF

▶ Is your level of diction suitable for your subject and audience? Is it consistent? If not, is every shift in level justified?

▶ Have you checked the dictionary for any word you're not quite sure how to use?

▶ Do your words denote exactly the meaning you want to express?

▶ Do your words connote what you want them to?

▶ Does your writing combine general and specific words, the abstract and the concrete?

▶ Have you enlivened your writing with figurative language?

▶ Have you avoided mixed metaphors?

▶ Have you avoided clichés, jargon, pretentious words, and euphemisms?

▶ Have you used idioms correctly?

▶ Is your language gender-inclusive?

▶ Are your terms respectful of others?

▶ Have you cut all words that you don't need to deliver your meaning?

9 Revising Your Text

9.1 WHY REVISE?

Revising literally means "looking again." Why do you need to revise—to look again at what you have written? The main reason is that to produce an effective text, you must put yourself in the place of the reader. You must see what the text presents to a reader and check its effect against your purpose. Since a first draft seldom if ever realizes the writer's aims perfectly, you must consider what it needs.

A draft usually needs more than tinkering, more than small corrections in spelling, grammar, punctuation, or usage. That is what we call *editing*, and it is treated in chapter 10. This chapter deals with revising, which means looking again at the whole of your text: its tone, the development of its main point, and its appeal to the reader for whom it is written. In revising, try to make big changes before turning to little ones. If you try to do both at the same time, you may find yourself laboring over a particular sentence and then deciding to rewrite or cut out altogether the whole paragraph that contains it. So we suggest you revise and edit your text in two stages.

Revising works best when you have set your draft aside for two or three days so that you can read it with fresh eyes, as if it had been written by someone else. In addition, you may need some guidance from your instructor, your fellow students, or both. The following section explains the kind of comments you may get from another student as well as the kind of comments you may be asked to make on another student's paper.

9.2 MAKING AND RECEIVING COMMENTS ON A DRAFT

If you are asked to comment on another student's draft, you may be expected to answer a set of questions such as those in the box below. Note that none of the questions involves grammar, punctuation, or spelling. All those things should be considered later—in the editing phase. In reviewing another student's draft, give credit wherever it is due. If a word seems particularly well chosen, or if a phrase or sentence seems notably well crafted, mark it as a hit. Be considerate in expressing your criticism. If you spot a weakness or a problem, you should certainly identify it, but rather than saying what the writer has failed to do, try to say what you missed—or what you need—as a reader: "This point left me confused" or "I felt the need for more detail here." Bear in mind that your comments should help the writer to revise. Besides serving for peer review, the following questions can also be applied to a draft of your own.

If your instructor is reading your draft, you should consider her comments carefully since she is your most experienced reader. Ask questions if you don't understand a comment.

Peer Review Questionnaire

1. What did you like best about this text?
2. Where did you find hits: well-chosen words, well-crafted phrases, or strikingly good sentences?
3. Can you find the thesis or state the main point of the text in a single sentence?
4. If not, why not?
5. Where do you feel the need for more information or development?
6. Where did you find the text confusing or hard to follow, and why?
7. Did the author write with full respect for readers of different sexes, classes, races, and nationalities?

Following is a set of answers to these questions made by a student who was asked to comment on the first draft of Carmen's paper. (For the paper itself, together with the teacher's comments on it, see 9.7.)

1. I liked the subject and the idea of women being "sexy" without being sex objects.

2. Hit sentences: "If they scream, it's because they have to scream in order to be heard. If they shock people, it's because they want to shock others into feeling something—into being aware of life with all its pleasures and suffering."

3. "Feminist punk music challenges consumer culture and traditional male/female relationships, leading to new ways of looking at women's power."

4. I found the thesis.

5. More examples of the last point—women's power and ways of expressing themselves—would be helpful.

6. The thesis sentence suggests that challenging "consumer culture and male/female relationships" will "lead" to new ways of looking at female power. I don't see the cause/effect relationship in the text.

7. I think so.

9.3 CLARIFYING YOUR PURPOSE

Whether your thesis is explicit or implicit, you should now be able to say what it is and to see how well your text develops it. But as you think about your thesis, ask yourself again about your purpose. Do you chiefly want to express your own feelings, to explain something outside yourself, or to persuade your reader?

When you revise a draft, you can clarify and refine your purpose. Carmen's purpose was primarily to explain something—feminist punk music. At the same time, since she listened to the music and attended punk concerts, she was also able to express her feelings about the music and its message. Carmen's revision more effectively *explained* feminist punk music by offering definitions and examples in the second paragraph. At the same time, she made her explanation more vivid and personal by giving a personal example of her family's misconceptions about her generation's politics and feminism.

EXERCISE 1   **Clarifying Your Purpose**

Do three things: (1) state the thesis of your text in its present form; (2) identify your purpose; and (3) if necessary, rewrite the thesis to make it fit the aim.

9.4 REVISING FOR TONE AND SENSE OF AUDIENCE

The best way to hear the tone of your first draft is to read it aloud to yourself or ask someone to read it aloud to you. As you listen, consider these questions: Does the writing sound too personal for your topic and aim, or too impersonal? Is the tone consistent? Does it help you develop your thesis and realize your aim? To see how you might answer such questions, consider this opening paragraph of a student's first draft:

> Going to college for most people means the onset of new freedoms and many responsibilities. The acquisition of these new responsibilities helps to develop values and maturity in an individual. This makes the prospect of attending college appealing. Going home for the Christmas break, I felt not so much a kid as a grownup guest.

The final sentence of this paragraph leads to a statement of thesis. But the detached, impersonal tone of the opening sentences, which refer to "most people" and "an individual," hardly prepares us for the personal tone of the final sentence. To bridge the gap between the two, the student made the middle sentences sound personal, so that the paragraph read this way:

> For most people, going to college means the onset of new freedoms and many responsibilities. In my first semester of college, new responsibilities helped me to develop values and maturity. The chance to mature is what drew me to college in the first place, and I especially noticed the change in myself at the end of the first semester. Going home for the Christmas break, I felt not so much a kid as a grownup guest.

Now the paragraph moves from the impersonal tone of the opening generalization to a personal tone in the middle sentences, which lead the way to the distinctly personal statement of thesis. Thus the tone of the paragraph enhances its most important point.

Reconsidering Tone

EXERCISE 2

Read the passage below and then say whether or not the tone is consistent. If not, identify the inconsistencies, and then revise the passage to make its tone consistent.

> As Patrick Henry once delivered fiery speeches that roused American colonists to revolution in the 1770s, so Martin Luther King Jr. inspired many Americans during the 1960s. Many people in this period struggled to bring blacks and whites together, but no one expressed the ideal of integration more movingly than King when he stood in front of the Lincoln Memorial and declared to the thousands of people gathered there, "I have a dream." King spoke straight from the heart. He didn't hide his feelings, as politicians often do. Of course, the reason they hide their feelings is that they can't get elected any other way. That's the problem with straightforward speaking; it doesn't win elections. But I still like to hear an honest speech now and then. It's refreshing.

9.5 REVISING FOR STRUCTURE

To see how well your text is constructed, consider the following questions:

1.   CAN YOU STATE THE THESIS—THE MAIN POINT—OF YOUR TEXT?   A well-structured text is unified by its emphasis on one main point, the thesis of the text as a whole. Even a personal narrative should strive to answer a basic question such as "What did I learn from this experience?" If you can't state the thesis of your text, you should rethink the relation between or among the points it makes, decide which point you want to stress most, and subordinate the other points to that one.

2.   DOES YOUR INTRODUCTION ANNOUNCE OR FORECAST YOUR THESIS?   The introduction should tell the reader where the text is headed. It should end by stating your thesis or clearly leading the reader toward your implied thesis.

3.   CAN YOU STATE THE MAIN POINT OR IDENTIFY THE MOST IMPORTANT IMAGE IN EACH PARAGRAPH?   If you can't do either, the paragraph must be split up, reconstructed, or both. (For more on this topic, see 7.2.)

4.   DOES EACH PARAGRAPH HELP TO DEVELOP THE THESIS?   If the main point of any paragraph departs from or works against the thesis, you should cut the paragraph, write a new one that helps develop the thesis, or revise the thesis to make it fit the new point you've discovered.

5.   AFTER THE FIRST PARAGRAPH, IS EACH NEW PARAGRAPH LINKED TO THE ONE BEFORE IT?   Readers look for a chain of connections as they move through a text. The chain breaks when the opening sentence of a new paragraph has no connection to the closing sentence of the one before it, or begins by simply saying, "Another point to consider is X." You can forge a link between two paragraphs by repeating a key word or phrase from the first one in the opening sentence of the second, or by opening the second with a transitional word or phrase (see 7.5). In her revision, Carmen linked the first paragraph to the second by repeating "feminist punk music" in the second paragraph's opening sentence. She used the word "finally" in the opening sentence of the fifth paragraph to signal that she was raising her last point.

6.   DOES EACH NEW PARAGRAPH REVEAL SOMETHING NEW ABOUT THE TOPIC?   Besides continuity, readers expect to see progression. If a new paragraph mainly repeats the point made by the one before, you should either cut the paragraph altogether or find a way to stress whatever is new in it.

7.   DOES THE ENDING REAFFIRM, REFLECT UPON, OR EXTEND THE MAIN POINT OF THE TEXT?   When Carmen revised her draft, she ended by returning to differences between feminists of her generation and those of her mother's—the same topic she raised in her introduction.

Reconsidering Your Structure   IN BRIEF

1. Can you state your thesis?
2. Does your introduction state or forecast your thesis?
3. Can you state the main point of each paragraph?
4. Does each paragraph help develop the thesis?
5. Are the paragraphs linked to each other?
6. Does each new paragraph reveal something new?
7. Does the ending reaffirm, reflect upon, or extend the main point of the text?

9.6   STRENGTHENING TEXTURE

You can strengthen the texture of your writing by interweaving general ideas with specific details. Writing that lacks specific detail will seem abstract, colorless, and vacant, like a big empty windowless room with cinderblock walls. Writing that lacks any generalizations will seem dense and confusing, like a newspaper without headlines. To strengthen texture, do two things:

1.   ADD SPECIFICS TO MAKE GENERALIZATIONS (IN ITALICS) VIVID AND TANGIBLE:

Laughter takes many different forms. The nervous giggle, the cackle, the chuckle, and the guffaw are just a few of its variations.

In his first year as a rock musician, he had a hard time. He could not afford heat or hot water in his apartment, so he slept under a pile of heavy blankets and washed and shaved each morning in the men's room at McDonald's.

2.   ADD GENERALIZATIONS TO SHOW THE SIGNIFICANCE OF SPECIFIC DETAILS:

FIRST DRAFT: Getting dressed in the locker room, we said nothing to each other beyond "What's your name?" and "Where are you from?" We dressed quickly, finishing the job while running onto the field. Each of us wanted to get there first. One guy spoke my thoughts. Leaning my way, he said in a low voice, "These guys are massive. I don't stand a chance of playing."

REVISED (additions shown in italics): *On the first day of practice, competitiveness made us all tense and wary.* Getting dressed in the locker room, we said nothing to each other beyond "What's your name?" and "Where are you from?" We dressed quickly, finishing the job while running onto the field. Each of us wanted to get there first. *Everyone seemed to be checking over the rest of the team, measuring himself against the others.* One guy spoke my thoughts. Leaning my way, he said in a low voice, "These guys are massive. I don't stand a chance of playing."

EXERCISE 3   **Recognizing Generalizations and Specifics**

Identify the shifts between generalizations and specifics in the following passage:

Practically no aspect of the cultural lives of the Romans went untouched by Greek influence. Latin literary history begins with an adaptation of the *Odyssey*. By the second century, most educated Romans knew Greek and thus studied Homer. Inevitably, Rome challenged its dependence upon a superior but alien culture, calling the Greeks unreliable, crooked, sycophantic, deceptive, clever, garrulous, and even a bit effeminate. Romans raised their voices against Greek influence and affectation—the satirist Juvenal and the epigrammaticist Martial penned hysterically harsh caricatures of Hellenized Romans as unmanly, unpatriotic, and untraditional. A good Roman was expected to appreciate Greek classical culture but *never* to become too tainted by current Greek fads—much like the later attitude of the English towards the French.
—Victor David Hanson and John Heath, *Who Killed Homer?*

EXERCISE 4   **Furnishing Specifics**

Add specific details or examples to each of the following generalizations:

1. College students of my generation are *not* apathetic.

2. Rising costs have made getting a college education difficult for many.

3. Popular TV shows reflect our culture's values.

Furnishing Generalizations

Suppose you are writing a booklet to be used in recruiting young people for the U.S. Army. What attractive generalization about the army could you make on the basis of the following details?

After completing basic training in obedience, privates are assigned to an advanced training unit, where they learn a particular specialty such as mechanics, radio operation, or infantry tactics. Privates who learn their specialties exceptionally well have the chance to become noncommissioned officers (NCOs) after training in leadership and supervisory skills.

Revising with Specifics

Add specific details or examples to any passage in your first draft that leans too heavily on generalizations.

Revising with Generalizations

Add one or more generalizations to any passage in your first draft that is not sufficiently clear in its overall significance

Revising Your Text

Following the suggestions made in this chapter and illustrated by the instructors comments in 9.7, reexamine the aim, structure, tone, and texture of your text and revise where necessary. Do not worry now about correcting errors in spelling, grammar, or punctuation. Those can wait.

9.7 SAMPLE STUDENT PAPER

DRAFT

Different Worlds, Different Struggles

People my age have grown up hearing that my generation is apathetic and that feminism is dead. I think of this almost every time my parents tell me to turn down my CD player. Maybe if they listened, they

Good
statement
of thesis,
but can
you better
explain
what you
mean by
"attitudes
about my
generation"
—perhaps
provide an
example?

You may
need to
define
feminist
punk music
for people
who are
unfamiliar
with it.

Good
examples!

wouldn't have these attitudes about my generation. People can define a new vision of the world only from where they stand. Feminist punk music challenges consumer culture and traditional male/female relationships, leading to new ways of looking at women's power.

Feminist punkers write about commercialization turning people, feelings, and relationships into products. This is the message of Bikini Kill's "Jet Ski." In this song, Kathleen Hanna screams her rejection of a woman being used as a substitute for material objects.

—Weak
transiti

> I'm not yr oilwell
>
> I'm not yr bloodbank
>
> I'm not yr bullet proof vest
>
> Or yr visa card

Sometimes people associate punk with violence *but often that violence comes from the urge to break out of commercial culture. How do we break out of a culture where we are "determined by many," as Tobi Vail sings in "Distinct Complicity," without an act of violence? I think that is what Hanna is suggesting in "No Backrub": "No Pleasure / No Time / Don't Need To / Feel fine / Dirty Kitchen / Broken car / Trying to Breathe in / Through a Scar / (these are the things / I give myself) / . . . Loads of execution." Hanna seems to be saying that we are so programmed into believing that commercial culture will give us all the "good things" in life that all we seem to be able to give ourselves is "bad things." Many punk groups are so serious about resisting commercial culture that they have *they're own mail order services to distribute cheap CDs and 'zines *and they offer bands free information on how to inexpensively cut their own CDs. Making noncommercial music and distributing it on small labels, punkers try to create an alternative economic network, one that hasn't been absorbed by the corporate music industry.

A lot of women my age feel that my mother's generation of feminists tried to reject men. This is one very important difference between older feminism and the feminism of punk groups like Bikini Kill, Huggy Bear, and Sleater-Kinney. Most feminist punkers believe women can be strong and self-determining and still fall in love, *they don't believe that men should determine women's images of themselves. Sleater-Kinney has a good example of this in "Burn, Don't Freeze":

> You're the truest light I've known,
>
> but someday I'll learn I don't need your fuel to burn.
>
> (I'm the one who decides who I am
>
> I'm the one who will shed this old skin.)

In the "new renegade girl/boy hyper-nation" that Huggy Bear sings about, a woman can be sexy without making herself a sex object, and the guy who is dumb enough to confuse the two probably won't do it a second time. Feminist punk music affirms a *womens right to be sexually aggressive and rejects the negative stereotypes and labels that used to be attached to sexually aggressive women.

Feminist punkers don't believe in putting a lid on things. They believe women's power resides in following their impulses. *And expressing themselves in as many different ways as they can imagine. If they scream, it's because they have to scream in order to be heard. If they shock people, *its because they want to shock others into feeling something—into being aware of life with all its pleasures and suffering. This is one reason feminist punk (like all punk) is loud, repetitive, and often shocking. As Bikini Kill puts it in "Distinct Complicity," life is the struggle against being "determined by many" by "those who refuse to conquer hesitation." Sometimes their messages aren't very optimistic. This song doesn't end by saying it is possible to escape being determined. But by crying out, feminist punkers are at least saying that they aren't giving up.

Being radical for feminist punkers means living radically. This point is expressed well in a quote on the liner notes to Huggy Bear's "Taking the Rough with the Smooch." According to Raoul Vaneigem, it is impossible to "talk about revolution and class struggle without referring explicitly to everyday life, without understanding what is subversive about love and what is positive in the refusal of constraints." We believe there can be a better world and we're trying to create one, *we have to find it ourselves, for our own time.

UNEDITED REVISION

Different Worlds, Different Struggles

It's like a yearly rerun, though I don't know if it is a sit-com or a soap opera. In December we will visit my mother's parents, *my grandmother will fix a huge meal. After we eat, my parents, my aunt, my uncle and his wife will sit around the living room talking about the 60s. They will open a couple of bottles of wine, and with every sip their roles in student protests will grow more important. By the time they go to bed, you'd think my uncle started Earth Day and my mother started the feminist movement. Sometimes they try to be careful about what they say, knowing I might be listening. But I've heard it all before: "Young people today are apathetic." "The feminist movement is dead." I just readjust my headphones and turn up "Her Jazz" by Huggy Bear: "mental . . . men-torn . . . you had your way, baby, you had your say and had your way with that girl now come on outta yr world . . . this is happening without yr permission the arrival of a new renegade girl/boy hyper-nation." Of course, if I were playing Huggy Bear on their CD player, they'd tell me to turn it down—or off; and when they do that, they don't hear the voice of my generation.

Good point!

Can you establish more clearly the relationship between your thesis statement and the topic of this paragraph?

-Strengthen transition.

Can you bring your conclusion back around to the generational differences you raise in your introduction?

We aren't apathetic, and I consider myself a feminist—even if I occasionally *wear* a Wonderbra instead of burning it on the steps of the campus administration building. The feminist movement isn't dead; it's just taken
new forms, and one place it can be found is in feminist punk music.

Feminist punk music isn't easy to define. People who listen to punk
music identify it with the Riot Grrrls, which is another difficult category to
define, and the Riot Grrrl image lives on in groups like Bikini Kill, Huggy
Bear and Sleater-Kinney. Whether or not feminist punkers are equated
with Riot Grrrls, feminist punk music challenges consumer culture and
traditional male/female relationships, leading to new ways of looking at
women's power.

My generation grew up saturated in consumer culture—the same
cartoon characters who taught us the alphabet also sold us cereal. Punk
feminist music challenges the commercialization of people, feelings, and
relationships. In Bikini Kill's "Jet Ski," Kathleen Hanna screams her rejection of being a woman who is just a substitute for material objects.

> I'm not yr oilwell
>
> I'm not yr bloodbank
>
> I'm not yr bullet proof vest
>
> Or yr visa card

Sometimes people associate punk with violence *but often that violence
comes from the urge to break out of commercial culture. How do we escape a culture where we are "determined by many," as Tobi Vail sings in
"Distinct Complicity," without an act of violence? I think that is the
message in Bikini Kill's "No Backrub": "No Pleasure / No Time / Don't
Need To / Feel fine / Dirty Kitchen / Broken car / Trying to Breathe in /
Through a Scar / (these are the things / I give myself) / . . . Loads of execution." Hanna seems to be saying that if we think all "good things" must
come from commercial culture, then all we seem to be able to give ourselves is "bad things." Many punk groups resist by creating *they're own
mail order services to distribute cheap CDs and 'zines *and some offer
bands free information on cutting CDs in the most economical way. Making noncommercial music and distributing it on small labels, punkers try
to create an alternative economic network, one that hasn't been absorbed
by the corporate music industry.

Many women my age feel that the feminism of my mother's generation often rejected men; in contrast, a lot of feminist punk music focuses
on women's relationships with men, affirming women's sexuality. Most
feminist punkers believe women can be strong and self-determining and
still fall in love; they don't believe that men should determine women's
images of themselves. Sleater-Kinney has a good example of this in "Burn,
Don't Freeze":

You're the truest light I've known,

but someday I'll learn I don't need your fuel to burn.

(I'm the one who decides who I am

I'm the one who will shed this old skin.)

In the "new renegade girl/boy hyper-nation" that Huggy Bear sings about, a woman can be sexy without making herself a sex object, and the guy who is dumb enough to confuse the two probably won't do it a second time. Because feminist punkers affirm women's right to be sexually aggressive, their lyrics might be considered obscene by some people. In Bikini Kill's "Finale," which is a mild example of these lyrics, the band repeats: "we're the girls with the bad reputations." Their point is that women are not going to play by other *peoples' rules about sex and morality. They are going to redefine what it means to be a "bad" woman—and the labels they wear will be labels they've chosen for themselves.

Finally, feminist punkers challenge commercial culture and traditional male/female relationships because they believe both repress women's self-expression. Feminist punkers believe women's power resides in following their impulses. *And expressing themselves in as many different ways as they can imagine. Being radical is about living radically. This point is summarized in a quotation in the liner notes to Huggy Bear's "Taking the Rough with the Smooch," which says that it is impossible to "talk about revolution and class struggle without referring explicitly to everyday life, without understanding what is subversive about love and what is positive in the refusal of constraints." The same idea is expressed in Bikini Kill's "Distinct Complicity": life is the struggle against being "determined by many" by "those who refuse to conquer hesitation." If feminist punkers scream, *its because they feel they have to scream in order to be heard. If they shock people, it's because they want to shock others into feeling—into being aware of life with all its pleasures and suffering. Feminist punk music may not be very optimistic about women's ability to escape repression, but by crying out—often in loud, repetitive, and *sometime shocking ways—feminist punkers are at least saying that they aren't giving up.

Sometimes I think about my mother's generation when I listen to these groups. I know many of the advantages I have as a *women are the result of battles fought for equal rights by *mother's generation. I only wish the older feminists could see that we aren't apathetic. Like the women of my mother's generation, we are looking for ways to create a better world. But since the world we have to change is different, our struggle will be different too.

NOTE: For models of how to format essays and research papers in MLA and APA styles, see chapter 12; for a sample research paper in the humanities, see chapter 40; for sample essays about literature, see chapter 41.

10 *Editing and Proofreading*

10.1 WHY EDIT AND PROOFREAD?

Editing followed by **proofreading** is the final stage of writing, the final chance to ensure that your writing makes the best possible impression on your reader. While revising treats the substance and structure of the piece as a whole, editing concentrates on the construction of individual sentences, on punctuation, grammar, spelling, and word choice. These things make up the face of your text. No matter how well organized the text may be, small errors can mar its clarity and weaken its credibility, and awkward sentences can weaken its rhetorical impact. Careful editing helps you win the good opinion of your reader and, with it, your reader's willingness to see things your way.

What follows is a series of brief suggestions designed to guide you through the editing process. To learn more about any point listed here, see the chapter or section noted in parentheses.

10.2 MAKING YOUR SENTENCES RHETORICALLY POWERFUL

Good writing is made of sentences that are not just grammatically correct but also **rhetorically powerful**: vigorous, concise, emphatic, well-balanced, and varied. To achieve these effects with your own sentences, consider the following suggestions:

1. **USE SUBORDINATION TO BREAK THE MONOTONY OF SHORT, SIMPLE SENTENCES AND TO STRESS YOUR MAIN POINTS** (chapter 18):

   ▶ ~~One~~ When one clown took a roundhouse swing at the other, ~~He~~ and wound up punching himself in the nose, ~~The~~ the children roared.

168

2. **VARY THE LENGTH AND STRUCTURE OF YOUR SENTENCES (27.1):**

    ▶ Ultimately, it is not for our teams, our schools, or our coaches that we
      love to score, ~~but~~ for ourselves. *. It is*

3. **USE VERBS OF ACTION (24.3).** Wherever possible, replace forms of the
    verb *be*—forms such as *is, are, was, were, has been,* and *had been*—with verbs
    denoting action:

    ▶ Many children ~~are afraid of~~ the dark. *fear*

    ▶ Harry ~~was a source of interruption~~ throughout the meeting. *continually interrupted*

4. **CHANGE PASSIVE-VOICE VERBS TO THE ACTIVE WHENEVER NO GOOD REASON
    JUSTIFIES THE PASSIVE (24.2):**

    ▶ In Japanese families, all of the husband's salary ~~is taken by the wife,~~ *the wife takes*
      and all household expenditures ~~are managed by her.~~ *manages .*

5. **USE PARALLEL CONSTRUCTION TO ENHANCE THE COORDINATION OF TWO OR
    MORE ITEMS (chapter 16):**

    ▶ To score a goal is for one shining moment to conquer all frustration,
      ~~Anxiety has been banished~~, and ~~we~~ rule the world. *to banish anxiety,   to*

6. **CUT WORDS YOU DON'T REALLY NEED TO DELIVER YOUR MEANING (8.13):**

    ▶ ~~There are many~~ things ~~that~~ make me laugh. *Many*

7. **IF A SENTENCE IS TOO TANGLED TO BE UNDERSTOOD ON THE FIRST READING,
    BREAK IT UP AND REORGANIZE IT (18.2):**

    ▶ Due to the progress in military weaponry over the years, there has been
      an increased passivity in humankind that such advancements bring as
      wars are easier to fight resulting in a total loss of honor in fighting.

      EDITED: Since progress in military weaponry over the years has made
      humankind more passive and wars easier to fight, fighting has lost all
      honor.

10.3 CHECKING YOUR CHOICE OF WORDS

1. **REPLACE WORDS TOO HIGH OR LOW FOR THE LEVEL OF DICTION PREVAILING AROUND THEM** (8.4):

    ▶ After debating it for more than an hour and considering various
    amendments, the faculty finally ~~blew off~~ *rejected* the proposal.

2. **REPLACE WORDS OR PHRASES THAT ARE MISUSED:**

    ▶ Fortunately, the earthquake had no ~~a~~ffect *e* on the city.

You may need help from your teacher to spot misused words or phrases. See 8.5–8.6, 8.14, and the Glossary of Usage.

3. **REPLACE VAGUE ABSTRACTIONS WITH CONCRETE, SPECIFIC, OR FIGURATIVE TERMS** (8.7–8.8):

    ▶ Going to college ~~involves learning many new things.~~ *is like exploring a big city for the first time.*

4. **REPLACE PRETENTIOUS VERBIAGE AND JARGON** (8.12) **WITH WORDS THAT PLAINLY DELIVER YOUR MEANING:**

    ▶ ~~Upwardly mobile~~ *Ambitious* young lawyers and doctors often work ~~in excess of~~ *more than*
    seventy hours a week.

5. **REPLACE CLICHÉS** (8.10):

    ▶ I ~~was busy as a bee~~ *worked steadily* all week long.

10.4 CHECKING YOUR GRAMMAR

Watch for the following errors, which are explained in the designated chapter or section of part 2:

1. THE SENTENCE FRAGMENT (chapter 19)

   ▶ Feminist punkers believe women's power resides in following their impulses, ~~And~~ *and* expressing themselves in as many different ways as they
   can imagine.

   ▶ If feminist punk musicians shock people, it's because they want to
   shock others into feeling, ~~Into~~ *into* being aware of life with all its pleasures
   and suffering.

2. THE DANGLING MODIFIER (14.17)

   ▶ After exercising a swim *we took* ~~was taken.~~

3. THE MISPLACED MODIFIER (14.15–14.16)

   ▶ *While sitting in the tub,* I thought about the speech I had to give in French class ~~while sitting in the tub.~~

4. THE RUN-ON (FUSED) SENTENCE (15.7)

   ▶ The quake struck without warning *, and* in minutes it leveled half the town.

5. UNCLEAR REFERENCE OF PRONOUNS (20.4)

   ▶ When I took the Walkman back to the store, ~~they~~ *the manager* told me I couldn't get
   a refund.

6. FAULTY SHIFTS IN PRONOUN REFERENCE (20.8)

   ▶ When a college requires drug testing of ~~their~~ *its* athletes, does the testing
   violate their rights?

7. INCORRECT PRONOUN CASE FORMS (20.9–20.12)

   ▶ ~~Him~~ *He* and I always disagreed.

   ▶ The race between Paul and ~~I~~ *me* left me exhausted.

8. **FAULTY AGREEMENT OF SUBJECT AND VERB** (chapter 21)

▸ Anyone with small children ~~know~~ how demanding they are.
knows

9. **FAULTY TENSE SHIFTS** (23.5)

▸ As soon as I saw the coat, I ~~recognize~~ it.
recognized

10.5 CHECKING YOUR PUNCTUATION

For guidance on punctuation, see part 3. Make a list of any punctuation errors that your teacher notes in your writing so that you can learn to spot them for yourself. Watch especially for the following comma errors:

1. **THE COMMA SPLICE** (15.6)

▸ Temperatures dropped below zero, *and* the big pond froze for the first time in ten years.

2. **COMMAS MISUSED WITH RESTRICTIVE ELEMENTS** (29.6)

▸ Cars/equipped with airbags/can save the lives of drivers/who fail to wear safety belts.

3. **COMMA AFTER A CONJUNCTION** (29.2)

▸ We walked all over town, but/we couldn't find the store.

4. **COMMA SEPARATING THE BASIC PARTS OF A SENTENCE** (29.13)

▸ Poisonous gas from a pesticide factory in India/killed more than two thousand people in 1984.

10.6 CHECKING YOUR SPELLING, CAPITALIZATION, AND APOSTROPHES

Check the following:

1. **YOUR OWN SPELLING DEMONS**   These are words you have trouble spelling correctly. Your computer spell checker will catch some of them, but it will not catch mistakes such as misusing homonyms, words that sound alike: *right/write, there/their, here/hear* (see 34.5).

> ▸ Of course, if I were playing Huggy Bear on ~~there~~ *their* CD player, they'd tell me to turn it down—or off; and when they do, they don't ~~here~~ *hear* the voice of my ~~genaration~~ *generation*.

To find the correct spelling of a word marked *sp.*, look it up in a dictionary. Then analyze the misspelling as explained in 34.2 and correct it.

2.   APOSTROPHES NEEDED OR MISUSED (34.9–34.10)

> ▸ The town's police force consisted of the sheriff and his dog/s.

3.   CAPITALIZATION NEEDED OR MISUSED (35.1)

> ▸ Theodore Roosevelt became president of the United States when William McKinley was assassinated in 1901.

10.7   PROOFREADING YOUR TEXT

Technically, **proofreading** is the reading of proof sheets—what the printer submits for the author's final corrections before a piece of writing is published. As you read your text once more, imagine it is going to be published. Reread every word carefully, watching particularly for errors in grammar, spelling, and punctuation. If you make more than five corrections on a page, retype or reprint the page.

Editing Checklist

Sentence Rhetoric

▪   Do you use subordination to stress your main point?

▪   Do your sentences vary in length and structure?

▪   Do you frequently use verbs of action and the active voice?

▪   Do you use parallel construction whenever suitable?

▪   Have you cut all words you don't really need to deliver your meaning?

▪   Is any sentence tangled?

Word Choice

▬ Is any word too high or too low for your level of diction?

▬ Is any word or phrase misused?

▬ Do you see vague abstractions that could be replaced with concrete terms?

▬ Do you see pretentious words that could be replaced with plain ones?

▬ Do you find any cliches?

Sentence Grammar

▬ Does any sentence sound incomplete?

▬ Does any part of a sentence seem out of place?

▬ Is the reference of each pronoun clear?

▬ Does the form of each verb agree with its subject?

▬ Is the tense of each verb correct?

Punctuation and Mechanics

▬ Have you used commas where they belong, and only where they belong?

▬ Have you marked the end of every sentence correctly?

▬ Are you sure that each word is correctly spelled?

▬ Have you fixed all typographical errors?

EXERCISE 1   **Proofreading**

We have deliberately mutilated this passage from Mark Twain's "Advice to Youth" so that it contains three misspellings, a sentence fragment, and a comma splice. Find the errors and correct them.

> You want to be very careful about lying, otherwise you are
> nearly sure to get caught. Once caught, you can never again be, in
> the eyes of the good and the pure, what you were before. Many a
> young person has injured himself pernamently through a single
> clumsy and ill-finished lie. The result of carelessness born of incom-   5
> plete training. Some authorities hold that the young ought not to lie
> at all. That, of course, is puting it rather stronger than necessary; still,
> while I cannot go quite so far as that, I do maintane, and I believe I
> am right, that the young ought to be temperate in the use of this
> great art until practice and experience shall give them that confi-   10
> dence, elegance, and precision which alone can make the accomplish-
> ment graceful and profitable.

Proofreading

Following is a paragraph from the next-to-last version of the essay by Andrew Lyle cited in earlier chapters. Correct any errors you find.

> For over half an hour we tried to snag the rope on an overhanging rock. We never did make it. We tried other, longer routes, giving each other boosts with our hands, but the top layre of copper sediment was so thick. That what we thought was a firm handhold would often crumble in our grasp. So we couldnt trust the climbing surface. We even explored old mine shafts in hopes that they would lead us out, they only led us deeper into the mine. As we explored one shaft, however, we stumbled over an eight-foot iron rod and then a six-foot metal tube. With some dificulty, we found a way to fit the rod into the tube, forming a crude but relativly sturdy pole of about thirteen feet. Bracing the pole to the ground next to the precipece, we climbed it and made our way out of the cave.

5

10

10.8   EDITED REVISION OF STUDENT TEXT

DIFFERENT WORLDS, DIFFERENT STRUGGLES

It's like a yearly rerun, though I don't know if it is a sit-com or a soap opera. In December we will visit my mother's parents. My grandmother will fix a huge meal. After we eat, my parents, my aunt, my uncle and his wife will sit around the living room talking about the 60s. They will open a couple of bottles of wine, and with every sip their roles in student protests will grow more important. By the time they go to bed, you'd think my uncle started Earth Day and my mother started the feminist movement. Sometimes they try to be careful about what they say, knowing I might be listening. But I've heard it all before: "Young people today are apathetic." "The feminist movement is dead." I just readjust my headphones and turn up "Her Jazz" by Huggy Bear: "mental . . . mentorn . . . you had your way, baby, you had your say and had your way with that girl now come on outta yr world . . . this is happening without yr permission the arrival of a new renegade girl/boy hyper-nation." Of course, if I were playing Huggy Bear on their CD player, they'd tell me to turn it down—or off; and when they do that, they don't hear the voice of my generation. We aren't apathetic, and I consider myself a feminist—even if I occasionally *wear* a Wonderbra instead of burning it on the steps of the campus administration building. The feminist movement isn't dead; it's just taken new forms, and one place it can be found is in feminist punk music.

Feminist punk music isn't easy to define. People who listen to punk music identify it with the Riot Grrrls, which is another difficult category to define, and the Riot Grrrl image lives on in groups like Bikini Kill, Huggy Bear and Sleater-Kinney. Whether or not feminist punkers are equated with Riot Grrrls, feminist punk music challenges consumer culture and traditional male/female relationships, leading to new ways of looking at women's power.

My generation grew up saturated in consumer culture—the same cartoon characters who taught us the alphabet also sold us cereal. Punk feminist music challenges the commercialization of people, feelings, and relationships. In Bikini Kill's "Jet Ski," Kathleen Hanna screams her rejection of being a woman who is just a substitute for material objects.

> I'm not yr oilwell
>
> I'm not yr bloodbank
>
> I'm not yr bullet proof vest
>
> Or yr visa card

Sometimes people associate punk with violence, but often that violence comes from the urge to break out of commercial culture. How do we escape a culture where we are "determined by many," as Tobi Vail sings in "Distinct Complicity," without an act of violence? I think that is the message in Bikini Kill's "No Backrub": "No Pleasure / No Time / Don't Need To / Feel fine / Dirty Kitchen / Broken car / Trying to Breathe in / Through a Scar / (these are the things / I give myself) / . . . Loads of execution." Hanna seems to be saying that if we think all "good things" come from commercial culture, then all we seem to be able to give ourselves is "bad

things." Many punk groups resist by creating ~~they're~~ *their* own mail order ser-

vices to distribute cheap CDs and 'zines, and some offer bands free infor-

mation on cutting CDs in the most economical way. Making noncommer-

cial music and distributing it on small labels, punkers try to create an

alternative economic network, one that hasn't been absorbed by the cor-

porate music industry.

Many women my age feel that the feminism of my mother's genera-

tion often rejected men; in contrast, a lot of feminist punk music focuses

on women's relationships with men, affirming women's sexuality. Most

feminist punkers believe women can be strong and self-determining and

still fall in love; they don't believe that men should determine women's

images of themselves. Sleater-Kinney has a good example of this in "Burn,

Don't Freeze":

> You're the truest light I've known,
>
> but someday I'll learn I don't need your fuel to burn.
>
> (I'm the one who decides who I am
>
> I'm the one who will shed this old skin.)

In the "new renegade girl/boy hyper-nation" that Huggy Bear sings about,

a woman can be sexy without making herself a sex object, and the guy

who is dumb enough to confuse the two probably won't do it a second

time. Because feminist punkers affirm women's right to be sexually aggres-

sive, their lyrics might be considered obscene by some people. In Bikini

Kill's "Finale," which is a mild example of these lyrics, the band repeats:

"we're the girls with the bad reputations." Her point is that women are not

going to play by other ~~peoples'~~ *people's* rules about sex and morality. They are

going to redefine what it means to be a "bad" woman—and the labels they

wear will be labels they've chosen for themselves.

Finally, feminist punkers challenge commercial culture and traditional

male/female relationships because they believe both repress women's self-

expression. Feminist punkers believe women's power resides in following their impulses. And expressing themselves in as many different ways as they can imagine. Being radical is about living radically. This point is summarized in a quotation from Raoul Vaneigem in the liner notes to Huggy Bear's "Taking the Rough with the Smooch," which says that it is impossible "talk about revolution and class struggle without referring explicitly to everyday life, without understanding what is subversive about love and what is positive in the refusal of constraints." The same idea is expressed in Bikini Kill's "Distinct Complicity": life is the struggle against being "determined by many" by "those who refuse to conquer hesitation." If feminist punkers scream, it's because they feel they have to scream in order to be heard. If they shock people, it's because they want to shock others into feeling—into being aware of life with all its pleasures and suffering. Feminist punk music may not be very optimistic about women's ability to escape repression, but by crying out—often in loud, repetitive, and sometimes shocking ways—feminist punkers are at least saying that they aren't giving up.

Sometimes I think about my mother's generation when I listen to these groups. I know many of the advantages I have as a woman are the result of battles fought for equal rights by my mother's generation. I only wish the older feminists could see that we aren't apathetic. Like the women of my mother's generation, we are looking for ways to create a better world. But since the world we have to change is different, our struggle will be different too.

NOTE: For models of how to format essays and research papers in MLA and APA styles, see chapter 12; for a sample research paper in the humanities, see chapter 40; for sample essays about literature, see chapter 41.

Persuasion and Argument **11**

11.1 WHAT IS PERSUASION?

Persuasion is the art of leading people to do something or to believe something without compelling them to do so. It is an art practiced with pictures and gestures as well as with spoken and written words, and it is practiced all around us. Persuasive appeals spring from billboards, magazines, newspapers, television, radio, the Internet, and even our own telephones whenever we lift the receiver to hear the voice of a salesperson. To survive and succeed in this world, we must be able to recognize persuasion, to judge it, and to use it ourselves.

Persuasion never occurs in a vacuum. It always rests on a base of shared assumptions. Suppose, for instance, that the zoning board of Amityville has been asked to approve a request that a house on Elm Street be used as a residence for people recovering from mental illness, who would live there under the supervision of a nurse. If Jane E. Homeowner, who now lives on Elm Street, doesn't like this idea, she might say to the zoning board that the presence of such patients on her street would reduce the value of her property. If that point persuaded the zoning board to vote against the request, she and a majority of its members must have shared one assumption: maintaining property values is more important than helping the recovering mentally ill readjust to living in a normal environment.

Occasionally, persuasion may also be fueled by some form of power. Suppose that one member of the zoning board mentioned above is the automobile dealer from whom Jane Homeowner normally buys her cars. While considering her point about property values, he knows very well what this good customer might do if he votes to approve the new residence. She doesn't even have to remind him of the power she holds.

Just as persuasion may be fueled by some form of power, it is commonly lubricated by an appeal to the feelings—especially in selling and advertising. Over a big color picture of a farming family gathered around a tractor, an insurance ad proclaims:

> **There are people more famous we insure.**
> **But none more important.**

Under the picture the ad continues:

> For over a hundred years, we've tried to keep personal insurance from becoming too impersonal.
> When you do business with ____, it's with one of our independent agents. So when you have a question about auto, health, home or life insurance, you deal with someone who is close to you and your situation.
> You can easily find an independent ____ agent in the Yellow Pages.
> ____ is one of the world's largest insurance companies, a size that doesn't diminish our big concern for the individual.

As in many ads, picture and text together seek to persuade readers that the advertiser cares about each of them. The means of persuasion are essentially emotional. With the family picture reinforcing the point, the reader is told that the company deals in "personal insurance," that the company agent will be "someone who is close to you and your situation." The tone is warm and reassuring; the statement is the verbal equivalent of a friendly handshake.

Since feelings play a part in the formation of almost every opinion, you need to understand as well as you can the feelings of your readers. But you can seldom persuade an audience by appealing to their feelings alone. If you respect the intelligence of your readers, you will also appeal to their minds. And to do that successfully, you must construct an argument.

11.2   WHAT IS AN ARGUMENT?

We commonly think of an argument as a quarrel—a shouting match in which tempers flare and necks turn red. But the word *argument* can also mean "a rational way of persuading." It differs from exposition because it seeks to convince, not just to explain, and it differs from emotional persuasion because it seeks to convince by appealing to the mind. To see these differences more clearly, consider the following three passages:

Exposition

1. The bear population of Maine is 7,000 to 10,000 animals, and the annual "harvest," or kill, averages 930. State wildlife biologists estimate that the number killed falls short by 120 of the "allowable harvest," i.e.,

"the harvest level that takes only the annual increase and does not affect the population size."

—Jonathan Evan Maslow, "Stalking the Black Bear"

2. Every year, bloodthirsty hunters go into the Maine woods and ruthlessly shoot to death hundreds of bears. The hunters care nothing for the suffering they cause, for the blood they spill, or for the harm they do to creatures who have done no harm to them. Hunters kill for a thrill, and that is all they care about. No one seems to care anything for the bears.

Emotional appeal

3. Though some people may think hunting is nothing more than wholesale and wanton destruction of living creatures, hunters actually help to ensure the health and survival of wildlife. Take bear-hunting in Maine as a case in point. Out of the 7,000 to 10,000 bears that roam the Maine woods, hunters kill an average of 930 a year. State wildlife biologists estimate that this is 120 fewer than the annual population increase. If the bear population were allowed to grow unchecked, it would increase well over 1,000 a year, and the food available for any one bear would correspondingly decrease. By killing an average of 930 bears a year, hunters keep the annual increase down, and therefore help to ensure an adequate food supply for the bear population as a whole.

Argument

These three passages treat the same topic in fundamentally different ways. The first calmly explains the relation between the number of bears born and the number killed in Maine each year. The second tries to make the reader feel outrage at hunters and pity for bears. The third tries to prove that hunting is beneficial to wildlife.

Note the difference between passage 2 and passage 3. Passage 2 relies on words like *bloodthirsty* to stir the reader's feelings; passage 3 relies on facts, figures, and authoritative estimates to gain the reader's agreement. Purely emotive words may appeal to a reader who already tends to feel the way the writer does, but they are unlikely to change an opponent's mind. On the other hand, the argument of passage 3 is thought-provoking. It won't persuade all readers, but it will give even fervent conservationists something to think about. To combat such an argument effectively, conservationists would have to challenge its facts, figures, and estimates in a manner such as this:

4. Hunting advocates try to justify the killing of bears by arguing that it limits the annual increase in the bear population and thereby helps to ensure an adequate food supply for the bears that remain. But this argument rests on the assumption that wildlife biologists can reliably estimate the size of the population increase, which is said to be 120 more than the number of bears killed each year. Can we be sure it is? If estimates of the bear population range from 7,000 to 10,000, how can we

accurately calculate the annual increase in that population? Do we even know how many bears die each year of natural causes? If we don't know that, we cannot determine what the net annual increase in the bear population would be in the absence of hunters. And even if we knew this figure exactly, it would not tell us just how well an unregulated bear population would manage to feed itself. Without hunters threatening them, bears might well become more venturesome and thus more successful in their quest for food. We can hardly be certain, therefore, that bears are better off with hunters than they would be without them.

Like passage 2, this passage aims to convince the reader that bear-hunting is unjustified. But unlike passage 2, it does not try to stir pity for bears or outrage at hunters. Instead, it calmly exposes the weaknesses in the pro-hunting argument, and thus appeals to the reader's mind.

Just as argument differs from emotional persuasion, so also does it differ from exposition. In exposition, every statement is offered as a matter of accepted fact. In argument, only some statements are offered as matters of fact, and these are given as reasons to make us believe assertions or claims. For example, the assertion in passage 3 that "hunters actually help to ensure the health and survival of wildlife" is disputable and needs defending. Instead of assuming that we will believe it, the writer must give us reasons for doing so.

An effective argument is the product of an imaginary conversation between the writer and a skeptical, questioning reader. The conversation starts with a **claim**, which is a statement of what the writer intends to prove:

1. CLAIM: Hunters help to ensure the health and survival of bears.
   QUESTION: How?

2. EVIDENCE: They limit the growth of the bear population.
   QUESTION: But how does that help the bears?

3. ASSUMPTION: Fewer bears means more food per bear.

The **evidence** for a claim includes the specific facts or data on which the claim rests. But statements of fact can often be challenged, as passage 4 shows, especially when they depend on estimates rather than precise measurement. To build an effective argument, therefore, you must be sure that your statements of fact are true.

Besides evidence, most arguments include one or more **assumptions**, which are beliefs or principles—often unstated—that the writer takes for granted. An assumption binds the evidence to the claim. To prove that hunters help ensure the health and survival of bears, it's not enough to say that hunters limit population growth among bears; you must also ask readers to assume that fewer bears means more food per bear. To argue effectively, therefore, you should know what your assumptions are and whether or not your readers are likely to share them.

Basic Elements of an Argument

▶ **Claim:** statement that needs defending

▶ **Evidence:** statements of fact made to support the claim

▶ **Assumption:** belief or principle (often unstated) that the writer takes for granted

---

11.3   SUPPORTING CLAIMS WITH EVIDENCE

Effective arguments support general claims with specific evidence. Giving evidence means doing one or more of the following things:

GIVING STATEMENTS OF FACT AND EXAMPLES

A statement of fact is a statement of what the writer takes for certain because it is well known ("George Washington was the first president of the United States"), readily verifiable by experiment ("Heat makes gases expand"), or set down in public record ("Martin Luther King Jr. won the Nobel Peace Prize in 1963").

An example is a particular object, event, or condition that is said to represent something larger than itself. Statements of fact often serve as examples. The statement about Martin Luther King Jr. could readily serve as an example of the international recognition he achieved. But not all examples are statements of fact. In 11.1, to show how persuasion depends on shared assumptions, we offered an imaginary example. We asked you to *suppose* a set of circumstances.

The persuasive force of an imaginary example depends on its plausibility—that is, on whether or not the reader can imagine that it could be true or that something like it could actually happen. The persuasive force of a factual example depends in part on its plausibility (you would not readily accept the statement that a tribe of pygmies has been discovered living underwater), but also on its specificity, and sometimes on the sources or authorities that are said to stand behind it (as explained in "Citing Sources and Authorities," below).

To see how an argument may be strengthened by examples and statements of fact, which we'll simply call *facts* from now on, compare these two passages written by first-year college students:

Claim supported only by broad generalizations

> My feeling is that all people are equal. Neither sex is superior to the other. In the times of today, men and women both have an equal opportunity for education. They can pursue any career that they are qualified for. Schools are now getting away from trying to make certain things for boys and vice versa. Children are growing up as equals.

Claim supported only by specific facts and examples

> There are differences between men and women, but none that make either sex inferior. Athletic performance is a case in point. A major study by a West German doctor has shown that because of different skeletal leverage in men and women, muscles of identical strength will produce about 5 percent greater apparent strength in men. In sports such as running and mountaineering, however, women show greater endurance and resistance to stress. Several years ago, when I assisted a friend running the Boston Marathon, I noticed that although many of the male runners were literally collapsing at the finish or at least in need of help, the women rarely needed any help at all.

The persuasive force of an argument generally grows with the weight of evidence presented. See how the following argument gains rhetorical power as it gathers facts and examples to support its opening claim:

> Nuclear power plants are fundamentally unsafe. The history of nuclear power is a list of major accidents and near catastrophes. At Windscale, England, in 1957, a fire and a partial meltdown of a nuclear core spread radioactivity across miles of pastureland, and thousands of gallons of contaminated cows' milk had to be dumped. In 1966 another partial meltdown occurred at Unit One of the Fermi plant near Detroit. In 1970 fifty thousand gallons of radioactive water and steam escaped from the reactor vessel of the huge Commonwealth Edison plant near Chicago. At Browns Ferry, Alabama, in 1975, a single candle started a fire at a nuclear power plant that burned for seven hours, caused 150 million dollars' worth of damage and loss to the plant, and—according to some experts—very nearly caused a catastrophic release of radiation. Even after the Rasmussen report supposedly analyzed everything that could go wrong with a nuclear reactor, a malfunctioning water gauge led to yet another near meltdown at Three Mile Island, Pennsylvania, in 1979. Finally, in April 1986, an explosion and fire in the graphite core of a nuclear reactor at Chernobyl in the Soviet Ukraine caused more than 25 fatalities, spread radioactive dust over much of Europe, contaminated food supplies in Scandinavia, and may lead to more than 30,000 cancer-related deaths over the next 70 years.

Taken together, all of these accidents show that the risks we run in operating nuclear power plants are intolerably high.

Statements of established fact ("Heat makes gases expand") or of public record (like the statements of fact made in the passage above) can usually stand by themselves. But for some other kinds of evidence, you must cite your sources (as explained in "Citing Sources and Authorities," below).

CITING STATISTICS

Statistics help to make an argument persuasive by providing what appears to be "hard" evidence. If, for instance, you want to argue that hunters help bears, you can strengthen your case by stating that hunters hold the net growth of the bear population to 120 each year. If you want to argue that American highways have grown steadily more dangerous in the past forty-five years, you can state that auto fatalities in 1989 were eighteen thousand higher than they were in 1945.

But figures and statistics alone will not make your argument for you. If the figures on the bear population are only an estimate, this "hard" piece of evidence turns soft. If the number of automobile fatalities has risen since 1945, what about the number of cars and drivers on the road? If they've risen also—and they have—the number of fatalities doesn't tell the whole story. Other figures tell a different story: the *rate* of fatalities per 100 million vehicle miles actually *fell* after 1945, from 9.8 in 1946 to 2.25 in 1989. The meaning of the number of fatalities at Chernobyl must likewise be interpreted. If more than twenty-five people were killed by the Chernobyl explosion, does this mean that every nuclear power plant is a disaster waiting to happen? Not necessarily, since (as a matter of fact) the design of the Chernobyl reactor is fundamentally different from the design of most commercial reactors in the West.

To make figures and statistics serve as evidence, then, you must clearly explain what they mean and you may also have to establish their reliability by citing their source.

CITING SOURCES AND AUTHORITIES

Cite sources for statistics and authorities for estimates and opinions.

1. STATISTICS ARE NOT MATTERS OF FACT.   They are products of calculation. Their reliability depends on who calculated them, how they were calculated, and for what purpose. So you should cite your source for any statistics you use, and you can do so in one of two ways:

a.   SOURCE CITED IN PASSING

According to the U.S. Bureau of Census, the proportion of working women who are mothers of children under 6 rose from 11.9 percent in 1950 to 56.8 percent in 1987.

b.   SOURCE CITED IN PARENTHESES

The rate of fatalities per 100 million vehicle miles fell from 9.8 in 1946 to 4.24 in 1973 (National Safety Council).

These are both *informal* ways of citing sources. For detailed guidance on *formally* citing a source, see chapters 39 and 42.

2.   THE VALUE OF AN ESTIMATE OR OPINION IS ONLY AS GOOD AS THE AUTHORITY WHO STANDS BEHIND IT.   Before citing an authority, ask yourself the following questions:

a.   WHO IS THE AUTHORITY?   Is he or she an unnamed "expert" or a named, established specialist in a particular field? A "major study" of anatomical differences between men and women made "by a West German doctor" carries less weight than "a thorough study of nuclear power plants made at a cost of four million dollars under the supervision of Norman Rasmussen, professor of nuclear engineering at M.I.T."

b.   IS THE AUTHORITY SPEAKING ON A TOPIC IN HIS OR HER FIELD OF EXPERTISE? If a specialist in the study of alcohol says that a driver with a blood alcohol content of .05 percent is twice as likely to have an accident as a driver who is perfectly sober, that statement carries the weight of special authority. But if the alcohol expert says that teenagers should not be allowed to drive until they are eighteen, he or she no longer speaks with special authority, because the topic has changed.

c.   GIVEN THE FACTS AVAILABLE ON A PARTICULAR QUESTION, CAN ANY EXPERT ANSWER IT WITH CERTAINTY?   Predictions are notoriously unreliable, and experts on some subjects—the stock market, for instance—frequently miscalculate what will happen. No amount of authority can give to a prediction or an estimate the weight of an established fact.

d.   DOES ANY OTHER AUTHORITY AGREE WITH THE ONE YOU CITE? Experts often disagree. If the expert you cite is alone in his or her testimony, it will carry less weight than testimony backed by other experts.

Evidence

► Use statements of fact that are reliable and relevant to your claim.

► Cite statistics that are reliable and meaningful.

► Cite sources for statistics.

► Cite authorities for estimates and opinions after considering these questions:

Who is the authority?
Is he or she an expert on the topic?
Given the available facts on this topic, can any expert give a wholly reliable opinion on it?
Does any other authority agree with the one you are citing?

11.4 DEDUCTION AND INDUCTION

Successful argumentation requires a basic understanding of logic, which is the art of drawing inferences or conclusions. Whether you realize it or not, you make inferences every day. If, for instance, you accidentally slide your finger along the edge of a piece of paper and then discover a thin line of dark red on the fingertip, you will probably infer that you have cut yourself. That is a logical inference because it is based on a credible set of assumptions (the edge of a paper can be sharp enough to cut; a dark red line on the fingertip is more likely to be blood than anything else) and a known fact (you have indeed run that fingertip along the paper's edge).

If we all make inferences every day, why do we need logic? Why do we need rules of inference? We need them because it is all too easy to make mistakes in drawing inferences, and arguments based on mistaken inferences are like buildings resting on cracked foundations. At best they will totter; at worst they will fall.

Without logic to rein us in, we commonly jump to conclusions. How often have you heard two or three people complain about a proposal and then concluded that *everyone* dislikes it? How often have you seen a member of a particular group do something odd or offensive and then concluded, "That's the way they all are"? If you are sensible enough to avoid such obvious mistakes in inference as those, you may nonetheless fall into more subtle traps. Suppose you were with the police at Berkeley in 1964 when they entered the office of President Emeritus Robert Gordon Sproul to remove student demonstrators who had broken into it during the Free

Speech Movement. After the demonstrators were taken out, police found papers strewn all over the floor of Sproul's office. Surely, they thought, this was the work of the demonstrators. But in fact it wasn't. The papers had been strewn about by Sproul himself, who often liked to do his work on the floor.

To avoid subtle as well as obvious traps in the construction of your own arguments, you need to know something about inference—the process of drawing conclusions from assumptions and evidence. It commonly takes one of two forms—*deduction* or *induction*.

DEDUCTION AND VALIDITY

Deduction applies a general principle to a specific case. In formal logic, deduction is sometimes illustrated by a syllogism, a set of categorical statements that looks like this:

> MAJOR PREMISE (ASSUMPTION): All those who limit the growth of the bear population help bears.
>
> MINOR PREMISE (EVIDENCE): Bear hunters limit the growth of the bear population.
>
> CONCLUSION (CLAIM): Bear hunters help bears.

In a syllogism, the claim supported by an argument appears last, as a conclusion. The conclusion is deduced or inferred from the major premise (a general principle the writer assumes), and the minor premise (normally evidence—a statement of fact). When a deduction is valid, the conclusion follows *necessarily* from the premises. The above syllogism is valid because the minor premise puts bear hunters within the category of "all those who limit the growth of the bear population." Since what applies to all members of this category must apply to every group within it, the conclusion is validly drawn. But if this syllogism were to conclude that bear hunters help all animals, the conclusion would be invalidly drawn, for it would then have strayed outside the category established by the premises.

MAKING DEDUCTIVE ARGUMENTS PERSUASIVE

Validity alone will not make an argument persuasive. The persuasiveness of an argument depends on the credibility of its assumptions.

Take, for instance, the assumption (major premise) made by the syllogism above. If we don't know how many bears die each year from natural causes, how do we know that anyone who limits the growth of their population is helping them? So long as the assumption can be questioned in this way, any conclusion drawn from it will be questionable also. A conclusion validly drawn from premises that are questionable or false is like a route carefully followed in strict obedience to a faulty compass. The route is only as good as the compass that determines it, and the argument is only as credible as the assumption that stands behind it.

Consider the assumption made by this deductive argument:

> In spite of the widespread fear and resistance they often generate, nuclear power plants are fundamentally safe. From 1972 to 1975, a thorough study of nuclear power plants was made at a cost of four million dollars under the supervision of Norman Rasmussen, professor of nuclear engineering at M.I.T. Given the time, money, and expertise devoted to this study, its results must be reliable. And in fact they are not only reliable; they are also reassuring. After examining, identifying, and—with computer analysis—establishing the risk of every possible accident that could release radiation from a nuclear power plant, the Rasmussen study concluded that in any given year the odds against a single death from a nuclear plant accident are five billion to one. Obviously, therefore, nuclear power plants are at least as safe as anything on earth can be.

This argument rests on an assumption about authority: any prolonged, expensive study supervised by a recognized expert in the field being studied must be reliable. Since the Rasmussen study fits these requirements, the conclusion ("its results must be reliable") is validly drawn. But the conclusion is credible only if the assumption is credible. Can anyone—no matter how authoritative—reliably calculate the odds against a nuclear plant fatality? And even apart from accidents, what about the dangers caused by radioactive wastes?

To make such an argument persuasive, you would have to reformulate the assumption on which it is based. Try this one: any enterprise that has functioned for more than thirty years without causing a single death or injury is fundamentally safe. If that assumption is credible—and it is certainly more credible than the assumption about authority—it could help to build a persuasive argument for the safety of nuclear power plants in the United States. (Such an argument would not have to explain the fatalities caused by the Chernobyl explosion, which occurred outside the United States—and after the Rasmussen study was made.)

INDUCTION AND PROBABLE CONCLUSIONS

While deductive arguments draw *necessary* conclusions (as explained in "Deduction and Validity," above), inductive arguments draw *probable* conclusions, which are commonly generalizations based on specific examples. Thus, to support the claim that nuclear power plants are unsafe, the author of the argument on pp. 184–85 cites six major accidents that have occurred at such plants since 1957. These examples do not prove that all nuclear power plants are unsafe, but they could help to make this general claim seem probable.

MAKING INDUCTIVE ARGUMENTS

The chief advantage of an inductive argument lies in the cumulative impact of successive examples. Because of this impact, an inductive argument can sometimes feel strongly persuasive, and the argument against nuclear power plants (above, pp. 184–85) may feel that way to you. But would the argument bring any new supporters to the no-nuke side, or merely bolster the morale of the old ones? To answer questions like these, you must not only weigh the impact of the examples but also consider the unstated assumption linking them to the claim that nuclear power plants are fundamentally unsafe.

Consider first the number of examples cited. Given all the nuclear power plants throughout the world, does a record of six accidents in thirty years justify this claim? Behind the imposing facade of examples lurks an unstated and shaky assumption: if six nuclear power plants have suffered major accidents, all such plants are unsafe. Is this any better than assuming that six defective washing machines prove all washing machines to be defective?

Whether or not the writer states the assumption that stands behind an argument, he or she should know what the assumption is and how well it binds the evidence to the general claim. Is a fatal disaster at Chernobyl relevant to a general claim about the safety of nuclear power plants? Prior to the Chernobyl disaster, no one had been killed or injured in any of the accidents cited, and the Chernobyl accident was caused (as we have already noted) by a reactor fundamentally different from those in the United States. Given that difference, and given also the absence of any nuclear fatalities in the West, the unstated assumption does not adequately bind the evidence to the general claim.

To make an inductive argument persuasive, state your claim with caution, and be sure that your evidence can be linked to the claim by a credible assumption. The inductive argument about nuclear power plants, for instance, would be more persuasive like this:

CLAIM: It is probably impossible to guarantee the safety of nuclear power plants.

EVIDENCE: Six nuclear power plants have suffered major accidents in the past thirty years.

ASSUMPTION: If major accidents have repeatedly occurred at nuclear power plants, it is probably impossible to guarantee that no more accidents will occur.

COMBINING INDUCTION AND DEDUCTION

By itself, a deductive argument will seldom persuade your reader. Here, for instance, is a purely deductive version of an argument that Martin Luther King Jr. made for the rights of African Americans in 1963:

MAJOR PREMISE (ASSUMPTION): A people repeatedly abused and humiliated should not be required to wait any longer for their rights.

MINOR PREMISE (FACT): African Americans are repeatedly abused and humiliated.

CONCLUSION: African Americans should not be required to wait any longer for their rights.

What King actually wrote implies the above assumption and uses induction—generalization drawn from a set of examples—to prove the minor premise (fact) stated above. The combination of induction and deduction makes a highly persuasive argument:

Perhaps it is easy for those who have never felt the stinging darts of segregation to say, "Wait." But when you have seen vicious mobs lynch your mothers and fathers at will and drown your sisters and brothers at whim; when you have seen hate-filled policemen curse, kick, and even kill your black brothers and sisters; when you see the vast majority of your twenty million Negro brothers smothering in an airtight cage of poverty in the midst of an affluent society; when you suddenly find your tongue twisted and your speech stammering as you seek to explain to your six-year-old daughter why she can't go to the public amusement park that has just been advertised on television, and see tears welling up in her eyes when she is told that Funtown is closed to colored children, and see ominous clouds of inferiority beginning to form in her little mental sky, and see her beginning to distort her personality by developing an unconscious bitterness toward white people; when you have to concoct an answer for a five-year-old son who is asking, "Daddy, why do white people treat colored people so mean?"; when you take a cross-country drive and find it necessary to sleep night after night in the uncomfortable corners of your automobile because no motel will accept you; when you are humiliated day in and day out by nagging signs reading "white" and "colored"; when your first name becomes "nigger," your middle name becomes "boy" (however old you are) and your last name becomes "John," and your wife and mother are never given the respected title "Mrs."; when you are harried by day and haunted by night by the fact that you are a Negro, living constantly at tiptoe stance, never quite knowing what to expect next, and are plagued with inner fears and outer resentments; when you are forever fighting a degenerating sense of "nobodiness"—then you will understand why we find it difficult to wait. There comes a time when the cup of endurance runs over, and men are no longer willing to be plunged into the

abyss of despair. I hope, sirs, you can understand our legitimate and un-
avoidable impatience.

—"Letter from Birmingham Jail"

King's examples help to persuade us not only because of their number but
also because of their appeal to our feelings, as in the pictures of the weep-
ing child and of black men "smothering in an airtight cage of poverty."
(For more on appealing to the feelings, see 11.7.)

EXERCISE 1   **Spotting Assumptions**

Identify the assumptions made by each of the following arguments. Judge
how credible the assumptions are.

1. The Microsoft anti-trust trial reminds us that the U.S. attorney
general's office—in principle and, on occasion, in practice—does not
look kindly on unchecked monopolies. But just outside Washington,
in another federal office, it seems our government has been handing
out commercial monopolies on everything from specific medical
treatments to concepts as broad as the "idea of Internet commerce."
   The culprit is our patent system. Once restricted to protecting the
rights of inventors to the designs of particular, novel innovations, the
Patent Office today has stretched the definitions of "innovation" and
"novel" to the point where they are pushing more than one ethical
envelope, according to Seth Shulman in *The Sciences* (Jan./Feb. 1999).
   Shulman makes the case that the government's system of intellectual property rights has become simply absurd—granting creator
and owner status over unique life forms (whether genetically engineered or, in some cases, simply newly identified), as well as particular colors, fragrances, even sounds. Shulman also argues—with more
profound concern—that the system is allowing a dangerous concentration of control over the technological and medical know-how that
"make up the lifeblood of the new economy." . . . The only solution is
for the government—either Congress or the courts—to establish
guidelines, he argues. "Unless society tackles the issue head-on, the
privatization of knowledge assets will choke productivity, magnify in-
equities, and erode our democratic institutions." In the very murky
waters of intellectual property rights, that is about all that seems clear.
                              —"Patently Absurd: Will Ideas Become the Next Hot
                                       Commodity?" *Utne Reader*, May–June 1999

2. At this year's annual meeting of the prestigious American Association for the Advancement of Science in Anaheim, California, in a symposium titled "The Precautionary Principle: A Revolution in Environmental Policymaking?", environmentalist advocates and academics insisted that a principle of ultimate precaution should trump all other considerations in future environmental and technological policy making. . . . The Principle was formalized last year by environmentalist advocates who convened at the Wingspread Conference Center in Wisconsin. . . .

What did the Wingspread activists finally recommend? The actual text of the Principle . . . reads: "When an activity raises threats of harm to human health or environment, precautionary measures should be taken even if some cause-and-effect relationships are not fully established scientifically."

The Wingspreaders and their followers on the AAAS (American Association for the Advancement of Science) panel want to apply the Principle solely to environmentalist concerns, but, in fact, their formula is essentially an empty vessel into which anyone can pour whatever values they prefer. It simply codifies a very risk-averse version of standard cost-benefit analysis; the Wingspread participants think that certain activities, such as manufacturing plastics or burning fossil fuels, are unacceptably risky. In other words, very conservative environmentalist values are being privileged over what, to other people, may be equally or more compelling values.

—Ronald Bailey, "Precautionary Tale," *Reason*, April 1999

Using Deduction

EXERCISE 2

This exercise has three steps: (1) formulate an assumption that could be used in a deductive argument that supports or attacks one of the following propositions; (2) write a syllogism containing the assumption; (3) write a short deductive argument based on the syllogism.

1. The government should control the kind of material posted on the Internet.

2. All U.S. citizens should be guaranteed healthcare by the government.

3. The private lives of elected officials should not be reported on by the media.

4. Personal morality is essential for effective public leadership.

Using Induction

This exercise has four steps: (1) make a general claim about any one of the topics listed below; (2) make a list of facts that could be used to establish the probability of the claim; (3) explain what assumption links the facts to the claim; (4) use this material to write a brief inductive argument.

violence in video games	minimum wage
product liability	Internet censorship
sweatshops	international trade agreements
school voucher programs	women's professional sports
public funding for the arts	advertising in public elementary and high schools

Combining Induction and Deduction

Use induction to strengthen the deductive argument you made in exercise 2.

11.5 AVOIDING FALLACIES

Fallacies are mistakes in reasoning. Here are the most common of them.

ARGUING BY ASSOCIATION

According to Senator Blank, all parents of school-age children should be given vouchers that may be used at any school of their choice. Leading conservatives also support the voucher system. Obviously, therefore, Senator Blank is a conservative.

The fact that Senator Blank shares *one* opinion with leading conservatives does not mean that she shares any other opinions with them. She may disagree with conservatives on every other issue.

SHIFTING THE MEANING OF A KEY TERM

Criminals do everything possible to avoid and obstruct arrest, prosecution, and conviction. Likewise, liberal lawyers try in every possible way to obstruct the work of police. They are the ones responsible for things like the Miranda rule, which says that the police can't even interrogate anyone they've arrested until they tell the person what his or her rights are, and if they forget to do so, the case can be thrown out of court. Obviously, then, liberal lawyers are no better than criminals themselves.

This argument uses the word *obstruct* in two different senses. Criminals obstruct the police by hiding out, resisting arrest, or refusing to answer questions. Lawyers obstruct the police only insofar as they demand respect for the constitutional rights of the suspect, who—under the U.S. system of justice—must be presumed innocent until proven guilty. Since the writer uses the word *obstruct* to identify what lawyers and criminals have in common, the shift in the meaning of this key term invalidates the argument.

BEGGING THE QUESTION (CIRCULAR ARGUMENT)

Anyone who cannot afford to pay for basic medical care should be treated at government expense, because it's the government's responsibility to see that poor people get the medical help they need.

The second part of this sentence (starting with *because*) is offered as a reason for us to accept the first, but this would-be "reason" is just another way of saying what the writer is trying to prove—which is stated in the first part of the sentence. Rather than proving this point by means of other points, the writer circles back to it in different words. Thus the writer begs us—not persuades us—to accept it.

FALSE ALTERNATIVE

If guns are outlawed, only outlaws will have guns.

This slogan assumes that the disarming of all law-abiding citizens—including the police—is the only alternative to allowing everyone to own a gun. But of course there are many other alternatives.

FALSE ANALOGY

A college has no right to fire a popular teacher. To do so is like throwing out of office a public official who has just been reelected by a majority of voters. Colleges that fire popular teachers violate the basic principles of democracy.

But a college is not a democracy. While teachers and college administrators like to know what students think of teachers—just as public officials like to know what voters think of them—teaching is not an elective office.

We said earlier in this book that analogy may be used to explain. If you wanted to *explain* what teachers do, you might well compare them to public officials because both groups must be able to speak effectively to

195

various audiences. But you cannot use analogy to argue unless the two things compared are essentially similar. (For more on this point, see 6.5.)

PERSONAL ATTACK

> In *The American Way of Death*, Jessica Mitford dissects the American funeral industry. She criticizes the rituals of embalming, the elaborateness of wakes, the cost of burials, and the ways in which funeral directors manipulate the bereaved. But anyone who reads this book should first of all know that both Jessica Mitford and her husband were members of the Communist party. Her book, therefore, is essentially a left-wing assault on private enterprise and the American way of life.

This line of would-be reasoning tries to divert our attention from the substance of an argument to the character of the person making it. (Technically, this is arguing *ad hominem*—"to the person.") But there is no necessary connection between the two.

FALSE CAUSE

> To protect the habitat of the northern spotted owl, a federal judge last month ordered a stop to all logging in old-growth national forests. Now, just one month later, the price of wholesale lumber is up 30 percent. Is saving the owl worth that much?

This kind of argument equates sequence with causality: because event A (the judge's order) was followed by event B (the price increase), the first caused the second. (Technically, this fallacy is called *post hoc, ergo propter hoc*—"after this, therefore because of it.") But sequence and causality are two different things. By itself, the fact that one event follows another proves nothing at all about a causal link between them.

IRRELEVANT CONCLUSION

> As everyone knows, the U.S. Constitution gives all American citizens the right to bear arms. Furthermore, there is far too much crime in the streets and subways of our major cities. So anyone faced with a mugger should have the right to kill the mugger on the spot.

After stating a fact and then a common opinion, this writer lurches to an irrelevant conclusion. Neither the right to bear arms nor crime in the streets gives anyone the right to shoot anyone else. To make a persuasive case for the right to retaliate against muggers, the writer should focus on life-threatening situations; this approach would allow him to introduce the highly relevant topic of self-defense.

HASTY GENERALIZATION

> Keating won by a landslide, so it is obvious that everyone in the state supports his plan to reduce the deficit in the state budget. Regardless of complaints about what his plan will do to housing for the elderly and other state-supported welfare programs, Keating's plan is clearly what the people want.

In politics, winning by a "landslide" means winning by a decisive majority of the votes cast. Yet this writer tries to identify Keating's supporters with "everyone"—not just with all of the voters, but with all of "the people" in the state, whether or not they voted at all (and whether or not they may be hurt by this plan). This argument would be more persuasive with a restricted claim based on specific evidence, such as the claim that Keating's plan is supported by 58 percent of voters polled about his deficit-reduction plan.

Spotting, Explaining, and Eliminating Fallacies

EXERCISE 5

Identify and explain the fallacy in each of the following statements. Then, if you can, eliminate the fallacy by revising the statement. If you can't salvage the argument, say so.

EXAMPLE: Since 1968, when a federal gun control act made it illegal to order a handgun by mail, the crime rate has risen substantially. So any attempt to regulate guns simply aggravates crime.

FALLACY: False cause.

EXPLANATION: This statement does not prove that the gun control act *caused* the increase in the crime rate, even though the increase followed the act. What the first sentence does show is that gun control laws are sometimes ineffectual. So a more workable version of the statement would look as follows:

REVISION: Since 1968, when a federal gun control act made it illegal to order a handgun by mail, the crime rate has risen substantially. Gun control laws, therefore, do not necessarily reduce crime.

1. The U.S. Supreme Court ruled recently that no state could penalize anyone for expressing opinions offensive to members of a particular religion or race. This decision has been applauded by racist organizations such as the American Nazi Party and the Ku Klux Klan. Obviously, therefore, the Supreme Court is racist.

2. "If divorce becomes legal in Ireland, it will spread through the country like the radiation that started at Chernobyl and then covered all of Europe."   —Archbishop of Dublin

3. On December 7, 1941, shortly after the United States government received Japanese envoys who had come to discuss peace, the Japanese bombed the U.S. naval base in Pearl Harbor. That event plainly shows that a willingness to discuss peace simply encourages the enemy to attack.

4. The only way to make the tax law truly fair is to cancel all deductions and exemptions. Everyone knows that the government squanders billions of our tax dollars on expensive and unnecessary trips for legislators and their spouses, on lavish official parties, and on military equipment for which the Pentagon is grossly overcharged. Something must be done to stop the waste in government spending.

5. Since we know that cigarette smoking has caused cancer in some cases, it is clearly dangerous to the health of the nation and should be banned altogether.

IN BRIEF   **Fallacies**

▶ Arguing by association (if A and B each have the attribute C, A is B)

▶ Shifting the meaning of a key term

▶ Begging the question (taking for granted what is to be proved)

▶ False alternative (the *only* alternative to A is B)

▶ False analogy (A is like B in some ways, so A is like B in every way)

▶ Personal attack (the argument is bad because the arguer is bad)

▶ False cause (B followed A; therefore, A caused B)

▶ Irrelevant conclusion

▶ Hasty generalization

11.6 TREATING THE OPPOSITION WITH RESPECT

Persuasive writing never appears in a vacuum. It springs not only from the desire to defend a particular belief but also from the recognition that others hold a contrary belief, that conflicting claims compete for public support—like rival products in the marketplace or rival candidates in a political campaign. If there is no room for disagreement, there is no need for persuasion.

How do you deal with the opposition in a persuasive essay? To ignore it entirely is to risk antagonizing the reader or provoking objections that may undermine your argument. To argue effectively, you must first reckon with the opposition, and thereby anticipate objections. You can do one of two things: *make concessions* or *fairly explain the position you plan to oppose.*

MAKING CONCESSIONS

A concession is a point granted to the other side: an expression of concern for the feelings of those who may disagree with you, of respect for the reasons that prompt them to do so, or of positive agreement with them on one or more aspects of the topic in dispute. Starting with concession is a good way to overcome the reader's resistance to an unpopular argument and gain a hearing for even the most controversial point of view. Compare these two ways of arguing that everyone applying to college should be interviewed by an admissions officer:

> NO CONCESSIONS:
> No one should be admitted to college without a personal interview. What can admissions people tell from a piece of paper? They can't really tell anything. Only when they see a student face to face can they decide what kind of a person he or she is.

> WITH CONCESSIONS:
> Admissions officers can tell some things from a piece of paper. They can tell how well a person writes and what he or she is interested in, factors that go a long way toward determining if a student is capable of using the college resources to the fullest extent. However, there are things that an application cannot bring forth, things that can be seen only in a personal meeting. The way a person talks, answers questions on the spot, and reacts to certain pieces of information are all important signs of personality that cannot be found on a written piece of paper.

In the second paragraph, the transitional word *However* marks the shift from concession to contrasting assertion. (For another good example of the concessive opening, see p. 75, item 6; on transitional words in the paragraph, see 7.4.)

DEFINING THE POSITION YOU WILL OPPOSE

To begin with a concession is to express sympathetic concern for those you plan to disagree with or even partial agreement with them. But if you see no reason for sympathetic concern or partial agreement, you can nonetheless begin your essay by fairly defining the position you aim to oppose, by letting the reader know that you understand and respect the views of your adversaries. Here is the opening paragraph of an essay written to defend the high salaries of corporate executives:

> Ralph Nader stands at the end of a long line of critics who assail the high incomes of top corporate executives. Nader and his associates suggest that "in the absence of judicial limitations, excessive remuneration has become the norm." They observe that the average top executive in each of the fifty largest industrial corporations earns more salary in a year than many of the corporate employees earn in a lifetime. Salaries are only part (albeit the major part) of the compensation the top executives receive. Bonuses, lavish retirements, stock options, and stock ownership combine to swell the incomes of corporate chief executives by another 50 to 75 percent of the executives' direct remunerations. Nader and his associates conclude that the top corporate executives receive "staggeringly large salaries and stock options."
>
> —Robert Thomas, "Is Corporate Executive Compensation Excessive?"

By respectfully defining his adversary's position, Thomas earns the right to a respectful hearing for his own.

You will seldom persuade anyone by simply expressing contempt for the position you oppose:

> Logic, common sense and public opinion are on the side of gun control, but America's firearms fanatics are insufferably relentless. Now, for pete's sake, they want their own political party.
>
> With their own blind, the gun lovers can offer us candidates promising not a chicken in every pot, but a pistol in every pocket. And carnage in every home. Someone else to vote against.
>
> —Richard J. Roth, "Despite Evidence and Reason, Pro-Gun Talk
> Won't Go Away"

To describe the opponents of gun control as "firearms fanatics" who promise "a pistol in every pocket" and "carnage in every home" is to antagonize any reader who is not already on the writer's side. This is not persuasive writing; it is a slapdash mix of invective and gross exaggeration. It will rouse the antigun faithful, but it is unlikely to make any converts.

EXERCISE 6   **Making Concessions**

Rewrite each of the following arguments in one of two ways: (1) support the writer's point of view but add one or more concessive sentences at the beginning, or (2) argue against the writer's point of view by first making a concession to it and then defending the other side. Whichever you choose to do, be sure to use a transitional word between your concession and the main point you are making.

1. Regional expressions are a hindrance to communication. Each part of the country has adopted many that cannot be found anywhere else. For instance, New England is the only part of the U.S. where you can order a "frappe" in a drugstore or ice cream parlor. Try ordering a frappe in Nebraska and see what kind of reaction you will get. The purpose of language is to make communication possible. By separating regions of the country from each other, nonstandardized forms of expression defeat this purpose.

—college student

2. American restaurants should abolish tipping and do what European restaurants do: add a service charge of 10 to 15 percent to every bill. The service charge would eliminate the worrying and wondering that goes into tipping: the customer worrying about how much to leave, and the waiter or waitress wondering how much is going to be left. Since the tip is always left at the end of the meal, not before, it can't really affect the quality of service provided, and shouldn't be left to chance.

Defining a Position You Oppose

EXERCISE 7

Choose from any printed source or the Internet an essay that defends a position you oppose. Then, using Thomas's introduction (p. 200) as a guide, write a paragraph defining this position.

11.7 APPEALING TO THE EMOTIONS

A working knowledge of argumentative technique is indispensable for the writer who wants to persuade. But readers are seldom persuaded by rational arguments alone. For this reason the writer should try to understand the reader's feelings and appeal to them. Though excessive or exclusive appeal to the reader's feelings weakens an argument, the combination of emotional appeal and rational support can be powerfully persuasive.

Consider the final paragraphs of Stephen Jay Gould's *Mismeasure of Man*. In the book as a whole, Gould demonstrates that biological determination has no basis in fact, that no characteristics of anyone's parents can determine what he or she will become, and therefore that laws requiring the sterilization of children born to allegedly feebleminded parents are scientifically unjustified. After making this argument by strictly rational means, Gould ends his book by citing the case of Doris Buck, whose fifty-two-year-old mother had been judged to have a mental age of seven, and who was sterilized under a Virginia law in 1928. Gould writes:

> She later married Matthew Figgins, a plumber. But Doris Buck was never informed. "They told me," she recalled, "that the operation was for an appendix and rupture." So she and Matthew Figgins tried to conceive a child. They consulted physicians at three hospitals throughout her child-bearing years; no one recognized that her Fallopian tubes had been severed. Last year [1979], Doris Buck Figgins discovered the cause of her lifelong sadness.
>
> One might invoke an unfeeling calculus and say that Doris Buck's disappointment ranks as nothing compared with millions of dead in wars to support the designs of madmen or the conceits of rulers. But can one measure the pain of a single dream unfulfilled, the hope of a defenseless woman snatched by public power in the name of an ideology advanced to purify a race? May Doris Buck's simple and eloquent testimony stand for millions of deaths and disappointments and help us to remember that the Sabbath was made for man, not man for the Sabbath: "I broke down and cried. My husband and me wanted children desperately. We were crazy about them. I never knew what they'd done to me."

Given at the very end of a strictly rational, analytic, and mathematically supported argument, the story and the words of Doris Buck powerfully appeal to our emotions. They move us to see that biological determinism is not just scientifically unjustified but unconscionably cruel.

EXERCISE 8   **Using Emotional Appeal**

From your own experience or the experience of someone you know, tell a story or describe a situation that could lend emotional appeal to an argument made for or against any one of the following:

1. living on campus

2. drug testing

3. cosmetic surgery

4. controlling content on the Internet

5. performance-enhancing drugs

11.8 USING RHETORICAL QUESTIONS

A **rhetorical question** is asked not to get information but to stir the reader. Typically, a rhetorical question prompts the reader to answer yes or no and thus draws the reader to side with the writer:

> Can any goal truly justify the torturing of animals?

> Should a woman's self-esteem depend wholly on the size and shape of her body?

> With air pollution rising every year, especially in large cities, isn't it high time we started driving electric cars?

> But can one measure the pain of a single dream unfulfilled, the hope of a defenseless woman snatched by public power in the name of an ideology advanced to purify a race?

> —Stephen Jay Gould

As these examples show, rhetorical questions may appeal to the mind, the feelings, or both. Their chief advantage lies in their provocative impact; they challenge the reader to think or feel in a particular way. But rhetorical questions are not a foolproof means of persuasion, because the writer cannot guarantee how the reader will answer them. The question about animals, for instance, is clearly meant to be answered "No," but some readers might answer it "Yes, the goal of combating disease in humans." To use a rhetorical question effectively, therefore, you should consider the possibility of more than one answer and be willing to explain—in statements—why your answer is the right one.

Using Rhetorical Questions

EXERCISE 9

Formulate a rhetorical question on a topic of your choice.

11.9 CONSTRUCTING AN ARGUMENTATIVE ESSAY

To see how various methods of argumentation can work together, consider this essay:

SAVING THE CULTURAL ENVIRONMENT

Introduction leads up to statement of thesis (claim) in last sentence.

[1] The Earth Summit in Rio de Janeiro that begins this week is a response to the piercing of the ozone layer, the despoiling of rain forests, the polluting of oceans and rivers, the endangering of species from the whales to the spotted owl. But a complete environmentalist should be concerned with more than damage to our natural habitat. Just as vulnerable as nature to a noxious environment are the artifacts of civilization.

Concession: danger to Earth itself seems more important than danger to monuments.

[2] A few years ago the plight of Venice attracted attention, because of the prospect of an enchanting city's being swallowed up by the waters over which it was so ingeniously constructed. But except for Venice, the apocalyptic scenarios that make the headlines tend to deal less with the risk to cultural monuments than with primal threats to the very existence of the Earth.

Emotional appeal: cherished masterworks being vandalized.

[3] As the 100 or so world leaders gathered in Rio work out their so-called Agenda 21, the issues of sheer survival must take priority. What is the eroding nose of the Sphinx compared to the greenhouse effect? Yet the havoc wreaked on cherished and irreplaceable masterworks by the vandalism of a polluted environment should not be ignored. The great expressions of culture are themselves integral parts of humankind's moral and spiritual environment.

Evidence (three examples), rhetorical questions, and authoritative estimate cited.

[4] June, the month of the Earth Summit, is also the month when tourists by the millions begin their pilgrimages to cultural shrines, from medieval cathedrals to Stonehenge, from the Acropolis to the Pyramids. But how many of those who visit Chartres know that Europe's medieval stained-glass windows are turning opaque and slowly disintegrating because they are susceptible to the gases from automobile exhausts and coal-burning factories? Of the 6,000 tourists a day who gaze in awe at the Parthenon, how many are aware of the vandalism committed upon it by the smog rising from Athens, known by the Greeks as "the Cloud"? In Cairo, where the Sphinx crumbles, scholars estimate that up to 90 percent of the historic structures in the city should be classified as in desperate need of restoration—some undermined by sewage leaks, some shaken by the vibration from new construction.

Claim restated as conclusion, with final emotional appeal in "precious treasures."

[5] Nature knows nothing of national boundaries. A poisoned environment affects all living things on the planet. This is the theme at Rio. Art—built upon the power of symbolism—can and should reinforce the theme, illustrating by every deteriorating work of expression that the toxic byproducts of civilization assault not only nature, but also the precious treasures of civilization itself.

—editorial, *Christian Science Monitor,* June 2, 1992

This essay states its claim in the first paragraph and restates it as a conclusion in the final paragraph: our toxic wastes damage masterworks of civilization as much as they damage nature.

Recognizing the opposition that this claim might provoke, the essay makes a concession: combating environmental damage to the Earth itself "must take priority" over combating damage to cultural monuments. But the plight of the monuments is stressed by emotional appeal on behalf of these "irreplaceable masterworks" that are parts of our "moral and spiritual environment."

After making this emotional appeal, the essay presents its evidence: environmental pollution is now seriously damaging three major cultural monuments in different parts of the world. These examples are presented with the aid of two rhetorical questions and one authoritative estimate.

So the basic argumentative strategy here is induction, with an implied deduction standing behind it:

IMPLIED ASSUMPTION: If pollution is damaging major monuments in different parts of the world, then it threatens not only nature but also the masterworks of civilization, which are essential to our moral and spiritual environment.

EVIDENCE: Pollution is damaging the medieval stained-glass windows of Europe, the Parthenon in Athens, and the Sphinx in Cairo.

CONCLUSION: Pollution threatens not only nature but also the masterworks of civilization, which are essential to our moral and spiritual environment.

Since the implied assumption is credible, and since the evidence is both reliable and relevant to the conclusion, the argument is plausible. Together with the emotional appeal made in the third paragraph, the final appeal to our feelings helps to make this essay persuasive.

Composing an Argumentative Essay

EXERCISE 10

Using at least ten of the following items plus any others that you can gather from printed sources, compose an argumentative essay that defends or attacks the need for more gun-control laws. The argument should be chiefly based on evidence and assumptions, but you may reinforce it with one or more emotional appeals, and you should reckon with the opposition before introducing your claim.

When you have written the essay, identify as well as you can the assumptions it makes—both explicit and implicit.

1. Lincoln, McKinley, and John F. Kennedy were all killed by guns. No American president has ever been stabbed or clubbed to death.

2. Article II of the United States Bill of Rights says, "A well-regulated militia being necessary to the security of a free state, the right of the people to keep and bear arms shall not be infringed."

3. There are now almost two hundred million guns in the United States, and fifty million of those are handguns.

4. On April 20, 1999, two teenage boys stormed Columbine High School in Littleton, Colorado, and in a five-hour rampage used guns and bombs to kill thirteen people and wound twenty-three others before killing themselves. The weapons found at the school after the killings included two sawed-off twelve-gauge shotguns, one nine-millimeter semiautomatic rifle, and one semiautomatic pistol, none of which the boys could legally own.

5. Rifle and shotgun barrels can be sawed off with a fifty-nine-cent hacksaw blade, and the resulting weapons are more lethal than most handguns.

6. John F. Kennedy, assassinated by rifle shots in 1963, was a member of the National Rifle Association who strongly believed in the citizens' right to bear arms.

7. Theodore Roosevelt, who was wounded by a pistol shot in the chest while making a speech, recovered from the wound and afterward joined the National Rifle Association, which he staunchly supported.

8. Guns are used in 250,000 crimes each year, and 20,000 of those are homicides.

9. On April 6, 1999, in the first referendum on concealed weapons ever held in the U.S., Missouri voters decisively rejected a proposal that would have lifted a century-old ban on the carrying of such weapons.

10. Hunters kill an estimated two hundred million birds and fifty million other animals each year.

11. On September 15, 1999, a forty-seven-year-old gunman named Larry Ashbrook used two legally obtained semiautomatic handguns to kill seven people and wound seven more at the Wedgewood Baptist Church in Fort Worth, Texas. With a shot in the head he then killed himself.

12. According to a report released by the FBI on October 17, 1999, serious crimes reported to the police in 1998 fell for the seventh year in a row, and in 1998 there were nearly sixteen hundred fewer homicides committed with firearms than in 1997.

13. On June 18, 1999, Congress defeated a bill that would have required all vendors at gun shows to perform a background check on anyone seeking to purchase a gun.

14. The National Rifle Association claims that legislation designed to restrict criminals' access to firearms will also curtail the rights of law-abiding citizens.

15. Together with the federal gun control acts of 1968, 1993, and 1994, many state laws already regulate ownership of handguns. In the states of New York and Massachusetts, for instance, persons convicted of carrying unlicensed handguns—regardless of what they are carried for—must go to jail for a year.

16. On November 30, 1993, President Clinton signed the Brady Handgun Violence Prevention Act, which requires a five-day waiting period for anyone seeking to buy a gun. Though the Supreme Court ruled in 1997 that local police may not be forced to check the backgrounds of gun buyers during that time, as the act originally required, most police departments have voluntarily continued to do so.

17. While Maryland, South Carolina, Virginia, and California all restrict the number of guns that any one person may buy in a month, no such limit applies anywhere else in the U.S.

18. In 1998, a team of doctors compared crime in Seattle with crime in Vancouver from 1980 through 1986, a period in which handguns were far less regulated in the American city than in the Canadian one. While the rates of homicide by means other than guns proved substantially the same in both cities for the period studied, the risk of being killed by a handgun was almost five times higher in Seattle.

19. According to the U.S. Bureau of Alcohol, Tobacco, and Firearms, more than five thousand of the guns used in crimes committed in the state of Indiana alone in 1998 were bought from licensed gun dealers.

20. In June 1999, the state of Illinois enacted a law (1) requiring that any gun accessible to children under the age of fourteen have a safety lock or be stored in a childproof location, and (2) making gun owners responsible if children under fourteen used their weapons in a crime. According to the Illinois Council against Handguns, sixteen other states have similar laws.

21. High-powered semiautomatic rifles can fire thirty rounds in a clip. About fifty thousand of these weapons in the United States are privately owned.

22. On February 11, 1999, a New York City jury found gun manufacturers liable for seven shootings performed with guns that had been illegally sold in New York State, which has strict gun control laws.

23. During the six months from November 1998 to June 1999, some seventeen hundred people banned by law from buying guns managed to buy them anyway from federally licensed dealers—in spite of background checks made by the FBI and local police.

24. On April 1, 1999, a U.S. District Court judge in Lubbock, Texas, found unconstitutional a federal law forbidding anyone under a restraining order to own a gun. The judge said the law infringed on Second Amendment rights.

25. According to a study published in the October 7, 1993, issue of the *New England Journal of Medicine,* homicides are more likely to occur in households that have guns than in households that don't. Rather than protecting families from intruders, guns increase the chances that one family member or acquaintance will kill another.

26. In a recent study of incarcerated felons made by the National Institute of Justice, 38 percent said they had decided not to commit a particular crime because they were afraid the potential victim might be armed.

Document Design

For a simple illustration of the importance of good document design, think of an addressed envelope. If most envelopes have two different addresses, how does a postal worker determine where to deliver each letter? How, for that matter, do we know where to put the correct mailing and return addresses?

When we address an envelope, we show that we already know something about document design. Specifically, we know that *where* we place information on a writing surface (whether it be a page, a computer screen, a blackboard, etc.) often can be as important as *what* we place there. Moreover, we sometimes show that the very surface on which the words appear can be important. Think of wedding invitations. Few people would send out invitations using plain white typing paper and envelopes they bought at the drugstore. Instead, they use paper of a heavier weight, often in colors such as ivory or pink or gray. The writing surface itself conveys a sense of the formality of the occasion.

When most of us think about the act of writing, we probably think about such things as word choice, paragraph development, and thesis statements. We have been encouraged to think about the meaning of words rather than their appearance on a page or screen. As our addressed envelope and invitation illustrate, however, we often should think about more than *what* we are writing.

Jane Doe
123 This Street
Hertown ST

John Doe
456 That Street
Histown ST

An addressed envelope illustrates the importance of document design.

Document design serves two purposes: informative and heuristic. Good design not only informs us; it also helps us solve problems and make discoveries (the Greek word *hueriskein* means "to discover"). This chapter briefly shows you how to maximize the communicative impact of your document by effectively using the basic elements of design: *layout, typographics,* and *color.*

A WORD ABOUT WEB PAGE DESIGN   A number of Web designers, including Roger Black, Patrick J. Lynch, and Sarah Horton, have noted that the basics of document design apply equally to print and electronic texts. In many cases, therefore, the information and suggestions offered in this chapter apply to Web pages as well as printed documents. Distinctions will be made when appropriate.

12.1   ELEMENTS OF DESIGN: A WRITER'S BASIC MATERIALS

You have a number of elements to work with when you design a text—regardless of whether your design will appear on paper, a computer screen, or some other surface. Those materials include

- ▶ the writing surface
- ▶ the marks and images that appear on that surface
- ▶ the colors defining those marks and images

LAYOUT

Design begins with a space, or surface.[1] Whether you are an architect, a dancer, a painter, an engineer, or a writer, you must have a space in which (or surface on which) to create. The nature of that space depends, of course, on the type of design you are creating. When you are writing, your surface will most likely be a piece of paper or a computer screen. Whatever the surface, you must decide how to *arrange* your words on it, how to lay out your text. In doing so, you must consider *margins, justification, columns,* and *orientation.*

---

[1] Jay David Bolter uses the term *writing space* in his book *Writing Space: The Computer, Hypertext, and the History of Writing* (Hillsdale, NJ: Erlbaum, 1991).

MARGINS Establish your margins, the spaces between the edges of the paper and the text. On paper, margins should be about one inch unless your instructor asks for more. On a computer screen, where text can sometimes be difficult to read, consider ample margins, especially if the screen is mainly filled with words, as shown below.

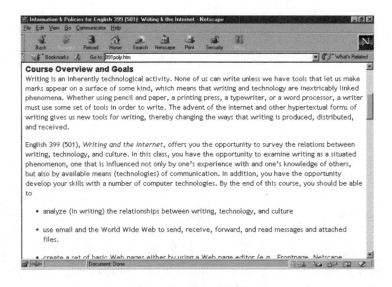

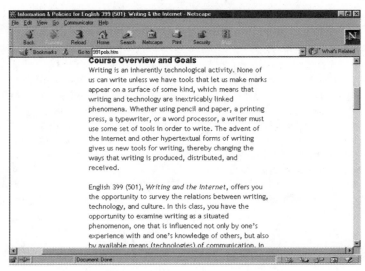

Which Web page looks more readable?

JUSTIFICATION

Justification is the arrangement of text so that it forms a straight line along the left or right side. Normally the left side of a text is justified and the right is ragged, as shown below in the upper left box. Alternatives are shown in the other three boxes.

Full justification (with both sides justified) looks tidy, but word processors put varying amounts of space between words to keep the margin straight. That variable spacing can leave awkward gaps in your text.

Centering text on the page works well for titles or highlighted elements, but centering a whole text makes it hard for the reader to find each new line. The same is true for text that is right justified.

Justification is the arrangement of text so that it forms a straight line along the left or right side. Normally the left side of a text is justified and the right is ragged, as shown below in the upper left box. Alternatives are shown in the other three boxes.

Full justification (with both sides justified) looks tidy, but word processors put varying amounts of space between words to keep the margin straight. That variable spacing can leave awkward gaps in your text.

Left Justification

Justification is the arrangement of text so that it forms a straight line along the left or right side. Normally the left side of a text is justified and the right is ragged, as shown below in the upper left box. Alternatives are shown in the other three boxes. Full justification (with both sides justified) looks tidy, but word processors put varying amounts of space between words to keep the margin straight. That variable spacing can leave awkward gaps in your text.

Right Justification

Justification is the arrangement of text so that it forms a straight line along the left or right side. Normally the left side of a text is justified and the right is ragged, as shown below in the upper left box. Alternatives are shown in the other three boxes. Full justification (with both sides justified) looks tidy, but word processors put varying amounts of space between words to keep the margin straight. That variable spacing can leave awkward gaps in your text.

Centered

Justification is the arrangement of text so that it forms a straight line along the left or right side. Normally the left side of a text is justified and the right is ragged, as shown below in the upper left box. Alternatives are shown in the other three boxes. Full justification (with both sides justified) looks tidy, but word processors put varying amounts of space between words to keep the margin straight. That variable spacing can leave awkward gaps in your text.

Full Justification

Four types of justification: Which looks better? Which is easiest to read?

COLUMNS Most teachers expect a single column of text with margins of about one inch on all sides. But if you are writing things such as Web pages, newsletters, or brochures, you might use two or more columns. (For more on this point, see 12.3.)

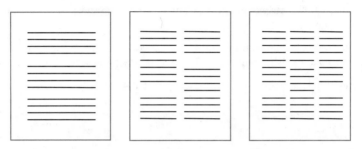

One-, two-, and three-column page layouts

ORIENTATION Normally lines of text run across the width of the page, as shown at left (*portrait orientation*). But they may also run across the length of the page, as shown at right (*landscape orientation*). Landscape orientation is commonly used for fliers, banners, and materials accompanying an oral presentation: materials created, for instance, with software such as PowerPoint or Freelance Graphics.

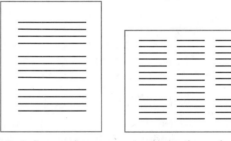

Portrait, one column   Landscape, three columns

Two types of page orientation
(with sample column formats)

TYPOGRAPHY

Typography includes letters, numbers, punctuation marks, and other related marks such as the ampersand (&) and the asterisk (*). A complete set of such marks is called a *font,* and each font has its own look. In this book, headings appear in the Arial font, while the rest of the text is Times New Roman.

Fonts generally come in one of these four categories:

▶ SERIF   A serif is a small stroke at each end of a letter, such as appear at the ends of this capital letter S. Serifs help readers distinguish individual letters and are therefore preferable for longer printed works.

213

▶ SANS SERIF   Since *sans* means "without" in French, sans serif fonts lack serifs. Though such fonts can be difficult to read in long texts, they are useful for headlines and headings.

▶ DECORATIVE AND SCRIPT FONTS   These convey a certain kind of mood. A decorative font such as Park Avenue conveys a sense of elegance and formality, while a script font such as Mistral conveys a sense of informality and intimacy.

▶ DINGBATS AND SYMBOLS   are images such as bullets (which we have used to distinguish each item in this list) and the paragraph symbol (¶).

The table below presents examples of the first three types of fonts.

Serif	Sans Serif	Decorative and Script
Times New Roman	Arial	Park Avenue
Bookman Old Style	Helvetica	Kaufmann
Garamond	Geneva	Mistral
Courier	Comic Sans MS	

Three fonts (all in 11-point size)

When choosing a font for your text, consider readability and appropriateness. For example, a serif font such as Times New Roman, Palatino, or Garamond probably would be more readable in a double-spaced, five-page paper than would a sans serif font such as Arial or Geneva. You can save yourself time by finding one font that works well for you when writing academic papers. If you want to experiment with different types of fonts, be sure to look carefully at copies of your work to determine readability.

Likewise, you should format your semester-long research paper on the lingering effects of the Vietnam War in a formal-looking font rather than an informal, playful one such as Alley Cat ICG. The playful look of that font would clash with the seriousness of the research topic.

Some fonts have been specifically designed for the World Wide Web. Among them is Trebuchet MS, a sans serif font well suited for reading on a computer screen.

Besides choosing a font, you can determine the size, slant, and boldness of its letters. You can increase the font size for a title, for instance, and you can use *italics* or **boldface** to emphasize certain words:

Motherhood is in trouble, and it ought to be. A rude question is long over-due: Who needs it? The answer used to be (1) society and (2) women. But now, with the impending horrors of overpopulation, society desperately *doesn't* need it.

—Betty Rollin, "Motherhood: Who Needs It?"

There are old pilots, and there are bold pilots, but there are not many **old, bold** pilots.

Use boldface and italics for emphasis sparingly. If overused they lose their punch. But italics and underlining should be regularly used for certain ti-tles, as explained in chapter 39, "Documenting the Research Paper."

When choosing a font for your text, consider readability and appropriateness. For example, a serif font such as Times New Roman, Palatino, or Garamond probably would be more readable in a double-spaced, five-page paper than would a sans serif font such as Arial or Geneva.	When choosing a font for your text, consider readability and appropriateness. For example, a serif font such as Times New Roman, Palatino, or Garamond probably would be more readable in a double-spaced, five-page paper than would a sans serif font such as Arial or Geneva.	When choosing a font for your text, consider readability and appropriateness. For example, a serif font such as Times New Roman, Palatino, or Garamond probably would be more readable in a double-spaced, five-page paper than would a sans serif font such as Arial or Geneva.
Times New Roman (11 pt)	**VAG Rounded Thin (10 pt)**	**Franklin Gothic Demi Extra Compressed (12 pt)**

Which passage is most readable? What makes one font easier to read than another?

215

GRAPHICS

PHOTOS

Photos can reveal details in a landscape or building better than words. They can be used to supplement, enhance, or even contrast with a text. And, of course, they can show us what an author or a biographical subject looks (or looked) like.

Vaulted interior of Modena Duomo, Italy

LINE DRAWINGS

Line drawings are useful when you want to reveal details that would otherwise be hidden in a photo. For example:

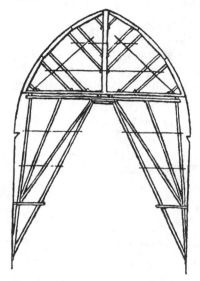

Diagrammatic scheme of framing and undergirding the half-frame
of gothic ribbed vault centering

CLIP ART

Clip art consists of ready-made images that you can use in your own work. These images can be found in many word processing and presentation programs and in numerous sites on the Internet. Be sure you have permission to use any clip art you select, and be sure to acknowledge its source in your paper. (Follow the style manual for your discipline. On MLA, see 39.1; on *CMS,* 42.5; on APA, 42.7; on CBE, 42.9.)

TABLES

Tables make certain types of information easy to read and search by presenting it in a series of rows and columns, as shown here.

Student Extracurricular Involvement Over the Past Five Years

Academic year	% currently involved	% formerly involved	% never involved
1998–1999	15	32	53
1997–1998	18	32	50
1996–1997	23	29	48
1995–1996	24	30	46
1994–1995	27	27	46

LINE GRAPHS These can show trends. The downward slope of the line in the first graph below, for instance, illustrates the decline in the percentage of students doing extracurricular activities. In the second graph, two lines show two different trends and thereby let us compare the two. (Avoid using more than two lines, which can make a graph cluttered and confusing.)

Notice also that the graph is clearly labeled with both a descriptive main title and labels for each axis. Since the point of this graph is to illustrate the decline of involvement, rather than to give exact percentages, the graph lacks grid lines, which could clutter the image.

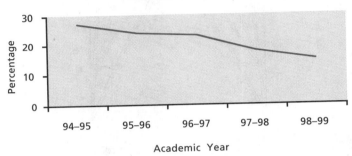

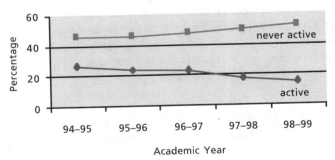

BAR GRAPHS AND COLUMN GRAPHS

Bar graphs and column graphs use horizontal or vertical blocks (respectively) to show trends and comparisons. For example, the column graph to the right (the blocks stand vertically, like columns) shows the same trend that the previous line graph shows. A bar graph (with horizontal blocks) could be used to compare inactive versus active membership.

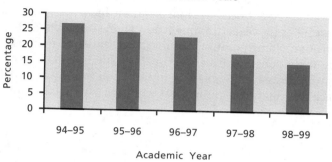

**Student Extracurricular Involvement
Over the Past Five Years**

PIE CHARTS

Pie charts let readers compare the parts of a whole. For example, a pie chart can let readers compare the percentages of currently active, formerly active, and uninvolved students.

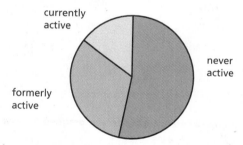

A Comparison of Student Activity and Inactivity in 98–99

A FEW FORMAT TIPS As with the writing of any text, you should consider your purpose and audience before creating or inserting a graphic. Ask yourself, "What point do I want to make with this graphic?" (Each graphic should make only one main point. If you have more than one point to make, create more than one graphic.) "What do my readers expect? What do they need to know?" To help convey your point, include a descriptive title and proper labels. This information should help your graphic stand on its own. That is, in many cases, a reader should be able to see a graphic and determine its main point without referring to the text.

COLOR

The advent of relatively inexpensive color printers has made it possible for more and more of us to use color. Although one can easily use too much, a little color—used judiciously—not only brightens the look of a text but also can help readers comprehend its organization. For example, a writer may choose to present headings in red and the main body in black. In this way, color helps the reader comprehend the organization of a text by seeing its major dividing points. Color may also be used to reinforce a mood. Wedding invitations, for instance, usually come in colors such as ivory, light gray, or dusty rose. Sometimes just one color on a white background with black text can speak strongly—as when red is used for headings.

> The Parents of
> Robert and
> Rachel
> invite you to
> celebrate an
> exchange
> of wedding
> vows.

> The Parents of
> Robert and
> Rachel
> invite you to
> celebrate an
> exchange
> of wedding
> vows.

Which invitation seems more appropriate for a wedding?

12.2 BASIC PRINCIPLES OF EFFECTIVE DESIGN

Effective design means arranging individual elements in a unified whole that readers can see—like the circle made from individual stars in Betsy Ross's design for the first U.S. flag. To design a document effectively, we suggest you do as follows:

▶ Remember your readers' habits.

▶ Signal differences visually.

▶ Group related elements visually.

▶ Make text and figures stand out from the background.

▶ Balance your elements.

Do you see one circle or thirteen separate stars?

REMEMBER YOUR READERS' HABITS

Readers normally read from left to right and from top to bottom, so they are likely to read the left column of a table first. But since readers also expect to see familiar information before learning something new, they may be a little confused to find unfamiliar information in the left column, as in the table *on* the left. As the table on the right shows, it's better for the weeks (the familiar information) to appear in the left column and the attendance numbers (the unfamiliar information) to appear in the right column.

Club Attendance for the Past Five Weeks			Club Attendance for the Past Five Weeks	
Attendance	Week		Week	Attendance
43	1		1	43
40	2		2	40
34	3		3	34
39	4		4	39
31	5		5	31

Likewise, the line graph on the left makes more sense to most of us than the one on the right because we normally read a time sequence from left to right—not from bottom to top.

Remember, though, that the figure on the left still would not make as much sense to someone who had been taught to read from right to left, or to read lines that proceed from bottom to top. Good design always depends on how well you meet your readers' expectations.

Club Attendance for the Past Five Weeks

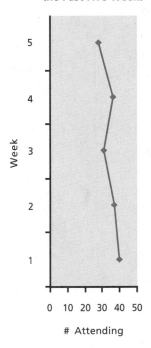

Club Attendance for the Past Five Weeks

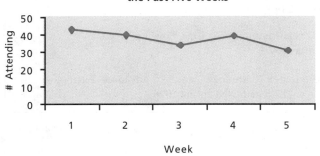

GROUP RELATED ELEMENTS VISUALLY

Each of the boxes below contains the same information. But the second is more readable than the first because the writer has grouped her degrees into three separate units. The third is the most readable of all because blank lines divide the three units, larger type and boldface accentuate the headings, and indentation subordinates the whole text to the main heading.

Regarding my education: I am currently working on a bachelor's degree in computer technology at Western Kentucky University in Bowling Green, Kentucky. I expect to graduate in the year 2000 after the fall semester. Before working on my bachelor's, I earned an associate of science degree at Bowling Green Community College in the spring of 1997, and I earned a certificate in computer technology from the Kentucky Advanced Technology Institute in the spring of 1996. Both institutions are located in Bowling Green.

Education
B.S. Computer Technology, Western Kentucky University, Bowling Green, KY
Expected Graduation Fall 2000
A.S. Bowling Green Community College, Bowling Green, KY
Graduated Spring 1997
Certificate, Computer Technology, Kentucky Advanced Technology Institute,
Bowling Green, KY, Graduated Spring 1996

Education

    B.S. Computer Technology, Western Kentucky University, Bowling Green, KY
    Expected Graduation: Fall 2000

    A.S. Bowling Green Community College, Bowling Green, KY
    Graduated Spring 1997

    Certificate, Computer Technology, Kentucky Advanced Technology Institute, Bowling Green, KY, Graduated Spring 1996

Careful document design can reveal the organization of information and make a reader's job easier.

MAKE TEXT AND FIGURES STAND OUT FROM THE BACKGROUND

Text and figures should contrast sharply with the background—whether it's a solid color, a picture, or a watermark.

> Make text and figures stand out from the background.

> Make text and figures stand out from the background.

Create a clear contrast.

BALANCE YOUR ELEMENTS

A balanced layout looks tidy and helps clarify the organization of your text. In the top row, for instance, the left-hand page shows its three-part organization more clearly than the right-hand one does. In all three rows, the left-hand pages show how to group elements into a few manageable chunks and how to spread text and graphics evenly over the page.

Why do the examples in the left column look more balanced than those in the right?

223

12.3 PUTTING THE PIECES TOGETHER: A SAMPLING OF FORMATS AND TEXTS

Now that you have read about the basic elements of design and principles for combining those elements, consider the following examples of formats and texts. What are their strong points? Their weak points?

HEADINGS

Headings represent one of the most basic combinations of design elements, namely typography and spacing. Well-worded headings help readers see the organization of a text, and they let busy readers search for important information. When you use headings, make them descriptive. Consider the differences between these headings:

▶ Principles

▶ Six Design Principles

▶ A Graphic Designer's Six Most Important Principles

After reading the first heading, a reader will most likely be unable to tell exactly what kind of principles will be discussed. The second heading mentions design, but what kind? The third heading gives readers a much clearer picture of the type of principles to be covered.

BULLETED AND NUMBERED LISTS

Lists represent another basic combination of design elements. They are helpful when you have a group of closely related facts, such as the names of team members, items needed for an experiment, or steps necessary for completing a project. Use numbered lists when order is important—for example, when readers should follow the steps of a process in a specific order or when you want to present a ranking of some sort. Use bulleted lists when the order of the information is not particularly important or is merely alphabetical—as with a list of team members' names.

When you create a list, be sure that all items are parallel. (See chapter 16, "Parallel Construction.")

ACADEMIC DOCUMENTS

ESSAY IN MLA STYLE
Format with Title on First Page of Text

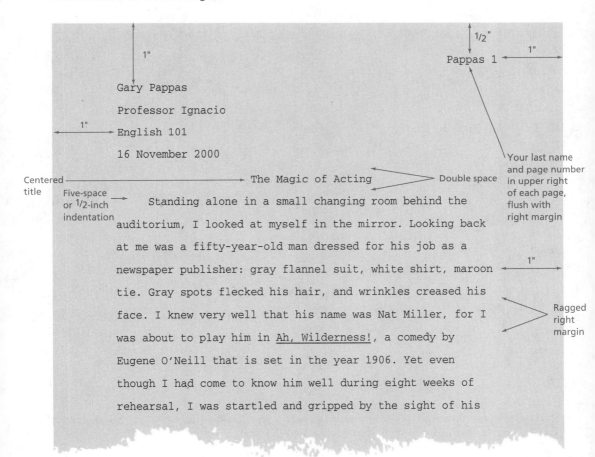

Pappas 1

½"   1"

1"

Gary Pappas

Professor Ignacio

1"   English 101

16 November 2000

Centered title — The Magic of Acting ← Double space

Your last name and page number in upper right of each page, flush with right margin

Five-space or ½-inch indentation →   Standing alone in a small changing room behind the

auditorium, I looked at myself in the mirror. Looking back

at me was a fifty-year-old man dressed for his job as a

newspaper publisher: gray flannel suit, white shirt, maroon   1"

tie. Gray spots flecked his hair, and wrinkles creased his

face. I knew very well that his name was Nat Miller, for I

Ragged right margin

was about to play him in Ah, Wilderness!, a comedy by

Eugene O'Neill that is set in the year 1906. Yet even

though I had come to know him well during eight weeks of

rehearsal, I was startled and gripped by the sight of his

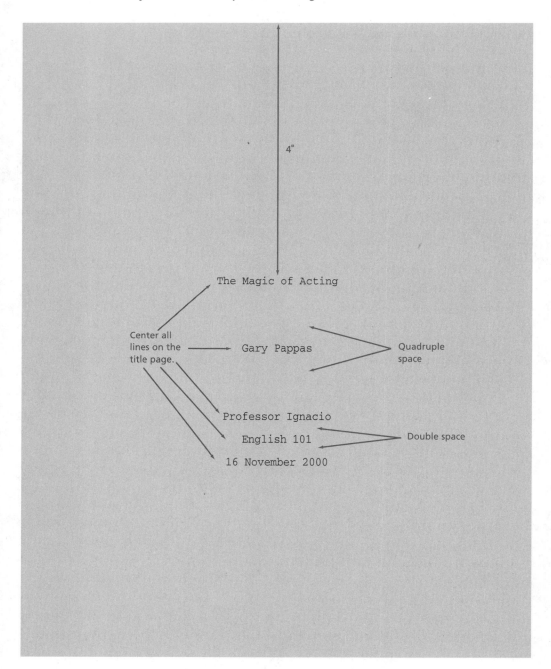

4"

The Magic of Acting

Center all
lines on the
title page.

Gary Pappas

Quadruple
space

Professor Ignacio

English 101

Double space

16 November 2000

First Page of Text Following Separate Title Page (note repeating title)

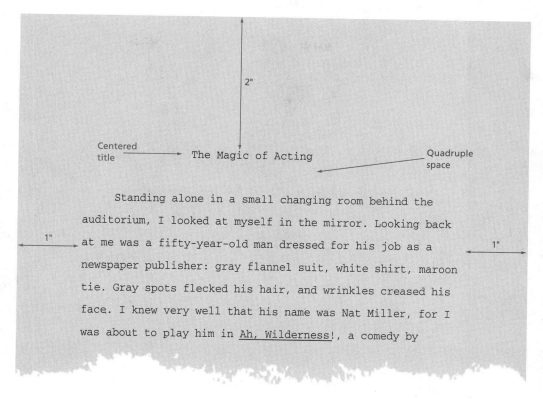

2"

Centered title → The Magic of Acting ← Quadruple space

1"

          Standing alone in a small changing room behind the
auditorium, I looked at myself in the mirror. Looking back
at me was a fifty-year-old man dressed for his job as a
newspaper publisher: gray flannel suit, white shirt, maroon
tie. Gray spots flecked his hair, and wrinkles creased his
face. I knew very well that his name was Nat Miller, for I
was about to play him in Ah, Wilderness!, a comedy by

1"

Second and Succeeding Pages of Text

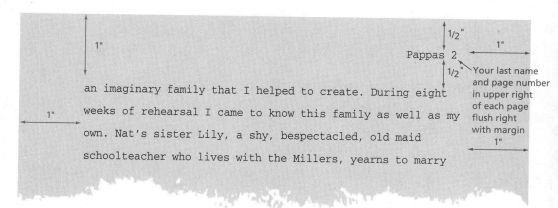

1"

1/2"   1"

Pappas 2 ←

1/2" Your last name
and page number
in upper right
of each page
flush right
with margin

an imaginary family that I helped to create. During eight
weeks of rehearsal I came to know this family as well as my
own. Nat's sister Lily, a shy, bespectacled, old maid
schoolteacher who lives with the Millers, yearns to marry

1"

1"

RESEARCH PAPER IN MLA STYLE
Format with Title on First Page of Text

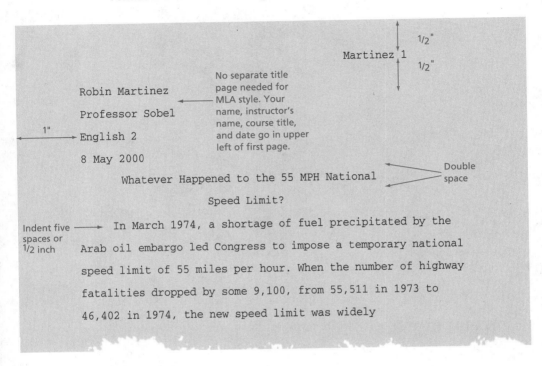

Martinez 1

½"

½"

Robin Martinez

Professor Sobel

No separate title page needed for MLA style. Your name, instructor's name, course title, and date go in upper left of first page.

1"

English 2

8 May 2000

Whatever Happened to the 55 MPH National

Double space

Speed Limit?

Indent five spaces or ½ inch

In March 1974, a shortage of fuel precipitated by the Arab oil embargo led Congress to impose a temporary national speed limit of 55 miles per hour. When the number of highway fatalities dropped by some 9,100, from 55,511 in 1973 to 46,402 in 1974, the new speed limit was widely

Second and Succeeding Pages of Text

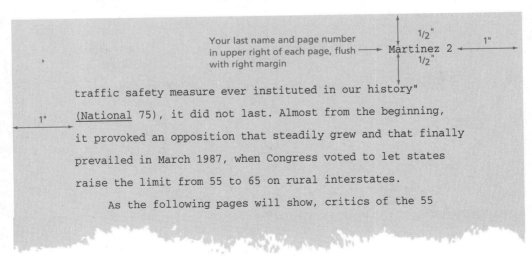

Your last name and page number in upper right of each page, flush with right margin

½"

Martinez 2

1"

½"

traffic safety measure ever instituted in our history"

1"

(National 75), it did not last. Almost from the beginning, it provoked an opposition that steadily grew and that finally prevailed in March 1987, when Congress voted to let states raise the limit from 55 to 65 on rural interstates.

As the following pages will show, critics of the 55

RESEARCH PAPER IN APA STYLE

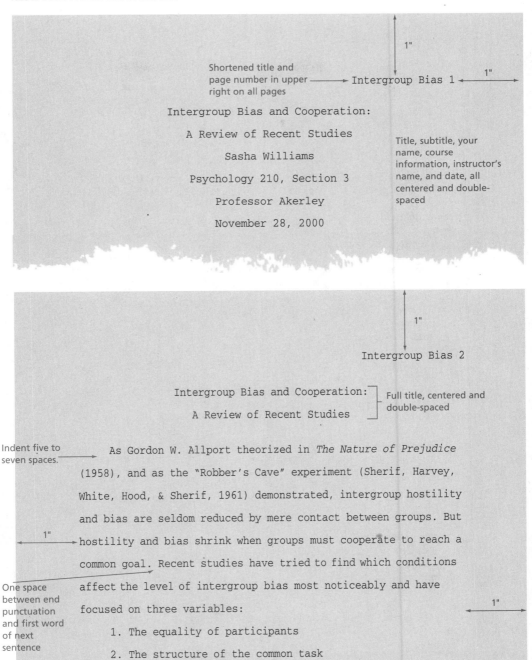

Shortened title and page number in upper right on all pages ⟶ Intergroup Bias 1 ◂

1"

1"

Intergroup Bias and Cooperation:

A Review of Recent Studies

Sasha Williams

Psychology 210, Section 3

Professor Akerley

November 28, 2000

Title, subtitle, your name, course information, instructor's name, and date, all centered and double-spaced

1"

Intergroup Bias 2

Intergroup Bias and Cooperation:

A Review of Recent Studies

Full title, centered and double-spaced

Indent five to seven spaces.

    As Gordon W. Allport theorized in *The Nature of Prejudice* (1958), and as the "Robber's Cave" experiment (Sherif, Harvey, White, Hood, & Sherif, 1961) demonstrated, intergroup hostility and bias are seldom reduced by mere contact between groups. But

1"

hostility and bias shrink when groups must cooperate to reach a common goal. Recent studies have tried to find which conditions

One space between end punctuation and first word of next sentence

affect the level of intergroup bias most noticeably and have focused on three variables:

1"

   1. The equality of participants

   2. The structure of the common task

RÉSUMÉS

Natalie Lucille Ravel
ravelnl@anyu.edu

Campus Address
#1413 Vistana Tower
Rutherford, IN 46464
(222) 283-4826
until May 20, 2000

Permanent Address
333 Bainbridge Road
Calloway, OH 44114
(111) 843-1234
after May 20, 2000

Objective
Co-op position in the computer industry that allows me to
work with programming, system setup or web development.

Computer Skills
- Languages: C++, Java
- Operating systems: Unix, Linux, Windows 95, 3.x, and NT
- Hardware: Scanners, Printers, RAM, Peripherals, Hard Drives
  and Communication Cards
- Software: Novell Netware 4.0, Microsoft Developing Studio,
  Netscape Communicator 4.5, Microsoft Office 97, Photoshop

Experience

Self-employed   1997–Present
Computer Consultant
Worked across two counties installing hardware and soft-
ware and instructing customers with general applications
and the Internet. Created Web site for Jackson County Humane
Society (http://www.jackson.us/~JCHS).

Ed Vallio's Pizza   June 1996–August 1999
Team Leader
Supervised crew of 5 employees through nightly closes.
Conducted nightly inventory and reconciled cash and regis-
ter receipts. Actively led employees to maintain cleanest
restaurant in Calloway (according to Calloway Chamber of
Commerce, 1999).

Happy Burger (Store #16)   October 1995–May 1996
Cashier

Education

Rutherford University   July 1999–Present
Double major in Computer Science and Mathematics.
34 credit hours completed.
GPA: 3.2 of 4.0

Jenny K. Johnson
_____

134 Upton Lane
Calloway, MN 43334
234-567-1234

OBJECTIVE
To obtain an administrative position in a social service
agency

EDUCATION
B.S., Psychology (cum laude), Western East University,
May 1999
Southtown, MN

SOCIAL SERVICE EXPERIENCE
Community Living Counselor   1997-Present
Southtown Assisted Living Center, Southtown, MN
• Assist individuals with independent living skills and de-
  velopmental activities.
• Report, record, and document all information pertaining to
  individuals in program.

Hotline Volunteer   1998-1999
Smith County Crisis Center
• Responded to calls from county residents regarding such
  situations as domestic violence, potential suicide, and
  despression. On call six hours per week.
• Trained eight new volunteers during 1999.

RETAIL EXPERIENCE
Sales Associate/Cashier
Laughing Girl Clothing, Calloway, MN   Summer, 1996
Dylan's Toys, Calloway, MN   1994-1995

ACTIVITIES
Volunteer, Calloway Multiple Sclerosis 10K Walk, 1999
Coordinator, Smith County Adopt-a-Grandparent Goodwill
  Fundraising Pageant, 1998
Volunteer, Western East University Fall Blood Drive, 1998

MEMOS

A memo is a form of written communication commonly used by people who work together. Its format looks official, but its language is commonly informal.

EXAMPLE OF MEMO FORMAT

MEMORANDUM

To: Dr. Mary Clyne, Advisor, Marketing Club
From: Harold Rivers, Club President
Date: September 18, 2000
Re: Possible Guest Speakers for Upcoming Marketing Meetings

An informal poll of our marketing club members suggests that the following topics would be popular:

- career placement
- internship & co-op opportunities
- marketing in nonprofit organizations
- what to expect in one's first year in marketing

Given these interests, I recommend that we invite three speakers for the spring semester.

Beverly Shaw is the director of the Monmouth College Career Placement Center. She has spoken to other groups on campus about résumé and letter writing, research in the job search, and related topics.

Ylce Lopez is a Monmouth College alumna and the current director of recruiting for Marketing Concepts in Chicago. She could speak on both job search strategies and what to expect in one's first year in marketing.

Ronald French, a Monmouth College alumnus, is the current assistant director of development for the Municipal Zoo. He could speak on marketing in nonprofit organizations.

Let me know if you like these choices. I will begin contacting them as soon as I have your approval.

Bullets can be used for items listed in no special order. →

BUSINESS LETTERS

BLOCK FORMAT

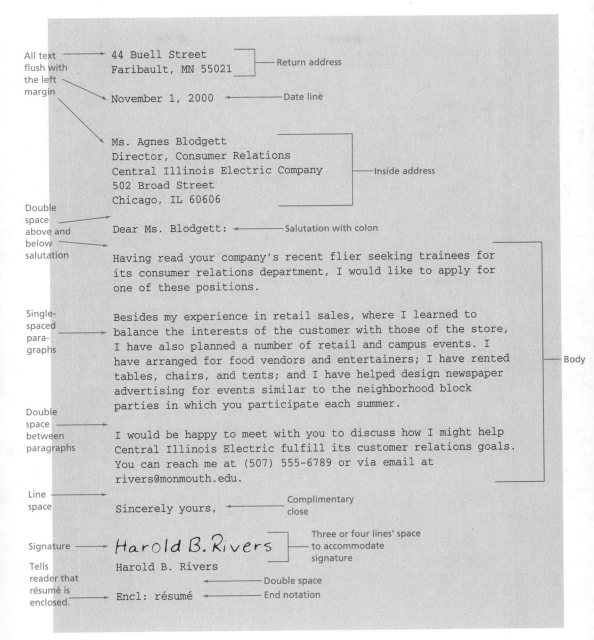

All text flush with the left margin

44 Buell Street
Faribault, MN 55021 ——— Return address

November 1, 2000 ←——— Date line

Ms. Agnes Blodgett
Director, Consumer Relations
Central Illinois Electric Company ——— Inside address
502 Broad Street
Chicago, IL 60606

Double space above and below salutation

Dear Ms. Blodgett: ←——— Salutation with colon

Having read your company's recent flier seeking trainees for its consumer relations department, I would like to apply for one of these positions.

Single-spaced paragraphs

Besides my experience in retail sales, where I learned to balance the interests of the customer with those of the store, I have also planned a number of retail and campus events. I have arranged for food vendors and entertainers; I have rented tables, chairs, and tents; and I have helped design newspaper advertising for events similar to the neighborhood block parties in which you participate each summer.

——— Body

Double space between paragraphs

I would be happy to meet with you to discuss how I might help Central Illinois Electric fulfill its customer relations goals. You can reach me at (507) 555-6789 or via email at rivers@monmouth.edu.

Line space

Sincerely yours, ←——— Complimentary close

Signature ——— *Harold B. Rivers* ——— Three or four lines' space to accommodate signature

Harold B. Rivers

Double space

Tells reader that résumé is enclosed.

Encl: résumé ←——— End notation

233

MODIFIED BLOCK FORMAT

Indent
approximately five ———→ 44 Buell Street
inches from the   Faribault, MN 55021
left margin.
                       November 1, 2000

Include
your reader's   Ms. Agnes Blodgett
title, if you   Director, Consumer Relations
know it.   Central Illinois Electric Company
                502 Broad Street
                Chicago, IL 60606

Dear Ms. Blodgett:

Having read your company's recent flier seeking trainees for its
consumer relations department, I would like to apply for one of
these positions.

Besides my experience in retail sales, where I learned to balance
the interests of the customer with those of the store, I have
also planned a number of retail and campus events. I have ar-
Tie your   ranged for food vendors and entertainers; I have rented tables,
experience   chairs, and tents; and I have helped design newspaper advertising
to the job   for events similar to the neighborhood block parties in which you
you are   participate each summer.
seeking.

I would be happy to meet with you to discuss how I might help
Central Illinois Electric fulfill its customer relations goals.
You can reach me at (507) 555-6789 or via email at
rivers@monmouth.edu.

                       Sincerely yours,

                       Harold B. Rivers ←—— Triple
                                                space to
                       Harold B. Rivers   accommo-
                                                date
                                                signature

Encl: résumé

234

BROCHURES

Typical letterfold brochure, opening from the right, like a book

Common layout patterns for inside of three-panel brochure

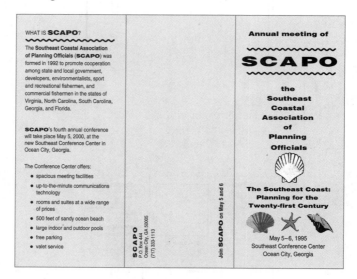

Panels A, B, and C of brochure
(outside panels, with cover panel at right and address panel in middle)

Panels D, E, and F of brochure
(inside panels)

Panel A when brochure is unfolded,
with cover panel at right

Panel A when brochure is folded

WHAT IS **SCAPO**?

The **Southeast Coastal Association of Planning Officials** (**SCAPO**) was formed in 1992 to promote cooperation among state and local government, developers, environmentalists, sport and recreational fishermen, and commercial fishermen in the states of Virginia, North Carolina, South Carolina, Georgia, and Florida.

SCAPO's fourth annual conference will take place May 5, 2000, at the new Southeast Conference Center in Ocean City, Georgia.

The Conference Center offers:

- spacious meeting facilities
- up-to-the-minute communications technology
- rooms and suites at a wide range of prices
- 500 feet of sandy ocean beach
- large indoor and outdoor pools
- free parking
- valet service

Panel B when brochure is
unfolded, with cover panel at right

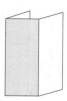

Panel B when brochure is folded

SCAPO
P.O. Box 444
Ocean City, GA 50005
(717) 333-1113

Join **SCAPO** on May 5 and 6

Panel C when brochure is
unfolded, with cover panel at
right

Panel C (cover panel) when
brochure is folded

Annual meeting of

SCAPO

the
Southeast
Coastal
Association
of
Planning
Officials

The Southeast Coast:
Planning for the
Twenty-first Century

May 5–6, 2000
Southeast Conference Center
Ocean City, Georgia

Planning for the Twe

FRIDAY EVENING SESSION

Welcome: Max Winston, SCAPO Chair

Panel Discussion

Tourism, Economic Development, and the Environment: An Overview

Sandra Alberg, Alberg Enterprises

Barry Jones, South Carolina Office of Coastal Zone
Management

Olivia DiGregorio, Seaside City Planning Director

Dana Schwartz, Virginia Economic Development
Commission

SATURDAY MORNING SESSION

Panel Discussions

Recreational Uses and Coastal Ecosystems

Walter Talltrees,
Save Our Shores

Abner Mahlon,
Southeast Association
of Sport Fishermen

Andrea Finkelstein,
Department of
Marine Biology,
Tidewater University

Steven Beaumont, South Carolina Department of
Tourism

OR

Single-Family Development: The Hidden Costs

Jordan Atkins, Edgewater County Zoning Commission

Melanie Zimmer, Department of Urban Planning,
Sunbelt University

Hubie Whiteside, Metropolitan Development Corporation

Atha Poulakis, Affordable Housing Initiative

photo

Panel D when brochure is unfolded (inside of brochure)

Panel D when brochure is folded

Panel E when brochure is unfolded
(inside of brochure)

Panel E when brochure is folded

nty-first Century

SATURDAY AFTERNOON SESSIONS

Workshops

Environmental Regulation Update

Leader:
Carol Neslow, EPA

photo

Preparing the Environmental Impact Statement

Leader: Jonathan Wong, Wong and Bell Associates

Innovative Zoning in Coastal Tourist Areas

Leader: Luella Gaskins, Alton County Zoning Board

Using the Design Review Process to Preserve Community Character

Leader: Calvin Walden, Seaside City Planning Department

SATURDAY EVENING SESSION

Video Presentation and Discussion

Sunrise Township: A Model for Partnerships between Developers, Environmentalists, and Local Government

Leader: Max Winston, Outer Banks Association

REGISTRATION FORM
Registration deadline: April 14

I plan to attend the following sessions:
____ Friday, May 5, 5 to 10 p.m. (includes dinner) $80
____ Saturday, May 6 , 9 a.m. to 5 p.m. (includes continental breakfast and full lunch) $100
____ Saturday, May 6, 5 to 10 p.m. (includes dinner) $80
____ Amount Enclosed or Charged

I am paying by
____ check (make payable to **SCAPO**)
____ Mastercard   ____ VISA
   Acct #_____
   Exp. Date _____
   Cardholder name_____
   Signature _____

Name: _____
Address: _____
City: _____
State: _____   Zip: _____
Phone, with area code: _____

Mail to:
   SCAPO
   P.O. Box 444
   Ocean City GA 50005

Fax credit card payment only to:
   (717) 333-1111

Panel F when brochure is unfolded (inside of brochure)

Panel F when brochure is folded

12.4 FURTHER READING

Black, Roger (with Sean Eldred). *Web Sites That Work*. San Jose, CA: Adobe, 1997.

Lynch, Patrick J., and Sarah Horton. *Web Style Guide: Basic Design Principles for Creating Web Sites*. New Haven, CT: Yale UP, 1999.

Parker, Roger C. *Looking Good in Print,* 10th Ed. Chapel Hill, NC: Ventana, 1998.

Tufte, Edward R. *The Visual Display of Quantitative Information*. Cheshire, CT: Graphics, 1992.

Analyzing Documents and Web Pages   EXERCISE 1

1. Collect several types of printed documents, such as newsletters, fliers, instructions, or newspapers. Analyze the use of space, text, graphics, and color. Share examples with the class. Solicit people's preferences, and determine why some examples are preferred over others.

2. Do the same thing with specific types of Web pages. Compare and contrast favored prints and electronic examples.

Considering Messages   EXERCISE 2

Visit a place where you are likely to find a lot of text—a place such as a museum, a cemetery, or a shopping mall. Consider the messages being conveyed by particular types of text on specific types of writing surface. What sorts of emotions do they elicit? How do fonts, writing surfaces, and colors influence your response to the various texts you find?

2

Crafting Sentences

The Simple Sentence   13

The **sentence** is a fundamentally human creation. Like the human beings who write them, sentences come in a seemingly endless variety of shapes and sizes: some stretch out for line upon line; others stop short after two or three words. Yet for all its variety, the sentence has a definable structure.

How much do you need to know about this structure to write well? If you can speak and write English, you already know a good deal about the structure of the English sentence. But to make your sentences both grammatically correct and rhetorically effective, you may need to know more about the basic parts.

13.1 THE SUBJECT AND THE PREDICATE

A sentence consists of at least one **clause**—a word group with a subject and a predicate. The **subject** identifies a person, place, or thing. The **predicate** tells what the subject does or is, where it is, what it has, or what is done to it. In statements the subject often comes first:

SUBJECT	PREDICATE
Economists	study the production and consumption of goods and services.
The American economic system	rewards individual initiative.
Control of production	is private.
Consumers	have a variety of choices.
Prices of goods and services	are largely determined by supply and demand.

In this chapter we consider the basic parts of the one-clause sentence (the **simple sentence**) because all other sentences are based on this structure.

13.2 VERBS AND VERB PHRASES

The predicate always includes a **verb**, which may be one word or a phrase:

> The comet *is* visible now.
>
> A solar eclipse *will be* visible in October.

> Napoleon's victory *revived* his dream of political domination.
>
> Dreams *can revive* old memories.

> Over 80 percent of the first inhabitants *perished* in 1607.
>
> All of the early settlers *would have perished* without help from the natives.

> *Is* the ceremony a humane one?
>
> *Do* the initiation rites *include* bloodletting?

> *Are* interest rates *falling?*
>
> The recession *has* not *ended* yet.

Every **verb phrase** consists of a base verb and at least one "helping" verb or auxiliary. Auxiliaries include forms of *be (is, are, was, were), have, has, had, do, does, may, might, can, could, will, shall, would,* and *should.*

13.3 TYPES OF VERBS

Verbs may be *linking, intransitive,* or *transitive.*

(i) LINKING VERBS

A **linking verb** connects the subject to a word or phrase that identifies, classifies, or describes it:

> John Marshall *was* the fourth chief justice of the United States.
>
> Pyrite *is* a mineral chiefly used as a source of sulfur.
>
> The primaries *are* testing grounds for the candidates of political parties.
>
> Primary campaigns soon *become* expensive.

The most widely used linking verb is a form of *be,* such as *am, is, are, was,* or *were.* Other linking verbs include *seem, become, feel, sound,* and *taste.*

248

The word or phrase that follows a linking verb is called a subject complement. If the word is a noun, such as *mineral,* it is called a predicate noun. If the word is an adjective, such as *expensive,* it is called a predicate adjective.

ⓘ INTRANSITIVE VERBS

An intransitive verb names an action that has no direct impact on anyone or anything named in the predicate:

> The Earth *turns* on its axis.

> All symptoms of the disease *vanished.*

> The volcano *could erupt* at any time.

As the examples show, <u>intransitive verbs do not have objects.</u> Compare them with transitive verbs, shown in the next section.

ⓘ TRANSITIVE VERBS

A transitive verb names an action that directly affects a person or thing mentioned in the predicate. The word or phrase naming this person or thing is called the direct object (DO):

> DO
> An enthusiastic crowd *greeted* the president at the airport.

> DO
> Gamblers *lose* money.

> DO
> A fungus *has been threatening* maples in the region.

④ Some verbs take an indirect object (IO), which may go before or after the direct object:

> IO   DO
> The president *gave* his staff a stern warning.

You could also write:

> DO   IO
> The president *gave* a stern warning to his staff.

Other verbs that give you this option include *make, send, offer, show, write,* and *tell.* But whatever the verb, you must put the direct object first whenever both objects are pronouns:

> DO   IO
> Ellen offered it to them.

Another kind of transitive verb takes an **object complement** (OC), a word or phrase that follows the direct object and classifies or describes it:

DO   OC

Many scientists *considered* the experiment a disaster.   *(consider it a disaster)*

DO   OC

Unfair accusations *make* most people angry.   *(make sb. angry)*

DO   OC

The jury *found* the defendant guilty of treason.   *(found him guilty)*

Other verbs of this kind include *name, elect, appoint, think, judge,* and *prove.*

active vs passive voice ∘   You can use a transitive verb in either the active or the passive voice. When the subject performs the action named by the verb, the verb is **active**:

> Farmers *plow* fields.
> Vandals *defaced* the queen's portrait.

When the subject undergoes, receives, or suffers the action named by the verb, the verb is **passive**:

> Fields *are plowed* by farmers.
> The queen's portrait *was defaced* by vandals.

For a full discussion of voice, see chapter 24.

Types of Verbs

A **linking verb** connects the subject to a word or phrase that identifies, classifies, or describes it:

> Lima *is* the capital of Peru.
> Some professional athletes *become* wealthy.

An **intransitive verb** names an action that has no effect on a person or thing mentioned in the predicate:

> Children *giggle.*
> Palm trees *were swaying* in the moonlight.

A **transitive verb** in the **active voice** names an action performed by the subject and affecting a person or thing mentioned in the predicate:

> Winston Churchill *inspired* the people of Great Britain during World War II.
> Traffic jams *inhibit* the flow of goods and services.

A **transitive verb** in the **passive voice** names an action affecting the subject. The person or thing performing the action may be mentioned in the predicate after the word *by* or left unmentioned:

> During World War II the people of Great Britain *were inspired* by Winston Churchill.
> The flow of goods and services *is inhibited* by traffic jams.
> Traces of mercury *were found* in the water.

13.4   WRITING THE SUBJECT

The **subject** of a simple sentence can be a noun, a noun phrase, a pronoun, or a verbal noun.

1. A **noun** is a word naming one or more persons, creatures, places, things, activities, conditions, or ideas:

SUBJECT	PREDICATE
Children	thrive on loving care.
Freedom	entails responsibility.
Dinosaurs	became extinct some sixty-five million years ago.

2. A **noun phrase** is a group of words consisting of a main noun (MN) and the words that describe, limit, or qualify it:

SUBJECT (NOUN PHRASE)   PREDICATE

MN
The price of gold   has dropped sharply.

                MN
Long-standing labor disputes   can be difficult to settle.

     MN
The sound of snoring in the audience   distracted the performers.

3. A **pronoun** (PR) takes the place of a noun (N):

SUBJECT   PREDICATE

N
Investors   have become cautious

PR
They   fear a recession.

N
Traffic   moved briskly at first.

PR
It   soon slowed to a crawl.

For a full discussion of pronouns, see chapter 20.

Verbal nouns can serve as
0) the subject in a sentence
0) a predicate noun after a linking verb in Pattern 1.
(0) DO in Pattern 3

4. A **verbal noun** is a word or phrase formed from a verb and used as a noun. It can function as the subject in a sentence:

SUBJECT   PREDICATE

To err   is human.

Splitting logs   takes muscle.

Verifying the testimony of witnesses   can be a time-consuming process.
to an accident

the purpose of using verbal nouns.

Verbal nouns enable you to treat actions as things, and thus to get more action into your sentences. There are two types: the **gerund**, which ends in *-ing,* and the **infinitive**, which is usually marked by *to.* A verbal noun may also serve

a. as a predicate noun (PN) after a linking verb:

PN
Their aim is *to obstruct justice.*

PN
The most common mishap of all is *breaking a test tube.*

b. as the direct object (DO) of a transitive verb:

DO
Gourmands love *to eat.*

DO
Few enjoy *my singing of the national anthem.*

Writing the Subject

The subject of a simple sentence may be—

▶ a noun:

Children thrive on loving care.

▶ a noun phrase:

All the children of the world thrive on loving care.

▶ a pronoun:

They need our help.

▶ a verbal noun:

To work is to pray.
Seeing is believing.

13.5 PUTTING THE SUBJECT AFTER THE VERB

The subject of a **declarative** sentence—a sentence that makes a statement—usually precedes the verb. But the subject follows the verb in sentences like these:

There were *riots* in the occupied territories.

[handwritten: Riots were in the occupied territories.]

It is hard to *read small print.*

[handwritten: To read small print is hard. subject; verbal noun]

In these sentences *there* and *it* are introductory words or **expletives**. They are not part of either the subject or the predicate.

The subject also follows the verb when the word order is inverted:

In the center of the painting stands *a white unicorn with a golden horn.*

[handwritten: In the center of the (Uffizi Gallery displays the painting titled The Spring)]

The inversion of subject-verb order gives special prominence to the subject, so you should use inversion sparingly—and only when you want this special effect.

In most questions the subject (S) follows a verb so that the predicate (P) is divided:

P	S	P
Can	we	find a cure for AIDS?
Have	we	the will and the means?

13.6 OMITTING THE SUBJECT

A sentence that gives a command or makes a request often omits the subject, which is understood to be *you:*

Keep off the grass.

Please don't litter.

Submit your application before June 1.

For more on this type of sentence, which is called imperative, see 25.3.

13.7 USING MODIFIERS

The complete subject and the complete predicate of a sentence normally include modifiers. A modifier is a word, phrase, or clause that describes, limits, or qualifies another word or word group. The italicized words are all modifiers in this sentence:

SUBJECT   PREDICATE

The price *of gold*   had dropped *sharply.*

The words modifying *price* form part of the subject; the word modifying *had dropped* forms part of the predicate. Here are further examples:

S   P
A negligent workman   spilled lye *over the oriental rug.*

S   P
The equivocal statements of the *prime minister*   are sending *mixed* signals *to the opposition.*

S   P
The brightly painted masks *used in the hunting rituals*   *are sacred* objects *representing tribal ancestors.*

S   P
Grandfather   sat *in his rocker, watching the children.*

For a full discussion of modifiers, see chapter 14.

Recognizing Subjects and Predicates

In each of the following sentences, identify the subject and the predicate, using brackets around the complete subject and parentheses around each part of the predicate.

EXAMPLE:

[A fool's brain] (digests philosophy into folly, science into superstition, and art into pedantry).

—G. B. Shaw

1. [As a television news correspondent, I] (am a watchdog for the images of black people.)

—Farai Chideya

2. [It (occurred to me] that we had not been listening much to children in these recent years of "summit conferences" on education, of severe reports and ominous prescriptions.]

—Jonhathan Kozol

3. [Outside literature, the main motive for writing] (is to describe the world.)

—Northrop Frye

4. [White Americans] (find it as difficult as white people elsewhere do to divest themselves of the notion that they are in possession of some intrinsic value that black people need, or want.]

—James Baldwin

5. [Reading James Baldwin's early essays in the fifties] (had stirred me with a sense that apparently "given" situations like racism could be analyzed and described and that this could lead to action, to change.)

—Adrienne Rich

6. At once [a black fin] (slit the pink cloud on the water, shearing it in two.)

—Annie Dillard

7. [A work of art] (expresses a conception of life, emotion, inward reality.)

—Susanne K. Langer

8. [Who] (will compute the lonely nights made less lonely by your songs, or the empty pots made less tragic by your tales?)

—Maya Angelou

handwritten margin notes:

modifier

I, = a television news correspond, am a . . . .

verb: occurred
what occurred to me?
we had not been . . .

[The main motive for writing, outside literature,]
(is to describe the world.)

[CP] for this type of sentence.

255

13.8 USING COMPOUND PHRASES

Compound phrases help to turn short, meager sentences into longer, meatier ones. A compound phrase joins words or phrases to show one of the following things:

1. **ADDITION**

   Presidential election campaigns have become long.

   Presidential election campaigns have become expensive.

   COMBINED: Presidential campaigns have become *long and expensive.*

   The dancer was lean.

   The dancer was acrobatic.

   The dancer was bold.

   COMBINED: The dancer was *lean, acrobatic, and bold.*

   Ants crawled over the floor.

   They crawled up the wall.

   They crawled onto the counter.

   They crawled into the honey pot.

   COMBINED: Ants crawled *over the floor, up the wall, onto the counter, and into the honey pot.*

   The witness blushed.

   He cleared his throat.

   He began to speak in a halting manner.

   COMBINED: The witness *blushed, cleared his throat, and began to speak in a halting manner.*

2. **CONTRAST**

   Marketing U.S. products in Japan is difficult.

   But it is not impossible.

   COMBINED: Marketing U.S. products in Japan is *difficult but not impossible.*

3. CHOICE

The government must reduce its spending.

Or it must raise taxes.

COMBINED: The government must *either reduce its spending or raise taxes.*

The senator had not anticipated the setback.

Her staff had not anticipated the setback.

COMBINED: *Neither the senator nor her staff* had anticipated the setback.

Both the senator & her staff had not anticipated the setback.
Or
(The senator had not anticipated the setback, nor had her staff.)

For advice on punctuating the items in a compound phrase, see 29.7–29.8.

Sentence Combining and Compound Phrases   EXERCISE 2

Combine the sentences in each of the following sets by using compound phrases.

EXAMPLE:

Proud nations have gradually fallen into dust.

Great civilizations have gradually fallen into dust.

COMBINED: Proud nations and great civilizations have gradually fallen into dust.

1. The painting was savage.
   The painting was sensuous.
   The painting was brilliant.

   The painting was savage, sensuous, & brilliant

2. It cost the artist hundreds of hours.
   It demanded all of her skill.
   It left her exhausted.
   It left her elated.

   It cost the artist hundreds of hrs, & demanded all of her skill
   It left her exhausted, but elated.

3. She had feared the demands on her strength.
   She could not spare herself.

4. She devoted the summer to sketching.
   She devoted the fall to painting.
   She devoted the winter to repainting.

5. An artist must use her powers.
   Otherwise she must lose them.

   An artist must either use her power or lose them.

13.9 EDITING MIXED CONSTRUCTIONS

A **mixed construction** is a combination of word groups that do not fit together grammatically or meaningfully:

MODIFIER MISUSED AS SUBJECT

1. *Fearful of the dark

PREDICATE

kept the boy awake all night.

To correct a sentence like this, you can do one of two things:

a. Turn the modifier into a noun:

SUBJECT   PREDICATE

EDITED: Fear of the dark / kept the boy awake all night.

b. Furnish a noun as the subject:

MODIFIER   SUBJECT   PREDICATE

EDITED: Fearful of the dark, the boy / lay awake all night.

The boy who is fearful of the dark lay lay awake all night.

2. *The head of the shipbuilding company congratulated the achievement
of the workers.

An *achievement* cannot be congratulated; only people can be. To correct the
error, change the verb or the object so that the two things fit together:

EDITED: The head of the shipbuilding company congratulated the workers
on their achievement.
[or] The head of the shipbuilding company praised the achievement of the
workers.

3. *Of the two hundred persons questioned, no correct answer was given.

The first part of this sentence leads us to expect that the second part will
say something about the *persons questioned.* Since the second part says
nothing about them, it leaves us confused:

EDITED: Of the two hundred persons questioned, none answered correctly.

Editing Mixed Constructions

In each of the following a word or phrase is misused in relation to other parts of the sentence. Edit the wording to produce an acceptable sentence.

EXAMPLE: *Raised in Wyoming has made Polly love the West.

EDITED: Raised in Wyoming, Polly loves the West.

1. By climbing with sneakers in subzero weather nearly froze my toes.
2. Numbed with the cold often made me stumble.
3. But on reaching a heated cabin before sundown restored circulation to my feet.
4. Loaned a pair of insulated boots helped me get back down the mountain safely the next day.
5. Out of all the trips in my experience, I was challenged the most.

13.10 EDITING FAULTY PREDICATION

Faulty predication using a linking verb between two words that are not equivalent or compatible:

1. *Another kind of flying is a glider.

The sentence classifies an activity (*flying*) as an object (*a glider*). But an activity is not an object. To correct the sentence, make the verb link two activities or two objects:

EDITED: Another type of flying is gliding. (two activities)
[or] Another type of aircraft is a glider. (two objects)

2. *According to the senator, his greatest achievement was when he persuaded the president not to seek reelection.

An achievement is not a time, a *when*. It is an act:

EDITED: According to the senator, his greatest achievement was persuading the president not to seek reelection. (two acts)

3. *The reason for the evacuation of the building was because a bomb threat had been made.

This sentence equates *reason* with *because*. Those two words are related but not equivalent. *Reason* is a noun, and *because* is not.

> EDITED: The reason for the evacuation of the building was that a bomb threat had been made. (noun plus noun equivalent)
> [or] The building was evacuated because a bomb threat had been made.

This sentence contains an adverb clause; for more on adverb clauses, see 17.8.

EXERCISE 4   **Editing Faulty Predication**

Rewrite each of the following sentences to make the words after the linking verb compatible with the subject. If the sentence is correct as it stands, write *Correct*.

EXAMPLE: *A picnic is when you eat outdoors.

EDITED: A picnic is an outdoor meal.

1. Successful campaigning is where you attract a wide range of voters.

2. The main fault of Claghorn's speeches was how they offended votes over sixty.

3. Claghorn's worst mistake was when he recommended large cuts in Social Security payments.

4. The reason for the proposal was because he wanted to balance the federal budget.

5. Another cause of his unpopularity with older voters was his endorsement of mandatory retirement at age sixty.

13.11 ADDING THE POSSESSIVE BEFORE A GERUND

Normally a noun or pronoun used before a gerund should be in the possessive case:

▶ Jake winning surprised everyone.

▶ Everyone was surprised by him winning.

The possessive shows that what concerns you is not the person but the action—the winning. When the gerund is followed by a noun, you can use *of* to clarify the meaning:

> Jake's winning of the marathon surprised everyone.

> Everyone was surprised by his winning of the marathon.

For more on the apostrophe, see 34.9–34.10. For more on the possessive case of pronouns, see 20.10.

Adding the Possessive before a Gerund

Revise each of the following sentences in which the writer fails to use the possessive case with a noun or pronoun followed by a gerund. If a sentence is correct as it stands, write *Correct*.

EXAMPLE: Helen shouting startled me.

EDITED: Helen's shouting startled me.

1. Davy Crockett defending the Alamo is one of the great heroic feats in American history.

2. Along with approximately 180 Texans, he chose to fight to the death against an army numbering in the thousands.

3. There was no chance of Davy emerging from the battle alive.

4. With the defenders refusing to raise the white flag, Santa Anna's soldiers would take no prisoners.

5. Since that fateful day in 1836, Americans faced with overwhelming odds have been inspired to hold firm by someone shouting, "Remember the Alamo!"

14 *Modifiers*

14.1 WHAT MODIFIERS DO

A **modifier** is a word or word group that describes, limits, or qualifies another word or word group. Consider this sentence:

> The stag leapt.

This is a **bare-bones sentence**. It has a subject *(stag)* and a predicate *(leapt)*, but no modifiers (except *The*), no words to tell us what the stag looked like or how he leapt. Modifiers can show the reader the size, color, and shape of a thing, or the way an action is performed. Thus they can help to make a sentence vivid, specific, emphatic, and lively:

> *Startled and terrified,* the stag leapt *suddenly from a high rock, bounding and crashing through the dense green woods.*

Modifiers also let you add information without adding more sentences. If you had to start a new sentence for every new piece of detail, you would begin to sound monotonous:

> The stag *leapt.*
>
> He was *startled.*
>
> He leapt *suddenly.*
>
> He leapt *from a rock.*
>
> The rock was *high.*

The stag which is startled & terrified leapt suddenly ··· .

Instead of serving up information in bite-size pieces like these, you can arrange the pieces in one simple sentence, putting each piece where it belongs:

> The *startled* stag leapt *suddenly from a high rock.*

14.2 USING ADJECTIVES AND ADJECTIVE PHRASES

Adjectives modify nouns, specifying such things as what kind and which ones:

> *Complex* problems require *careful* study.

> Investors were *jubilant*.

> The prosecutor, *intense and aggressive*, jabbed her forefinger at the witness.

Adjective phrases begin with a preposition—a word like *with, under, by, in, of,* or *at:*

> Applicants *with experience* found jobs immediately.

> From our house *on the hill* we could see the whole town.

• a probationary faculty with good student evaluations converts to a continuing one automatically

• From my apt. on the 11th floor, I have a good view.

> It was Seymour, *with a big bottle of champagne in his hand, a mile-wide grin on his fat, jolly face, and a triumphant gleam in his eye.*

14.3 OVERUSING NOUNS AS ADJECTIVES

A noun used before another noun often serves as an adjective:

> Cars may not travel in the *bus* lane.

> A *stone* wall surrounded the *dairy* farm.

> An orthopedist is a *bone* doctor.

But the overuse of nouns as adjectives makes a sentence confusing:

> The *fund drive completion target date* postponement gave the finance committee *extension* time to gather *area business* contributions.

In this sentence, too many nouns are lined up, and the reader is left to figure out how they relate to one another. To clarify the statement, turn some of the nouns into ordinary adjectives, and use prepositional phrases:

> Postponement of the final date of the fund drive gave the finance committee more time to gather contributions from local businesses.

14.4 USING ADVERBS AND ADVERB PHRASES

An **adverb** tells such things as how, when, where, why, and for what purpose:

The delegates cheered *loudly.* (adverb modifying verb)

Two bolts were *dangerously* loose. (adverb modifying adjective)

Light travels *amazingly* fast. (adverb modifying another adverb)

Unfortunately, acid rain has damaged many forests. (adverb modifying entire clause)

To form most adverbs, you add *-ly* to an adjective. Thus *quick* becomes *quickly,* and *gruff* becomes *gruffly.* Exceptions are as follows:

1.   A few words (such as *fast, far, well,* and *little*) keep the same form when they turn from adjectives into adverbs:

We made a *fast* stop. (adjective)

We stopped *fast.* (adverb)

2.   Adjectives ending in *-y* must be made to end in *-ily* when they become adverbs:

A *lucky* guess saved me. (adjective)

Luckily, I knew the answer. (adverb)

3.   Adjectives ending in *-ly* do not change their endings when they become adverbs:

A *deadly* blow struck him. (adjective)

He looked *deadly* pale. (adverb)

4.   Some adverbs—such as *never, soon,* and *always*—are not based on adjectives at all and have their own special forms:

The injured child *never* cried.

She will *soon* be walking again.

An **adverb phrase** begins with a preposition—a word such as *at, with, in, or like*—and works like an adverb, telling how, when, or where:

In 1885 a severe drought forced some farmers to increase their mortgages.

The production of machine tools has fallen *behind schedule.*

Tyson used his right fist *like a sledgehammer.*

14.5 MISUSING ADJECTIVES AS ADVERBS

When the adjective form differs from the adverb form, do not use the first in place of the second. In conversation you might say that a car *stopped quick* or that its driver *talked gruff,* but formal writing requires *stopped quickly* and *talked gruffly.* Most adverbs require the *-ly* ending. On *good* and *well, bad* and *badly, poor* and *poorly,* see the Glossary of Usage.

14.6 FORMING AND USING COMPARATIVES AND SUPERLATIVES

The comparative lets you compare one person or thing with another; the superlative lets you compare one person or thing with all others in a group of three or more:

> Jake is *tall.*

> Jake is *taller* than Steve. (comparative)

> Jake is the *tallest* man on the team. (superlative)

COMPARATIVES

A comparative adjective starts a comparison that normally must be completed by *than* plus a noun or noun equivalent:

> Dolphins are *smarter* than sharks.

To form a comparative adjective, add *-er* to most short adjectives. To form the comparative of adjectives ending in *-y,* such as *risky,* change the *-y* to *i* before adding *-er:*

> Skiing is *riskier* than skating.

With a long adjective, form the comparative by using *more* rather than *-er:*

> Are women *more observant* than men?

Use *less* with an adjective of any length:

> Are they any *less quick?*

To form a comparative adverb, use *more* before an adverb ending in *-ly;* otherwise, add *-er.* Use *less* before any adverb:

> The north star shines *more brightly* than any other star.

> Does anything move *faster* than light?

> Roberts campaigned *less effectively* than Johnson did.

SUPERLATIVES

To form a superlative adjective, add *-est* to most short adjectives:

> St. Augustine, Florida, is the *oldest* city in the United States.

> The blue whale is the *largest* of all living creatures.

With a long adjective, form the superlative by using *most* rather than *-est:*

> Forest Lawn Meadow Memorial Park in Los Angeles has been called "the *most cheerful* graveyard in the world."

Use *least* with an adjective of any length:

> According to the *Guinness Book of World Records,* the *least successful* author in the world is William A. Gold, who in eighteen years of writing earned only fifty cents.

Use *most* or *least* to form a superlative adverb:

> The *most lavishly* decorated float in the parade came last.

> Of all grammatical forms, the superlative adverb is perhaps the one *least commonly* used.

IN BRIEF   **Forming Comparatives and Superlatives**

Positive	Comparative	Superlative
high	higher	highest
confident	more confident	most confident
anxious	less anxious	least anxious
carefully	more carefully	most carefully
commonly	less commonly	least commonly

SPECIAL FORMS

Some modifiers have special forms for the comparative and superlative:

	POSITIVE	COMPARATIVE	SUPERLATIVE
good well	[adjective] [adverb] }	better	best
bad badly	[adjective] [adverb] }	worse	worst
little	[adjective and adverb, for quantity]	less	least
much	[adjective and adverb]	more	most
far	[adjective and adverb]	farther	farthest

14.7 MISUSING COMPARATIVES AND SUPERLATIVES

Do nor use -er and *more* or -est and *most* at the same time:

▶ Anthracite is ~~more~~ harder than bituminous coal.

▶ Mount Everest is the ~~most~~ highest peak in the world.

14.8 DOUBLE NEGATIVES

A **double negative** occurs when the writer uses two negative words to make one negative statement:

*The patient didn't want no sleeping pills.

To correct a double negative, remove or change one of the negative words:

EDITED: The patient did not want any sleeping pills.
[or] The patient wanted no sleeping pills.

Negative words include *not (n't), never, hardly, scarcely, barely, none, nothing, no one, no, neither,* and *nor.* Here are further examples of the double negative, with corrections:

▶ People sitting in the back could~~n't~~ hardly hear the speaker.

▶ The foreman ~~didn't give~~ *gave* me nothing but grief.

▶ [or] The foreman didn't give me ~~nothing~~ *anything* but grief.

▶ The other team didn't follow the rules ~~neither.~~ *either.*

For advice on **could care less,* see the Glossary of Usage.

14.9 USING APPOSITIVES

An **appositive** is a noun or noun phrase that identifies another noun phrase or a pronoun:

> Graduation, *the hush-hush magic time of frills and gifts and congratulations and diplomas,* was finished for me before my name was called.
> —Maya Angelou

> Could I, *a knock-kneed beginner,* ever hope to ski down that icy slope without breaking a leg?

An appositive is usually placed right after the word or phrase it identifies. But it may sometimes come just before:

> *A chronic complainer,* he was never satisfied.

Most appositives are set off by commas, as in all the examples above. But you can set off an appositive with dashes if you want to emphasize it, and you should use dashes if the appositive consists of three or more nouns in a series:

> Two athletes—Brandi Chastain and Briana Scurry—helped the U.S. win the Women's World Cup soccer championship.

Use no commas when the appositive identifies the noun just before it and the noun is not preceded by *a* or *the:*

> Reporters questioned city employee *Frank Mason* about the fire. (COMPARE: Reporters questioned a city employee, Frank Mason, about the fire.)

> Film producer *Brenda Budget* has a new project underway.

14.10 USING PARTICIPLES AND PARTICIPLE PHRASES

A **participle** is a word formed from a verb and used to modify a noun; it can enrich any sentence with descriptive detail:

The *sobbing* child stared at the *broken* toy.

A **participle phrase** is a group of words based on a participle:

Her father, *taking her in his arms,* promised to fix it.

Participles may be present, past, or perfect:

1. The **present participle**, formed by the addition of *-ing* to the bare form of the verb, describes a noun as *acting:*

Athletes from fifty nations entered the stadium with *flaming* torches.

Building contractors watch for *falling* interest rates.

Present participles can be expanded into phrases:

Planning every minute of the journey, she studied maps and tourist guides.

The prospector stared in disbelief at the gold dust *shining brightly in his palm.*

2. The **past participle**, commonly formed by the addition of *-d* or *-ed* to the bare form of the verb, describes a noun as *acted upon:*

A *sculpted* figure graced the entrance to the museum.   A figure which was sculpted graced the entrance to the museum.

Past participles can be expanded into phrases:

Politicians *influenced by flattery* talk of victory at receptions *given by self-serving backers.*

In the last sentence, the past participle *given* ends in *-n* because it is formed from an irregular verb, *give.* The past participles of other irregular verbs have various other forms, such as *seen, bought, flung,* and *bred.* (For the past participles of commonly used irregular verbs, see 22.11.)

3. The **perfect participle**, formed with *having* plus a past participle, describes the noun as *having acted—having completed some action:*

Having struck a reef, the supertanker dumped over ten million gallons of oil into the waters of Prince William Sound.

PUNCTUATING PARTICIPLES

Punctuate participles and participle phrases as follows:

1.   Normally, use one or more commas to set off a participle or participle phrase from the word or phrase it modifies:

> *Stalking her prey noiselessly,* the cat crept up to the mouse.

> The mouse, *frightened by a shadow,* darted into a hole.

> The cat squealed, *clawing the hole in vain.*

2.   Don't use commas to set off a single participle when it is part of a noun phrase or when it immediately follows a verb:

> The *exhausted* fighter sank to his knees.

> Let *sleeping* dogs lie.

> Steve walked *muttering* out of the room.

3.   Don't use commas to set off a participle phrase when it restricts—limits—the meaning of the word or phrase it modifies:

> Students *majoring in economics* must take one course in statistics.

For more on restrictive modifiers, see 17.6 and 29.6.

14.11   MISFORMING THE PAST PARTICIPLE

The past participle is misformed in these sentences:

> *For lunch I ate nothing but yogurt and *toss* salad.

> **Prejudice* persons see no difference between one Chicano and another.

If you write this way, it may be because you speak this way, not pronouncing the final *-d* and *-ed* when they are needed. To hear the difference those endings make, see if you can make them audible as you read the following sentences aloud:

> EDITED: For lunch I ate nothing but yogurt and *tossed* salad.

> EDITED: *Prejudiced* persons see no difference between one Chicano and another.

Participles

Present participle:	planning
Present participle phrase:	planning every minute of the journey
Past participle:	influenced
Past participle phrase:	influenced by flattery
Perfect participle:	having lost
Perfect participle phrase:	having lost the election

Sentence Combining with Modifiers

Combine the sentences in each of the following sets by using the first sentence as a base and adding modifiers from the others. Some modifiers may have to be combined with each other before they can be joined to the base sentence. Combine the sentences of each set in at least two different ways. Then, if you prefer one of the combinations, put a check next to it.

EXAMPLE:

The bird sailed.
He did so for hours.
He was searching the grasses.
The grasses were blanched.
The grasses were below him.
He was searching with his eyes.
The eyes were telescopic.
He was gaining height.
He was gaining it against the wind.
He was descending in swoops.
The swoops were mile-long.
The swoops were gently declining.
—deliberately altered from a sentence by Walter Van Tilburg Clark

COMBINATION 1: The bird sailed for hours, searching the blanched grasses below him with his telescopic eyes, gaining height against the wind, descending in mile-long, gently declining swoops.
—Walter Van Tilburg Clark

COMBINATION 2: Searching the blanched grasses below him with his telescopic eyes, gaining height against the wind, descending in mile-long, gently declining swoops, the bird sailed for hours.

(Continued on p. 272.)

1. Wally sang.
   He was soulful.
   He was swaying.
   He was sensuous.
   He was dressed in a skinsuit.
   The skinsuit was glittering.
   The skinsuit was white.
   The skinsuit was satin.
   He was stroking his guitar.
   The guitar was blue.
   The guitar was electric.
   He stroked with fingers.
   The fingers were long.
   The fingers were pink.
   The fingers were nimble.

2. The spotlight illuminated his form.
   The spotlight was dim.
   His form was slender.
   The illumination was faint.
   The spotlight drew him out of the darkness.
   He looked like an apparition.
   The darkness was clammy.

3. He sang about a woman.
   The woman was young.
   She had red hair.
   She was dressed in a raincoat.
   The raincoat was shiny.
   The raincoat was black.
   She was standing on a street corner.
   The street corner was in New York.
   The street corner was crowded.
   She was waiting for a bus.

4. She waited in a certain mood.
   Her mood was restless.
   She clutched a suitcase.
   It was big.
   It was vinyl.
   It was white.
   Stickers covered it.
   They were marked "Broadway or Bust."

5. She had just arrived from a town.
   The town was little.
   It was in Oregon.
   It was in the eastern part.
   She was filled with ambition.
   She was dreaming of a career.
   The career would be great.
   It would be in the theater.

Sentence Expanding with Modifiers

Expand five of the following sentences by adding as many modifiers as possible. Let your imagination go.

1. The gorilla roared.

2. The flames crackled.

3. The clown danced.

4. The rock-climber slipped.

5. The building shook.

6. The waiter stumbled.

7. The piñata cracked.

8. The boy cried.

9. The dog growled.

10. The curtain rose.

14.12 USING INFINITIVES AND INFINITIVE PHRASES

The **infinitive** (usually made by placing *to* before the bare form of the verb) can be used to modify various parts of a sentence:

> Civilization has never eradicated the urge *to hunt.*

> My favorite time *to run* is early in the morning.

> Determined *to succeed,* she redoubled her efforts.

> In every situation Chester plays *to win.*

Infinitives can form phrases:

> *To write grammatically,* you must know something about sentence structure.

> On August 27, 1966, Sir Francis Chichester set out *to sail a fifty-three-foot boat single-handedly around the world.*

Infinitives with *have* and *have been* plus a participle identify an action or condition completed before another one:

> The work to be done that morning seemed enormous. Sandra was glad *to have slept* a full eight hours the night before. But she was annoyed *to have been told* nothing of this work earlier.

EXERCISE 3   **Supplying Infinitives**

Complete each of the following sentences with a suitable infinitive or infinitive phrase.

EXAMPLE: The sheer will ____ brought him through the operation.

to live

1. Throughout history a compelling desire ____ the unknown has led men and women ____.

2. Almost eight hundred years ago Vikings sailed west ____.

3. In recent years adventurous explorers like Jacques Cousteau have developed special underwater equipment ____.

4. The wish ____ has taken astronauts to the moon, and may someday take others beyond the solar system.

5. The growth of the Internet has vastly improved our ability ____.

6. Now that genetic engineers have cloned a sheep, will they ever have the power ____?

14.13 AVOIDING THE SPLIT INFINITIVE

When one or more adverbs are wedged between *to* and a verb form, the infinitive is split:

> Detectives needed special equipment to *thoroughly and accurately* investigate the mystery.

This sentence is weakened by the cumbersome splitting. The adverbs should go at the end of the infinitive phrase:

> EDITED: Detectives needed special equipment to investigate the mystery *thoroughly and accurately.*

Sometimes an infinitive may be split by a one-word modifier that would be awkward in any other position:

> The mayors convened in order to *fully* explore and discuss the problems of managing large cities.

A construction of this type is acceptable nowadays to most readers. But unless you are sure there is no other suitable place in the sentence for the adverb or adverb phrase, do not split an infinitive with it.

Editing Split Infinitives

EXERCISE 4

Each of the following sentences contains a split infinitive. If you find the split awkward, revise the word order to get rid of it. If you find the split necessary, write *Acceptable.*

EXAMPLE: He was sorry to have ~~rudely~~ answered/ *rudely.*

1. The nurse took a deep breath before starting to gently remove the bandage from the child's stomach.

2. The child, in turn, began to with strong determination resist her.

3. He exercised all of his cunning to quickly distract her attention from the task.

4. Then, after running out of distractions, he decided to at the last moment grab her hands and bite them.

5. To fully control the little boy, the nurse had to ask an aide for help.

14.14 USING ABSOLUTE PHRASES

An **absolute phrase** usually consists of a noun or noun phrase followed by a participle. It can modify a noun, a pronoun, or an entire clause:

> Donna laughed, *her eyes flashing with mischief.*

> *Its fuel line blocked,* the engine sputtered to a halt.

The participle may sometimes be omitted:

> *Head down,* the bull charged straight at the matador.

> *Nose in the air,* she walked right past me.

You can form compounds with absolute phrases, and you can use them in succession anywhere in a sentence:

> *Its freshly painted walls gleaming in the sunlight and dazzling the beholder,* the factory symbolized economic progress.

> The village was silent, *its shops closed, the streets deserted.*

> The skaters are quick-silvering around the frosty rink, *the girls gliding and spinning, the boys swooping, their arms flailing like wings.*
> —college student

EXERCISE 5   **Sentence Combining with Absolute Phrases**

Combine the sentences in each of the following sets by using the first sentence as a base and turning the others into absolute phrases.

EXAMPLE:

Finch dozed.

His chin was resting on his chest.

COMBINED: Finch dozed, his chin resting on his chest.

1. Janet rode the big wave.
   Her shoulders were hunched.
   Her hair was streaming in the wind.
   Her toes were curled over the edge of the board.

2. The board sped forward.
   Its slender frame was propelled by surging water.

3. Janet yelled with delight.
   Her heart was pounding.
   Her eyes were sparkling with excitement.

4. Meanwhile, the lifeguard gripped the arms of his chair.
   His knuckles were white.
   His hair was standing on end.
   His stomach was heaving.

14.15 PLACING MODIFIERS

One of the hardest things about writing an effective sentence is that unless you can plan it out completely in your head beforehand, you may not know at once the best way to arrange all of its parts. You know by habit, of course, that an adjective usually comes before the noun it modifies. You don't write *leaves green* or *fumes smelly* or *brass hot;* you write *green leaves, smelly fumes,* and *hot brass.* But the placing of other modifiers—especially modifying phrases—may call for some thought. Often, in fact, you will not be able to decide where to put a particular modifier until *after* you have written out the whole sentence in which it appears.

While you are writing a sentence, therefore, don't worry right away about where to place the modifiers. You can often start with the base sentence and put the modifiers at the end, using one modifier to lead you to another. See how this sentence grows:

> Mary traveled.

Where from?

> Mary traveled *from* Denver.

Where to?

> Mary traveled *from Denver to San Francisco.*

How?

> Mary traveled *from Denver to San Francisco by hitchhiking.*

Did she hitchhike all the way?

> Mary traveled *from Denver to San Francisco by hitchhiking to the house of a friend in Salt Lake City.*

And how did she finish the trip?

> Mary traveled *from Denver to San Francisco by hitchhiking to the house of a friend in Salt Lake City and then borrowing his motorcycle to make the rest of the trip.*

Now, having written your base sentence and added as many modifiers as you want, you can think about where to place those modifiers. You may decide, for instance, that you want to put most of them up front instead of at the end. In that case, bracket the words you want to move and use an arrow to show where they are to go:

> Mary traveled from Denver to San Francisco [by hitchhiking to the house of a friend in Salt Lake City and then borrowing his motorcycle to make the rest of the trip].

When you rewrite the sentence, it will look like this:

> By hitchhiking to the house of a friend in Salt Lake City and then borrowing his motorcycle to make the rest of the trip, Mary traveled from Denver to San Francisco.

Do you like this version better than the other? That's the kind of question you will have to answer for yourself. If you want to state a simple point and then develop it, you will lead with that point and then put the modifiers after it. But if you want to create suspense, you will put all or most of your modifiers first. In that position they signal that the main point is coming at the end, where it gets special emphasis. (For more discussion of how to emphasize your main point, see 17.1 and 17.10.)

Placing a modifier well means connecting the modifier to its **headword**—the word or phrase it modifies. If the modifier doesn't clearly point to its headword, the modifier is *misplaced;* if the headword is missing from the sentence, the modifier *dangles.*

14.16 EDITING MISPLACED MODIFIERS

A **misplaced modifier** does not point clearly to its headword—the word or phrase it modifies:

1. *I asked her for the time while waiting for the bus to start a conversation.

The sentence seems to say that the bus was ready to start a conversation. To get the meaning straight, put the modifying phrase right before its headword—*I:*

> EDITED: To start a conversation, I asked her for the time while waiting for the bus.

2. *The college librarian announced that all fines on overdue books will be doubled yesterday.

The sentence puts the future into yesterday or yesterday into the future. Either way, it makes no sense:

> EDITED: The college librarian announced yesterday that all fines on overdue books will be doubled.

EDITING SQUINTING MODIFIERS

A squinting modifier is one placed where it could modify either of two possible headwords:

> *The street vendor she saw on her way to school occasionally sold wild mushrooms.

Did she see the vendor occasionally, or did he sell wild mushrooms occasionally?

> EDITED: The street vendor she occasionally saw on her way to school sold wild mushrooms.
>
> [or] The street vendor she saw on her way to school sold wild mushrooms occasionally.

EDITING MISPLACED RESTRICTERS

A restricter is a one-word modifier that limits the meaning of another word or a group of words. Restricters include *almost, only, merely, nearly, scarcely, simply, even, exactly, just,* and *hardly.* Usually a restricter modifies the word or phrase that immediately follows it:

1. *Only* the Fabulous Fork serves brunch on Sundays.

2. The Fabulous Fork serves *only* brunch on Sundays.

3. The Fabulous Fork serves brunch *only* on Sundays.

A restricter placed at the end of a sentence modifies the word or phrase just before it:

4. The Fabulous Fork serves brunch on Sundays *only.*

If you place *only* carelessly, you will confuse your reader:

> *The Fabulous Fork only serves brunch on Sundays.

Is brunch the only meal it serves on Sundays, or is Sunday the only day on which it serves brunch? The meaning becomes plain only when *only* stands right next to *brunch* or *on Sundays,* as shown above in sentences 2, 3, and 4.

Editing Misplaced Modifiers

Revise each of the following sentences that includes one or more misplaced modifiers, squinting modifiers, or misplaced restricters. If a sentence is correct, write *Correct*.

EXAMPLE: An article describes the way skunks eat ~~in this magazine.~~
in this magazine

1. Alvin Toffler states that young Americans are becoming consumers of disposable goods in a well-known essay.

2. After just keeping an item for a few months, children want to throw it out and get something new.

3. I have learned that this practice marks a change from conversations with my grandparents.

4. In their childhood, a girl only played with one doll for years.

5. Then, wrapped in tissue paper, she would put it away against the day when she would present it to a daughter or a niece with fond memories.

6. Likewise a boy would keep his electric train so that he could one day give it to his children carefully boxed.

7. There are several reasons why children no longer keep toys in this way according to Toffler.

8. One is the impact of industrialization and in particular of mass production.

9. Most toys were made by craftspeople who devoted years to just mastering their trade and hours to carefully shaping each product by hand until the late 1800s.

10. Toys were expensive and hard to get as a result; but each was a treasure, a unique creation.

11. Today large machines make toys in seconds, and each looks just like all the others of its kind.

12. Most of these mass-produced toys only captivate children for a short time and then wind up in the trash.

13. Another reason why modern toys soon lose their appeal is that they are made of plastic commonly.

14. Plastic almost costs nothing to make; and when painted in bright, vivid colors, it can seem shiny and desirable.

15. But unlike such materials as leather and wood, plastic does not mellow with age.

16. Finally, children are pressured to be habitual consumers by advertising.

17. With TV and catalogs continually showing them new toys, how can they learn to cherish their old ones?

14.17 EDITING DANGLING MODIFIERS

A modifier dangles when its headword is missing. Since a modifier always needs a headword, it will attach itself to a false one if the true one is not in the sentence.

> *After doing my homework, the dog was fed.

And any dog that can do your homework for you certainly deserves his food! Unless the dog is unusually clever, though, this sentence contains a dangling modifier. You can eliminate it by saying who actually did the homework:

> EDITED: After I did my homework, the dog was fed.

But this version still doesn't tell us who fed the dog. It fails to do so because *The dog was fed* is in the passive voice and does not mention the agent—the one *by whom* the dog was fed. That agent should be named:

> The dog was fed by me.

Once you've named the agent, you can turn this sentence from the passive to the active voice (chapter 24):

> I fed the dog.

Now you can write:

> After I did my homework, I fed the dog.

Or you can drop the first *I* and change *did* to *doing*:

> After doing my homework, I fed the dog.

Here is one more example:

> *Based on the gradual decline in College Board scores over the past twenty years, American high school education is less effective than it used to be.

There is a miscombination of two sentences:

> American high school education is less effective than it used to be. This conclusion is based on the gradual decline of College Board scores over the past twenty years.

So how can you combine these two sentences and not leave *Based* dangling? We suggest you kick the *Based* habit altogether. To combine sentences like these, use *shows that, indicates that,* or *leads to the conclusion that:*

> EDITED: The gradual decline of College Board scores over the past twenty years indicates that American high school education is less effective than it used to be.

Spotting Misused Modifiers

Misplaced modifier:

> *I asked her for the time while waiting for the bus *to start a conversation.*

Squinting modifier:

> *The street vendor she saw on her way to school *occasionally* sold wild mushrooms.

Misplaced restricter:

> *The Fabulous Fork *only* serves brunch on Sundays.

Dangling modifier

> **After doing my homework,* the dog was fed.

Editing Dangling Modifiers

Revise each of the following sentences that includes a dangling modifier. Either supply a suitable headword as best you can or reconstruct the whole sentence. If a sentence is correct as it stands, write *Correct.*

EXAMPLE: After checking the figures, the new budget was rejected.

EDITED: After checking the figures, the voters rejected the new budget.

1. At six each morning, the ringing of my alarm clock stirs me from a sound sleep.

2. Crawling from my bed, my black wool cycling shorts are put on, along with my green-and-black shirt.

3. I grope my way into the kitchen and unlock the back door onto the breezeway connecting the house to the garage.

4. As I face the early morning light, my breath is visible, chilled by the cold air.

5. Hastily pulling on my shoes and tightening my helmet strap, no help from my brain seems to be needed by my hands.

6. My legs begin to wake up wheeling the bicycle out of the garage.

7. Once peddling along the road, my circulation quickens, and I no longer feel cold.

8. Turning left at Bank Street and beginning the rapid descent to River Road, the air rushes through my helmet and causes my eyes to water uncontrollably.

9. My senses are fully awakened, and I hear the swishing sound made by the tires speeding over the pavement.

10. Exhilarated, my bike is pushed forward, eager to outrace the sun.

11. Sixty minutes later I am becoming tired, straining to push myself up every hill.

12. Reaching the top of a long rise, a short break is taken before turning back and heading home.

13. The morning sun has won the race, just as it always does when pedaling to the point of exhaustion.

Editing Misused Modifiers

EXERCISE 8

Edit the following passage by correcting all misused modifiers:

The *New York Times Magazine* publishes often striking advertisements. One example is an ad for Movado watches, which are made in Switzerland from a recent issue of the magazine. Standing in the center of a ten-by-fifteen-inch page, with pitch-black fur, the ad shows a cat focusing its bright golden eyes on a fishbowl filled with sand, water, and white coral. But the fishbowl contains no fish. Resting among the pieces of coral, it only contains two Movado watches. Below the fishbowl are a brief description of the watches and the words "Movado, a century of Swiss Watchcraft" printed in large white letters.   10

The ad designer has created an eerie effect by almost covering half the page in black, hiding the body of the cat in darkness, and only showing its head in a dim glow of light. Looking down at the fishbowl, the watches are being eyed by the cat as if they were fish. But the watches also look like the cat. Set in a gold case, one has a   15
black face, while the other has a gold face set in a black case. Thus both watches match the colors of the cat's eyes and fur.

The ad succeeds because it catches the reader's attention. Leafing through the magazine, the mysterious-looking cat will strike the average reader, and, submerged in a fishbowl, he or she will certainly   20
examine the watches. The combination of gold and black under water will make them look like treasures discovered at the bottom of the sea.

15 *Coordination: Compound Sentences*

To coordinate two or more parts of a sentence is to give them the same rank and role by making them grammatically alike. As we noted in 13.8, you can coordinate words or phrases to make a compound phrase. In this chapter we show how you can coordinate simple sentences to make a *compound sentence.*

15.1 MAKING COMPOUND SENTENCES

A compound sentence consists of two or more independent clauses joined by conjunctions, semicolons, or conjunctive adverbs. Each clause is called independent (IC) because each could stand by itself as a complete sentence:

IC	JOINED TO	IC	JOINED BY
They acquired horses	and	their ancient nomadic spirit was suddenly free of the ground. —N. Scott Momaday	conjunc
History does not stutter	;	it rhymes.	semicol
The average age for women to marry in Ireland is twenty-six;	in contrast,	women of India marry at an average age of fourteen.	conjunc adverb

15.2 COMPOUNDING WITH CONJUNCTIONS

Conjunctions include the set of words commonly known as "A. B. Fonsy": *and, but, for, or, nor, so,* and *yet.* They show the following relations:

1. SIMPLE ADDITION

   The economists considered budget cuts, *and* the politicians thought of votes.

2. ADDITION OF A NEGATIVE POINT

   Many of the settlers had never farmed before, *nor* were they ready for the brutal Saskatchewan winters.

3. CONTRAST

   The delegates came to discuss world trade, *but* the protestors wanted to stop them.

   All the candidates claim to understand Europeans, *yet* none has ever lived in Europe.

4. LOGICAL CONSEQUENCE

   My father never attended the military parades in the city, *for* he hated war.

   During World War II, Americans of Japanese descent were unjustly suspected of disloyalty, *so* they were placed in detention camps.

For introduces a reason; *so* introduces a consequence.

5. CHOICE

   Nelson could keep his ships near England, *or* he could order them to attack the French in Egypt.

PUNCTUATION WITH CONJUNCTIONS

A conjunction used between independent clauses normally needs a comma just before it, as shown by all the examples above. But there are two exceptions.

1. You can omit the comma when the clauses are short:

   Many are called but few are chosen.

2.   You can replace the comma with a semicolon when there are commas elsewhere in the sentence:

> On the morning of June 28, 1969, the weather finally cleared; but the climbers, wearied by their efforts of the previous days, could not attempt the summit.

You can use a comma without a conjunction when there are more than two clauses, but you should normally use a conjunction between the last two:

> The sun shone, a stiff breeze ruffled the bay, the sails bellied out, and the bow cut the water like a knife.

15.3   OVERUSING *AND*

Use *and* sparingly in compound sentences. A series of clauses strung together by *and* can become boring:

> I was born in Illinois, and the first big city I ever saw was Chicago, and was I ever excited! I went there with my father and mother, and we stayed in a big hotel in the Loop, and I saw lots of interesting sights. We spent a whole day just walking around the city, and I got a stiff neck from looking up at the skyscrapers, and my feet got sore too from walking down so many streets. I was glad to go back to the hotel and take a long soak in the Jacuzzi.

To break the monotony of compounding with *and,* substitute other linking words—or other constructions:

> Since I was born in Illinois, the first big city I ever saw was Chicago. Was I ever excited! My father and mother took me to a big hotel in the Loop. On the day after our arrival, we spent eight hours just walking around the city to see the sights. It was exhausting. In fact, I got a stiff neck from looking up at all the skyscrapers and sore feet from walking down so many streets. I couldn't wait to take a long soak in the Jacuzzi at our hotel.

For alternatives to the overuse of *and* constructions, see chapter 17.

15.4 COMPOUNDING WITH THE SEMICOLON

A semicolon alone can join two independent clauses when the relationship between them is obvious:

Some books are undeservedly forgotten	;	none are undeservedly remembered

—W. H. Auden

Too much, perhaps, has been said of his silence	;	too much stress has been laid upon his reserve.

—Virginia Woolf

15.5 COMPOUNDING WITH CONJUNCTIVE ADVERBS

A conjunctive adverb—sometimes called a sentence adverb—is a word or phrase that shows a relation between the clauses it joins, as a conjunction does. But a conjunctive adverb is usually weightier and more emphatic than a conjunction:

The Iron Duke had complete confidence in his soldiers' training and valor; *furthermore,* he considered his battle plan a work of genius.

Conjunctive adverbs indicate the following relations between one clause and another:

1. ADDITION *(besides, furthermore, moreover, in addition)*

   Some economists oppose legislation restricting foreign trade; *in addition,* they attack proposals to increase corporate taxes.

2. LIKENESS *(likewise, similarly, in the same way)*

   Many young Englishmen condemned the English war against France in the 1790s; *likewise,* many young Americans condemned the American war against North Vietnam in the 1960s.

3. CONTRAST *(however, nevertheless, still, nonetheless, conversely, otherwise, instead, in contrast, on the other hand)*

   Einstein's theory of relativity was largely the product of speculation; experiments made within the past fifty years, *however,* have confirmed many of its basic points.

4. **CAUSE AND EFFECT** (*accordingly, consequently, hence, therefore, as a result, for this reason*)

> Chamberlain made an ill-considered peace treaty with Hitler after the German invasion of Czechoslovakia; *as a result,* England was unprepared for the German invasion of Poland.

5. **A MEANS-AND-END RELATION** (*thus, thereby, by this means, in this manner*)

> Florence Nightingale organized a unit of thirty-eight nurses for the Crimean War in the 1850s; *thus* she became a legend.

6. **REINFORCEMENT** (*for example, for instance, in fact, in particular, indeed*)

> Public transportation will also be vastly improved; a high-speed train, *for instance,* will take passengers from Montreal to Toronto in less than two hours.

7. **TIME** (*meanwhile, then, subsequently, afterward, earlier, later*)

> At first, members of the audience were overtly hostile to the speaker; *later,* they cheered her as one of their own.

As items 3 and 6 show, you may use a conjunctive adverb *within* a clause, not just before its subject.

PUNCTUATION WITH CONJUNCTIVE ADVERBS

A conjunctive adverb normally takes punctuation on either side of it. The punctuation depends on where the conjunctive adverb is used:

1.   When used *between* two independent clauses, the conjunctive adverb is normally preceded by a semicolon and followed by a comma:

> Townspeople consider the covered bridge a link to a golden age; *as a result,* they have voted funds for its restoration.

2.   Some conjunctive adverbs (including *thus, then, still, otherwise,* and *hence*) may begin a clause with no comma after them:

> The rise of the dollar against foreign currencies drives up the price of our exports; *thus* we lose customers abroad.

3.   When used *within* the second clause, the conjunctive adverb is normally set off by commas:

> Jackson did not get the nomination; he managed, *however,* to win the votes of over one thousand delegates.

EXCEPTION: Some conjunctive adverbs, including *therefore, nevertheless, nonetheless, instead,* and those mentioned above in entry 2, may be used without commas when they are placed just before the main verb:

> The hole in the ozone layer is steadily growing; we must therefore stop sending fluorocarbons into the atmosphere.

Joining Independent Clauses

IN BRIEF

The independent clauses (IC) of a compound sentence are normally joined in one of the following three ways:

1. __IC__ ; __IC__ when the relation between clauses is obvious.
2. __IC__ , conjunction __IC__ to make the relation explicit.
3. __IC__ ; conjunctive adverb, __IC__ to make the relation emphatic. (Placement of the conjunctive adverb is optional)

Sentence Combining to Make Compound Sentences

EXERCISE 1

Using a semicolon, a conjunction, or a conjunctive adverb, combine the sentences in each of the following sets into a single sentence. Whenever you use a conjunction or conjunctive adverb, state in parentheses the relationship it shows.

EXAMPLE:

We are all in the gutter.
Some of us are looking at the stars.

COMBINED: We are all in the gutter, but some of us are looking at the stars. (contrast)   —Oscar Wilde

1. In sixteenth-century England women with literary talent undoubtedly wrote.
   None was encouraged to publish her work.

2. In the nineteenth century, Jane Austen earned little acclaim for her novels.
   Today they are considered masterpieces.

3. Some writers gain fame with their first major work.
   Others win fame later or possibly never.

4. Harriet Beecher Stowe became widely known with the publication of *Uncle Tom's Cabin* in 1852.
   Emily Dickinson remained unacclaimed until fifty years after her death.

(Continued on p. 290.)

5. James Joyce was a painstaking writer.
   He once spent half a day on the composition of a single sentence.

6. Ernest Hemingway would have sympathized with Joyce.
   Hemingway rewrote the last page of *A Farewell to Arms* thirty-nine times.

7. In his later years John O'Hara is said to have disregarded revision altogether.
   He typed his pages and mailed them untouched to his publisher.

8. Fictions become reality for some writers.
   Balzac's characters walked about on his desk, speaking, striving, suffering.

9. Georges Simenon used to impersonate his main characters before writing about them.
   His wife had to cope with a series of strangers.

10. Joseph Conrad's native language was Polish.
    He wrote his novels and short stories in English.

15.6 EDITING COMMA SPLICES

The **comma splice** is the error of joining two independent clauses—two possible sentences—with nothing but a comma:

> *One of the runners suffered from heat exhaustion, she collapsed two miles from the finish.

When you use the comma to join or splice two distinct statements, you are probably trying to keep two related points together in one sentence. But the comma alone cannot do that for you. You should therefore do one of four things:

1. PUT A CONJUNCTION AFTER THE COMMA:

   EDITED: One of the runners suffered from heat exhaustion, so she collapsed two miles from the finish.

2. REPLACE THE COMMA WITH A SEMICOLON:

   EDITED: One of the runners suffered from heat exhaustion; she collapsed two miles from the finish.

3. **REPLACE THE COMMA WITH A SEMICOLON AND A CONJUNCTIVE ADVERB:**

    EDITED: One of the runners suffered from heat exhaustion; as a result, she collapsed two miles from the finish.

4. **REPLACE THE COMMA WITH A PERIOD, MAKING TWO SENTENCES:**

    EDITED: One of the runners suffered from heat exhaustion. She collapsed two miles from the finish.

Sometimes a comma splice occurs when the second clause in a sentence begins with a conjunctive adverb:

> *Most working people get at least one raise a year, nevertheless, inflation often leaves them with no increase in buying power.

A conjunctive adverb used between two clauses must be preceded by a semicolon:

> EDITED: Most working people get at least one raise a year; nevertheless, inflation often leaves them with no increase in buying power.

Alternatively, you can use a period, making two sentences:

> EDITED: Most working people get at least one raise a year. Nevertheless, inflation often leaves them with no increase in buying power.

Editing Comma Splices

Some of the following entries contain a comma splice. If you find one, correct it. If the punctuation is correct, write *Correct*.

> EXAMPLE: The chemicals lodge in soil ; they also enter streams and ponds.

1. The sculpture represents Don Quixote and his horse Rocinante, the Don is the most famous knight in Spanish literature.

2. The knight looks ready for adventure, perhaps he has spotted giants disguised as windmills.

3. His left hand is grasping a shield, his right hand holds a sturdy lance.

4. The appeal of the small work lies in its materials, they could have been the contents of a mechanic's trash can.

(Continued on p. 292.)

5. The sculptor has used bolts, screws, washers, and scraps of sheet metal, they are all painted a flat black.

6. Rocinante's head, neck, and muzzle are a single unit made from a small elbow joint; and her body is an L-shaped allen wrench, with the smaller part forming a tail.

7. Welded to the body are four legs, they are made from socket head cap screws.

8. Slanting outward and to the rear, they give an impression of movement.

9. The Don's body is a threaded carriage bolt, one end is welded to the back of Rocinante.

10. The top of the bolt is rounded, and it represents a Spanish sombrero.

11. The Don's arms are made from two allen wrenches, in fact, they curve around his back to create the image of shoulders.

12. Two more allen wrenches form legs. Bent at the knees, they end in small globs of welding rods, the rods are molded to resemble boots with tiny spurs.

13. The knight's shield is a thin metal plate, its rough edges and solder marks give it a battle-scarred look.

14. The lance is not particularly long, nonetheless, it looks like a potent weapon.

15. Supporting both the horse and the man is a hefty-looking washer, the base of the piece.

15.7 EDITING RUN-ON (FUSED) SENTENCES

A run-on sentence, sometimes called a fused sentence, joins two independent clauses—two possible sentences—with no punctuation or conjunction between them:

> *Emily listened to the lobster boats chugging out to sea from the cove she watched the gulls sailing overhead.

Here the first independent clause simply pushes into the second one. We cannot tell for sure where the first one ends. Is its last word *sea* or *cove?*

You make this error when your thoughts come in a rush, outrunning your hand. You are most likely to find the error by reading your sentences aloud, listening for the drop in your voice to tell you where one statement (or independent clause) ends and another begins. When you find that point and see no punctuation to mark it, do one of four things:

1. **USE A COMMA AND A CONJUNCTION BETWEEN THE CLAUSES:**

   EDITED: Emily listened to the lobster boats chugging out to sea from the cove, and she watched the gulls sailing overhead.

2. **USE A SEMICOLON BETWEEN THE CLAUSES:**

   EDITED: Emily listened to the lobster boats chugging out to sea from the cove; she watched the gulls sailing overhead.

3. **USE A SEMICOLON AND A CONJUNCTIVE ADVERB BETWEEN THE CLAUSES:**

   EDITED: Emily listened to the lobster boats chugging out to sea from the cove; then she watched the gulls sailing overhead.

4. **USE A PERIOD AT THE END OF THE FIRST CLAUSE.** You will then have two sentences:

   EDITED: Emily listened to the lobster boats chugging out to sea from the cove. She watched the gulls sailing overhead.

Editing Comma Splices and Run-on (Fused) Sentences

EXERCISE 3

In some of the following sentences, the punctuation is faulty. Correct any mistakes you find, adding words where necessary. If a sentence is correct as it stands, write *Correct*.

EXAMPLE: Cloudy days tend to make us gloomy⁄sunny days, in contrast, make us cheerful.

1. On the coast of Maine is the small town of Pirates Cove it resembles the old New England seaports depicted in paintings hanging in country inns and seafood restaurants.

2. The narrow streets are paved with irregularly shaped bricks these make walking an adventure.

3. Most of the buildings have a weathered look the shingles are gray and the blue of the shutters is faded from exposure to the salt air.

4. At the harbor picturesque rock formations glisten in the sunlight, and the hulls of freshly painted fishing boats bob in the waves.

5. Completing the scene is a welcome touch of wildness large white gulls swoop over the boats and various clam shells lie on the sand.

6. Walking on the beach I collect the shells, they slide and rattle in my bucket as I step over rocks.

16 *Parallel Construction*

16.1 WHY CHOOSE PARALLELISM?

Parallel construction, also called **parallelism**, shows that two or more ideas are equally important by stating them in grammatically parallel form: noun lined up with noun, verb with verb, phrase with phrase. Parallelism can lend clarity, elegance, and symmetry to what you say:

> I *came;*
>
> I *saw;*
>
> I *conquered.*
>
> —Julius Caesar

Using three simple verbs to list the things he did, Caesar makes coming, seeing, and conquering all equal in importance. He also implies that for him, conquering was as easy as coming and seeing.

> In many ways writing is the act *of saying* I,
> *of imposing* oneself upon
> other people,
> *of saying listen* to me,
> *see* it my way,
> *change* your
> mind.
>
> —Joan Didion

Didion gives equal importance to saying *I*, imposing oneself, and voicing certain commands. Furthermore, she builds one parallel construction into another. Using a series of imperative verbs, she puts equal weight on *listen, see,* and *change.* The result is a rhetorically commanding definition of the act of writing.

We look for signs in every strange event; we search for heroes in every unknown face.

—Alice Walker

Walker stresses our searching by making the second half of this sentence
exactly parallel with the first.

16.2 WRITING PARALLEL CONSTRUCTIONS

To write parallel constructions, put two or more coordinate items into the
same grammatical form:

I have nothing to offer but *blood, toil, tears,* and *sweat.*

—Winston Churchill

Churchill uses four nouns to identify what he offers the British people in
wartime.

. . . and that government *of the people, by the people, for the people* shall not
perish from the earth.

—Abraham Lincoln

Lincoln uses three prepositional phrases to describe the essential characteristics of American democracy.

On all these shores there are echoes *of past and future: of the flow of time,
obliterating* yet *containing* all that has gone before.

—Rachel Carson

Carson uses two prepositional phrases about time, and then a pair of
participles to contrast its effects.

We must indeed all hang together, or most assuredly *we shall all hang
separately.*

—Benjamin Franklin

Franklin uses two parallel clauses to stress the difference between two
equally pressing alternatives.

A *living dog* is better than a *dead lion.*

—Ecclesiastes

The likeness in form between the two phrases lets us clearly see how much
they differ in meaning.

16.3   USING CORRELATIVES WITH PARALLELISM

Correlatives are words or phrases used in pairs to join words, phrases, or clauses. The principal correlatives are *both . . . and, not only . . . but also, either . . . or, neither . . . nor,* and *whether . . . or.* When using correlatives to highlight a parallel construction, be sure that the word or word group following the first member of the pair is parallel with the word or word group following the second:

> Before the Polish strikes of 1980, *both* the Hungarians *and* the Czechs tried in vain to defy Soviet authority.

> His speech *not only* outraged his opponents, *but (also) cost* him the support of his own party. (*Also* is optional here.)

> Near the end of the story Daniel Webster threatens to wrestle with the devil *either* on Earth *or* in hell.

> In the nineteenth century, tuberculosis spared *neither* the wealthy *nor* the poor.

EXERCISE 1   **Recognizing Parallel Elements**

Each of the following sentences contains one or more parallel constructions. Write down the parallel elements.

EXAMPLE: Crawling down a mountain is often harder than climbing up.

Crawling down, climbing up

1. The cosmic ulcer comes not from great concerns but from little irritations.

   —John Steinbeck

2. She was impervious to lies or foolish excuses or the insufferable plea of not knowing any better.

   —Eudora Welty

3. I went to the woods because I wished to live deliberately, to front only the essential facts of life.

   —Henry David Thoreau

4. I open my eyes and I see dark, muscled forms curl out of water, with flapping gills and flattened eyes.

   —Annie Dillard

5. What is written without effort is in general read without pleasure.

   —Samuel Johnson

16.4 EDITING FAULTY PARALLELISM

When two or more parts of a sentence are parallel in meaning, you should coordinate them fully by making them parallel in form. If you don't, the faulty parallelism may jar your reader:

▶ The Allies decided to invade Italy and then ~~that they would~~ *to* launch a

massive assault on the Normandy coast.

Here are further examples:

▶ I like swimming, skiing, and ~~to hike~~ *hiking* in the mountains.

▶ [or] I like ~~swimming, skiing,~~ *to swim, ski,* and ~~to~~ hike in the mountains.

▶ Either we must make nuclear power safe*, we must* or stop using it.

▶ [or] ~~Either~~ *W* we must make nuclear power safe *either* or stop using it.

In sentences made with correlatives, each correlative goes just before one of the parallel items.

▶ The more I see of men, *the more likable* I find dogs. ~~more likable.~~

—Madame de Staël

▶ My idea of heaven is a great big baked potato, and ~~I would like~~

someone to share it with.

—Oprah Winfrey

▶ They fought in the streets, *in* the fields, and in the woods.

In a series of phrases beginning with a word such as *to* or *in*, repeat the word before each phrase or don't repeat it at all after the first one (*in the streets, the fields, and the woods*).

                   Editing Faulty Parallelism

Revise each of the following sentences that is marred by faulty parallelism. If a sentence is correct as it stands, write *Correct*.

> EXAMPLE: You can improve your performance ~~if you master~~ *by mastering* the fundamentals and by training daily.

1. Ancient Greek myths often describe the exploits of heroes confronting threats from violent men, evil monsters, and the gods sometimes menace them as well.

2. The heroes seek undying fame, not to become wealthy or live peacefully.

3. They generally display their remarkable prowess at an early age both by performing difficult tasks and they show bravery in the face of danger.

4. The infant Hercules, for example, strangles not only two venomous serpents in his crib but laughs without fear at the menace.

5. Young Theseus enters the dreaded labyrinth on Crete determined either to slay the Minotaur or he will die in the attempt.

6. Besides demonstrating bravery and strength in fighting deadly foes of many kinds, heroes often undertake dangerous journeys.

7. A companion travels with the hero, and sometimes the companion is not mortal but a god.

8. Athene, in perhaps the most famous story of all, guides young Telemachos not only during a voyage from Ithaca to Pylos, the home of Nestor, but also helps him to win the regard of kings.

9. Even for heroes, meeting a challenge can be as dangerous as to play Russian roulette.

10. In a major test of strength and courage, Jason has to yoke a pair of fire-breathing bulls, seed a field with dragons' teeth, and there is a climactic battle to be won against armed men sprouting from the seeds.

Sentence Combining

Combine the sentences in each of the following sets into a single compound sentence, using parallel construction where possible.

EXAMPLE:

Much of the land was arid.
The presence of many rocks was another feature.
To the Moabites the land was beautiful.
They loved it passionately.
They fought to keep it.

COMBINED: Much of the land was both arid and rocky; nonetheless, the Moabites found it beautiful, loved it passionately, and fought to keep it.

1. Most tarantulas live in the tropics.
   The temperate zone, however, is home to some species of them.
   A few species commonly occur in the southern United States.

2. Some tarantulas have large bodies.
   Their fangs are powerful.
   They can bite hard.
   They can cause deep wounds.
   But they don't attack human beings.
   Their bite harms only certain small creatures.
   These include insects.
   Mice can be harmed by their bite too.

3. Tarantulas come out of their burrows at dusk.
   Dawn is the time of their return to their burrows.
   At night the mature males look for females.
   Sometimes they become intruders in people's homes.

4. A fertilized female tarantula lays several hundred eggs at one time.
   Her next act is to weave a cocoon of silk to enclose them.
   She does nothing more for her young.

5. When hatched, the young walk away.
   They live alone.
   They are unlike ants in this respect.
   They also differ from bees.
   They do not live in colonies.

17 *Subordination: Complex Sentences*

Subordination lets you show the relative importance of the parts of a sentence. Suppose you want to describe what a dog did on a particular night, and you want your description to include the following points:

The dog lived next door.

The dog was scrawny.

The dog barked.

The dog was old.

The dog howled.

The dog kept me awake.

I was awake all night.

What is the best way to arrange these isolated facts in a sentence? Part of the answer is to coordinate facts that are equally important to the point you want to make:

The dog was scrawny and old, and he lived next door; he barked and howled and kept me awake all night.

This sentence puts all the facts together, but it fails to show which fact is most important to the writer—to you.

Which *is* the most important? That depends on the topic of your essay. If you're writing about yourself, for instance, the most important fact about the dog is that it kept you awake all night. To highlight that fact, you could rewrite the sentence like this:

300

The scrawny old dog next door kept me awake all night by barking and howling.

This sentence emphasizes just one statement: the dog kept me awake. By turning all the other statements into modifiers of *dog* or *kept me awake*, it subordinates them to the point that is most important to you. You can stress this point even more by placing it at the end of the sentence—the stress position:

By barking and howling, the scrawny old dog next door kept me awake all night.

Alternatively, you can subordinate all the other facts about the dog to the fact that it lived next door:

The dog *that kept me awake all night with its barking and howling* lived next door.

The entire group of italicized words modifies *dog*. So all the other facts about the dog are now subordinated to the fact that it lived next door.

Finally, suppose you want to subordinate all of these facts about the dog to a brand-new fact. Suppose you mainly want to tell what happened to you *as a result* of that sleepless night. Then you might write a sentence like this:

Because the barking and howling of the scrawny old dog next door had kept me awake all night, I fell asleep in the middle of the chemistry final.

Subordination helps make a sentence fit its context. Consider these paragraphs:

For me, the one big problem with dogs is noise. On the night before I had to take a final exam in chemistry, "man's best friend" turned out to be my worst enemy. I got to bed at eleven, but I didn't sleep a wink. *What kept me awake all night was the barking and howling of the scrawny old dog next door.*

The Bible tells us all to love our neighbors, but I have always had trouble even liking most of mine. When I was about six years old, I climbed over the fence in our backyard, wandered into Mr. O'Reilly's flower garden, and sat down in the middle of some big yellow daffodils. Mr. O'Reilly came up from behind and whacked me so hard I can still feel it now. We've moved a few times since then, but I have yet to find neighbors that I love. On the contrary, many of the things I don't love seem to come from across a fence. In El Paso, for instance, *a scrawny old dog that kept me awake all night with its barking and howling lived next door.*

In the chemistry course I managed to do just about everything wrong. To begin with, I bought a used textbook at a bargain price, and then found out that I was supposed to buy the new edition. Trying to get along instead with the old one, I almost always wound up reading the wrong pages for the assignment and giving the wrong answers to quiz questions. I did no better with beakers and test tubes; the only thing my experiments showed is that I could have blown up the lab. But the worst came last. *Because the barking and howling of the scrawny old dog next door had kept me awake all night, I fell asleep in the middle of the final.*

The sentence about the dog is written three different ways to emphasize three different things: the noise it made, the fact that it lived next door, and the fact that something happened because of its noise. In each case, the methods of subordination make the sentence fit the particular paragraph for which it is written. The three ways of writing the sentence also illustrate three different kinds of subordinate clauses. We consider these in the next sections.

17.2 WHAT SUBORDINATE CLAUSES ARE

A subordinate clause (SC), also called a dependent clause, is a group of words that has its own subject and predicate but cannot stand alone as a simple sentence. It must be included in or connected to an independent clause (IC)—one that can stand by itself as a sentence:

SC	IC
Before she spoke to reporters,	she conferred with her advisers.

IC	SC
Medical researchers have long been seeking a cure for a disease	that takes thousands of lives each year.

IC	SC	SC
Pavarotti was cheered	as he finished the beautiful aria	in which Rodolfo declares his love to Mimi.

A sentence containing one independent clause and at least one subordinate clause is called complex. Complex sentences are made with various kinds of subordinate clauses, as explained below.

17.3 USING ADJECTIVE (RELATIVE) CLAUSES

An adjective clause, sometimes called a relative clause, normally begins with a relative pronoun—*which, that, who, whom,* or *whose*. The relative pronoun refers to a noun or noun phrase that is called its antecedent. The adjective clause modifies this antecedent, which usually appears just before the relative pronoun:

> The dog *that* kept me awake all night lived next door.

An adjective clause can say more about its antecedent than a single adjective does. Compare these two sentences:

> Medical researchers have long been seeking a cure for a *fatal* disease.

> Medical researchers have long been seeking a cure for a disease *that takes thousands of lives every year.*

An adjective clause also enables you to subordinate one set of facts to another set. See how these two sentences can be combined:

> Amelia Earhart disappeared in 1937 during a round-the-world trip. She set new speed records for long-distance flying in the 1930s.

> COMBINATION 1: Amelia Earhart, *who set new speed records for long-distance flying in the 1930s,* disappeared in 1937 during a round-the-world trip.

> COMBINATION 2: Amelia Earhart, *who disappeared in 1937 during a round-the-world trip,* set new speed records for long-distance flying in the 1930s.

Combination 1 subordinates Earhart's record-setting to her disappearance; combination 2 subordinates her disappearance to her record-setting. Which combination the writer chooses depends on which fact the writer wants to emphasize in a particular context.

17.4 CHOOSING RELATIVE PRONOUNS

The relative pronoun you choose depends chiefly on the antecedent—the noun or pronoun the clause modifies.

1.   Use *who, whom, whose,* or *that* when the antecedent is one or more persons:

> Women *who* miscalculate are called "mothers."   —Abigail Van Buren

Millard Fillmore, *whom* almost nobody remembers, was president of the United States from 1848 to 1852.

Never trust a doctor *whose* office plants have died.   —Erma Bombeck

Pedestrians *that* ignore traffic lights are living dangerously.

The case endings of *who, whom,* and *whose* depend on what the pronoun does in the clause it introduces. (For a full discussion of case endings, see 20.11.)

2.   Use *which* or *that* when the antecedent is one or more things:

A mind *that* is stretched to a new idea never returns to its original dimensions.   —Oliver Wendell Holmes

A team of shipwreck hunters recently found the wreck of the *S.S. Leopoldville,* *which* was sunk by a German torpedo on Christmas Eve 1944.

We must preserve the freedoms for *which* our ancestors fought.

3.   Use *which* when the antecedent is an entire clause—but only when nothing else can be mistaken for the antecedent:

Tim cackled maliciously, *which* infuriated Paul.

The accident could have been avoided, *which* made it all the harder to bear.

For more on this use of *which,* see 20.4, "Broad Reference."

4.   Do not use *that* when the antecedent is a proper name, a clearly identified person, or a clearly identified thing:

▶ The world's greatest jumpers include Carl Lewis, ~~that~~ *who* has cleared nearly twenty-nine feet.

▶ The Verrazano-Narrows Bridge, ~~that~~ *which* links Brooklyn to Staten Island, has the longest suspension span in the world.

▶ Passengers on Flight 89 commended the pilot, ~~that~~ *who* had guided the plane to safety despite the blizzard.

▶ The town's library, ~~that~~ *which* was built in 1850, holds over one hundred thousand volumes.

5. You may use *whose* with any antecedent to avoid writing *of which:*

> The children worked in a schoolroom *whose* windows were never opened.
> (COMPARE: The children worked in a schoolroom *of which* the windows
> were never opened.)

> She landed a helicopter *whose* pilot had collapsed over the controls.

6. You may use *where* or *when* as a relative pronoun when the antecedent
is a place or a time:

> That morning we drove to the town of Appomattox Court House, Virginia,
> *where* Lee surrendered to Grant at the end of the Civil War.

> Her favorite season was spring, *when* the Earth seemed born again.

> She felt a chill as she stood on the very spot *where* the murderer had been
> hanged.

17.5 PLACING THE ADJECTIVE CLAUSE

Place the adjective clause so that the reader can clearly see its connection to
the antecedent of the relative pronoun. Observe the following guidelines:

1. Whenever possible, place the adjective clause immediately after the
antecedent of the relative pronoun:

> Students *who cheat* poison the atmosphere of the college.

> Newhouse made a proposal *that nobody else liked.*

> The police shot a raccoon *that appeared to be rabid.*

2. If an adjective phrase gets between the relative pronoun and its antecedent, you can sometimes turn the phrase into another adjective clause:

> ▶ Mothers ~~of small children~~ who work ⌄must juggle conflicting
> *and who have small children*
>
> responsibilities.

Alternatively, you can reconstruct the sentence:

> Working mothers of small children must juggle conflicting responsibilities.

For more on the placement of modifying phrases, see 14.14–14.17.

3.   If the adjective clause is long, you can move the antecedent (in bold print here) to the end of the main clause:

> **Leonardo da Vinci,** *whose knowledge of sculpture, painting, architecture, engineering, and science made him the intellectual wonder of his time,* painted the *Mona Lisa* in Florence about 1504.

> EDITED: The *Mona Lisa* was painted in Florence about 1504 by **Leonardo da Vinci,** *whose knowledge of sculpture, painting, architecture, engineering, and science made him the intellectual wonder of his time.*

The second version keeps both parts of the main clause together.

EXERCISE 1   **Placing Adjective Clauses**

To each of the sentences add the adjective clause written within parentheses. Reword the sentence and add punctuation as necessary so as to connect the clause clearly to the italicized item.

EXAMPLE: *Psychologists* have been studying the mental effects of prolonged weightlessness. (who work for NASA)

NEW SENTENCE: Psychologists who work for NASA have been studying the mental effects of prolonged weightlessness.

1. Workers are busy cleaning a *statue* in Cedar Park. (that was designed by Phidias Gold in 1953)

2. The *statue* has been discolored by pollutants emitted by motor vehicles and nearby cement factories. (which represents the American farmer)

3. City officials want to honor *Gold* with a parade and a banquet on Labor Day. (whose works have earned him a reputation for bold designs)

4. The sculptor recently described a *memorial* in an interview with reporters. (that will honor the astronauts killed in the explosion of the space shuttle *Challenger*)

5. The *Challenger* blew up within minutes of its launching on January 28, 1986. (whose crew included the first schoolteacher ever sent into space)

17.6   PUNCTUATING ADJECTIVE CLAUSES

1.   Use commas to set off an adjective clause only when it is nonrestrictive—that is, not needed to identify the antecedent. A nonrestrictive adjective clause has a well-identified noun as its antecedent:

Linda Watson, *who earned a cumulative grade-point average of 3.8,* was graduated with highest honors.

This adjective clause is not needed to identify the antecedent because she is already identified by name. Without the adjective clause, some details would be lacking, but the essential information would remain:

Linda Watson was graduated with highest honors.

Well-identified nouns include not only names of persons but also names of things, job titles, and any other phrases that plainly identify one of a kind:

The Lincoln Memorial, *which was dedicated in 1922,* attracts visitors from all over the world.

We attended a reception for the dean of the business school, *who will retire in June.*

My youngest brother, *who seldom opened a book as a teenager,* has just been appointed head librarian of Wakefield University.

In all of these examples, the adjective clauses are nonrestrictive. They give information about the antecedents but do not identify them.

EXCEPTION: When the antecedent is the proper name of a group, the clause may restrict its meaning to certain members of the group and would therefore require no commas:

Most Canadians *who speak French* live in the province of Quebec.

2.   Do not use commas to set off a **restrictive** adjective clause—one that *does* identify the antecedent:

Students *who earn a cumulative grade point average of 3.7 or more* will be graduated with highest honors.

This adjective clause restricts the meaning of the antecedent, specifying which students are eligible for highest honors. Without the clause the sentence would say something quite different:

Students will be graduated with highest honors.

Since a restrictive clause is essential to the meaning of the antecedent and of the sentence as a whole, it must not be set off from the antecedent by commas. Here is one more example:

Tree surgeons may have to remove the oak *that towers over the new greenhouse.*

17.7 OVERUSING ADJECTIVE CLAUSES

Do not use adjective clauses starting with phrases like *who is* and *which are* when you don't need them. Cut the excess words:

▶ Some of the compact cars ~~that are~~ sold by American companies are manufactured in Japan.

▶ Joseph P. Kennedy, ~~who was the~~ father of President John F. Kennedy, made a fortune in banking and real estate.

EXERCISE 2 Sentence Combining with Adjective Clauses

Combine the sentences in each of the following pairs by turning one sentence into an adjective clause and using it in the other. Then underline the adjective clause and in parentheses state whether it is restrictive or nonrestrictive.

EXAMPLE:
Employees of a certain kind will be fired.
Those employees arrive late.

COMBINED: Employees *who arrive late* will be fired. (restrictive)

1. On Interstate 70 in Colorado, a stretch offers tourists many attractive sights.
   The stretch extends from Idaho Springs to Glenwood Springs.

2. At Idaho Springs the countryside is dotted with the entrances to old silver mines.
   One hundred years ago, the mines were making people rich.

3. Farther along, the highway enters Vail.
   Vail draws thousands of skiers to its beautiful trails every winter.

4. Glenwood Canyon is another rewarding place.
   Its colorful walls rise steeply above a winding river.

5. Here, in the spring, men and women ride the rapids in rubber rafts.
   The men and women relish adventure and spectacular scenery.

Sentence Combining with Adjective Clauses

Combine the sentences in each of the following sets by using one or more adjective clauses.

EXAMPLE:
Ronald Reagan governed the state of California from 1967 to 1975.
Six years later, he became president of the United States.
He first made his name in the movies.

COMBINED: Ronald Reagan, who governed the state of California from 1967 to 1975 and became president of the United States six years later, first made his name in the movies.

1. Susan B. Anthony was arrested on a certain day in 1872.
   On that day she led a group of women to the polls in Rochester, New York.
   Women owe their voting rights to early feminists like Susan B. Anthony.

2. Feminism in the nineteenth century was also strongly promoted by Elizabeth Cady Stanton.
   She organized the first U.S. women's rights convention in 1848.
   She presided over the National American Woman Suffrage Association from 1890 to 1892.

3. In the early twentieth century, Carrie Chapman Catt led the fight for women's rights.
   She became president of the National American Woman Suffrage Association in 1900.

4. She achieved her goal in 1920.
   At that time Congress passed the Nineteenth Amendment.
   That amendment gave women the right to vote.

5. Since the 1960s, the spirit of feminism has been revived by the National Organization for Women.
   This organization has demanded for women certain rights and opportunities.
   Those rights and opportunities once were granted only to men.

17.8 USING ADVERB CLAUSES

An adverb clause begins with a subordinator—a word like *when, because, if,* and *although.* Modifying a word, phrase, or clause, an adverb clause tells such things as why, when, how, and under what conditions. Normally it gives more information than a simple adverb does:

ADVERB
Then I hit the brakes.

ADVERB CLAUSE
As the deer leaped onto the road, I hit the brakes.

An adverb clause also enables you to subordinate one point to another:

As he was being tackled, he threw the ball.

This sentence highlights the throwing of the ball and is designed to fit into a paragraph like this:

> The line wavered, and Keene knew it would break in seconds. But he dropped back, dancing around until he spotted a receiver. *As he was being tackled, he threw the ball.* Polanski made a leaping catch at the twenty-five-yard line, came down running, zigzagged past the Iowa safety, and crossed the goal line. The crowd went wild.

On the other hand, if the most important thing is not the pass but the tackle, the sentence should emphasize that:

> Keene looked desperately for a receiver, sensing the seconds ticking away. Suddenly his blocking broke down, and he was surrounded. *As he threw the ball, he was being tackled.* The pass went nearly straight up, then fell to Earth behind him. The game was over.

In each version of the italicized sentence, the adverb clause lets you indicate which of two points is more important.

17.9 CHOOSING SUBORDINATORS

A **subordinator** is a word or phrase that subordinates the clause to whatever it modifies. Subordinators signal a variety of relations:

1. TIME

   The factory closed *when* the owner died.

   Until power was restored, we cooked our meals in the fireplace.

   While Marian sang, Zachary played the piano.

2. CAUSALITY

   Kate was happy *because* she had just won her first case.

   Since I had no money, I walked all the way home.

3. **CONCESSION AND CONTRAST**

Money cannot make you happy, *though* it can keep you comfortable.

Though money cannot make you happy, it can keep you comfortable.

Although the mosquitoes were out in force, we spent an enjoyable hour fishing before sundown.

In my new car, I am averaging over thirty-five miles per gallon of gas, *whereas* I got only twenty in my old one.

While Finnegan himself never ran for any office, he ran many successful campaigns.

4. **CONDITION**

If battery-powered cars become popular, the price of gas will drop.

He ran *as if* he had a broken leg.

5. **PURPOSE**

I worked in a department store for a year *so that* I could earn money for college.

6. **PLACE**

Where federal funds go, federal regulations go with them.

7. **RESULT**

We are *so* accustomed to adopting a mask before others *that* we end by being unable to recognize ourselves.

—William Hazlitt

She fixed the clock *so that* it worked.

8. **RANGE OF POSSIBILITIES**

Whatever the president wants, Congress has a will of its own.

You can also signal general possibility with *whenever, wherever, whoever, whichever,* and *however:*

I can't pronounce the name *however* it is spelled.

9. **COMPARISON**

The river is cleaner now *than* it was two years ago.

311

Relations Signaled by Subordinators

Time

after
as
as long as
as soon as
before
ever since
until
when
whenever
while

Concession and Contrast

although
even though
though
whereas
while

Condition

as if
as though
if
provided that
unless

Range of Possibilities

however
whatever
whichever
whoever

Place

whence
where
wherever

Purpose

in order that
lest
so that

Causality

because
since

Result

so that
that

Comparison

than

17.10 PLACING ADVERB CLAUSES

An adverb clause of result and comparison normally follows the main clause. But most other adverb clauses are movable. So where do you put them?

To be clear-cut and straightforward, lead with your main clause and let the adverb clause follow:

The colonel ordered an investigation as soon as he heard the complaint of the enlisted men.

I worked in a department store for a year so that I could earn money for college.

This kind of order has a brisk, no-nonsense effect, and you will seldom go wrong with it. But it is not always the best order. To create suspense, or to build up to your main point, put the adverb clause at the beginning and save the main clause for the end. Consider these two versions of a sentence spoken by Winston Churchill in 1941, when the Germans had occupied most of Europe and were threatening to invade England:

> We shall not flag or fail even though large tracts of Europe and many old and famous states have fallen or may fall into the grip of the Gestapo and all the odious apparatus of Nazi rule.

> Even though large tracts of Europe and many old and famous states have fallen or may fall into the grip of the Gestapo and all the odious apparatus of Nazi rule, we shall not flag or fail.

There is nothing grammatically wrong with the first sentence, which starts with a main clause and finishes with a long adverb clause. But this sentence has all the fire of a wet match. Because the crucial words *we shall not flag or fail* come first, they are virtually smothered by what follows them. By the time we reach the end of the sentence we may even have forgotten its main point. The arrangement of the second sentence—the one Churchill actually wrote—guarantees we will remember it. Precisely because we are made to wait until the end of the sentence for the main clause, it strikes with telling effect.

17.11 PUNCTUATING ADVERB CLAUSES

Introductory adverb clauses are followed by a comma:

> *Even though I knocked loudly on the door,* the storekeeper would not open it.

> *When the gate opened,* the bull charged into the ring.

Ordinarily, an adverb clause coming at the end of a sentence is not preceded by a comma:

> The bull charged into the ring *when the gate opened.*

> A wall collapsed *because the foundation was poorly constructed.*

If the adverb clause at the end of a sentence is nonrestrictive—not essential to the meaning of the sentence—a comma may precede it:

> We planted the trees in the fall of 1984, *just after we bought the house.*

| EXERCISE 4 | **Sentence Combining with Adverb Clauses** |

Combine the sentences in each of the following pairs by turning one sentence into an adverb clause and attaching it to the other. Be sure to begin the adverb clause with a suitable subordinator, and in parentheses state the relation that the subordinator shows.

EXAMPLE:
I see roses.
Then my nose starts to itch.

COMBINED: Whenever I see roses, my nose starts to itch. (time)

1. Assume that commercial airlines will offer regular flights to the moon by the year 2050.
   The moon may become the new playground of the super-rich.

2. This prospect is unlikely.
   But scientists may eventually establish some kind of observatory on the moon.

3. The moon has no atmosphere.
   Therefore it affords a perfectly clear view of the stars.

4. Even without a lunar observatory, we may be able to put a telescope in a permanently orbiting space station.
   As a result, we will get an equally clear view.

5. We will be able to study the stars without the least interference from atmospheric disturbance.
   Then our understanding of them will dramatically increase.

17.12 MAKING ADVERB CLAUSES COMPLETE: AVOIDING FAULTY COMPARISONS

1.   Do not use an incomplete adverb clause when a complete one is needed to make a comparison clear:

▶ The river is as clean now as ^it was two years ago.

The original sentence seems to compare the river with *two years*.

2.   Do not skip any word that is essential to a comparison:

▶ Roger moves faster than any ^other player on the team~~does~~.

If Roger himself is a player on the team, the original sentence seems to compare him with himself as well as others.

▶ Tokyo's population is larger than New York. *'s is.*

The original seems to compare a population with a city. Another way of correcting the sentence is this:

Tokyo's population is larger *than that of New York.*

3. You may skip any words in a comparison that can be easily supplied by the reader:

The exhaust system emits less sulphur dioxide *than the original system (did).*

Some writers think more about plot *than (they do) about characters.*

Ever since I began swimming every day, I have felt better *(than I did before I began swimming).*

Roger moves faster than any other player on the team *(does).*

Tokyo's population is larger than New York's *(is).*

Correcting Faulty Comparisons

EXERCISE 5

Each of the following sentences makes a comparison. Revise any sentence in which the comparison is not clear and complete. If a sentence is correct as it stands, write *Correct.*

EXAMPLE: The Federal Reserve Bank in New York City holds more gold

than any bank in the United States.

1. The old house on the bay at St. Anthony's Island looks just as good as twenty years ago.

2. At that time, however, the sand was much whiter.

3. Also, the water in the bay was clearer than any bay in the islands.

4. Now the bay gets more sewage than any septic system on St. Anthony's.

5. And fishermen are not catching nearly as many cod and haddock as twenty years ago.

17.13 USING NOUN CLAUSES

A noun clause is used as a noun within a sentence. Normally it gives more information than a simple noun can. Compare the following:

Government officials did not anticipate the *problem.*

Government officials did not anticipate *that protestors would occupy the presidential palace.*

A noun clause can serve as subject, object, or predicate noun.

1. NOUN CLAUSE AS SUBJECT

   What Sylvia did amazed me.

   Whoever wins the nomination will be running against a popular incumbent.

2. NOUN CLAUSE AS OBJECT

   I feared *(that) we would never get out alive.* (*That* is optional.)

   The police have not discovered *how the prisoner escaped.*

   No one knew *whether or not interest rates would rise.*

   We will plug the leaks with *whatever is handy.*

   Alexandra wondered *what marriage would do to her.*

3. NOUN CLAUSE AS PREDICATE NOUN

   The main reason for the change is *that all in the company will benefit.*

   A computer with the brain of a genius is *what I need right now.*

   The most puzzling mystery of all is *why she abdicated at the height of her power.*

Subordinate Clauses

The **adjective (relative) clause** begins with a relative pronoun—*which, that, who, whom,* or *whose.* The relative pronoun refers to its antecedent, the noun or noun phrase that normally appears just before it:

All *that glitters* is not gold.

The **adverb clause** begins with a subordinator—a word like *when, because,* or *although*—and tells such things as why, when, or how something happened:

I missed class *because I had to go out of town for a job interview.*

The **noun clause** is used as a noun within a sentence:

Many people want *what they cannot afford.*

Noun clauses may begin with

▶ a pronoun: No one knows exactly *who* built Stonehenge.

▶ an adverb: Astronomers can explain *how* stars are born.

▶ *that:* Many workers fear *that* they will lose their jobs.

That may be omitted if the meaning is clear without it:

Many workers fear they will lose their jobs.

Using Noun Clauses

Underline the noun clause(s) in the following sentences. Then write a sentence that resembles the form of the original one.

EXAMPLE: I have sometimes wondered <u>how automatic elevators respond to conflicting signals</u>.

Children often ask how bears survive winter.

1. Whoever tries to resolve a conflict soon learns that nothing pleases everybody.

2. What solves one problem often causes another.

3. No one knows whether gains will be greater than losses.

4. It soon becomes evident that progress is elusive.

5. Who can explain why negotiations sometimes take months?

Sentence Combining: Review of Subordination

Combine the sentences in each of the following sets by using at least two of the three different kinds of subordinate clauses—noun clauses, adjective clauses, and adverb clauses.

EXAMPLE:
Frank Waters was a powerful man.
He could not lift the big stove.
It weighed over four hundred pounds.

COMBINED: Though Frank Waters was a powerful man, he could not lift the big stove, which weighed over four hundred pounds.

1. The Sioux Indians settled down near the Black Hills in 1867.
   Soon after, the Black Hills were invaded by white men.
   The white men were searching for gold.

2. A U.S. treaty forbade white men to enter the Black Hills.
   Army cavalrymen entered the Black Hills in 1874 under General George Custer.
   Custer had led the slaughter of the Southern Cheyenne in 1868.

3. Red Cloud led the Sioux.
   Red Cloud denounced Custer's invasion.
   The invasion violated the treaty.

4. This violation led to disaster in 1876 at Little Bighorn River.
   At that time the Sioux attacked Custer ferociously.
   As a result, he and all his men were killed.

5. Custer's extraordinary exploits in the Civil War made him the youngest general in the Union Army.
   But most people know only one thing about Custer.
   He was the central figure in "Custer's last stand."

Coordination and Subordination

18

18.1 USING COORDINATION AND SUBORDINATION TOGETHER

Using coordination and subordination together, you can arrange all the parts of a sentence according to their relative importance and the desired emphasis. For example:

1. No one had the guts to raise a riot.

2. But suppose a European woman went through the bazaars alone.

3. Somebody would probably spit betel juice over her dress.

> COMBINED: No one had the guts to raise a riot, but if a European woman went through the bazaars alone somebody would probably spit betel juice over her dress.
>
> —George Orwell

In the combined sentence, both sentence 1 and sentence 3 remain independent clauses, though they are now joined by *but*. The result is a compound sentence. Within it, sentence 2 becomes a subordinate clause introduced by *if*. Here is another example:

> When Matthew heard about the accident, he molded his face into a mask as he had seen actors do, and he holed up in his bedroom, where he unplugged his stereo and tried to cry.
>
> —college student

Using coordination and subordination together, make one sentence from each of the following sets of sentences. Include all the information given, but feel free to change the wording or arrangement of the sentences. Combine the sentences of each set in at least two different ways. Then, if you prefer one of the combinations, put a check next to it.

EXAMPLE:
The snow melts in the spring.
The dirt roads in the region turn into muddy streams.
Certain people live in isolated houses.
Those people use old footpaths to reach Bridgeton.
Bridgeton has two grocery stores.
It has one gas pump.

COMBINATION 1: The snow melts in the spring, so the dirt roads in the region turn into muddy streams; certain people live in isolated houses, and those people use old footpaths to reach Bridgeton, which has two grocery stores and one gas pump.

COMBINATION 2: When the snow melts in the spring, the dirt roads in the region turn into muddy streams, so people who live in isolated houses use old footpaths to reach Bridgeton, which has two grocery stores and one gas pump.

1. According to some, the source of evil lies in society's institutions.
   These are said to nurture evil behavior in otherwise good people.
   According to others, evil springs directly from human nature.
   This is said to be inherently corrupt.

2. William Golding states his opinion in a novel.
   The novel is called *Lord of the Flies.*
   He nowhere states his opinion directly.
   But the setting, plot, and characters of his novel clearly reveal it.

3. The action is set on a beautiful South Pacific island.
   It has a bountiful supply of fruit trees.
   It has springs of fresh water.
   It has wild pigs.
   They run freely through the thick vegetation.

4. The only human inhabitants are a group of British schoolchildren.
   The children survived the crash of a plane.
   The plane was shot down during World War II.

5. Ralph is the leader of the boys.
   Ralph summons them to meetings in a certain way.
   He uses a large shell.
   The shell makes a loud noise at a certain time.
   He blows into it at that time.
   The boys respond to the sound for a certain reason.
   The shell is a symbol of authority.
   It is also a symbol of order.

6. At first the older boys follow Ralph's lead.
   They agree to perform certain tasks.
   One task is to build shelters.
   Another task is to care for the youngest.
   A third is to keep a fire burning.
   The fire burns on a hilltop.
   Its purpose is to serve as an SOS signal for crews of passing ships.

7. But trouble develops shortly.
   Ralph's leadership is challenged by Jack.
   Jack has been a leader of choirboys.
   He wants to be the chief again.
   Then he can give orders.
   He will not take them.

8. Jack forms his own band of followers.
   They walk out on Ralph.
   They want to stop working on the signal fire.
   They want to hunt wild pigs.
   They like the excitement of the chase.
   They like the excitement of the kill.
   They stab the squealing pig with a wooden spear.

9. Jack's followers attack Ralph's group one night.
   They take Piggy's glasses.
   They want the lenses for a purpose.
   They will use the lenses.
   The lenses will concentrate the sun's rays on firewood.
   The lenses will make a fire.
   The fire will cook the pig meat.

10. In the end, the boys are discovered by a strong naval officer.
    The naval officer scolds the boys.
    The boys look like savages.
    The boys have been fighting among themselves.
    Yet he has been fighting too.
    He has come ashore from a warship.
    The warship aims to sink enemy warships and their crews.

Writing One-sentence Summaries

Using coordination, subordination, or both, write a one-sentence summary of each of the following passages.

EXAMPLE:

More than ever before in American politics, language is used not as an instrument for forming and expressing thought. It is used to prevent, confuse, and conceal thinking. Members of each branch and agency of government at every level, representing every hue of political opinion, habitually speak a language of nonresponsibility.
—Richard Gambino, "Through the Dark, Glassily"

ONE-SENTENCE SUMMARY: More than ever before, American politicians and government workers use language not to express thought but to prevent, confuse, and conceal it; they speak a language of non-responsibility.

1. The average person has many worries, but there is one thing he does not generally worry about. He does not worry that somewhere, without his knowledge, a secret tribunal is about to order him seized, drugged, and imprisoned without the right of appeal. Indeed, anyone who worries overmuch about such a thing, and expresses that worry repeatedly and forcefully enough, would probably be classified as a paranoid schizophrenic.
—Hendrik Hertzberg and David C. K. McClelland, "Paranoia"

2. Every grown-up person expects to pay a price for his pleasures, but seldom is the price as vast as the one endured "however happily" by most mothers. We have mentioned the literal cost factor. But what does that mean? For middle-class American women, it means a life style with severe and usually unimagined limitations; i.e., life in the suburbs, because who can afford three bedrooms in the city? And what do suburbs mean? For women, suburbs mean other women and children and left-over peanut-butter sandwiches and car pools and seldom-seen husbands.
—Betty Rollin, "Motherhood: Who Needs It?"

3. Historically, clutter is a modern phenomenon, born of the industrial revolution. There was a time when goods were limited; and the rich and fashionable were few in number and objects were precious and hard to come by. Clutter is a 19th century esthetic; it came with the abundance of products combined with the rise of purchasing power, and the shifts in society that required manifestations of status and style.
—Ada Louise Huxtable, "Modern-Life Battle: Conquering Clutter"

4. I have described imagination as the ability to make images and to move them about inside one's head in new arrangements. This is the faculty that is specifically human, and it is the common root from which science and literature both spring and grow and flourish together.
—Jacob Bronowski, "The Reach of Imagination"

5. To lie habitually, as a way of life, is to lose contact with the unconscious. It is like taking sleeping pills, which confer sleep but blot out dreaming. The unconscious wants truth. It ceases to speak to those who want something else more than truth.
—Adrienne Rich, "Women and Honor: Some Notes on Lying"

18.2 UNTANGLING SENTENCES

It is sometimes hard to put several ideas into a single sentence without getting them tangled up in the process. Consider this sentence:

*Due to the progress in military weaponry over the years, there has been an increased passivity in humankind that such advancements bring as wars are easier to fight resulting in a total loss of honor in fighting.

If you come across such a sentence in your own writing, you should first of all break it up into single ideas:

1. There has been progress in military weaponry over the years.

2. There has been increased passivity in humankind.

3. Such advancements bring passivity.

4. The passivity is due to the progress.

5. Wars are easier to fight.

6. This results in a total loss of honor in fighting.

Once you have broken up the sentence into single ideas, you can use coordination and subordination to put them back together clearly:

Since progress in military weaponry over the years has made humankind more passive and wars easier to fight, there has been a total loss of honor in fighting.

[or] Since progress in military weaponry over the years has made humankind more passive and wars easier to fight, fighting has lost all honor.

Sentence Untangling—A Challenge

This may well be the toughest exercise in the book. All of the following sentences were written by students who had a lot to say but who got into a tangle when they tried to say it. So you will probably have trouble even figuring out what the writers meant. But we're asking you to do just that—and more. We're asking you to untangle each sentence in the same way we untangled the sentence about weaponry in the preceding discussion. First, cut up each tangled sentence into a series of short, simple sentences; second, using coordination, subordination, or both, recombine these into one long sentence that makes sense.

1. Thoreau spent much of his time outdoors in nature, which he loved, so he saw no reason to keep it out of his cabin, and he symbolized a door-mat as the mistake of avoiding natural things like dirt and leaves like his neighbors.

2. The bean field made him self-sufficient, which was one of his beliefs, and he could also see it as an extension of himself, through the bean field, into nature in returning to a natural state.

3. The author of "The Cold Equations" is saying, in effect, that the main difference of life on the frontier for people living there after living in settled communities is that their lives are now ruled by the laws of nature instead of people making the laws.

4. For fifty years the people prospered under his rule; then, feeling a personal responsibility for the welfare of his subjects and their safety, the old king fought another monster which he was severely injured and soon died.

Sentence Fragments   **19**

Complete sentences help the writer to sound well organized and the reader to grasp the writer's point. Sentence fragments often do just the opposite. Unless skillfully used, they give the impression that the writer's thoughts are incomplete or disorganized, and they may confuse the reader.

19.1 USING AND MISUSING SENTENCE FRAGMENTS

A **sentence fragment** is part of a sentence punctuated as if it were a whole one:

> A new mountain to be climbed.

In conversation we often use fragments that make perfectly good sense:

> "When is she leaving?"
>
> "Tomorrow."
>
> "Really?"
>
> "No question about it."
>
> "Rats!"

Occasionally, sentence fragments also occur in writing:

> For so many years college had seemed far-off, but all of a sudden it was there, staring me in the face. A new mountain to be climbed.
>
> —college student

This passage ends with a sentence fragment whose meaning is perfectly clear in its context. In fact, the fragment highlights a point that might not have been made so effectively with a complete sentence.

But sentence fragments must be handled with care. If you don't know how to use them sparingly and strategically, your writing will look disorganized:

> In conclusion I feel Falstaff proves to be a most likable and interesting character. Showing an ability to think quickly in tight spots. But above all he lends a comical light to the play. Which I feel makes it all the more enjoyable.
>
> —college student

This passage includes two fragments—one after the first sentence and one at the end. Alternating with sentences of about equal length, they seem improvised and arbitrary, as if the writer could only now and then form a complete thought.

If you know how to use fragments effectively, do so. If you don't, or if your instructor will not accept any fragments at all, make sure all of your sentences are complete.

19.2   SPOTTING AND EDITING SENTENCE FRAGMENTS

How can you tell whether a particular word group is a sentence fragment? Here are some useful questions to ask if you aren't sure.

1. DOES THE "SENTENCE" START WITH A SUBORDINATOR OR A RELATIVE PRONOUN? A clause that starts with a subordinator or a relative pronoun and stands by itself is a fragment. It should be attached to an independent clause:

   a. On Halloween night some years ago, a full-grown man with a sick sense of humor disguised himself as a ghost. *So that he could terrify little children. (fragment starting with subordinator)

   EDITED: On Halloween night some years ago, a full-grown man with a sick sense of humor disguised himself as a ghost so that he could terrify little children.

   b. The British and French developed a supersonic plane called the Concorde. *Which can fly from New York to London in three hours. (fragment starting with relative pronoun)

   EDITED: The British and French developed a supersonic plane called the Concorde, which can fly from New York to London in three hours.

2. **DOES THE "SENTENCE" LACK A SUBJECT?**

    Lancelot won fame as a knight because of his prowess in battle. *Defeated the other great warriors in the kingdom.

    EDITED: He defeated the other great warriors in the kingdom.

3. **DOES THE "SENTENCE" LACK A PREDICATE?**

    *The common cold. It strikes everyone at least once a year.

This fragment should be combined with the sentence following it:

    EDITED: The common cold strikes everyone at least once a year.

4. **IS THE "SENTENCE" MERELY A MODIFYING PHRASE?**

    They went to a ski lodge. *With a view of the Rockies.

This fragment should be combined with the sentence preceding it:

    EDITED: They went to a ski lodge with a view of the Rockies.

Spotting Sentence Fragments

Word group starting with a subordinator:

*So *that* he could terrify little children.

Word group starting with a relative pronoun:

Which can fly from New York to London in three hours.

Word group missing a subject:

*Defeated the other great warriors.

Word group missing a predicate:

*The common cold.

Word group that is merely a modifying phrase:

*With a panoramic view of the Rockies.

Each of the following passages includes several sentence fragments. Make whatever changes are necessary to remove them.

EXAMPLE: assumption that mentally (line 2)

1. The directors of social programs like Special Olympics make the accurate assumption. That mentally and physically disabled kids need to develop self-confidence. If they are going to function in society. According to Evelyn West, handicapped children need "to develop a strong, realistic sense of self." Society hinders this development. Children tease handi- 5
capped classmates. Separate facilities and special education classes are all clues to the handicapped. That they are different. Because they cannot succeed in regular classrooms or gyms. They feel incompetent. Now any child who feels incompetent is not ready to compete. This is where competitive programs fail. Wanting to foster confidence, 10
Special Olympics demands it of the contestants. Who are already sure they are going to lose out. Because they lack a vital prerequisite for any competition. Confidence.

   The kids' lack of confidence is, ironically, nurtured by Saturday morning practices. For which the kids are unequally skilled. The 15
qualifications for enrollment in Special Olympics are nebulous at best. Supposedly, only children with a ninety or lower on an I.Q. test are considered eligible. Few, however, are actually tested, and no one is turned away. Consequently, many mothers with several children send all of their brood to Saturday practices. For the free, supervised care. 20
Some of these kids are barely handicapped. So that their competing with the severely disabled clearly loads the dice. With unfortunate consequences for all. The least handicapped kids—the winners—gain a feeling of superiority. Based on a false measure of their skills. The severely handicapped—the losers—feel shunned again. This time in 25
their own program. None emerges with the sense of pride and respect for others. That the program's founders hoped to instill.

2. Most of the people who eat at a fast-food restaurant like McDonald's fall into one of four subgroups. The regulars, the families, the groups of kids, and the travelers.

   Unlike all the others. Regulars actually enjoy the restaurant. They talk to the servers about personal matters. While waiting for their 5
meals. They eat carefully. Placing french fries one by one into their mouths. And sipping their drinks slowly. Their meals are an opportunity. To relax after a strenuous day on the job.

Groups of kids often come to celebrate a birthday. Under the supervision of a mother. Who leaves them at a table. While she orders identical meals. For all of them. The kids play with straws. As they wait. Blowing them through the air and shooting the wrappers at each other. When the food comes to the table, they argue over who gets what. Even though all their meals are the same. During the meal they talk loudly. Despite the mother's efforts to control the volume. They also stare at nearby adults. Who wish the kids were sitting someplace else.

20 *Using Pronouns*

A **pronoun** is a word that commonly takes the place of a noun or noun phrase:

> Brenda thought that *she* had lost the dog, but *it* had followed *her.*

She and *her* take the place of *Brenda,* a noun; *it* takes the place of *the dog,* a noun phrase. Pronouns thus eliminate the need for awkward repetition.

20.1 USING PRONOUNS WITH ANTECEDENTS

The word or word group that a pronoun refers to is called its **antecedent**. *Antecedent* means "going before," and this term is used because the antecedent usually goes before the pronoun that refers to it:

1. The old man smiled as he listened to the marching band. Its spirited

   playing made him feel young again.

2. To build city districts that are custom-made for crime is idiotic. Yet

   that is what we do.

   —Jane Jacobs

In the second example, the antecedent of the first *that* is *city districts.* The antecedent of the second *that* is a whole word group: *To build city districts that are custom-made for crime.*

The antecedent sometimes follows the pronoun that refers to it:

> By the time he was three, Coleridge could read a chapter of the Bible.

20.2 USING PRONOUNS WITHOUT ANTECEDENTS

Some pronouns have no antecedent, and others may sometimes be used without one.

1. Indefinite pronouns have no antecedents. Compare these two sentences:

> Ellen said that *she* wanted privacy.

> *Everyone* needs some privacy.

She is a definite pronoun. It refers to a particular person, and its meaning is clear only if its antecedent has been provided—that is, if the person has already been identified. But *everyone* is an indefinite pronoun. Because it refers to no one in particular, it has no antecedent. Other widely used indefinite pronouns include *everybody, one, no one, each, many,* and *some.*

2. The pronouns *I* and *you* have no antecedent because they are understood to refer to the writer and the reader or to the speaker and the listener.

3. The pronoun *we* sometimes appears without an antecedent—for example, in newspaper editorials, where the writer clearly speaks for a group of people.

20.3 USING PRONOUNS CLEARLY

The meaning of a definite pronoun is clear when readers can identify the antecedent with certainty:

> People who saw the Tall Ships sail up the Hudson River in 1976 will long remember the experience. It gave them a handsome image of a bygone era.

The antecedent of each pronoun is obvious. *Who* clearly refers to *People; It* refers to *the experience; them* refers to *People who saw the Tall Ships.*

20.4 AVOIDING UNCLEAR PRONOUN REFERENCE

The meaning of a definite pronoun is unclear when readers cannot identify the antecedent with certainty. The chief obstacles to clear reference are as follows:

AMBIGUITY

A pronoun is **ambiguous** when it has more than one possible antecedent:

> *Whenever Mike met Dan, he felt nervous.

Does *he* refer to *Mike* or to *Dan?* The reader cannot tell. The simplest way to eliminate the ambiguity is to replace the pronoun with a noun:

> EDITED: Whenever Mike met Dan, Mike felt nervous.

To avoid repeating the noun, you can put the pronoun before it:

> EDITED: Whenever he met Dan, Mike felt nervous.

BROAD REFERENCE

Pronoun reference is **broad** when *that, this, which,* or *it* refers to a whole statement containing one or more possible antecedents within it:

> *The senator supports the bottle bill, which rankles many of his constituents.

Are they rankled by the bill or by the senator's support for it?

> EDITED: The senator's support for the bottle bill rankles many of his constituents.

> *Some people insist that a woman should have a career, while others say that she belongs in the home. This is unfair.

What is unfair? *This* could refer to the whole sentence that precedes it, to the first half, or to the second:

> EDITED: This contradictory set of demands is unfair.

MUFFLED REFERENCE

Pronoun reference is **muffled** when the pronoun refers to something merely implied by what precedes it:

> A recent editorial contained an attack on the medical profession. *The writer accused them of charging excessively high fees.

Who is meant by *them?* Before using *them,* the writer should clearly establish its antecedent:

> EDITED: A recent editorial contained an attack on hospital administrators and doctors. The writers accused them of charging excessively high fees.

> *Lincoln spoke immortal words at Gettysburg, but most of the large crowd gathered there couldn't hear it.

The writer is thinking of Lincoln's address, of course, but the word *address* is missing. It must be inserted:

> EDITED: Lincoln gave an immortal address at Gettysburg, but most of the large crowd gathered there couldn't hear it.

> [or] Lincoln spoke immortal words at Gettysburg, but most of the large crowd gathered there couldn't hear his address.

> [or] . . . couldn't hear them.

The last way of editing the sentence changes the *number* of the pronoun to match the number of its antecedent; see 20.6.

FREE-FLOATING *THEY* AND *IT*

They and *it* are free-floating when they are used as pronouns but have no definite antecedents:

> *In the first part of the movie, it shows clouds billowing like waves.

What shows clouds? The pronoun *it* has no antecedent. The writer is probably thinking of the *it* that simply fills out a sentence, such as *It was cloudy,* meaning *There were clouds.* That kind of *it* (called an expletive) needs no antecedent. But the pronoun *it* does. If you can't readily figure out a way to furnish one, reconstruct the sentence:

> EDITED: The first part of the movie shows clouds billowing like waves.

> Traveling in Eastern Europe used to be difficult. *At some checkpoints they held foreigners for questioning.

The word *they* needs an antecedent:

> EDITED: Traveling in Eastern Europe used to be difficult because of the *security police.* At some checkpoints they held foreigners for questioning.

Alternatively, you can replace the pronoun with a noun:

> EDITED: At some checkpoints the security police held foreigners for questioning.

Or you can use the passive voice:

> EDITED: At some checkpoints foreigners were held for questioning.

INDEFINITE *YOU* AND *YOUR*

You and *your* are indefinite when used to mean anything but the reader. Though writers sometimes use *you* to mean "people in general," you will increase the precision of your sentences if you use *you* and *your* for your reader alone.

> *You didn't have microphones in Lincoln's day.

> EDITED: There were no microphones in Lincoln's day.

> One of Orwell's contradictions is the unperson, a man who existed once, but doesn't anymore, so he never existed. *But by defining someone as an unperson, you are saying that he once existed.

> EDITED: But to define someone as an unperson is to say that he once existed.

REMOTE REFERENCE

Pronoun reference is remote when the pronoun is so far from the antecedent that readers cannot find their way from one to the other:

> Bankers have said that another increase in the prime lending rate during the current quarter would seriously hurt their major customers: homeowners, small-business personnel, and self-employed contractors using heavy equipment. *It would keep all of these borrowers from getting needed capital.

> EDITED: Such an increase would keep all of these borrowers from getting needed capital.

EXERCISE 1   Editing Unclear Pronouns

In some of the following sentences, the italicized pronoun has been used confusingly. Briefly diagnose what is wrong and then clarify the sentence. If the sentence is correct as it stands, write *Correct*.

> EXAMPLE: The boy and the old man both knew that *he* had not much longer to live.

DIAGNOSIS: *He* is ambiguous; it can refer to either the boy or the old man.

CURE: The boy and the old man both knew that the old man had not much longer to live.

1. Archimedes discovered the principle of displacement while he was taking a bath. *It* made him leap out of the water with excitement.

2. Shouting "Eureka!" over and over, he ran naked through the streets of Syracuse. *They* must have been amazed to see him—or at least amused.

3. But in any case, Archimedes had found the solution to a problem assigned to him by King Hieron II. *He* would surely be pleased.

4. Hieron wanted Archimedes to investigate a crown that had been recently made for the king from an ingot of gold. The king wanted to know if *it* was pure gold.

5. The weight of the crown exactly matched the weight of the original ingot, *which* pleased the king.

6. But the goldsmith could have taken some of the gold for himself and added copper in *its* place.

7. Since the resulting alloy would look just like pure gold and weigh as much as the original ingot, *you* couldn't tell by appearance or weight what the goldsmith had done.

8. Gold, however, is denser than copper. So any given weight of pure gold takes up less space than the same weight of copper, or of gold mixed with *it*.

9. To learn whether or not the crown was pure gold, therefore, *they* had to see whether its volume matched the volume of a pure gold ingot that weighed the same.

10. But the crown was so intricately shaped that no way of measuring known in Archimedes' time could establish *it*.

11. Only when Archimedes got into the tub did a solution strike *him*.

12. By measuring the water displaced by the crown, and then measuring the water displaced by the ingot, he could easily tell whether or not *they* matched in volume, and thus whether or not the crown was pure gold.

Obstacles to Clear Pronoun Reference

Ambiguity:

*Whenever Mike met Dan, *he* felt nervous.

Broad reference:

*The senator supports the bottle bill, *which* rankles many of his constituents.

Muffled reference:

A recent editorial contained an attack on the medical profession. *The writer accused *them* of charging excessively high fees.

Free-floating *they* and *it:*

*In the first part of the movie, *it* shows clouds billowing like waves.

*Traveling in Eastern Europe used to be difficult. *At some checkpoints *they* held foreigners for questioning.

Indefinite *you* and *your:*

You didn't have microphones in Lincoln's day.

Remote reference: see p. 334.

20.5 MAKING ANTECEDENTS AND PRONOUNS AGREE IN GENDER

In some languages, many words change in form to indicate **gender.** In French, for instance, the word for *the* is *le* when used of a male (as in *le garçon,* the boy) and *la* when used of a female (as in *la femme,* the woman).

In English, gender affects only personal pronouns referring to a single being or thing in the third person. (*I* and *we* are first-person pronouns; *you* is the second-person pronoun; third-person pronouns include *he, she, it,* and *they.*) The gender of a personal pronoun in the third-person singular depends on the gender of its antecedent.

> When Marie Curie outlined the first steps of the award-winning research to *her* husband, *he* encouraged *her* to complete *it.* Though *he himself* was an eminent chemist, *he* wanted *her* to gain credit for *it.*

When the antecedent is a word of unspecified gender such as *doctor* or *lawyer,* you should use something other than a singular masculine pronoun (see 8.2).

20.6 MAKING ANTECEDENTS AND PRONOUNS AGREE IN NUMBER

An antecedent is singular if it refers to one person or thing and plural if it refers to more than one. A singular antecedent calls for a singular pronoun; a plural antecedent calls for a plural pronoun:

The boy saw that he had cut his hand.

The Edmonton Oilers believed that they could win the Stanley Cup in

1988, and they did.

20.7 RESOLVING PROBLEMS IN NUMBER

Some antecedents can be hard to classify as either singular or plural. Here are guidelines:

1. TWO OR MORE NOUNS OR PRONOUNS JOINED BY *AND* ARE USUALLY PLURAL:

Orville and Wilbur Wright are best known for *their* invention of the airplane.

Nouns joined by *and* are singular only if they refer to one person or thing:

The chief cook and bottle washer demanded *his* pay.

2. WHEN TWO NOUNS ARE JOINED BY *OR* OR *NOR*, THE PRONOUN AGREES WITH THE SECOND NOUN:

Neither Pierre LaCroix nor his boldest followers wanted to expose

themselves to danger.

3. A NOUN OR PRONOUN FOLLOWED BY A PREPOSITIONAL PHRASE IS TREATED AS IF IT STOOD BY ITSELF:

In 1980 Canada, together with the United States and several other countries, kept *its* athletes from participating in the Moscow Olympics.

The antecedent of *its* is *Canada.* Unlike the conjunction *and,* a phrase like *together with* or *along with* does not make a compound antecedent.

337

The leader of the strikers said that *he* would get them a new package of benefits.

The pronoun *he* agrees with *leader*. The antecedent of *them* is *strikers*.

4.   COLLECTIVE NOUNS CAN BE EITHER SINGULAR OR PLURAL, DEPENDING ON THE CONTEXT:

The team chooses *its* captain in the spring.

Since the captain is a symbol of unity, the writer treats *the team* as singular, using the singular pronoun *its*.

The audience shouted and stamped *their* feet.

Since each person in the audience was acting independently, the writer treats *the audience* as plural, using the plural pronoun *their*.

5.   SOME INDEFINITE PRONOUNS ARE SINGULAR, SOME ARE PLURAL, AND SOME CAN BE EITHER SINGULAR OR PLURAL:

ALWAYS SINGULAR

anybody	either	one
anyone	neither	another
anything		
each	nobody	somebody
each one	none	someone
	no one	something
everybody	nothing	
everyone		whatever
everything		whichever
		whoever

ALWAYS PLURAL

both	few	others	several

SOMETIMES SINGULAR
AND SOMETIMES PLURAL

all	many	some
any	most	

As this list indicates, *each* by itself is always singular:

Each of the men brought *his* own tools.

But *each* does not change the number of a plural subject that it follows:

The men each brought *their* own tools.

Though some writers treat *everybody* and *everyone* as plural, *we* suggest you treat them as singular or simply avoid using them as antecedents:

Everyone in the cast had to furnish *his* or *her* own costume.

All cast members had to furnish *their* own costumes.

The number of a pronoun in the third group depends on the number of the word or phrase to which it refers:

Some of the salad dressing left *its* mark on my shirt.

Some of the students earn *their* tuition by working part-time.

Many of the customers do not pay *their* bills on time.

Many a man learns to appreciate *his* father only after *he* has become one *himself.*

6. **THE NUMBER OF A RELATIVE PRONOUN DEPENDS ON THE NUMBER OF THE ANTECEDENT:**

Mark is one of those independent carpenters who *want* to work for *themselves.*

Marilyn is the only one of the gymnasts who *wants* to compete in the Olympics.

Recognizing Agreement in Number

Each of the following consists of two sentences. In one sentence the number of the pronoun matches that of its antecedent; in the other it doesn't. Say which sentence is correct—and why.

EXAMPLE:
(a) Twenty years ago, a woman who kept her own name after marriage was hardly considered married at all.
(b) Twenty years ago, a woman who kept their own name after marriage was hardly considered married at all.

Sentence (a) is correct because the singular pronoun *her* matches the singular antecedent *woman.*

1.(a) On the first day of summer, the members of the Smith family found a rude surprise behind its house.
  (b) On the first day of summer, the members of the Smith family found a rude surprise behind their house.

2.(a) A raccoon or the neighbor's dogs had left their tracks on the freshly painted deck in the backyard.
  (b) A raccoon or the neighbor's dogs had left its tracks on the freshly painted deck in the backyard.

3.(a) Every one of the boards showed their trace of the intruders.
  (b) Every one of the boards showed its trace of the intruders.

4.(a) Ordinarily Mr. Smith is one of those stoical types who can control his temper.
  (b) Ordinarily Mr. Smith is one of those stoical types who can control their temper.

5.(a) But this time, he, along with his wife and sons, vented his rage.
  (b) But this time, he, along with his wife and sons, vented their rage.

6.(a) Everyone in the neighborhood has their own version of the uproar that followed.
  (b) Everyone in the neighborhood has his or her own version of the uproar that followed.

7.(a) But every animal within shouting distance of the Smiths' house was put in terror of losing its life.
  (b) But every animal within shouting distance of the Smiths' house was put in terror of losing their lives.

8.(a) For weeks, in fact, neither of the neighbor's two dogs would show its head.
  (b) For weeks, in fact, neither of the neighbor's two dogs would show their head.

20.8 AVOIDING FAULTY SHIFTS IN PRONOUN REFERENCE

To make sure pronouns fit their antecedents, do as follows:

1. Avoid using *they, them,* or *their* with a singular antecedent:

   ▶ No one should be forced into a career that ~~they do~~ *he or she does* not want to pursue.

2. Avoid shifting the reference of a pronoun from one grammatical person to another:

   *When one [third person] is alone, one is free to do whatever you [second person] want.

   EDITED: When one is alone, one is free to do whatever one wants. [or] When you are alone, you are free to do whatever you want.

For the correct use of *you,* see p. 334, "Indefinite *You* and *Your.*"

Revising a Passage with Inconsistent Pronoun Usage

EXERCISE 3

Each of the following passages is marred by shifts in the number and person of pronouns referring to the same antecedent. Make these pronouns consistent in number and person.

1. The job of being a counselor in a girls' summer camp is not an easy one. You have to meet your responsibilities twenty-four hours a day, and they may include such things as making sure her girls attend all the camp meetings, overseeing the cleaning of your cabin, and giving our campers archery lessons. Because of the demands on us, we sometimes become tired and even cross. At these times everybody wants a break—a chance to go someplace else and relax. In a well-run camp you can do this; the director gives everybody a day off. After that we resume our duties with a cheerful, positive attitude.

2. Our body language often expresses our emotions. Through gestures, postures, facial expressions, and other visible signs, we indicate our feelings. If you are elated, for example, you tend to speak with more tonal fluctuations and with more arm movement than when a person is depressed. In a good mood, our eyes sparkle, our posture is erect, and you smile a lot. When someone is angry, their body language tells the tale. Our faces scowl, our jaws are clenched, one's gestures look aggressive, and sparks flash from your eyes. When you are sad, the feeling shows in your downcast eyes, limp shoulders, and shuffling walk.

20.9 PRONOUN CASE FORMS

The form of a pronoun referring to a person depends partly on its case—that is, on the grammatical role it plays in a sentence. Consider this passage:

> The Kiowas are a summer people; *they* abide the cold and keep to themselves, but when the season turns and the land becomes warm and vital *they* cannot hold still; an old love of going returns upon *them*. The aged visitors who came to my grandmother's house when I was a child were made of lean and leather, and they bore *themselves* upright. *They* wore great black hats and bright ample shirts that shook in the wind. *They* rubbed fat upon *their* hair and wound *their* braids with strips of colored cloth.
>
> —N. Scott Momaday, *The Way to Rainy Mountain*

They, them, themselves, and *their* all have the same antecedent, *Kiowas.* But these four pronouns differ in form because they play different roles: subject (*they* abide), object (upon *them*), reflexive object (bore *themselves*), and possessive (*their* braids). Because each form signifies a different case, the difference between one case form and another helps this writer show exactly what his pronouns mean.

Case Forms of Pronouns

Personal Pronouns

	I	*he*	*she*	*it*	*we*	*you*	*they*
SUBJECT CASE	I	he	she	it	we	you	they
OBJECT CASE	me	him	her	it	us	you	them
POSSESSIVE CASE	my, mine	his	her, hers	it	our, ours	your, yours	their, theirs
REFLEXIVE/ EMPHATIC CASE	myself	himself	herself	itself	ourselves	yourself, yourselves	themselves

Pronouns Used in Questions and Adjective Clauses

	who	*whoever*
SUBJECT CASE	who	whoever
OBJECT CASE	whom	whomever
POSSESSIVE CASE	whose	

20.10 USING PRONOUN CASE

SUBJECT CASE

Use the subject case when the pronoun is the subject of a verb:

> When Adam and Eve were accused of eating the forbidden fruit, *they* each excused themselves; *he* blamed Eve for tempting him, and *she* blamed the serpent for tempting her.

OBJECT CASE

1.   Use the object case when the pronoun is the object of a verb:

> We heard birds but could not see *them.*

2.   Use the object case when the pronoun is the object of a gerund, infinitive, or participle:

> GERUND   INFINITIVE
> Hearing *them* made us eager to see *them.*
>
> PARTICIPLE
> Seeing *them,* we could hardly believe our eyes.

3.   Use the object case when the pronoun is the object of a preposition:

> I hate to spread rumors, but what else can one do with *them?*
> —Amanda Lear

4.   Use the object case when the pronoun comes immediately before an infinitive:

> A sentry ordered *us* to leave the area.

POSSESSIVE CASE

1.   Use the possessive case of the pronoun—with *no* apostrophe—to indicate ownership of an object or close connection to it:

> *My* car has a dent in *its* right rear door.
>
> The car with the new paint job is *hers.*

343

2.   Use the possessive case of the pronoun before a gerund—an *-ing* word used as the name of an action:

> Joan hoped that *her* leaving the class early would not be noticed.

For more on this point, see 13.11.

REFLEXIVE/EMPHATIC CASE

Use the reflexive/emphatic case of the pronoun when

1.   the object of a verb or preposition is a pronoun referring to the subject:

> He gazed at *himself* in the mirror as she dressed *herself*.

2.   you want to stress the antecedent of the pronoun:

> The governor *herself* conceived the new plan.

EXERCISE 4   **Choosing Case Forms**

Choose the correct form for the pronoun or pronouns in each of the following sentences, and explain each choice.

EXAMPLE: The coach watched Rosenberg and (I, me) run.

Me (object case) is correct because the pronoun is the direct object of the verb *watched*.

1. (Me, My) brother Frank and (him, his) wife, Rhonda, love to play poker; it's (them, their) favorite pastime.

2. (My, Mine) is pool.

3. Frank and (I, me) sometimes argue about which of the two is more interesting.

4. Since Frank and (me, I) seldom agree on anything, I don't expect (we, us) to settle this question soon—if ever.

5. Frank (him, himself) realizes that (him, his) arguing will never convince (I, me) and that the dispute between (we, us) may continue indefinitely.

6. But Frank and Rhonda don't realize what (them, they) are missing.

7. While poker takes only a good head, pool takes good hands as well. Every shot depends on (their, them) steadiness.

8. Though Frank will admit this, Rhonda always objects to (me, my) saying that poker is mainly a game of luck.

9. In reply, I point out to (they, them) that pool is a game of nothing but skill.

10. But that statement is never the last word. In fact, we would talk (us, ourselves) to exhaustion on this subject if Rhonda did not finally tell Frank and (I, me) to stop.

20.11 USING *WHO, WHOM, WHOSE, WHOEVER,* AND *WHOMEVER*

The form you need depends on which grammatical role the pronoun plays in the sentence or clause that contains it. Observe the following guidelines:

1. Use *who* or *whoever* whenever the pronoun is a subject:

    Some people *who* attended the concert were lucky.

    Tickets were given away to *whoever* wanted them.

2. Use *whom* or *whomever* when the pronoun is an object:

    To *whom* can we turn?

    Some voters will support *whomever* their party nominates.

    They back a candidate *whom* others have selected.

A sentence like this last one can be tightened by the omission of *whom:*

    They back a candidate others have selected.

And if you find w*homever* stiff, you can replace it with *anyone:*

    Some voters will support *anyone* their party nominates.

3. Use *whose* whenever the pronoun is a possessor:

    The colt *whose* picked skeleton lay out there was mine.
    —Wallace Stegner

20.12 MISUSING PRONOUN CASE FORMS

To avoid misusing the case forms of pronouns, observe the following guidelines:

1.   Use the same case forms for pronouns linked by *and:*

     a. *Her and I went swimming every day.

Her is in the object case; *I* is in the subject case. Since they are linked by *and,* both should be in the same case. To see which case that should be, test each pronoun by itself:

     TEST: Her went swimming every day. I went swimming every day.

     EDITED: She and I went swimming every day.

     b. *He and myself took turns driving.

     TEST: He took turns driving. Myself took turns driving.

     EDITED: He and I took turns driving.

     c. *There was little to choose between them and we.

     TEST: There was little to choose between them. There was little to choose between we.

     EDITED: There was little to choose between them and us.

2.   Avoid using *me, him, myself, himself, herself,* or *themselves* as the subject of a verb:

     *Me and Sally waited three hours for a bus.

     TEST: Me waited three hours for a bus. Sally waited three hours.

     EDITED: Sally and I waited three hours for a bus.

3.   Avoid using a *-self* pronoun as the object of a verb unless the pronoun refers to the subject:

     ▸ The director chose Laura and ~~myself~~ *me* for two minor parts, and then cast herself in the leading role.

4. Avoid using a *-self* pronoun as the object of a preposition:

    ▶ The letter was addressed to ~~myself.~~ *me.*

    ▶ The director had to choose between Laura and ~~myself.~~ *me.*

EXCEPTION: A *-self* pronoun may be the object of *by:*

Diana organized the exhibition by herself.

5. Avoid using the forms **hisself,* **theirself,* or **theirselves* under any conditions in academic English.

6. Avoid using *I, he, she, we,* or *they* as the object of a verb or preposition:

    ▶ My uncle always brought presents for my sister and ~~I.~~ *me.*

    ▶ We rarely gave anything to my aunt or ~~he.~~ *him.*

7. When a pronoun after *than* or *as* is compared with a subject, use the subject case:

    ▶ Pete [subject] dribbles faster than ~~me.~~ *I.*

8. Use the object case after *than* or *as* when the pronoun is compared to an object:

    *The manager pays a veteran like Bob [object] more than I [subject case].

    EDITED: The manager pays a veteran like Bob more than he pays me.

9. Avoid confusing *its* and *it's;* or *their, there,* and *they're;* or *whose* and *who's.* For help distinguishing these words, see the Glossary of Usage.

Editing Mistakes in Case

Each of the following sentences may contain one or more mistakes in case. Correct every mistake you find by writing the correct form of the pronoun. If a sentence contains a compound, test it as shown in 20.12. If a sentence is correct as it stands, write *Correct*.

EXAMPLE: The argument between Paul and I is unimportant.

1. Every spring my Aunt Mary and me go fishing in the mountains.

2. We put two sets of camping gear in the truck—mine and her.

3. Sometimes a forest ranger shows us where to look for trout.

4. The rangers theirselves have never fished with us; they just want to help ourselves get our quota.

5. Once my cousin Roger asked if he could go fishing with Aunt Mary and I.

6. Aunt Mary had to decide who to take—him or myself.

7. There wasn't room for we two in the truck, and neither him nor me had a car.

8. That spring her and Roger caught the biggest trout she had ever seen.

9. I heard all about it when Roger arrived home; nobody talks more than him.

10. He can hardly wait until Aunt Mary and him go fishing again.

Subject-Verb Agreement 21

21.1 WHAT IS AGREEMENT?

To say that a verb agrees in form with its subject is to say that a verb has more than one form and that each form matches up with a particular kind of subject. Here are three parallel sets of examples:

	STANDARD ENGLISH	FRENCH	SPANISH
SINGULAR	I live	je vis	(yo)† vivo
	you live	tu vis	(tú) vives
	he lives	il vit	(él) vive
	she lives	elle vit	(ella) vive
PLURAL	we live	nous vivons	vivimos
	you live	vous vivez	vivis
	they live	ils vivent [masc.]	(ellos) viven [masc.]
		elles vivent [fem.]	(ellas) viven [fem.]

In this example, Spanish has six different verb forms, French has five, and Standard English has just two: *live* and *lives*.

To write Standard English correctly, you need to know which form goes with each type of subject, where to find the subject in a clause, and whether the subject is singular or plural.

---

†In Spanish, when the subject is a pronoun, it is sometimes omitted.

349

21.2 MAKING VERBS AGREE WITH SUBJECTS

In most cases, the subject affects the form of the verb only when the verb is in the present tense. Except for the verb *be* (21.3) and for subjunctive verb forms (25.4 and 25.5), the rules of agreement in the present tense are as follows:

1. With third-person singular subjects, add *-s* or *-es* to the bare form of the verb:

> Peggy *wants* to study economics.
>
> She *works* at the bank.
>
> It *serves* over two thousand depositors.
>
> Each of them *holds* a passbook.
>
> Marvin Megabucks *owns* the bank.
>
> He *polishes* his Jaguar once a week.

EXCEPTION: **The verb *have* becomes *has:***

> Everyone *has* moments of self-doubt.
>
> Uncertainty *has* gripped all of us.

2. With all other subjects, use the bare form of the verb:

> Economists *study* the stock market.
>
> They *evaluate* the fluctuation of prices.
>
> Like the experts, we *want* to make profitable investments.
>
> My brother and his wife both *work* on Wall Street.
>
> I *do* other things.

3. Whatever the subject, use the bare form of any verb that follows an auxiliary, such as *does, can,* or *may:*

> Does she *play* the sax?
>
> She can *sing.*
>
> She may *become* famous.

21.3 MAKING THE VERB *BE* AGREE WITH SUBJECTS

1. When *be* is a main verb, its forms are as follows:

PRESENT TENSE

I *am* cold.

You *are* cold.

She
He
It · *is* cold.
Everyone
The student

We
You
They · *are* cold.
Many
The students

PAST TENSE

I *was* busy.

You *were* busy.

She
He
It · *was* busy.
Everyone
The student

We
You
They · *were* busy.
Many
The students

2. When *be* is an auxiliary, its form depends on the subject, just as when *be* is a main verb:

I *am annoyed* by most tax forms.

The current one *is written* in incomprehensible language.

The pages *are covered* with small print and confusing diagrams.

What *were* the experts *thinking* of when they designed the form?

21.4 AVOIDING DIALECTAL MISTAKES IN AGREEMENT

The rules of agreement in academic English differ from the rules of agreement in regional and ethnic dialects. To write academic English correctly, observe the following guidelines:

351

1.   If you're writing about what anyone or anything does now, make sure you add -s or -es to the verb:

> ▶ My brother work *s* for the post office.

> ▶ He live *s* with a couple of his friends.

2.   If you're writing about what you or they (any group of two or more) do now, use only the bare form of the verb:

> ▶ I need~~s~~ a job.

> ▶ Politicians love~~s~~ to make promises.

> ▶ They want~~s~~ votes.

3.   The only verb to use between *I* and a verb with -*ing* added is *am* or *have been:*

> ▶ I ~~be~~ *am* taking calculus this semester.

> ▶ I *have* been living in Seattle since 1998.

4.   If you're writing about what anyone or anything is at present, use *is:*

> ▶ Veronica ~~be~~ *is* my best friend.

> ▶ Smoking ~~be~~ *is* risky.

5.   If you're writing about what two or more persons or things are, use *are:*

> ▶ Banks ~~be~~ *are* closed on holidays.

6.   Use *has* after any one person or thing:

> ▶ My sister ~~have~~ *has* a new apartment.

> ▶ It ~~have~~ *has* two bedrooms.

7.   Use *have* after *I, you,* or any words naming more than one:

> ▶ I ~~has~~ *have* a lot of bills to pay.

> ▶ My feet ~~has~~ *have* been hurting.

8. Before *been,* always use *has, have,* or *had:*

>   *has*
> ▶ Everyone ⌃ been hurt by the layoffs.

>   *have*
> ▶ I ⌃ been studying chemistry.

>   *had*
> ▶ I ~~done~~ ⌃ been watching the news when the phone rang.

Using Correct Verb Forms   EXERCISE 1

For each verb in parentheses, write down a verb form that agrees with the subject. The correct form will sometimes be the same as the one in parentheses. Use the present tense.

EXAMPLE: A cold drink (taste) good on a hot day when you (be) working outside.

tastes, are

1. In Charles Dickens's well-known tale *A Christmas Carol,* Scrooge (be) a coldhearted miser.

2. He (drive) a hard bargain in business and (spend) less on food, lodging, and clothing than any other inhabitant of London (do).

3. The needs of others (do) not concern him; in his opinion, the poor and the homeless may (find) shelter in the public workhouses or prisons.

4. Or they can (die) and thereby help to reduce the surplus population.

5. It (be) not surprising, therefore, that no one (like) to visit with him.

6. Nor (do) he enjoy the company of others; to his way of thinking, all their socializing (have) no value whatsoever.

7. Any moment lost from moneymaking, he thinks, (be) misspent: nobody (get) rich if he or she (devote) even one moment in the day to speaking with friends, helping the needy, or caring for families.

8. Scrooge's outlook (be) vividly illustrated by his behavior on Christmas Eve.

9. He (make) his underpaid clerk work until dark; he (do) not contribute a penny to a subscription for the poor; he (chase) a caroler from the office; and he cannot (speak) a civil word to his only nephew, who (invite) Scrooge to spend Christmas Day with his family.

10. To the miser, all talk of a happy holiday (be) "humbug," and people (be) fools not to spend the hours making money.

21.5 FINDING THE SUBJECT

You can find the subject easily when it comes right before the verb:

> s
> Alan Paton / has written movingly about life in South Africa.

> s
> Many readers / consider *Cry, the Beloved Country* a classic.

But the subject follows the verb in sentences of the following kinds:

1. Sentences starting with *There* or *Here* plus a form of the verb *be:*

> s
> There was once / a thriving civilization in the jungles of the Yucatán.

> s
> Here is / a translation of *Popol Vuh,* the Mayan book about the dawn of life.

2. Sentences with inverted word order:

> s
> Visible near Monte Alban in southern Mexico are / massive pyramids constructed over two thousand years ago.

3. Some questions:

> s
> Have / archeologists / identified the builders of the pyramids?

> s
> Are / you / going to Egypt this year?

> s
> Will / the travel agent / book you on a charter flight?

21.6 RECOGNIZING THE NUMBER OF THE SUBJECT

To make a verb agree with the subject, you must know whether the subject is singular or plural. Observe the following guidelines for various kinds of subjects:

NOUNS MEANING ONE THING

A noun meaning one thing is always singular, even if it ends in *-s:*

> The *lens* was cracked.
>
> *The Grapes of Wrath* is John Steinbeck's greatest novel.
>
> *Gas* is cheaper this summer than it was last fall.

NOUNS MEANING MORE THAN ONE THING

A noun meaning more than one thing is always plural:

> The *lenses* were cracked.
>
> His *teeth* are crooked.
>
> *Women* deserve to be paid as much as *men* are.
>
> The new *data* require study.
>
> *Mice* like cheese.
>
> *Cats* like mice.

PRONOUNS FIXED IN NUMBER

Most pronouns are fixed in number. They include the following:

ALWAYS SINGULAR

he	each	one
she	each one	another
it		
	everybody	somebody
this	everyone	someone
that	everything	something
anybody	either	whatever
anyone	neither	whichever
anything		whoever
	nobody	
	none	
	no one	
	nothing	

ALWAYS PLURAL

we	these	both	few
they	those	others	several

355

PRONOUNS VARIABLE IN NUMBER

The pronouns *all, any, many, more, most, some, who, that,* and *which* are variable in number. The number of such a pronoun depends on the number of the word or phrase to which it refers:

Most of the sand *is* washed by the tide.

Most of the sandpipers *are* white.

Some of the oil *has* been cleaned up.

Some of the problems *have* been solved.

Titan is one of the fifteen known satellites that *revolve* around Saturn.

Titan is the only one of the satellites that *has* an atmosphere.

Many is singular only when used with *a* or *an:*

Many of the artists *visit* Florence.

Many an artist *visits* Florence.

Other pronouns are not affected in number by the phrases that modify them; see "Modified Nouns and Pronouns," p. 357.

VERBAL NOUNS AND NOUN CLAUSES

Verbal nouns are always singular:

> *Reassembling the broken pieces of a china bowl* is difficult.

> *To fit the fragments together* takes considerable patience.

Noun clauses are always singular too:

> *What one also needs* is steady hands.

NOUNS FOLLOWED BY A FORM OF THE VERB *BE*

The verb agrees with what comes before it, no matter what comes after it:

> *Newspapers* are his business.

> His *business* is newspapers.

MODIFIED NOUNS AND PRONOUNS

Except for pronouns variable in number (see above), the number of a modified noun or pronoun depends on the noun (N) or pronoun (PR) itself—not on any of the modifiers (M) attached to it:

M N   M

A ship carrying hundreds of tourists enters the narrow harbor every Friday.

PR   M

Each of the tourists has a credit card, traveler's checks, and the phone number of the local consulate.

M   M   N   M

Any gold ornament, together with silver bracelets and earrings, always attracts a crowd.

COMPOUNDS MADE WITH *AND*

1. Compound subjects made with *and* are plural when they are used before the verb and refer to more than one thing:

> *The lion and the tiger* belong to the cat family.

> *Bach and Beethoven* are among the greatest composers of all time.

2. When a compound subject made with *and* follows the verb, and the first item in the compound is singular, the verb may agree with that:

> There was *a desk and three chairs* in the room.

Strictly speaking, the verb should agree with both items: There *were* a desk and three chairs in the room. But since *There were a desk* sounds odd, no matter what follows *desk*, the verb may agree with *desk* alone—the first item. If the first item is plural, the verb always agrees with it:

> At the entrance stand *two marble pillars and a statue of Napoleon.*

3. A compound subject that is made with *and* and refers to only one thing is always singular:

> *The founder and first president of the college* was Eleazor Wheelock.

ITEMS JOINED BY *OR, EITHER . . . OR,* AND SO ON

When items are joined by *or, either . . . or, neither . . . nor, not . . . but,* or *not only . . . but also,* the verb agrees with the item just before it:

> *Neither steel nor glass* cuts a diamond.

> *Not a new machine but new workers* are needed for the job.

NOUNS SPELLED THE SAME WAY IN SINGULAR AND PLURAL

A noun spelled the same way in the singular and the plural depends for its number on the way it is used:

> A *deer* was nibbling the lettuce.

> *Two deer* were standing in the middle of the road.

> *One means* of campaigning is direct mail.

> *Two other means* are TV advertising and mass rallies.

COLLECTIVE NOUNS AND NOUNS OF MEASUREMENT

Collective nouns and nouns of measurement are singular when they refer to a unit, and plural when they refer to the individuals or elements of a unit:

> *Half of the cake* was eaten.

> *Half of the jewels* were stolen.

> *Statistics* is the study and analysis of numerical information about the world.

> *Recent statistics* show a marked decline in the U.S. birthrate during the past twenty years.

> *Fifty dollars* is a lot to ask for a cap.

SUBJECTS BEGINNING WITH *EVERY*

A subject beginning with *every* is normally singular:

> *Every cat and dog in the neighborhood* was fighting.

But if the subject includes plural items, treat it as plural:

> *Every cat and two of the dogs* were fighting.

THE WORD *NUMBER* AS SUBJECT

The word *number* is singular when it follows *the,* plural when it follows *a:*

> *The number of applications* was huge.

> *A number of teenagers* now hold full-time jobs.

FOREIGN WORDS AND EXPRESSIONS

When the subject is a foreign word or expression, use a dictionary to find out whether it is singular or plural:

> The *coup d'état* has caught diplomats by surprise.

> The *Carbonari* of the early nineteenth century were members of a secret political organization in Italy.

Correcting Faulty Agreement

EXERCISE 2

In some of the following sentences the verb does not agree with its subject. Correct every verb you consider wrong and then explain the correction. If a sentence is correct as it stands, explain why.

EXAMPLE: One of the insurance agents are a graduate of my university.

ANSWER: The verb should be *is* because the subject is *one,* a singular pronoun.

1. Members of the city's transportation department is seeking a solution to the traffic problem on Main Street.

2. There has been many complaints from merchants and shoppers.

3. An attorney representing five store owners are preparing to sue the city for negligence and economic harassment.

4. Each of the five companies have lost money in the last ten months.

5. A number of shoppers is circulating a petition calling for the resignation of the mayor.

6. She, along with the heads of the transportation department, are feeling the heat.

7. Three-quarters of the gripes is justified.

8. Thirty minutes are too long for any motorist to drive two blocks.

9. No one with important errands wants to spend most of a lunch hour looking for a parking space.

10. A new and improved means of traffic control need to be found.

Singular nouns ending in -*s*:

    The *lens* needs to be polished.

Plurals not ending in -*s*:

    The new *data* require study.

Pronouns variable in number:

    Hospital patients like doctors *who* listen.

    My aunt has a doctor *who* listens.

Modified nouns and pronouns:

    Each of the chairs is an antique.

Subjects joined by *either . . . or, not only . . . but also,* and so on:

    Not only the managers but also the umpire was at fault.

    Neither the pitcher nor his teammates were responsible.

Collective nouns and nouns of measurement:

    The *jury* has a private room.

    The *jury* are unable to agree on a verdict.

Modified nouns and pronouns:

    One-third of the seniors are planning to study medicine.

    Each of them has applied to medical school.

The word number as subject:

    A number of women have applied for the job.

    The number of applications has exceeded expectations.

Correcting Faulty Agreement

This exercise will give you practice in dealing with subject-verb agreement in an extended passage. In the following paragraphs, we have deliberately inserted some errors in agreement. We hope you can spot and correct them.

> EXAMPLE: efficiency and level . . . are usually measured (lines 3–4)

Cognition is the process by which the individual acquires knowledge about an object or an event. It includes perceiving, recognizing, judging, and sensing—the ways of knowing. The efficiency and level of the acquisition of knowledge is usually measured in older children and adults by the use of tests which requires language. Studies of   5
infant cognition, of what and how babies "know," have begun to appear only in the last decade, with the development of new techniques which provides insights into what and how babies learn.

In spite of the persistent belief that babies differ along sex lines—for example, that girl babies vocalize more and boy babies are   10
more active—sex differences in cognitive functions in the first two years of life has not been demonstrated (Maccoby and Jacklin, 1974). Measurements of intellectual ability, learning, and memory does not differ on the average for boys and girls. However, patterns of performances are different for the two sexes, as are the consistency (thus   15
the predictability) of the measures as the infants get older. A longitudinal study of 180 white, first-born infants, 91 boys and 89 girls, each of whom were tested in the laboratory at four, eight, thirteen, and twenty-seven months, offers some evidence concerning these patterns (Kagan, 1971). One of the behaviors for which different patterns   20
were observed for boys and girls were vocalization; the infant's response when aroused or excited by an unusual or discrepant stimulus.

—Juanita H. Williams, *Psychology of Women*

22 *Verbs: Tense*

If English is your native language, you probably have a good working knowledge of tenses. You know how to describe what someone or something did in the past, is doing in the present, or will do in the future. But you may not know just how to describe an action that doesn't fall neatly into one time slot. For instance, how do you describe the action of a character in a novel or a play? How do you describe an action that started in the past but is still going on now? How do you write about an action that will be completed at some time in the future? This chapter is chiefly meant to answer questions like these.

The chapter is limited to verbs in the indicative mood (the mood of fact or matters close to fact) and in the active voice (in which the subject performs the action, as in "Whales eat plankton"). For a full discussion of mood, see chapter 25; for a full discussion of voice, see chapter 24.

22.1 TENSE AND TIME

The tense of a verb helps to indicate the time of an action or condition:

PAST: The sun *rose* at 6:03 this morning.

PRESENT: As I *write* these words, the sun *is setting*.

FUTURE: The sun *will rise* tomorrow at 6:04.

But tense is not the same as time. A verb in the present tense, for instance, may be used in a statement about the future:

The bus leaves tomorrow at 7:30 A.M.

The time of an action or state is often indicated by a word or phrase like *tomorrow, next week,* or *last month.*

22.2 FORMING THE TENSES

The tenses of all but a few verbs are made from the four **principal parts**. The principal parts of regular verbs are formed by the addition of *-ing* or *-ed* to the bare form, as shown here:

PRESENT (BARE FORM)	PRESENT PARTICIPLE	PAST	PAST PARTICIPLE
cook	cook*ing*	cook*ed*	cook*ed*
lift	lift*ing*	lift*ed*	lift*ed*
polish	polish*ing*	polish*ed*	polish*ed*

Verbs with some principal parts formed in other ways are called irregular:

eat	eating	ate	eaten
write	writing	wrote	written
go	going	went	gone
speak	speaking	spoke	spoken

For the principal parts of other commonly used irregular verbs, see 22.11.

FORMING THE PRESENT

With most subjects, the form of a verb in the present tense is simply the bare form:

> Seasoned traders *drive* hard bargains.

> I *polish* my shoes every day.

But after a singular noun or a third-person singular pronoun, such as *she, it, this, each,* or *everyone,* you must add *-s* or *-es* to the bare form of the verb:

> Helen *drives* a cab.

> She *polishes* it once a week.

For more on this point, see 21.1–21.4.

FORMING THE PAST

The past tense of regular verbs is formed by the addition of *-d* or *-ed* to the bare form:

> Helen *liked* her work.

> She *polished* her cab regularly.

For the past tense of commonly used irregular verbs, see 22.11.

FORMING TENSES WITH AUXILIARIES

Besides the present and the past, there are four other tenses. You form these by using certain auxiliary verbs, such as *will, has,* and *had:*

	REGULAR VERB	IRREGULAR VERB
FUTURE	She will work.	She will speak.
PRESENT PERFECT	She has worked.	She has spoken.
PAST PERFECT	She had worked.	She had spoken.
FUTURE PERFECT	She will have worked.	She will have spoken.

USING THE COMMON AND PROGRESSIVE FORMS

The common forms shown above indicate an action viewed as momentary, habitual, completed, or expected. The progressive forms indicate that the action named by the verb is viewed as continuing. Either form may be used with each tense:

PRESENT

COMMON: Coluntuano *runs* two miles every morning.

PROGRESSIVE: Coluntuano *is running* for mayor.

PAST

COMMON: Charles Dickens *wrote* many novels.

PROGRESSIVE: Charles Dickens *was writing* a mystery novel when he died.

FUTURE

COMMON: In the years ahead, many cars *will run* on batteries.

PROGRESSIVE: Many of us *will be driving* electric cars.

Writing Principal Parts

For each of the following sentences write out the principal parts of the italicized verb, listing in sequence the present, the present participle, the past, and the past participle. Whenever you are unsure of a form, refer to your dictionary or to the list of irregular verbs in 22.11.

EXAMPLE: The concert *begins* at 8 P.M.

begin, beginning, began, begun

1. In 1927 Charles A. Lindbergh *flew* nonstop from New York to Paris.

2. On his return New Yorkers *gave* him a hero's welcome.

3. Some spectators *had slept* on the sidewalk in order not to miss the parade.

4. No one who *witnessed* the triumphant procession ever *forgot* the spectacle.

5. The young American *had laid* to rest the fear of crossing the Atlantic in a plane. (For a full discussion of the verbs *lay* and *lie,* see the Glossary of Usage.)

6. He *had broken* a barrier with his record flight.

22.3 USING THE PRESENT

1. USE THE *COMMON PRESENT*

a. To report what happens regularly:

Concert pianists usually *practice* every day.

Leaves *change* color in autumn.

b. To state a fact or widely held belief:

Water *freezes* at 32°F.

Opposites *attract.*

c. To describe characters, events, or other matters in an aesthetic work, such as a painting, a piece of music, a work of literature, a movie, or a television show:

In *Jaws,* a vicious shark *attacks* and *terrifies* swimmers until it is finally killed.

In the first chapter of *Far from the Madding Crowd,* Gabriel *sees* the beautiful Bathsheba, but she *does* not *see* him.

d. To say what a writer or a creative artist does in his or her work:

Many of Georgia O'Keeffe's paintings *convey* the stark contrasts of the harsh and beautiful desert.

In *The Wealth of Nations* (1776), Adam Smith *argues* that an "invisible hand" regulates individual enterprise for the good of society as a whole.

In his Fifth Symphony, Beethoven *reveals* the power and fury of his imagination.

e. To describe an opinion or idea:

In the Marxist vision of history, the ruling classes ceaselessly *oppress* the working class.

f. To indicate that a condition or situation is likely to last:

My sister *loves* chocolate ice cream.

g. To describe a future action that is definitely predictable:

The fair *opens* on Wednesday.

h. To report a statement of lasting significance:

"All art," *says* Oscar Wilde, "is quite useless."

2. USE THE *PRESENT PROGRESSIVE*

a. To indicate that an action or state is occurring at the time of the writing:

The sun *is setting* now, and the birches *are bending* in the wind.

b. To indicate a gradual process that need not be taking place at the exact moment of the writing:

Suburban life *is losing* its appeal. Many young couples *are moving* out of the suburbs and into the cities.

22.4 USING THE PRESENT PERFECT

1. USE THE *COMMON PRESENT PERFECT*

a. To report a past action or state that touches in some way on the present:

> I *have* just *finished* reading *Gone with the Wind.*

> A presidential commission *has* already *investigated* the causes of one nuclear accident.

The words *just* and *already* are often used with the present perfect.

b. To report an action or state begun in the past but extending into the present:

> Engineers *have begun* to explore the possibility of harnessing the tides.

> Since the invention of the automobile, traffic accidents *have taken* many thousands of lives.

c. To report an action performed at some unspecified time in the past:

> I *have seen* the Statue of Liberty.

2. USE THE *PROGRESSIVE FORM* OF THE *PRESENT PERFECT* when you want to emphasize both the continuity of an action from the past into the present and the likelihood of its continuing into the future:

> Some instrumental satellites *have been traveling* through space for years.

> The cost of routine medical care *has been growing* at a staggering rate.

22.5 USING THE PAST

1. USE THE *COMMON PAST*

a. To report an action or state that was definitely completed in the past:

> Thomas Edison *invented* the phonograph in 1877.

> The city *became* calm after the cease-fire.

b.   To report actions repeated in the past but no longer occurring at the time of the writing:

The family always *went* to church on Sundays.

2.   USE THE *PAST PROGRESSIVE*

a.   To emphasize the continuity of a past action:

His insults *were becoming* unbearable.

b.   To state that one action was being performed when another occurred:

I *was pouring* a glass of water when the pitcher suddenly cracked.

22.6   USING THE PAST PERFECT

1.   USE THE *COMMON PAST PERFECT*

a.   To state that an action or state was completed by a specified time in the past:

By noon we *had gathered* three hundred bushels.

b.   To indicate that one past action or state was completed by the time another occurred:

By the time Hitler sent reinforcements, the Allies *had* already *taken* much of France.

I suddenly realized that I *had left* my keys at home.

By the age of thirty, she *had already borne* seven children.

c.   To report an unfulfilled hope or intention:

Mary *had planned* to travel as far as Denver, but her money ran out while she was still in Chicago.

2.   USE THE *PROGRESSIVE FORM* OF THE *PAST PERFECT*   to indicate that the first of two past actions or states went on until the second occurred:

Before Gloria entered Mark's life, he *had been spending* most of his time with books.

22.7 USING THE FUTURE

1. **USE THE** *COMMON FUTURE*

a. To report a future event or state that will occur regardless of human intent:

> The sun *will rise* at 6:35 tomorrow morning.
>
> I *will be* nineteen on my next birthday.

b. To indicate willingness or determination to do something:

> The president has declared that he *will veto* the bill.

c. To report what will happen under certain conditions:

> If you get up early enough, you *will see* the sunrise.

d. To indicate future probability:

> The cost of a college education *will increase*.

In the preceding examples, the auxiliary *will* is used. Years ago, *will* generally went with *you, they, he, she, it,* and noun subjects, and *shall* was used with *I* and *we* to express the simple future. When *will* was used with *I* and *we*, it signified the speaker's (or writer's) determination: "We will stop the enemy." The use of *shall* with *you, they, he, she, it,* or a noun subject had the same function: "You shall pay the tax." But in current usage *shall* and *will* mean about the same thing, and most writers use *will* with all subjects to express the simple future. Some writers substitute *shall*, again with all subjects, to express determination or certainty: "We shall overcome."

2. **USE THE** *FUTURE PROGRESSIVE*

a. To say that an action or state will be continuing for a period of time in the future:

> Twenty years from now, many Americans *will be driving* electric cars.
>
> In doing so, they *will be helping* to reduce our consumption of fuel and our pollution of the air.

b.   To say what the subject will be doing at a given time in the future:

Next semester I *will be taking* Sociology 101.

Also, I *will be auditing* two other social science classes.

22.8 USING THE FUTURE PERFECT

1.   **USE THE *COMMON FUTURE PERFECT***

a.   To say that an action or state will be completed by a specified time in the future:

At the rate I'm living, I *will have spent* all my summer earnings by the end of October.

b.   To say that an action or state will be completed by the time something else happens:

By the time an efficient engine is produced, we *will have exhausted* our supplies of fuel.

2.   **USE THE *PROGRESSIVE FORM* OF THE *FUTURE PERFECT*** to say that an activity or state will continue until a specified time in the future:

By 2000 the *Pioneer 10* probe *will have been traveling* through space for more than twenty-five years.

No one *will have been tracking* its progress longer than Dr. Stellar.

22.9 MISUSING TENSES

1.   **USE THE *COMMON PRESENT***—not the present progressive—to report what happens regularly:

> ▶ Usually my day ~~is starting~~ at 7:00 A.M.

starts

2. USE THE *PAST PERFECT*—not the simple past—for action completed by the time something else happened:

▶ By the time the game ended, many of the spectators ⟨had⟩ left.

3. USE THE *PRESENT PERFECT*—not the past—for action continuing into the present:

▶ Ever since the steel plant closed, the town ⟨has⟩ suffered.

22.10 MANAGING TENSE AND TIME WITH PARTICIPLES AND INFINITIVES

Participles and infinitives have two tenses: the present and the perfect:

	PRESENT	PERFECT
INFINITIVE	to dance	to have danced
PARTICIPLE	dancing	having danced

1. USE THE *PRESENT TENSE* when the action or state named by the participle or infinitive occurs at or after the time of the main verb:

> We spend hours in conference with individual students, hours *meeting* together and with counselors, *trying to teach* ourselves how *to teach* and *asking* ourselves what we ought *to be teaching*.
>
> —Adrienne Rich

2. USE THE *PERFECT TENSE* when the action or state named by the participle or infinitive occurred before the time of the main verb:

> *Having lost* his cargo during the hurricane, the captain faced bankruptcy when his vessel finally reached port.

> Several reporters are sorry *to have missed* the president's impromptu press conference.

22.11 FORMING THE PRINCIPLE PARTS OF COMMONLY USED IRREGULAR VERBS

Following is a selected list of irregular verbs—those with special forms for the past, the past participle, or both. When more than one form for a principal part is shown, the first is more commonly used (except for *was* and *were,* which are used with equal frequency). For verbs not listed here, see your dictionary.

PRESENT (BARE FORM)	PRESENT PARTICIPLE	PAST	PAST PARTICIPLE
arise	arising	arose	arisen
awake	awaking	awoke, awaked	awoke, awaked, awoken
be†	being	was / were	been
bear [bring forth]	bearing	bore	born, borne
bear [carry]	bearing	bore	borne
beat	beating	beat	beaten, beat
begin	beginning	began	begun
bid [command]	bidding	bade	bid, bidden
bid [offer to pay]	bidding	bid	bid
bite	biting	bit	bitten
bleed	bleeding	bled	bled
blend	blending	blended, blent	blended, blent
blow	blowing	blew	blown
break	breaking	broke	broken
bring	bringing	brought	brought
buy	buying	bought	bought
catch	catching	caught	caught
choose	choosing	chose	chosen
clothe	clothing	clothed, clad	clothed, clad
come	coming	came	come

†In this case the bare form *(be)* is not the same as the present *(am, is, are).*

PRESENT (BARE FORM)	PRESENT PARTICIPLE	PAST	PAST PARTICIPLE
cost	costing	cost	cost
creep	creeping	crept	crept
dig	digging	dug	dug
dive	diving	dived, dove	dived
do	doing	did	done
draw	drawing	drew	drawn
drink	drinking	drank	drunk, drunken
drive	driving	drove	driven
eat	eating	ate	eaten
fall	falling	fell	fallen
feel	feeling	felt	felt
fight	fighting	fought	fought
find	finding	found	found
fly	flying	flew	flown
forbid	forbidding	forbade, forbad	forbidden, forbid
forget	forgetting	forgot	forgotten, forgot
freeze	freezing	froze	frozen
get	getting	got	got, gotten
give	giving	gave	given
go	going	went	gone
grow	growing	grew	grown
hang [execute]	hanging	hanged	hanged
hang [suspend]	hanging	hung	hung
have	having	had	had
hear	hearing	heard	heard
hide	hiding	hid	hidden, hid
hit	hitting	hit	hit

PRESENT (BARE FORM)	PRESENT PARTICIPLE	PAST	PAST PARTICIPLE
hold	holding	held	held
keep	keeping	kept	kept
know	knowing	knew	known
lay	laying	laid	laid
lead	leading	led	led
learn	learning	learned, learnt	learned, learnt
leave	leaving	left	left
let	letting	let	let
lie [recline]	lying	lay	lain
lie [tell a falsehood]	lying	lied	lied
lose	losing	lost	lost
make	making	made	made
pay	paying	paid	paid
prove	proving	proved	proved, proven
ride	riding	rode	ridden
ring	ringing	rang	rung
rise	rising	rose	risen
run	running	ran	run
saw	sawing	sawed	sawed, sawn
see	seeing	saw	seen
seek	seeking	sought	sought
shake	shaking	shook	shaken
shine	shining	shone	shone
show	showing	showed	shown, showed
shrink	shrinking	shrank, shrunk	shrunk, shrunken
sing	singing	sang	sung

PRESENT (BARE FORM)	PRESENT PARTICIPLE	PAST	PAST PARTICIPLE
sink	sinking	sank, sunk	sunk, sunken
slay	slaying	slew	slain
sleep	sleeping	slept	slept
smell	smelling	smelled, smelt	smelled, smelt
speak	speaking	spoke	spoken
spin	spinning	spun, span	spun
spring	springing	sprang	sprung
steal	stealing	stole	stolen
stride	striding	strode	stridden
strike	striking	struck	struck, stricken
strive	striving	strove	striven
swear	swearing	swore	sworn
sweep	sweeping	swept	swept
swim	swimming	swam	swum
take	taking	took	taken
teach	teaching	taught	taught
tear	tearing	tore	torn
throw	throwing	threw	thrown
tread	treading	trod	trodden, trod
wake	waking	woke, waked	woke, waked, woken
wear	wearing	wore	worn
weave	weaving	wove	woven
wed	wedding	wed, wedded	wed, wedded
weep	weeping	wept	wept
wind	winding	wound	wound
work	working	worked, wrought	worked, wrought
write	writing	wrote	written

Picturing the Tenses

Simple Present

NOW

PAST—○ ○ ○ ○ ⊕ ○ ○ ○ ○—FUTURE

Water *freezes* at 32°F.
My sister *loves* ice cream.

Present Progressive

NOW

PAST——○ ○ ○│○ ○ ○——FUTURE

Sam *is cooking* linguine.

Simple Past

NOW

PAST—○————│————FUTURE

Edison *invented* the phonograph in 1877.

Past Progressive

NOW

PAST—○⌒⌒⌒○——│————FUTURE

I *was pouring* water when the pitcher cracked.

Simple Future

NOW

PAST————│———○——FUTURE

The cost of a college education *will increase*.

Future Progressive

NOW

PAST————│——○ ○ ○ ○—FUTURE

Next semester I *will be taking* Sociology 101.

Present Perfect

NOW

PAST—○⌒⌒⌒⊕————FUTURE

Up to now, traffic accidents *have taken* many lives.

Present Perfect Progressive

NOW   (probably)

PAST——○ ○ ○ ⊕ ○ ○ ○——FUTURE

The cost of medical care *has been growing*.

Past Perfect

NOW

PAST—○———○—│————FUTURE

I suddenly realized that I *had left* my keys at home.

Past Perfect Progressive

NOW

PAST—○⌒⌒⌒○——│———FUTURE

Before Gloria entered Mark's life, he *had been spending* his time with books.

Future Perfect

NOW

PAST————│—○———○——FUTURE

By the time we arrive, she *will have gone*.

Future Perfect Progressive

NOW

PAST—○⌒⌒⌒⌒⊕⌒⌒⌒○——FUTURE

By June I *will have been taking* courses for six quarters in a row.

Using Tenses

In the following passage, we have replaced nearly every verb with a blank and put the bare form of the verb in parentheses. Write out the passage with the appropriate tense of each verb.

EXAMPLE: When he _____ (arrive) in London in 1900, the twenty-six-year-old magician _____ (do) not have a single booking.

arrived, did

In 1901, when Houdini _____ (take) on the Imperial Police, he _____ (is) not _____ (whistle) in the dark. By the time he _____ (leave) America at the end of the nineteenth century he _____ (dissect) every kind of lock he _____ (can) find in the New World, and whatever he _____ (can) import from the old one. Arriving in London, Houdini _____ (can) write that there _____ (are) only a few kinds of British handcuffs, "seven or eight at the utmost," and these _____ (are) some of the simplest he _____ (have) ever _____ (see). He _____ (search) the markets, antique shops, and locksmiths, buying up all the European locks he _____ (can) find so he _____ (can) dismantle and study them.

—Daniel Mark Epstein, "The Case of Harry Houdini"

23 Verbs: Sequence of Tenses

23.1 UNDERSTANDING SEQUENCE OF TENSES

When a passage has more than one verb, the relation between the tenses of the verbs is called the sequence of tenses. Various sequences are possible.

When all the verbs in a sentence describe actions or states that occur at or about the same time, their tenses should be the same:

> Whenever the alarm clock *rings*, I *yawn*, *stretch*, and *roll* over for another fifteen minutes of sleep. (all present tense)

> The prima donna *opened* her arms to the audience, *smiled*, and *bowed* deeply. (all past tense)

On the other hand, a sentence may describe actions that happen at different times. It will then have verbs in different tenses:

> Beth *had been working* on the research project for almost three years before she *made* the first discovery. (past perfect and past)

> Recently the largest bank in the area *lowered* its interest rate on loans; the directors *want* to stimulate borrowing. (past and present)

23.2 SEQUENCES IN COMPOUND SENTENCES

A compound sentence consists of two or more independent clauses. Since the clauses are independent, the tenses of the verbs may be independent of each other:

In the past, most Americans *wanted* big cars, but now many *drive* small ones. (past and present)

The number of finback whales *is decreasing;* as a result, they *will be added* to the list of endangered species. (present and future)

I *wanted* a big raise, but I *will be getting* a small one. (past and future)

23.3 SEQUENCES IN COMPLEX SENTENCES

A complex sentence consists of one independent clause and at least one subordinate clause (see chapter 17). In this kind of sentence, which often deals with two different times, many sequences are possible. The sequence chiefly depends on the tense of the main verb.

MAIN VERB IN THE PRESENT

MAIN VERB	SUBORDINATE VERB
Some Americans *are* so poor	that they *suffer* from malnutrition. (present)
Most children *learn* to talk	after they *have learned* to walk. (present perfect)
Greg *likes* to boast about the marlin	that he *caught* last summer. (past)
Astronomers *predict*	that the sun *will die* in about ten billion years. (future)

MAIN VERB IN THE PRESENT PERFECT

MAIN VERB	SUBORDINATE VERB
Scientists *have studied* the rings of Saturn	ever since Galileo *discovered* them. (past)

SUBORDINATE VERB	MAIN VERB
Although drivers *have complained* about the heavy traffic, (present perfect)	the police *have done* nothing to alleviate the problem.

MAIN VERB IN THE PAST

MAIN VERB	SUBORDINATE VERB
Centuries ago most people *believed*	that the sun *revolved* around the Earth. (past)
Copernicus *discovered*	that the Earth *revolves* around the sun. (present, for statements of timeless truth)
Recently archaeologists working in Egypt *opened* a tomb	that *had been sealed* in about 2500 B.C. (past perfect)

SUBORDINATE VERB	MAIN VERB
When the crewmen *saw* land, (past)	they cheered.

MAIN VERB IN THE PAST PERFECT

SUBORDINATE VERB	MAIN VERB
By the time Columbus *sighted* land, (past)	most of his crew *had lost* all hope of survival.

MAIN VERB INDICATING FUTURE

MAIN VERB	SUBORDINATE VERB
People *will buy* new homes	when interest rates *are* (or *have been*) *lowered*. (present or present perfect)
Students *will get* their diplomas	only after they *pay* (or *have paid*) their library fines. (present or present perfect)
I *start* my summer job	just as soon as I *take* (or *have taken*) my exams. (present or present perfect)

As the examples show, the subordinate verb in this kind of sequence is never future in form:

▶ The building will be demolished when the school year ~~will end.~~ *ends.*

▶ [or] The building will be demolished when the school year ~~will end.~~ *has ended.*

MAIN VERB IN THE FUTURE PERFECT

MAIN VERB

SUBORDINATE VERB

Workers *will have completed* repairs   by the time the airport *reopens*.
(present)

On the sequence of tenses in the indirect reporting of discourse, see 26.2.

Transforming Tenses   **EXERCISE 1**

In each of the following sentences, change the italicized verb to the past tense if it is in the present, and to the present tense if it is in the past. Then, if necessary, change the tense of the subordinate verb.

EXAMPLE: We ~~want~~ to take a walk before it ~~starts~~ raining.
                     wanted   *started*

1. On April 9, 1865, when Lee's Army of Northern Virginia has already been defeated, Ulysses S. Grant *meets* Robert E. Lee at Appomattox Court House, Virginia.

2. Historians *believed* that this meeting ended the Civil War.

3. The Confederate government *struggles* to survive for a short time even after Lee formally surrenders to Grant.

4. But Grant and Lee both *know* that the war is over.

5. They *realize* that the time for peace has come.

23.4 USING SEQUENCES IN PARAGRAPHS

A paragraph normally includes many verbs and often several different tenses. But you should shift tenses in a paragraph only when you have a good reason for doing so.

A well-written paragraph is usually dominated by just one tense. Consider the following example:

> Before I *set* my world record, I *was* a great fan of *The Guinness Book of World Records* and *read* each new edition from cover to cover. I *liked* knowing and being able to tell others that the world's chug-a-lug champ *consumed* 2.58 pints of beer in 10 seconds, that the world's lightest adult person *weighed*

only 13 pounds, that the largest vocabulary for a talking bird *was* 531 words, spoken by a brown-beaked budgerigar named Sparky. There *is*, of course, only a fine line between admiration and envy, and for awhile I *had been* secretly *desiring* to be in that book myself—to astonish others just as I *had been astonished*. But it *seemed* hopeless. How could a nervous college sophomore, an anonymous bookworm, perform any of those wonderful feats? The open-throat technique necessary for chug-a-lugging *was* incomprehensible to my trachea—and I *thought* my head alone must weigh close to 13 pounds.

—William Allen, "How to Set a World Record"

The author is describing a past condition, so the dominant tense here is the simple past, as in *was, read, liked, consumed, weighed,* and *seemed*. Midway through the paragraph the author shifts out of the simple past, to express a general truth in the present tense (there *is* a fine line) and two conditions that existed before the simple past *(had been desiring, had been astonished)*. Then the author returns to the simple past with *seemed, was,* and *thought*.

Now consider this paragraph:

February 2, 1975. Wasps *begin* to appear in country houses about now, and even in some suburban houses. One *sees* them dart uncertainly about, *hears* them buzz and bang on window panes, and one *wonders* where they came from. They probably *came* from the attic, where they *spent* the early part of the winter hibernating. *Now* with longer hours of daylight, the wasps *begin* to rouse and *start* exploring.

—Hal Borland, "Those Attic Wasps"

This passage describes not a past condition but a recurrent one—something that happens every year. The dominant tense of the verbs, therefore, is the present: *begin, sees, hears, wonders, begin, start*. Since the presence of the wasps calls for some explanation, the writer shifts tense in the middle of the paragraph to tell us where they *came* from and where they *spent* the early part of the winter. But in the final sentence, *now* brings us back to the present, and the verbs of this sentence, *begin* and *start,* are in the present tense.

23.5 CORRECTING FAULTY TENSE SHIFTS IN SENTENCES

The shift of tenses in a sentence is faulty when the tense of any verb differs without good reason from the tense of the one before it, or when the tense of a subordinate verb is inconsistent with the tense of the main verb:

▶ The novel describes the adventures of two immigrant families who

enter the United States at New York, withstand the stresses of culture

shock, and ~~traveled~~ *travel* to the Dakota Territory to make their fortune.

▶ Marthe likes to display the miniature spoons she ~~had~~ *has* collected since

her marriage to an antique dealer.

Correcting Faulty Tense Shifts in a Sentence   EXERCISE 2

In some of the following sentences, the tense of one or more verbs does not properly correspond to the tense of the italicized verb. Correct those sentences. If a sentence is correct as it stands, write *Correct*.

EXAMPLE: A roll of thunder *announced* the coming of the storm; then drops of rain ~~begin~~ *began* to pelt the earth.

1. Filters *are being installed* in water systems that had been threatened by pollutants from industrial wastes.

2. The pollutants *were* first *discovered* last July when inspectors from the city's water department have checked the systems.

3. At that time, inspectors *found* that pollutants have already made the water unsafe to drink.

4. The water *will be* drinkable after the filters had been installed.

5. But until the installation was complete, residents *will drink* bottled water.

23.6 CORRECTING FAULTY TENSE SHIFTS IN PARAGRAPHS

The shift of tenses in a paragraph is faulty when the tense of a verb differs without good reason from the dominant tense of the paragraph. Consider two examples, the first a commentary on *Green Mansions,* a novel by W. H. Hudson:

[1] On his return to the once peaceful woods, Abel *is horrified* to learn that his beloved Rima *has been slain* by savages. [2] Rage and grief *swell* within him as Kua-kó *tells* how Rima *was forced* to seek refuge in a tree and how

the tree *became* a trap when the savages *sent* searing flames and choking smoke high into the branches. [3] As Abel *hears* of her final cry—"Abel! Abel!"—and fatal plunge to earth, he *fought* against a wild impulse to leap upon the Indian and tear his heart out.

Since the present tense is normally used in the summary of a literary work (see 22.3), the dominant tense is the present *(swell, tells,* and *hears).* There is one shift to the present perfect *(has been slain* in sentence 1) and four shifts to the past *(was forced, became, sent* in sentence 2; *fought* in sentence 3). The shifts in sentences 1 and 2 are correct; the shift in sentence 3 is not. In sentence 1, *has been slain* tells what has just happened before Abel is horrified to learn about it. In sentence 2, the past-tense verbs describe what happened well before Kua-kó *tells* about it. But in sentence 3, the verb *fought* tells what Abel does when he *hears* of Rima's death. *Fought* should be *fights.*

[1] To understand Marx, we *need* to know something about the times in which he *lived*. [2] The period *was characterized* by revolutionary pressures against the ruling classes. [3] In most of the countries of Europe, there *was* little democracy, as we *know* it. [4] The masses *participated* little, if at all, in the world of political affairs, and very fully in the world of drudgery. [5] For example, at one factory in Manchester, England, in 1862, people *work* an average of 80 hours per week. [6] For these long hours of toil, the workers generally *receive* small wages. [7] They often *can do* little more than feed and clothe themselves. [8] Given these circumstances, it *is* little wonder that revolutionary pressures *were* manifest.

—Deliberately altered from Edwin Mansfield, *Economics*

In sentence 1 the writer correctly shifts from the present tense *(need),* which signifies the writer's time, to the past tense *(lived),* which signifies Marx's time. In the last part of sentence 3, he correctly returns to the present tense *(know)* to signify his own time, and then shifts back to Marx's time with the past tense *(participated).* But in sentences 5, 6, and 7, the shifts to the present tense *(work, receive, can do)* are wrong because the verbs refer to past actions; they should be *worked, received,* and *could do.* In sentence 8 both tenses are correct. The present tense *is* signifies the writer's time, while the past tense *were* signifies Marx's time.

Correcting Faulty Tense Shifts in a Paragraph   **EXERCISE 3**

Each of the following paragraphs is a rewritten version of a paragraph from the source cited after it. Into each paragraph, we have deliberately introduced one or more faulty shifts in tense. Correct them.

EXAMPLE: manfully thrashes (line 3)

1. However violent his acts, Kong remains a gentleman. Whenever a fresh boa constrictor threatens Fay, Kong first sees that the lady is safely parked, then manfully thrashed her attacker. (And she, the ingrate, runs away every time his back was turned.) Atop the Empire State Building, ignoring his pursuers, Kong places Fay on a ledge as tenderly as if she were a dozen   5 eggs. He fondled her, then turned to face the Army Air Force. And Kong is perhaps the most disinterested lover since Cyrano: his attentions to the lady were utterly without hope of reward. After all, between a five-foot blonde and a fifty-foot ape, love can hardly be more than an intellectual flirtation. His forced exit from his jungle, in chains, results directly from   10 his single-minded pursuit of Fay. He smashes a Broadway theater when the notion entered his dull brain that the flashbulbs of photographers somehow endanger the lady. His perilous shinnying up a skyscraper to have plucked Fay from her boudoir is an act of the kindliest of hearts. He was impossible to discourage even though the love of his life can't lay   15 eyes on him without shrieking murder.

   —Deliberately altered from X. J. Kennedy, "Who Killed King Kong?"

2. Since graduating from college, Susan has held a variety of political jobs. Her warm, friendly manner, together with her capacity for hard work, makes her an ideal employee. Three years ago, she managed the reelection campaign of a New England governor. She has to talk with people in all parts of the state, trying to build support. Soon after the election, which   5 turns out successfully for the governor, Susan goes to Washington, D.C., to work for a senator. She had a high-paying position; but, being more interested in working creatively than in making money, she soon re-signed, proclaiming, "Never have so many people done so little work for so much money." Because she has had so much experience, finding a   10 new job was easy. She becomes an adviser to the New England Gover-nors' Conference on Energy.

   —Deliberately altered from Mark Bartlett, "A Political Woman"

    Avoiding Faulty Tense Shifts

In discussing literary works, use the common present—not the past—as the dominant tense:

> As Macbeth *ponders* the prophecies, a desire to be king *rises* within
>
> him. He ~~envisioned~~ [envisions] the crown upon his head and ~~imagined~~ [imagines] how the
>
> Scots ~~would~~ [will] cheer when he *sits* upon the throne.

In writing about past events from the vantage point of the present, use the past tense for what applies to the past, and the present tense for what applies to the present:

> Today many Democrats *like* to swap stories about Harry Truman, who
>
> *was* noted for his plain speech. He *is* especially *remembered* for what
>
> he ~~threatens~~ [threatened] to do after he *reads* a harsh review of a concert *given*
>
> by his daughter.

Verbs: Active and Passive Voice

24.1 WHAT VOICE IS

The *voice* of a verb depends on the relation between the verb and its subject. When the subject of a verb *acts*, the verb is in the *active voice*; when the subject is *acted upon*, the verb is in the *passive voice*.

The active voice stresses the activity of the subject and helps to make a sentence direct, concise, and vigorous:

The old woman *threatened* me with her umbrella.

The tornado *flattened* entire houses.

You can't *steal* second base and *keep* one foot on first.
—Anonymous

The passive voice presents the subject as the target of an action:

Entire houses *were flattened* by the tornado.

The barn *was struck* by a bolt of lightning.

In Moulmein, in Lower Burma, I *was hated* by large numbers of people—the only time in my life that I have been important enough for this to happen to me.
—George Orwell

In passive constructions, the performer of the action is called an *agent*. In the examples above, *a bolt of lightning* and *large numbers of people* are agents.

24.2 FORMING THE ACTIVE AND THE PASSIVE VOICE

Verbs in the active voice can take many forms: the bare form, the past-tense form, the *-ing* form with *be,* and the form with *have:*

My sisters often *chop* logs for exercise.

Last week they *stacked* firewood for the stove.

But today they *are lifting* weights.

They *have done* wonders.

Verbs in the passive voice are formed from their past participle and some tense of *be:*

The burglar alarms *were chosen* by a security guard.

They *will be installed* next week.

They *will be tested* every month.

CHANGING FROM ACTIVE TO PASSIVE

You can change a verb from active to passive only if it has a direct object (DO):

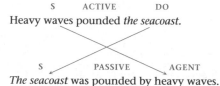

       S   ACTIVE   DO
Heavy waves pounded *the seacoast.*

       S   PASSIVE   AGENT
The seacoast was pounded by heavy waves.

If the performer of an action is not important to your point, you don't need to mention the agent:

       S   ACTIVE   DO
Workers installed burglar alarms.

       S   PASSIVE   AGENT OMITTED
Burglar alarms were installed.

CHANGING FROM PASSIVE TO ACTIVE

To change a verb from the passive to the active voice, turn the subject of the passive verb into the direct object of the active one:

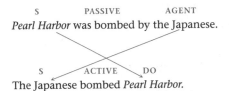

<small>S   PASSIVE   AGENT</small>
Pearl Harbor was bombed by the Japanese.

<small>S   ACTIVE   DO</small>
The Japanese bombed *Pearl Harbor.*

If the passive version does not include the agent, you must either keep the passive or supply the agent itself before changing to the active:

The city of Washington was planned in 1791. (passive, no agent)

The city of Washington was planned in 1791 by Pierre-Charles L'Enfant. (passive, agent supplied)

Pierre-Charles L'Enfant planned the city of Washington in 1791. (active)

PASSIVE VOICE VERSUS PROGRESSIVE FORM

Passive-voice verbs look something like verbs in the progressive form, because both types of verbs include a form of *be*. But don't confuse the types. The passive voice includes a form of *be* and the *past* participle, which usually ends in *-ed;* the progressive form includes a form of *be* and the *present* participle, which always ends in *-ing.* The progressive form is never used in the passive and often used in the active:

<small>PROGRESSIVE FORM</small>
<small>ACTIVE VOICE</small>
Ellen *was washing* her dog when I arrived.

<small>PASSIVE VOICE</small>
The dog *was washed* as I watched.

24.3 CHOOSING THE ACTIVE VOICE

To make your writing forceful, direct, and concise, you should use the active voice frequently. Compare these sentences:

> Through her studies of child-rearing and culture, world fame was achieved by Margaret Mead. (passive)

> Through her studies of child-rearing and culture, Margaret Mead achieved world fame. (active)

The active version ditches the excess verbal baggage—*was* and *by*—and highlights the action of the subject. To a great extent, the life and energy of your writing will depend on what the subjects of your sentences do.

24.4 CHOOSING THE PASSIVE VOICE

Forceful as the active voice is, you should know when to use the passive.

1.   Use the passive when you want to keep the focus on someone or something that is acted upon:

> On August 13, 1927, while driving on the Promenade des Anglais at Nice, Isadora Duncan met her death. She *was strangled* by her colored shawl, which became tangled in the wheel of the automobile.
>
> —Janet Flanner

> If our heads swim occasionally, if we grow giddy with change, is it any wonder? We *are urged* to take our rightful place in the world of affairs. We *are* also *commanded* to stay at home and mind the hearth. We *are lauded* for our stamina and *pitied* for our lack of it. If we run to large families, we *are told* we are overpopulating the earth. If we are childless, we *are damned* for not fulfilling our functions. We *are goaded* into jobs and careers, then warned that our competition with men is unsettling both sexes.
>
> —Phyllis McGinley,

2.   Use the passive when the agent is unknown or unimportant to your point:

> Traces of the oil spill *were found* as far away as Newfoundland.

3. Use the passive when you want to put the agent at the end of a clause, where you can easily attach a long modifier:

> A secret mission to help thousands of starving Cambodians was organized in the summer of 1979 by *Father Robert I. Charlesbois*, a forty-eight-year-old Catholic priest from Gary, Indiana, with twelve years of experience in the Vietnam war zone.

Active Voice and Passive Voice
IN BRIEF

In active-voice constructions, the subject of the verb *acts:*

> Wolfe *defeated* Montcalm on the Plains of Abraham in 1759.

In passive-voice constructions, the subject of the verb is *acted upon:*

> Montcalm *was defeated* by Wolfe on the Plains of Abraham in 1759.

Use the active voice to make your writing direct, forceful, and concise:

> Marie Curie *won* the Nobel Prize for Chemistry in 1911.

Use the passive voice to keep the focus on someone or something that is acted upon:

> She *was honored* for her discovery of polonium and radium.

24.5 MISUSING THE PASSIVE

Avoid switching from active to passive when you have no particular reason to do so:

> Usually I run two miles in the morning, but that morning it *was decided* that a four-mile run *should be taken.*

Who made the decision?

> EDITED: Usually I run two miles in the morning, but that morning I decided to run four.

The active voice snaps the sentence into shape and keeps the focus on the one who is acting. Switch to the passive only to gain a special advantage—such as keeping the focus on someone who is acted upon:

> Usually I run two miles in the morning, but that morning I *was kept* in bed by the flu.

EXERCISE 1   **Eliminating the Passive**

Rewrite any of the following sentences in which you find the passive voice misused. If the passive voice is justified, write *Acceptable*.

> EXAMPLE: Every year we cut a Christmas tree in the woods/ and ~~it is~~
>
>   *it*
> decorated ~~by us~~ on December 24.

1. A terrible conflict between a doctor and a child is dramatized by William Carlos Williams's short story "The Use of Force."

2. At the start of the story, the doctor enters the house of a blue-collar family knowing that a throat culture has to be obtained from a frightened girl.

3. No one in the family, however, gives him the cooperation that is needed by him.

4. His initial efforts to examine the girl are thwarted when his glasses are knocked to the floor by her.

5. The mother is visibly disturbed by the child's screams and lack of cooperation.

6. In addition, ambivalence over the examination is displayed by the father when his hold on his daughter's arms is first tightened and then loosened.

7. With no support from the family, the doctor wonders whether his visit should be ended.

8. He is troubled by a growing fear that he may lose his temper.

9. The idea of leaving is rejected, however, as his better judgment is overruled by his increasing anger and wounded pride.

10. The child must be defeated; her resistance must be overcome.

11. An attack is launched with the aid of a metal spoon that is jammed between her teeth and pressed down hard like a lever.

EXERCISE 2   **Gaining Vigor and Coherence
                                            with the Active Voice**

Passive verbs predominate in the following passage, and since almost every sentence has a different subject, the writing is not only tedious but unfocused. Wherever you find the passive voice unjustified, make the verb active.

At the sound of a bell, the huge red building was entered by me along with hundreds of others. Just inside the entrance, instructions were being yelled at us by a mean-looking old lady. My lunchbox was clutched, and a crowd of six-year-olds was followed down a long hallway, up some steps, and down another corridor. Mrs. Nearing's   5
room was being looked for by us. I knew our destination had been reached when I was greeted loudly by a tall, black-haired woman. I was asked my name by her. Then it was printed by her on a sticky tag, and the tag was pressed to my chest. Inside the room several other six-year-olds could be seen, some of them big. Finally the classroom   10
door was closed by Mrs. Nearing, and a loud bang was made in the process. The small pane of glass near the top was kept from shattering by a network of wires. To my imagination, the wires looked like the bars in a prison. I was back in school.

Using Active and Passive Effectively Together   EXERCISE 3

Following is a group of simple sentences, some with verbs in the active voice, others with verbs in the passive. Make one continuous passage out of these sentences by combining some of them and changing the voice of the verbs whenever such a change will tighten a sentence or improve its focus. Underline all changes in voice.

EXAMPLE:

1. As a prime minister of England from 1940 to 1945, Churchill led his country through World War II.

2. But immediately after the war people voted him out of office.

3. Later his position as prime minister was regained by him.

4. That office was left by him in 1955.

5. Great popularity for the rest of his life was enjoyed by him.

6. He died in 1965.

7. People acclaimed him as a national hero.

   COMBINED: As prime minister of England from 1940 to 1945, Churchill led his country through World War II, but immediately after the war he was voted out of office. Later he regained his position as prime minister. After he left that office in 1955, he enjoyed great popularity for the rest of his life, and when he died in 1965, he was acclaimed as a national hero.

1. The political structure of modern China was largely created by Mao Zedong.

2. Mao led the Chinese Communist revolution.

3. The theory behind it was formulated by him.

4. China was virtually ruled by him from 1949 to his death in 1976.

5. Mao worked for revolution throughout much of his early life.

6. In 1911 the Nationalist armed forces of Hunan Province were joined by him in their revolt against the Manchu dynasty.

7. He was then eighteen.

8. In 1921 he helped to found the Chinese Communist party.

9. In the spring of 1928, the Fourth Chinese Red Army was organized by him and a fellow revolutionary named Zhu De.

10. In 1934–35, he and Zhu De led a six-thousand-mile march of Chinese Communist forces to northwest China.

11. There a new base of operations was established by the two leaders.

12. The new base was established against the Kuomintang.

13. That was the Nationalist political organization.

14. Generalissimo Chiang Kai-shek headed it.

15. Mao and Chiang joined forces during World War II to fight their common enemy, the Japanese.

16. But in the summer of 1946 a full-scale civil war against the Nationalists was resumed by Mao.

17. Mao's forces won the war in three years.

18. On September 21, 1949, the establishment of the People's Republic of China was proclaimed by Mao.

19. A succession of increasingly powerful posts was then assumed by him.

20. The posts included chairmanship of the Government Council, chairmanship of the Republic, and, most important, chairmanship of the Chinese Communist party.

21. In effect, China was ruled by Mao for nearly thirty years.

22. For better or worse, a lasting change in that country was made by Mao.

23. People will long remember him as one of the most important revolutionaries of the twentieth century.

Verbs: Mood

25.1 WHAT MOOD IS

The mood of a verb or verb phrase indicates your attitude toward a statement as you make it. Do you think of it as a statement of fact? Then you will use the *indicative* mood. Do you think of it as a command? Then you will use the *imperative*. Do you think of it as a wish, a recommendation, or an imaginary condition? Then you will use the *subjunctive*.

25.2 USING THE INDICATIVE

The indicative mood is for statements of actuality or strong probability:

> The spine-tailed swift *flies* faster than any other bird in the world.
>
> The Missouri and Mississippi Rivers *rose* to record heights in 1993.
>
> Midwesterners *will remember* the flooding for many years to come.

Use *do, does,* or *did* with the indicative for emphasis.

25.3 USING THE IMPERATIVE

The imperative mood is for commands and requests made directly.

1. Use the bare form of the verb for commands addressed entirely to others:

> *Vote* for change.
>
> *Fight* pollution.

Be yourself.

Kindly *send* me your latest catalog.

2.   When a command or suggestion includes yourself as well as others, use *let us* or *let's* before the bare form of the verb:

Let us negotiate our differences in a spirit of mutual trust and respect.

Let's cooperate.

25.4   USING THE SUBJUNCTIVE: MODAL AUXILIARIES

The subjunctive mood is for statements of hypothetical conditions or of wishes, recommendations, requirements, or suggestions. To express the subjunctive, you often need one of the modal auxiliaries, which include *can, could, may, might, must, ought, should,* and *would.* Use them as follows:

1.   USE *CAN* TO EXPRESS

   CAPABILITY: *Can* the Israelis and the Palestinians ever make peace?

   PERMISSION: Why *can't* first-year college students live off campus?

In formal writing, permission is normally signified by *may* rather than *can,* which is reserved for capability. But *can* may be used informally to express permission and is actually better than *may* in requests for permission involving the negative. The only alternative to *can't* in such questions is the awkward term *mayn't.*

2.   USE *COULD* TO EXPRESS

   THE OBJECT OF A WISH: I wish I *could* climb Mount Everest.

   A CONDITION: If all countries of the world *could* set aside their antagonism once every four years, the Olympics would be truly international.

   A DISTINCT POSSIBILITY: A major earthquake *could* strike California within the next ten years.

On the distinction between *would* and *could,* see item 8 below.

3.   USE *MAY* TO EXPRESS

   A MILD POSSIBILITY: The next president of the United States *may* be a woman.

PERMISSION: Students who cannot afford tuition *may* apply for loans.

4. **USE *MIGHT* TO EXPRESS**

A REMOTE POSSIBILITY: Biogenetic experiments *might* produce some horribly dangerous new form of life.

THE RESULT OF A CONTRARY-TO-FACT CONDITION: If I had driven all night, I *might* have fallen asleep at the wheel.

5. **USE *OUGHT* TO EXPRESS**

A STRONG RECOMMENDATION: The Pentagon *ought* to eliminate waste in defense spending.

LIKELIHOOD: The new museum *ought* to be ready by next fall.

Ought is normally followed by the infinitive.

6. **USE *MUST* TO EXPRESS**

AN ABSOLUTE OBLIGATION: Firefighters *must* be ready for action at any hour of the day or night.

A FIRM CONCLUSION: William Bligh, who sailed a small boat nearly four thousand miles, *must* have been an extraordinary seaman.

7. **USE *SHOULD* TO EXPRESS**

ADVICE: Students who hope to get into medical school *should* take biology.

EXPECTATION: By the year 2050, the population of the world *should* exceed eight billion.

8. **USE *WOULD* TO EXPRESS**

THE RESULT OF A CONDITION OR EVENT: If a one-kiloton neutron bomb were exploded a few hundred feet over the Earth, it *would* kill everyone within a radius of three hundred yards.

THE OBJECT OF A WISH: Some people wish the federal government *would* support them for the rest of their lives.

Both *would* and *could* may be used to express the object of a wish. But "I wish you could go" means "I wish you were able to go"; "I wish you would go" means "I wish you were willing to go."

MISUSING MODAL AUXILIARIES

Avoid putting two or more modal auxiliaries together:

▶ I might ~~could~~ move to Calgary.

▶ [or] I ~~might~~ could move to Calgary.

EXERCISE 1   **Supplying Modal Auxiliaries**

Complete the following sentences with suitable modal auxiliaries. Identify in parentheses their meanings.

EXAMPLE:
Students hoping to attend medical school ____ take biology.

Students hoping to attend medical school <u>should</u> take biology. (advice)

1. Helen ____ leave the hospital for the weekend; the doctor has just given her permission.

2. She ____, however, avoid going up or down stairs.

3. And she ____ limit her walking to ten steps every two hours.

4. She ____ eat whatever she likes, provided she limits the size of the portions.

5. Although complications ____ develop, she ____ be strong enough to spend Thanksgiving at home.

25.5 USING THE SUBJUNCTIVE: SPECIAL VERB FORMS

The subjunctive mood is sometimes indicated by a special verb form instead of by a modal auxiliary.

1. The *present subjunctive* is the same in form as the bare form (infinitive form) of the verb, and it is the same with every subject. Use the present subjunctive to express a hope, a requirement, a recommendation, a demand, a request, or a suggestion:

INDICATIVE	SUBJUNCTIVE
God *has* mercy on us.	God *have* mercy on us!
The queen *lives*.	Long *live* the queen!
A premed student normally *takes* biology.	The college requires that every student *take* first-year English.
The toxic dump *is* still open.	Protesters demand that the dump *be* closed.
The trustees' meetings *are* closed.	The students demand that those meetings *be* open.

The present subjunctive of the verb *be* is *be* with every subject (dump *be* closed; meetings *be* open).

2. The *past subjunctive* is the same in form as the common past, except that the past subjunctive of *be* is *were* with every subject. Use the past subjunctive to express a wish for something in the present:

INDICATIVE (FACT)	SUBJUNCTIVE (WISH)
I *have* five dollars.	I wish (that) I *had* a hundred dollars.
I *am* a pauper.	I wish (that) I *were* a millionaire.
I *am taking* Math 36.	I wish (that) I *were taking* Math 23.
I *live* in Ottawa.	I wish (that) I *lived* in Vancouver.
I *am* in New York.	I wish (that) I *were* in Texas.
It *is* summer.	I wish (that) it *were* winter.

3. The *past perfect subjunctive* is the same in form as the common past perfect. Use it to express a wish for something in the past:

INDICATIVE (FACT)	SUBJUNCTIVE (WISH)
I *saw* the second half of the game.	I wish (that) I *had seen* the first. [or] I wished (that) I *had seen* the first.
I *was* there for the second half.	I wish (that) I *had been* there for the first.
I *had* no binoculars with me.	I wish (that) I *had had* them.

25.6 FORMING AND USING CONDITIONAL SENTENCES

A conditional sentence normally consists of an *if* clause, which states a condition, and a result clause, which states the result of that condition. The mood of the verb in the *if* clause depends on the likelihood of the condition.

THE POSSIBLE CONDITION

If the condition is likely or even barely possible, the mood is indicative:

> [condition] If electric cars *replace* gas-powered cars in our cities, [result] urban air will be much cleaner than it is now.

THE IMPOSSIBLE OR CONTRARY-TO-FACT CONDITION

If the condition is impossible or contrary to fact, the mood of the verb in the *if* clause is subjunctive, and the result clause usually includes a modal auxiliary, such as *would* or *might*. The tense of the verb in the *if* clause depends on the tense of the condition.

1.   A *condition contrary to present fact* should be stated in the past subjunctive:

> If the federal government *spent* no more than it collected, interest rates would plunge.

> If I *were* a millionaire, I would buy an airplane.

> The new clerk acts as if he *were* the owner.

The expression *as if* always signals a condition contrary to fact. Some writers now use *was* instead of *were* in sentences like the second and third, but in formal writing you should use *were*.

2.   A *condition contrary to past fact* should be stated in the past perfect subjunctive:

> After the fight, the former champion looked as if he *had been put* through a meat grinder.

> If Montcalm *had defeated* Wolfe in 1759, the Canadian province of Quebec might now belong to France.

MISUSING *WOULD HAVE* IN CONDITIONAL CLAUSES

Avoid using *would have* to express a condition of any kind:

> *If I *would have* attended the meeting, I would have attacked the proposal.

Use *would have* only to express the *result* of a condition:

> EDITED: If I had attended the meeting, I *would have* attacked the
> proposal.

Supplying Verbs in Conditional Sentences   EXERCISE 2

Using the facts in brackets as a guide, complete each of the following
sentences by supplying a suitable verb or verb phrase.

EXAMPLE: If Ross Perot ____ the presidency in 1992, he would have
fundamentally altered the two-party system. [Ross Perot did not win
the presidency in 1992.]

had won

1. If high-speed trains ____ all major cities in the United States, Americans
   could travel much more often without their cars. [High-speed trains
   serve hardly any cities in the United States.]

2. If my father ____ five hundred shares of Microsoft in 1980, he would
   be a millionaire today. [Alas, my father never bought any shares of
   Microsoft.]

3. If the prime rate ____ unemployment may go up also. [The prime rate
   goes up and down regularly.]

4. After winning the match, Joan felt as if she ____ the world. [She did not
   actually conquer the world.]

5. If the Continental Army ____ to the British at Yorktown, George
   Washington might never have become president of the United States.
   [The Continental Army did not lose to the British at Yorktown.]

Supplying Verbs in a Paragraph

For each of the blanks in the following passage, supply a suitable verb or verb phrase.

EXAMPLE: were (line 1)

Many students wish that the Thanksgiving recess _____ one week long, or that the fall term _____ completely before Thanksgiving, so that they could stay home between Thanksgiving and Christmas. But the students have not asked for either of those things. They have asked only that the Thanksgiving recess _____ on the Wednesday be-   5
fore Thanksgiving. If the recess _____ on Wednesday, students would have one full day to travel home before Thanksgiving Day itself. Many students need that time. If every student _____ rich, he or she could fly home in an hour or two. But most students are not rich.

Direct and Indirect Reporting of Discourse

26

Any statement, whether spoken or written, can be reported *directly*—by quotation of the actual words. Or it can be reported *indirectly*—by a paraphrase of those words. In this chapter we explain when and how to use each method of reporting discourse.

26.1 DIRECT REPORTING

Use **direct reporting** when the exact words of the original statement are memorable or otherwise important. Enclose the words in quotation marks:

> "The vilest abortionist," writes Shaw, "is he who attempts to mould a child's character."

> Frost puts four stresses in his opening line: "The well was dry beside the door."

For a full discussion of how to punctuate quotations, see chapter 32.

USING TENSES IN TAGS

Since no statement can be reported until after it has been made, you should normally use the past tense for the verb in the accompanying tag:

> "No child should be homeless," *said* the nurse.

> "I agree with you completely," *answered* the orderly.

> In 1782 Thomas Jefferson *wrote:* "There must doubtless be an unhappy influence on the manners of our people produced by the existence of slavery among us."

But use the present when you are quoting an undated statement of lasting significance or a statement made by a character in a work of literature:

> "In every work of genius," *observes* Emerson, "we recognize our own rejected thoughts."

> In the first chapter of *Huckleberry Finn*, Huck *says*, "I don't take no stock in dead people."

QUOTING EXTENDED DIALOGUE

In reporting an exchange between two speakers, you should first indicate clearly who is speaking and in what order. You can then omit tags until the dialogue ends or is interrupted:

> "Our market surveys indicate," Hurts said, "that there are also a lot of kids who claim their parents don't listen to them. If they could rent a gun, they feel they could arrive at an understanding with their folks in no time."
>
> "There's no end to the business," I said. "How would you charge for Hurts Rent-A-Gun?"
>
> "There would be hourly rates, day rates, and weekly rates, plus ten cents for each bullet fired. Our guns would be the latest models, and we would guarantee clean barrels and the latest safety devices. If a gun malfunctions through no fault of the user, we will give him another gun absolutely free. . . ."
>
> "Why didn't you start this before?"
>
> "We wanted to see what happened with the gun-control legislation. . . ."
>
> —Art Buchwald, "Hurts Rent-A-Gun"

Paragraph indentations mark the shift from one speaker to another.

QUOTING SEVERAL LINES OF PROSE OR POETRY

When you quote more than four lines of prose or three lines of poetry, you should indent instead of using quotation marks, as described in sections 32.4 and 32.5.

26.2 INDIRECT REPORTING OF STATEMENTS

Use indirect reporting when the exact words of a statement are less important than their content:

> During the campaign, the senator said that she favored federal subsidizing of daycare.

Form indirect statements as shown here:

ORIGINAL STATEMENT: I want you to play the lead.

DIRECT REPORT (QUOTATION):   The director said, "I want you to play the lead."

INDIRECT REPORT: The director said that she wanted me to play the lead.

As this example shows, an indirect report does the following:

1.   It refers to the speaker or writer.

2.   It uses no quotation marks.

3.   It often puts *that* just before the reported statement. But *that* may be omitted:

> The director said she wanted me to play the lead.

4.   It changes the pronouns in the reported statement where necessary. In this example, *I* becomes *she,* and *you* becomes *me.*

5.   It may change the tense of the verb in the original statement so that it matches the tense of the introductory verb. Thus *want* in the original statement becomes *wanted* in the indirect report. But if the original statement has continuing force at the time it is reported, the indirect report may keep the original tense:

> The director said that she wants me to play the lead.

Generalizations may be reported with the present tense for both verbs:

> Farmers say that rain before seven means sun by eleven.

> They also say that when cows lie down, a storm is coming.

Transforming Reports of Statements

EXERCISE 1

Each of the following consists of a statement, with the speaker and (in two cases) the listener identified in brackets. Write a direct and an indirect report of the statement. Then put a check next to the version you think is more suitable, and say why you prefer it.

EXAMPLE: You will have to take a breath test. [*Speaker:* police officer; *listener:* me]

DIRECT: "You will have to take a breath test," said the police officer to me.

(Continued on p. 406.)

> ✔ INDIRECT: The police officer told me that I would have to take a breath test.
> (Since the content is more important than the exact words, the indirect version is preferable.)
>
> 1. You will have to earn your own spending money. [*Speaker:* my father; *listener:* me]
>
> 2. I do not mind lying, but I hate inaccuracy. [*Writer:* Samuel Butler]
>
> 3. I will pay you $3.50 an hour. [*Speaker:* manager; *listener:* me]
>
> 4. You have been baptized in fire and blood and have come out steel. [*Speaker:* General Patton; *listeners:* battle survivors]
>
> 5. Nothing in education is so astonishing as the amount of ignorance it accumulates in the form of inert facts. [*Writer:* Henry Adams]
>
> 6. Fanaticism consists in redoubling your efforts when you have forgotten your aim. [*Writer:* George Santayana]

26.3 DIRECT REPORTING OF QUESTIONS

To report a question directly, you normally use a verb of asking (such as *ask, request,* or *inquire*) in the past tense:

> The Sphinx asked, "What walks on four legs in the morning, two legs at noon, and three legs in the evening?"

> "Have you thought about college?" my father inquired.

> "When did the plane leave?" I asked.

Use the present tense when you are reporting a question of standing importance or a question asked by a literary character:

> The consumer advocate asks, "How can we have safe and effective products without government regulations?"

> The business owner asks, "How can we have free enterprise with government interference?"

> When Tom Sawyer proposes to form a gang that will rob and kill people, Huck asks, "Must we always kill the people?"

26.4 INDIRECT REPORTING OF QUESTIONS

To report a question indirectly, you normally introduce it with a verb of asking and a word like *who, what, whether, how, when, where, why,* or *if:*

ORIGINAL QUESTION: Why do birds migrate each year?

INDIRECT REPORT: The teacher asked why birds migrate each year.

The indirect report drops the auxiliary verb *do,* which is commonly used in questions. Also, the question mark becomes a period.

Use the present tense for the introductory verb when reporting a question of continuing importance or a question asked by a literary character:

> The consumer advocate asks how we can have safe and effective products without government regulation.

> When Tom Sawyer proposes to form a gang that will rob and kill people, Huck asks whether they must always kill the people.

After a past-tense verb of asking, you must normally use the past tense in the reported question:

> The interviewer asked me what I knew about programming.

> She also asked if I had an advanced degree.

But you may use the present tense if the reported question is essentially timeless:

> The utilitarian asks what practical purpose poetry serves.

> The romantic asks how we could live without it.

26.5 CONFUSING THE DIRECT AND INDIRECT REPORTING OF QUESTIONS

1.   Do not use a question mark to punctuate the indirect report of a question:

> *The customer sat down at the counter and asked did we have any scruples?

The **direct report** of a question repeats its actual words and ends in a question mark:

> EDITED: The customer sat down at the counter and asked, "Do you have any scruples?"

The **indirect report** of a question states that a question has been asked. It must end with a period:

> EDITED: The customer sat down at the counter and asked if we had any scruples.

2.   When reporting a question indirectly, do not use interrogative word order:

> *The police officer asked when was the car stolen.

The direct report of a question preserves its word order, putting the auxiliary verb before the subject:

> EDITED: The police officer asked, "When was the car stolen?"

The indirect report uses declarative word order, putting the subject first:

> EDITED: The police officer asked when the car was stolen.

26.6 FITTING QUOTATIONS INTO YOUR OWN PROSE

The combination of your own prose and a quotation should always make a complete, coherent sentence:

> According to Phyllis Rose, "We shop to cheer ourselves up."

> Ambrose Bierce defines achievement as "the death of endeavor and the birth of disgust."

> Barbara Garson writes: "The crime of modern industry is not forcing us to work, but denying us real work."

MISFITTED QUOTATIONS

A quotation is misfitted when it fails to combine with your own prose to make a complete, coherent sentence:

> *According to Orwell, "When there is a gap between one's real and one's declared aims."

This sentence fragment lacks a main clause, and it leaves the reader guessing about what happens "when there is a gap." To correct the error, do one of the following:

1. Quote a complete sentence:

   EDITED: According to Orwell, "When there is a gap between one's real and one's declared aims, one turns as it were instinctively to long words and exhausted idioms, like a cuttle fish squirting out ink."

2. Make the quoted matter part of a complete sentence:

   EDITED: According to Orwell, one resorts to obscure language "when there is a gap between one's real and one's declared aims."

Fitting Quotations into Your Own Prose

Take a sentence from any printed source and do three things: (1) copy it out and put the author's name in parentheses after it; (2) write a sentence in which you quote it all; (3) write a sentence in which you quote part of it.

EXAMPLE:

1. Taught from infancy that beauty is woman's sceptre, the mind shapes itself to the body, and roaming around its gilt cage, only seeks to adorn its prison. (Mary Wollstonecraft)

2. Mary Wollstonecraft writes: "Taught from infancy that beauty is woman's sceptre, the mind shapes itself to the body, and roaming around its gilt cage, only seeks to adorn its prison."

3. When a woman has been conditioned to worry constantly about her appearance, her mind, says Mary Wollstonecraft, "shapes itself to the body, and roaming around its gilt cage, only seeks to adorn its prison."

27 *Invigorating Your Style*

Nearly all of the chapters in parts 2 and 3 of this book aim to help you improve your **style:** to write not just correctly but cogently, to shape your sentences with coordination and subordination, to enhance them with parallel structure, to enrich them with modifiers, and to perfect them with well-chosen words. In this chapter, we focus specifically on what you can do to invigorate your style.

Good writing exudes vitality. It not only sidesteps awkwardness, obscurity, and grammatical error; it also expresses a mind continually at work, a mind seeking, discovering, wondering, prodding, provoking, asserting. Whatever else it does, good writing keeps the reader awake.

Unfortunately, much of what gets written seems designed to put readers to sleep. In most college writing you are expected to sound thoughtful and judicious, but no reader wants you to sound dull. To enliven your writing on any subject, here are five specific things you can do.

27.1 VARY YOUR SENTENCES

Take a hard look at one of your paragraphs—or at a whole essay. Do all of your sentences sound about the same? If most are short and simple, combine some of them to make longer ones. If most are lengthened out with modifiers and dependent clauses, break some of them up. Be bold. Be surprising. Use a short sentence to set off a long one, a simple structure to set off a complicated one. Though you need some consistency in order to keep the reader with you (did you notice that all of our last five sentences are imperatives?), you can and should spurn the monotony of assembly-line sentences.

To see what you can do with a variety of sentences, consider this example:

Someone is always at my elbow reminding me that I am the grand-daughter of slaves. It fails to register depression with me. Slavery is sixty years in the past. The operation was successful and the patient is doing well, thank you. The terrible struggle that made me an American out of a potential slave said "On the line!" The Reconstruction said "Get set!"; and the generation before said "Go!" I am off to a flying start and I must not halt in the stretch to look behind and weep. Slavery is the price I paid for civilization, and the choice was not with me. It is a bully adventure and worth all that I have paid through my ancestors for it.

—Zora Neale Hurston

Among the many things that invigorate the style of this passage is the variety of sentence types that Hurston uses—simple, compound, complex, and compound with a subordinate clause:

SIMPLE: It fails to register depression with me.
          Slavery is sixty years in the past.

COMPOUND: The operation was successful *and* the patient is doing well, thank you.
            I am off to a flying start *and* I must not halt in the stretch to look behind and weep.

COMPLEX: Someone is always at my elbow reminding me *that I am the granddaughter of slaves.*
           It is a bully adventure and worth all *that I have paid through my ancestors for it.*

COMPOUND WITH SUBORDINATE CLAUSE: Slavery is the price *that I paid for civilization,* and the choice was not with me.

Now consider this passage:

This looking business is risky. Once I stood on nearby Purgatory Mountain, watching through binoculars the great autumn hawk migration below, until I discovered that I was in danger of joining the hawks on a vertical migration of my own. I was used to binoculars, but not, apparently, to balancing on humped rocks while looking through them. I reeled.

—Annie Dillard, *Pilgrim at Tinker Creek*

Dillard varies both the structure and the length of her sentences. She moves from five to thirty-five words, then down to just two at the end. When a very short sentence follows one or more long ones, it can strike like a dart.

27.2 USE VERBS OF ACTION INSTEAD OF *BE*

Verbs of action show the subject not just *being* something but *doing* something. At times, of course, you need to say what your subject *is* or *was* or *has been,* and these words can speak strongly when used to express equality or identity, as in *Beauty is truth.* But verbs of action can often replace verbs of being:

▶ Sheila ~~was the winner of~~ the nomination.
    (won)

▶ Frederick's desire to learn reading would have ~~been a shock to~~ other slaveholders.
    (shocked)

▶ Mr. Ault believed that learning would ~~be the~~ ruin ~~of~~ Frederick as a slave.

27.3 USE THE ACTIVE VOICE MORE OFTEN THAN THE PASSIVE

Use the active voice as much as possible. Verbs that tell of a subject acting usually express more vitality than verbs that tell of a subject acted upon:

PASSIVE: After a big hole was dug and sprinkled with fertilizer, the tree *was planted.*

ACTIVE: After digging a big hole and sprinkling it with fertilizer, I *planted* the tree.

While some sentences work better in the passive voice, overuse of the passive can paralyze your writing. This is a problem *to be seriously considered by anyone who has ever been asked* to write an essay in which a subject of some sort is *to be analyzed, to be explained, or to be commented upon by him or her.* That sentence shows what overuse of the passive will do to your sentences: it will make them wordy, stagnant, boring, dead. Whenever you start to use the passive, ask yourself whether the sentence might sound better in the active. Often it will. (For a full discussion of the active and passive voice, see chapter 24.)

27.4 ASK QUESTIONS

Break the forward march of your statements with an occasional question:

> He falls back upon the bed awkwardly. His stumps, unweighted by legs and feet, rise in the air, presenting themselves. I unwrap the bandages from the stumps, and begin to cut away the black scabs and the dead, glazed fat with scissors and forceps. A shard of white bone comes loose. I pick it away. I wash the wounds with disinfectant and redress the stumps. All this while, he does not speak. What is he thinking behind those lids that do not blink? Is he remembering a time when he was whole? Does he dream of feet?
>
> —Richard Selzer, "The Discus Thrower"

Questions like these can draw the reader into the very heart of your subject. And questions can do more than advertise your curiosity. They can also voice your conviction. In conversation you sometimes ask a question that assumes a particular answer—don't you? Such a question is called rhetorical, and you can use it in writing as well as in speech. It will challenge your readers, prompting them either to agree with you or to explain to themselves why they do not. And why shouldn't you challenge your readers now and then?

27.5 CUT ANY WORDS YOU DON'T NEED

Cut out all needless repetition and strive to be concise (see 8.13):

▶ During their tour of Ottawa, they saw the Parliament buildings/and ~~they saw~~ the National Art Center.

▶ ~~The reason for~~ _He decided_ ~~his decision~~ to ~~make a~~ visit ~~to~~ Spain ~~was his desire~~ _because he wanted_ to see a bullfight.

▶ [or] ~~The reason for his decision to make a visit~~ _He went_ to Spain ~~was his desire~~ to see a bullfight.

Invigorating Your Style

▶ Vary the length and structure of your sentences:

I was used to binoculars but not, apparently, to balancing on humped rocks while looking through them. I reeled.

—Annie Dillard

▶ Use verbs of action instead of *be*:

Sheila won the nomination.

▶ Use the active voice as much as possible.

▶ Ask questions:

What on earth is *our* common goal? How did we ever get mixed up in a place like this?

—Lewis Thomas

▶ Cut unneeded words:

He went
~~The reason for his decision to make a visit~~ to Spain ~~was his desire~~ to
                                          ∧
see a bullfight.

Rewriting to Invigorate Style

Using verbs of action and the active voice as much as possible, asking at least one question, cutting all unneeded words, and varying the length and structure of your sentences, rewrite each of the following paragraphs to invigorate its style.

1. The French culture is greatly respected by the French. No other culture, in their opinion, is even close to theirs in value, worth, or overall quality. And they want to keep things that way. Strenuous efforts are made to be sure there is protection against a loss of excellence from contamina- tion. One of the greatest fears is the fear of words which are a threat   5 to come into the country from American English. According to the defenders of French culture, it is a fact that a purity of the French language will be tainted if words used by the uncouth speakers of the American tongue are uttered by French men and women. Since 1945 many important electronic machines have been made by Americans,   10 and given American English names. The computer is one such ma- chine, and *computer* has become an important, widely used word in American society along with many other related words. Among the French, however, there has been no willingness to use these American

words, so French words have been created. A computer is called an 15
ordinateur, software is called *le logiciel,* and data processing is called
l'informatique. For the guardians of French culture, there must be a
French sound to the words that are spoken and written by them.

2. Critics of detective stories have three complaints. First, there is too
much senseless violence. Lots of characters are killed. Others are
badly beaten. In *The Lonely Silver Rain* by John D. MacDonald over
twenty people are killed. The violence and deaths are not "senseless," however. A purpose is served by them. Clues are furnished to 5
the detective. Second, detective stories are said to be filled with old,
lifeless plots. The age of the plots is a problem, but a youthful vitality
is usually imparted to them by writing which is conducive to a dramatic effect with regard to both places and characters. Interiors are
described in vivid detail by Rex Stout. In the dialogues of Ed McBain, 10
the words spoken by his characters sound just like the words of real
people. This vitality is ignored by critics. They have a third complaint.
The detectives, they say, are cardboard cutouts. The characters are
likened to wooden statues. In reality, fictional detectives are like real
human beings. There are real problems in their lives. Agatha Christie's 15
Hercule Poirot is faced with the problem of being an old man. A failed
marriage is a haunting memory in the mind of Ross MacDonald's Lew
Archer. There is almost no end to the examples. So it may be asked
whether the critics ever read the stories they criticize.

3. In the modern city there is no safety for decent people. They are in a
situation of continual exposure to crime. But it is my belief that a solution
to this problem is attainable. The solution may sound strange, even crazy.
New ideas often sound that way. Here is my proposal. Criminals and
law-abiding city dwellers must switch places—literally. Criminals should 5
be released from prison. They will live in the perilous freedom of our
cities. They will become victims of their own robberies, muggings, and
killings. Eventually self-destruction will result. Meanwhile the prisons
will be remodeled for all decent people. A cell will be allotted to each
single person. Families will be housed in multicell units. With regard to 10
those who prefer to live in solitude, applications for solitary confinement may be submitted on a first-come, first-served basis. Food and
medical services will be available for the inmates. Educational programs
will be broadcast to large TV screens in every cell. For entertainment
there will be block parties. There will be games for children to play. 15
Dances for adults will be arranged. At the end a movie will be shown.
It will be about the bad old days. It will be a reminder of the dangers before the big switch.

(Continued on p. 416.)

4. In "The American Scholar" the wise use of books is discussed by
   Emerson. Unwise uses are also considered. The use is unwise, Emerson
   says, when the contents of books are taken as final truth by readers.
   They are deficient in their ability to see something. Truth in one
   period of time is not necessarily truth at a later time. There is another 5
   problem. Mistakes are made by authors. What is said in a book may
   be false to begin with. There is another unwise use. Some readers
   become bookworms. They enter the paper and binding of a book. No
   thought is given to its contents. But the behavior of wise readers is
   different. Emerson says that books can be studied by the wise reader 10
   for knowledge of history. They are also a source of scientific facts
   that can be absorbed. There is an additional good use. Inspiration
   can be gained from books. If books are used properly, they can be
   wonderful instruments for readers.

Academic English for Nonnative Speakers

28

This chapter discusses some features of American English that often cause trouble for students of English as a second language. Though it includes explanations of key grammatical points, it should be supplemented with a good English–English dictionary and a grammar-reference guide, such as Jocelyn M. Steer and Karen A. Carlisi's *Advanced Grammar Book,* 2nd ed. (Boston: Heinle & Heinle, 1997), or Betty Schrampfer-Azar's *Understanding and Using English Grammar,* 3rd ed. (Paramus, NJ: Prentice-Hall, 1998). The *Newbury House Dictionary of American English,* 3rd ed. (Boston: Heinle & Heinle, 2000), speaks to ESL students and comes with a CD-ROM demonstrating pronunciation and usage.

28.1 ARTICLES AND OTHER DETERMINERS

DETERMINERS DEFINED

A **determiner** (D) is a type of modifier: a modifier that always precedes the noun (N) it modifies and marks it as such:

> D   D   D   N   D   N   D   N
> We spent *the first two* weeks of *our* trip in *a* village.

Though an adjective (A) can follow the noun it modifies, a determiner must always precede it:

> D   A   N
> It was *a* remote village.

D   N   A   A
It was *a* village remote from modern development.

Unlike adjectives, determiners have no comparative (C) or superlative (S) forms:

D   A   N   A(C)   D   D   N
It was also *a* poor village, poorer than *any other* village in the province.

D   A(S)   N
It was *the* poorest village I had ever seen.

COUNTABLE AND UNCOUNTABLE NOUNS

To choose the right determiner, you must know whether the noun it modifies is *countable* or *uncountable*.

Countable nouns may be singular or plural:

car, cars

book, books

woman, women

course, courses

Uncountable nouns are normally singular. They include:

WORDS NAMING A MASS OF SOMETHING, SUCH AS	WORDS NAMING ABSTRACT IDEAS, SUCH AS
cement	fortune
wheat	luck
dirt	justice
rice	advice
mud	knowledge
air	cowardice
cotton	bravery

Some nouns are countable in one sense and uncountable in another:

We added *sand* [a mass] to the mixture.

The sands of time [individual grains] are running out.

Life is full of surprises.

What is the value of *a life?*

418

USING *A, AN,* AND *THE*

A and *an* are Group 1 determiners (see pp. 426–27). Use *a* or *an* before a noun that is singular, countable, and indefinite:

> Recent labor statistics in the U.S. show that *a woman* earns seventy-five cents for every dollar earned by *a man* doing the same job.

> According to *an old story,* Sir Isaac Newton discovered the principle of gravity when *an apple* fell on his head.

If you refer again to a noun introduced by *a* or *an,* use *the:*

> I have often wondered if Newton ever ate *the apple.*

The second sentence refers to something that has been made definite by the first one. *An* apple is now *the* apple *that fell on Newton's head.*

Use *a/an* in expressions of measurement where the meaning is "each":

> Swordfish now costs four dollars *a pound.*

> In my new job I work just four days *a week.*

In choosing between *a* and *an,* look only at the first letter of the next word. Use *a* when the first letter of the next word is a consonant, including an *h* that is pronounced:

> a *c*ar

> a *b*ig apple

> a *b*ook

> a *g*reen umbrella

> a *w*oman

> a *h*acienda

> a *h*istory book

Use *an* when the first letter of the next word is a vowel or an unpronounced *h:*

> an *a*pple

> an *a*bsorbing book

> an *o*range car

> an *i*mbecile

> an *i*njured woman

> an *h*eir

MISUSING OR MISTAKENLY OMITTING *A/AN* Do not use *a/an* before an uncountable noun:

- I asked my uncle for ~~an~~ advice.

- The medal was awarded for ~~a~~ bravery.

- My question provoked ~~a~~ laughter.

- The room needs ~~a~~ new furniture.

Do not use *a/an* before any plural noun:

- ~~A~~ paperback books are cheaper than ~~a~~ hardbound books.

- ~~A~~ women generally earn less than ~~a~~ men.

Do not omit *a/an* before a singular, countable, definite noun:

- Marie Curie was ^a^ brilliant scientist.

- Every undergraduate studies ^a^ variety of subjects.

USING *THE* *The* is a Group 1 determiner (see pp. 426–27). Use *the* before a noun referring to one or more specific persons or things:

The first woman in *the* U.S. Senate was Hattie Caraway of Arkansas, who served out her husband's term after his death in 1931. She gained *the* seat on her own in *the* election of 1932.

In this instance, *the* voters of Arkansas were more progressive than *the* voters of any northern state.

The present form of *the* Great Wall of China largely originated in *the* Ming dynasty.

To commemorate *the* American Revolution, *the* Statue of Liberty was given to *the* United States by *the* Franco-American Union in 1886.

Use *the* with superlatives:

Many basketball fans consider Michael Jordan *the* greatest player in *the* history of the game.

Soccer is still *the* most popular sport in many countries.

Use *the* with any adjective or participle used as a noun:

The rich cannot understand the misery of *the* poor.

The sick, *the* suffering, and *the* neglected all need our help.

The real and *the* ideal have little in common.

The British transferred Hong Kong to *the* Chinese in the 1990s.

MISUSING *THE*   Do not use *the* before nouns used in a generalized sense. In the sample sentences below on the left, the italicized words particularize the nouns they modify; the sample sentences on the right contain no such particularizing words.

PARTICULAR	GENERAL
The men and the women *in my office* often have trouble understanding each other.	Men and women often have trouble understanding each other.
The dog *next door to me* barks at everyone.	When a dog is happy, it wags its tail.
The mistake *made by a ticket agent* cost me $250.	Scientists often make discoveries by making mistakes.

Some nouns follow neither *the* nor *a* when used in a general sense. They include *night, prison, school, court,* and the names of meals:

The breakfast *I had this morning* was nothing but coffee.	I take coffee with breakfast and wine with lunch and dinner.
I saw her on the night *before she left.*	She takes classes at night.
The school *I once attended* is now closed.	Most American children start going to school at the age of five.
The prison *on Alcatraz Island* is a ruin.	No one wants to go to prison.
Ellen never forgot the court *where she won her first case.*	In court, judges wear black.

EXCEPTIONS:

Some nouns—such as *morning, afternoon, evening,* and *hospital*—regularly follow *the,* even when used in a generalized sense:

I take classes in *the morning* and work in *the afternoon.*

A night in *the hospital* can be very expensive.

421

As nouns, *left* and *right* follow *the* except when used with *at:*

> *On the left* stood the church; *on the right* was the school.
>
> *At left* stood the church; *at right* was the school.

USING *THE* WITH PROPER NOUNS   Use *the* with names of the following:

POLITICAL/ECONOMIC UNIONS	RIVERS
the United States	the Mississippi River
the British Commonwealth	the Colorado River
the European Union	the Amazon River

GEOGRAPHICAL REGIONS	MOUNTAIN RANGES
the Arctic	the Rocky Mountains
the South Pole	the Appalachians
the Canary Islands	the Himalayas
the Southwest	the Adirondacks

OCEANS	BUILDINGS AND MONUMENTS
the Pacific	the Empire State Building
the Atlantic	the Washington Monument
the Indian Ocean	the Eiffel Tower
the Mediterranean	the World Trade Center

Do not use *the* with names of persons, churches, languages, countries, political regions, lakes, or ponds:

▶ ~~The~~ Simón Bolívar liberated a great part of ~~the~~ Latin America from ~~the~~ Spain.

▶ In parts of San Francisco, ~~the~~ Chinese is spoken more often than ~~the~~ English.

▶ When recession struck ~~the~~ China, the Chinese government could not pay its debts.

▶ ~~The~~ Lake Michigan is much larger than ~~the~~ Walden Pond.

▶ The pastor of ~~the~~ Trinity Church was invited to deliver a sermon at ~~the~~ St. Patrick's Cathedral.

EXCEPTIONS:

Use *the* before *Church* when referring to a religious organization:

The Roman Catholic Church strongly opposes abortion.

Use *the* before *Church* or *Cathedral* when a name follows either of those words:

The Cathedral of St. John the Divine is in New York.

Use *the* before the name of a language when the word *language* follows the name:

The English language is widely spoken.

Using *A*, *AN*, and *THE*

EXERCISE 1

In the following passage, make an acceptable change wherever you find *a*, *an*, or *the* misused or needed. Write a clean copy of your version and give it to your instructor. We have edited the first mistake for you.

Three summers ago I became interested in ~~the~~ plants and the gardening. I began to plan garden. It would include three flower beds, small sundial, and stone wall. In center of garden, I wanted to put lily pool. By end of summer, I had constructed the pool and laid stone wall around it. Beyond wall were three flower beds, each of   5
which was shaped like a arc circling one part of pool. My sundial rested on top of large rock between two of flower beds. Because of drought, the soil was driest it had been in the ten years, so only few of plants grew well.

During the following winter, I had the many new ideas. I taught   10
myself about the gardening in general and a water gardening in particular by reading lots of the books. In spring I redid lily pool and three flower beds, adding waterfall, water lilies, and the many other aquatic plants, as well as stocking pool with the goldfish. I enlarged flower beds and fertilized soil with a compost, a peat, and a manure,   15
working material into soil with my hands and small trowel. During summer, which was wetter than one before, the every single plant quadrupled in size and stayed healthy.

USING *SOME, ANY, NO,* AND *NOT*

Some, any, no, and *not* are all Group 1 determiners (see pp. 426–27). *Some* denotes an unknown or unspecified amount or number. Use it in affirmative and imperative sentences:

> *Some people* are always lucky.

> Please give us *some help.*

Any denotes an unknown or unspecified small amount or number. Use it in sentences that are negative or express uncertainty:

> The box office did not have *any tickets.*

> I asked if there was *any standing room.*

Use *no* to negate a noun:

> *No tickets* were left.

> I saw *no animal* in the cage.

NOTE: Do not use *not* to negate a noun. Use it only to negate a verb:

> ▶ There was ~~not~~ ^{no} solution [noun] to the problem.

> ▶ I could ~~no~~ ^{not} solve [verb] the problem.

USING THE DEMONSTRATIVES *(THIS, THAT, THESE, THOSE)*

Demonstratives (Group 1 determiners, pp. 426–27) are words that point to one or more particular persons or things. Use them as follows:

Use *this* and *that* with singular nouns, whether countable or not. *This* suggests nearness *(this weekend, this room)* while *that* suggests distance in space or time *(that weekend, that room).*

Use *these* and *those* with plural countable nouns *(these men, those women).* As with *this* and *that, these* suggests nearness while *those* suggests distance.

USING NUMBERS, *MUCH, MANY, LITTLE, FEW*

Ordinal numbers (Group 2 determiners, pp. 426–27) refer to the order of the items in a group *(first, second, third . . .).* Use the ordinals after a Group 1 word or by themselves:

> The *third chapter* of the novel describes the groom.

> Marilyn's story won *first prize.*

Cardinal numbers (Group 3 determiners, pp. 426–27) refer to the quantity of items in a group (*one, seven, forty-three, two hundred,* etc.); words denoting quantity include *many, much,* and *few.*

Use any of these numerical determiners after words from Group 1 and Group 2 or by themselves before a noun:

> The first *three men* had tickets.
>
> *Three men* were waiting at the airport gate.
>
> Those *three tickets* cost a lot of money.
>
> *Ten poems* were in the book.
>
> Her first *few poems* were short.
>
> The anthology included *many poems.*

Use *much* and *little* (Group 3) with uncountable nouns and singular countable nouns:

> much wisdom
>
> little creativity
>
> much land
>
> little industry

Use *few, several,* and *many* with plural countable nouns:

> few settlers
>
> several farms
>
> many animals

When *little* means "small in stature," it can be used with countable nouns: *little boys, little girls.*

USING *ALL, BOTH, HALF,* AND OTHER PREDETERMINERS

Predeterminers are words and phrases that can be used before some Group 1 determiners:

> 1   2   3
>
> *All* the first five runners beat the record.
>
> *Half* a   loaf is better than none.
>
> *Both* these   nations have suffered.

Both and *all* can also be used before a noun:

> *Both women* won congressional seats.

> At night *all cats* are gray.

Some, any, none, and any Group 3 determiner may be used with *of* as a **predetermining phrase:**

> *None of the first five passengers* had tickets.

> *Much of our confusion* was due to inaccurate reports.

> We did not hear *any of the latest news.*

> *Some of the food* was missing.

> *Three of the women* left the room.

IN BRIEF   **Using *A, AN, THE,* and Other Determiners**

A **determiner** is a word marking a noun that follows it. Determiners come in three groups corresponding to the order in which they may be used:

> 1
> *Some* applicants had interviews.

> 1   2
> *The first* applicants had interviews.

> 1   2   3
> *The first five* applicants had interviews.

Group 1

a, an	with singular countable nouns: *a boy, a mistake, an orange*
the	with nouns referring to particular persons or things: *the Statue of Liberty, the owner of that car, the people of Nicaragua, the capital of Arkansas*
	with superlatives: *the greatest athlete in the world*
some	with nouns in affirmative sentences: *Some people are always lucky.*
any	with nouns in negative sentences: *I never have any luck.*

no	to negate any noun: *No tickets were left.*
this, that	with singular nouns, countable or not: *this college, this courage, that movie, that fear*
these, those	with plural countable nouns: *these men, those women*
my, your, his, her, its, our, their	with any noun: *my car, her job, his letter, their property, our town, your house, its roof*

Group 2

the ordinal numbers: *first, second, third,* etc.	after a Group 1 word or by themselves: 1 2 2 *the first chapter, first prize*

Group 3

the cardinal numbers: *one, two, three,* etc., and words denoting measurement	after words from Group 1 and Group 2 or by themselves with a noun: 1 2 3 3 *the first three men, three men* 1 2 3 3 *the last few sheep, few sheep*
much, little	with uncountable nouns: *much land, little industry*
few, several, many	with countable nouns: *few settlers, several farms, many animals*

Predeterminers

all, both, half	before some Group 1 determiners:
	    1 1
	all the first five runners, half a loaf,
	    1
	both the women
	all and *both* may be used right before a noun: *all runners, both women*

In the following passage, make an acceptable change wherever you find a determiner misused or needed. Write a clean copy of your version and give it to your instructor. We have edited the first mistake for you.

           the
In evening of the April 18, 1775, any British troops occupying the Boston prepared to make this surprise attack on the American colonists who lived in some nearby villages. As soon as the night fell, much small boats began to ferry British soldiers across Charles River from the Boston to the Cambridge. British believed that they were   5
acting in a secret. In reality, however, much agents of American patriots were watching all move of redcoats. On discovering enemy's plan, agents dispatched several messengers, who hoped to warn villagers of threat to safety.

    At the ten o'clock one of messengers, the Paul Revere by name,   10
left his home and hastened to the Christ Church in the Boston. From there he hurried to Charles River, which he crossed in small rowboat using the muffled oars. Then he reported to another agent, who gave him horse and wished him a Godspeed. Although the Paul Revere was almost captured much times by these British patrols, he   15
managed to elude his pursuers and to reach the Lexington shortly after the midnight. Shouting with many excitement, he warned any townspeople about British soldiers and then rode to the Concord, where he repeated message.

    The Revere's work was well done. As a result of now-famous ride   20
in dark, these American colonists living in the Lexington were ready to defend themselves when British soldiers reached a village.

28.2 VERBS

VERB TENSE

For a full presentation on using English verb tenses, including those for irregular verbs, see chapters 22 and 23.

NUMBER AND AGREEMENT

For a full presentation on agreement of verb forms (person and number) with subjects, see chapter 21.

MODAL AUXILIARIES

For a full presentation on modal auxiliary verbs, see chapter 25, especially 25.4.

FORMING VERB PHRASES

A phrase is a group of words that functions as a single part of speech. A verb phrase therefore contains two or more words, including an auxiliary verb. These words function together as the predicate of a sentence, not as a complete sentence.

EXAMPLES:

The workers *have gone* home for the day.

She *might have told* me her name, but I *don't remember* it.

Professor Casey *will be giving* a lecture next Friday.

USING *DO* AND *DOES*

Do is used as a main verb and as a helping (auxiliary) verb.

DO AS A MAIN VERB   As a main verb, *do* takes the following forms:

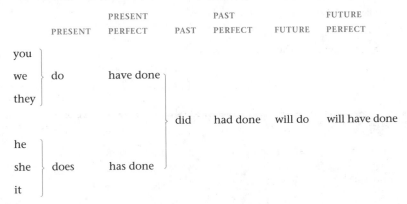

	PRESENT	PRESENT PERFECT	PAST	PAST PERFECT	FUTURE	FUTURE PERFECT
you we they	do	have done				
			did	had done	will do	will have done
he she it	does	has done				

As a main verb, *do* can serve any one of the following purposes:

It can be a transitive verb:

Carmen *does* many things.

The storm *did* no damage to the house.

It can finish a comparison:

> Andrea speaks French better than Mark *does.*

It can take the place of a verb used in the preceding sentence:

> Carpenters recently renovated the cafeteria. They *did* it [the work] in just three weeks.

It can help to form an interrogative tag at the end of a statement:

> The soloist played well, *didn't* she?

> Guards never admit strangers, *do* they?

DO AS A HELPING VERB   Use *do* as a helping verb in questions and negative statements:

> *Does* money grow on trees?

> *Do* jobs fall from the sky?

> ▶ Money ^ *does* not grow on trees, and jobs ^ *do* not fall from the sky.

You could also write *doesn't* and *don't,* which are both less formal than *does not* and *do not.*

MISUSING *S* WITH *DOES*   When using *does* as a helping verb, never add *s* to the base form of the main verb (MV):

> ▶ *Does* smoking causes̸ cancer?
>
>   MV

> ▶ It certainly *does* not serves̸ the cause of health.
>
>   MV

EXERCISE 3   **Using *DO* and *DOES***

The following sentences may be flawed because a form of *do* is missing or a verb phrase is miswritten. Edit the mistakes and write out the new sentences. If a sentence is correct as it stands, write "correct."

EXAMPLE: My uncle ^ *does* not phone me very often.
My uncle does not phone me very often.

1. My basketball coach not look like a typical coach.

2. He is short and overweight, and he does not wears gym shoes or sneakers.

3. During practice he sometimes does not brings a ball, and he not have a whistle.

4. What we players think?

5. We not think that he is a good coach.

6. But we play hard for him, no matter what he do during practice.

PHRASAL VERBS

A phrasal verb is a verb combined with certain adverbs *(away, forward)* or one or more prepositions. When combined with the verb, these adverbs and prepositions no longer function as such and instead are known as *particles*. The addition of a particle can dramatically change the meaning of the verb.

> NO PARTICLE: When I *dropped* [let fall] the glass, I was lucky it didn't break.

> PHRASAL VERB: We *dropped in on* [visited] Alonzo over the weekend.

> NO PARTICLE: She *broke* [injured] her leg in a skiing accident.

> PHRASAL VERB: Keiko and James *broke up* [ended a relationship] last year.

Phrasal verbs are usually less formal than single-word verbs or verbs with auxiliaries, but they are commonly used in writing and speech.

SEPARABLE PHRASAL VERBS   Some phrasal verbs may be separated to make way for a direct object (DO) of one or two words:

> DO
> After the party, he *cleaned* the kitchen *up*. (Also acceptable: . . . he cleaned up the kitchen.)

Whenever a separable phrasal verb has a pronoun (PR) for its object, the pronoun goes between the verb and the particle:

> PR
> Since the kitchen was a mess, he *cleaned* it *up*.

> PR
> As soon as I got the application, I *filled* it *out*.

Some phrasal verbs (such as *care about*) may not be separated by a noun or pronoun.

COMMON PHRASAL VERBS: A BRIEF LIST Following is a list of common phrasal verbs, with daggers marking those that should never be separated by a noun or pronoun.

agree

The negotiators have †*agreed to* [accepted] changes in the plan.

They have †*agreed with each other* [concurred] *on* some points.

Some shellfish †*doesn't agree with me* [makes me sick].

approve

The governor †*approved of* [accepted] the new proposal.

believe

Many people †*believe in* [accept the reality of] ghosts.

Magda was the only one who †*believed in* [accepted the value of] Jorge.

break

When she heard the news, she *broke down* [collapsed] and cried.

Finally, the relentless salesman *broke down* [overcame] my resistance.

In 1990, the Soviet Union *broke up* [disintegrated].

In the same year, Maria and Jose *broke up* [ended their relationship].

bring

I hated to *bring up* [raise for discussion] the question again.

Without help, how can a single parent *bring up* [nurture] a child?

burn

One night someone *burned down* [leveled by fire] the police station.

call

She was so sick that she decided to *call off* [cancel] the party.

She had to *call up* [telephone] all her friends.

The president has *called up* [summoned to duty] the reserves.

care

He †*cared about* [loved/carefully considered] his family.

He often †*cared for* [tended] his children when they were sick.

clean

We *cleaned up* [cleaned thoroughly] the house before moving into it.

come

Rounding the bend, we †*came across* [encountered, found] a dog in the middle of the road.

I †*come from* [originate from] Costa Rica.

consist

My apartment †*consists of* [includes altogether] two bedrooms, a little kitchen, a bathroom, and a sitting area.

depend

I †*depend on* [need] my alarm clock to wake me each morning.

drop

On my way home, I †*dropped in on* [visited] my cousin.

I told her that I had decided not to †*drop out of* [quit] school.

Then I *dropped off* [left] my shirts at the laundry.

get

My sister and her husband try to †*get along* [subsist] on one salary.

People of different races often do not wish to †*get along with* [cooperate with, coexist with] each other.

Police say that the robbers †*got away with* [stole] a million dollars.

How many students †*get away with* [escape punishment for] cheating?

She *got up* [rose from bed] at 7:00 A.M.

give

The rebels refused to †*give in* [submit] or †*give up* [surrender].

keep

Whatever happens, I will †*keep on* [continue] trying.

I aim to *keep up* [maintain] my studies.

Can American companies †*keep up with* [compete effectively with] the Japanese?

I am trying to †*keep up with* [meet the requirements of] all my courses.

Some private clubs *keep out* [exclude] women.

look

My brother †*looked after* [tended] my apartment while I was away.

We †*looked at* [examined] many photographs.

We were †*looking for* [seeking] pictures of my grandfather.

Reporters are †*looking into* [investigating] the scandal.

Public radio †*looks to* [solicits] its listeners for financial support.

Egotists †*look down on* [despise] most other people.

While in the city, I *looked up* [arranged to meet] my cousin.

Children †*look up to* [admire] superstar athletes.

I †*looked over* [surveyed] the books quickly.

make

The ink was so blurred that I couldn't *make out* [decipher] the words.

In spite of setbacks, she *made out* [succeeded] handsomely. (slang)

To celebrate, she *made over* [redecorated] her office.

Arriving hours late, he *made up* [invented] a ridiculous excuse.

After feuding for years, they *made up* [agreed to be friendly].

The five superstar players *made up* [constituted] a "dream team."

The professor let me *make up* [do at a time later than originally specified] the exam I had missed.

put

At the end of the day, the carpenter *put away* [stored] her tools.

She also *put back* [replaced] the broom she had taken from the closet.

The army soon *put down* [suppressed] the rebellion.

Whenever I say anything, he *puts me down* [criticizes me].

The committee voted to *put off* [postpone] a final decision.

The manager *put off* [dismissed] all my objections.

His indifference *put* me *off* [irritated me].

I felt thoroughly *put out* [annoyed].

Midnight was high time to *put out* [place outside] the cat.

The Acme Tire company *puts out* [produces] ten thousand tires a day.

When asked to serve a third time, she felt †*put upon* [overburdened].

There is no reason to †*put up with* [endure] bad service.

refer

In a lecture on civil disobedience, the professor †*referred to* [mentioned] Henry David Thoreau.

run

While reading the paper, I †*ran across* [met by chance] a strange word.

At the party she †*ran into* [met by chance] an old friend.

While backing up the car, I *ran into* [collided with] a truck.

I was afraid the gas would †*run out* [be wholly consumed].

By noon the store had †*run out of* [exhausted its supply of] milk.

Spending lavishly, he *ran up* [incurred] big debts.

take

My sister and I sometimes †*take care of* [tend] my baby brother.

The hot weather led me to *take off* [remove] my coat.

Did you ever hear her *take off* [impersonate] the boss? (colloquial)

After the meeting he *took* me *out* [escorted me] to dinner.

After just three months on the job, she was ready to *take over* [assume control or management of] the shipping room.

think

When asked to †*think about* [consider] the problem, she tried to *think of* [devise] a solution.

What do you †*think of* [how do you judge] her proposal?

Do you need time to *think* it *over* [consider it]?

Using Phrasal Verbs

Choose the correct particle or set of particles from those given in parentheses, and then write out the whole sentence.

EXAMPLE: All she cared (on, <u>about</u>) was her cat.
All she cared about was her cat.

1. Most corporations want their employees to get (along with, away with) each other.

2. Friendly employees help one another keep (on, up) working efficiently.

3. They even look (for, to) ways to reduce waste and increase production.

4. As a result, the corporations can keep (up, up with) their competitors.

5. No worker can be fully effective if he or she is made to put (down, up with) troublesome coworkers.

6. For this reason good managers regularly look (into, to) complaints whenever they are made to a supervisor.

7. Some companies devise training programs to break (up, down) hostility between workers.

8. Every month a few trainees drop (off, out of) the programs.

9. The dropouts cannot put (out, up with) the demands being placed upon them.

10. But most trainees learn to (keep out, keep up with) those demands.

Phrasal Verbs (Verb-Particle Combinations)

A **phrasal verb** is a single verb combined with one or more *particles*. A particle is part of the verb and strongly affects its meaning. For example:

NO PARTICLE: When I *dropped* [let fall] the glass, I was lucky it didn't break.

PHRASAL VERB: We *dropped in on* [visited] Alonzo over the weekend.

NO PARTICLE: She *broke* [injured] her leg in a skiing accident.

PHRASAL VERB: Keiko and James *broke up* [ended a relationship].

In a few cases, the same combination can produce different meanings in different sentences:

He *made up* [invented] a ridiculous excuse.

The five superstar players *made up* [constituted] a "dream team."

After their quarrel Helen and Bob soon *made up* [restored good relations, became friends again].

Some phrasal verbs may be separated to make way for a word or short phrase. Whenever a separable phrasal verb has a pronoun (PR) for its object, the pronoun goes between the verb and the particle:

PR
Since the kitchen was a mess, he *cleaned* it *up*.

Some phrasal verbs (such as *care about*) may not be separated. For a brief list of common phrasal verbs, see above.

28.3 GERUNDS, INFINITIVES, PARTICIPLES, PROGRESSIVE VERBS

GERUNDS AND INFINITIVES

A **gerund** (G) is a word or phrase made from a verb (V), ending in *-ing,* and used as a noun:

V
I run every day.

G
Running keeps me fit.

V
At night I play the piano.

G
I like *playing the piano.*

G
But my upstairs neighbor complains about *losing sleep.*

Words made from a verb and ending in *-ing* are gerunds only when they serve as nouns. A word made from a verb and ending in *-ing* may also be used as a **participle** (PART) modifying a noun and as part of a **verb phrase**:

VERB
PART   PHRASE
For one *shining* moment, we *were basking* in the sun.

An **infinitive** (I) is a phrase made from a verb and starting with *to*. It is often used as a noun:

$$\overset{\text{V}}{\text{Some pray;}} \quad \overset{\text{V}}{\text{others work.}}$$

Some pray; others work.

$$\overset{\text{I}}{\textit{To work}} \text{ is } \overset{\text{I}}{\textit{to pray.}}$$

To work is *to pray*.

$$\qquad\qquad\qquad \overset{\text{I}}{\textit{to publish}}$$

Paula hopes *to publish* her poems.

CHOOSING BETWEEN GERUNDS AND INFINITIVES   Use gerunds—*not* infinitives—as objects of prepositions (PREP):

▶ What are the advantages of ~~to live~~ *living* in Miami?   (PREP)

▶ Nothing matches the excitement of ~~to see~~ *seeing* New York.   (PREP)

▶ The cost of ~~to live~~ *living* rises steadily.   (PREP)

▶ The professor explained the purpose of ~~to study~~ *studying* sociology.   (PREP)

▶ I like to take a walk after ~~to eat~~ *eating* lunch.   (PREP)

▶ I read about the movie before ~~to see~~ *seeing* it.   (PREP)

▶ Without ~~to take~~ *taking* her hat off, she sat down at the table.   (PREP)

Use infinitives after nouns (N), participles (PART), adjectives (A), and most verbs (V):

$$\overset{\text{N}}{\text{I felt a desire}} \textit{ to roam.}$$

I felt a desire *to roam*.

N

The urge *to wander* possessed me.

PART

I was determined *to travel*.

A

It was hard *to get* a passport.

A

It was easy *to buy* a plane ticket.

A

Eager *to see* the rest of the world, I boarded the plane.

PART

I was dismayed *to lose* my passport.

A

I was glad *to find* it.

V

I want *to explore* Latin America.

V

I hope *to become* a journalist.

N

My wish *to work* has been granted.

Some verbs may be followed by *either* a gerund *or* an infinitive:

I love *dancing*.
I love *to dance*.

I like *singing*.
I like *to sing*.

I hate *to wait*.
I hate *waiting*.

A few verbs may be followed by the gerund but *not* by the infinitive:

▶ I enjoy ~~to walk.~~ *walking.*

▶ I dislike ~~to jog.~~ *jogging.*

▶ She didn't mind ~~to work~~ *working* late.

▶ She finished ~~to write~~ *writing* the report at two in the morning.

Other verbs of this type are *avoid, delay, miss, practice, risk, resent,* and *suggest.*

EXERCISE 5   **Using Gerunds and Infinitives**

In the following sentences, choose between a gerund and an infinitive. In some sentences, only one of the two is correct. In other sentences, either one can be used. Write out each sentence with your choice included.

EXAMPLE: The cost of (to live, living) rises steadily.

The cost of living rises steadily.

1. Juanita usually exercises before (having, to have) supper.

2. She dislikes (to go, going) without a workout at the end of a day.

3. On weekends she often has an urge (taking, to take) a long hike.

4. After (to work, working) at the office all week, she enjoys (roaming, to roam).

5. She sometimes walks for hours without (to stop, stopping).

6. She likes (looking, to look) for elk and deer.

7. The thrill of (to see, seeing) wild birds and animals delights her.

8. Juanita's friends never grow tired of (to hear, hearing) her stories of life in the woods.

9. They are always ready (to hear, hearing) a new tale.

10. They enjoy (to know, knowing) her.

PARTICIPLES

A **participle** is a word made from a verb and ending in *-ing* or *-ed*. It can serve as part of a verb phrase and as a modifier. We treat each use in turn.

USING PRESENT AND PAST PARTICIPLES IN VERB PHRASES When you want to say how someone or something is, was, or will be act*ing*, use the present participle, which ends in *-ing*:

My cousin is *studying* economics.

He will be *taking* an exam next week.

Last week he was *preparing* for a sociology exam.

Next week he will be *visiting* me.

When you want to say how someone or something is, was, has been, had been, or will be act*ed upon,* use the past participle, which ends in *-ed, -d, -n,* or *-t:*

My car is *washed* once a week.

It was *washed* yesterday.

It has been *washed* regularly since I bought it.

Before then, it had never been *washed.*

It will be *washed* regularly as long as I own it.

The simple past (SP) of many verbs is the same in form as the past participle (PP):

PP
My car is *washed* once a week.

SP
I *washed* it yesterday.

For more on the use of participles in verb phrases, see chapters 22 and 24.

USING PAST AND PRESENT PARTICIPLES AS MODIFIERS Whenever a present participle is used to modify a noun, it tells what the noun is do*ing:*

I woke up to the sound of *laughing* children.

A *singing* waiter brought our food.

Whenever the past participle is used to modify a noun, it tells what has been *done to* the noun:

Lincoln left behind a *stricken* nation, a people *divided* by civil war.

After the long walk, Raul was *tired.*

For more on the use of participles as modifiers, see sections 14.10 and 14.11.

PRESENT AND PAST PARTICIPLES COMMONLY CONFUSED Confusion of past and present participles leads to sentences like these:

▶ The movie was ~~excited.~~ *exciting.*

▶ I was very ~~exciting~~ *excited* by it.

To avoid mistakes like these, you need to know the difference between present and past participles that are commonly confused.

NOUN/PRONOUN SAID TO BE ACT*ING*	NOUN/PRONOUN SAID TO BE ACT*ED* UPON
N The mosquitos were annoy*ing*.	PR We were all annoy*ed* by them.
N The bor*ing* speech lasted two hours.	N The bor*ed* listeners fell asleep.
N The explanation was confus*ing*.	N It left the students confus*ed*.
N The news is often depress*ing*.	N The economy is often depress*ed*.
N The song was excit*ing*.	N The crowd was excit*ed* by it.
N An exhaust*ing* day began the week.	PR Exhaust*ed*, I crawled into bed.
N She told a fascinat*ing* story.	N Her fascinat*ed* listeners loved it.
N The robber was frighten*ing*.	N The frighten*ed* onlookers froze.
N We ate a satisfy*ing* meal.	PR It made us all feel satisfi*ed*.
N A surpris*ing* sight greeted us.	N A surpris*ed* raccoon sat on our porch.

PROGRESSIVE VERBS

The progressive form of the verb combines a form of *be* with the present participle.

USING THE PROGRESSIVE FORMS   Use the present progressive to indicate

▶ what is happening as you write:

I *am* now *sitting* at my desk.

▶ what is in progress as you write, whether or not it is occurring at the moment of writing:

The public school teachers in Los Angeles *are planning* a protest march.

Use the **present perfect** progressive to indicate what continues from the past into the present:

They *have been planning* the march for several weeks.

On the progressive forms of other tenses, see 22.5–22.8.

MISUSING THE PROGRESSIVE FORMS Do not use the present progressive with any phrase referring to past action that is continued up to the present. Use the perfect progressive:

> *have been*
> ▶ I ~~am~~ living in San Diego for six months.

You can also use the simple perfect:

I have lived in San Diego for six months.

Do not use the present progressive for any action or condition that has become habitual and is likely to continue indefinitely. Use the simple present:

> *live*
> ▶ I ~~am living~~ in San Diego.

> *work*
> ▶ I ~~am working~~ for the telephone company

Editing Mistakes in the Use of Participles   **EXERCISE 6**

In the following sentences, correct every mistake in the use of a participle, writing out each sentence in full. The participle may be a part of a verb phrase or the modifier of a noun or pronoun. We have made the first correction for you.

1. Children were ~~waded~~ *wading* in the cold water of a brook.

2. The water was swirling about in a small pool shaping by boulders from the ice age.

3. As the glacier covering the region was receded, it left behind a trail marking by boulders, sand beds, and narrow gorges.

4. The children, of course, were not thought of such things as they frolicked in water that only moments earlier had been tumbled down the mountainside.

(Continued on p. 444.)

5. They were wiggled their toes against moss-covering rocks and splashing friends with handfuls of sparkled water.

6. Squeals of laughter echoed in the clear air as busy hands scooping beneath the surface sent yet another shower cascaded into the sunlight.

7. Earlier that day the children had been hiked up a trail covering with roots, loose stones, and pine needles.

8. At first, they had been pleasing with the adventure and delighting to be carrying backpacks like the grown-ups.

9. But as the minutes passed and the sun's rays became hotter, they grew weary of the ever-risen trail.

10. The pool of cold water had appearing just in time to restore their flagged spirits and their pleasure in the day.

28.4 PRONOUNS

A pronoun (PR) is a word that takes the place of a noun. Usually the noun (N) comes before the pronoun referring to it:

> N   PR
>
> Arturo smiled when he recognized the old man.

You need a pronoun only when referring to a noun mentioned in a different clause:

> CLAUSE 1   CLAUSE 2
>
> Arturo smiled   when   he recognized the old man

Do not use a pronoun to refer to something already mentioned in the same clause:

> ▶ Arturo he smiled.

> ▶ The store it belongs to my grandfather.

Do not mistake the second half of an *interrupted* clause for a *new* clause:

> CLAUSE 1
>
> CLAUSE 2
>
> ▶ The store [that was burglarized] it belongs to my grandfather.

CLAUSE 1

CLAUSE 2

▶ The town [where I was born] ~~there~~ is near Cartagena.

Do not use two pronouns referring to the same noun as objects of one verb:

CLAUSE 1   CLAUSE 2

▶ Gabriella wore the kind of dress that I have always loved.~~it.~~

Since *that* and *it* both refer to *dress,* they cannot both be objects of *loved.*

For a full presentation on pronoun use, see chapter 20.

USING THE POSSESSIVES

Possessives (Group 1 determiners, pp. 426–27) are pronouns in the possessive case, such as *my* and *your.* Use them as follows:

Use *my, your, his, her, its, ours,* and *their* before any noun:

my car	their properties	its roof
her job	our town	their courage
his letters	your house	her wisdom

Use the other possessives—*mine, yours, hers, ours,* and *theirs*—after any noun and a linking verb (LV):

LV
The house was *mine.*

LV
The car was *hers.*

On the possessive case of *nouns,* see *case* in the Glossary of Grammatical Terms; also see 34.9.

Editing Redundant Pronouns

EXERCISE 7

The following sentences may or may not contain redundant pronouns. If you find any, remove them and write out the new sentences. If a sentence is correct as it stands, write "correct."

EXAMPLE: Peggy ~~she~~ laughed when she heard the joke.

Peggy laughed when she heard the joke.

(Continued on p. 446.)

1. Phillipa she wants to find a new apartment that it overlooks the city park.

2. Her present apartment, which she has rented it for two years, has too many drawbacks.

3. For one thing, the plumbing it keeps breaking down; for another thing, the landlords they keep raising the rent.

4. The rent that she now has to pay it comes to more than half of what she earns it at work.

5. With any luck, the new place it will cost her less money than she has to spend it on the old one, and the facilities they will function without a hitch.

28.5 PREPOSITIONS

The use of prepositions is one of the most highly idiomatic features of the English language. Few easily explained rules govern prepositions, though the section above on phrasal verbs does provide information about one aspect of preposition use. As you encounter other uses, write them down in order to learn the idioms.

Listed below are some idiomatic uses for the common prepositions *in* and *on* and for *adjective-preposition combinations:*

IN: *in the summer, in December, in the evening, in the library, in San Francisco, in 2001, in California, in Japanese, in class, in school, in your hair, in the hospital, in the sun, in love, in bed, in time, in order, in a letter, in the office*

ON: *on top of, on time, on Broadway, on the table, on the menu, on a chair, on the moon, on Earth, on her head, on paper, on TV, on the Internet, on the phone, on a plane, on purpose, on foot*

ADJECTIVE + PREPOSITION: *afraid of, ashamed of, aware of, capable of, careful of, independent of, full of, proud of, tired of, bored with, cooperate with, satisfied with, dependent on, responsible for, responsible to, interested in, worried about*

28.6 TIPS ON SENTENCE STRUCTURE AND STYLE

SENTENCE COMPLETENESS

SUPPLYING A SUBJECT In some languages the subject may be part of the verb. In Spanish, for instance, *vivo* means "I live," a complete sentence. But an English sentence normally requires a subject that is separate from the verb:

> *I* live in Miami.
>
> *She* works in Chinatown.
>
> *We* need jobs.
>
> *They* are scarce.
>
> *You* are thin.

EXCEPTION: Sentences that make commands omit the subject and start with the verb:

> *Watch* the conductor.
>
> *Lift* the handle.
>
> *Use* the seat belt in your car.
>
> *Close* the door.

In sentences like these, the subject is understood as *you.*

For more on subjects, see 13.4.

USING LINKING VERBS *(IS, ARE, WAS, WERE)* A linking verb (LV) is so called because it links the subject (S) to an adjective (A) or noun (N):

>   S LV A
> The house is old.

>   S   LV   N
> The men were thieves.

In some languages, the subject may be linked by position alone to a word that follows it (*My brother a police officer). In English the link must be made by a verb:

▶ The walk long.
(was)

▶ The people tired and hungry.
(were)

▶ My brother a police officer.
(is)

USING *THERE* AND *IT* (EXPLETIVES) TO START A SENTENCE   An expletive (E) is a word typically used at the beginning of a sentence whenever the subject (S) follows the verb:

E   S
There are alligators in the Florida everglades.

E   S
It is dangerous to skate on thin ice.

Normally, you must start with an expletive whenever the subject follows the verb:

▶ ~~Is~~ hard to climb a mountain.
(It is)

▶ ~~Is~~ no fool like an old fool.
(There is)

When an opening *It* refers to the weather, the temperature, the date, or the time, *It* is the subject:

S
It is always cold in the Arctic.

It was Friday, July 2, when the earthquake struck.

It was noon when I felt the first tremor.

WORD ORDER

Subject-verb-object (SVO): The most common sentence pattern in English is subject, verb, direct object, as in *She enjoys sports*.

Time and place: Expressions of time and place should come at the beginning or end of a clause, but not between the verb and the direct object.

INCORRECT: *Hakim saw yesterday his brother.*

CORRECT: *Hakim saw his brother yesterday.*

CORRECT: *Yesterday Hakim saw his brother.*

Using Subjects, Linking Verbs, and Expletives

In the following passage, the writer omitted some subjects, linking verbs, and expletives. Provide these as needed, writing out the corrected passage in full. We have done the first bit of editing for you.

Electricity ^is very important in our lives. Yet rarely think about it. Take it for granted until something wrong. When is nothing we can do, we realize we helpless without its power. In the summer of 1959, everyone in New York City unhappy when the city's power plant broke down for many hours. Electric fans and air conditioners ⁵ stopped working. Apartments and offices soon hot. Elevators motionless, and subways stopped on their tracks. That night, streets dark and gloomy. People scared. In the emergency, little the police could do. They helpless too. Then was a sudden change. Lights shone again, trains began moving, and fans stirred the air in hot, stuffy ¹⁰ rooms. All of the people glad. They safe. Had their precious electricity again.

3

Punctuation and Mechanics

The Comma **29**

29.1 USING COMMAS WITH CONJUNCTIONS

1. Use a comma before a conjunction *(and, but, for, or, nor, so, yet)* linking two independent clauses:

> Canadians watch America closely, *but* most Americans know little about Canada.

> The prospectors hoped to find gold on the rocky slopes of the Sierra Madre, *so* they set out eagerly.

> Cowards never started on the long trek west, *and* the weak died along the way.

2. Use a comma before a conjunction linking the last two items in a series:

> She loved life, liberty, and the happiness of being pursued.

For more on conjunctions, see 15.2 and 15.3. For more on punctuating items in a series, see 29.7.

29.2 MISUSING COMMAS WITH CONJUNCTIONS

1. Do not use a comma before a conjunction within a series of just two items:

▶ The manager was genial/but shrewd.

▶ She checked my weekly sales/and asked to speak with me.

The Comma

EXCEPTION: You may use a comma to set off a contrasting phrase:

She liked running her own business, but not working on weekends.

2. Do not use a comma after a conjunction:

   ▶ The speaker coughed, studied his notes, and/ frowned.

   ▶ He was scheduled to discuss Rembrandt. But/ the notes treated the etchings of Picasso.

EXCEPTION: Use a pair of commas after a conjunction to set off a word, phrase, or clause:

But, he sadly realized, the notes treated the etchings of Picasso.

EXERCISE 1   **Using Commas with Conjunctions**

Each of the following may require the addition or removal or moving of a comma. Make any changes necessary. If an entry is correct as it stands, write *Correct*.

EXAMPLE: We can stop for the night in Moose Jaw, or we can push on.
                                                          ^

1. Odysseus longs to return to his home on the island of Ithaca but he does not reach it for ten years.

2. He blinds the son of the sea-god Poseidon so, he must endure Poseidon's avenging wrath.

3. Poseidon's son is a one-eyed giant named Polyphemus and he lives alone in a cave with herds of sheep, and goats.

4. Odysseus enters the cave with his men one day, for, he expects to find hospitality there.

5. Instead the giant blocks the exit with a massive stone, eats two of Odysseus's men, and threatens to devour the rest.

6. Odysseus and his men seem doomed but, Odysseus blinds the giant, and escapes with his men.

7. They escape by hiding under the bellies of rams for the giant does not see the men when he lets his herds out of the cave.

8. Odysseus then recklessly shouts his name to the giant so, the giant asks Poseidon to make Odysseus's homecoming as painful as possible.

29.3 MISUSING COMMAS BETWEEN INDEPENDENT CLAUSES: THE COMMA SPLICE

Do not use a comma alone between two independent clauses:

▶ The beams have rotted,/they can no longer support the roof.

▶ [or] The beams have rotted, ^so^ they can no longer support the roof.

▶ [or] ~~The~~ ^Since the^ beams have rotted, they can no longer support the roof.

For a full discussion of the comma splice, see 15.6.

29.4 USING COMMAS AFTER INTRODUCTORY ELEMENTS

1.   Use a comma after an introductory clause, phrase, or word:

Whenever it rains hard, the roof leaks.

To stop the leak, we have been replacing old shingles with new ones.

Unfortunately, last night's thunderstorm showed us that we still have more work to do.

2.   Use a comma after a conjunctive adverb at the beginning of a sentence or clause:

The kitchen was drenched; *in fact,* an inch of water covered the floor.

Nevertheless, the living room remained dry.

For more on conjunctive adverbs, see 15.5.

EXCEPTION: To accelerate the pace of their sentences, writers sometimes skip the comma after an introductory adverb or short introductory phrase:

Today students protest individually rather than in concert.
                                                            —Caroline Bird

Throughout the 1930s the number of addicts remained about the same in both England and the United States.
                                                            —Edward Bunker

Using Commas after Introductory Elements

Each of the following sentences may require a comma after an introductory element. Add a comma if needed. If the sentence is correct as it stands, write *Correct*.

EXAMPLE: Furthermore, an increase in property taxes would severely limit the number of young adults who could live here.

1. After Odysseus and his men escape from the giant's cave they sail to the island of Aeolus, god of winds.

2. From Aeolus Odysseus gets a bag of winds that is supposed to ensure his safe return to Ithaca.

3. Having sailed for nine days Odysseus and his men actually catch sight of Ithaca; nevertheless they are swept away by a storm when the men foolishly open the bag.

4. As a result they must sail on to further adventures.

5. On the island of Aiaia they find an enchantress named Circe.

6. When a group of Odysseus's men go to see her she turns them into pigs.

7. On learning of their fate Odysseus decides to see her for himself.

8. His remaining companions are terrified; in fact they fear that he will never return.

9. Fortunately he obtains a magic potion from Hermes.

10. With the aid of that, he withstands Circe's magic and persuades her to change the pigs back into men.

29.5 USING COMMAS WITH NONRESTRICTIVE ELEMENTS

Use a comma or a pair of commas to set off **nonrestrictive** elements: words, phrases, and clauses that are not essential to the meaning of the sentences in which they appear. Compare these two sentences:

Anyone *who publishes a book at the age of six* must be remarkable. (restrictive)

Dorothy Straight of Washington, D.C., *who published her first book at the age of six,* was a remarkable child. (nonrestrictive)

In the first sentence, the *who* clause is essential to the meaning of the sentence because it restricts the meaning of *anyone* to a certain person. The clause tells *which one* is remarkable. In the second sentence, the *who* clause is nonrestrictive and nonessential because it does not identify *Dorothy Straight*. She has already been identified by her name.

Now compare these two sentences:

> At the microphone stood a man *wearing a green suit.* (restrictive)

> At the microphone stood the master of ceremonies, *wearing a green suit.* (nonrestrictive)

In the first sentence, the italicized phrase is restrictive because it identifies *a man*. In the second sentence, the italicized phrase is nonrestrictive because the man has already been identified by his title. The italicized phrase just adds further information about him.

The distinction between restrictive and nonrestrictive is commonly applied to adjective clauses, such as *who publishes a book at the age of six,* and participle phrases, such as *wearing a green suit.* Broadly speaking, however, nonrestrictive elements include anything that supplements the basic meaning of the sentence, anything not essential to that meaning. Here are further examples:

> The surgeon, *her hands moving deftly,* probed the wound.

> Fearful, *not confident,* he embarked on his journey.

> At midnight, *long after the final out of the game,* the losing manager was still shaking his head in disbelief.

> In October of 1987, *however,* stock prices plummeted.

A single comma sets off a nonrestrictive element that comes at the end of the sentence:

> The tour includes three days in Toronto, *which must be one of the cleanest cities in the world.*

> Celia stood in the wings, *waiting for her cue.*

29.6 MISUSING COMMAS WITH RESTRICTIVE ELEMENTS

Do not use commas with restrictive elements: with words, phrases, or clauses essential to the meaning of the sentences in which they appear:

▶ All entries/ postmarked later than July 1/ will be discounted.

▶ Plants/ that aren't watered/ will die.

(Adjective clauses starting with *that* are always restrictive.)

▶ No one/ without a ticket/ will be admitted.

▶ Film director/ François Truffaut/ died of cancer in 1984.

A name that follows a common noun or noun phrase is restrictive and should not be set off by commas. But when the name comes first, the common noun that follows it is nonrestrictive and should be set off by commas:

François Truffaut, *the film director,* died of cancer in 1984.

EXERCISE 3

Punctuating Restrictive and Nonrestrictive Elements

Decide whether each of the italicized elements is restrictive or nonrestrictive, and add or remove commas where necessary. If a sentence is correct as it stands, write *Correct.*

EXAMPLE:

All motorists, *who drive recklessly,* should have their licenses suspended for six months.

DECISION: restrictive.

EDITED: All motorists who drive recklessly should have their licenses suspended for six months.

1. My brother's car *a 1979 Ford Fiesta* looks like a gooey red marshmallow.

2. The interior *which has never been cleaned* is sticky with grime.

3. Nobody could close the front ashtray *which is stuffed with bottle caps, Kleenex tissues, and wads of chewing gum.*

4. The dashboard, another disaster area, has all but disappeared beneath the dust *that has built up over the months.*

5. The speedometer is barely visible, and it's impossible for anyone, *with normal vision,* to read the fuel gauge.

6. The driver's seat *which is covered with a piece of worn vinyl* smells like a loaf of moldy bread.

7. The exterior *with its layers of grime, rust spots, and dents* looks no better than the inside.

8. The rear window *lacking a windshield wiper* looks like one of those gray boards, *that collect dust in the corners of old barns.*

9. The front windshield *on the other hand* has a clear spot, *made by an ice scraper.*

10. For the past month, my brother has been looking for a used-car dealer, *who will take the car off his hands without charging him.*

11. He's not sure, though, whether he'll find a dealer who wants a car, *that stands little chance of ever being sold.*

29.7   USING COMMAS WITH COORDINATE ITEMS IN A SERIES

1. Use commas to separate three or more coordinate items in a series:

> Maples, oaks, and sycamores have been afflicted.

> The leaves shrivel, wither, and fall to the ground before autumn.

> Scientists are seeking to learn what is causing the blight, how it enters the trees, and whether it can be halted.

2. Use commas to separate two or more coordinate adjectives modifying the same noun:

> A big, old, dilapidated house stood on the corner.

> Its owner always spoke in a low, husky voice.

For more help with punctuating items in a series, see 29.1, item 2.

29.8   MISUSING COMMAS WITH COORDINATE ITEMS IN A SERIES

1. Do not use a comma to separate adjectives when they are not coordinate—that is, when they do not modify the same word:

> ▶ His deep/blue eyes stared at me.

Deep modifies *blue; blue* modifies *eyes.* Coordinate adjectives can be reversed. A *low, husky* voice can become a *husky, low* voice. But *deep blue* eyes cannot become *blue deep* eyes.

2.   Do not use a comma before a conjunction when there are just two items:

▶ Her hair was black/and long.

(For an exception, see 29.2, item 1.)

EXERCISE 4   **Using Commas with Items in a Series**

Each of the following sentences may require the addition or removal of a comma or commas. Make the necessary changes. If an entry is correct as it stands, write *Correct*.

EXAMPLE: Under the circumstances, only an intelligent discreet and experienced official should be assigned to the case.

1. Last summer my brother, my father, and, I visited a busy, logging camp in a rugged, picturesque, largely uninhabited part of Maine.

2. From dawn to dusk, hardy skilled lumberjacks felled trees, cut them into logs, and cleared the thick, green underbrush.

3. Our guide was a slow-moving infirm old man with dark brown eyes; but he could still repair broken, or sputtering chain saws.

4. Dressed in his bright, red, flannel jacket, he had a sturdy, workbench in a pleasant, shaded area next to the large, equipment shed.

5. Inside the shed were various things, including coils of thick heavy rope, stacks of wooden, axe handles, and bright, yellow, slickers for rainy days.

6. Our guide's worn, carpenter's chest contained pliers, screwdrivers with hard, rubber handles, a set of galvanized, steel, wrenches, two copper oil cans, and bolts of many different sizes.

7. Carefully expertly, and patiently he worked on each, broken chain saw until its motor coughed, wheezed, and sputtered into life.

8. Then, with a deft, and clever adjustment of the carburetor, he would soon have the motor purring like a cat stretched out before a warm cozy fire.

9. My father, my brother and I wondered how many kinds of discarded appliances might be thus revived, and saved from the trash can, and the dump.

29.9 USING COMMAS TO PREVENT A MISREADING

Use a comma when you need one to prevent a misreading of your sentence:

▶ On the left‚ walls of sheer ice rose over five thousand feet into the
ᐱ
clouds.

29.10 USING COMMAS WITH DATES, ADDRESSES, GREETINGS, NAMES, AND LARGE NUMBERS

1. Use commas to set off parts of dates and addresses that appear within a sentence:

On the afternoon of July 1, 1963, the fighting began.

The return address on the letter was 23 Hockey Street, Lexington, Kentucky 40502.

EXCEPTION: Use no comma to separate parts of a date that begins with the day:

The atomic bomb was first dropped on 6 August 1945.

2. Use commas to set off the names of someone directly addressed in a sentence:

A few weeks ago, Mr. Taplow, I spoke to you on the telephone about the possibility of a summer job.

3. Use a comma after the greeting in a friendly or informal letter, and after the closing in a letter of any kind:

Dear Mary,   Sincerely,

Dear Uncle Paul,   Yours truly,

4. Use commas to set off titles or degrees after a person's name:

Barbara Kane, M.D., delivered the commencement address.

But *Jr., Sr.,* and *III* may be written without commas:

Sammy Davis Jr. started his singing career at age four.

5.   Use a comma after the last part of a proper name when the last part comes first:

> Lunt, George D.

6.   Use commas to mark groups of three digits in large numbers, counting from the right:

> Antarctica is 5,400,000 square miles of ice-covered land.

29.11   MISUSING COMMAS WITH DATES AND ADDRESSES

1.   Do not use a comma to separate the name of the month from the day:

> ▶ October/ 22   ▶ 15/ May

2.   Do not use a comma to separate the name of the month from the year:

> ▶ January/ 1988   ▶ 22 April/ 1939

3.   Do not use a comma to separate a street number from the name of the street:

> ▶ 15/ Amsterdam Avenue

4.   Do not use a comma before a zip code or anywhere else in an address that is written out on an envelope:

> ▶ 24 Mechanic Street   ▶ 35 Rosemount Avenue
>   Lebanon/ NH/ 03766   Montreal/ Que./ H3Y3G6
>   Canada

(On the abbreviations used here, see 35.4.)

29.12   USING COMMAS WITH QUOTATION MARKS

For a full discussion of how to use commas with quotation marks, see 32.3.

Using Commas   IN BRIEF

Generally, use a comma before a conjunction linking independent clauses:

> Canadians watch America closely, *but* most Americans know little about Canada.

Generally, do not use a comma after a conjunction:

> The speaker coughed, studied his notes, and/frowned.

Do not use a comma alone between two independent clauses:

> The beams have rotted/they can no longer support the roof.

Generally, use commas after an introductory item:

> Whenever it rains hard, the roof leaks.

> Unfortunately, we haven't yet fixed it.

Use commas with nonrestrictive elements:

> Dorothy Straight of Washington, D.C., *who published her first book at the age of six,* was a remarkable child.

Do not use commas with restrictive elements:

> Anyone/who publishes a book at the age of six/must be remarkable.

Generally, use commas to separate three or more coordinate items in a series:

> We played cards, told stories, and sang old songs.

29.13 MISUSING THE COMMA BETWEEN BASIC PARTS OF A SENTENCE

1. Do not use a comma between a subject and its predicate:

    ▶ In August, all the members of the Johnson clan/ gathered for their annual picnic.

EXCEPTION: Use a *pair* of commas to set off a phrase or clause that comes between the subject and the predicate:

In August, all the members of the Johnson clan, from little Susie to ancient Winona, gathered for their annual picnic.

2.   Do not use a comma between a verb and its object:

▶ Altogether we ate/forty hamburgers and six big watermelons.

▶ I don't know/how many ears of corn we consumed.

EXERCISE 5   **Editing Commas—A Review**

In the following passage, we have deliberately introduced some errors in punctuation. Remove all misused commas, add any that are needed, and leave any that are correctly used.

Many early American homes, were decorated with block-printed wallpapers. Imported from England, and France, the papers made the arrival of ships from abroad an exciting event for Colonial home-makers. Merchants, looking for sales, advertised that papering was cheaper than whitewashing, and, they urged would-be customers to   5
examine the endless variety of brightly colored patterns. Indeed by today's standards the colors in many Colonial papers seem vibrant, intense, and, even gaudy. One wonders whether the citizens of Boston Massachusetts and Providence Rhode Island, yearned for bright reds, greens, and, blues because of the grey, New England winters.   10

The process of reproducing historic wallpapers, requires the finesse of a craftsman. To establish a particular paper's full pattern, the expert may have to fit together the fragments of surviving samples, that he finds in museums in the attics of old houses and even under layers of other papers. He determines the original hue of   15
the colors in various ways: he runs chemical tests, or, he matches a fragment to a fresh original in some museum, even then he must be careful before proceeding to the next step printing the design. As a final precaution therefore he makes, a blacklight examination knowing it may reveal otherwise indistinguishable elements of the   20
pattern.

One of the leading experts in America is Dorothy Waterhouse cofounder of Waterhouse Hangings. She first became interested in historic wallpapers in 1932 when she was restoring, an old house on Cape Cod Massachusetts. While stripping the walls in one room she   25
got down to the eighth, and bottom layer of paper. She became very excited, she knew it had to be over 140 years old. That discovery was the first of many. Today she has a collection of some three hundred historic wallpapers, all carefully stored in her Boston home.

—Peter M. Lincoln, "Documentary Wallpapers"   30

The Semicolon and the Colon

30

30.1 USING THE SEMICOLON

1.   You may use a semicolon to join two independent clauses that are closely related in meaning:

> Insist on yourself; never imitate. —Ralph Waldo Emerson

2.   You may use a semicolon to join two independent clauses when the second begins with or includes a conjunctive adverb:

> Shakespeare's plays are four hundred years old; nevertheless, they still speak to us.

> Many of his characters resemble people we encounter or read about daily; a few, in fact, remind us of ourselves.

For more on semicolons and conjunctive adverbs, see 15.5.

3.   You may use a semicolon before a conjunction to join two independent clauses that contain commas:

> By laughing at our faults, we can learn to acknowledge them graciously; and we can try to overcome them in a positive, even cheerful way, not grimly and disagreeably.

4.   Use semicolons to emphasize the division between items that include commas:

> There were three new delegates at the meeting: Ms. Barbara Smith from Boulder, Colorado; Ms. Beth Waters from Omaha, Nebraska; and Mr. James Papson from Greenwood, Arkansas.

30.2   MISUSING THE SEMICOLON

1.   Do not use a semicolon between a phrase and the clause to which it belongs:

▶ The climbers carried an extra nylon rope; to ensure their safe descent from the cliff.

▶ Proceeding cautiously down the rock face; they neared the floor of the canyon.

2.   Do not use a semicolon between a subordinate clause and the main clause:

▶ Most of the crowd had left; before the concert ended.

▶ Although the hall was almost empty; she came out for a second bow.

▶ Ticket sales had been good; which made both her agent and her manager happy.

3.   Do not use a semicolon to introduce a list. Use a colon:

▶ The prophets denounced three types of wrongdoing; idolatry, injustice, and neglect of the needy.

For more on colons, see the next section.

EXERCISE 1   **Using Semicolons**

Each of the following sentences requires the addition or removal of one or more semicolons. Make any necessary changes, adding other punctuation if necessary.

EXAMPLE: Some people give others take.

1. The Gateway Arch in St. Louis symbolizes opportunity, in particular, it represents the soaring aspirations of America's pioneers who ventured into unknown lands throughout the nineteenth century.

2. The pioneers consisted of many subgroups: New England farmers seeking richer soil, immigrants fleeing a nation's slums, shy trappers from the north; lusty mountain men, failed merchants, and adventurers with an eye for danger.

3. For all of these people St. Louis was a gateway, it was the entrance to a new and prosperous life somewhere beyond the Mississippi River.

4. Few of the pioneers realized how difficult their new lives would be, on the contrary, they thought of the west as a vast land flowing with milk and honey.

5. They would live high on the hog they would live like kings and queens.

30.3 USING THE COLON

1.   Use a colon after an independent clause to introduce a list:

Success depends on three things: talent, determination, and luck.

2.   Use a colon to introduce an example or an explanation related to something just mentioned:

The animals have a good many of our practical skills: some insects make pretty fair architects, and beavers know quite a lot about engineering.
—Northrop Frye

3.   Use a colon to introduce one or more complete sentences quoted from formal speech or writing:

In the opening sentence of his novel *Scaramouche*, Rafael Sabatini says of his hero: "He was born with the gift of laughter, and a sense that the world was mad."

4.   Use a colon to follow the salutation in a formal letter:

Dear Mr. Mayor:

Dear Ms. Watson:

To Whom It May Concern:

5.   Use a colon to separate hours from minutes when the time of day is shown in numerals:

8:40   6:30   11:15

30.4 MISUSING THE COLON

1. Do not use a colon after *such as, including,* or a form of the verb *be:*

    ▶ On rainy days at camp, we played board games such as/ Monopoly, Scrabble, and Trivial Pursuit.

    ▶ One morning I woke up to find that someone had taken all of my valuables, including/ my watch, my camera, and my money.

    ▶ Still in my locker were/ my toilet kit, my flashlight, and my wallet— now empty.

2. Do not use a colon between a verb and its object or between a preposition and its object:

    ▶ Before heading home, we stopped at/ the supermarket, the hardware store, and the gas station.

    ▶ We needed/ pasta, a window screen, and a tank of gasoline.

EXERCISE 2   **Using Semicolons and Colons**

In the following passage, we have deliberately removed some of the author's punctuation. Add a semicolon or a colon wherever necessary.

EXAMPLE: 10:00 (line 1)

The events on Good Friday are tragic. At 10 00 a grim-looking priest conducts a solemn service Christ is removed from the Cross and placed in a tomb. All work ceases flags fly at half mast. Soldiers carry their rifles reversed as they do during funeral processions. Offices and shops close everyone goes to church. The church bells will toll all day   5 long. After the service the young girls of the parish perform a bittersweet task they decorate the bier of Jesus with flowers from 11 00 to 1 00. By that time it is a mass of flowers.

Lunch consists of simple fare boiled lentils, which represent the tears of the Virgin, and vinegar, which represents the vinegar given   10 to Christ on the Cross.

On Friday evening the church is filled to overflowing. All in the city are present old men and women, officials, husbands and wives, children. The songs of mourning are lovely in their sadness for

example, in one of them Mary refers to her dead son as a child who   15
was as sweet as spring. After the service, which usually ends at 9 00, a
kind of funeral procession takes place. It follows a definite order first
comes a band playing a funeral march next comes a priest carrying
the Cross then comes the bier accompanied by girls in white, the Boy
Scouts, and a detachment of soldiers then come the other priests. The   20
people follow, each one carrying a brown candle. The gathering has
spiritual meaning. It is also deeply human.

—Ismene Phylactopoulou, "Greek Easter"

31 *End Marks*

31.1 USING THE PERIOD

1. Use a period to mark the end of a declarative sentence, a mild command, or an indirect question:

    The days are growing shorter, and the nights are becoming cool.

    On some mornings a hint of frost chills the air.

    Nature is proceeding at her accustomed pace.

    Note her ways closely.

    I wonder what she will do next.

When typing on a computer, skip one space after the period before beginning the next sentence. (On a typewriter, skip two spaces.)

2. Use a period to mark the end of some abbreviations:

    Dr. Boyle

    500 Fifth Ave.

    Kate Fansler, Ph.D.

    Mr. G. H. Johnson

    Mrs. L. S. Allingham

    Ms. N. A. Stephens

    3:28 P.M.

    350 B.C.

(NOTE: MLA recommends not using periods in abbreviations that include capital letters, such as PhD and BC.)

Generally, you don't need periods with acronyms (words formed from the initials of a multiword title), with capital-letter abbreviations of technical terms, or with abbreviated names of states, agencies, and organizations:

CBS	ROTC	IBM
NATO	TVA	IQ
FM	ID	KP
NY	CIA	VISTA

But you do need periods with abbreviations standing for the names of political entities:

U.S.A.   U.K.   C.I.S.

For guidance, see your dictionary.

3.   Use a period to mark letters or numerals used in vertical lists:

Woven into the history of the world is the history of its four great religions:

1. Buddhism

2. Judaism

3. Christianity

4. Islam

If you give the information in a sentence, enclose the letters or numbers within parentheses and omit the periods:

Woven into the history of the world is the history of its four great religions: (1) Buddhism, (2) Judaism, (3) Christianity, and (4) Islam.

31.2   MISUSING THE PERIOD

1.   In formal writing, do not use a period to separate the different parts of a sentence. If you do, you will create a sentence fragment:

▶ Customers should be treated courteously, ~~Even~~ if they are extremely rude.

even

End Marks

For more on sentence fragments, see chapter 19.

2. Do not use a period after another period or other end mark:

▶ To please our customers, we have ordered scarce materials from Home Supplies Company, Inc./

▶ We don't want customers saying, "Why don't you have what I want?"/

31.3 USING THE QUESTION MARK

Use a question mark—

1. To mark the end of a direct question:

   Must the problems of farmers be ignored?
   To what agency can they go for legal aid?

2. To indicate uncertainty within a statement:

   Some exotic dish—pheasant under glass?—was served at the banquet.
   The host must have paid a lot of money (fifty dollars?) for each meal.

31.4 MISUSING THE QUESTION MARK

Do not use a question mark at the end of a question reported indirectly:

▶ I wonder who wrote this song?.

▶ She asked if I wanted more cheese?.

For more on this topic, see 26.4.

31.5 USING THE EXCLAMATION POINT

Use the exclamation point to mark an expression of strong feeling:

> What a spectacular view!

> Impossible!

Because exclamation points make a special appeal to the reader, you should use them sparingly.

Using Periods and Question Marks

EXERCISE

Improve the punctuation in the following paragraph by adding a period or question mark wherever necessary; also make any accompanying change in capitalization that may be required. As you make these corrections, write out the entire paragraph.

How do historians rate the contributions of General Gordon to his country their opinions differ some consider him a military genius, one of the greatest soldiers in British history others criticize him severely in their opinion General C G Gordon, or "Chinese" Gordon as he was popularly known, acted impulsively he was rash he was   5 dangerous he was not fit to hold a command did he seek death on January 26, 1885 historians give conflicting answers

32 Quotation Marks and Quoting

32.1 QUOTING WORDS, PHRASES, AND SHORT PASSAGES OF PROSE

Use double quotation marks (" ") to enclose any words, phrases, or short passages quoted from speech, writing, or printed matter:

> After the murder of the old king in Shakespeare's *Macbeth,* Lady Macbeth imagines there is blood on her hand and cries, "Out, damned spot!"

> "Look before you leap" is particularly good advice for divers.

> "An agnostic," writes Clarence Darrow, "is a doubter."

Quoted passages must normally be accompanied by tags identifying the speaker or writer; see 26.1.

32.2 USING DOUBLE AND SINGLE QUOTATION MARKS

1.   Use double quotation marks to enclose the words of speakers engaged in dialogue (conversation), and start a new paragraph each time the speaker changes:

> "How did the interview go?" Bob asked.

> "It's hard to say," said Helen. "At first I was nervous. Then I relaxed and spoke clearly. I began to enjoy myself."

> "Well, it sounds as if you might get the job. If you do, let's celebrate."

2. Use single quotation marks (' ') to enclose a quotation within a quotation:

> At the beginning of the class, the teacher asked, "Where does Thoreau speak of 'quiet desperation,' and what does he mean by this phrase?"

32.3 USING QUOTATION MARKS WITH OTHER PUNCTUATION

1. To introduce a quoted sentence with a phrase, use a comma:

> According to G. B. Shaw, "Economy is the art of making the most of life."

2. To introduce a quoted sentence with a clause, use a comma or colon:

> Winston Churchill said, "To jaw-jaw is always better than to war-war."

> In his first Inaugural Address, Lincoln asked: "Why should there not be a patient confidence in the ultimate justice of the people?"

> June Callwood writes, "Canadians are not Americans who live in a colder climate; they are different people."

Some writers use a comma after a short introductory clause and a colon after a long one. Other writers use a comma before quoting informal speech and a colon before quoting formal speech or writing.

3. Use quotation marks alone to introduce a quoted word or phrase or any quoted words introduced by *that:*

> According to Jung, the "something greater" is the unconscious, which he defines as "a natural phenomenon producing symbols that prove to be meaningful."

> The professor said Jung's theories have been "seminal."

> Margaret Atwood writes that "in fact, a character in a book who is consistently well-behaved probably spells disaster for the book."

4. To end a quoted statement that is followed by a tag, use a comma:

> "It's time for you to leave," said Mimi.

But do not use the comma if the quoted sentence ends in a question mark or an exclamation point:

"What's your problem?" John asked.

"Get out!" she yelled.

The tag begins with a lowercase letter unless its first word is a proper name.

5.   To set off an interruptive tag, use a pair of commas:

"Ideas," writes Carl Jung, "spring from something greater than the personal human being."

The word "spring" is lowercased because it simply continues the quoted sentence.

6.   To end a quoted statement that ends a sentence, use a period:

The governor stated, "I will not seek reelection."

7.   A closing comma or period goes inside the closing quotation mark:

"High school," writes Ellen Willis, "permanently damaged my self-esteem."

8.   A closing semicolon or colon goes outside the closing quotation mark:

The head of the union announced, "The new contract is a good one for management and labor"; then she left the room. Later she told reporters that the new contract "has major benefits for women": payment for overtime, maternity leave, and seniority privileges.

9.   A quotation mark or an exclamation point that belongs to the quotation goes inside the closing quotation mark:

Who wrote, "What's in a name?"

A new idea about the universe always prompts the scientist to ask, "What's the evidence for it?"

Suddenly he bellowed, "Get out!"

10. A question mark or exclamation point that does not belong to the quotation goes outside the closing quotation mark:

Should a 1 percent drop in unemployment be called "a decisive sign of recovery"?

> Though two hundred thousand workers have lost their jobs in the past year, one congressman calls the economy "robust"!

For advice on fitting quotations smoothly into your own sentences, see 26.6.

32.4 QUOTING LONG PROSE PASSAGES

To quote more than four lines of prose, use indentation instead of quotation marks, and follow the format shown here:

> Vicki Hearne invokes the idea of artistry to explain why a horse is willing to jump a high fence:
>
>> There are various ways to talk about what could possibly motivate a horse, or any animal, to such an effort. Fear certainly does not do it. Courage, joy, exaltation are more like it, but beyond that horses have, some of the time, a strong sense of artistry. . . . When I say artistry, I mean that the movements of a developed horse, the figures and leaps, mean something, and an artistic horse is one who is capable of wanting to mean the movements and the jump perfectly. (43)

Keep the punctuation of the original. For use of the ellipsis dots, see 32.6. On citing sources at the end of quotations, see 39.1.

When quoting one or more paragraphs, follow this format:

At the end of his Inaugural Address, John F. Kennedy declared:

Indent ⟶ And so, my fellow Americans: ask not what your
thirteen
spaces.   country can do for you, ask what you can do for

Indent ⟶ your country.
ten
spaces.   My fellow citizens of the world: ask not what

              America will do for you, but what together we can

              do for the freedom of man.

32.5 QUOTING VERSE

1.   Quotations of verse must look like verse, not prose. Keep all capital letters that you find at the beginning of lines, and if you quote more than a line, use a slash (/), with a space on each side, to show where one line ends and another begins:

Elsewhere, Sylvia Plath writes: "Mother to myself, I wake

swaddled in gauze, / Pink and smooth as a baby." This

preoccupation with herself and her own baby . . .

---

2. To quote more than three lines of verse, double-space them and indent each line ten spaces from the left margin:

William Blake's "The Tyger" begins with the lines:

          Tyger! Tyger! burning bright

          In the forests of the night,

          What immortal hand or eye

          Could frame thy fearful symmetry?

If the lines are long, you may indent fewer than ten spaces. If a single line is long, let it run to the right-hand margin and put the overflow under the right-hand side:

Ruefully alluding to his own ill-fated marriage, Byron rhetorically asks,

          I don't choose much to say upon this head

          I'm a plain man, and in a single station,

          But--Oh! ye lords of ladies intellectual,

          Inform us truly, have they not hen-peck'd

                        you all?

For more on quoting verse, see 39.2, items 26–27.

32.6 USING BRACKETS AND ELLIPSIS DOTS TO MARK CHANGES IN A QUOTATION

To quote effectively, you must quote accurately, keeping every word of the original or plainly indicating any changes you have made. Use brackets to mark any words you have added and ellipsis dots to show where you have left words out.

USING BRACKETS TO MARK WORDS ADDED TO A QUOTATION

1.   Use brackets to insert a clarifying detail, comment, or correction of your own into a quotation:

> "In the presidential election of 1993 [1992], Bill Clinton defeated George Bush."

> "When we last see Lady Macbeth [in the sleepwalking scene], she is obviously distraught."

> "Most remarkably, the Motherhood Myth [the notion that having babies is instructive and enjoyable] persists in the face of the most overwhelming maternal unhappiness and incompetence."
>
> —Betty Rollin

2.   Use brackets to note a misspelling with the Latin word *sic* ("thus") or to correct the misspelling:

> "There were no pieces of strong [sic] around the boxes," one witness wrote.

> [or] "There were no pieces of strong [string] around the boxes," one witness wrote.

3.   Do not use brackets when inserting comments into your own writing. Use parentheses or dashes. (See 33.1–33.3.)

USING ELLIPSIS DOTS (. . .) TO MARK WORDS LEFT OUT OF A QUOTATION

1.   Use three spaced dots to signal the omission of a word or words from the middle of a quoted sentence:

> It matters not where or how far you travel . . . but how much alive you are.
>
> —Henry David Thoreau

In all cases, the material left out should be nonessential to the meaning of what is quoted. Here, for example, the words omitted are "—the farther commonly the worse—."

In typing, leave one space before the first dot, between each pair of dots, and after the last one.

2.   Use a period and three spaced dots:

a.   To show that you are omitting the end of a quoted sentence:

> Thoreau wrote: "We must learn to reawaken and keep ourselves awake, not by mechanical aids, but by an infinite expectation of the dawn. . . ."

The period follows the last quoted word without a space, and the fourth dot comes before the closing quotation mark. Normally you may cut off the end of a quoted sentence in this way only if what remains makes a complete sentence.

b.   To show that you have omitted one or more whole sentences:

> "In other words," as Percy Marks says, "the spirit of football is wrong. 'Win at any cost' is the slogan of most teams, and the methods used to win are often abominable. . . . In nearly every scrimmage the roughest kind of unsportsmanlike play is indulged in, and the broken arms and ankles are often intentional rather than accidental."

3.   Use an entire line of spaced dots to signal that a line (or more) of poetry has been omitted:

> Under the cooling shadow of a stately elm
>
> Close sat I by a goodly river's side,
>
> Where gliding streams the rocks did overwhelm;
>
> . . . .
>
> I once that loved the shady woods so well,
>
> Now thought the rivers did the trees excel.
>
> And if the sun would ever shine, there would I dwell.
>
> > —Anne Bradstreet,
> > "Contemplations," no. 21

32.7 SPECIAL USES OF QUOTATION MARKS

1.   Use quotation marks to enclose certain titles, as explained in 35.3.

2.   Use quotation marks to define words:

As a verb, *censure* generally means "find fault with" or "reprimand."

3.   Use quotation marks to set off common words and phrases that you don't take at face value:

When a man and woman decide to live together without being married, are they "living in sin"?

4.   Use quotation marks to identify a word that you are treating as a word:

In the America of the 1990s the word "liberal" became a political insult.

You may also use italics or underlining for this purpose, as explained in 35.2, item 2, and as shown in item 2, above.

32.8 MISUSING QUOTATION MARKS

1.   Do not use quotation marks in the indirect reporting of discourse:

▶ The lieutenant said that /her platoon had finished ahead of schedule./

▶ Clients are asking /when the rates will go down./

For more on the indirect reporting of discourse, see 26.2 and 26.4.

2.   Do not use quotation marks for emphasis:

*Joe's restaurant serves "fresh" seafood.

Quotation marks used in this way cast doubt on the truth of the word or words they enclose.

Punctuating with Quotation Marks   EXERCISE

Add quotation marks and any other punctuation needed in the following sentences.

EXAMPLE: "We are all strong enough," wrote La Rochefoucauld, "to

endure the misfortunes of others."

1. What writer asked, Who has deceived thee so oft as thyself

2. Did Ambrose Bierce define a bore as a person who talks when you wish him to listen.

3. Alexander Pope wrote, True wit is nature to advantage dressed, What oft was thought, but ne'er so well expressed

4. The history of the earth says Rachel Carson has been a history of interaction between living things and their surroundings.

5. *Continual* means going on with occasional slight interruptions. *Continuous* means going on with no interruption.

6. Perhaps the poet John Donne was right when he wrote: One short sleep past, we wake eternally / And Death shall be no more.

7. My roommate torments me by repeating trite sayings like better safe than sorry.

8. "This song, which was composed by Bailey in 1928 1930, reflects the influences of his five years in New Orleans."

   [The second date represents your correction of a mistake in a sentence written by someone else.]

9. "The most popular recording of the song featured Bix Dandy on the trumpit trumpet."

   [The second spelling represents your correction of a misspelling in a passage written by someone else.]

10. [The following sentence has been taken from George Orwell's "Politics and the English Language." Using ellipsis dots to mark the omission of words we have italicized, copy the sentence.]

   "Each of these passages has faults of its own, but, *quite apart from avoidable ugliness,* two qualities are common to all of them."

(Continued on p. 484.)

11. [The following sentences appear near the start of Orwell's essay. Select two successive sentences to copy, using ellipsis dots to mark the omission of words from the end of the first sentence you copy.]

   "Now, it is clear that the decline of a language must ultimately have political and economic causes; it is not due simply to the bad influence of this or that individual writer. But an effect can become a cause, reinforcing the original cause and producing the same effect in an intensified form, and so on indefinitely. A man may take to drink because he feels himself to be a failure, and then fail all the more completely because he drinks. It is rather the same thing that is happening to the English language."

The Dash, Parentheses, the Slash

33

33.1 USING THE DASH

1. Use a dash to introduce a word, phrase, or clause that summarizes or restates what comes just before:

> Terns, geese, and warblers—all migratory birds—fly hundreds of miles each year.

> But ideas—that is, opinions backed with genuine reasoning—are extremely difficult to develop.
>
> —Wayne Booth

2. Use a dash to set off an interruption that is important to the meaning of the sentence but not grammatically part of it:

> It matters not where or how far you travel—the farther commonly the worse—but how much alive you are.
>
> —Henry David Thoreau

Less important interruptions may be set off by parentheses (as explained in 33.3).

3. Use dashes to set off a series of specific items:

> The wings of the natural extant flying vertebrates—the birds and the bats—are direct modifications of the preexisting front limbs.
>
> —Michael J. Katz

4. Use a dash in dialogue to indicate an unfinished remark:

> "You wouldn't dare to—" Mabel gasped in disbelief.

"But I would," he said. "In fact, I—"

"No!" she screamed.

When the dash is used to indicate an unfinished remark, it should be followed only by quotation marks, not by a comma or period.

5.   If dashes set off a parenthetical remark that asks a question or makes an exclamation, put the question mark or the exclamation point before the second dash:

> During the American bicentennial of 1976, Canada's gift to the United States was a book of superb photographs of—what else?—scenery.
>
> —June Callwood

6.   In typing, make a dash with two hyphens (--) and leave no space on either side.

33.2   MISUSING THE DASH

The main misuse is overuse. Too many dashes can make your writing seem breathless or fragmented:

> The new baseball stadium—with its luxury boxes, shopping malls, and restaurants—went seriously over budget—straining the local economy and threatening to alienate the city's residents. The mayor—criticized in the local media—tried to convince her constituents that the stadium would stimulate the economy—bringing in tourists from a three-state region. But local citizens—disappointed in the cost overruns and the tax breaks given to the team's owners—remained skeptical about—even resentful of—the stadium, the mayor, and their hometown team.

33.3   USING PARENTHESES

1.   Use parentheses to enclose words, phrases, or complete sentences that offer a side comment or help to clarify a point:

> All this does not mean, what I should be the last man in the world to mean, that revolutionists should be ashamed of being revolutionists or (still more disgusting thought) that artists should be content with being artists.
>
> —G. K. Chesterton

> Why would parents want to go to such expense (treatment with bio-synthetic hGH costs roughly $10,000 a year), cause their children pain (the shots hurt a bit), and risk unknown long-term side effects?
> —Thomas Murray

Parentheses placed *within* a sentence do not change any other punctuation, and a parenthesized sentence within a sentence (such as *the shots hurt a bit*) does not need a capital or a period. But a freestanding parenthetical sentence needs both:

> No Allied leader would have flinched at assassinating Hitler, had that been possible. (The Allies did assassinate Heydrich.)
> —Michael Levin

2.   Use parentheses to enclose numerals or letters introducing the items of a list:

> Motherhood is in trouble, and it ought to be. A rude question is long overdue: Who needs it? The answer used to be (1) society and (2) women.
> —Betty Rollin

3.   Use parentheses to enclose numerals clarifying or confirming a spelled-out number:

> The law permits individuals to give no more than one thousand dollars ($1,000) to any one candidate in a campaign.

Like material put between dashes, a parenthetical insertion interrupts the flow of a sentence. Parentheses make the interruption less emphatic than dashes do, but since they do in fact break up the sentence, you should use them sparingly.

33.4 USING THE SLASH

1.   Use a slash, or virgule, to indicate alternative items:

> Every writer needs to know at least something about his/her audience.

Leave no space before or after a slash used in this way.

2.   Use a slash to mark off lines of poetry when you run them on as if they were prose:

Coleridge introduces the mariner in the very first stanza: "It is an ancient Mariner, / And he stoppeth one of three."

Leave one space before and after a slash used in this way.

3.   Use a slash in typing a fraction that is not on the keyboard of your typewriter or computer:

2 1/2   5 7/8   15/16

EXERCISE   **Using the Dash, Parentheses, and the Slash**

Each of the following sentences requires a dash or dashes, parentheses, or a slash. Using the comment in brackets as a guide, add the appropriate punctuation.

EXAMPLE: The asking price for the clock a whopping $500,000 has not deterred some collectors from attending the auction.
[The explanatory phrase is important to the meaning of the sentence.]

1. Somalia officially the Somali Democratic Republic is a country of over nine million 9,000,000 people located on the east coast of Africa just south of the Arabian Peninsula.
   [The numerals clarify the spelled-out numbers.]

2. The country is made up of dry but varying terrain, with coastal lowlands rising to an inland plateau that is generally about 3,000 feet 910 meters high and reaches to the highlands in the north and west.
   [Feet and meters are alternative units of measurement.]

3. Herding of animals they include camel, sheep, goats, and cattle is the chief occupation.
   [The interruption is important to the rest of the sentence.]

4. Somalia chiefly exports live animals, hides, skins, and clarified butter it is known as ghee.
   [The last words are relatively unimportant to the rest of the statement.]

5. Somali they constitute more than 80 percent of the population are Sunni Muslims, and Islam is the state religion.
   [The interruption contains important information.]

6. In the nineteenth century, the region now known as Somalia was colonized by Italy and Britain, which conquered Italian Somaliland in World War II; renamed Somalia, the former colony gained full independence in 1960 it had already gained internal autonomy in 1956.
   [The last words are relatively unimportant to the rest of the statement.]

7. In 1969, an army coup engineered by Major General Muhammad Siyad Barre led to a socialist government that was supported by the Soviet Union until 1977, when the Soviet advisors six thousand in all were expelled.
   [The interruption is important.]

8. In the late 1970s, the Somali army invaded the Ogaden region of Ethiopia it borders Somalia on the west but was driven back by Ethiopian forces.
   [The interruption offers a side comment.]

34 *Spelling, Hyphen, Apostrophe*

34.1 CHECKING YOUR SPELLING WITH A COMPUTER PROGRAM

If you're writing with a computer and have access to a spell-check program, use it. The program will check every word in your essay against the words in its own dictionary; it will list or "flag" every word of yours that its dictionary doesn't have; and in some cases, it will tell you which words in its dictionary resemble yours. If you've written *complament,* for instance, the program will furnish two correctly spelled alternatives: *compliment* and *complement.*

Spell checkers, however, will not proofread your essay or correct your misspellings for you. The programs can merely tell you which of your words does not appear in the program dictionary, and suggest one or more similar words that do. Also, spell checkers can seldom identify a word misspelled for its context. If you write a *peace of pie,* most programs will accept the phrase—simply because each of its words appears in the program dictionary. Likewise, when the program suggests *compliment* and *complement* as correctly spelled alternatives to *complament,* you must still choose between these alternatives. If you don't know what each means, you will need to consult a printed dictionary or perhaps our Glossary of Usage.

Spell checkers can save you time and help you spot misspellings that you might have overlooked. But since no such program is foolproof, you should keep a good dictionary within easy reach of the computer screen. And to improve your spelling generally, you may also want to use one or more of the pre-electronic methods explained below.

34.2 LISTING YOUR SPELLING DEMONS

Keep an analytical list of your spelling demons—words you have trouble spelling. Beside each of the words, write out the correct spelling, as shown in your dictionary. Then, beside the correct spelling of the word, write the letter or letters involved in the error. Your list will look like this:

MISSPELLED	CORRECTLY SPELLED	ERROR
alot	a lot	al / a l
goverment	government	erm / ern
defensable	defensible	able / ible
imovable	immovable	im / imm
defenite	definite	en / in

34.3 LEARNING HOW TO ADD SUFFIXES

Learn how to add suffixes—extra letters at the end of a word.

1. Change final *y* to *i* before adding a suffix:

    beauty + ful = beautiful

    bury + ed = buried

    tricky + est = trickiest

    carry + es = carries

    EXCEPTION: *If y follows a vowel or if the suffix is -ing, keep the y:*

    joy + ful = joyful

    carry + ing = carrying

    bury + ing = burying

2. Drop silent *e* before adding *-able* or *-ing:*

    love + able = lovable

care + ing = caring

restore + ing = restoring

If any other suffix is added, keep the *e:*

care + ful = careful

aware + ness = awareness

EXCEPTION: If the silent *e* follows *c* or *g,* keep the *e* before *-able:*

change + able = changeable

peace + able = peaceable

3.   If the word ends in a single consonant after a single vowel *(forget)* and the accent is on the last syllable *(for get'),* double the consonant before adding *-ing, -ed, -or,* or *-er:*

for get' + ing = forgetting

re fer' + ed = referred

bet' + or = bettor

If the accent is not on the last syllable, do not double the consonant:

ham' mer + ing = hammering

a ban' don + ed = abandoned

al' ter + ing = altering

34.4   LEARNING HOW TO ADD PREFIXES

Learn how to add prefixes—extra letters at the beginning of a word. When adding a prefix, be careful to add all of its letters, and only those:

dis + satisfaction = dissatisfaction

mis + fire = misfire

mis + spell = misspell

un + necessary = unnecessary

34.5 RECOGNIZING HOMONYMS

1. Distinguish between homonyms—words that sound alike but have different meanings and different spellings, such as these:

bare	bear	
brake	break	
capital	capitol	
cite	site	sight
peace	piece	
principal	principle	
right	write	rite
there	their	they're

If you aren't sure how to spell a homonym, see your dictionary.

2. Distinguish between partial homonyms—words with syllables that sound alike but are spelled differently, such as these:

tole*r*ate   sep*a*rate

super*sede*   ex*ceed*   con*cede*

domin*ance* (think of domin*ate*)   exist*ence* (think of existe*ntial*)

incred*ible* (think of cred*it*)   irrit*able* (think of irrit*ate*)

34.6 PLURALIZING SIMPLE NOUNS

1. Form the plural of most nouns by adding -*s:*

book, books

2. Form the plural of nouns ending in *ch, s, sh, x,* and *z* by adding -*es* (pronounced as a syllable):

church, churches   business, businesses   tax, taxes

EXCEPTIONS: crisis, crises; basis, bases; ox, oxen

3. Form the plural of nouns ending in *fe* by changing *f* to *v* before adding *-es:*

wife, wives   life, lives

4. Form the plural of nouns ending in *f* by changing the *f* to *v* and then adding *-es:*

leaf, leaves   thief, thieves

EXCEPTION: Some nouns ending in *f* need only *-s* to become plural:

chief, chiefs   belief, beliefs   proof, proofs

5. Form the plural of some nouns ending in *o* by adding *-es:*

hero, heroes

Most nouns ending in *o* need only an *-s* to become plural:

piano, pianos   solo, solos

mosquito, mosquitos (*or* mosquitoes)   banjo, banjos (*or* banjoes)

6. Form the plural of words ending in a consonant plus *y* by changing the *y* to *-ies:*

vacancy, vacancies   authority, authorities

Words ending in a vowel plus *y* need only an *-s* to become plural:

day, days   attorney, attorneys

7. Form the plural of some nouns in special ways:

datum, data   criterion, criteria   woman, women

The forms *data* and *criteria* reflect the derivation of the words from Latin and Greek respectively.

8. Form the plural of figures, numbers written as words, capitalized letters, undotted abbreviations, and isolated words by adding *-s* or an apostrophe plus *-s:*

the 1990s / the 1990's

three YMCAs / three YMCA's

twos and threes / two's and three's

four Cs / four C's

no *ifs* or *buts* / no *if's* or *but's*

9. Form the plural of lowercase letters and dotted abbreviations by adding an apostrophe and *-s:*

six *s's* and five *m's*   three M.A.'s   two c.o.d.'s

10. Some nouns are spelled the same in the plural as in the singular:

deer, deer   fish, fish   barracks, barracks

34.7 PLURALIZING COMPOUND NOUNS

Compound nouns are written as separate words *(master chef)*, as words linked by a hyphen *(self-esteem)*, or as one word *(notebook)*. Here are guidelines.

1. If the compound is written as one word, pluralize the final word:

notebook   notebooks

blueberry   blueberries

EXCEPTION: passerby, passersby

2. If the compound is hyphenated or written as separate words, pluralize the major word:

mother-in-law   mothers-in-law

editor in chief   editors in chief

A few compounds have alternative plurals: *attorney general,* for instance, may be pluralized as *attorneys general* or *attorney generals.*

3. If the compound has no noun within it, pluralize the final word:

also-ran   also-rans

4. If the compound ends in *-ful,* add *s:*

mouthful   mouthfuls

In the following passage, we have deliberately misspelled some words. Find these words and make the necessary corrections.

Mr. Bunten's farm is sucessful largely because he has kept the size within reason and because he is a skilful farmer. His heard is relatively small, consistting of only thirty-five milkers plus thirty more cows, including the heifers. When most farmers in the region expanded there oparation after World War II by building expensive   5 silos and milking systemes, Mr. Bunten kept his farm about the same size. Within a few years, many of his neighbors had gone into debt, and some had failed alltogether. It was a sad sceen for just about everybody.

We milk the cows both mourning and night. Mr. Bunten gets up   10 at 5:30, and I arive at 6 p.m. After geting down a dozen bales of hey, I dash around, feeding the cows and prepareing the milking machines. I literaly run to complete the chores in the shortest time posible. He never askes me to do them quickly; however, if I should be moveing slowly, he'll exclaim, "Geeze, boy, what took ya!" Usualy   15 he doesn't have to say anything because he's the type of person one wants to please—some one on the go all the time. For a man of sixty-four Mr. Bunten has unbeleivable endurence. Viewing his efforts as a challenge, I try to keep up and win his respect. Fortunetely, he gives me the benifit of the doubt much of the time.   20

—Andrew Evans

34.8 USING THE HYPHEN

1.   Use a hyphen to divide a long word at the end of a line:

The long black centipede walked across the sand with an enor-
mous limp.

Normally you divide a word at the end of a syllable. But do not put syllables of one or two letters on either side of a hyphen, as in *i-tem* and *end-ed*. If you aren't sure what the syllables of a word are, see your dictionary.

2. Use a hyphen to form a compound of three or more words:

> The older citizens don't want a Johnny-come-lately for mayor.

> But they don't want a stick-in-the-mud either.

3. Use a hyphen to form a compound adjective:

> Enrico Caruso was a world-famous tenor.

> I wouldn't touch cocaine with a ten-foot pole.

> Spike Lee is a well-known movie director.

> Twentieth-century writers include Faulkner and Hemingway.

4. Do not use a hyphen:

a. Between an adjective and a noun in a noun phrase:

> The twentieth century will soon come to an end.

b. In a compound predicate adjective:

> Spike Lee is *well known.*

c. In compounds made with an adverb ending in *-ly,* such as *widely held.*

FORMING COMPOUND NOUNS

Generally, use a hyphen in a compound noun when both items serve as nouns:

> city-state

> poet-critic

> teacher-scholar

Generally, use no hyphen when the first noun serves as an adjective modifying the second:

> stone wall

> city hall

> master chef

> police officer

EXCEPTIONS: Some compound nouns are made with neither a hyphen nor a space *(paintbrush, notebook),* and some make it hard to tell whether the first item is serving as an adjective or not *(beer drinker, cattle prod).* If in doubt about hyphenating a particular noun compound, see your dictionary.

ATTACHING PREFIXES

Use a hyphen to join a prefix to a *capitalized* word:

> un-American
>
> post-Renaissance
>
> pre-Reformation

Generally, use no hyphen to join a prefix to an *uncapitalized* word:

> deemphasize
>
> nonprofit
>
> antibodies

EXCEPTIONS: Some words made with prefixes may be written with or without hyphens, but the choice of one or the other affects the meaning of the word; *re-cover,* for instance, does not mean the same as *recover.* For words such as this, see your dictionary.

WRITING OUT NUMBERS

Use a hyphen in a number written as two words, provided it is below one hundred:

> Twenty-five applicants have requested interviews.
>
> Two-thirds of the trees had been cut.
>
> One-half of the design is complete.

Do not attach a hyphen to the word for any number over ninety-nine:

> Some cars can run over three hundred miles on a tank of gas.
>
> One speaker earned eight thousand dollars for a single lecture.
>
> Thirty-five thousand spectators watched the game.

Thirty-five, which is below one hundred, is hyphenated, but no hyphen is attached to *thousand.*

Using the Hyphen

Each of the following sentences may require the addition of one or more hyphens. Add one as needed. If an entry is correct as it stands, write *Correct.*

EXAMPLE: Running high speed trains between major cities would

definitely reduce traffic on major highways.

1. The long distance runners looked buoyant as they passed the fifteen mile mark.

2. Organized by a well known sponsor, the race had attracted a number of world renowned athletes to compete before an all European audience.

3. Over three-quarters of the contestants were from Germany and Russia.

4. Many had come from medium sized towns with populations ranging from twenty one thousand to over fifty five thousand.

5. The front runners moved so fast that even spectators on ten speed bicycles had trouble keeping up with them.

6. After the race the winner told reporters of his long term plans for acquiring more trophies.

34.9 USING THE APOSTROPHE

1. To form the possessive of nouns and abbreviations that do not end in *s,* use an apostrophe plus *-s:*

a girl's hat	Bill's car	a team's mascot
NATO's future	the C.O.'s orders	Dr. T.'s patients
men's activities	children's toys	someone's coat

If a singular noun ends in *s* (as in *James*) you may form the possessive by adding an apostrophe plus *-s* (James's apartment) or by adding just the apostrophe (James' apartment). Custom calls for the latter form with Zeus, Moses, Jesus, and ancient Greek names ending in *es:* Zeus' thunderbolts, Moses' staff, Jesus' teachings, Sophocles' plays.

2. To form the possessive of plural nouns ending in *s,* add just an apostrophe:

players	players' uniforms
animals	animals' eating habits
the Joneses	the Joneses' car

3. To indicate that two people possess something jointly, add an apostrophe, and -*s* if necessary, to the second of the two nouns:

Ann and James' apartment

Tim and Susan's wedding album

To indicate that two people possess two or more things separately, use the apostrophe, and -*s* if necessary, with both of the nouns:

Paul's and Marysa's cars

Kitty's and James' tests

4. To form the possessive with singular compound nouns, add an apostrophe plus -*s* to the last word:

my sister-in-law's career   the editor in chief's policy

5. To form the possessive of certain indefinite pronouns, add an apostrophe plus -*s:*

someone's coat   no one's fault   everybody else's jokes

With indefinite pronouns that do not take the apostrophe, form the possessive with *of: the plans of most, the hopes of many, the triumphs of few.*

6. Use the possessive case with nouns or pronouns followed by gerunds:

The *crowd's cheering* could be heard a mile away.

Everyone who hears the young violinist admires *her playing.*

For more on this point, see 13.11.

7. Use an apostrophe, and -*s* when necessary, in common phrases of time and measurement:

four o'clock	five dollars' worth

two weeks' notice   a day's work

our money's worth   a stone's throw

8. Use an apostrophe plus -*s* to form the plurals shown above in 34.6, items 8 and 9.

9. Use an apostrophe to mark the omission of a letter or letters in a contraction:

I have finished.   I've finished.

He is not here.   He's not here.

This does not work.   This doesn't work.

They will not stop.   They won't stop.

You should have written.   You should've written.

10. Use an apostrophe to mark the omission of numbers in dates:

the election of '92   the Great Crash of '29

34.10   MISUSING THE APOSTROPHE

1. Do not use an apostrophe to form the plural of nouns:

▶ Five girl's went swimming.

▶ Two houses' need paint.

2. Do not use an apostrophe with the possessive forms of the personal pronouns:

▶ This is our thermos; that one is their's.

▶ Ben's notes are incomplete; your's are thorough.

3. Do not confuse the possessive pronoun *its* with the contraction *it's* (for *it is*). Use *its* as you use *his;* use *it's* as you use *he's:*

his success   he's successful

its success   it's successful

4.   Do not confuse the possessive *whose* with the contraction *who's* (for *who is*):

Whose notebook is this?   *This is his notebook.*

No one knows whose painting this is.

Who's going to the concert?

No one has heard of the pianist who's scheduled to play.

5.   Do not use the apostrophe and *-s* to form a possessive when the construction would be cumbersome:

WEAK: Questions about the candidate's husband's financial dealings hurt her campaign.

EDITED: Questions about the financial dealings of the candidate's husband hurt her campaign.

EXERCISE 3   **Using the Apostrophe**

Improve the punctuation in the following passage by adding or removing apostrophes wherever necessary. As you make these corrections, write out the entire passage.

Everyones talking about Frank Smiths novel. Its plot seems to be based on something that happened to him during his freshman year. Its weird to read about characters youve seen in class or in the students lounge. I dont think there are many of his classmate's who wont be annoyed when they discover theyve been depicted as thugs'   5 and moron's. Its as if Frank thought that his experiences were the same as everyones—Juanitas, Murrays, and Mikes. That kind of thinking can be overlooked in someone whos in his early teen's, but it isnt all right for someone in his twenties'.

Mechanics

Mechanics are conventional rules such as the one requiring capitalization for the first word of a sentence. You need to follow the conventions so that your writing will look the way formal writing is expected to look.

35.1 USING CAPITAL LETTERS

1. Capitalize the first word of a sentence:

    The quick brown fox jumped over the lazy dog.

    Where do bears hibernate in the winter?

Here and elsewhere in the chapter, to *capitalize* a word means to capitalize its first letter.

2. Capitalize proper nouns and proper adjectives. Unlike a common noun, which names one or more in a class or group, a proper noun names a *particular* person, place, thing, or event. Proper adjectives are based on common nouns. Here are examples:

COMMON NOUNS	PROPER NOUNS	PROPER ADJECTIVES (also serve as proper nouns)
country	Canada	Canadian
person	Jefferson	Jeffersonian
state	Texas	Texan
river	Mississippi River	
revolution	the French Revolution	
party	the Republican Party	

Mechanics

east (direction)	the East (particular region)
corporation	the Rand Corporation
economics	Economics 101
day	Wednesday

Do not capitalize words such as *a* and *the* when used with proper nouns, and do not capitalize the names of the seasons *(fall, winter, spring, summer)*.

3. Capitalize a personal title when it is used before a name or when it denotes a particular position of high rank:

the president	President Clinton
	the President of the United States
	the Pope
the senator	Senator Mosely-Braun
the mayor	Mayor Bradley
the colonel	Colonel Templeton

4. Capitalize a term denoting kinship when it is used before a name:

my uncle   Uncle Bob

5. Capitalize titles as explained in 35.3.

6. Always capitalize the pronoun *I:*

When I heard the news, I laughed.

EXERCISE 1   **Using Capitals**

Improve each of the following sentences by capitalizing where necessary:

1. the grand canyon extends over 270 miles from east to west, measures 18 miles from rim to rim at its widest point, and reaches a depth of approximately 1 mile.

2. the canyon has been formed over billions of years by a combination of forces, including wind, erosion, and, in particular, the action of the mighty colorado river.

3. some of the canyon's most spectacular sights are to be found within grand canyon national park, which lies in northwestern arizona.

4. to protect the canyon from commercial development, president theodore roosevelt declared it a national monument in 1908; then, in 1919 the congress of the united states proclaimed it a national park.

5. today the park attracts visitors from all of the fifty states as well as from countries far and near, including japan, south korea, france, and canada; the tourists prefer to arrive in july and august.

6. all who view the canyon marvel at the extraordinary rock formations, many of which have impressive names like thor temple, dragon head, and cheops pyramid.

7. according to one report, the canyon received its present name from major john wesley powell, who in 1869 was the first to travel through the canyon by boat. a brave man, he had lost part of an arm in the civil war.

8. he began the journey in wyoming with nine companions and four boats; he ended the journey three months later at the virgin river near lake mead with only three boats and six men.

9. modern tourists have an easier time, hiking along well-marked trails or riding in automobiles to scenic spots like powell memorial and hopi point.

10. like the other national parks in the united states, grand canyon national park is maintained by the national park service of the u.s. department of the interior.

35.2 USING ITALICS OR UNDERLINING

Use italics or underlining as explained below. (If you're writing with a typewriter or word processor that can print *italic type like this,* use italics. Otherwise use underlining.)

1.   Use italics or underlining to emphasize a word or phrase in a statement:

```
If an inspired guess turns out to be correct, it is not

reported as an inspired guess.

                                        --Isaac Asimov
```

Use this kind of emphasis sparingly. When overused, it loses its punch. (If you add your own emphasis to any word in a passage you are quoting, you must say so.)

2. Use italics or underlining to identify a letter or a word treated as a word:

> Neither the term <u>sexism</u> nor the term <u>racism</u> existed fifty
>
> years ago.   --Casey Miller and Kate Swift

You may also use quotation marks to identify a word as such; see 32.7, no. 4.

3. Use italics or underlining to identify a foreign word or phrase not absorbed into English:

> <u>omerta</u>   <u>jouissance</u>   <u>dumkopf</u>   <u>a la page</u>

4. Use italics or underlining to identify the name of a ship, an airplane, or the like:

> <u>Queen Elizabeth II</u> [ship]
>
> <u>Spirit of St. Louis</u> [airplane]
>
> <u>Apollo 2</u> [spaceship]

5. Use italics or underlining for titles as explained in 35.3.

EXERCISE 2   **Using Underlining**

Each of the following sentences may require the addition or removal of underlining. Make any necessary changes. If an entry is correct as it stands, write *Correct.*

1. Carol and Alex have named their <u>motorboat</u> The Calex.

2. They wanted to call it Paradise, but couldn't agree whether the last consonant should be an s or a c.

3. They also argue about whether the <u>drink</u> known as a frappé is the same as the one called a frost.

4. But they do see eye to eye on some things, like <u>yoga</u> and <u>karate</u> classes, pasta and <u>pizza</u>, and the way to spell harassment.

5. When their first child was born, Alex gave Carol a dozen roses with a card explaining that the English word mother derives from the Middle English word moder and is akin to the Latin word mater.

6. Carol gave Alex a copy of the <u>first edition</u> of All Quiet on the Western Front.

35.3 USING TITLES

1. Capitalize the first and last word of a title, whatever they are. Also capitalize all the words in between except articles (such as *a* and *the*), prepositions (such as *for, among, between,* and *to*), and coordinating conjunctions (such as *and, but,* and *or*):

    Zen and the Art of Motorcycle Maintenance [book]

    "Ode on a Grecian Urn" [poem]

2. Use italics or underlining for the titles of books, scholarly journals, magazines, newspapers, government reports, plays, musicals, operas or other long musical compositions, films, television shows, radio programs, or long poems:

    The Grapes of Wrath [book]

    The American Scholar [journal]

    Newsweek [magazine]

    New York Times [newspaper]

    Uniform Crime Reports for the United States
       [government publication]

    Hamlet [play]

    Oklahoma [musical]

    The Barber of Seville [opera]

    Star Wars [film]

    Friends [television show]

    Morning Pro Musica [radio program]

    Song of Myself [long poem]

3. Use double quotation marks for titles of works like these:

    "Seal Hunting in Alaska" [magazine article]

    "Bullfighting in Hemingway's Fiction" [essay]

"The Tell-Tale Heart" [short story]

"Mending Wall" [short poem]

"Burn, Don't Freeze" [song]

"The American Scholar" [speech]

"Winning the West" [chapter in a book]

4. Change double to single quotation marks when the title appears within another title that needs quotation marks, or is mentioned within a quotation:

"Fences and Neighbors in Frost's 'Mending Wall' " [title of an essay on the poem]

"Frost's 'Mending Wall,' " said Professor Ainsley, "is a gently disarming poem."

5. Do not use both underlining and quotation marks unless the title *includes* an underlined title:

"Experience" [essay]

<u>Gone with the Wind</u> [novel]

"On Sitting Down to Read <u>King Lear</u> Again" [poem]

6. Do not use italics or quotation marks in a title of your own unless it includes a reference to another title:

What to Do with Nuclear Waste

Bullfighting in Hemingway's *The Sun Also Rises*

Art and Sex in Pope's "Rape of the Lock"

EXERCISE 3   **Writing Titles**

Each of the following titles requires capitalization and may also require underlining or quotation marks. Make the necessary changes.

1. carmen [opera]
2. politics and leadership [speech]
3. my old kentucky home [song]

4. washington post [newspaper]

5. what freud forgot [essay]

6. 60 minutes [television show]

7. the will of zeus [history book]

8. john brown's body [long poem]

9. the mismatch between school and children [editorial]

10. natural history [magazine]

11. solutions to the energy problem [your report]

12. the role of fate in shakespeare's romeo and juliet [your essay]

13. imagery in the battle hymn of the republic [your essay]

14. barefoot in the park [play]

15. the age of innocence [novel]

35.4 USING ABBREVIATIONS

Writers differ about how they use abbreviations, but we recommend the following procedures:

1. Abbreviate most titles accompanying a name:

    Dr. Martha Peters

    Martha Peters, Ph.D.

    Robert Greene Jr.

    Ms. Elizabeth Fish

    Joseph Stevens, M.D.

But do not abbreviate when referring to people with religious, governmental, academic, and military titles:

> the Reverend Leonard Flischer
>
> Senator Nancy Kassebaum
>
> the Honorable George Pataki, governor of New York
>
> Professor Pamela Pinckney
>
> General H. Norman Schwarzkopf

2. Abbreviate terms that help to specify a date or a time of day:

350 B.C.   12 B.C.E.   8:30 A.M.

A.D. 1776   186 C.E.   2:15 P.M.

Note that A.D. precedes the date. (Also note that MLA recommends not using periods in abbreviations that include capital letters.)

3. Abbreviate the *United States of America* as "U.S.A."

a. When abbreviating *United States* as an adjective, write "U.S." alone:

the U.S. Supreme Court

U.S. elections

b. In writing to a U.S. address from outside the country, or in writing your own return address on a letter going to another country, write "USA" (undotted) on a separate line:

28 Foster Street

Cambridge MA 02138

USA

4. Abbreviate the name of a state, province, or district when it forms part of an address:

Austin TX

Long Beach CA

Washington DC

Sherbrooke Que.

Abbreviate names of U.S. states, the District of Columbia, and Puerto Rico with just two capital letters and no periods. Here are standard abbreviations:

Alabama	AL	Kentucky	KY	North Dakota	ND
Alaska	AK	Louisiana	LA	Ohio	OH
Arizona	AZ	Maine	ME	Oklahoma	OK
Arkansas	AR	Maryland	MD	Oregon	OR

California	CA	Massachusetts	MA	Pennsylvania	PA
Colorado	CO	Michigan	MI	Puerto Rico	PR
Connecticut	CT	Minnesota	MN	Rhode Island	RI
Delaware	DE	Mississippi	MS	South Carolina	SC
District of Columbia	DC	Missouri	MO	South Dakota	SD
Florida	FL	Montana	MT	Tennessee	TN
Georgia	GA	Nebraska	NE	Texas	TX
Hawaii	HI	Nevada	NV	Utah	UT
Idaho	ID	New Hampshire	NH	Vermont	VT
Illinois	IL	New Jersey	NJ	Virginia	VA
Indiana	IN	New Mexico	NM	Washington	WA
Iowa	IA	New York	NY	West Virginia	WV
Kansas	KS	North Carolina	NC	Wisconsin	WI
				Wyoming	WY

5. You may use undotted abbreviations in referring to well-known firms and other organizations:

> NBC   YMCA
>
> IBM   NAACP

6. If an abbreviation comes at the end of a declarative sentence, use the period marking the abbreviation as the period for the sentence:

> The rocket was launched at 11:30 P.M.

If an abbreviation ends a question, add a question mark:

> Was the rocket launched at 11:30 P.M.?

7. Most abbreviations must be marked by periods, but you need no periods to abbreviate the names of U.S. states and of well-known organizations, as shown above, or to abbreviate well-known phrases:

> mph
> mpg

35.5 MISUSING ABBREVIATIONS

1.   In formal writing, avoid using abbreviations for the days of the week and the months of the year:

Sunday   August

2.   Avoid using abbreviations for the names of most geographical entities when they are not part of an address:

New England   the Snake River   Lake Avenue   Canada

You may, however, use *Mt.* before the name of a mountain, as in *Mt. McKinley,* and *St.* in the name of a place, as in *St. Louis.*

3.   Avoid using abbreviations for the names of academic subjects and the subdivision of books:

French 205   biology   chapter 10   page 45

EXCEPTION: In parenthetical citations of books and articles, "page" is commonly abbreviated as "p." and "pages" as "pp."

4.   Avoid using abbreviations for units of measurement (such as size and weight) unless the accompanying amounts are given in figures:

The new guard is six feet seven inches tall.

This box must weigh over fifty pounds.

A 50 lb. bag of fertilizer costs $24.50.

5.   Avoid using any abbreviation that is not widely known without first explaining its meaning:

* The MISAA was passed in 1978.

EDITED: The Middle Income Student Assistance Act (MISAA) was passed in 1978.

After you have explained its meaning, you may use the abbreviation on its own. But beware of crowding too many abbreviations into a sentence or passage. If you don't keep them under control, your reader may end up drowning in alphabet soup:

* In 1971 Congress established the BEOG program, and the EOGs were renamed SEOGs.

EDITED: In 1971 Congress established the Basic Educational Opportunity Grant (BEOG) program, and the Educational Opportunity Grants (EOG) were renamed Supplemental Educational Opportunity Grants (SEOG).

If you aren't sure how to abbreviate a particular term, see your dictionary. If you don't know whether you should abbreviate a term at all, don't. In formal writing, most terms should be spelled out in full.

35.6 USING NUMBERS

When you refer to a number in your writing, you have to decide whether to use a figure or to spell it out as a word. In much scientific and technical writing, figures predominate; in magazines and books of general interest, words are common, though figures are also used. In this section, we offer some guidelines for nontechnical writing.

1. Spell out a number when it begins a sentence:

    Eighty-five dignitaries attended the opening ceremony.

    Two hundred dignitaries had been invited.

Rearrange the sentence if spelling out the number would require more than two words:

    The opening ceremony was attended by 157 dignitaries.

    Invitations were sent to 218 dignitaries.

2. Spell out a number that can be written in one or two words, except as noted in item 4, below:

    A batter is out after three strikes.

    The firefighters worked without relief for twenty-two hours.

    She owns seven hundred rare books.

    Twenty-five thousand people were evacuated.

A hyphenated number may be counted as one word.

3.   Use numerals if spelling out a number would require more than two words:

The stadium can hold 85,600 spectators.

Attendance at last Saturday's game was 79,500.

4.   Use numerals for addresses, dates, exact times of day, exact sums of money, and exact measurements such as miles per hour, scores of games, mathematical ratios, fractions, and page numbers:

22 East Main Street

October 7, 2001

44 B.C.

11:15 A.M.

$4.36

65 mph

a ratio of 2 to 1

$5\frac{7}{8}$

page 102

However, when a time of day or a sum of money is given as a round figure, spell it out:

Uncle Ben always gets up at six.

I reached the border at around eight o'clock.

He used to earn two dollars for ten hours of work.

It's hard to believe that fifty cents can no longer buy a cup of coffee.

Using Abbreviations and Numbers

Each of the following sentences may include incorrectly written abbreviations and numbers. Make any necessary changes. If an entry is correct as it stands, write *Correct*.

> EXAMPLE: "Why," said the White Queen to Alice, "sometimes I've
> believed as many as 6̲ impossible things before breakfast."
>   six
>   —Adapted from Lewis Carroll

1. We plan to spend part of our vacation on a Miss. Riv. steamboat and the rest in the Cascade Mts.

2. 1st, however, we must attend a meeting of the Young Women's Christian Association that is expected to attract an audience of 25 hundred members in Alexandria, Virginia.

3. The Rev. Ann Proctor, Doctor of Divinity, will be one of the speakers; her talk is scheduled to begin at seven-fifteen P.M.

4. All of the speakers have said they will contribute 3/4 of their honorarium to the Assoc.

5. The combined amounts should come to exactly seven hundred dollars and seventy-two cents.

6. Following the meeting, we will head west, doing our best to make time with a speed limit of sixty-five miles per hour.

7. If all goes well, we should arrive in St. Lou. on Fri., Aug. nine.

Research and Writing

4

The Research Process 36

36.1 WHY DO RESEARCH?

You already do research for many reasons. Well before high school graduation, you probably tried to learn all you could about the colleges you might attend. Before you vote in an election, you may read about candidates and issues to help you make informed choices. When you buy something expensive, such as a computer or a car, you try to learn which models and brands are the most dependable and affordable.

In one sense, research is simply a process of finding the information to make life better for you and others. But doing effective research means doing more than just locating information. It also means critically evaluating information—making judgments about accuracy, validity, and objectivity.

All kinds of information—not just what is found on the Internet—must be evaluated. The *National Geographic* wall map of the world that your family bought in 1988, for example, is an inadequate source of information today about Russia because that country's political boundaries have changed.

36.2 UNDERSTANDING A RESEARCH ASSIGNMENT, DEFINING A TOPIC, AND POSING A RESEARCH QUESTION

Research assignments in college usually have at least two purposes: to help you learn something new about a specific subject and to help you learn the methods used in an area of study to discover and present new knowledge. When you are assigned a research project in college, you must take care to *understand what your instructor expects.* Your next steps are usually to *define your topic* and then *pose a question* that will guide your research.

UNDERSTANDING A RESEARCH ASSIGNMENT

A research assignment for a college course usually calls for you to consider these four questions:

1. **WHAT IS THE PURPOSE OF THE PAPER?** Does your instructor expect you to use research to discuss a topic or to support a persuasive thesis?

2. **WHAT KINDS OF RESEARCH SOURCES DOES YOUR INSTRUCTOR EXPECT YOU TO USE?** The kinds of sources you use will depend on your subject. For example, if you are writing a paper on a Shakespeare play, your instructor probably will not expect you to study current newspapers and magazines. Instead, you will be expected to locate books and scholarly journals in your college library. If you are writing a paper on the funding of education in your state, you will have to examine current newspapers and magazines.

3. **WHAT ROLE DOES YOUR INSTRUCTOR EXPECT INTERNET SOURCES TO PLAY IN YOUR PAPER?** Any good researcher incorporates a variety of sources. Although the Internet is a good resource for information on current issues, don't assume that you can do all your research on the Web.

4. **WHAT IS THE EXPECTED LENGTH OF THE PAPER?** Knowing the expected length will help you judge the amount of research you must do. For example, a twenty-page paper will probably require more sources than a ten-page paper.

Check with your instructor if you are unable to answer any of these questions.

DEFINING A TOPIC

Even if your instructor assigns a topic, you may still need to make it more specific. The two sets of questions below can help you do that by helping you both build on what you already know and understand your topic in context.

1. **BUILD ON WHAT YOU ALREADY KNOW.**

   ▶ Why do you care about the topic? Does it affect you personally? Does it raise questions you want to answer or problems you want to explore?

The more you know about why the topic interests you, the more interesting your research will be.

▶ What do you already know about the topic? What you already know is the starting point for what you will learn.

▶ What are the sources of your present knowledge? As soon as you ask yourself this question, you begin to think like a researcher. Suppose you "know," for instance, that AIDS can be transmitted by physical contact. But so far as you can recall, your source for this bit of information—actually misinformation (since it is HIV, the virus believed to cause AIDS, that can be transmitted)—was a stranger you met at a party; and you have no idea what credentials she possessed or what basis she had for making that judgment.

2. **UNDERSTAND YOUR TOPIC IN ITS VARIOUS CONTEXTS.** Research topics don't exist in a vacuum. They have histories and usually social, political, or economic implications. They are also discussed, argued about, and explored in one or more contexts. For example, both psychologists and educators discuss Howard Gardner's theory of multiple intelligences. Psychologists discuss the theory to judge how well it explains human abilities, while educators discuss it to see how it might help them develop better teaching methods.

Different groups can also view a topic in very different ways. For example, Scott decided to research the Native American Graves Protection and Repatriation Act, a law passed in 1990, which was still debated in Congress in 1998 (see 40.2). The law places restrictions on anthropologists and archaeologists who, for research purposes, dig up Native American burial sites. The law also requires museums and universities to return human remains and burial artifacts to Native American peoples. Clearly, different groups have very different views on this issue. Some Native Americans see excavation of their burial sites as a violation of their culture and religion. Archaeologists and anthropologists view the law as an impediment to scientific inquiry. Museum curators view the law as the imposition of work at a time when their resources are scarce.

The media in which a topic is discussed are also an important part of its context. For example, Juan wanted to research a topic that had been the subject of controversy in his state: financing public schools with state lotteries. He was particularly interested in exploring the question of whether or not state lotteries encouraged gambling—something that foes of lotteries had argued. He soon learned that very little serious research had been done on the question he originally wanted to explore. Most of the sources he located on state lotteries came from either newspaper articles or Web sites that were sponsored by companies that states hired to administer their lotteries. The kind of media in which he found information affected his approach to the topic. He decided to explore a new question: How do lottery companies influence a state's debate on instituting a lottery?

Use the following questions to help you explore your topic's contexts:

▶ How would you classify your topic? Is it a subject of personal interest, public controversy, or professional and academic research?

▶ Is your topic a local issue with global connections? Suppose a jeans manufacturer closes its factory in your hometown. You might investigate this local incident for its global context. Did that manufacturer move the factory to another country? What were the company's reasons? How different is that company's operation in another country?

▶ Is your topic a global issue with local connections? You have probably heard people discuss "globalization" and international trade agreements (like NAFTA), but you may have little idea of what these mean. You could study business and manufacturing in your community and state to see if meaningful changes had been made since NAFTA went into effect, on January 1, 1994.

▶ Who is talking, writing, or arguing about your topic? When you write a research paper, you are taking a first step toward entering a conversation about a particular topic. In order to enter a conversation, you need to know something about other participants in the conversation.

▶ In what different media is the topic being discussed? Some topics may be discussed primarily in popular media or newspapers, and knowing that will make a difference in how you conduct your research.

POSING A RESEARCH QUESTION

The best research projects seek answers to questions you find important. When a question guides your research, it not only pushes you to make new discoveries but also limits your subject, making it more manageable. If you have been answering the questions above, you have laid the groundwork for posing a question. Your question may change as you learn more about your topic, but beginning with a question will help guide your research.

Use the following guidelines as you craft your research question:

1. A GOOD RESEARCH QUESTION IS OPEN-ENDED.   It cannot be answered with a yes or a no.

2. A GOOD RESEARCH QUESTION IS ONE THAT YOU AS A STUDENT CAN REALISTICALLY ADDRESS.   Research projects help you on the road to becoming an expert in an area. For example, Ellen, an astronomy major, wants to

do a research project on "superclusters," the apparent "clumping together" of galaxies. As a new science student, she can hardly formulate her own theory of order among galaxies—or even make a case for or against an astronomer's theory. However, Ellen still can ask questions that she can answer for other nonexperts—such as "What does the theory of superclusters suggest about the development of galaxies?"

Choosing Topics and Posing Questions

EXERCISE 1

The following exercise has two steps:

1. Write a potential research topic for each of the following categories:
   ▶ a hobby
   ▶ a public debate
   ▶ an issue or subject of study in your major

2. Write a research question for each of the topics you listed.

36.3 DEVELOPING A RESEARCH STRATEGY

Starting off on a research project without a strategy would be like setting out on an ocean voyage without a map or navigation instruments. A research strategy can serve as your map and compass; it is more than a schedule or list of things to do. Developing a research strategy means understanding what kind of information you are looking for and deciding where to look for it.

KNOW WHAT KINDS OF SOURCES ARE AVAILABLE

Research sources can be divided into four types:

1. Firsthand Research

This means collecting information yourself. It includes:

   ▶ Field research (also called ethnographic research)

   ▶ Interviews

   ▶ Surveys

For information on each of these activities, see 3.5.

2. Reference Sources

    ▶ General dictionaries, encyclopedias, and almanacs

    ▶ Specialized dictionaries, encyclopedias, and almanacs

3. Print Sources

    ▶ Books

    ▶ Periodicals

        ▶ Popular magazines

        ▶ Scholarly journals

        ▶ Newspapers

    ▶ Government documents

Print sources are generally found on your library shelves and in its periodical and government-document rooms.

4. Online Sources

    ▶ Documents (World Wide Web and File Transfer Protocol)

        ▶ Personal home pages

        ▶ Professional, commercial, and business sites

            ▶ Online versions of print sources

                ▶ Books

                ▶ Periodicals

                ▶ Government documents

    ▶ Electronic communication

        ▶ Asynchronous communication

            ▶ Email

            ▶ Listservs

            ▶ Usenet

        ▶ Synchronous communication

            ▶ MUDs, MOOs

            ▶ Chat forums

The Internet provides a whole new realm of research resources. By using FTP, telnet, gopher, or the Web (see 36.6), you can access online versions of many traditional print sources, as well as current information and reports from groups involved in your topic. You may even be able to communicate via email with experts and others who are studying your topic.

DETERMINE WHICH SOURCES YOU NEED FIRST

Understand where you're starting, so you know where to go next.

If you are new to a subject	→	consider beginning with a general reference work.
If you have basic knowledge	→	consider reading a specialized reference work or skimming an introductory book.
If you have a solid background	→	look for articles, online resources, and books that deal with your topic.

36.4 STARTING WITH GENERAL AND SPECIALIZED REFERENCE WORKS

DICTIONARIES AND ENCYCLOPEDIAS

General reference dictionaries and encyclopedias provide easy-to-locate background information. Specialized dictionaries and encyclopedias, such as the *Oxford Classical Dictionary,* provide more detailed information for readers familiar with a general subject. To find the specialized encyclopedia (sometimes spelled *encyclopaedia*) for your subject, ask the reference librarian or see the *Guide to Reference Books* (1986), edited by Eugene P. Sheehy, which lists specialized guides to research in all fields; the *Supplement to the Tenth Edition* (1992), edited by Robert Balay, covers material from 1985 to 1990. You might also consult the following general and specialized encyclopedias:

GENERAL ENCYCLOPEDIAS

▶ *The Canadian Encyclopedia*

▶ *Compton's Encyclopedia Online* <www.comptons.com> A subscription service that offers a free trial.

▶ *Concise Columbia Encyclopedia*

525

▶ *Encarta* <www.encarta.msn.com> A concise edition; the full edition is available by subscription.

▶ *Encyclopedia Americana*

▶ *Encyclopaedia Britannica* Available both in print and online: <www.britannica.com.>

▶ *Research-It!* <www.itools.com/research-it/> Includes search functions for language (dictionary, thesaurus, translation), library (people, quotations), geography (maps, telephone numbers), finance (currency, stock markets), shipping and mailing, and the Internet.

SPECIALIZED ENCYCLOPEDIAS
Business

▶ *Encyclopedia of Banking and Finance*

▶ *McGraw-Hill Dictionary of Modern Economics*

History

▶ *American Voices: Significant Speeches from American History*

▶ *Cambridge Ancient History*

▶ *Cambridge History of Africa*

▶ *Cambridge Medieval History*

▶ *Dictionary of Asian American History*

▶ *Encyclopedia of African-American Culture and History*

▶ *Encyclopedia of American Social History*

▶ *Encyclopedia of Asian History*

▶ *Encyclopedia of the Renaissance*

Humanities

▶ *American Writers*

▶ *Asian and American Studies*

▶ *Contemporary Literary Criticism*

▶ *Dictionary of the History of Ideas*

▶ *Dictionary of Literary Biography*

▶ *Encyclopedia of Architecture*

▶ *Encyclopedia of Philosophy*

▶ *Encyclopedia of Religion*

▶ *Encyclopedia of World Art*

▶ *Handbook of Hispanic Culture*

▶ *Handbook of North American Indians*

▶ *Multicultural Encyclopedia*

▶ *New Grove Dictionary of Music and Musicians*

▶ *New Oxford History of Music*

▶ *Notable American Women*

▶ *Oxford Companion to the Theater*

▶ *Women's Studies Encyclopedia*

Sciences

▶ *CRC Handbook of Chemistry and Physics*

▶ *Encyclopedia of Astronomy and Astrophysics*

▶ *Encyclopedia of Bioethics*

▶ *Encyclopedia of Computer Science*

▶ *Encyclopedia of Computer Science and Technology*

▶ *Encyclopedia of Physical Science and Technology*

▶ *Encyclopedia of Physics*

▶ *McGraw-Hill Encyclopedia of Engineering*

▶ *McGraw-Hill Encyclopedia of Environmental Science*

▶ *McGraw-Hill Encyclopedia of Science and Technology*

Social Sciences and Education

▶ *Annual Review of Anthropology*

▶ *Atlas of World Cultures*

▶ *Encyclopedia of Anthropology*

▶ *Encyclopedia of Cultural Anthropology*

▶ *Encyclopedia of Education*

▶ *Encyclopedia of Psychology*

▶ *Encyclopedia of Sociology*

The Research Process

- *Encyclopedia of World Cultures*

- *International Encyclopedia of Communications*

- *International Encyclopedia of the Social Sciences*

COMPILATIONS OF FACTS AND STATISTICS

Compilations of facts and statistics include almanacs, yearbooks, and other sources that document current events. These include such works as:

- *Britannica Book of the Year*

- *Facts on File*

- *Fedstats* <www.fedstats.gov> Statistics from government agencies.

- *Information Please Almanac*   Available both in print and online: <www.infoplease.com>.

- *Statistical Abstract of the United States*

- *World Almanac and Book of Facts*

ATLASES

Current atlases provide geographic and demographic information. Bear in mind that geographical boundaries change with political and historical events. Consult historical atlases when you want to research political and geographical boundaries that no longer exist, such as the Roman Empire or the Soviet Union. Otherwise, be sure the atlas you consult is current.

- *Historical Atlas*

- *National Geographic Atlas of the World*

- *The New International World Atlas*

- *The New York Times Atlas of the World*

- *Rand McNally Cosmopolitan World Atlas*

BIOGRAPHICAL GUIDES

Biographical guides offer background information on individuals both living and deceased. They are particularly useful when you find names you do not recognize in your research sources.

- *African American Biographies*

- *Biography Index*

- *Biography.com* <www.biography.com>

▶ *Chambers's Biographical Dictionary*

▶ *Contemporary Authors*

▶ *Current Biography*

▶ *Dictionary of American Biography* (covers deceased Americans)

▶ *Dictionary of Canadian Biography* (covers deceased Canadians)

▶ *Dictionary of National Biography* (Britain)

▶ *International Who's Who*

▶ *Notable American Women*

▶ *Who's Who in America*

▶ *Who's Who in Canada*

Using Print Reference Sources

Read an article in a standard encyclopedia about a research topic you used for exercise 1 and jot down any questions this article raises for you. Then find a specialized encyclopedia that contains an article on your topic. Explain how the second article differs from the first and whether or not the second answers all the questions raised by the first.

36.5 LOCATING BOOKS AND PERIODICALS

SUBJECT HEADINGS AND KEYWORDS

Your library is filled with sources you need for your research. The Internet has useful sources as well. But what connects you to the books, articles, and online sources you need? You are connected to these research resources through:

▶ card catalogs

▶ indexes and bibliographies

▶ Internet search engines

In order to use these resources, you must know how your topic is classified (*subject headings*) and what specific terms (*keywords*) are used for your topic. In other words, your first link to sources is *subject headings and keywords*.

One of the most important steps in developing a research strategy is learning how to make the connection between your language for your topic and the language of the research sources you need. That connection is made in two ways:

subject headings: classifications or categories for your topic

keywords: synonyms for your topic

When you look up something in the yellow pages of your telephone book, you use subject classifications and keywords to find what you want. Suppose you want to call movie theaters to find out what's playing. If you look up "movie" in many yellow pages, you won't find anything between "movers" and "moving companies." "Movies" simply isn't the subject heading used in most yellow pages. If you have user-friendly yellow pages, you might find between "movers" and "moving companies" a small note that says "Movies—see Theaters—Movie." This note gives you the synonym for "movies" used by your yellow pages ("theaters"); it thus directs you to another subject classification, "Theaters," under which you'll find the subclassification "Theaters-Movie."

This process isn't all that different from the one you follow when you do research. Card catalogs, periodical indexes, and Internet search engines all require you to translate your name for your topic into the language used to connect you to research sources.

LIBRARY OF CONGRESS SUBJECT HEADINGS

The Library of Congress Subject Headings is the classification system used by most libraries and many periodical indexes. These subject headings are found online and in large, hardbound books, owned by virtually every library and usually located in the reference area.

In the opening pages of each volume, you'll find a page that explains the symbols and abbreviations used inside (see, for example, p. 531).

Begin with the terms you are using for your subject. If your terms do not correspond to a subject heading in the book, either follow the suggested term or try other closely related terms.

Understanding what your research subject is called is critical in finding the books you need. For example, when Scott began his library research he looked in *The Library of Congress Subject Headings,* first, for the full name "Native American Graves Protection and Repatriation Act" and, next, for the law's acronym: NAGPRA. Neither of these terms was listed in the subject headings. When he looked up "Native American," the book referred him to "Indians of North America." He looked through the categories under that heading to find subcategories related to his subject.

Symbols

UF   Used For
BT   Broader Topic
RT   Related Topic
SA   See also
NT   Narrower Topic

Use of these symbols in the expression of relationships between headings is explained in the introduction.

For those libraries maintaining manual card catalogs, the following may be used as a guide.

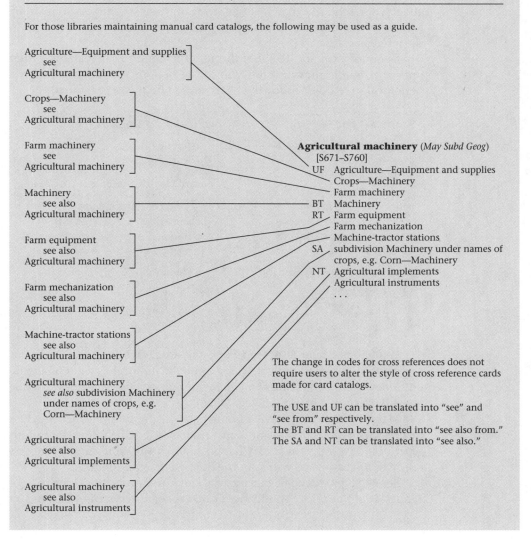

Agriculture—Equipment and supplies
   see
Agricultural machinery

Crops—Machinery
   see
Agricultural machinery

Farm machinery
   see
Agricultural machinery

Machinery
   see also
Agricultural machinery

Farm equipment
   see also
Agricultural machinery

Farm mechanization
   see also
Agricultural machinery

Machine-tractor stations
   see also
Agricultural machinery

Agricultural machinery
   see also subdivision Machinery
   under names of crops, e.g.
   Corn—Machinery

Agricultural machinery
   see also
Agricultural implements

Agricultural machinery
   see also
Agricultural instruments

Agricultural machinery (*May Subd Geog*)
   [S671–S760]
UF   Agriculture—Equipment and supplies
      Crops—Machinery
      Farm machinery
BT   Machinery
RT   Farm equipment
      Farm mechanization
      Machine-tractor stations
SA   subdivision Machinery under names of
      crops, e.g. Corn—Machinery
NT   Agricultural implements
      Agricultural instruments
      . . .

The change in codes for cross references does not require users to alter the style of cross reference cards made for card catalogs.

The USE and UF can be translated into "see" and "see from" respectively.
The BT and RT can be translated into "see also from."
The SA and NT can be translated into "see also."

Finding Subject Headings

Find one or more Library of Congress Subject Headings for either the topic you have used in previous exercises or the topic of the paper you will write.

LEARNING ABOUT YOUR SCHOOL'S LIBRARY

Each library has a slightly different method for helping you locate books and periodicals. The smartest way to begin a research project is to learn about your school's library either by taking an orientation tour or by reading material about your library, which you should be able to find in the reference area.

Generally, you locate books through the library's card catalog, either online or in file drawers; and you locate periodical articles through a periodical index. The following chart should help you get started:

Source Type	Ways to Locate
general and specialized reference sources	reference area of your library, the Internet
books	card catalogs: online or file drawer
periodicals • popular magazines • scholarly journals • newspapers	periodical indexes located in online databases, CD-ROM databases, or printed books
online books, periodicals, and government documents	online indexes and databases
Web sites	search engines

Your library may also keep book-and-article bibliographies on your topic—print guides to both articles and books. To locate such a bibliography, check your subject heading in the online catalog or the card catalog or ask a reference librarian to help you.

Many libraries now have a home page on the Internet that provides links both to the card catalog and to databases, which contain various types of indexes. If your library has an Internet site, you can probably do research off-campus, as well as in the library reference room.

Below is an example of a library home page from the University of Tennessee at Knoxville. This library's card catalog is accessed by clicking on either "UTK Catalogs & Collections" near the top of the page or "UTK Library Catalog" at the bottom. Databases and indexes for journals and periodicals can also be accessed through the home page.

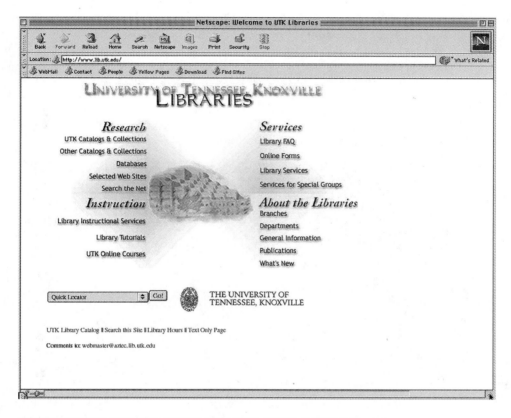

LOCATING SOURCES IN YOUR LIBRARY CARD CATALOG

Whether your card catalog is online or not, books will generally be cataloged in three ways:

▶ by title

▶ by author

▶ by subject (usually Library of Congress Subject Heading)

Many online catalogs make the Library of Congress Subject Headings easier to use by allowing you to do keyword searches, which will lead you to the Library of Congress headings.

The online catalog for the University of Tennessee Library allows searches by:

▶ keywords or Library of Congress Subject Heading

▶ title

▶ author

(Options available through other catalogs include author and title combined, journal or serial title, words from title or subject, and words from content notes or organization names.) Because this catalog allows searches using either keywords or Library of Congress Subject Headings, the entire name of the law Scott researched (Native American Graves Protection and Repatriation Act) can serve as keywords.

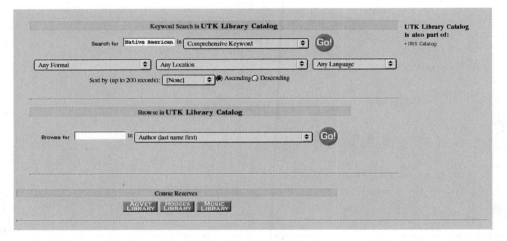

These keywords bring up four listings (see p. 535). The first, second, and fourth are government documents. The second is a book edited by Nina Swidler and others. Clicking on the title for this source brings up a list of appropriate Library of Congress Subject Headings (under "Subject"), beginning with "United States. Native American Graves Protection and Repatriation Act."

The full record also provides the call number (E98.M34 N37 1997). Call numbers are used to locate books on your library shelves (also called "stacks").

The record also provides author and publication information about the book, including a link to the book's home page, which provides its table of contents.

UTK Library Catalog (1 -4)

SAVE ALL

SAVE 1. Native American Graves Protection and Repatriation Act : hearing before the Committee on Indian Affairs, United States Senate, One Hundred Third Congress, first session, on oversight hearing on understanding how the Native American Grave Protection and Repatriation Act is being implemented, May 27, 1993, Washington, DC.
Author: United States. Congress. Senate. Committee on Indian Affairs (1993-) **Date of Publication:** 1993
Summary Holdings:
Y 4.IN 2/11:S.HRG. 103-198 This document title held in Documents and Microforms in the Hodges Library.

SAVE 2. Native Americans and archaeologists : stepping stones to common ground / Nina Swidler ... [et al.], editors.
Date of Publication: 1997
Holdings
Hodges stacks E98.M34 N37 1997 checked in

SAVE 3. Implementation of the Native American Graves Protection and Repatriation Act : hearing before the Committee on Indian Affairs, United States Senate, One Hundred Fourth Congress, first session ... December 6, 1995, Washington, DC.
Author: United States. Congress. Senate. Committee on Indian Affairs (1993-) **Date of Publication:** 1996
Holdings
Hodges DocMic microfiche Y 4.IN 2/11:S.HRG. 104-399 checked in

SAVE 4. Native American Graves Protection and Repatriation Act : hearing before the Committee on Indian Affairs, United States Senate, One Hundred Sixth Congress, first session, on Public Law 101-601, to provide for the protection of Native American graves, April 20, 1999, Washington, DC.
Author: United States. Congress. Senate. Committee on Indian Affairs (1993-) **Date of Publication:** 1999
Holdings
Hodges DocMic microfiche Y 4.IN 2/11:S.HRG. 106-57 checked in

---

UTK Library Catalog (2)

SAVE

Title Native Americans and archaeologists : stepping stones to common ground / Nina Swidler ... [et al.], editors.

Imprint Walnut Creek : AltaMira Press, c1997.

Call Number E98.M34 N37 1997

Description 289 p. : ill., maps ; 24 cm.

Subject United States. Native American Graves Protection and Repatriation Act. Indians of North America -- Material culture Indians of North America -- Antiquities -- Law and legislation Indians of North America -- Civil rights Human remains (Archaeology) -- Law and legislation -- United States. Archaeologists -- United States -- Attitudes. Cultural property -- Repatriation -- United States.

Notes "Published in cooperation with the Society for American Archaeology."

URL http://lcweb.loc.gov/catdir/toc/97-4593.html ; http

Bibliography Includes bibliographical references (p. 253-266) and index.

Other Authors Swidler, Nina. Society of American Archaeology.

ISBN 0761989005 (cloth : acid-free paper) 0761989013 (pbk : acid-free paper) 0761989048 (cloth : acid-free paper) 0761989056 (pbk : acid-free paper)

Holdings Hodges stacks E98.M34 N37 1997 checked in

Native Americans and Archaeologists : Stepping Stones to Common Ground / edited by Nina Swidler, Kurt Dongoske, Roger Anyon, and Alan Downer

Bibliographic record available from Z39.50 Gateway

Frontispiece
Dedication
Foreword: Living Human Values, by William V. Tallbull and Sherri Deaver
Preface
Introduction
Acknowledgments
Biographical Sketches

SECTION I: HISTORICAL OVERVIEW
Archaeologists Native American Relations, by Alan S. Downer

GETTING BOOKS YOUR LIBRARY DOESN'T HAVE

If you can't find a book in the card catalog, see the person in charge of interlibrary loan. If you can wait at least a week, your library may be able to borrow the book for you from another library.

Search Tips

- Online catalogs will not correct your spelling. If you enter a misspelled word, you may get "0" results.

- If your online catalog does not connect keywords to Library of Congress Subject Headings, you must use the Library of Congress subject guide to find the correct heading.

LOCATING PERIODICALS

You can locate periodicals through indexes that may be online, on CD-ROM, or in print. If your library's catalog is online, subject-specific indexes may give you books as well as periodicals.

PRINT INDEXES

General Indexes These indexes are the best place to begin for many research topics.

▶ *The Magazine Index* lists chiefly by subject matter articles from over four hundred magazines.

▶ *The New York Times Index* lists selected articles published in the *Times* from 1851 to 1912, and all articles published in the *Times* thereafter. Issued twice a month with quarterly cumulations and then bound into annual volumes, this index is a prime source of up-to-date information.

▶ *The Newspaper Index* lists articles from the *Chicago Tribune, Los Angeles Times, New Orleans Times-Picayune,* and *Washington Post.*

▶ *The Readers' Guide to Periodical Literature,* issued every month and cumulated quarterly as well as annually, is an author-and-subject index to articles of general (rather than scholarly) interest published in over a hundred American magazines.

Specialized Indexes   Specialized indexes list articles in one or more specified fields. Most of these articles were written by specialists for other specialists. But if you have a solid background in the specific field, you should
find them helpful. Ask the reference librarian to help you find an index on
your topic.

▶ *The Art Index* lists articles from close to three hundred journals on art
  and architecture.

▶ *The Bulletin of the Public Affairs Information Service* (PAIS) covers articles
  on public affairs and public policy as well as government documents
  and books.

▶ *The Environment Index* lists articles as well as books and technical reports under subject headings such as "Oil Spills." Many of the articles
  are briefly summarized in a companion volume, *Environment Abstracts*.

▶ *The General Science Index* lists articles under subject headings in fields
  such as astronomy, botany, genetics, mathematics, physics, and
  oceanography.

▶ *The Humanities Index* lists articles by author and subject in fields such as
  archaeology, folklore, history, language, literature, the performing arts,
  and philosophy.

▶ *The Modern Language Association International Bibliography* lists books
  and articles in the fields of literature and linguistics.

▶ *The Social Sciences Index* lists articles by author and subject in fields such
  as anthropology, economics, law, criminology, medical science, political science, and sociology.

Finding Articles   Once you've identified articles on your topic, you need to
locate them in your library. If the article is in a book of articles or essays,
find the call number of the book by looking up its title in the card catalog.
If the article appears in a periodical, ask the reference librarian where to
find it. Some libraries list all periodicals under their titles (like book titles)
in the card catalog; others list periodicals in a separate file, often called a
"serials list." If your library doesn't have the periodical, the librarian may
be able to get a photocopy of the article from another library, or you may
be able to find it in an online database.

Government Publications   The United States government produces a vast amount of printed matter on a wide range of subjects. Here is a sample of the guides to this material, which can often be found in the microfiche collections of many large libraries (see 37.5). Much of this material can also be found online.

▶ The *ASI* (*American Statistics Index*) consists of two volumes, Index and Abstracts. The first is a subject index to statistical documents produced by hundreds of government offices; the second describes the documents more fully.

▶ The *CIS*, published by the *Congressional Information Service*, also consists of two volumes, Index and Abstracts. They index and describe working papers of Congress: reports, documents, and other special publications of nearly three hundred House, Senate, and joint committees and subcommittees.

▶ The *Monthly Catalog of United States Government Publications*, indexed semiannually, lists government publications by author, title, and subject.

▶ *RIE* (*Resources in Education*), issued monthly and indexed semiannually by the Educational Resources Information Center (ERIC), lists books, pamphlets, and conference papers on educational topics under subject headings, author, and title, and also summarizes every document it lists. Though *RIE* does not list journal articles on education, you will find these in the *CIJE* (*Current Index to Journals in Education*), also produced by ERIC.

ELECTRONIC INDEXES

Databases for Books and Articles   Most of the print indexes above are available on CD-ROM and online databases. For example, *The Readers' Guide* is available online, and the *MLA International Bibliography* is available on CD-ROM. Many of these databases will give you citations for books as well as periodicals. Some of them even provide the full text of articles, which you can download and save or print out. The most well-known "full-text" databases are:

▶ *Dow Jones Interactive*

▶ *Lexis-Nexis*

▶ *ProQuest Research Library*

 If your library has online databases, you can probably access them through your library's Web page. Selecting "Databases" from the menu brings up a list of databases by subject. Selecting a subject area will bring up a list of specific databases, and many of these combine different indexes. Selecting the subject area "Art & Architecture," for instance, may bring up a list of databases that includes online versions of *Art Index* and *Avery Index to Architectural Periodicals.*

▶Research   Services   Instruction   About the Libraries

[UTK Catalogs & Collections] - [Other Catalogs & Collections] - [Databases] - [Selected Web Sites] - [Search ▶

Databases

● Database Finder
● Database Titles A-Z
● New & Trial Subscriptions

Full-Text :	Dow-Jones Interactive | Lexis-Nexis Academic Universe | ProQuest Research Library | More . . .
Multidisciplinary :	General Topics | Current Contents, etc. | News | Dissertations | UnCover@UTK | Web of Science
Arts & Humanities :	Art & Architecture | History & Classics | Literature & Language | Music | Philosophy & Religion
Sciences :	Agriculture & Veterinary Medicine | Biology | Earth Sciences & the Environment | Engineering | Physical & Chemical Sciences | Mathematics & Computer Science | Health Sciences
Social Sciences :	Anthropology | Business & Economics | Education | Journalism & Mass Communications | Political Science & Law | Psychology | Social Work & Sociology
Government Documents :	General Topics | Energy & Transportation | Criminal Justice | Health & Environment | International | Laws & Legislation | Patents & Trademarks | Rules, Regulations, Taxation | Statistics |
Reference Resources :	Almanacs & Statistics | Biographies | Books, Book Reviews & Periodical Directories | Dictionaries & Encyclopedias | Directories

DATABASE FINDER
Search for Databases by name or description
[   ] FIND! Reset

UTK Library Catalog ▪ Search this Site ▪ Library Hours ▪ Suggestions & Comments

Comments to: webmaster@aztec.lib.utk.edu
Copyright © 1999 UTK Libraries

▶Research   Services   Instruction   About the Libraries

[UTK Catalogs & Collections] - [Other Catalogs & Collections] - [Databases] - [Selected Web Sites] - [Search ▶

Access Restrictions: CDROM Workstation, All UTK Libraries, On-Campus/IERA, Off-Campus/PH, All Users

Arts & Humanities | Art & Architecture | History & Classics | Literature & Language | Music | Philosophy & Religion |

Art & Architecture	About	Access Info
Art Index ERL *1984+* Access to 290 art, architecture and classics journals --also available in a Non-Web version within the UTK Libraries.		
Avery Index to Architectural Periodicals *1977+* Access to 1,000+ architecture, landscape and interior design journals.		
Bibliography of the History of Art (BHA) *1973+* Access to 3,000 post-classical art journals in 45 languages.	❓	⚠

also see:

AKL - World Biographical Dictionary of Artists Indexes 275,000 artists and 4,000 groups based on three 20th C. German biographical dictionaries.	❓	⚠
Art and Architecture Thesaurus A controlled vocabulary that can be used to improve access to cultural heritage information in the global networked environment.	❓	⬤

Not all databases are subject specific. For example, *ProQuest,* a commercial site, indexes sources in a number of fields, allowing you to customize your search by journals, fields, and modules.

ALTERNATIVE WAYS TO ACCESS RESEARCH DATABASES

You don't have to go through a library to have access to the many databases that are available. For a fee, you can access them directly, and database services, such as *www.allonesearch.com,* can help put you in touch with the most useful database.

Database Research Tips

■ Choose the database that's best for you. Your library's list of databases probably changes often, so ask a librarian if you're unsure which one to choose.

■ Some databases charge a fee.

■ Many databases do not index the full life of a periodical. Some databases, for example, begin with the year 1980, though many of the periodicals they index may have been publishing since 1900.

ONLINE GOVERNMENT DOCUMENT SITES   Many government documents can now be found and downloaded online. Other sites can help you locate a wide variety of government publications.

▶ *The Center for Information, Law, and Policy* <www.law.vill.edu> *CILP* links you to federal and state courts, tax law, and federal and state Web sites.

▶ *Federal Web Locator* <www.infoctr.edu/fwl> An extensive list of online resources related to the federal government, maintained by the Center for Information Law and Policy.

▶ *FedWorld Information Services* <www.fedworld.gov> As they say on their Web site, "FedWorld can offer . . . a comprehensive central access point for searching, locating, ordering, and acquiring government and business information."

▶ *The National Archives and Records Administration* <www.nara.gov> Through *NARA,* you can view copies of historic documents such as the Declaration of Independence and the Emancipation Proclamation. You can also view data from the Federal Register.

▶ *Thomas* <http://thomas.loc.gov> Maintained by the Library of Congress, *Thomas* archives legislation pending in the U.S. Congress, congressional historical records, and committee information.

▶ *The U.S. Census Bureau* <www.census.gov> The Census Bureau Web site links you to their demographic reports, including reports on educational attainment, income, and population trends.

Visiting Your Library   EXERCISE 4

Visit your college library to answer the following questions:

1. Is the card catalog online or in file drawers?
2. What general periodical indexes (print or online) does your library have?
3. What specialized indexes (print or online) does your library have?

Locating Books and Articles   EXERCISE 5

Locate two books and five articles on your research topic.

36.6 USING THE INTERNET AS A RESEARCH RESOURCE

USING THE INTERNET WISELY

The Internet allows you to do many forms of research in your home or dorm room, such as searching online card catalogs and locating and downloading articles. In addition, through email and discussion groups you can ask questions of experts. However, the Internet won't meet all your research needs. Relatively few books are presently online, for example, and the Web contains many sites and articles whose authors are difficult to determine and evaluate. In contrast, most of the material in your college library—university-press books and scholarly journals, in particular—has already been judged worthwhile and reliable by experts. While the Web contains a great deal of worthwhile and reliable information, you have to work much harder to find out if that is the case. You have to know *more* to judge the merits of what is on the Web.

RECOGNIZING WAYS OF COPYING DATA FROM ONE COMPUTER TO ANOTHER

When you use the Internet for research, you are essentially gathering copies of data from other computers around the world. To make your way through the Internet with minimal confusion, recognize ways that data is copied and transferred. By knowing this, you can anticipate what the data will look like, and how you can best work with it, when it reaches your computer.

A number of methods have been devised for transferring information from computer to computer.

▶ File Transfer Protocol (FTP) is an application that allows you to transfer a file (such as a text document or an image) from one computer to another. Using software such as *Fetch, WS-FTP,* or a Web browser, you can transfer individual files to your computer. If you use the Web and see ftp:// . . . at the beginning of a Web address, that tells you the file is being copied to your computer via FTP. FTP is preferable when you're copying larger files because it is less likely to corrupt during the transfer than files transferred using the hypertext transfer protocol (http:// . . .).

▶ Telnet is an application that lets your computer act like a terminal for another computer. A terminal usually consists of a keyboard and monitor connected to a remote computer. You can't physically access the computer from the terminal, but you can read information or run programs for viewing on your monitor. With telnet, your computer acts like a terminal, giving you text-only access to the information on a distant computer. (Many electronic card catalogs are still accessed through telnet.)

▶ Gopher is similar to telnet because it gives you text-only access to information on another computer. However, gopher can be easier to use because it arranges information through a series of searchable menus. Your choice of an option from one menu will lead you to another menu or perhaps to the text you seek. You can also search gopher indexes.

▶ The Web is an advance over telnet and gopher because it combines text and graphics, because it is hypertextual (that is, you often can link to one page from within another, rather than only through menus), and because you can use it for many gopher and FTP applications. For example, you may be presented with the option of downloading a file via the standard Hypertext transfer protocol (http:// . . .) or via FTP (ftp:// . . .). Which standard you choose should depend on the type of text you hope to receive.

USING WEB-BASED SEARCH ENGINES

A search engine helps you make the connection between your online browser (such as Netscape or Explorer) and sites on the World Wide Web. Most browsers contain a "Search" menu that will link you to the most popular search engines. If your college library has an Internet home page, you will probably find a menu of search engines there as well.

KEYWORDS AND CATEGORIES Using search engines is not unlike using your library's card catalog. A search engine will produce a list of URLs (Uniform Resource Locators). URLs resemble library call numbers in that they indicate where on the Web you can locate a particular site. When a search engine produces a list of results, however, all you have to do is to click on either the URL or the title of the Web site to be linked to the page.

Searching on the Web is also like searching in a card catalog because it involves making decisions about keywords (also called search terms) and subject headings (on the Internet, most frequently called categories and directories). Most search engines allow you to combine keyword searches with category searches. Some engines, such as *Yahoo!* (see p. 544), work primarily through category searches. The search engine *Excite* (see p. 545) begins with a keyword search; then it produces categories in a directory before providing "Web Results."

What's New   Check Email   Personalize   Help

Yahoo! Auctions   **Yahoo! Mail**
coins, cards, stamps   free email for life

[   ]   **Search**   advanced search

Shopping - Auctions - Yellow Pages - People Search - Maps - Travel - Classifieds - Personals - Games - Chat - Clubs
Mail - Calendar - Messenger - **Companion** - My Yahoo! - News - Sports - Weather - TV - Stock Quotes - more...

Yahoo! Shopping - Thousands of stores. Millions of products.

Departments		Stores	Products
· Apparel	· Flowers	· Toys R Us	· Digital cameras
· Bath/Beauty	· Food/Drink	· Gap	· Pokemon
· Computers	· Music	· Vermont Teddy Bear	· MP3 players
· Electronics	· Video/DVD	· Macy's	· DVD players

Arts & Humanities
Literature, Photography...

Business & Economy
Companies, Finance, Jobs...

Computers & Internet
Internet, WWW, Software, Games...

Education
College and University, K-12...

Entertainment
Cool Links, Movies, Humor, Music...

Government
Elections, Military, Law, Taxes...

Health
Medicine, Diseases, Drugs, Fitness...

News & Media
Full Coverage, Newspapers, TV...

Recreation & Sports
Sports, Travel, Autos, Outdoors...

Reference
Libraries, Dictionaries, Quotations...

Regional
Countries, Regions, US States...

Science
Animals, Astronomy, Engineering...

Social Science
Archaeology, Economics, Languages...

Society & Culture
People, Environment, Religion...

In the News
· Iran's reformers say poised for election win
· Winter storm hits Midwest, Northeast
· NASA releases NEAR asteroid images
more...

Marketplace
· Y! Travel - plan a vacation
· Yahoo! Bill Pay - free 3-month trial
· Y! Careers - resume database, 500,000+ jobs
more...

Inside Yahoo!
· Weekend's top movies
· Y! Mobile - Yahoo! on your phone
· Play free Fantasy Auto Racing
· Y! Greetings - free greeting cards
more...

World Yahoos   *Europe* : Denmark - France - Germany - Italy - Norway - Spain - Sweden - UK & Ireland
                  Pacific Rim : Asia - Australia & NZ - China - Chinese - HK - Japan - Korea - Singapore - Taiwan
                  Americas : Brazil - Canada - Mexico - Spanish

Yahoo! Get Local   LA - NYC - SF Bay - Chicago - more...   [   ]   Enter Zip Code

Other   Autos - Careers - Digital - Entertainment - Greetings - Health - Invites - Local Events - Net Events
           Message Boards - Movies - Music - Real Estate - Small Business - Y! Internet Life - Yahooligans!

Yahoo! prefers

How to Suggest a Site - Company Info - Privacy Policy - Terms of Service - Contributors - Openings at Yahoo!

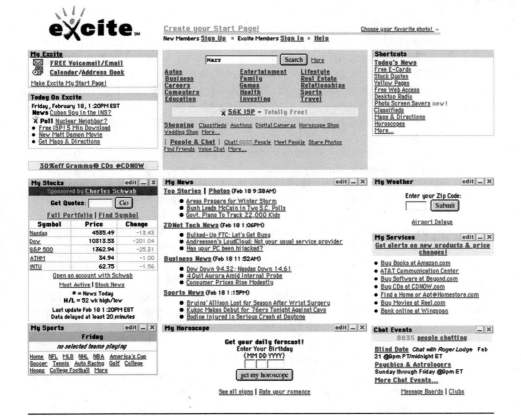

RESTRICTED OR INCLUSIVE SEARCHES   Consider your subject and purpose when you choose between these two general approaches to searching the Internet. Using both types of searches will help you find relevant Web sites.

Restricted searches are *category* or *directory* searches. When the quality of the sites is very important to you, begin with a restricted category search. Bear in mind, though, that category searches often exclude useful sites either because particular sites don't fall neatly into the category or because the person classifying the sites was not very familiar with the subject.

Inclusive searches are *keyword* searches. These searches return all Web sites that contain the keywords you have entered, but all such searches are not the same. Some engines search the entire Web site, while others search only keywords in the name listed in the Web page's head.

To get an idea of the range of sites a keyword search can produce, look at the "Top 10 Web Results" produced by the keyword "Mars" in an *Excite* search (see p. 547). The first Web site is NASA's official site, with information on Mars exploration. However, the search also produced URLs for a society dedicated to settling Mars and for something called the Unofficial Biker Mice from Mars Fan Club. ("Next Results," not shown here, include a church named Mars Hill and a Web site for couples counseling, sponsored by the author of *Men Are from Mars, Women Are from Venus*.)

ADVANCED WEB SEARCHES   Every search engine has options for customizing searches, usually found under the heading "Advanced Search." These options can make both keyword and category searching more effective.

The most common advanced search is an improved keyword search, often called a *Boolean* or *word filter* search. Here you can include and/or exclude certain words associated with your search term.

For example, one of the most popular keyword search engines is *HotBot* (see pp. 548–51). While using the keyword *Mars* yields many interesting scientific sites in the first twenty results, it also yields Web pages for M&M/Mars, a heavy metal band called Mars, and a ninety-chapter novel called *Underground Beneath the Dust of Mars*. To filter out these sites, you can do an advanced search for all the sites that contain the word *Mars* but exclude sites in which *Mars* occurs together with other words, such as *attacks* (to eliminate sites devoted to the movie *Mars Attacks!*). You also can limit the search by date and location (or *domain*; see "Evaluating Web sites," below).

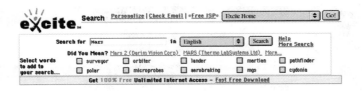

Search for Mars **in** English | Search | Help More Search

Did You Mean? Mars 2 (Darim Vision Corp)　MARS (Thermo LabSystems Ltd)　More...

Select words to add to your search...
☐ surveyor　☐ orbiter　☐ lander　☐ martian　☐ pathfinder
☐ polar　☐ microprobes　☐ aerobraking　☐ mgs　☐ cydonia

Get 100% Free Unlimited Internet Access – Fast Free Download

✕ Search Results

| Try These First | Directory | Web Results | Web News |

Go to Mars, Inc.'s web site

✕ Directory

Education > Science & Nature > Astronomy & Space > Celestial Bodies > Planets ✕
Recommended Web sites and Excite resources about Planets

Education > Science & Nature > Astronomy & Space > Celestial Bodies > Planets > **Mars** ✕
Recommended Web sites and Excite resources about **Mars**

Education > Science & Nature > News & Magazines > News Topics > **Mars** ✕
Recommended Web sites and Excite resources about **Mars**

Reference > News & Magazines > Current Events > Science & Technology > **Mars** ✕
Recommended Web sites and Excite resources about **Mars**

✕ Web Results

Top 10 matches.
Show: Titles only　View by: Web site

69% Center for Mars Exploration Home Page – The Center for Mars Exploration (CMEX) WWW server is constantly being updated, so keep checking this page for many new features including historical references to Mars, previous Mars mission information, tools to analyze Mars, current Mars news, and much more.
http://cmex-www.arc.nasa.gov/
Search for more documents like this one

67% West to Mars–Support MarsDirect Worldwide – "... if they decide to do so, our descendents can create a New Earth – perhaps a New Eden – on the next world outwards from the Sun."Arthur C.
http://www.marswest.org/
Search for more documents like this one

67% The Case for Mars – The Case for Mars Conference Program and Abstracts – The Case for Mars VI Conference, July 17-20, 1996 Add your name to the Case for Mars Mailing List
http://spot.colorado.edu/~marscase/Home.html
Search for more documents like this one

66% Unofficial Biker Mice from Mars Fan Club – Unofficial Biker Mice From Mars Fan Club
http://www.bikermice.com/
Search for more documents like this one

66% Mars Pathfinder Home – We are now processing data acquired during the extended mission. The latest information will be released as it becomes available. Main Topics General Information
http://mars.pgd.hawaii.edu/default.html
Search for more documents like this one

Get 100% Free Unlimited Internet Access – Fast Free Download

65% Welcome to the Mars Academy – Relive the history of Mars exploration, from the early days of blurred images to Mars Polar Lander. Participate in exciting activities with students all over th world on and before December the 3rd in preparation for the landing.
http://www.marsacademy.com/
Search for more documents like this one

65% Mars Today – Mars Today, created by Howard Houben of the Mars Global Circulation Model Group, is a poster produced daily by the Center for Mars Exploration at NASA's Ames Research Center.
http://www.mgcm.arc.nasa.gov/
Search for more documents like this one

65% MarsNews.com – NewsWire for the New Frontier – MarsNews.com – NewsWire for the New Frontier. A comprehensive news and information resource with the latest news about the Red Planet from all over the Internet. Details about current, past, and future missions, the search for life on Mars, technology, and planetology. Brought to you by the Mars Society.
http://www.marsnews.com/
Search for more documents like this one

64% Mars-Watch.com – The Site for Mars Enthusiasts – The site for Mars enthusiasts. Find the latest information, news, and photographs about Mars, interesting Martian facts, and an outstanding Mars photo archive.
http://www.mars-watch.com/
Search for more documents like this one

64% Mars-Watch.com – The Site for Mars Enthusiasts – The site for Mars enthusiasts. Find the latest information, news, and photographs about Mars, interesting Martian facts, and an outstanding Mars photo archive.
http://www.mars-watch.com/index.shtml
Search for more documents like this one

[Next Results]

WEB RESULTS **Top 10 Matches**   next >>

1. Center for Mars Exploration Home Page
The Center for Mars Exploration (CMEX) WWW server is constantly being updated, so keep checking this page for many new features including historical references to Mars, previous
http://cmex-www.arc.nasa.gov/
See results from this site only.

2. Mars Missions
Welcome to the ! Mars Pathfinder - Landed July 4, 1997 Mars Global Surveyor - In Orbit Around Mars Mars Surveyor 98 - Launches December 1998 Mars Surveyor 2001 - Launches March
http://www.sun.com/mars/nav.html
See results from this site only.

3. The Daily Martian Weather Report
from the Cape Canaveral Air Station took place on November 7, 1996. After a ten-month cruise to Mars, the MGS spacecraft executed its orbit insertion maneuver on September 12,
http://nova.stanford.edu/projects/mgs/dmwr.html
See results from this site only.

4. NSSDC Master Catalog Display: Experiment
The Mars Global Surveyor Mars Orbital Camera (MOC) experiment is designed to obtain images of the surface and atmosphere of Mars for studying the meteorology/climatology and
http://nssdc.gsfc.nasa.gov/cgi-bin/database/www-nmc?96-062A-01
See results from this site only.

5. The Whole Mars Catalog [tm]
The Whole Mars Catalog. An online guide to Mars
http://www.reston.com/astro/mars/catalog.html
See results from this site only.

6. Exploring Mars
Mars exploration, from Pathfinder to manned landing--the very best of what there is has landed here in concise style.
http://silkscape.com/mars/
See results from this site only.

7. Mars-Watch.com - The Site for Mars Enthusiasts
The site for Mars enthusiasts. Find the latest information, news, and photographs about Mars, interesting Martian facts, and an outstanding Mars photo archive.
http://www.mars-watch.com
See results from this site only.

8. Life from Mars: Video Animations
A NASA research team of scientists at the Johnson Space Center and at Stanford University has found evidence that strongly suggests primitive life may have existed on Mars more
http://spaceart.com/solar/eng/marslif3.htm
See results from this site only.

9. JPL Mars Missions
Mars Pathfinder & Sojourner Rover Mars Global Surveyor Mars Surveyor '98 Martian Chronicle Electronic Newsletter for Mars Exploration Mars Exploration Education Web Page Go to: JPL
http://www.jpl.nasa.gov/mars/
See results from this site only.

10. Mars Orbiter Camera Views "Face on Mars"
Shortly after midnight Sunday morning (5 April 1998 12:39 AM PST), the Mars Orbiter Camera (MOC) on the Mars Global Surveyor (MGS) spacecraft successfully acquired a high
http://mars.jpl.nasa.gov/mgs/msss/camera/images/4_6_face_release/index.html
See results from this site only.

next >>

SECOND OPINION
try your search for "Mars" with **LYC○S**

About Us | Advertise | Jobs | Privacy Statement | Feedback | Help | Submit a Web site | Text-only version

HOTBOT

Advertisement

Results for mars   [SEARCH] ■ *Search within these results*

NEW SEARCH | REVISE OPTIONS | ADVANCED SEARCH

Search Partners

· See Deja.com ratings or info on "mars."
· Find books on "mars" at bn.com.
· Chat about "mars" at Talk City.

WEB RESULTS   more than 100,000   << back   11 - 20   next >>

11. M&M/Mars
Another famous candy company! Snickers, Milky Way, M&Ms
/director.asp?target=http%3A%2F%2Fwww%2Em%2Dms%2Ecom&id=11&userid=40qjefJkEaAE&query=MT=mars&rsource=ODS
More like this: Shopping/ Food/ Candy

12. Mars
Home page of the metal band. Includes news, lyrics, photos, links, and ordering info.
/director.asp?target=http%3A%2F%2Fwww%2Eairplaying%2Fmars%2Ehtml&id=12&userid=40qjefJkEaAE&query=MT=mars&rsource=ODS
More like this: Arts & Entertainment/ Music/ Bands and Artists/ M

13. Underground Beneath the Dust of Mars
A 90 chapter novel by Erie poet, Ron Androla, "Poet Laureate of the Millennium."
/director.asp?target=http%3A%2F%2Fwww%2Ebscan%2Ecom%2Fesp%2Frandrola&id=13&userid=40qjefJkEaAE&query=MT=mars&rsource=ODS
More like this: Arts & Entertainment/ Poetry/ Contemporary

14. Mars Muppet Page
Mar's Muppet Page, Links to the Best Muppet and Jim Henson Web Pages
/director.asp?target=http%3A%2F%2Fwww%2Egeocities%2Ecom%2FPittsburgh%2FFarm%2F4164%2Findex%2Ehtml&id=14&userid=40qjefJkEaAE&query=MT=mars
More like this: Arts & Entertainment/ Performing Arts/ Puppetry/ Muppets

15. Mars Scales
Manufacturers of electronic weighing scales, precision balances, bench scales, load cells, weight indicators for a wide range of weighing applications.
/director.asp?target=http%3A%2F%2Fwww%2Emarsscale%2Ecom%2F&id=15&userid=40qjefJkEaAE&query=MT=mars&rsource=ODS
More like this: Business & Money/ Industries/ Industrial Supply/ Scales

16. Mars & Co.
Focuses upon organizational strategy.
/director.asp?target=http%3A%2F%2Fwww%2Emarsandco%2Ecom%2F&id=16&userid=40qjefJkEaAE&query=MT=mars&rsource=ODS
More like this: Business & Money/ Management/ Consulting

17. Medical Accounts Receivable Solutions (MARS)
Consulting services in A/R and reimbursement operations specializing in the collection of old insurance claims.
/director.asp?target=http%3A%2F%2Fwww%2Emarsadvantage%2Ecom&id=17&userid=40qjefJkEaAE&query=MT=mars&rsource=ODS
More like this: Business & Money/ Financial Services/ Medical Billing

18. Conspiracy Revealed: Mars Pathfinder Mission
These slightly adjusted genuine pictures from the Mars Pathfinder Mission reveal a government conspiracy. There is life on Mars.
/director.asp?target=http%3A%2F%2Finternettrash%2Ecom%2Fusers%2Fmarstraveller%2F&id=18&userid=40qjefJkEaAE&query=MT=mars&rsource=ODS
More like this: Travel & Recreation/ Humor/ Stories

19. Cats Are From Mars
Cats Are From Mars! Masquerading as "finicky and solitary" earth creatures all these years, these wiley beings have been skillfully manipulating the hum
centuries, coaxing handouts, shredding furniture, cleansing their home planet of toxic waste cleverly disguised as "hairballs."
/director.asp?target=http%3A%2F%2Fhome%2Etampabay%2Err%2Ecom%2Fdapage%2Fmars%2Fmarscats%2Ehtm&id=19&userid=40qjefJkEaAE&query=MT=mars&
More like this: Travel & Recreation/ Pets/ Cats/ Humor

20. Mars Pathfinder Mission - Genuine Pictures
These slightly adjusted pictures prove that there is life on Mars [ed: contains parodies of NASA images of Mars and of Mars exploration].
/director.asp?target=http%3A%2F%2Fwww%2Egeocities%2Ecom%2FArea51%2FDunes%2F2035%2F&id=20&userid=40qjefJkEaAE&query=MT=mars&rsource=ODS
More like this: Science & Technology/ Astronomy/ Personal Home Pages

<< back   11 - 20   next >>

SECOND OPINION
try your search for "mars" with LYC◯S

Advertisement

Advertisement

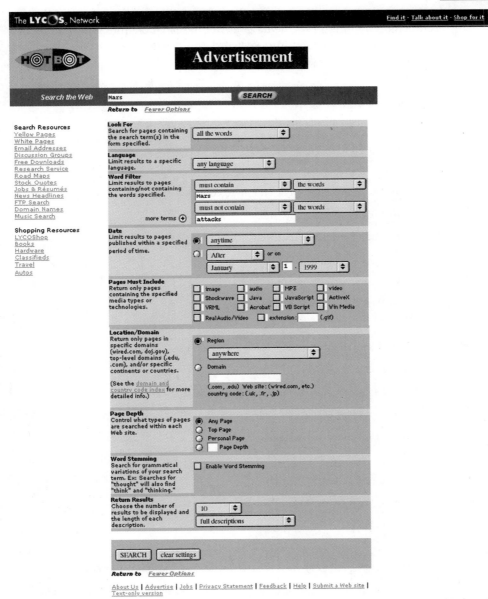

WORLD WIDE WEB SEARCH ENGINES   The following list provides URLs for the most common and the most powerful search engines. Though the first two groups are divided into keyword and category searches, most search engines offer some combination of the two.

Common Search Engines for Keyword Searches

▶ *AltaVista* <www.altavista.com>

▶ *Argus Clearinghouse* <www.clearinghouse.net>

▶ *Excite* <www.excite.com>

▶ *Fast Search* <www.ussc.alltheweb.com>

▶ *Google* <www.google.com>

▶ *HotBot* <http://hotbot.lycos.com>

▶ *GO.com* <http://infoseek.go.com>

▶ *Lycos* <www.lycos.com>

▶ *Webcrawler* <www.webcrawler.com>

Common Search Engines for Category Searches

▶ *DMOZ Open Directory Project* <www.dmoz.org>

▶ *Librarians' Index to the Internet* <www.lii.org>

▶ *LookSmart* <www.looksmart.com>

▶ *Yahoo* <www.yahoo.com>

Keyword and Category Search Engines

▶ *Skworm* <www.skworm.com>

▶ *Snap* <http://home.snap.com>

Multiple Database Searches   Search other engines simultaneously.

▶ *Ask Jeeves* <www.ask.com> A keyword search engine in a question/ answer format.

▶ *Dogpile* <www.dogpile.com>

▶ *Go 2 Network Metacrawler* <www.go2net.com>

- ▶ *Metacrawler* <www.metacrawler.com>

- ▶ *Northern Light* <www.northernlight.com> A keyword search engine that allows results to be saved in folders organized by categories.

- ▶ *Oneseek* <www.oneseek.com>

- ▶ *ProFusion* <www.profusion.com>

- ▶ *SavvySearch* <www.savvysearch.com>

Search Engine Tips

- Most search engines are commercial ventures. Research suggests that searches may be influenced by the engine's sponsors and/or advertisers.

- Companies producing search engines make money by selling advertising. Watch out for ads that appear to be URLs produced by your search.

- Computer companies often make deals with or are part owners of search engines. The browser installed on your computer may automatically bring up only one search engine. If your browser doesn't easily give you a variety of search engines, bookmark the list of search engines provided above.

EVALUATING WEB SITES   As we suggested, Web sites require more critical reading and thinking skills than the average university-press book from your school's library. In order to judge the credibility and usefulness of information you find on the Web, you have to understand who put it there and why. The following questions should help:

What is the Web site's domain?   A Web site's domain, usually indicated by the last three letters of its URL, will help tell you why a Web site exists by indicating, in part, how it was created.

- ▶ .com designates commercial sites. Such sites exist because (1) someone paid to have his or her home page placed on the Internet, (2) a commercial enterprise offered an individual server space for a page, or (3) a commercial enterprise paid to market a product or service online.

- ▶ .edu designates sites maintained by educational institutions. Most of these sites exist to promote learning and research. Individual students and teachers often have home pages in this domain. While some of these sites are academically oriented, others are no different from home pages in a commercial domain.

▶ .gov refers to government agencies.

▶ .mil refers to military groups.

▶ .org designates sites maintained for nonprofit organizations, such as charity fund-raising, special-interest, and political-party groups.

▶ .net refers to commercial networks.

Who is sponsoring the site?   A Web site's domain gives you only a general idea of its nature and purpose. Specific URLs are sponsored by individuals, groups, or businesses. Many different organizations sponsor Web sites to further their causes, get new members, and communicate with members they already have. Businesses sponsor Web sites primarily to sell you something. Generally, .edu sites sponsored by universities contain reliable information because they exist primarily for educational purposes. Web sites maintained by reliable sources generally present the credentials of the site's sponsor. Reputable businesses, institutions, and individuals stand behind the material they post on the Internet. A good rule of thumb: If you can't figure out who is sponsoring the site, be careful.

How recently was material posted?   Many sites are constructed and then abandoned, sometimes leaving behind outdated information. Again, a responsible Web site will make clear, usually on the home page, when the last material was posted. The results of most search engines will also indicate when the site was last updated.

EXERCISE 6   **Using Online Reference Sources**

Find an online source for the topic you used in exercise 2. Which of the two sources—print and online—do you find easier to use, and why? What kinds of information are furnished by one source and not the other?

ADDITIONAL ONLINE REFERENCE SOURCES   The sites below contain information, statistics, bibliographies, and some online articles.

The Columbia Guide to Online Style
<http://www.columbia.edu/cu/cup/cgos> Although the complete guide appears in print form, this page presents basic advice on citing online sources.

The Internet Public Library <www.ipl.org> Hosted by the School of Information at the University of Michigan, this site collects useful information resources on the Web, including periodicals and online texts.

Arts and Humanities

▶ *All-music Guide* <www.allmusic.com> Searchable database of information about music in all genres.

▶ *Arts Journal* <www.artsjournal.com> Daily digest and archive of news about dance, media, music, publishing, theater, and the visual arts.

▶ *Artsource* <www.ilpi.com/artsource> Links to general resources, bibliographies, and sites related to arts and architecture.

▶ *Internet Movie Database* <http://us.imdb.com> Searchable archive of cast, production, and historical information about movies and television.

▶ *Literature and Composition Resources* <www.frostburg.edu/dept/engl/gartner/Litcomp.htm> A guide to primary and secondary resources on the Web, including lists, biographical and bibliographical information, analytical articles, reference works, instructional materials, electronic texts, databases, archives, literary history, journals, magazines, and newspapers.

Business, Commerce, Economics, and Labor

▶ *American Federation of Labor* <www.aflcio.org> Find information on working conditions, union efforts, salaries, worker training.

▶ *Bureau of Labor Statistics* <www.bls.gov> Government site containing survey data and information on workplace conditions, the economy, and worker demographics.

▶ *Commerce Department* <www.doc.gov> Government site containing information on trade, economic indicators, and Department activities.

▶ *Federal Reserve Board* <www.bog.frb.fed.us> Find information on the Board of Governors of the Federal Reserve System, its structure, its activities, and its research data.

▶ *FreeEDGAR* <www.freeedgar.com> Database of companies from the Securities and Exchange Commission.

▶ *International Monetary Fund* <www.imf.org> Learn about IMF activities and standards. Search the IMF status of any country.

▶ *Public Register's Annual Report Service* <www.prars.com> Search the annual reports of over thirty-six hundred public companies.

▶ *Stat-USA* <www.stat-usa.gov> A service of the U.S. Department of Commerce, this site provides business, economic, and trade information from the U.S. federal government.

▶ *World Bank Group* <www.worldbank.org> Read about the World Bank Group and its projects.

Gender, Culture, and Ethnicity

▶ *Archives for Research on Women and Gender* <www.lib.utsa.edu/Archives/arwg.html> Describes an archival collection at the University of Texas at San Antonio and provides links to other archives.

▶ *Asia Society* <www.asiasociety.org> Learn about the structure and activities of one of the primary institutions devoted to an understanding of Asia.

▶ *Center for Afroamerican and African Studies* <www.umich.edu/~iinet/caas/index.html> Presents information on the Center for Afroamerican and African Studies at the University of Michigan.

▶ *Center for Judaic Studies—University of Pennsylvania* <www.cjs.upenn.edu> Search the exhibits and library holdings of the Center for Judaic Studies. Learn about fellowships and activities related to the center.

▶ *Center for World Indigenous Studies* <www.cwis.org> Information about and from the Center for World Indigenous Studies.

▶ *Chicana/o Latina/o Net* <http://latino.sscnet.ucla.edu> A site devoted to REFORMA, a group devoted to library services for Spanish-speaking citizens.

▶ *Harvard Center for Jewish Studies* <www.fas.harvard.edu/~cjs> Information about and from a "focal point for the study and teaching of Judaica."

▶ *Indigenous Women's Network* <www.honorearth.com/iwn> Information about and from "a coalition of Native women who work in rural and urban communities applying Indigenous values to resolve contemporary problems."

▶ *Internet Resources in Native American Studies* <www.library.pima.edu/native.htm> An index of Web sites, newsgroups, and listservs.

▶ *Latino Internet Sites* <http://clnet.ucr.edu/latinos.links.html> An index of Web sites, gophers, newsgroups, and listservs.

▶ *Native Web: An Internet Community* <www.nativeweb.org> A collection of resources for indigenous cultures throughout the world.

▶ *Womanist Theory and Research* <www.uga.edu/~womanist> Presents indexes to the journal of the same title and information on related consortia, fellowships, and grants.

Law

▶ *FindLaw* <www.findlaw.com> A categorized index (similar to Yahoo) devoted to legal topics.

News

▶ *ABC News* <abcnews.go.com> Web site of the ABC television network's news program.

▶ *BBC News* <http://news.bbc.co.uk> Web site of the British Broadcasting Corporation. A good source for world news.

▶ *CNN* <www.cnn.com> Web site of the Cable News Network.

▶ *C-Span* <www.c-span.org> Information on politics and the network's current programming.

▶ *New York Times* <www.nytimes.com> Online version of a leading American newspaper. A good source for breaking news of all kinds.

▶ *PBS* <www.pbs.org> Presents links to breaking news as well as in-depth coverage of selected issues covered by PBS programs such as *Frontline*.

Politics, Special-interest Groups

▶ *All Politics* <cnn.com/ALLPOLITICS> Sponsored by *Time* and CNN, *All Politics* presents current political news.

▶ *American Civil Liberties Union* <www.aclu.org> Contains reports and statements relating to civil rights.

▶ *American Jewish Committee* <www.ajc.org> Information about and from a group that aims to "safeguard the welfare and security of Jews in the United States, in Israel, and throughout the world" by strengthening "the basic principles of pluralism . . . as the best defense against anti-Semitism and other basic forms of bigotry."

▶ *B'nai B'rith Interactive* <bnaibrith.org> Information about and from the international Jewish service organization.

▶ *The Cato Institute* <www.cato.org> Web site of an organization dedicated to "individual liberty, limited government, free markets, and peace."

▶ *Children's Defense Fund* <www.childrensdefense.org> Contains information and resources relating to children's health, safety, education, and growth.

▶ *Congressional Black Caucus Foundation* <www.cbcfonline.org> Information about and from a group that aims to "broaden and elevate the influence of African Americans in the political, legislative and public policy arenas."

▶ *Democracy Network* <www.democracynet.org> Sponsored by the League of Women Voters, this site covers elections throughout the United States.

▶ *Electronic Policy Network* <www.epn.org> EPN "is the front door to progressive policy on the Web," providing information "about the policies and politics that shape our world." Includes links to over sixty progressive organizations.

▶ *Federal Election Commission Info* <www.tray.com/fecinfo> The site links you to reports on campaign contributions and spending.

▶ *The Federalist Society* <www.fed-soc.org> Web site of "a group of conservatives and libertarians interested in the current state of the legal order."

▶ *The Jefferson Project* <www.capweb.net/classic/jefferson> Sponsored by Net.Capitol, this site links you to news about the federal government as well as information from such resources as local government agencies, federal agencies, and political watchdog groups. The site also includes information on political action.

▶ *NAACP* <www.naacp.org> Information about and from a group dedicated to ensuring "the political, educational, social, and economic equality of minority group citizens of the United States."

▶ *National Organization for Women* <www.now.org> Contains information about politics, health, and the economy. Also presents information on NOW.

▶ *National Urban League* <www.nul.org> Information about and from a group that assists "African Americans in the achievement of social and economic equality."

▶ *Opensecrets.org* <www.opensecrets.org/home/index.asp> Sponsored by the Center for Responsive Politics, this site offers information on campaign spending and contributions.

▶ *Rainbow/PUSH Coalition* <www.rainbowpush.org> Information about and from the "multiracial, multi-issue, international membership organization founded by Rev. Jesse L. Jackson, Sr."

▶ *Web Active* <www.webactive.com> Links to liberal media (print, radio, and video).

Science

▶ *National Aeronautics and Space Administration* <www.nasa.gov> News and information from NASA.

▶ *UniSci* <www.unisci.com> Information on university scientific research.

Sports

▶ *ESPN* <espn.go.com> Scores, features, and special sections.

Using Search Engines

EXERCISE 7

Use two keyword and two category search engines to research your topic. Pull up at least twenty-five results, then list the sites that appear in both search results.

Using a Multiple Search Engine

EXERCISE 8

Research your topic using one multiple search engine.

Evaluating Web Sites

EXERCISE 9

Use the questions given on pp. 553–54 to evaluate sites that recurred with all search engines.

36.7 USING OTHER ELECTRONIC SOURCES

EMAIL

You probably already use email to communicate with friends and family. It can also link you to others doing research on the topic you are exploring.

You may find the following email directories useful:

▶ *InfoSpace* <www.infospace.com>

▶ *Internet Address Finder* <www.iaf.net>

▶ *InterNIC Internet directory and database services* <www.internic.net>

▶ *Switchboard.com* <www3.switchboard.com>

▶ *WhoWhere?* <www.whowhere.lycos.com>

LISTSERVS

Listservs are mailing lists for either organizations or people interested in a specific issue or project. They allow a single text to be distributed to all those who have subscribed to the list. (*Listserv* is a particular brand of software for managing lists; other brands are *majordomo* and *listproc*. However, people use "listserv" generally to mean electronic mailing lists, as in "Do you know of any listservs for feminist punk?")

Information on these listservs can be found at the following Web sites:

▶ *Lizst* <www.liszt.com>

▶ *Tile.Net* <www.tile.net>

▶ *Topica* <www.topica.com>

BULLETIN BOARDS, NEWSGROUPS, AND USENET

Bulletin boards, newsgroups, and Usenet provide public email forums on specific issues. The *Lizst, Tile.Net,* and *Topica* Web sites above can provide you with a directory of these forums. They are also collected at the following sites:

▶ *CyberFiber Newsgroups* <www.cyberfiber.com>

▶ *Deja.com* <www.deja.com>

▶ *Usenet Info Center* <http://metalab.unc.edu/usenet-i/home.html>

Finding Electronic Sources

Locate at least one listserv and one bulletin board, newsgroup, or Usenet on your research topic.

37 *Notetaking*

37.1 KEEPING TRACK OF YOUR SOURCES

As you learn about sources from reference books, record the authors, titles, and other information (such as names and dates of periodicals) so that you can find the sources in your library. The simplest way to keep track of books is to print information directly from an online catalog entry. But if you can't make printouts, fill out a three-by-five-inch source card on each book you plan to consult. You'll also need a source card for each article you plan to see.

SOURCE CARD FOR A BOOK

NA958
+T96X
1992
(LC)

Tzonis, Alexander, and Liane Lefaivre.

Architecture in Europe since 1968: Memory and Innovation

New York: Rizzoli, 1992

Library call number

Name(s) of author(s) starting with last name of first author

Title and subtitle (if any)

Place of publication, publisher, date of publication

SOURCE CARD FOR AN ARTICLE

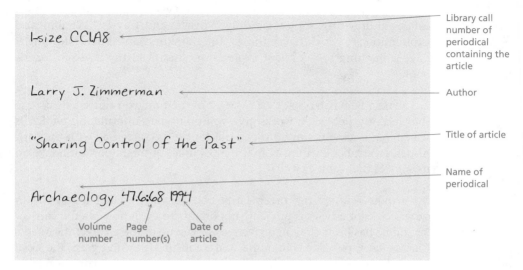

l-size CCIA8 ⟵ _____ Library call number of periodical containing the article

Larry J. Zimmerman ⟵ _____ Author

"Sharing Control of the Past" ⟵ _____ Title of article

_____ Name of periodical

Archaeology 47.6:68 1994
    Volume   Page   Date of
    number number(s) article

Once you actually get a particular source, make sure that the information on your source card is accurate and complete. Checking all this information now can save you trouble later, when you may not have the source in hand but will have to cite it fully and accurately.

Making Source Cards

EXERCISE 1

Using the card catalog and the list of serials, get the call numbers of one book and of one periodical containing an article that you would like to use in your research. Fill out a card for each source as shown above.

37.2 CHOOSING WHICH SOURCES TO CONSULT

As you work your way through reference books and catalogs, look for the following:

1. WORKS WITH OBVIOUS RELEVANCE TO YOUR TOPIC If your topic is whaling, you would certainly want to consult a book titled *Whale Hunt*, by

Nelson Cole Haley. But if your topic is nineteenth-century exploration in the South Pacific, you can ignore this book, even though you may find it cataloged under the subject heading "Voyages and Travels." Whaling and exploration are two different things, and the slim chance that Haley might have something to say about exploration doesn't justify a search for his book.

2. WORKS PUBLISHED RECENTLY   Most of the time you can safely assume that recently published works give you up-to-date information, which is valuable not just for current topics but for topics concerned with the past. Also, a recent book will usually cite most or all of the important books on its subject that came before it.

3. WORKS FREQUENTLY CITED   Any book or article cited frequently in other books or articles is probably important. To learn how often a particular source has been cited in a given year, see one of these three: the *Science Citation Index,* published bimonthly and cumulated every five years; the *Social Science Citation Index,* published three times a year and cumulated annually; and the *Arts & Humanities Citation Index,* published in the same way.

4. PRIMARY AND SECONDARY SOURCES   *Primary* means "first," and a primary source is one on which later, or secondary, sources are based. Depending on the subject, primary sources may be more or less valuable than secondary ones.

There are two kinds of primary sources: informational and authorial. An informational primary source is any firsthand account of an experience or discovery—an interview, a survey, an Arctic explorer's diary of an expedition, a scientist's report on the results of an experiment, a news story on a disaster written by someone who has seen it. Authorial primary sources are the writings of the individual you are studying. If you were writing a paper on James Baldwin, for instance, Baldwin's novels, essays, and letters would be your primary sources, and the critical essays that have been written *about* Baldwin's work would be your secondary sources.

If you are investigating a particular author or thinker, you should normally start by reading at least some of what he or she has written. But if you are investigating a person's life, an event, or a problem not tied to any particular works of literature, you do best to start with secondary sources and let them lead you to the primary ones. Secondary sources are further than primary sources from what they describe, but for that reason, they may give you a more detached, objective point of view.

5. **BOOKS WITH BIBLIOGRAPHIES** As shown in 36.5, the library catalog tells you whether or not the book has a bibliography—a list of related books and articles.

Sources You Should Consult

▶ Works with obvious relevance to your topic

▶ Works published recently

▶ Works frequently cited

▶ Primary and secondary sources

▶ Books with bibliographies

37.3 EXAMINING AND EVALUATING YOUR SOURCES

1. **ORGANIZE YOUR READING TIME.** List in order of importance the books and articles you plan to consult, and set up a reading schedule. Plan to finish all your reading and notetaking at least a week before the paper is due.

2. **READ SELECTIVELY.** If your source is a book, read the preface to get an idea of its scope and purpose. Then scan the table of contents and the index for specific discussions of your topic.

3. **READ RESPONSIBLY.** Respect the context of what you quote. Reading selectively doesn't mean reading carelessly or lifting statements out of context. To understand what you are quoting and to judge it adequately, you may have to read a good part of the section or chapter in which it appears—enough, at least, to familiarize yourself with the context.

4. **READ CRITICALLY.** If the writer gives opinions without facts to support them, or makes statements of "fact" without citing sources, you should be suspicious. (For more on this point, see p. 42, "Judging the Supporting Points in an Essay.") You should also compare your sources. If you find one of them more reliable or more persuasive than another, you're already beginning to see how you will present them in your paper.

37.4 TAKING NOTES

IDENTIFYING YOUR SOURCES

Before photocopying or taking notes on any source, be sure you have a source card or catalog printout on it (see 37.1). Then mark every copy or note with a short reference to the source and the pages you've used:

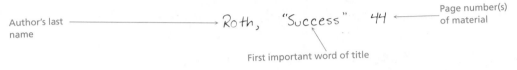

Author's last name ⟶ *Roth, "Success" 44* ⟵ Page number(s) of material

First important word of title

Every note you take must be marked with this information. Without it, you won't be able to cite the source of the note, and if you use the material without citing the source, you will be guilty of plagiarism (see 37.8).

PHOTOCOPYING

The simplest way to gather material for a research paper is to photocopy it. Copy completely any articles you plan to read. If you copy any pages from a book, be sure to mark them with a short reference to their source, as shown above. If you can't quickly decide what pages of a book you'll want to read, check it out of the library.

With all the convenience of photocopying, bear in mind that it's no substitute for reading, annotating, and highlighting or underlining the material you have thus gathered. Collecting source material is one thing; *digesting* it is another. (On exploring through reading, see 3.6.)

TAKING NOTES WITH A COMPUTER

Whether or not you have photocopied part of or all the material you plan to read, you will need to break it up into chunks small enough to use in your paper. The simplest way of doing so is with a computer. Once you've typed a note into the computer, you can call it up for use anywhere in your paper without retyping it. If you label each note with a headline, your notes will be much easier to arrange when you start writing. Each note is followed by a short reference to its source. If you add a comment of your own, you can begin to think about how you will use the note in your paper.

Whether or not you add a comment, however, you must be *absolutely certain to record your source.* If you fail to do so, you may confuse the source

```
COOPERATION:                                               ——— Headline

BETWEEN MUSEUMS AND NATIVE PEOPLES ◄


Alaska State Museum and Tlingets:

▶ joint ownership of some objects

▶ artifacts loaned to museums
                                                           ——— Source


(Roth 44) ◄
--------------------------------------------------------   ◄— Line of dashes
                                                               divides the
COOPERATION:                                                   notes.

ATTITUDE TOWARD REMAINS


Steve Henrikson, museum curator, on skeletal remains:


"We've obtained all the information the state of technology ◄——— Quotation

will allow. . . . There is the potential for advancement in

technology, but we don't believe that is sufficient reason

to keep the remains."

(Roth 45)
                                                           Student
Comment: Good to get a museum guy saying this. ◄——————      comment
```

material with your own words when you later call up the file for use in writing your paper.

You must also record the source of any material that you transfer to your computer electronically from a database. For such material you should create a separate file so that it cannot be confused with work of your own. Once this material is on your disk in a file of its own, you can easily transfer portions of it into your file of notes for the research paper, using headlines and short references just as if you were typing the passages from a printed text.

As you make your notes, you can add the information from each source card to a separate file called "Sources." Putting the author's last name first, enter each new item in alphabetical order:

Redhouse, David. <u>World Archaeological Congress-Home Page</u>.

22 March 1995. Updated 20 Oct. 1997. 2 Dec. 1998

<http://avebury.arch.soton.ac.uk/wac/>

Roth, Evan. "Success Stories." <u>Museum News</u> 71.1 (1991): 43-45.

Zimmerman, Larry J. "Sharing Control of the Past." <u>Archaeology</u>

47.6 (1994): 68.

For detailed guidance on writing the list of your sources in the research paper itself, see chapter 39.

TAKING NOTES ON INDEX CARDS

If you don't have access to a computer, the simplest way of taking notes is with a stack of index cards. Putting each note on a separate card considerably simplifies the task of arranging your notes when you start to organize your paper.

Use one whole card (four-by-six or five-by-seven inches) for each note. The larger size makes it easy to keep note cards separate from source cards and leaves room for comments of your own. (If a note is long, continue it on a second card, which can be stapled to the first.)

Headline ⟶ *Cooperation--attitude toward remains*

Quoted material ⟶ *"We've obtained all the information the state of technology will allow. . . . There is potential for advancements in technology, but we don't believe that is sufficient reason to keep the remains."*

--Steve Henrikson in Roth

Short reference to source ⟶ *Roth 45*

Student comment ⟶ *respectful attitude--*

37.5 USING MICROTEXTS

Because of storage problems, libraries have increased their use of micro-texts—printed material photographically reduced in size and readable only with the aid of mechanical viewers. Some excellent sources, such as complete files of major newspapers and magazines, may be available only in this form.

37.6 CONDUCTING AN INTERVIEW

An interview can enliven both the process of research and the finished product. Anyone with a special knowledge of your topic can be a living source of information that might not be readily available anywhere else. In addition, quotes and paraphrases from an interview can bring a special vitality to your paper.

To get as much as possible from an interview, we suggest you follow these steps:

1.   FIND THE RIGHT PERSON TO INTERVIEW.   Ask your instructor or the reference librarian if anyone working on the college staff or living in your area specializes in your topic. When Rick Harris asked a reference librarian for help in finding sources on sexual harrassment, for example, he was referred to the college's manager of personnel training and development.

2.   ARRANGE THE INTERVIEW BEFOREHAND.   Telephone the person to make an appointment. A face-to-face interview is best, but if that's not possible, make an appointment for a telephone interview. And however you conduct the interview, you should get advance permission if you plan to use a tape recorder.

3.   PREPARE YOUR QUESTIONS.   A good interviewer comes prepared with some preliminary knowledge of the topic gleaned from printed sources, and—most important—with a list of productive questions. Productive questions generally call for more than yes/no answers, and also for more than a simple expression of personal feeling. They call for information. Compare these questions:

a. How do you feel about smoking in restaurants?

b. Should smoking be banned in restaurants?

c. If all restaurants are required to maintain separate sections for smokers and nonsmokers, how will this requirement affect the restaurant business?

Question (a) invites a statement of personal feeling such as "I hate it," and question (b) invites a one-word answer: "yes" or "no." While such an answer can be helpful, only question (c) calls for the kind of information likely to enrich your paper.

Productive questions can be open-ended or pinpointed. An open-ended question stimulates a wide-ranging response, while a pinpointed question calls for a specific piece of information:

OPEN-ENDED: How have tobacco companies responded to the growing body of evidence that links smoking to cancer?

PINPOINTED: At what point—at what number of cigarettes a day—does smoking begin to pose a serious danger to health?

4. ASK FOLLOW-UP QUESTIONS WHENEVER YOU NEED TO CLARIFY A POINT. Though you should come to the interview with a list of questions prepared in advance, you should also be ready for surprises. If your interviewee says something unexpected or puzzling, ask for clarification.

5. TAKE CAREFUL NOTES OR TAPE THE INTERVIEW. The best way to record the whole interview is to get it on tape (with the permission of the interviewee) and then transcribe it. But if you don't have or can't use a tape recorder, make sure your notes are accurate and thorough.

6. AFTER THE INTERVIEW, CHECK YOUR QUOTATIONS WITH THE INTERVIEWEE. Make sure they are accurate and consistent with the context from which you've taken them. It's also courteous to send the interviewee a note of thanks and a copy of your paper.

EXERCISE 2   **Preparing an Interview**

Describe the kind of person you would most like to interview for your research paper and then make a list of at least six questions you would ask.

Conducting an Interview

- ▶ Find out who at your college or in your area specializes in your topic.
- ▶ Arrange the interview beforehand.
- ▶ Prepare your questions.
- ▶ Ask follow-up questions whenever you need to clarify a point.
- ▶ Take careful notes or tape the interview.
- ▶ After the interview, check your quotations with the interviewee.

37.7 FILLING GAPS IN YOUR RESEARCH

While you are rereading and sorting your notes, or even after you have decided what kind of paper you will write and what its thesis will be, you may discover that you need to know more about one or two things. You may suddenly realize that you have failed to consult an important source—one that several of your sources often refer to—or have failed to answer an important question. While sorting his own notes, for instance, Brandon noticed that one of his sources cited a promising article in *Archaeology*, but he had never seen the article itself. So he got a copy and made further notes before starting to write.

37.8 AVOIDING PLAGIARISM

Plagiarism is presenting the words or thoughts of another writer as if they were your own. When you submit a paper that is wholly or partly plagiarized, you are taking credit—or asking your teacher to give you credit—for work done by someone else. This is fundamentally dishonest and therefore wrong.

You commit plagiarism whenever you use a source *in any way* without precisely acknowledging what you have taken from it. Consider first this passage:

If the waking world has certain advantages of solidity and continuity, its social opportunities are terribly restricted. In it we meet, as a rule, only the neighbors, whereas the dream world offers the chance of intercourse, however fugitive, with our distant friends, our dead, and our gods. For normal men it is the sole experience in which they escape the offensive and incomprehensible bondage of time and space.

—E. R. Dodds, *The Greeks and the Irrational*
(1951; Boston: Beacon, 1957) 102.

Following are four ways of plagiarizing from this passage, with plagiarized material appearing in color. After three of the plagiarized passages we show the same material with correct acknowledgment, using the parenthetical form of citation that is explained in 39.1.

1. WORD-FOR-WORD, CONTINUOUS COPYING WITHOUT QUOTATION MARKS OR MENTION OF THE AUTHOR'S NAME:

Dreams help us satisfy another important psychic need—our need to vary our social life. This need is regularly thwarted in our waking moments. If the waking world has certain advantages of solidity and continuity, its social opportunities are terribly restricted. In it we meet, as a rule, only the neighbors, whereas the dream world offers the chance of intercourse, however fugitive, with our distant friends. We awaken from such encounters feeling refreshed, the dream having liberated us from the here and now.

CORRECT ACKNOWLEDGMENT

Dreams help us satisfy another important psychic need—our need to vary our social life. This need is regularly thwarted in our waking moments. "If," as one critic observes, "the waking world has certain advantages of solidity and continuity, its social opportunities are terribly restricted. In it we meet, as a rule, only the neighbors, whereas the dream world offers the chance of intercourse, however fugitive, with our distant friends" (Dodds 102). We awaken from such encounters feeling refreshed, the dream having liberated us from the here and now.

2. CITING THE AUTHOR BUT COPYING MANY WORDS AND PHRASES WITHOUT QUOTATION MARKS, SO THAT THE READER HAS NO WAY OF KNOWING WHO HAS WRITTEN WHAT:

Dreams help us satisfy another important psychic need—our need to vary our social life. In the waking world our social opportunities are terribly restricted. As a rule, we usually encounter only the neighbors. In the dream world, on the other hand, we have a slight chance of meeting our distant friends. For most of us it is the sole experience in which we escape the bondage of time and space (Dodds 102).

We show no correct acknowledgment in this case because a passage stuffed with short quotations needs more than quotation marks. Such a passage needs rewriting to make the quotation more selective.

3. PARAPHRASING THE PASSAGE—EXPRESSING ITS MEANING IN YOUR OWN WORDS—WITHOUT MENTION OF THE AUTHOR'S NAME:

> Dreams help us satisfy another important psychic need—our need to vary our social life. When awake, we are creatures of this time and this place. Those we meet are usually those we live near and work with. When dreaming, on the other hand, we can meet far-off friends. We awaken refreshed by our flight from the here and now.

CORRECT ACKNOWLEDGMENT

> Dreams help us satisfy another important psychic need—our need to vary our social life. E. R. Dodds observes that when we are awake, we are creatures of this time and this place. Those we meet are usually those we live near and work with. When dreaming, however, we can meet far-off friends (102). We awaken refreshed by our flight from the here and now.

4. TAKING THE AUTHOR'S IDEA WITHOUT ACKNOWLEDGING THE SOURCE:

> Dreams help us satisfy another important psychic need—the need for a change. They liberate us from the here and now, taking us out of the world we normally live in.

CORRECT ACKNOWLEDGMENT

> Dreams help us satisfy another important psychic need—the need for a change. According to E. R. Dodds, they liberate us from the here and now, taking us out of the world we normally live in (102).

This summary of Dodds's passage includes the word *world*, which also appears in the original. Generally, an individual word can be taken from the source without quotation marks unless the author of the source has coined it or used it in a special way. But any string of two or more words from the source must appear with quotation marks.

Read this two-paragraph passage. Then read the summary that follows, and indicate whether any part of the summary—besides the word *motifs*—should be in quotation marks.

> And, speaking more generally, it is plain foolishness to believe in ready-made systematic guides to dream interpretation, as if one could simply buy a reference book and look up a particular symbol. No dream symbol can be separated from the individual who dreams it, and there is no definite or straightforward interpretation of any 5 dream. Each individual varies so much in the way that his unconscious complements or compensates his conscious mind that it is impossible to be sure how far dreams and their symbols can be classified at all.
>
> It is true that there are dreams and single symbols (I should prefer to call them "motifs") that are typical and often occur. Among 10 such motifs are falling, flying, being persecuted by dangerous animals or hostile men, being insufficiently or absurdly clothed in public places, being in a hurry or lost in a milling crowd, fighting with useless weapons or being wholly defenseless, running hard yet getting nowhere. A typical infantile motif is the dream of growing infinitely 15 small or infinitely big, or being transformed from one to the other— as you find it, for instance, in Lewis Carroll's *Alice in Wonderland*. But I must stress again that these are motifs that must be considered in the context of the dream itself, not as self-explanatory ciphers.
>
> —Carl G. Jung, "Approaching the Unconscious,"
> *Man and His Symbols*, ed. Jung and M.-L. von Franz
> (Garden City: Doubleday, 1964) 53.

SUMMARY: According to Carl G. Jung in "Approaching the Unconscious," it would be just plain foolishness for anyone to think he or she could interpret dreams reliably by buying a ready-made reference book. No such guide has value because it is impossible to separate a dream symbol from the person who dreams it, and the unconscious of everyone is unique. Jung does admit that certain dreams and symbols come often to many. Calling these "motifs," he lists several, including falling, fighting with useless weapons, and running hard yet getting nowhere. But he emphasizes that even the motifs cannot be understood properly unless considered in the context of each dream itself.

Writing the Research Paper 38

38.1 FORMULATING YOUR THESIS

The best way to formulate a thesis is to review all of your notes, especially if you've taken them with headlines and comments (see 37.4). Rereading your notes gives you a concentrated view of all your research, and thus helps you decide—if you haven't already—what basic question you will try to answer. In rereading his notes, Scott observed that the NAGPRA debate among Native Americans, scientists, and museum curators tended to bring out the best and the worst in these groups. When groups on different sides of the issue approached each other with respect, they were able to create solutions. When groups insisted on only defending their position, they weren't even able to hold a productive dialogue. After writing several versions of his thesis, he decided that the following sentence best summarized his insight: "NAGPRA has produced conflict stalemate when parties have insisted on furthering only their own interests and conflict resolution when each party has been willing to respect the interests of the others."

38.2 MAKING AN OUTLINE

Once you have made a collection of notes and formulated a thesis, you may feel no strong need for an outline—especially if your notes are labeled with headlines for quick reference. But even though you may have plenty of clearly labeled notes, you must still decide how to organize the argument that will incorporate the material from those notes. In other words, you must still decide the order of your main points. This is what the making of an outline helps you to do.

To prepare yourself to make an outline, arrange your notes under separate headings. If your notes are in a computer file, print them out so that you can see their connections; then rearrange them on the screen so that notes about related points are grouped together. If your notes are on index cards, sort them into separate piles for each heading of your topic.

Once you have established your main headings, you must decide what arrangement of them will best serve to develop your thesis. To plot the arrangement, you can draft a *branching diagram* or a *topic outline*. Then, if you want to make your plan quite definite or if your teacher requires it, you can draft a *full-sentence outline*. We illustrate all three below, together with some revisions of the thesis and the adding of a conclusion in the sentence outline.

BRANCHING DIAGRAM

THESIS: The Native American Graves Protection and Repatriation Act has produced conflict stalemate when parties have insisted on furthering only their own interests and conflict resolution when each party has been willing to respect the interests of the others.

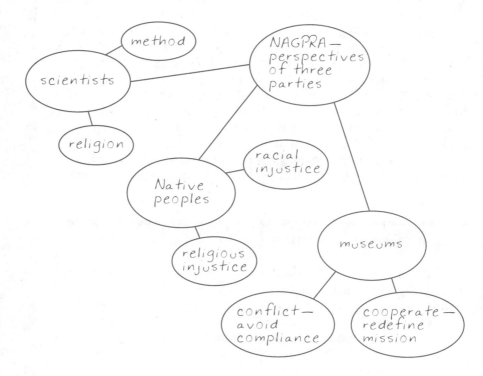

TOPIC OUTLINE

THESIS: The Native American Graves Protection and Repatriation Act has produced conflict stalemate when parties have insisted on furthering only their own interests and conflict resolution when each party has been willing to respect the interests of the others.

I. The scientific community
    A. NAGPRA prevents scientific inquiry and offers unfair protection to Native American religion
    B. American Committee for Preservation of Archaeological Collections (ACPAC)
    C. Meighan's perspective
II. The Native American community
    A. NAGPRA redresses racial injustice
    B. NAGPRA redresses religious injustice
    C. Native American approach to cultural preservation
    D. Conflict between Hopi tribe and museums
III. Museums
    A. Museums that resist complying
    B. Museums that comply and redefine their cultural mission
    C. World Archeological Congress—cooperation with Native peoples
IV. Conflict resolution/conflict stalemate
    A. Resolution—museums working with Native groups
        1. University of Nebraska at Omaha and Omaha tribes
        2. Alaska State Museum and Tlinget tribes

FULL-SENTENCE OUTLINE

THESIS: The Native American Graves Protection and Repatriation Act has produced conflict stalemate when parties have insisted on furthering only their own interests and conflict resolution when each party has been willing to respect the interests of the others.

I. The scientific community has been the most vocal in protesting NAGPRA.
    A. It maintains that the law prevents scientific inquiry and offers unfair protection to a specific religious perspective.
    B. The American Committee for Preservation of Archaeological Collections (ACPAC) has been the most powerful voice representing scientists' interests where NAGPRA is concerned.

C. From the perspective of archeologists like Meighan, the knowledge gained from scientific study is beneficial to everyone, no matter their race or religious creed.

II. Native Americans see NAGPRA as both restitution for past injustices and public confirmation of the legitimacy of their culture and history.

A. Native Americans have suffered racial injustices at the hands of scientists.

B. Native Americans have suffered religious injustices as well.

C. The argument that scientists are helping to preserve Native American culture through excavation and study is not very convincing to most Native peoples.

D. Further conflict between scientists and Native groups has arisen as provisions in the law have been implemented.

III. NAGPRA has caused both work and turmoil for museums.

A. Some museums are perpetuating the conflict. Believing that NAGPRA is preventing them from preserving heritage by taking away materials and information, some have refused to comply with the sanctions imposed by NAGPRA.

B. While some museums perpetuate the problem, other museums are adapting to the law and reestablishing their positions as the preservers of heritage.

C. Many museums are responding to Zimmerman's (WAC) call to action and working closely with Native American tribes.

IV. Conclusion: As with any action involving several parties, NAGPRA works best when all parties approach it in good faith.

A. The museums and Native American tribes who are working together are splendid examples of conflict resolution.

B. Some of the responses to NAGPRA illustrate the kind of stalemate that can result when there is no good-faith effort to right the wrongs of the past; other responses demonstrate what can happen when different parties are willing to respect the interests of others and together create a better future for everyone.

Documenting the Research Paper

39

In the final draft of your research paper, you must clearly identify all the sources you have quoted from, summarized, or paraphrased. To do this you will need a style of documentation.

Styles of documentation are established by professional societies and journals to regularize the citing of sources in each field. Though each field has its own special requirements, scientists and social scientists often cite their sources by parenthetical reference rather than numbered notes, and parenthetical citing has been adopted by many humanists also. This chapter explains just one kind of parenthetical citation; it offers a simplified version of the MLA style, which has been recommended by the Modern Language Association for research papers on literature, philosophy, art, and other subjects in the humanities. For styles of documentation in the social sciences and natural sciences, see chapter 42.

39.1 THE MLA PARENTHETICAL STYLE: BASIC PROCEDURES

Complete information on the MLA style appears in the fifth edition of the *MLA Handbook for Writers of Research Papers,* by Joseph Gibaldi (New York: MLA, 1999). Here we explain briefly how to use the MLA style with the kinds of sources you are likely to cite in a research paper written for a college course.

Citing with parentheses calls for two steps: citing each source in parentheses as you use it, and making a list of Works Cited at the end of your paper—an alphabetical list of all the sources you have used. We treat each step in turn.

PARENTHETICAL CITING

1. Cite the source in parentheses immediately after the material used:

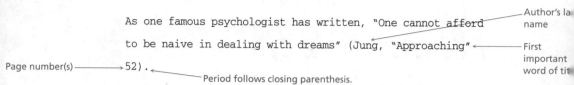

As one famous psychologist has written, "One cannot afford

to be naive in dealing with dreams" (Jung, "Approaching"

52).

Author's last name

First important word of title

Page number(s)

Period follows closing parenthesis.

2. If the author of your source has written no other work cited in your paper, give just the author's last name and the page number(s):

As one traffic analyst observes, no police force can arrest

everyone who violates a traffic law (Gardiner 5).

3. If you use the author's name to introduce the source, do not repeat the name in parentheses. Give just the page number(s):

As Carl Jung says, "One cannot afford to be naive in dealing

with dreams" (52).

But use a title word before the page number(s) if you are citing another work by the same author elsewhere in the paper:

According to Margaret Mead, all of us need to define our-

selves by making some mark on the place we occupy or putting

a special object there (Blackberry 12).

4. When quoting a passage that must be indented from your text because it is more than four lines long, put the citation one space *after* the final punctuation mark:

Virginia Woolf writes as follows about the role of women in

literature and history:

> A very queer, composite being thus emerges.
>
> Imaginatively she is of the highest importance;
>
> practically she is completely insignificant. She

pervades poetry from cover to cover; she is all

but absent from history. She dominates the lives

of kings and conquerors in fiction; in fact she

was the slave of any boy whose parents forced a

ring upon her finger. (60)

5. If all your quotations come from just one source, as in a paper written about a work of fiction, cite the source by page number(s) alone—*after* mentioning the author and title in your text:

Meridel Le Sueur's "The Girl" is the story of what hap-

pens when a prim, unmarried, unnamed schoolteacher sets out

to drive alone from Southern California to San Francisco.

. . . But the story makes it clear that in rejecting his

desires, she also stifles her own, dooming herself to a life

of repressive order in which she will "never never change"

(212).

For guidance in treating plays and poems, which are often *not* cited by page number(s), see 39.2, items 25–27.

6. If your use of source material ends in the middle of a sentence, you may put the citation there:

During the ride itself, neither her fear of being touched

nor her annoyance at being flattered "just as if she were

any common slut" (209) can altogether keep her from showing

off.

LISTING THE WORKS CITED

Start the list on a separate page at the end of your paper. All the works you have cited should be listed alphabetically by the author's last name, or by the title if the source is unsigned:

Author's last name first, starting at margin

Deacon, Terence W. The Symbolic Species: The Co-Evolution of

Language and the Brain. New York: Norton, 1997.

Book title and subtitle (if any) underlined

Title of article in quotation marks

Kermode, Frank. "Sensing Endings." Nineteenth Century

Fiction 33 (1978): 144-58.

Journal title underlined

Volume and year of journal

Place of publication, publisher, date of publication

Le Sueur, Meridel. "The Girl." Ripening: Selected Work,

1927-1980. Ed. Elaine Hedges. Old Westbury: The

Feminist Press, 1982. 204-12.

Edited by

Page numbers of work in edited book

Mead, Margaret. Blackberry Winter. New York: Morrow, 1972.

Three hyphens plus a period signify another work by the same author.

Woolf, Virginia. The Death of the Moth and Other Essays. New

York: Harcourt, 1942.

---. A Room of One's Own. New York: Fountain, 1929.

The simplest way to use parenthetical citation is to compile your Works Cited while making parenthetical references in your paper. Some software, such as *Norton Textra Writer,* offers a special Works Cited function. With other software, you can create a "Workcit" file for your Works Cited. Then split the screen each time you make a parenthetical reference, switch to the "Workcit" file, and write the full reference there, as explained in the following section. If you keep the alphabetical order as you insert each new entry in the "Workcit" file, your list of Works Cited will be ready to print just as soon as you've finished writing the paper.

If you aren't using a computer or can't split the computer screen, make a source card for each work you cite (as explained earlier in 37.1). When you've finished the paper, alphabetize the cards and then write the list according to the instructions given here.

Following are guidelines for parenthetically citing and then listing various kinds of sources. Most of what you need to know is *illustrated* by examples rather than explained by detailed commentary, so you should study each example carefully.

39.2 CITING AND LISTING VARIOUS SOURCES

(For *CMS*, APA, and CBE styles, see part 5.)

BOOK

1. **BOOK BY ONE AUTHOR**

One argument in <u>Rethinking the Rhetorical Tradition</u> is that "in the standard account in the histories of rhetoric Gorgias either exemplifies bad philosophy or, at best, makes the trivial point that the practice of rhetoric can be abused" (Kastely 30).

Kastely, James L. <u>Rethinking the Rhetorical Tradition</u>. New
Haven: Yale UP, 1997.

University Press

2. **BOOK BY TWO OR THREE AUTHORS**

One school of thought holds that "the most complicated as-pect of race relations in America today concerns attitude" (Kinder and Sanders 6).

Kinder, Donald R., and Lynn M. Sanders. <u>Divided by Color:
Racial Politics and Democratic Ideals</u>. Chicago: U of
Chicago P, 1996.

All lines after the first in each entry are indented five spaces.

3. **BOOK BY FOUR OR MORE AUTHORS**

Some contend that the "cold war, like its 'hot' counterpart, is a contest" (Medhurst et al. 19).

Medhurst, Martin J., Robert L. Ivie, Philip Wander, and
Robert L. Scott. <u>Cold War Rhetoric: Strategy, Metaphor,
and Ideology</u>. New York: Greenwood, 1990.

Double-space between and within entries.

583

or

Medhurst, Martin L., et al. <u>Cold War Rhetoric: Strategy,</u>
    <u>Metaphor, and Ideology</u>. New York: Greenwood, 1990.

4. **MORE THAN ONE BOOK BY THE SAME AUTHOR**

Cornell West critiques religious fundamentalism as an elite
form of nationalism that is "fanned by elites within nation-
states" (<u>Prophetic Reflections</u> 134). West also maintains
that the "prophetic Christian tradition" offers a "moral vision and ethical norms (that) propel human intellectual activity to account for and transform existing forms of dogma-
tism, oppression and despair" (<u>Keeping the Faith</u> 134).

West, Cornel. <u>Keeping Faith: Philosophy and Race in America</u>.
    New York: Routledge, 1993.

---. <u>Prophetic Reflections: Notes on Race and Power in</u>
    <u>America</u>. Monroe: Common Courage, 1993.

5. **BOOK WITH EDITOR**

Green explains that "full and free public discussion and debate is an absolute prerequisite to any process of democratic decision making" (164).

Green, Philip, ed. <u>Democracy: Key Concepts in Critical</u>
    <u>Theory</u>. Atlantic Highlands: Humanities, 1993.

6. **MULTIVOLUME WORK**

"Having witnessed the corruption of the English government
at first hand," Smith writes, colonists who had visited England "were determined to preserve America from exploitation
and repression" (1: 151).

————————————————————————————— Volume number

Smith, Page. <u>A New Age Now Begins</u>. 2 vols. New York: McGraw,

1976.

7. **MATERIAL QUOTED BY YOUR SOURCE**

Robert G. Templin, Jr., dean of instruction at Piedmont Community College in Virginia, says that better-off students
are "squeezing out the poor, disadvantaged, and minority
students who once called the community college theirs" (qtd.
in Watkins 1).

Watkins, Beverly T. "2-Year Colleges Told They're Becoming
Institutions for Middle Class Students." <u>Chronicle of
Higher Education</u> 11 Apr. 1984: 1.

8. **AN INTRODUCTION, FOREWORD, OR AFTERWORD**

Rhetoric is both a discipline and a cultural practice,
"profoundly implicated in a large array of other disciplines
and practices, from politics to literature to religion"
(Rebhorn ix).

Rebhorn, Wayne. Introduction. <u>Rhetoric Reclaimed: Aristotle
and the Liberal Arts Tradition</u>. By Janet M. Atwill.
Ithaca: Cornell UP, 1998.

9. **EDITION AFTER THE FIRST**

"The most important feature of the nucleus is the genetic material" (Lewin 41).

Lewin, Benjamin. <u>Genes VI</u>. 6th ed. Oxford: Oxford UP, 1997.

10. **REPRINT**

"During the crisis," Angelou writes, "Black people had often made more money in a month than they had seen in their whole lives" (2).

Angelou, Maya. <u>Gather Together in My Name</u>. 1974. New York: Bantam, 1993.

Date originally published

11. **TRANSLATION**

The main character, Chantal, has a dream that disturbs her: "Her discomfort from the dream was so extreme that she went to some effort to figure out the reason for it" (Kundera 4).

Kundera, Milan. <u>Identity</u>. Trans. Linda Asher. New York: HarperCollins, 1998.

12. **CORPORATE AUTHOR**

<u>Resources for Teaching Middle School Science</u> describes how students can perform complicated experiments that "explore the melting points and conductivity of ionic and covalent compounds" (14).

National Science Resource Center. <u>Resources for Teaching</u>

<u>Middle School Science</u>. Washington: National Academy P,

1998.

13. GOVERNMENT PUBLICATION

In any case, a census taken in 1982 showed that less than
half the working mothers of young children had them supervised by a relative other than their father (USBC 9-10).

Beyond such formalities and regulations, some organizations
require that managers set an example of fairness in their
own behavior. As one training manual notes, their "doing"
will be closely scrutinized by employees sensitive to non-
verbal messages (USDI 38).

U.S. Bureau of Census [USBC]. <u>Child-Care Arrangements of</u>

<u>Working Mothers: June 1982</u>. Washington: GPO, 1983.

U.S. Department of the Interior [USDI]. <u>Training in the</u>

<u>Prevention of Sexual Harassment</u>. Rept. 637. Washington:

GPO, 1987.

14. BIBLE

Edith Wharton based <u>House of Mirth</u> on the biblical saying
"The heart of the wise is in the house of mourning; but the
heart of fools is in the house of mirth" (Ecclesiastes
7.4).

<u>Holy Bible</u>. King James Version. Nashville: Regency, 1973.

ARTICLE OR ESSAY

15. ESSAY OR ANY OTHER SHORT WORK IN BOOK

"Jefferson," writes Cox, "sees his life as a history of
himself" (133).

Hemingway's description of Macomber's death is coolly technical. Firing a 6.5 Mannlicher, we are told, Mrs. Macomber
"hit her husband about two inches up and a little to one
side of the base of his skull" (36).

Cox, James M. "Recovering Literature's Lost Ground Through
    Autobiography." Autobiography: Essays Theoretical and
    Critical. Ed. James Olney. Princeton: Princeton UP,
    1980. 123-45.

Hemingway, Ernest. "The Short Happy Life of Francis
    Macomber." The Short Stories of Ernest Hemingway. New
    York: Scribner's, 1938. 3-37.

16. ARTICLE IN A MONTHLY MAGAZINE

Sharp believes that "with a double platinum album already
under his belt, Silkk the Shocker is on the verge of super-
stardom" (136).

Sharp, Sean Lewis. "Love or Money." The Source Mar. 1999:
    130-38.

Abbrevi
month
names
longer t
four let

17. **ARTICLE IN A SCHOLARLY JOURNAL**

Professor Noland thinks that primary education cannot take
sole responsibility for the decline in poetry in the classroom but that "the very rhythm of academic life would seem
to dictate a shift away from poetry toward prose" (40).

Noland, Carrie. "Poetry at Stake: Blaise Cendrars, Cultural
    Studies, and the Future of Poetry in the Literature
    Classroom." <u>PMLA</u> 112 <u>(1997)</u>: 40-55.

Volume
number

18. **ARTICLE IN A REFERENCE BOOK**

The city of Chattanooga is situated "on a bend in the
Tennessee River, near a natural opening in the southern
Appalachians" (Ezzell 139).

Ezzell, Timothy P. "Chattanooga." <u>The Tennessee Encyclopedia</u>
    <u>of History and Culture</u>. 1998 ed.

19. **ARTICLE IN A DAILY NEWSPAPER, SIGNED**

A reporter from the <u>New York Times</u> reports that "a biparti-
san group of Senators will propose a plan on Thursday to
deal with Social Security's looming problems . . . an issue
that had seemed all but dead this year" (Stevenson).

Stevenson, Richard W. "Congress and White House Try to Break
    Social Security Deadlock." <u>New York Times</u> 20 May 1999,
    natl. ed.: A23.

Specify the
edition.

20. ARTICLE IN A DAILY NEWSPAPER, UNSIGNED

Use the first few words of the title as your in-text parenthetical citation.

> William H. Gates and his wife, Melinda, donated $5 million
> to the United Way of Santa Clara County ("Microsoft Head").

> "Microsoft Head Donates to Silicon Valley Causes." <u>New York</u>
>   <u>Times</u> 20 May 1999, natl. ed.: A23. ◄─────────────── Page
>   number of
>   section A
>   ─ Edition

21. EDITORIAL

Signed editorial:

> Historian Warren Goldstein maintains that "historians
> haven't figured out how to articulate the values and methods
> of our discipline so that non-historians are even faintly
> interested in them" (" 'Dutch' " A80).

> Goldstein, Warren. " 'Dutch': an Object Lesson for History
>   and Biography." Editorial. <u>Chronicle of Higher</u>
>   <u>Education</u> 15 Oct. 1999: A80.

Unsigned editorial:

> As an editorial in the <u>New York Times</u> observes, "hundreds of
> thousands of displaced ethnic Albanians need to be safely
> resettled in Kosovo before freezing temperatures return to
> the Balkans" ("Before Winter" A28).

> "Before Winter Arrives in Kosovo." Editorial. <u>New York Times</u>
>   20 May 1999, natl. ed.: A28.

22. **WORK FROM AN ANTHOLOGY**

"Every native of every place is a potential tourist,"
Kincaid explains, "and every tourist is a native of somewhere" (Kincaid 321).

Kincaid, Jamaica. "The Ugly Tourist." <u>The Norton Reader</u>.
>Linda H. Peterson, John C. Brereton, and Joan E.
>Hartman. New York: Norton, 1999. 320-22.

23. **WORK IN A COLLECTION WITH MORE THAN ONE EDITOR**

In <u>Birth of a Nation'hood</u>, Morrison and Lacor observe that
"the story of O.J. Simpson on trial sold well" (3).

Morrison, Toni, and Claudia Broadsky Lacor, eds. <u>Birth of a</u>
>   <u>Nation'hood: Gaze, Script, and Spectacle in the O.J.</u>
>   <u>Simpson Case</u>. New York: Pantheon, 1997.

24. **WORKS BY DIFFERENT AUTHORS CITED FROM ONE BOOK**

As St. John and Byce observe, the Department of Education
helps college students in two ways: through Pell Grants
and Guaranteed Student Loans (24). According to one
investigator, students are reluctant to borrow because
of "deep-seated fears about excessive repayment burdens"
(Hauptman 70).

List the book under the name of its editor and use that name for cross-
reference.

Hauptman, Arthur M. "Shaping Alternative Loan Programs."
>   Kramer 69-82.

Kramer, Martin, ed. <u>Meeting Student Aid Needs in a Period of</u>
<u>Retrenchment</u>. New Directions for Higher Education 40. San
Francisco: Jossey-Bass, 1982.

St. John, Edward P., and Charles Byce. "The Changing Federal
Role in Student Aid." Kramer 21-40.

LITERARY WORK

25. PLAY WITH ACT, SCENE, AND LINE NUMBERS

Don't cite page numbers. Use arabic numerals with periods between them
to indicate act, scene, and line number(s).

In Shakespeare's <u>Romeo and Juliet</u>, Romeo sees Juliet as "the
sun" of his universe (2.2.3).

If you're asked to cite plays with roman numerals, use uppercase for the
act, lowercase for the scene, and arabic numeral(s) for the line number(s).

Shakespeare's Romeo sees Juliet as "the sun" of his universe
(II.ii.3).

Shakespeare, William. <u>Romeo and Juliet</u>. Ed. John E. Hankins.
Baltimore: Penguin, 1970.

26. POEM WITH NUMBERED LINES

Cite it by the lines, not by page number.

In Robert Frost's "Death of the Hired Man," one character
speaks of home as "the place where, when you have to go
there / They have to take you in" (lines 118-19).

Use the whole word "line" or "lines" in the first reference. Then just give
the numbers.

But his wife calls home "something you somehow haven't to deserve" (120).

Frost, Robert. "The Death of the Hired Man." <u>The Poetry of Robert Frost</u>. Ed. Edward Connery Lathem. New York: Holt, 1969. 34–40.

27. **POEM WITH NUMBERED SECTIONS AND NUMBERED LINES**

A poem without numbered lines may be cited by its title alone.

In "Cape Breton," Bishop speaks of mist hanging in thin layers "like rotting snow-ice sucked away / almost to spirit."

Bishop, Elizabeth. "Cape Breton." <u>The Complete Poems</u>. New York: Farrar, 1969. 75–77.

ELECTRONIC SOURCE

Here is the general format for citing online sources:

1. Author of Web site should come first, if it is available.
2. Title of Web site. (If author's name is not available, begin with title of Web site.)
3. Publication dates.
   ▶ If site is an online version of a published journal, give date of original publication first, then online publication second.
   ▶ If no date is provided, indicate with *n.d.*
4. Date site was accessed.
5. Web site address.

On *The Columbia Guide to Online Style,* see p. 554, "Additional Online Reference Sources."

28. WORLD WIDE WEB

Personal Web site:

Mostern, together with other scholars in cultural, literary, and ethnic studies, maintains that many of the concerns of postmodernism are compatible with traditional Marxist thought.

Mostern, Kenneth. Home page. 25 August 1998. 8 Nov. 1999
<http://web.utk.edu/~kmostern/hybridmarx.html>.

Professional Web site with no author:

A great deal of recent scholarship in classical studies focuses on gender roles in ancient Greece ("What's New?").

"What's New?" Diotoma. 25 Oct. 1999. 8 Nov. 1999
<http://www.uky.edu/AS/Classics/nova.html>.

29. ONLINE JOURNAL

Signed article:

The educational pilot project is "based on the conviction that public education is an important way to increase under-standing and appreciation for the past" (Krass).

Krass, Dorothy Schlotthauer. "Archaeology Education Coordi-nator Pilot Project Enters Second Year." Society for American Archaeology Bulletin 14.5 (1996). 24 June 1999
<http://www.sscf.ucsb.edu/SAABulletin/14.5/SAA11.html>.

Unsigned article:

> The Confederated Tribes of the Umatilla Indian Reservation
> claimed the 9,300-year-old skeletal remains because they
> were uncovered in Umatilla aboriginal land ("9,300-Year-Old
> Skeleton").

"9,300-Year-Old Skeleton Sparks Controversy in Northwest."
> Society for American Archaeology Bulletin 14.5 (1996).
> 24 June 1999 <http://www.sscf.ucsb.edu/SAABulletin/
> 14.5/SAA5.html>.

30. ONLINE NEWSPAPER

> A reporter from Seattle Times observes that "anthropologists
> and tribes across the nation have their eyes cast on this
> unfolding drama on the University of Nebraska-Lincoln (UNL)
> campus, where the conflict between scientific research
> and respect for Native traditions is being played out"
> (Henderson).

Henderson, Diedtra. "Human Bones: What to Do With Them?"
> Seattletimes.com 11 Oct. 1998. 24 June 1999
> <http://www.seattletimes.com/news/health-
> science/htm198/bone_101198.html>.

31. ONLINE EDITORIAL

> The Chattanooga News Free Press takes a hard stance on what
> it describes as "the growing evils of expanded legalized
> gambling" ("Gambling").

"Gambling and Politics." Editorial. <u>Chattanooga News Free</u>
<u>Press Online</u> 24 June 1999 <http://207.69.235.40/
opinion/fpedit/1999/Jun/Jun241999fpedit2.html>.

32. ONLINE BOOK

Austen describes Emma Woodhouse as "handsome, clever, and
rich."

Austen, Jane. <u>Emma</u>. Sunsite Manager. University of California, Berkeley. 25 June 1999
<http://sunsite.berkeley.edu/Literature/Austen/Emma/
1emma1.html>.

33. EMAIL

When citing an email, the title of the email should be the subject line.

Swoope explains that one way to unravel the affirmative
action debate is to view opportunity in light of sociological theories of "life chances."

Swoope, Lenika. "Re: Affirmative Action Topic." Email to
Janet Atwill. 15 Nov. 1998.

34. ONLINE POSTING

Kent Strock observes that Pierre Bourdieu's theories of
culture are inadequate for a late-capitalist society.

Strock, Kent. "Re: Bourdieu and Phenomenology." Online
posting. 6 Aug. 1999. Bourdieu Forum. 8 Nov. 1999
<gopher://lists.village.virginia.edu:70/. . . s/
spoons/bourdieu.archive/bourdieu.9908>.

OTHER MEDIA OR SOURCE

35. CD-ROM

According to the CIA, Macedonia is faced with the prospect
of a "move down to a bare subsistence level of life
unless economic ties are reforged or enlarged with its
neighbors Serbia and Montenegro, Albania, Greece, and Bul-
garia."

The CIA Works Factbook. CD-ROM. Minneapolis: Quanta, 1993.

36. MOVIE

In Pirates of Silicon Valley, Noah Wyle plays Steve Jobs and
Anthony Michael Hall plays Bill Gates.

Pirates of Silicon Valley. Dir. Martyn Burke. Perf. Noah
    Wyle and Anthony Michael Hall. TNT Original, June 26,
    1999.

37. INTERVIEW

Marion King said that during the Depression "her family was
the only one to own their own home."

King, Marion. Personal interview. 15 January 1998.

38. MACHINE-READABLE DOCUMENT

"To err is human, and to write is to experience the human
inevitability of error" (Heffernan, Getting 4).

Heffernan, James A. W. Getting the Red Out: Grading without
    Degrading. ERIC, 1983. ED 229 788.

39. PERFORMANCE

A performance of Shakespeare's <u>Much Ado About Nothing</u> once again demonstrated how much his language can achieve theatrically without the aid of elaborate sets.

<u>Much Ado About Nothing</u>. By William Shakespeare. Dir. Terry Hands. Perf. Derek Jacobi, Sinead Cusack, and the Royal Shakespeare Company. Gershwin Theatre, New York. 19 Oct. 1984.

40. TELEVISION PROGRAM

This season, <u>Real World</u> takes place in Hawaii.

<u>Real World</u>. MTV, Knoxville. 26 June 1999.

41. LECTURE

According to Dr. Jameson, "social class" is a complex notion that includes attitudes as well as material resources.

Jameson, William. "Class Structure." Class lecture. Sociology 320. University of Tennessee, Knoxville. 26 Jan. 1998.

42. RECORDING

Frost's own reading of "Birches" fully exploits the resonance of its language.

Frost, Robert. "Birches." <u>Robert Frost Reads His Poetry</u>. Caedmon, 1956.

43. ARTWORK

The vortex that became Turner's trademark first appeared in

his <u>Snow Storm: Hannibal and His Army Crossing the Alps</u>.

Turner, J. M. W. <u>Snow Storm: Hannibal and His Army Crossing</u>

<u>the Alps</u>. 1812. The Tate Gallery, London.

44. SPEECH

Secretary-General Annan says, "Brazil has, in short, built

up and lived by a culture of peace."

Secretary-General Annan, Kofi. "Culture of Peace." Press

Release. Ministry for Foreign Affairs, Brasilia. 13

July 1998.

Citing with Parentheses—MLA Style

EXERCISE

Use the information given on each source to write two entries in the MLA style: a parenthetical citation as it would look in the text, and the entry as it would appear in a list of Works Cited.

EXAMPLE: The source is a book by Paul Fussell entitled *The Great War and Modern Memory.* It was published by Oxford University Press in 1975. The first place of publication listed is New York. Your reference is to material on pages 96 and 97. In the text you introduce the material without mentioning Fussell's name. You are using no other book by him.

PARENTHETICAL CITATION:

(Fussell 96–97)

IN WORKS CITED:

Fussell, Paul. <u>The Great War and Modern Memory</u>. New York:

Oxford UP, 1975.

(Continued on p. 600.)

1. Your source is a book titled *A Literature of Their Own,* subtitled *British Women Novelists from Brontë to Lessing.* It was published in 1977 by Princeton University Press, which is located in Princeton, NJ. You refer to material on pages 121, 122, and 123, and you use the author's name (Elaine Showalter) to introduce the material.

2. The source is a book by Joseph Conrad entitled *Lord Jim.* It was edited by Thomas C. Moser and published by W. W. Norton & Company, Inc., in 1995. The place of publication is listed as New York. Your reference, a direct quotation, is to something the editor states in the preface on page vi, and you mention him by name when introducing the quotation. You are using no other work edited or written by Moser.

3. Your source is a book by Ngũgĩ wa Thiong'o. It is called *Decolonizing the Mind: The Politics of Language in African Literature.* It was published in 1986 by Heinemann Educational Books, Inc., in London. You introduce the material without using the author's name, and the material comes from page 86.

4. The source is an essay by Stuart Levine entitled "Emerson and Modern Social Concepts." The essay is one of several essays by different authors in a book entitled *Emerson: Prospect and Retrospect.* The essay appears on pages 155 through 178 of the book. The editor of the book is Joel Porte. The book was published in 1982 by Harvard University Press. The place of publication is Cambridge, Massachusetts. Your reference is to page 156, and you mention Levine by name in the text.

5. The source is an article by George F. Kennan entitled "America's Unstable Soviet Policy." It appears on pages 71 through 80 of *The Atlantic Monthly,* a monthly magazine published by The Atlantic Monthly Company. The place of publication is Boston, MA. Kennan's article is printed in the November 1982 issue. You quote two sentences from page 79, but do not mention Kennan. You are using another work by him, *The Nuclear Delusion.*

6. The source is Victor Hugo's *Les Misérables* in the translation by Norman Denny. The edition is in two volumes, each with its own pagination; that is, each begins with a page 1. The edition was first published by the Folio Press in 1976, then by Penguin Books in 1980. The place of publication of the Penguin edition, which is the one you are using, is listed as Harmondsworth, Middlesex, England. Your reference is to an episode Hugo presents on pages 210 through 214 of volume 2.

7. The source is an editorial printed on page 15 of *The Christian Science Monitor* dated November 9, 1984. The editorial is unsigned; its title is "Polling Power."

8. The source is a recording of a poem as read by the author, T. S. Eliot. The title of the poem is "The Love Song of J. Alfred Prufrock." It is one of several poems on a record entitled *T. S. Eliot Reading Poems and Choruses.* The manufacturer is Caedmon Records, Inc., of New York City. The catalog number is TC 1045. A note on the record states that the recording was made in 1955. Your reference is to Eliot's portrayal of Prufrock in the entire poem. Since no parenthetical citation is required for this type of source, write out just the reference that would appear in your list of Works Cited.

Preparing the Final Copy of the Research Paper 40

40.1 BASIC PROCEDURES

If your teacher has special requirements for the final copy of a research paper, you should of course follow those. Otherwise, we suggest you do as follows:

1. Be sure your hard copy is clear and readable, with page breaks inserted where you want them.

2. Use double-spacing throughout, leave one-inch margins all around the text (top, bottom, and both sides), and indent paragraphs as shown on p. 228.

3. Print on one side of the paper only.

4. If your instructor requires a title page, follow the format shown on p. 226. Otherwise follow the format shown on p. 228. Do not underline the title or put it in quotation marks.

5. On each page, give your last name and the page number at upper right, as shown on p. 228.

6. Always keep a copy of what you have submitted.

Sweeten 1

Brandon Scott Sweeten

Professor Atwill

English 2

10 May 2001

Conflict Stalemate and Conflict Resolutions:

Implementing the Native American Graves and Repatriation Act

Many museums throughout America have exhibits displaying
the traditions of Native American Indians. These displays have
fascinated people of all ages interested in learning about those
who knew America before it was called America. Museums have
created rooms dedicated to Native American heritage. These rooms
contain materials excavated by archaeologists, ranging from
arrowhead and peace pipe collections to elaborate costumes worn
by shamans during religious festivals to the skeletal remains of
one Native American who used to roam the great frontier. For a
long time these displays were the pride of both archeologists
and museums. But what about the Native American tribes being
represented? Did Native Americans ever visit these museums,
wondering if the remains hanging in the glass display were those
of an ancestor?

Opening paragraph asks questions about the topic.

Only recently have these questions been confronted. Answering them has raised many scientific, cultural, and ethical questions, resulting in legislation in America and the international community. The culmination of this legislation in America was the Native American Graves Protection and Repatriation Act (NAGPRA). On November 16, 1990, President George Bush signed NAGPRA, a law that prohibits museums and institutions that receive federal aid from keeping cultural objects (human remains, funerary objects, sacred objects, and objects of cultural patrimony) belonging to Native American peoples. NAGPRA also protects burial sites belonging to Native Americans, making it illegal to disturb and develop land known to be Native American funeral grounds, Native American properties, or land owned by the federal government ("Native American Graves Protection and Repatriation Act"). This act ushered in a new era for the scientific community, Native American tribal organizations, and museums, creating a conflict among competing interests that has, at times, seemed irresolvable. For scientists, NAGPRA is an unconstitutional law that prevents them from conducting scientific inquiry. For the Native American community, NAGPRA is a law that attempts to redress past injustices, allowing them to reclaim the possessions, power, and pride of their heritage. Museums, faced with the daunting task of returning remains and artifacts, see

Writer summarizes the principal opposing views of the legislation he is examining.

NAGPRA as an expensive and time-consuming burden on their already scarce resources. NAGPRA is not perfect, for it in no way satisfies all the parties involved. Loopholes exist in the law—loopholes that may be exploited by any party not committed to the aims of the law. Because of these differences, NAGPRA has produced examples of both conflict stalemate and conflict resolution. NAGPRA has produced conflict stalemate when parties have insisted on furthering only their own interests and conflict resolution when each party has been willing to respect the interests of the others.

Writer introduces his thesis—his evaluation of the legislation and its effects on the conflict.

The scientific community has been the most vocal in protesting NAGPRA, arguing that it inhibits scientific inquiry and unfairly protects a specific religious perspective. By definition, scientific study generates hard fact from the analysis of physical materials, making a religious orientation virtually antithetical to science. Whereas religion involves faith, science involves rational explanation; consequently, science generally views religion as nothing more than myths and fables. Science cannot accept the Native American faiths that NAGPRA is founded upon, for to do so is to undermine the notion of scientific method.

Writer begins to detail one party's views.

The American Committee for Preservation of Archaeological Collections (ACPAC) has been the most powerful voice representing the interests of scientists. Formed specifically in order to combat laws such as NAGPRA, the ACPAC currently has over twelve

Writer develops the party's position.

hundred members, who are either professional archaeologists, museum curators, or students of the two fields (<u>ACPAC: Frequently Asked Questions</u>). Clement Meighan, emeritus professor of anthropology at the University of California and head of ACPAC, describes the impact of NAGPRA on the scientific community this way: "Repatriation is not merely an inconvenience but makes it impossible for scientists to carry out a genuinely scientific study of American Indian prehistory" (68). ACPAC has also charged that NAGPRA identifies the government with a particular religious perspective in violation of the First Amendment to the United States Constitution, which proclaims: "Congress shall make no law respecting an establishment of religion" ("Amendment I"). According to Meighan, "no other religious group in the United States has been given the same protection" (66). Meighan also argues that the basis of the law is flawed because "most Indians no longer hold these beliefs" (66).

From the perspective of archaeologists like Meighan, the knowledge gained from scientific study benefits all people, no matter their race or religious creed. By studying bodily remains, a scientist can determine the tribal origin, cause of death, and individual traits. Meighan claims that scientific research is especially important for people who are dependent on an oral tradition because without science, these "people remain without a history" (66). Science not only provides hard facts about heritage, but also guidance for the future when tribes

Sweeten 5

confront epidemics or other life-threatening forces of nature. With the knowledge of what went wrong yesterday, scientists claim, they can take preventive measures against recurrences. From their perspective, they are losing materials they view as invaluable sources of information. Meighan likens the repatriation of bodily remains and other objects to book burning or "a historian burning documents after he has studied them" (66). In other words, scientists insist that they cannot depend upon dreams and prophecies as given by the gods of Native Americans.

The Native American perspective, however, is quite compelling. Native Americans have long suffered injuries from the American government, and they see NAGPRA as both restitution for past injustices and public confirmation of the legitimacy of their culture and history. Native American resentment of the scientific community is easy to understand. In the 1860's the United States Surgeon General ordered the gathering of Native American bodies for a study that was used to support a "scientific" theory of white supremacy that was based on cranial size. This racially motivated study dehumanized Native Americans, depicting them as specimens; and it supported the then popular view that the Native Americans were soon to be an extinct race (Peck and Seaborne).

Native Americans have suffered not only racial but also religious injustices in the name of science. Minthorn, who is a

Writer introduces the other party's views.

606

religious leader with the Confederated Tribes of the Umatilla
Indian Reservation, states that removing a body from its resting
place in the ground is "a desecration of the body and a
violation of [a Native American's] most deeply-held religious
beliefs." Cecil Antone, of the Gila River Indian Tribes,
explains that once an individual has died, his or her body
should return to Mother Earth so the soul can travel to the next
world (in Pettifor). In the name of science, however, the bodies
of Native Americans have been exhumed, defiled by scientific
studies, then stored in cardboard boxes on laboratory shelves or
placed on display in glass cases in museums. According to
Antone, removing a body from the earth pollutes that body, and
the soul becomes trapped within the cardboard box or glass case.
He goes on to observe that Mother Earth does not let atrocities
go without punishment, and the implications for disturbing the
natural process are harmful to all of those involved (in
Pettifor).

The argument that scientists are helping to preserve Native
American culture through excavation and study is not very
convincing to most Native peoples. Many Native Americans have
little use for knowledge produced by the scientific community.
According to Minthorn, Native Americans preserve their heritage
orally: "We already know our history. It is passed on to us
through our elders and through our religious practices." This
strong oral tradition accounts for the past, the present, and

the future. The scientific community may be able to determine
which tribe was at a certain geographical location at a certain
time, but not all Native Americans want or need that
information.

Further conflict between scientists and Native groups has
arisen as provisions in the law have been implemented. NAGPRA
orders the return of the numerous bodily remains and objects
which were taken from the Native Americans over the years;
however, some tribes, such as the Hopi, interpret the law to
include any information gained from research, past, present, or
future. NAGPRA states that any scientific institution wishing
to study bodily remains or artifacts must first notify the
proper tribal authorities of their scientific intentions. The
Hopi Tribe is working toward reclaiming every set of Native
American bodily remains and objects, whatever their association
with the Hopi tribe. The Hopi have also formally placed a
moratorium on all scientific research utilizing Hopi archival
material (Masayesva in Grose 626). A scientist may research
Hopi materials, so not all scientific endeavor is lost;
however, the information gained from the research will be
censored by the Tribe. The Hopi are training their own people
in the ways of science so that they may conduct scientific
study on their own grounds. In the meantime, they insist that
their interests take precedence over those of non-Hopi
scientists.

Writer discusses
the effect of
legislation upon
the conflict.

Writer studies the role of museums in the conflict.

NAGPRA has caused both work and turmoil for museums. After NAGPRA was passed in 1990, the federal government released an outline of procedures that museums were to follow. Museums and institutions first had to inventory their Native American collections, and, by 1995, they were to have delivered detailed lists of holdings to both the tribes possibly affected by the collection and to the National Park Service, the governmental mediator of NAGPRA. Journalist Marie Porterfield notes that the required procedures have taxed the financial resources of both museums and Native American groups. Museums have been forced to take on the considerable task of inventorying their holdings without adequate funds to hire qualified personnel. Porterfield observes that Native American groups have also been given large tasks. When handed these lengthy lists, they have to sort through them and decide which items are theirs for repatriation.

Writer notes conflicting actions of some museums.

Some museums are perpetuating the conflict. Believing that NAGPRA prevents them from preserving heritage by taking away materials and information, some have refused to comply with the sanctions imposed by NAGPRA. In particular, those museums associated with scientific institutions or universities are ignoring NAGPRA because, in the opinion of the curators, returning an object for reburial is surrendering any hope for its preservation. Some of these museums delay the repatriation process by contesting tribes' claims. The contest must then be mediated by the National Park Service. A museum's protest of

Sweeten 9

repatriation could be based on scientific claims against tribal affiliation. A contest would consider the geographical location at which an item was found (if that information is available) as well as the dating ascribed to the item by the scientific community. These two points of contest could prove that a tribe requesting repatriation has no right to do so. Museums who are ordered to repatriate items and choose not to do so face punishment from the federal government in the form of heavy fines and loss of governmental funding. Perhaps the more serious consequence, however, is that they perpetuate the conflict by standing firm on the principle that created the conflict in the first place: The interests of science outweigh those of all other parties.

While some museums perpetuate the problem, other museums are adapting to the law and reestablishing their positions as the preservers of heritage. NAGPRA does not necessarily mean that museums are losing their entire Native American collections. The law gives museums and Native American tribal organizations the opportunity for discussion. The World Archaeological Congress (WAC) is an international organization that strives to collaborate with indigenous peoples. WAC is especially concerned with the ethics involved in scientific inquiry—"the ownership, conservation, and exploitation of the archaeological heritage" of a given people (Redhouse). Larry Zimmerman, University of South Dakota archaeologist and

Writer moves to study positive steps taken by other museums to reduce conflict.

610

executive secretary of WAC, notes that "if we, [the scientific community and museum professionals], do not take steps that are bold and creative in reinventing our profession, we continue to lose access to the artifacts, sites, and people we wish to study" (Zimmerman 68). The collaboration fostered by WAC attempts to combine scientific information with oral history in order to provide a more accurate and respectful picture of Native peoples.

Many museums are responding to Zimmerman's call to action and working closely with Native American tribes. The University of Nebraska-Lincoln is working with the Omaha tribal organization in a contract that gives the University the permission to study items for a limited amount of time. A member of the Omaha tribe is conducting the study with the University's scientific community. When the time period concludes, the University will repatriate the items to the Omaha tribe (Roth 43). The Alaska State Museum is working with the Tlinget tribal groups of Alaska. The Museum is allowed to retain possession of items as long as tribal officials have borrowing privileges; this scenario will continue until the Tlingets build their own museum (Roth 44). Other museums and institutions are trading material artifacts significant to a Native American tribe for replicas. Of course, the replicas do not carry the scientific significance of the originals, but they do add materials to a museum's collection. Cooperation between museums and Native

American tribes is meeting the needs of both parties. Museums
are being provided information concerning artifacts whose
purpose and context were unknown, and Native Americans are
reclaiming items that they had once believed to be lost forever.
The doors of communication have been opened. Working together,
both sides have profited from this new partnership.

As with any action involving several parties, NAGPRA works
best when all parties approach it in good faith. For the law to
succeed, each party must consider the consequences of its
actions on the other parties. Some members of the scientific
community, such as Meighan, are unwilling to consider anything
but the information produced from the scientific process. It was
precisely this kind of scientific attitude that created the
problem in the first place. On the other side of the coin are
Native American tribes such as the Hopi, who may be acting out
of resentment over the past. Because in the past they have been
denied access to these artifacts, the Hopi are reclaiming all
items and denying access to everyone else. Some Hopi are using
NAGPRA to exercise complete control over information on Native
peoples and how it is presented. As long as the parties involved
focus only on their interests, there is little hope for
reconciliation and progress.

The museums and Native American tribes who are working
together are splendid examples of conflict resolution. In
trying to settle their differences, both sides are

Writer begins his conclusion by uniting general truths of conflict resolution with details about the NAGPRA conflict.

participating in a give-and-take compromise that benefits all parties affected by NAGPRA. Museums are being allowed to preserve and present Native American culture to the public, and Native Americans are regaining possession of what was taken from them many years ago.

When legislation is passed, it is often designed to right a past wrong and prevent its recurrence. Laws can do that only when the parties involved can define similar aims and, at times, look beyond their own interests. Some of the responses to NAGPRA illustrate the kind of stalemate that can result when there is no good-faith effort to right the wrongs of the past. Other responses demonstrate what can happen when different parties are willing to respect the interests of others and work together to create a better future for everyone.

Writer closes with a restatement of his thesis.

Works Cited

"Amendment I." U.S. Constitution-Bill of Rights. n.d. 30 Nov.

    1998 <http://www.law.cornell.edu/constitution/

    constitution.billofrights.html>.

ACPAC: Frequently Asked Questions. 11 Nov. 1998. 2 Dec. 1998

    <http://www.adlestrop.com/acpac/faqs.html>.

Grose, Teresa Olwick. "Reading the Bones: Information Content,

    Value, and Ownership Issues Raised by the Native American

    Graves Protection and Repatriation Act." Journal of the

    American Society for Information Science 47.8 (1996): 626.

Horse Capture, George P. "Survival of Culture." Museum News 71.1

    (1991): 50.

Meighan, Clement. "Burying American Archaeology." Archaeology

    47.6 (1994): 66-68.

Minthorn, Armand. "Human Remains Should be Reburied." CTUIR

    Issues. Sept. 1996. 12 Sept. 1998

    <http://www.ucinet.com/~umatribe/kennman.html>.

"Native American Graves Protection and Repatriation Act." NAGPRA

    Legal Mandates: Native American . . . Repatriation Act, 25

    U.S.C. 3001 et seq. 16 Nov. 1990. 18 Oct. 1998

    <http://www.cast.uark.edu/other/nps/nagpra/nagpra.dat/

    lgm003.html>.

Peck, Danielle and Alex Seaborne. "Horizon—Bones of Contention."

    Horizon - 23.01.95. 23 January 1995. 12 Sept.1998

    <http://www.uiowa.edu/~anthro/reburial/bbcbones.html>.

Pettifor, Eric. <u>The Reburial Controversy</u>. 1995. 12 Sept. 1998

    <http://www.wynja.com/arch/reburial.html>.

Porterfield, K. Marie. "Tribes Sort Museum Inventories;

    Repatriation Law Brings Procedural Confusion Over Remains."

    <u>Dallas Morning News</u> 26 Nov. 1995, bulldog ed.: 40A.

Redhouse, David. <u>World Archaeological Congress-Home Page</u>.

    22 March 1995. Updated 20 Oct. 1997. 2 Dec. 1998

    <http://avebury.arch.soton.ac.uk/wac/>.

Roth, Evan. "Success Stories." <u>Museum News</u> 71.1 (1991): 43-45.

Zimmerman, Larry J. "Sharing Control of the Past." <u>Archaeology</u>

    47.6 (1994): 68.

5

Writing in Academic Contexts

Writing about Literature **41**

41.1 THE LITERARY WORK AS A CREATED WORLD

Literature is writing that can be read in many ways. We can read it as a form of history, biography, or autobiography. We can read it as an example of linguistic structures or rhetorical conventions manipulated for special effect. We can view it as a material product of the culture that produced it. We can see it as an expression of the ideology—beliefs and values—of a particular class. We can also see a work of literature as a self-contained structure of words—as writing that calls attention to itself, to its own images and forms.

Viewed in this light, literature differs from the three other kinds of writing treated elsewhere in this book: expressive, persuasive, and expository. Expressive writing aims to express the feelings of *the writer;* persuasive writing seeks to influence *the reader;* expository writing tries to explain *the outside world.* By contrast, a work of literature creates a world of its own:

INFANT SORROW

My mother groaned! My father wept.
Into the dangerous world I leapt,
Helpless, naked, piping loud;
Like a fiend hid in a cloud.

Struggling in my father's hands,
Striving against my swaddling bands;
Bound and weary I thought best
To sulk upon my mother's breast.

—William Blake

The first thing we're likely to notice about this text is its form. Instead of running all the way from the left margin to the right one, like a block of prose, it is broken up into two sets of four short lines, and the end words rhyme: *wept, leapt, loud, cloud, hands, bands, best, breast.* Besides these formal features, the text offers us striking images, like that of the "fiend hid in the cloud."

Since such an image makes no reference to the outside world as we normally know it, this is not expository writing. Nor is it quite the same as persuasive writing. Though the poem works on us rhetorically by exciting our sympathy for the desperate and frustrated speaker, it makes no direct appeal to us as audience, no systematic effort to shape our opinions on a specified point. Furthermore, while it looks like expressive writing, the "I" speaking here is not the writer but an infant, a figure the writer has created or imagined. What we have, then, is an independent little world made of words: a world of forms, images, and sounds (groans and "piping loud" screams) that are all designed to work together.

This does not mean that works of literature have nothing to do with the outside world. On the contrary, Walt Whitman's poems often address the reader directly; Mark Twain's *Huckleberry Finn* has everything to do with the history of American slavery; and when Emily Dickinson writes, "I never hear the word 'escape' / Without a quicker blood," she is surely expressing her own feelings. The world of literature is watered by many streams—by the writer's feelings, by the writer's desires to stir the reader, and by the writer's consciousness of the outside world. But in a work of literature, all of these streams flow through a world the writer creates.

41.2 LITERARY GENRE: POETRY, FICTION, DRAMA

To write effectively about a literary work, you need to know something about its genre—about the *kind* of literary work it is. Works of literature generally come in one of three genres: poetry, fiction, and drama.

POETRY

Most people think of **poetry** as writing arranged into lines with a uniform number of syllables, a regular pattern of stresses (called *meter*), and rhyming words at the end. The Blake poem quoted just above fits this definition nicely. But many poems have neither meter nor rhyme, and some of them look just like prose on the printed page. So poetry cannot simply be defined by its formal features.

You may consider a poem as the concentrated expression of a moment of feeling, a moment of vision, or both. This definition obviously excludes long poetic narratives such as the ancient epics, but probably includes most if not all of the poems you may be asked to write about.

In studying a poem that you plan to write about, use the following questions as a guide:

1.   WHO IS THE SPEAKER OF THE POEM?   Who is the "I"? Is it the poet or some character the poet has created? If the "I" is a created character, the title of the poem will often give you a clue to his or her identity. Blake's "Infant Sorrow," for instance, is spoken by an infant, and Langston Hughes's "Madam and the Phone Bill" is spoken by an angry woman talking to a telephone operator. But even if the speaker can be connected with the poet, the two are never identical. Wordsworth wrote his first-person "Tintern Abbey" while *walking* from the abbey to the city of Bristol; yet in the poem, he presents himself as *standing* on a riverbank a few miles north of the abbey. So we must ask ourselves why Wordsworth presents himself in this way and what sort of role he plays in the poem. Once you have identified the speaker, ask yourself what the poem tells us about his or her feelings and perceptions.

Poems such as Gwendolyn Brooks's "Mrs. Small" are spoken by a narrator who never becomes "I," a narrator speaking *about* someone or something in the third person. But even a third-person narrative can make us see a character or situation in a particular way—as "Mrs. Small" illustrates (see below, pp. 646–47).

2.   WHAT IS THE DOMINANT IMAGE?   An image is a word or phrase that calls to mind something we can experience with our senses, most often something we can imagine *seeing*, whether it is real or not. In Blake's "Infant Sorrow," the dominant image is that of the infant, who is first naked and then bound in "swaddling bands." The simile comparing the infant to "a fiend hid in a cloud" helps us to see infant energy trapped and smothered as if it were something diabolical—something threatening the established order.

3.   HOW DOES THE DOMINANT IMAGE EXPRESS THE THEME?   The theme of a poem is the product of a reader's interpretation—the abstract meaning that a reader infers from particular details and images. As the examples just cited show, to explain the dominant image of a poem is to begin to formulate its theme. If we take the swaddled infant as the dominant image of "Infant Sorrow," we can infer that the poem's theme is the conflict between infant energy and adult constriction (swaddling) of that energy. In Emily Dickinson's "I never hear the word 'escape,'" the dominant image is that of a prison, which plainly accentuates the urge to escape. In "Mrs.

Small," the dominant image is hot coffee, a symbol of the warmth, domesticity, and hospitality that Mrs. Small herself personifies.

4. **HOW IS THE DOMINANT IMAGE RELATED TO OTHER IMAGES?** In "Mrs. Small," the title character splashes coffee on an insurance salesman's white shirt. As explained in Cirri Washington's essay on the poem (pp. 641–45), these two images—the coffee and the white shirt—help define the chief conflict between the poem's two characters.

5. **HOW DOES THE POEM DEVELOP ITS THEME?** What sort of progression can you see as you move from the beginning to the end? Blake's "Infant Sorrow" consists of two verse paragraphs, or **stanzas**. The first reveals the primal energy of an infant leaping into life; the second shows weariness and resignation to confinement. The movement from one state to the other defines the speaker's state of mind.

6. **HOW DO RHYME AND METER (IF ANY) HELP TO EXPRESS MEANING?** **Meter** is the pattern of stresses made by a line of poetry. The first line of Blake's poem, for instance, consists of eight syllables divided into four "iambic feet," each containing an unstressed syllable (da) followed by a stressed one (DUM):

IAMBIC FOOT

da-DUM	da-DUM	da-DUM	da-DUM
My moth	er groaned!	My fa	ther wept.

The meter of this line—its pattern of stresses—helps to accentuate its two most important words, *groaned* and *wept*.

    Rhyme highlights a relation between words. The rhyme of *wept* and *leapt* in the first stanza of Blake's poem underscores the paradox that the speaker's birth dismays the speaker's father; the rhyme between *hands* and *bands* in the second stanza helps us see that both are used to confine the speaker.

FICTION

Fiction includes short stories and novels. All fiction is imaginary narrative, telling a series of events in which one or more characters do or experience something that leaves them changed. In William Faulkner's short story "Dry September," the rumor that a black man has accosted a white woman leads to his being lynched, and a barber who tries to stop the lynching is forced to discover how brutal his fellow townsmen can be.

In Ernest Hemingway's novel *A Farewell to Arms,* an American soldier wounded in Italy during the First World War falls in love with his nurse, recovers, and flees with her to neutral Switzerland; when she dies in childbirth, he is shattered.

In studying fiction, use the following questions as a guide:

1. WHAT DOES THE SETTING CONTRIBUTE? The setting of a piece of fiction—the place and time in which its central action originates—typically helps to explain how or why the action occurred. The setting is commonly established at the beginning, as in the opening sentences of Faulkner's "Dry September":

> Through the bloody September twilight, aftermath of sixty-two rainless days, it had gone like a fire in dry grass—the rumor, the story, whatever it was. Something about Miss Minnie Cooper and a Negro. Attacked, insulted, frightened: none of them, gathered in the barber shop on that Saturday evening where the ceiling fan stirred, without freshening it, the vitiated air, sending back upon them, in recurrent surges of stale pomade and lotion, their own stale breath and odors, knew exactly what happened.

The dryness and stagnation of the air helps to explain how and why the rumor could ignite a lynching, acting "like a fire in dry grass."

2. WHAT CENTRAL CONFLICT DRIVES THE PLOT? The plot of a fictional work is the sequence of events that it narrates. Typically the plot is driven by a conflict that is somehow resolved at the end. In "Dry September," for instance, a white barber who tries to use rational arguments on behalf of a black man is browbeaten and scorned by his enraged fellow whites, who end up lynching the man. Eudora Welty's "Why I Live at the P.O." is chiefly the tale of a young woman's feud with her sister, who has done everything possible to turn the rest of the family against her. But just as often, the conflict takes place *within* the central character. In David Leavitt's "Territory," for example, the main character is a young man who has invited his male lover to accompany him on a visit to his mother's house in California. Though his mother knows he is gay, he is torn between the urge to be openly affectionate with his lover in her presence and the fear of antagonizing her by doing so.

3. HOW IS THE STORY TOLD? By an undramatized narrator who plays no part in the story, by a dramatized observer (an "I") reporting largely the actions of others, or by a narrator-agent reporting his or her interaction with others? The story of J. D. Salinger's *Catcher in the Rye* is told by a narrator-agent named Holden Caulfield, the central figure in his own tale.

Nathaniel Hawthorne's *Scarlet Letter* is told entirely by an undramatized narrator. Some stories combine different techniques of narration. Joseph Conrad's *Heart of Darkness,* for instance, is begun by a dramatized observer and then largely taken over by a narrator-agent. In each case, the method of narration powerfully affects our experiences of the story. While an undramatized narrator often tells us what each of several characters thinks and feels, a narrator-agent makes us see the world of a story from his or her limited point of view. Thus we intimately share what one character does, suffers, and learns.

4.   HOW DOES THE STORY REVEAL ITS CHIEF CHARACTERS?   Fictional characters are revealed by the way they appear, by what they say, by what they do, and by what others say about them. In *Heart of Darkness,* a man who enters an African jungle seeking ivory on behalf of a European company is described by another character as a messenger of "progress," and later he says of himself, "I had immense plans." But we also learn that he has presided over human sacrifice and that his own body has been wasted by disease. To understand fictional characters, weigh the words spoken by and about them along with their actions and appearance.

5.   WHAT CHANGES DOES THE STORY REVEAL?   Plot requires not simply conflict but development, which usually means a change in one or more characters. Some characters change *for us* as we learn more about them; some change *in themselves* as they learn about themselves and the world around them; some do both. The would-be "emissary of pity . . . and progress" in *Heart of Darkness* changes for us when we learn how greedy and vicious he has become in the jungle; but he also changes in himself at the moment of his death, when he realizes the horror of what he has done.

6.   HOW DOES THE STORY DEVELOP ITS THEME?   Like the theme of a poem, the theme of a story is the product of a reader's interpretation: the general idea that a reader draws from the story as a whole. From "Dry September" we can draw the theme of racial hatred. The story develops this theme, we can say, by showing how blind and deaf such hatred can be to any voice of reason, and how murderous it finally becomes. This is a general statement about what the story *means.* But because a theme is the product of interpretation, different readers may have different ways of stating the theme. Some readers might say, for instance, that the theme of "Dry September" is the force of rumor, and that the story develops this theme by showing how uncontrollable and destructive rumor can be. In either case, the resolution of the conflict between the barber and the other white characters completes the development of the theme.

DRAMA

Drama is a kind of writing designed to be spoken by one or more characters on a stage. In the script of a play, stage directions often describe the appearance of a character or set, and sometimes they say what a character does (slams the door, sits down, leaps up). But otherwise the only description or narration to be found in a play is spoken by the characters themselves. Essentially, then, a play consists of speeches—dialogues, monologues, or both.

Since plays are written to be seen and heard, reading a play can never substitute for seeing it performed. If you're writing about a play that you've never seen performed, try to see a video of a performance or hear a recording of it. If you can't do either of those things, read at least parts of the play aloud to yourself. Try as well as you can to imagine how the play might look and sound on a stage, and use the following questions as a guide to your study of the text:

1. IS THE PLAY A COMEDY OR A TRAGEDY? Tragedy ends in death or disaster for the main character(s), as in William Shakespeare's *Romeo and Juliet*, where both the title characters die. Comedy ends by relieving the main characters of their problems, as in Eugene O'Neill's *Ah, Wilderness!*, where Richard finally overcomes the obstacles that stand between him and the young woman he loves. While some plays cannot readily be classified as either comic or tragic, this question can help you grasp the general shape of most plays.

2. WHAT IS THE CENTRAL CONFLICT? All plays—whether comic or tragic—turn on some kind of conflict. In *Romeo and Juliet*, the love between Romeo and Juliet is thwarted by the feud between their families. In Shakespeare's *Hamlet*, Hamlet's urge to avenge the murder of his father must contend with all the power embodied in the murderer, King Claudius, as well as with Hamlet's own reluctance to strike. In *Ah, Wilderness!*, the lovesick Richard must contend with the suspicions of the father of the young woman he loves.

3. WHAT SIDES OF THE CONFLICT DO THE CHARACTERS REPRESENT? Different characters in a play often stand for conflicting values, attitudes, or principles. In Henrik Ibsen's *Doll's House*, for instance, Torwald believes that his wife's duty is to obey him, amuse him, raise their children, and uphold his respectability. But she believes that her first duty is to herself as an independent human being.

4. HOW DO THE CHARACTERS DEVELOP?   While lesser characters may remain essentially the same, major characters often undergo a change. In the first act of Shakespeare's *King Lear,* for instance, the king impulsively disowns his daughter Cordelia for refusing to express her love for him in extravagant superlatives; in the last act, her death leaves him grief-stricken just before he dies himself. Does this sequence of events tell us that Lear has fundamentally changed? If so, when and how? And what does he learn? These questions will prompt different answers from different readers (and viewers), but they are the kinds of questions that lead to the heart of a play.

5. WHAT DOES THE SETTING CONTRIBUTE?   Though readers of older plays—Shakespeare's, for instance—must largely imagine the locale from hints in the dialogue, the scripts of modern plays usually include a detailed description of the set. *Where* the action occurs is often highly significant. In *Hamlet,* the shift from the dark night outside on the ramparts (where the ghost of Hamlet's father appears) to the bright inside light of Claudius's court symbolizes the contrast between dark vengeance and superficial gaiety. In Eugene O'Neill's *Long Day's Journey into Night,* the one living room where all the action takes place comes to epitomize the world in which all four major characters are trapped.

IN BRIEF   **Questions to Guide Your Study of Literature**

Questions to Ask about a Poem

Who is the speaker?
What is the dominant image?
How does the dominant image express the theme?
How is the dominant image related to other images?
How does the poem develop its theme?
How do rhyme and meter (if any) help to express the poem's meaning?

Questions to Ask about a Work of Fiction (Novel or Short Story)

What does the setting contribute?
What central conflict drives the plot?
How is the story told? Is the narrator part of the action?
How does the story reveal its chief characters?
What changes does the story reveal?
How does the story develop its theme?

Questions to Ask about a Play

Is the play a comedy or a tragedy?
What is the central conflict?
What sides of the conflict do the characters represent?
How do the characters develop?
What does the setting contribute?

41.3   NOTING SIGNIFICANT DETAIL

Provided you own the text you're reading, you should feel free to mark it up and make it your own. Watch for **significant detail:** words, phrases, and images that tell you something revealing about the main character, the theme, or the central conflict in the work. Underline or highlight these items and write your comments in the margin, as illustrated by these comments on the opening paragraphs of a short story by Meridel Le Sueur:

THE GIRL

She was going the inland route because she had been twice on the coast route. She asked <u>three times</u> at the automobile club how far it was through the Tehachapi Mountains, and she <u>had the route marked</u> on the map in red pencil. The car was running like a T, the garage man told her. All her dresses were back from the cleaner's, and there remained only the lace collar to sew on her black crepe so that they would be all ready when she got to San Francisco.

She had read up on the <u>history</u> of the mountains and <u>listed all the Indian tribes</u> and marked the route of the Friars from the Sacramento Valley. She was glad now that Clara Robbins, the math teacher, was not going with her. <u>She liked to be (alone)</u>, to have everything <u>just the way she wanted it</u>, exactly.

<u>There was nothing she wanted changed</u>. It was a remarkable pleasure to have everything just right, to get into her neat fine-looking little roadster, start out in the fine morning, with her map tucked into the seat, <u>every road marked</u>. She was lucky too, how lucky she was. She had her place <u>secure</u> at Central High, teaching history. On September 18, she knew she would be coming back to <u>the same room</u>, <u>to teach the same course in history</u>. It was a great pleasure. Driving along, <u>she could see her lean face in the windshield</u>. She couldn't help but think that she had <u>no double chin</u>, and her pride rode in her, a lean thing. She saw herself erect, a little caustic and severe, and the neat turn-over collar of her little blue suit. Her

[margin notes:]

wants to know exactly what's ahead of her—no surprises

a loner— and a perfectionist; likes her own way

loves security, sameness, pre- dictability

istory f?

t have wn!

res own ction

solitude again

something's bound to happen!

obsessed with orde[r]

likes looking good- wants to attract men

real ⟨lone⟩ self. This was what she wanted. <u>Nothing messy</u>. She had got herself up in the world. This was the first summer she had not taken a summer course, and she felt a little guilty; but she had had a good summer just being lazy, and now she was going to San Francisco to see her sister and would come back two days before school opened. She had thought in the spring that her skin was getting that papyrus look so many teachers had, and she had a little tired droop to her shoulders and was a little bit too thin. It was fine to be thin but not too thin. Now she looked better, brown, and she <u>had got the habit of a little eye shadow, a little dry rouge, and just a touch of lipstick</u>. It was really becoming.

Yes, <u>everything</u> was ideal.

41.4 RECORDING YOUR PERSONAL REACTIONS

It's often helpful to set down on paper your **first reactions** to a text: any thoughts or questions that occur to you as you read. Here, for instance, is what one student wrote after first reading the opening paragraphs of "The Girl":

What to make of this "girl"? She's something of a puzzle. Wants a little adventure, so she goes through the mountains, but has to be sure there'll be no surprises. So she's got to know just how many miles it is and have the route marked in red, "every road marked," and learn all the history. Nuts about order—"nothing messy" in her life. Just imagine what she'd say if she saw my room! And you'd think she'd be looking forward to seeing San Francisco—the Golden Gate—but no, she's looking forward to coming back—to teach the same course in the same room!

A loner, too. Doesn't even want her girl friend with her, and no thoughts of a man in her head. But she likes her looks, likes looking at herself in the mirror. Does she unconsciously fantasize about some sort of romantic adventure?

"Everything was ideal." Yes—perfect. Too perfect. She must be headed for some sort of mess.

41.5 CHOOSING AND REFINING YOUR TOPIC

Choosing a topic for an essay about a work of literature begins with choosing the work itself. If you're given a choice among those you have read in a course, take the work you like best—the work you find most interesting. That's the one you're most likely to enjoy writing about. If you're assigned a specific work to analyze, of course, you can proceed at once to the task of defining your approach to it.

The longer the work, the greater the need to concentrate on a specific part or feature of it. If you're writing a short essay on *Moby-Dick*, for instance, you can't possibly treat the novel as a whole, or trace the full development of its major character. You need to focus on a chapter, on a minor character, or on some recurrent feature of the whaling voyage, such as the "gams"—the occasional meetings between ships at sea. Whatever you choose to examine closely, ask yourself how it helps to reveal the theme of the work—as you interpret it—or one of its major conflicts.

Suppose you decide to write about chapter 36 of *Moby-Dick*, in which Captain Ahab tells his crew that their whole purpose must be to hunt the great white whale. This chapter dramatizes a conflict that is central to the development of the novel: the conflict between Ahab and Starbuck, his first mate. Ahab's obsession with revenge at any cost collides with Starbuck's practical concern for safety and profit. So your topic (and a working title) might be "Revenge versus Practicality in Chapter 36 of *Moby-Dick*."

Another way of approaching the choice of a topic for an essay on a long work is to think of the general ideas you want to explore, and then choose a specific part or feature of the work to explore them in. Suppose, for instance, you want to analyze Ahab's defiance of warnings against his pursuit of revenge. If you anchor this general topic to one or more of the chapters about gams, your topic might then be "Warning and Defiance in the Gams of *Moby-Dick*."

Besides looking for something specific to write about, look for something interestingly problematic: something that provokes a question you would really like to answer. If Ahab is obsessed with a purpose that is manifestly irrational and dangerous, how does he persuade the crew to follow him? If Starbuck makes good sense, why does he fail to match Ahab's influence on the crew? The search for answers to questions like these should lead you to a thesis that does far more than state the obvious. In fact, if such questions stir your own interest in the topic, you're much more likely to produce an essay that interests your reader.

If you're writing about a short story or short poem, you can certainly choose a topic that includes the whole work, but you will still need to identify the basic idea—or better still the basic conflict—that your paper will explore. After choosing Gwendolyn Brooks's poem "Mrs. Small" as the subject of her paper, Cirri Washington was struck by the very last word of the poem—"business." Since this word was applied to what the woman was doing in her house when she was visited by a business*man*, Cirri decided to see how the poem presents the contrast between two different kinds of business—male and female (see 41.11).

Choosing and Refining a Topic for a Paper on a Literary Work

If the work is long, identify a general issue or conflict that you can link to a specific part or feature of the text:

Ahab's obsession with revenge in chapter 36 of *Moby-Dick*

The cowardice of Falstaff in *1 Henry IV,* act 2, scene 4

Agamemnon's story of his bloody homecoming in book 11 of *The Odyssey*

Public law and private duty in act 3 of *A Doll's House*

Enlightenment and destruction in the fire images of *Heart of Darkness*

If the work is short enough to be treated as a whole in a short paper, identify the basic idea or basic conflict your paper will explore:

Male and female business in Gwendolyn Brooks's "Mrs. Small"

Desire and repression in Meridel Le Sueur's "The Girl"

Racial hatred in Faulkner's "Dry September"

41.6 CONSULTING SECONDARY SOURCES

If you are writing a short paper on a work of literature, you may not be asked to use or cite any secondary sources—just to cite the work you are writing about. If you *are* asked to use secondary sources, the first place to look for them is the text in which the work appears. Many editions of literary works include—sometimes in headnotes, more often in the back of the book—a bibliography of critical studies devoted to the work and its author. Some editions include critical essays or excerpts from them. The Norton Critical Edition of *Hamlet,* for instance, offers portions of twenty-three essays on the play.

The next place to look for secondary sources is the card catalog or online catalog of your college library (see 36.5). If you check the cards or computer listings under your author's name, you can readily find your way to all the books in the library written by or about your author.

For articles as well as books, see the *MLA International Bibliography* in the library reference room. Published annually, this is an author-and-subject index to books and journal articles on modern languages, literatures, folklore, and linguistics. If your library has the MLA file online, you can call up just about everything published on the work of your author since 1980.

Once you've located a book about your author, check the table of contents and the index to find discussion of the work or topic you're writing about. By itself, the title of an article will often tell you whether or not the article is worth tracking down and reading in full.

41.7 FORMULATING A THESIS

A good thesis about a literary work makes an arguable assertion about the meaning of the work or the way that meaning is shaped. It must be more than an inarguable statement of fact or a statement of your topic:

STATEMENT OF FACT: In chapter 36 of *Moby-Dick,* Ahab goads his entire crew to swear vengeance on the great white whale.

STATEMENT OF TOPIC: Chapter 36 of *Moby-Dick* is about the conflict between Ahab's lust for revenge and Starbuck's concern with practicality.

STATEMENT OF THESIS: In chapter 36 of *Moby-Dick,* Ahab's refusal to heed Starbuck's warnings about the folly of pursuing a single whale shows the intensity of Ahab's obsession with revenge.

STATEMENT OF FACT: In Gwendolyn Brooks's "Mrs. Small," the title character has to pay an insurance premium.

STATEMENT OF TOPIC: Gwendolyn Brooks's "Mrs. Small" is about the difference between male and female business.

STATEMENT OF THESIS: In Gwendolyn Brooks's "Mrs. Small," the superficial contrast between a man's business and a woman's absentmindedness gives way to the point that this woman's business is crucial to human life.

41.8 SUMMARIZING AND INTERPRETING: KNOWING THE DIFFERENCE

To summarize a work of literature is to tell its plot—the sequence of actions that it represents. Summarizing, in fact, is one way of writing about literature, and a good way to test your understanding of what happens in a literary narrative. Summarizing a story also helps you to identify crucial moments in its development. A good plot summary of "Dry September," for instance, would include the fact that the barber jumps out of the car on the way to the site of the lynching.

But to **interpret** a work of literature, you need to do some jumping of your own. You need to jump off the track of chronological sequence—one thing after another—and consider the **meaning** of particular events. How does the barber's action affect the development of the story? If the black man would have been lynched anyway, what difference does it make that the barber jumps from the car? To answer this question, you must consider the role that the barber has played in the story up to now, and particularly the ways in which he has tried to combat the mindless rage of his fellow whites. In moving back to find examples of what the barber said to them, you would be gathering material for an interpretation, which is a *logical* rather than *chronological* way of writing about the story. That is, interpretation aims not to retell the plot of the story but to show what conclusions we can draw about its meaning.

Many good essays on a work of literature include summary—enough to situate the reader in the world of the text so that he or she can follow the writer's argument about it. The opening paragraph of the sample essay in 41.10, for instance, summarizes Meridel Le Sueur's "The Girl" before stating a thesis about its meaning. But plot summary will not pass for interpretation. To see whether or not you're confusing the two as you write, check the first sentence of each of your paragraphs. If it merely states a fact about what happens in this story, you're falling into summary. Compare these openings:

PLOT SUMMARY: After hearing that Catherine will accept Linton's proposal, Heathcliff runs away into the night.

ANALYSIS: In running away after hearing that Catherine will accept Linton's proposal, Heathcliff reveals his bafflement and desperation.

PLOT SUMMARY: En route to the site of the lynching, the barber jumps from the car.

ANALYSIS: When the barber jumps from the car en route to the lynching, he shows us that hatred and fear have at last overpowered his rationality.

41.9 DEVELOPING YOUR INTERPRETATION: QUOTING AND CITING SOURCES

GIVING EVIDENCE

To make your points convincingly, you must support them with **evidence** from the text—references to specific incidents or images, quotations of particular words, phrases, or passages. In Meridel Le Sueur's "The Girl," a female schoolteacher sets out to drive alone from Southern California to San Francisco and reluctantly takes on a young male hitchhiker. In the following paragraph from an essay on this story, the author begins with an interpretative statement about the chief character and then develops it with significant detail:

> Her love of order goes hand in hand with an aversion to company. Initially, she is "glad" that Clara Robbins, the math teacher, is not with her, and she has no wish to take on anything or anyone else that might be "messy" (204). When she first sees the young man at the service station looking for a ride, she instantly decides that "she wouldn't pick him up, that was certain" (205). Even after the station owner tells her that he knows the young man's family and can "vouch for him," the sight of his smiling, eager face makes her feel only that he and the owner both "want something": something other than the "mite of education" that the owner "cunningly" suggests she could give the young man on the ride (207). "Men like that," she says to herself, "hate women with brains" (207). She trusts neither of them. Suddenly realizing "that she despised men and always had," she tells the station owner, "I don't like to drive with a strange man" (207).

The student author of this paragraph uses a series of brief quotations to develop the point made in the opening sentence. Here quotations and statements of fact about the story—such as the fact that the math teacher is not with the main character—constitute evidence for the author's interpretation. An effective interpretation combines evidence with interpretive points. Both are essential.

CITING SOURCES

Cite all sources in parentheses, observing these guidelines.

1.   Cite secondary sources by the author's last name and the page number(s) of the material quoted:

One critic says of <u>The Bean Eaters</u>, "There is much black

womanness in this book" (Lee 20).

2.   If you use the author's name in introducing the quoted material, give just the page number(s) in parentheses:

As Maria Mootry notes, her very name--Mrs. Small--"conforms to

the gender-based stereotype that women's lives are narrow and

that women are preoccupied with unimportant matters" (181).

3.   If you are writing about just one literary work, give the author's name and the title at the outset. You can then give just the page number(s) for each citation that follows:

> Meridel Le Sueur's "The Girl" is the story of what happens
> when a prim, unmarried, unnamed schoolteacher sets out to
> drive alone from Southern California to San Francisco on a
> bright, hot September day. . . . But the story makes it
> clear that in rejecting his desires, she also stifles her
> own, dooming herself to a life of repressive order in which
> she will "never never change" (212).

4.   In quoting more than one item from the same page within the same sentence, give the page number(s) for all the quoted items at the end of the sentence:

> Initially, she is "glad" that Clara Robbins, the math
> teacher, is not with her, and she has no wish to take on
> anything or anyone else that might be "messy" (204).

5.   In quoting plays and poems, follow the instructions given in 39.2, items 25–27.

6.   Finally, at the end of your finished paper, list all sources under the heading "Works Cited":

> Works Cited
>
> Le Sueur, Meridel. "The Girl." <u>Ripening: Selected Work,</u>
>   <u>1927-1980</u>. Ed. Elaine Hedges. Old Westbury: The Femi-
>   nist Press, 1982. 204-12.
>
> Lee, Don L. Preface. <u>Report from Part One</u>. By Gwendolyn
>   Brooks. Detroit: Broadside, 1972. 13-30.

Mootry, Maria. "'Tell It Slant': Disguise and Discovery as

Revisionist Poetic Discourse in <u>The Bean Eaters</u>." <u>A</u>

<u>Life Distilled: Gwendolyn Brooks, Her Poetry and</u>

<u>Fiction</u>. Ed. Maria K. Mootry and Gary Smith. Urbana:

U of Illinois P, 1987. 177–92.

For detailed guidance on the format of the Works Cited list, see 39.1.

41.10 SAMPLE ESSAY ON A SHORT STORY: NO SECONDARY SOURCES

The following essay illustrates a method of critical analysis that focuses on the elements of the literary work itself. Specifically, the student author tries to show how the actions, descriptive detail, and dialogue of a short story all work together with the reported thoughts of the main character to reveal a central conflict within her. For another way of treating Le Sueur's story—an approach that connects the story to the author's life and historical circumstances—see 41.12, where we explain how to link works of literature to the circumstances under which they are produced.

Arturo Garcia

Professor Payne

English 202

25 October 2001

Desire and Repression in Le Sueur's "The Girl"

Meridel Le Sueur's "The Girl" is the story of what happens
when a prim, unmarried, unnamed schoolteacher sets out to drive
alone from Southern California to San Francisco on a bright, hot
September day. Stopping for lunch at a service station, she
reluctantly takes on a passenger--a muscular, sunburnt young
farmhand who needs a lift to a bridge some fifty miles up the
road. His personal remarks disturb and frighten her. When she
stops the car at one point and he suggests that they lie down
together in the shade, she silently refuses, drives on until she
drops him off, and continues her trip. But the story makes it
clear that in rejecting his desires, she also stifles her own,
dooming herself to a life of repressive order in which she will
"never never change" (212).

Her love of order and predictability shows up at once.
Though taking the inland route in order to see something new (she
has taken the coast route twice before), she has done everything
she can to forestall surprises. Her neat little roadster is
"running like a T" and her dresses are freshly cleaned. She has
"asked three times at the automobile club how far it was through
the Tehachapi mountains," has carefully marked on her map every

road she will take, has studied the history of the region and made a list of its Indian tribes. Furthermore, rather than looking forward to any new experience, she relishes the thought that she will soon be returning to her job, "coming back to the same room, to teach the same course in history" at Central High (204).

Her love of order goes hand in hand with an aversion to company. Initially, she is "glad" that Clara Robbins, the math teacher, is not with her, and she has no wish to take on anything or anyone else that might be "messy" (204). When she first sees the young man at the service station looking for a ride, she instantly decides that "she wouldn't pick him up, that was certain" (205). Even after the station owner tells her that he knows the young man's family and can "vouch for him," the sight of his smiling, eager face makes her feel only that he and the owner both "want something": something other than the "mite of education" that the owner "cunningly" suggests she could give the young man on the ride (207). "Men like that," she says to herself, "hate women with brains" (207). She trusts neither of them. Realizing "that she despised men and always had," she tells the station owner, "I don't like to drive with a strange man" (207).

In taking the strange man on, however, she not only yields to the station owner's urging. She also reveals something she can hardly admit to herself, let alone anyone else: a desire to attract men. We get a hint of this earlier, when we learn that she takes pride in her appearance. Looking at herself in the windshield, she admires her own "lean" face ("no double chin"), lightly tanned skin, and deftly applied makeup: "a little eye shadow, a little dry rouge, and just a touch of lipstick. It was really becoming" (204). During the ride itself, neither her fear of being touched nor her annoyance at being flattered "just as if she were any common slut" (209) can altogether keep her from showing herself off. When she feels her passenger inching toward her "as if about to touch her leg" (208), she shrinks away and draws her skirt down sharply. But minutes later, "she let her skirt slip up a little. She knew she had good legs, tapering down swiftly to her ankles" (210).

The powerful appeal of sexuality in this story is symbolized by the heat of the day and the mountains, which are repeatedly de-scribed in terms that suggest the human body. Before the woman has even seen the young man, the sun shines "like a golden body" and she looks "into the fold upon fold of earth flesh lying clear to the horizon" (205). Like the muscular, sunburnt man himself, the contours of the sun-baked land repel and arouse her by turns. At first appalled by the "terrifying great mounds of earth and the sun thrusting down like arrows" (205), she is gradually entranced by "naked" mountains, by "bare earth curves, tawny and rolling in the heat" (208). At the same time, she feels the glowing pres-ence of the man like a force of nature, and she tries to slow down on the curves "so that his big body would not lounge down upon her like a mountain" (209).

Garcia 4

As that passage suggests, he never overcomes her fear. As long as he remains in the car, she feels "frightened as if they were about to crack up in a fearful accident" (209). Yet when she stops the car and he invites her to lie down with him, she is nearly overpowered by the combined effects of his body and the sunburnt landscape, which have now become virtually one:

> The rocks that skirted the road glistened like bone,
> . . . like the sheer precipice of his breast looming to-
> ward her so that she could feel the heat come from him
> and envelop her like fire, and she felt she was falling
> swiftly down the sides of him . . . and an ache, like
> lightning piercing stone, struck into her between her
> breasts. (211)

This moment leaves her to struggle with two desires—the man's and her own. She thwarts his desire by simply pulling back from him "in hard resistance" (211). As soon as she does so, he withdraws from her "completely" (212) and gets out of the car by himself to catch a ride with a man driving a truckload of melons. Yet the melon that he gives her as he says good-bye symbolizes all he might have given her, and all she has refused: "some sumptuous feast she had been unable to partake of, the lush passional day, the wheaty boy, some wonderful, wonderful fruit" (212). In rejecting the fruit of passion, she stifles her own desire.

Garcia 5

As a result, she feels both "safe" and withered. When she stops the car after dropping off the man, she looks in the mirror and sees something quite different from what she saw in the windshield at the beginning of her trip. While she earlier admired her lean, well-made-up face, now she feels "like a stick" and looks "like a witch" (212). She is "safe--safe" from violation (212), but she also realizes that she is stuck in a life of sterility. In the end, the prospect of order and sameness gives her only a grim satisfaction: "She would never never change, pure and inviolate forever; and she began to cry" (212).

Garcia 6

Works Cited

Le Sueur, Meridel. "The Girl." Ripening: Selected Work, 1927-1980. Ed. Elaine Hedges. Old Westbury: The Feminist Press, 1982. 204-12.

Cirri Washington

Professor Porter

English 201

8 March 2001

Male and Female Business in Gwendolyn Brooks's

"Mrs. Small"

Gwendolyn Brooks's poem "Mrs. Small" captures a revealing moment in the life of a housewife and mother. Visited by an insurance man who has come to collect a premium, she goes to the kitchen for her pocketbook, absentmindedly returns with a steaming pot of coffee instead of the money, and accidentally splashes his shirt before she finally gets around to paying him. On the surface, the poem presents the conflict between a woman's absentmindedness and the business of a man. As Maria Mootry notes, her very name--Mrs. Small--"conforms to the gender-based stereotype that women's lives are narrow and that women are preoccupied with unimportant matters" (181). But by the time we reach the end of this poem about a woman named Small, we have learned just how crucial to human life is "her part / Of the world's business" (lines 55-56).

The opening stanza perfectly expresses her preoccupation with the business of hospitality.

Going off for her pocketbook, she returns "with a peculiar look
/ And the coffee pot" (2-3). The rhyming "look" takes the place
of the pocket<u>book</u> she has forgotten about, and the next two
lines suggest that in the mind of the woman, "pocketbook" has
also been replaced with a word that sounds like its first syllable, "pot." But her substitution of one for the other is not
just an exercise in free association. Offering "a steaming coffee pot" is her instinctive way of treating a visitor "graciously" (15).

Coffee, however, is not what this particular visitor wants
or expects. As a businessman with a busy schedule, he shows her
a face that has "not . . . much time" for love "sublime" (8-9)
or even for getting acquainted. He can't stop to savor the
woman's company or sip her steaming brew, even if--as her
husband says--it's "the best coffee in town" (27). Coffee has
nothing to do with the money that the insurance man has come to
collect. That is why she looks almost crazy to him, with her
"half-open mouth and the half-mad eyes / And the smile half-
human" (11-12).

From his point of view, her actions must seem as crazy--or
at least as "peculiar"--as her look. Ironically, in coming "to
her senses" (16) about her first mistake, she makes a second one:
she jerks the pot and splashes coffee on the man. Thus she not

only forces him to take the coffee he didn't want; she also
stains the perfect whiteness of his shirt "with a pair of brown
/ Spurts" (24–25). "There is much black womanness in this book,"
says Don Lee of The Bean Eaters, the volume containing this poem
(20). Symbolically, this "little plump tan woman" (10) is dis-
rupting the orderly world of white male business, which is why
her mistake is called "unforgivable" (20).

But this word is ironic, for her mistake is hardly unforgivable when we realize how trivial it actually is and when we
see it from her point of view. She asks for no forgiveness.
Though she says, "I don't know where my mind is this morning"
(34), she knows her own mind. She scorns apologies because she
has no time to make them. Like the insurance man, she is in a
hurry, but she has more reason for haste because she has more
things to do than he does: "such / Mountains of things, she'd
never get anything done / If she begged forgiveness for each
one" (37–39).

We get a glimpse of those mountains when we learn (near
the end of the poem) that this woman is the mother of ten
children: six daughters scrambling and yelling in the hall, and
four sons who have run off beyond earshot, who "could not be
heard any more" (44). The size of the woman's family explains
why she is even now planning to bake some apple pies. In

the face of this job--just one of many to be done each day by
this hard-working mother--the payment of an insurance premium is
a truly small matter, something tersely set down in a stanza of
just three words: "she paid him" (40).

In doing so with brisk efficiency, she is anything but the
absentminded or slightly crazy woman the insurance man has seen.
In the end, it's the insurance man who glares "idiotically"
(47), not she. She knows how to cook and manage her children at
the same time, how to

> silence her six
>
> And mix
>
> Her spices and core
>
> And slice her apples, and find her four.
>
> (51-54)

The rhyming of "six" and "mix" and of "core" and "four"
shows just how she makes the parts of her working day fit together, how she mixes cooking and parenting, taking each in
stride. This "little plump tan woman" may look unimportant to
the insurance man, who symbolizes "the economic pressures of
white culture" (Melhem 120), and she may seem only an absentminded hindrance to his business. But his business finally
proves far less important than hers. In spite of her name, "her
part / Of the world's business" is demanding, essential, and big.

Washington 5

Works Cited

Brooks, Gwendolyn. "Mrs. Small." <u>The Bean Eaters</u>. New York:

    Harper, 1960. 27–28.

Lee, Don L. Preface. <u>Report from Part One</u>. By Gwendolyn Brooks.

    Detroit: Broadside, 1972. 13–30.

Melhem, D. H. <u>Gwendolyn Brooks: Poetry and the Voice</u>. Lexington:

    UP of Kentucky, 1987.

Mootry, Maria. "'Tell It Slant': Disguise and Discovery as

    Revisionist Poetic Discourse in <u>The Bean Eaters</u>." <u>A Life

    Distilled: Gwendolyn Brooks, Her Poetry and Fiction</u>. Ed.

    Maria K. Mootry and Gary Smith. Urbana: U of Illinois P,

    1987. 177–92.

MRS. SMALL

Mrs. Small went to the kitchen for her pocketbook
And came back to the living room with a peculiar look
And the coffee pot.
Pocketbook. Pot.
Pot. Pocketbook.   5

The insurance man was waiting there
With superb and cared-for hair.
His face did not have much time.
He did not glance with sublime
Love upon the little plump tan woman   10
With the half-open mouth and the half-mad eyes
And the smile half-human
Who stood in the middle of the living-room floor planning apple
    pies
And graciously offering him a steaming coffee pot.
Pocketbook. Pot.   15

"Oh!" Mrs. Small came to her senses,
Peered earnestly through thick lenses,
Jumped terribly. This, too, was a mistake,
Unforgivable no matter how much she had to bake.
For there can be no whiter whiteness than this one: 20
An insurance man's shirt on its morning run.
This Mrs. Small now soiled
With a pair of brown
Spurts (just recently boiled)
Of the "very best coffee in town."   25

"The best coffee in town is what *you* make, Delphine! There is
    none dandier!"
Those were the words of the pleased Jim Small—
Who was no bandier of words at all.
Jim Small was likely to give you a good swat
When he was *not*   30
Pleased. He was, absolutely, no bandier.

"I don't know where my mind is this morning,"
Said Mrs. Small, scorning
Apologies! For there was so much
For which to apologize! Oh such   35
Mountains of things, she'd never get anything done
If she begged forgiveness for each one.

She paid him.
But apologies and her hurry would not mix.
The six   40
Daughters were a-yell, a-scramble, in the hall. The four
Sons (horrors) could not be heard any more.

No.
The insurance man would have to glare
Idiotically into her own sterile stare   45
A moment—then depart,
Leaving her to release her heart
And dizziness
And silence her six
And mix   50
Her spices and core
And slice her apples, and find her four.
Continuing her part
Of the world's business.

—Gwendolyn Brooks

41.12 LINKING LITERATURE TO HISTORY

A work of literature may be treated as a self-sufficient world—something made of forms and images that can be wholly explained in terms of their relation to each other. But since no literary work is ever written in complete isolation from the material world, you can often enrich your study of a poem, play, or work of fiction by linking it to history. You can link it to the personal history of the author's own life or the historical period in which it was written; you can consider the social, political, cultural, or economic conditions that it may reflect.

Take, for example, Meridel Le Sueur's "The Girl." First published in 1936, this story of a woman who ends up feeling "like a stick" because she rejected the advances of a hitchhiker may seem peculiar to us now. Why should she be so repressed? Or more to the point, why shouldn't she feel perfectly free to send the sexy hitchhiker packing *without* feeling like a stick?

Some knowledge of Meridel Le Sueur's early life helps to answer these questions. Born in Nebraska in 1900, she grew up in a suffocatingly repressive household. According to Elaine Hedges, who has edited a volume of her writings, she inherited from her grandmother in particular a sense of guilt and shame about the human body. Against this repressive atmosphere she soon rebelled, and it was chiefly her need to escape what she called the "terrible purity" of her family background that prompted her to write about the sexual experience of women (qtd. in Hedges 6). In addition, at the time she wrote "The Girl," she was deeply influenced by the novels of D. H. Lawrence, which attack all forms of repression and glorify sexual fulfillment as a way of uniting oneself with nature. Significantly, the hitchhiker in "The Girl" comes across as a force of nature, and the contours of the mountainous landscape in the story resemble those of the human body.

To bring biography or history into your paper, of course, you will need to read some historical studies, consult secondary sources, or both. But to illustrate what history can bring to the analysis of literature, here is an excerpt from an essay on Jane Austen's novel *Emma* by a student named Julie Cusick:

Cusick 2

The poor people mentioned just once in <u>Emma</u> are not the
only figures who live outside the comfortable world of Highbury's landed gentry. Equally outcast--and more threatening--are
the gypsies. "Gypsies," writes David Simpson,

> had always been imaged as in a tense and
>
> contested relation to the rest of society.
>
> True gypsies had once been banned from
>
> Britain, by a statute of 1530, and . . .
>
> thirteen gypsies were executed under this
>
> law in the mid-seventeenth century. (44)

By the time <u>Emma</u> was written in the early nineteenth century,
gypsies were no longer banned. But as Simpson notes, they were
contemptuously classified with beggars, vagrants, thieves, pick-
pockets, and "the non-industrious poor" (44).

In <u>Emma</u> gypsies appear only briefly--just long enough to
show how their wandering, unsettled way of life can threaten the
established order. When Emma's friend Harriet Smith and another
young woman are out walking one day on the road from Highbury to
Richmond, they are suddenly accosted by a crowd of gypsies.
Though Harriet's companion scrambles away, she herself cannot
follow because her legs are cramped from dancing at the ball. As
a result,

> she was soon assailed by half a dozen
>
> children, headed by a stout woman, and a

> great boy, all clamorous, and impertinent
>
> in look, though not absolutely in word.
>
> More and more frightened, she immediately
>
> promised them money, and taking out her
>
> purse, gave them a shilling, and begged
>
> them not to want more, or to use her ill.
>
> She was then able to walk, though slowly,
>
> and was moving away--but her terror and her
>
> purse were too tempting; and she was
>
> followed, or rather surrounded, by the
>
> whole gang, demanding more. (305)

This is a fascinating passage, for it describes in detail how
gypsies strategically corner and attack their prey. Significantly, the gypsies are tempted quite as much by Harriet's "terror" as by her "purse." To know something of how despised and
marginal they were in early nineteenth-century England is to see
why they would relish this moment of power and control over one
of their superiors in rank and class. It is also to see how the
novel recognizes the social forces threatening the apparently
secure world of privilege in which Emma lives.

Cusick 4

Works Cited

Austen, Jane. <u>Emma</u>. New York: Bantam, 1981.

Simpson, David. <u>Wordsworth's Historical Imagination: The Poetry of Displacement</u>. New York: Methuen, 1987.

42 *Writing and Research in Different Disciplines*

Good writing does not stop at the borders of the English department. College courses in many different subjects require written work, and many of the qualities that make an essay on Shakespeare effective can also enhance a paper on the biology of adaptation or the influence of urban environment on family life. Whatever its subject, a good piece of writing is grammatically correct, lucid, precise, coherent, well focused on its main point, and—just as importantly—well designed to meet the expectations of its readers, the audience for whom it is written.

But different disciplines (which is what academic subjects are called) require different kinds of writing. Even when a humanist, a social scientist, and a natural scientist examine the same object, they approach it from fundamentally different points of view. For this reason, a highly specialized study can sometimes seem to be written in a language of its own: a language that sounds strange and difficult to the nonspecialist reader.

So if you plan to write a paper in a specialized discipline, or even to read specialized books and articles, you will have to learn something about the methods, assumptions, and above all the language of that discipline. In what follows, we first consider the kind of writing specialists produce when they are writing for other specialists. Then we explain how you can begin to write in various disciplines yourself. Bear in mind, however, that only your instructor can tell you exactly what he or she requires.

42.1 THREE DISCIPLINES ILLUSTRATED: SPECIALISTS WRITING FOR SPECIALISTS

To see the difference between writing in the humanities, writing in the social sciences, and writing in the natural sciences, consider how specialists from each of these three different fields of study approach a common topic.

1.   A literary critic writes about fictional treatments of cruelty to children:

> Any story will be unintelligible unless it includes, however subtly, the amount of telling necessary not only to make us aware of the value system which gives it its meaning but, more important, to make us willing to accept that value system, at least temporarily. It is true that the reader must suspend to some extent his own disbeliefs; he must be receptive, open, ready to receive the clues. But the work itself—any work not written by myself or by those who share my beliefs—must fill with its rhetoric the gap made by the suspension of my own beliefs.
>
> Even something as universally deplored as cruelty to children can be molded to radically different effects. When Huck's pap pursues him with the knife, or when the comic-strip father beats his child because he's had a bad day at the office; when Jim in "Haircut" and Jason in *The Sound and the Fury* disappoint the children about a circus; when Elizabeth Bowen's heroine experiences the death of the heart; when Saki's little pagan is punished by his aunt; when Medea kills her children; when Macbeth kills Lady Macduff's children; when Swift's Modest Proposer arranges to have the infants boiled and eaten; when Pip is trapped by Miss Havisham; when Farrington in Joyce's "Counterparts" beats his son; and, finally, when the child is beaten to death in *The Brothers Karamazov*, our reactions against the perpetrators range from unconcerned amusement to absolute horror, from pitying forgiveness to hatred, depending not primarily upon any natural relation between the bare events and our reaction but upon a judgment rendered by the author.
>
> —Wayne Booth, *The Rhetoric of Fiction*

Booth is writing for readers familiar with a wide variety of literary texts—with works ranging from *Huckleberry Finn* to *The Brothers Karamazov*. His object of study is "the work itself." He treats the individual work of literature as the source of meaning and value, as something that can make us react in a variety of ways to any theme—even cruelty to children.

2.   A sociologist writes about the family as a social group:

> The implications of conflict theory might best be considered from the perspective of an alternative theory. According to conflict theory, power pervades both the interactional and the societal levels of social life. Bierstedt (1974) elaborated on the theory of *social organization* by defining power as latent force, and identifying the sources of power as resources, numbers (especially majorities), and social organization (including authority, or institutionalized power). By implication, social organization

must be triadic, because authority entails command, either by a person or by a norm, and obedience; this points to the consensus of a majority, and a majority cannot exist in a detached dyad. Resources *per se* cannot influence social life unless they are given social definition (Bierstedt, 1974). The conception of the family as an institution holds that normative structures have crescively developed to meet the functional requirements of men, women, and children joined by ties of kinship. Women give birth and are more nurturant, children require a long period of dependency, and males exhibit greater aggressiveness and dominance the world over (Maccoby and Jacklin, 1974). These universal features gave rise to the traditional consensus regarding family statuses and the norms attached to them, whether in the conjugal family today or in the patriarchal family of the past. In summary, the view we have outlined sees social organization as triadic and hierarchical, instead of dyadic and polarized, and points to the principle that each person acts where he or she is strong (Weaver, 1948).

—Lawrence L. Shornack, "Conflict Theory and the Family"

Shornack is writing for readers familiar with sociological terms such as *interactional* (relating to behavior between persons), *dyadic* (twofold), *triadic* (threefold), and *crescively* (increasingly). He distinguishes between two rival theories that could be used to explain the family: conflict theory, which treats all social structures in terms of a two-sided (dyadic) struggle between oppressive top dogs and powerless underdogs; and organizational theory, which treats social structures as triangular (triadic), with a peak of power resting on a base of majority consent. As a sociologist, Shornack focuses on social groups. While Booth describes the many different forms that child abuse can take in various fictional families, Shornack seeks to explain the social structure of *the* family—that is, the social structure common to all family groups.

3.   A team of pediatricians and neurologists report on a study of children who suffered minor head injuries:

INTRODUCTION

Minor head injury is a common problem in the pediatric population. Yet, despite the relative frequency, it remains a source of concern often raising the spectra of serious sequelae and long-term neuropsychological problems. Relatively few data are available on the outcome of minor head trauma. Published studies have emphasized a substantial functional and behavioral morbidity and an increased incidence of headaches [1–6]. In general, however, these abnormalities have been established by comparing information obtained from individuals following head trauma with expected outcomes in healthy subjects.

The purpose of this study is to expand our knowledge of the physical and behavioral morbidity experienced by children with minor head injuries by comparing this population with individuals who had minor injuries to other parts of the body. All children were followed prospectively by telephone interviews. Our results have identified several short-term behavioral sequelae in a pediatric population treated in an emergency room for minor injuries, whether injuries affect the head or other body parts. Physician awareness of specific transient functional deficits following minor injuries can result in a reduction of parental anxiety.

—Mychelle Farmer et al., "Neurobehavioral Sequelae of
Minor Head Injuries in Children"

Farmer and her colleagues are writing for specialists in the fields of pediatrics and neurology—for readers familiar with terms such as *trauma* (wound), *morbidity* (illness), *sequelae* (abnormalities resulting from a wound), and *transient functional deficits* (short-term incapacities). They made their study to answer a specific question about a well-defined population: in children under thirteen, what special abnormalities can be expected to follow a minor head wound? To answer this question, they compared head-injured children with a "control group" of children suffering from other injuries. In this introduction to their report, they refer to what published studies have already shown; they explain the comparative method of their own study; and they note that what they have learned about minor head injuries can be used to reduce "parental anxiety."

Each of the three passages above considers children and the family—a topic everyone knows something about. Yet each is written to be read by specialists in a particular field. In addition, each also embodies a specialized way of thinking about its topic—a specialized kind of questioning.

42.2 ASKING THE QUESTION THAT FITS YOUR DISCIPLINE

The key to generating an effective piece of writing in any field is *to ask the kind of question that the field is organized to answer*. To learn what kind of question this is, consider the different things that humanists, social scientists, and natural scientists focus on when they write.

WRITING IN THE HUMANITIES: FOCUS ON THE WORK AND ITS CONTEXT

Specialists in philosophy and religion study what real people think and believe, but most other humanists—in spite of their generic name—do not study humans directly. They study works of literature, music, and visual art. In the process, they often try to analyze the *form* of individual works or to explain how such works evoke the *historical context* in which they were produced.

To study the form of an individual work is to consider how its parts collaborate to make a whole: how the ending of a novel recalls its beginning, how the last movement of a sonata recapitulates its first one, how a dark tree in the foreground of a landscape painting can set off a sunlit mountain in the background. To study the form of a work is also to see what that work shares with other works like it: with other novels, other sonatas, other landscape paintings. Wayne Booth, for instance, treats all works of fiction as *rhetorical,* written to persuade us that we should judge their characters in a certain way. But this general theory of fiction helps to show what is distinctive about each fictional work. If the theme of cruelty to children can be "molded to radically different effects," made to enrage us in one work and to amuse us in another, what explains these differences? Only a detailed analysis of the rhetorical strategies used in particular works can answer the question. Even as he explains a general theory of fiction, therefore, Booth shows us how to discover the uniqueness of individual works, how to formulate the kinds of questions that can lead us to their meanings, such as "Why are we amused when Huck's pap pursues him with a knife?" or "What makes us sympathize with Medea even when she kills her own children?"

Besides analyzing the form of an individual work, humanists may consider it biographically or historically. They may ask what it tells us about the life and artistic development of its creator; they may also ask how it evokes or reflects the political, cultural, or socioeconomic conditions of the time and place in which it was created. They may ask, for instance, not only how Mark Twain's *Huckleberry Finn* recalls the structure of classical epic, but also how it uses the author's personal experience as a Mississippi riverboat pilot, or how it reflects the history of American debates about slavery and Reconstruction. Alternatively, looking at a sixteenth-century portrait of a married couple in Amsterdam, they may ask what the picture tells us about the status of women, marriage, and property rights in Holland or Europe at that time. (For further discussion of the historical approach to the study of literature, see 41.12.)

Generally speaking, then, the humanities are organized to answer questions of this type about a work of music, literature, or art:

1. What kind of work is it?

2. How is it related to other works of its kind or other works by the same person?

3. How does it differ from other works like it?

4. What is the relation of any one of its parts to the whole?

5. How does it reflect the culture and ideas of the time and place in which it was produced?

WRITING IN THE SOCIAL SCIENCES: FOCUS ON SOCIAL GROUPS

While humanists often use categories and general terms to help them define something or someone unique, social scientists typically study groups. Shornack's approach to families differs from Booth's in two fundamental ways. Shornack is not only writing about real families rather than fictional ones; he is also generalizing, as sociologists typically do, about *the* family. Even when he distinguishes "the conjugal family" of today from "the patriarchal family of the past," he is still dealing with groups, with social categories rather than individuals.

This generalizing viewpoint is particularly evident in the kind of essay he has written—a review article focusing on theories of the family rather than on any personal observation of actual families. In case studies, social scientists study individuals, and you may be asked to do the same. But you will study an individual as a case—that is, an example of a definable group, or of a particular stage of development. In a psychology course, for instance, you may be asked to observe a particular child at a daycare center in order to answer a question such as "What is the relation between language learning and socialization in three-year-olds?"

Professional social scientists use similar methods of investigation. A recent study of child development set out to explain the relation between child abuse and illness in children under three. By studying such a relationship in a randomly drawn sample of this population, investigators tried to learn whether illness is typically one of the causes or the effects of abuse.

The questions raised by social scientists, then, are designed to generate information about groups and recurrent situations. Typical studies seek to answer questions like these:

1. What is the correlation between event or condition X and event or condition Y within population Z?

2. What norms and values are shared by a particular population?

3. What concept or theory will explain a particular form of behavior?

657

WRITING IN THE NATURAL SCIENCES: FOCUS ON PHYSICAL PROPERTIES

When we turn from the social sciences to the natural sciences, the focus shifts from social groups to physical properties. While social scientists try to answer a question about a group of human beings by observing or interviewing sample members of the group, physical scientists try to answer a question about the human body or the physical properties of the natural world. The kind of question that a scientific researcher sets out to answer will call for observation, experiment, or both.

Suppose, for instance, that a biologist wants to know whether hair condition in humans tells anything about protein or calorie deficiencies. This kind of question can be answered by observation and comparison—specifically by comparing hair samples taken from persons who don't have those deficiencies with hair samples taken from persons who do. Or suppose a neurologist wants to know whether or not minor head injuries in children produce any special long-term effects. This question too can be answered by observation and comparison, as shown by the article from which passage no. 3 is quoted above.

Like the authors of that article, physical scientists typically make controlled comparisons. To learn how one particular event or condition affects a certain population, they establish a control group that matches the group being tested in all but one respect—the one being studied. Controlled comparison allows researchers to focus on just one variable at a time and thus to see its effects clearly.

One other feature of this article about head injuries in children typifies scientific writing: the frequent use of the passive voice (see chapter 24). It appears twice in the introductory passage we quote *(these abnormalities have been established, all children were followed prospectively by telephone interviews),* and often thereafter. Scientists use the passive voice in order to sound as objective as possible: to keep the focus on what was done rather than on who did it. (Even if the study was conducted by a team of researchers, reports do not usually say which member of a team did anything in particular.) Also, by separating the action from the agent, the passive voice underscores the point that scientific experiments and procedures are repeatable: anyone who is properly trained should be able to do them.

In general, then, physical scientists try to answer questions like these:

1. What are the effects or causes of a particular physical condition or event?

2. What is the correlation between event or condition A and event or condition B?

3. If such a correlation may exist, what kind of experiment will confirm or disprove it?

Thinking Like a Humanist

Consider a work of literature, music, or visual art with questions such as these:

1. What kind of work is it?
2. How is it related to other works of its kind?
3. What is the relation of its parts to each other?
4. What does it tell us about the life and development of its creator?
5. How does it reflect the political, cultural, or socioeconomic conditions of the time and place in which it was created?

Thinking Like a Social Scientist

Investigate social groups with questions such as these:

1. What is the correlation between event or condition X and event or condition Y within population Z?
2. What are the norms and values shared by a particular population?
3. What concept or theory will explain a particular form of behavior?

Thinking Like a Physical Scientist

Investigate the natural world with questions such as these:

1. What are the effects or causes of a particular physical condition or event?
2. What is the correlation between event or condition A and event or condition B?
3. If such a correlation may exist, what kind of experiment will confirm or disprove it?

42.3 WRITING ON SPECIALIZED TOPICS FOR NONSPECIALISTS

Like good teachers, good specialists in any subject generally know how to explain it to nonspecialists, and—just as importantly—how to show why it matters to all of us. In the following paragraph, the author explains why some babies born with spina bifida (incomplete development of the verte-brae surrounding the spinal cord) are denied corrective surgery:

> The single most common cause of mental retardation in children with spina bifida is infection of the brain: either infection of the chambers

of the brain (ventriculitis) or of the linings and substance of the brain (meningoencephalitis). Such infection is most likely in those infants from whom corrective surgery is withheld. The parents of Baby Jane Doe, a child born with spina bifida, were told she would inevitably be severely retarded. For that reason they decided not to allow a surgeon to treat her. Because she was not treated, she acquired a brain infection, which means she is likely to be retarded. *This becomes a self-fulfilling prophecy.*

—David G. McLone, "The Diagnosis, Prognosis, and
Outcome for the Handicapped: A Neonatal View"

The author of this paragraph is a pediatric neurosurgeon who has treated hundreds of infants born with spina bifida. But since he is writing for a journal of general interest, he wants to reach more than just an audience of fellow specialists. So he explains such technical terms as *ventriculitis* and *meningoencephalitis.* He also explains—in language we can readily understand—exactly how the threat of retardation is used to justify the withholding of surgery from infants who need it.

This explanatory point serves a persuasive end. Elsewhere in his essay, McLone shows that no one can predict the life of an infant born with spina bifida until that infant has been treated. Here he shows what happens when a prediction of retardation is used to justify the withholding of corrective surgery: the withholding of surgery leads to infection and retardation, and the prediction becomes "self-fulfilling." Thus McLone converts his specialized knowledge into writing that can reach and persuade a general reader to accept his main point, which is that *all* infants born with spina bifida should be treated.

42.4   ORGANIZING A RESEARCH PAPER IN THE HUMANITIES

Sections 3.7 and 41.10 discuss and illustrate the organized analysis of a single work of literature. Likewise, section 41.11 illustrates how to use secondary sources in the analysis of a literary work. A research paper on one or more works of literature, art, music, or philosophy normally includes secondary as well as primary sources, and in general, you should organize this material as follows:

1.   In the introduction you identify the particular work or works you will consider in the paper. You also formulate the question you will try to answer: What do we learn about motherhood from Toni Morrison's *Beloved*—a novel about a black woman who kills her own infant daughter to save

her from a life of slavery? How does J. D. Salinger's *Catcher in the Rye* represent the passage from innocence to experience? Why does Mary Wollstonecraft attack Rousseau in *Vindication of the Rights of Women?* Why does Velázquez's *Las Meninas* include a self-portrait of the artist himself at work? How does the hard-boiled hero of the American detective novel reflect American notions of heroism? Here, for instance, is the introduction to a research paper by a first-year college student:

> Individual identity is a cherished ideal, and when institutions threaten to deny it, they provoke resentment. Nevertheless, in order to function in a society, individuals must be willing to compromise their personal moralities and assume certain prescribed roles. This conflict between the rights of the individual and those of society produces a sense of frustration, creating the need for an outlet. Consequently, we look to heroes, to strong individuals who will never compromise their values or surrender their identities. To nineteenth-century individuals, America offered a vast and challenging frontier—a place where individuals could preserve their identities. The question I want to answer is how the values of these frontier heroes survive in the hard-boiled heroes of American detective novels.
>
> —Neil Okun, "Heroism in the American Detective Novel"

2. In the body of the paper, you develop an answer to the basic question in terms of individual works, supplemented by comments drawn from secondary sources. Secondary sources—books and articles—help you to clarify the meaning of the works you discuss, to explain the connections between them, and to sharpen the edge of your argument. But the works themselves—not the secondary sources—should be the prime source of evidence for your argument:

> Dashiell Hammett's first novel, *Red Harvest,* pits the Continental Op against a town totally controlled by three mobs and a corrupt police force. As Robert Parker notes, Personville (pronounced "Poisonville") is the ultimate "symbol of the end of the frontier . . . a western city, sprung up on the prairie in the wake of the mines" (95). When the Op arrives in response to a call for his services, he discovers a dead client. At this point he could have left, since he had already received all the pay he would get. But in leaving, he would have sacrificed his heroic stature, so he stays to fight for what he sees as justice.
>
> He wins only a limited victory. Though he eventually cleans up the town by turning the various mobs against each other, the novel lets us see that evil will return. When the Op leaves, Personville is "nice and clean and ready to go to the dogs again" (178). Nevertheless, the detective has endured and upheld his own personal code of morality.
>
> —Neil Okun

3. In the conclusion of the paper, you restate the main point of your argument and indicate what the argument contributes to our understanding of the works of literature you have discussed:

> The demand for an individual who will not compromise on questions of morality produced the wilderness hero, a man who fled the corrupting influence of society for the freedom and challenge of the frontier. When the frontier closed, this man no longer had a refuge; he was forced to fight to retain his individuality and preserve his moral integrity. With a value system rooted in the nineteenth-century frontier, the hero of the detective novel must often confront the twentieth-century city. The reaction is often violent, and the hero can never impose his values on society. Yet he is personally victorious, for he always leaves uncorrupted, and he continually restores our faith in what Sisk calls "the American as rugged individualist and shaper of his own destiny" (368).
>
> —Neil Okun

42.5 DOCUMENTING SOURCES IN THE HUMANITIES

IN-TEXT PARENTHESES VERSUS NOTES

Authors of papers written in the humanities typically cite sources in either one of two ways—in parentheses within the text or in notes. The author of the paragraphs quoted above uses the MLA style of parenthetical citation, the parenthetical style normally used in the humanities (see chapter 39). But if your teacher asks you to cite your sources in notes, you should follow the note system explained in the *Chicago Manual of Style*, 14th ed. (Chicago: U of Chicago P, 1993). In the *CMS* system, each citation in the text is followed by a raised number referring to a note.[1]

USING THE *CMS* NOTE SYSTEM

CMS notes may be footnotes at the bottom of each page or endnotes at the end of the paper. While footnotes are easier for the reader to find, they are sometimes harder for the writer to manage because varying amounts of room must be left for them on each page. Some word processing programs will lay out footnoted pages for you. But in any case, you should find out which kind of note your teacher prefers and then use it *consistently*. Do not use footnotes and endnotes in the same paper.

---

1. This is the note. (Citation numbers *within* the text are raised, but note numbers are not.)

All notes written in *CMS* style—whether footnotes or endnotes—should be written as follows. The first reference to any book you cite should look like this:

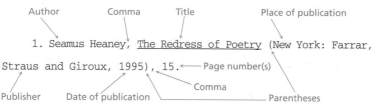

To cite again a source you have just cited in the previous note, use *Ibid.* (Latin for "in the same place"):

2. Ibid., 17.

To cite again a source you have cited more than one note earlier, use the author's last name:

3. Heaney, 17.

If your paper cites more than one work by the same author, a follow-up reference to any of his or her works should include a short version of its title:

4. Heaney, <u>Redress</u>, 17.

Specific in-text, footnote/endnote, and Bibliography-entry formats are illustrated below. For further variations, see the *CMS* or the student guide adapted from it, Kate L. Turabian's *Manual for Writers of Terms Papers, Theses, and Dissertations,* 6th ed. (rev. John Grossman and Alice Bennett [Chicago: U of Chicago P, 1987]).

1. **BOOK BY ONE AUTHOR**

Goldberg believes that "moral notions tend to be basic to each sociodiscursive order, for they are key in defining the interactive ways social subjects see and conceive [of] themselves."[1]

Raised number follows punctuation at end of sentence.

1. David Theo Goldberg, <u>Racist Culture: Philosophy and the Politics of Meaning</u> (Cambridge: Blackwell, 1993), 20.

First line of each footnote is indented five spaces.

Bibliographic entries are formatted as hanging-indent paragraphs.

Goldberg, David Theo. <u>Racist Culture: Philosophy and the</u> <u>Politics of Meaning</u>. Cambridge: Blackwell, 1993.

2. **BOOK BY TWO AUTHORS**

Kinder and Sanders maintain that "the most complicated aspect of race relations in America today concerns attitude."[2]

Footnotes, endnotes, and bibliographic entries are single-spaced, with a double space between them.

2. Donald R. Kinder and Lynne M. Sanders, <u>Divided by</u> <u>Color: Racial Politics and Democratic Ideals</u> (Chicago: University of Chicago Press, 1996), 6.

Kinder, Donald R., and Lynne M. Sanders. <u>Divided by Color:</u> <u>Racial Politics and Democratic Ideals</u>. Chicago: University of Chicago Press, 1996.

3. **BOOK BY THREE OR MORE AUTHORS**

Medhurst et al. argue that the "cold war, like its 'hot' counterpart, is a contest."[3]

3. Martin J. Medhurst, Robert L. Ivie, Philip Wander, and Robert L. Scott, <u>Cold War Rhetoric: Strategy, Metaphor,</u> <u>and Ideology</u> (New York: Greenwood, 1990), 19.

For subsequent references in text and footnotes, use *Medhurst et al.* (Latin *et alia,* "and others").

Medhurst, Martin J., Robert L. Ivie, Philip Wander, and Robert L. Scott. <u>Cold War Rhetoric: Strategy, Metaphor,</u> <u>and Ideology</u>. New York: Greenwood, 1990.

4. **BOOK, EDITED, WITH FOCUS ON ORIGINAL AUTHOR**

Thoreau says "we need to witness our own limits trans-
gressed, and some life pasturing freely where we never
wander."[4]

    4. Henry David Thoreau, <u>Walden</u>, ed. William Rossi (New
York: Norton, 1992), 212.

Thoreau, Henry David. <u>Walden</u>. Edited by William Rossi. New
    York: Norton, 1992.

CMS allows the abbreviations *Ed. (Edited by), Trans. (Translated by),* and
Comp. (Compiled by).

5. **BOOK, EDITED, WITH FOCUS ON EDITOR**

"For most of her life," writes J. Paul Hunter, "Mary Shelley
lived (apparently contentedly) in the shadow of her famous
parents and ultimately more famous husband."[5]

    5. J. Paul Hunter, ed., <u>Frankenstein</u>, by Mary Shelley
(New York: Norton, 1996), xi.

Hunter, J. Paul, ed. <u>Frankenstein</u>, by Mary Shelley. New
    York: Norton, 1996.

6. **BOOK WITH EDITOR(S)**

Gary Peller, one of the editors of <u>Critical Race Theory</u>,
thinks "the conflict between nationalists and integra-

tionists in the late sixties and early seventies represented a critical juncture in American race relations."[6]

    6. Kimberlé Crenshaw, Neil Gotanda, Gary Peller, and Kendall Thomas, eds., Critical Race Theory: The Key Writings That Formed the Movement (New York: New York University Press, 1995), 132–3.

For subsequent references in text and footnotes, use *Crenshaw et al.*

Crenshaw, Kimberlé, Neil Gotanda, Garry Peller, and Kendall
    Thomas, eds. Critical Race Theory: The Key Writings
    That Formed the Movement. New York: New York University
    Press, 1995.

7. **CHAPTER IN A BOOK**

"The basic issue in the classical period," according to Corbett, "was whether rhetoric or philosophy would be the dominant element in the Greek educational system."[7]

    7. Edward P. J. Corbett, "Classical and Modern Rhetoric: The Basic Issues," in Discourse Studies in Honor of James L. Kinneavy (Potomac, Maryland: Scripta Humanistica, 1995), 146.

Corbett, Edward P. J. "Classical and Modern Rhetoric: The
    Basic Issues." In Discourse Studies in Honor of James
    L. Kinneavy. Potomac, Maryland: Scripta Humanistica,
    1995.

8. **EDITION OTHER THAN THE FIRST**

As Petracca and Sorapure put it, "popular culture encompasses the most immediate and contemporary elements in our lives--

elements which are often subject to rapid changes in a highly technological world . . . by the ubiquitous mass media."[8]

8. Michael Petracca and Madeline Sorapure, eds., <u>Common Culture: Reading and Writing about American Popular Culture</u>, 2nd ed. (Upper Saddle River, New Jersey: Prentice Hall, 1998), 3.

Petracca, Michael, and Madeline Sorapure, eds. <u>Common Culture: Reading and Writing about American Popular Culture</u>, 2nd ed. Upper Saddle River, New Jersey: Prentice Hall, 1998.

9. REPRINT

"Women who had only known maid's uniforms and mammy-made dresses," Angelou writes, "donned the awkward men's pants and steel helmets."[9]

9. Maya Angelou, <u>Gather Together in My Name</u> (New York: Random House, 1974; reprint, New York: Bantam, 1993), 38.

Angelou, Maya. <u>Gather Together in My Name</u>. New York: Random House, 1974. Reprint, New York: Bantam, 1993.

▶ When you cite a reprint of a very old book, give only the year of the original publication along with full publication facts of the reprint.

▶ If the reprint adds something new or combines two or more volumes in one, give that information before the name of the city and publisher.

▶ If, as above, you give all the original publication data, you may omit the word *reprint,* though you may also retain it for clarity.

▶ Finally, if you give page references and are not certain that both editions have the same pagination, identify the edition used. For example: *(page citation is to the reprint edition).*

10. TRANSLATION

Albert Camus argues, "Capital punishment upsets the only indisputable human solidarity--our solidarity against death."[10]

    10. Albert Camus, <u>Resistance, Rebellion, and Death</u>, trans. Justin O'Brien (New York: Vintage, 1960), 222.

Camus, Albert. <u>Resistance, Rebellion, and Death</u>. Translated by Justin O'Brien. New York: Vintage, 1960.

11. CORPORATE AUTHOR

According to <u>Resources for Teaching Middle School Science</u>, "students explore the melting points and conductivity of ionic and covalent compounds."[11]

    11. National Science Resource Center, <u>Resources for Teaching Middle School Science</u> (Washington, D.C.: National Academy Press, 1998), 82.

National Science Resource Center. <u>Resources for Teaching Middle School Science</u>. Washington, D.C.: National Academy Press, 1998.

12. SELECTION FROM AN ANTHOLOGY

"My literary agenda," Mukherjee explains, "begins by acknowledging that America has transformed <u>me</u>. It does not end until I show how I (and the hundreds of thousands like me) have transformed America."[12]

12. Bharati Mukherjee, "A Four-Hundred-Year-Old Woman," in <u>The Norton Anthology of Short Fiction</u>, 6th ed., ed. R. V. Cassill and Richard Bausch (New York: Norton, 2000), 1704.

Mukherjee, Bharati. "A Four-Hundred-Year-Old Woman." In <u>The Norton Anthology of Short Fiction</u>, 6th ed., edited by R. V. Cassill and Richard Bausch. New York: Norton, 2000.

13. ARTICLE IN A MAGAZINE

"In South Florida," Martine Bury reports, "street gangs that represented most countries on the Caribbean, Central American and South American maps have created a blunt, broad geography to demarcate their turfs."[13]

13. Martine Bury, "Lost Ones," <u>The Source</u>, March 1999, 67.

Bury, Martine. "Lost Ones." <u>The Source</u>, March 1999, 67.

14. ARTICLE IN A JOURNAL WITH YEARLY VOLUME NUMBERS

Pamela L. Caughie states that "passing traditionally refers to the practice of representing oneself--for social, economic, or political reasons--as a member of a particular group not considered one's own."[14]

14. Pamela L. Caughie, "Let It Pass: Changing the Subject, Once Again," <u>PMLA</u> 112 (1997): 26-40.

Volume number

Caughie, Pamela L. "Let It Pass: Changing the Subject, Once Again." <u>PMLA</u> 112 (1997): 26-40.

15. ARTICLE IN A REFERENCE BOOK, SIGNED

Robert Brandt describes the Appalachian Trail as "a continuous marked footpath extending 2,140 miles through 14 states from Springer Mountain, Georgia, to Katahdin, Maine."[15]

15. Robert Brandt, "Appalachian Trail," in <u>The Tennessee Encyclopedia of History and Culture</u>, ed. Carroll Van West (Nashville: Tennessee Historical Society, 1998), 22.

Brandt, Robert. "Appalachian Trail." In <u>The Tennessee Encyclopedia of History and Culture</u>, edited by Carroll Van West. Nashville: Tennessee Historical Society, 1998.

16. ARTICLE IN A REFERENCE BOOK, UNSIGNED

"The bark and fruits" of the greenheart tree "contain bebeerine, an alkaloid formerly used to reduce fever."[16]

16. <u>Encyclopedia Britannica</u>, 15th ed., s.v., "greenheart."

In notes for well-known, alphabetically arranged reference books, as above, omit facts of publication (place, publisher, and date), volume, and page number. Cite the edition if it's not the first, then cite the item, preceded by *s.v.* (*sub verbo*, Latin for "under the word").

Do not list well-known reference books in your bibliography.

17. ARTICLE IN A NEWSPAPER

Wilgoren reports that "in retrospect, the name sounds a little menacing, now that it is linked to the two young men behind one of the deadliest school massacres in American history."[17]

17. Jodi Wilgoren, "Menacing 'Trench Coat Mafia' Was Just a Joke, at First," <u>New York Times</u>, 25 April 1999, national edition, sec. A, p. 1.

Wilgoren, Jodi. "Menacing 'Trench Coat Mafia' Was Just a Joke, at First." <u>New York Times</u>, 25 April 1999, national edition, sec. A, p. 1.

Specify the edition.

18. ONLINE BOOK

Austen describes Emma Woodhouse as "handsome, clever, and rich with a comfortable home and happy disposition."[18]

18. Jane Austen, <u>Emma</u>, Berkeley Digital Library Sun-SITE, University of California, Berkeley, May 15, 1997, <http://sunsite.berkeley.edu/Literature/Austen/Emma/1emma1.html> (25 June 1999).

Austen, Jane. <u>Emma</u>. Berkeley Digital Library SunSITE, University of California, Berkeley, May 15, 1997. <http://sunsite.berkeley.edu/Literature/Austen/Emma/1emma1.html> (25 June 1999).

19. ONLINE ARTICLE

An article in the <u>Society for American Archaeology Bulletin</u> states that the Confederated Tribes of the Umatilla Indian Reservation could claim the 9,300-year-old find because "the area in which the find was made is Umatilla aboriginal land."[19]

671

```
      19. "9,300-Year-Old Skeleton Sparks Controversy in

Northwest," Society for American Archaeology Bulletin 14,

no. 5 (November 1996), <http://www.sscf.ucsb.edu/

SAABulletin/14.5/SAA5.html> (24 June 1999).


"9,300-Year-Old Skeleton Sparks Controversy in Northwest."

      Society for American Archaeology Bulletin 14, no. 5

      (November 1996). <http://www.sscf.ucsb.edu/

      SAABulletin/14.5/SAA5.html> (24 June 1999).
```

The current *CMS* provides very limited coverage of online-source documentation. Until the appearance of the fifteenth edition, the *CMS* editors recommend that you consult any of several other style guides, including MLA (see chapter 39); APA (see 42.7); Xia Li and Nancy B. Crane, *Electronic Styles: A Handbook for Citing Electronic Information* (Medford, NJ: Information Today, 1996); and Andrew Harnack and Eugene Kleppinger, *Online! A Reference Guide to Using Internet Sources* (New York: St. Martin's, 1997), the basis for our formats. Ask your instructor about which style guide you should follow.

42.6 ORGANIZING RESEARCH PAPERS IN THE SOCIAL SCIENCES

Research papers in the social sciences are commonly based on the observation of particular cases or groups. If you are asked to write a case study or to report your findings on an assigned question, your most important primary source will be the record of your own observations, including the results of interviews you may conduct and questionnaires you may distribute. Together with published sources, these will provide the material for your paper.

A report of findings in the social sciences normally includes five parts:

1.   The introduction states the question you propose to answer and explains how the methods of a particular social science can help you answer it. Suppose the question is "Do children with disabilities gain more confidence from competitive sports (such as the Special Olympics) than from noncompetitive activities?" Having posed this question, the introduction

explains how the methods of developmental psychology can help you find and interpret the data needed to answer it.

2. The methods section of the paper indicates how you gathered the data for your study. Here you describe the particular characteristics of the group you studied, your methods of study (observation, interview, questionnaire), the questions you asked, and the printed sources you consulted, such as previous studies of children with disabilities who engage in competitive sports. You should describe your methods of gathering data in such a way that someone else can repeat your study and thus test its results.

3. The results section puts the raw data you have gathered into clearly organized form: into paragraphs, tabulated listings, illustrations, or graphs. (On tables and figures, see 42.10.)

4. The discussion section interprets the results of the study and explains its significance for an understanding of the topic as a whole. With reference to the sample question above, for instance, it could explain whether or not competitive sports actually benefit children with disabilities. If competition threatens their confidence rather than strengthening it, then programs like the Special Olympics should be reevaluated.

5. The conclusion briefly summarizes what the study has found and states the implications of its findings, including points to be further explored.

In addition to the paper itself, you may be asked to furnish an abstract of it. If so, read on.

WRITING ABSTRACTS FOR SOCIAL SCIENCE PAPERS

The abstract of a social science paper normally appears at the beginning. It consists of a single paragraph that succinctly explains what your paper tries to show. Here, for instance, is an abstract of a sociology article:

Pollution knows no frontiers: dirty or dangerous substances dumped in rivers or off the coast, or spewed into the atmosphere in one European country, have both direct and indirect harmful consequences for neighboring countries. Attempts by the capitalist democracies of Western Europe to clean up the local environment and avoid continental or even global ecological damage, have in the past been thwarted by the dirty, inefficient, and irresponsible modes of production adopted by the socialist countries of Eastern Europe. This was compounded by the political secrecy surrounding many of the polluting activities of the socialist military-industrial complex. Only recently, with the fall of socialism, has it been possible to envisage a full and free exchange of information about pollution and establish the basis for ecological cooperation throughout the entire continent.

> —Christie Davies, "The Need for Ecological Cooperation in Europe,"
> *International Journal on the Unity of the Sciences* 4 (1991):201–16.

This paragraph illustrates what every effective abstract should be: *succinct, informative, and comprehensive.*

First, the paragraph is succinct. Its first four words state one of the main points of the article: "Pollution knows no frontiers."

Second, the paragraph is informative. Using highly significant modifiers such as "dumped in rivers or off the coast" and "dirty, inefficient, and irresponsible," it tersely reveals how pollution moves from one country to another. Every sentence, in fact, is richly modified to deliver the maximum amount of information in a small number of words.

Third, the paragraph is comprehensive. It not only states the main point of the essay but shows how the point is developed. The recent history of pollution in Europe, we learn, is presented as a conflict between the cleanup efforts made by Western European democracies and the messes made by the socialist countries of Eastern Europe. Just as importantly, we learn what the article tells us about the latest development in this history: the fall of socialism may lead to full cooperation in the control of pollution throughout Western Europe.

42.7 DOCUMENTING SOURCES IN THE SOCIAL SCIENCES

USING APA STYLE

The *Publication Manual of the American Psychological Association*, 4th ed. (Washington, D.C.: APA, 1994), presents APA style, which is used in the behavioral and social sciences. If you are writing a paper for a psychology or sociology class, for example, check to see whether your instructor expects you to use APA. (On the APA format for typing a research paper, see p. 229. To obtain print publications or software devoted to APA style, visit <www.apa.org>.)

In APA style, parenthetical citations appear within the text, and full bibliographic entries appear in a list titled "References" at the end of the text.

CAPITALIZATION Within the body of your text, use standard capitalization. For the References page, follow this example:

Author's last name ———

Initials of first and middle names

Comma

Period

Capitalize first word of title and subtitle (if any), plus proper nouns.

Date of publication parenthesized ———

Erikson, E. H. (1964). <u>Insight and responsibility: Lectures on the ethical implications of psychoanalytic insight.</u>

Place of publication ———

New York: Norton.

Colon Publisher

Underlined period

IN-TEXT CITATION AND REFERENCE-PAGE FORMATS

1. BOOK BY ONE AUTHOR

Author's name used in discussion:

> Levine (1976) has found that "marriages in which the parents
> share responsibilities equally tend to be the happiest"
> (p. 176).

Author's name not used in discussion:

> One researcher has found that "marriages in which the par-
> ents share responsibilities equally tend to be the happiest"
> (Levine, 1976, p. 176).

> Levine, J. A. (1976). <u>Who will raise the children?</u> Philadel-
> phia: Lippincott.

All lines after the first are indented five spaces.

Double-space throughout.

2. BOOK BY TWO AUTHORS

If a work has two authors, give both authors' names each time the reference occurs in the text.

> According to one team of scholars, "Perhaps the most compli-
> cated aspect of race relations in America today concerns
> attitude" (Kinder & Sanders, 1996, p. 6).

Ampersand for <u>and</u>

Kinder, D. R., and Sanders, L. M. (1996). <u>Divided by color:</u>
<u>Racial politics and democratic ideas.</u> Chicago: Univer-
sity of Chicago Press.

3.   BOOK BY MORE THAN TWO AUTHORS

Give all the names in the **first citation** only:

Miller, Dellefield, and Musso (1980) have called for more
effective advertising of financial aid programs.

In **later citations** give just the first author's name followed by *et al.* (Latin
et alia, "and others"):

Miller et al. (1980) have studied the institutional management of financial aid.

Miller, S., Dellefield, W., & Musso, T. (1980). <u>A Guide to</u>
<u>selected financial aid management practices.</u> Washing-
ton, DC: U.S. Department of Education.

4.   MORE THAN ONE WORK BY THE SAME AUTHOR

On your References page, provide complete information for each work and
arrange entries by date, from earliest to most recent. If two or more works
by an author were published the same year, put them in alphabetical order
and assign a lowercase letter to each, placing that letter next to the date.

In <u>Keeping Faith: Philosophy and Race in America,</u> West concentrates on "cultural criticism" (1993a). In <u>Prophetic Re-</u>
<u>flections: Notes on Race and Power in America</u> (1993b), he
focuses on "cultural crisis."

West, C. (1993a). <u>Keeping faith: Philosophy and race in</u>
<u>America.</u> New York: Routledge.

West, C. (1993b). <u>Prophetic reflections: Notes on race and</u>
<u>power in America.</u> Monroe, ME: Common Courage Press.

5. **BOOK WITH EDITOR**

One author believes "full and free public discussion and
debate is an absolute prerequisite to any process of democratic decision making" (Green, 1993, p. 164).

Green, P. (Ed.). (1993). <u>Democracy: Key concepts in critical</u>
<u>theory.</u> Atlantic Highlands, NJ: Humanities Press.

6. **EDITION AFTER THE FIRST**

"If a therapist can arrange the situation so that the patient will concede that he is the authority on what the patient is <u>really</u> saying, then the therapist is in control of
what kind of relationship they have" (Haley, 1990, p. 79).

Haley, Jay. (1990). <u>Strategies of psychotherapy</u> (2nd ed.).
Rockville, MD: Triangle Press.

7. **TRANSLATION**

One author asks, "How and why is the practice of photography
predisposed to a diffusion so wide that there are few households, at least in towns, which do not possess a camera?"
(Bourdieu, 1990, p. 13).

Bourdieu, P. (1990). <u>Photography: A middle-brow art</u>
(S. Whiteside, Trans.). Stanford: Stanford University
Press. (Originally published in 1965)

8. **ARTICLE IN A REFERENCE BOOK**

According to the ancient Greeks, "emotional and physical health depended on a balance of four fluids, called humours" ("Personality," p. 311).

Personality. (1993). In <u>The new encyclopaedia Britannica</u> (15th ed., Vol. 10, pp. 311-312). Chicago: Encyclopaedia Britannica.

9. **ARTICLE IN A MAGAZINE**

Shacochis (1999) observes that the recent intervention of the American military in such international conflicts as Kosovo has produced the complicated notion of "military humanism" (p. 45).

Volume number — Shacochis, B. (1999, December). Soldiers of great fortune. <u>Harper's, 299,</u> 44-56.

10. **ARTICLE IN A SCHOLARLY JOURNAL**

Kamerman (1983, p. 36) reports that from 1967 to 1980, kindergarten enrollment rose by about a third, and from 1969 to 1980, nursery school enrollment more than doubled.

Kamerman, S. B. (1983). Child-care services: A national picture. <u>Monthly Labor Review, 106</u>(12), 35-39.

Issue number

11. **ARTICLE IN A NEWSPAPER**

<u>The New York Times</u> reports that "a bipartisan group of Senators will propose a plan on Thursday to deal with Social Se-

curity's looming problems . . . an issue that had seemed all
but dead this year" (Stevenson, 1999, p. A23). Page number
in section A

Stevenson, R. W. (1999, May 20). Congress and White House
try to break social security deadlock. The New York
Times, p. A23.

12. EDITORIAL, LETTER TO THE EDITOR, OR REVIEW

One commentator notes that although Dr. Robert Fiddes
"endangered the lives of study participants, and shows no
apparent remorse . . . he is sentenced to [only] 15 months
in prison" (Sims, 1999, p. A28).

Sims, Pat H. (1999, May 17). When drug trials hurt patients;
light sentence. [Letter to the editor]. The New York
Times, p. A28.

13. ONLINE[†] MAGAZINE

Provide author, year and issue of magazine, article title, magazine title,
URL, and date of access.

As Keegan (1999) notes, "Researchers and marketers have
known for decades that when it comes to kids and their toys,
speed sells. Give a child a choice between a storybook and a
television set, and guess which one will grab his attention"
(paragraph 10).

Keegan, P. (1999, November/December). Culture quake. Mother
Jones. [Magazine, selected stories on-line]. Available:
http://www.mojones.com/mother_jones/ND99/quake.html
[1999, December 6].

[†]Note that APA hyphenates *online,* though this handbook and Li and Crane's *Electronic
Styles* do not.

14. ONLINE SCHOLARLY JOURNAL

Follows pattern for magazine except volume and series numbers follow the journal's title.

> Crabtree (2000) asks:
>
> > Why is the unnoticed important? I would want to say
> > that is not just important but of <u>primordial</u> importance
> > in that, and precisely because, it is within the
> > practical actions that constitute our mundane reality
> > that the one and only real world, the one given through
> > perception, the one and only one that is experienced,
> > is inherently organised or structured. (paragraph 18)

> Crabtree, A. (2000, February). Remarks on the social
>   organisation of space and place. <u>Journal of Mundane Be-</u>
>   <u>havior</u> [Online], <u>1</u>(1). Available: http://www.mundane-
>   behavior.org/index2.htm [2000, March 1].

15. WEB SITE

Provide author's name if available, date of creation or last update of Web site, title of site, URL, and date of access.

> "Citistate is the name Neal Peirce and Curtis Johnson coined
> in 1993 to describe how metropolitan regions have begun to
> operate in the new, post-Cold War world economy" (<u>Citi-</u>
> <u>states,</u> 2000, paragraph 1).

> <u>Citistates</u> [Homepage of The Citistates Group], [Online].
>   (January 28, 2000). Available: http://www.citistates.
>   com/whatis.htm [2000, February 14].

The current APA guide provides very limited coverage of online-source documentation and follows Xia Li and Nancy B. Crane's *Electronic Style* (1993). Our formats are based on the updated version of Li and Crane's book, *Electronic Styles: A Handbook for Citing Electronic Information* (1996) and on the information at their Web site: <www.uvm.edu/~ncrane/estyles/apa.html>. Ask your instructor about which style guide you should follow.

42.8 ORGANIZING RESEARCH PAPERS IN THE NATURAL SCIENCES

Research papers in the natural sciences are generally of two kinds: review papers, which analyze the current state of knowledge on a specialized topic, and laboratory reports, which present the results of an actual experiment. Both kinds of papers normally begin with an abstract: a brief, one-paragraph summary of the paper's most important points. But the two kinds of papers differ in many respects.

The primary sources for a review paper are current articles in scientific journals, and the purpose of a review paper is not to make an argument or develop an original idea but to survey and explain what laboratory research has recently shown about the topic. A review paper normally does three things: (1) it introduces its topic, explaining why it is important and what questions about it have been raised by recent research; (2) it develops the topic by reviewing that research under a series of subheadings; and (3) it concludes by summarizing what has been discovered and stating what remains to be investigated.

A laboratory report explains how an experiment made in a natural science laboratory answers a question such as "How do changes in temperature affect the conductivity of copper?" Resembling in its format a report of findings in the social sciences, the lab report usually presents its materials as follows:

1. The *title* succinctly states what was tested. It might be, for instance, "The Effect of Temperature Changes on the Conductivity of Copper."

2. The *abstract* summarizes the report in about two hundred words.

3. The *introduction* explains the question that the lab test is designed to answer.

4. A section on *methods and materials* explains how the experiment was made, what apparatus was used, and how data were collected.

5. A section on *results* puts the data into clearly organized form, using graphs, tables, and illustrations where necessary. (See 42.10 on the presentation of tables and figures.)

6. The *conclusion* explains the significance of the results.

7. A *reference list* gives any published sources used, including any manuals or textbooks.

42.9 DOCUMENTING SOURCES IN THE SCIENCES

Each subject in the sciences has its own style of documentation, which is explained in one of the following style manuals:

BIOLOGY

Council of Biology Editors. *Scientific Style and Format: The CBE Manual for Authors, Editors and Publishers.* 6th ed. New York: Cambridge UP, 1994.

CHEMISTRY

Dodd, Janet S., ed. *The American Chemical Society Style Guide: A Manual for Authors and Editors.* 2nd ed. Washington, 1997.

GEOLOGY

Bates, Robert L., Rex Buchanan, and Marla Adkins-Heljeson, eds. *Geowriting: A Guide to Writing, Editing, and Printing in Earth Science.* 5th ed. Alexandria: American Geological Institute, 1995.

LINGUISTICS

Linguistic Society of America. *LSA Bulletin,* Dec. issue, annually.

MATHEMATICS

American Mathematical Society. *The AMS Author Handbook: General Instructions for Preparing Manuscripts.* Providence: AMS, 1997.

MEDICINE

Iverson, Cheryl, et al. *American Medical Association Manual of Style.* 9th ed. Baltimore: Williams and Wilkins, 1997.

PHYSICS

American Institute of Physics. *AIP Style Manual.* 4th ed. New York: AIP, 1990 (updated 1997).

Your instructor will tell you which scientific style of documentation you are expected to use. What follows is a brief guide to the style recommended by the Council of Science Editors (CSE), which until January 1, 2000, was called the Council of Biology Editors (CBE). Complete information on this style will be found in the CBE manual cited above; for more information on the CSE, visit <www.councilscienceeditors.org>.

USING CBE STYLE

The CBE style manual presents two documentation systems used in mathematics and the natural sciences. One is the *name-year* system; the other, illustrated below, is the citation-sequence system. In this system, each source is numbered in the text and then listed by number on a References page at the end of the paper. If a source is used more than once, the second use and any subsequent uses take the same number as the first. More than one number may appear in different places in a single sentence.

IN-TEXT CITATION AND REFERENCE-PAGE FORMATS

Raised number goes inside punctuation.

1. **SINGLE AUTHOR MENTIONED IN TEXT**

   According to Nagle[1], sunburn affects reproductive success only in rare instances.

2. **TWO OR MORE AUTHORS MENTIONED IN TEXT**

   Weiss and Mann[2] have shown that folate deficiency retards growth, causes anemia, and inhibits fertility.

3. **THREE OR MORE AUTHORS MENTIONED IN TEXT**

   Holick and others[3] exposed hypopigmented human skin to simulated solar unltraviolet radiation for various times and determined the photoproducts of 7-dehydrocholesterol.

4. **NO AUTHOR MENTIONED IN TEXT**

   This theory implies that ultraviolet radiation can penetrate more easily into lightly pigmented skin and will result in a greater production of vitamin D than will a heavily melanated skin subjected to the same light[4].

5. **SPECIFIC PAGES OR PARAGRAPHS CITED**

It is reasonable to assume that dark pigmentation was prominent among the ancient human populations[5].

6. **TWO OR MORE SOURCES CITED IN ONE REFERENCE**

How is the distribution of skin color among indigenous populations to be explained? One hypothesis is that heavily
melanated skin emerged in sundrenched countries as protection against sunburn[2,5].

Use only initials (without space or
punctuation between them) for
authors' first and middle names.

Capitalize only first word
of title.

References ←——————— Center.

Single-space
each entry,
double-space
between them.

1. Nagle JJ. Heredity and human affairs. St. Louis: Mosby;
   1974. 337 p.

Not underlined

2. Weiss MA, Mann AE. Human biology and behaviour: an an-
   thropological perspective. Boston: Little, Brown; 1985.
   274 p.

3. Holick MF, MacLaughlin JA, Dopplet SH. Regulation of cu-
   taneous previtamin D3 photosynthesis in man: skin pigment
   is an essential regulator. Science 1981;211:589-95.←——— No spaces
   between date
   volume numb-
   and pages

4. Loomis WF. Skin-pigment regulation of vitamin-D biosyn-
   thesis in man. Science 167;157:66-71.

5. Kottack CP. Anthropology: the exploration of human
   diversity. New York: Random House; 1978. p. 62.

table **42.10**

6. **ONLINE BOOK**

6. Young RM. Darwin's metaphor: nature's place in Victorian culture. [online] 1985. Available from: http://www.shef.ac.uk/~psych/darwin/dar.html. Accessed 1999 Nov 30.

7. **ONLINE JOURNAL**

7. Cukelly GJ, McNulty H, and Scott JM. Fortification with low amounts of folic acid makes a significant difference in folate status in young women: implications for the prevention of neural tube defects. Am J Clin Nutr [online] 1999;70:234-9. Available from: http://www.ajcn.org/cgi/content/full/70/2/234. Accessed 1999 Aug 30.

8. **WEB SITE**

8. Bry L. Visible human transverse section through the head [online]. 1998. Available from http://www.madsci.org/ cgi-bin/cgiwrap/~lynn/image?name=a_vm1110& show_this=brain&searc7/20/99. Accessed 1999 Jul 20.

42.10 TABLES AND FIGURES IN RESEARCH PAPERS

Research papers in the social and natural sciences often require tables (tabular data) or figures (graphs and illustrations). Tables and figures should be numbered consecutively (Table 1, Table 2; Figure 1, Figure 2) and accompanied by a descriptive caption, as shown below.

PRESENTING TABLES

Put the caption for a table above it as a heading. Use lowercase letters (a,b,c) for footnotes, and put the footnotes at the bottom of the table—not at the bottom of the page or the end of the paper. If the table is photo-

Table 5.1 Selected Indicators of Development in Eastern Europe and the USSR: Pre-WWII and 1950-70

	Pre-WWII	1950	1960	1970
ILLITERATES *(percent of total population)*				
Bulgaria	31.5% (1934)		(10.7%)[a]	
Czechoslovakia	4.1% (1930)			
Hungary	9.0% (1930)		3.8%	2.4%
Poland	23.1% (1931)	5.8%	2.7%	
Romania	42.9% (1930)	23.1%		
USSR	43.4% (1926)		1.5%	0.3%
Yugoslavia	44.6% (1931)	25.4%	21.0%	15.1%
INFANT MORTALITY *(rates per thousand live births)*				
Bulgaria	147 (1935)	94.5	45.1	27.3
Czechoslovakia	130 (1935)	77.7	23.5	22.1
Hungary	157 (1935)	85.7	47.6	35.9
Poland	137 (1935)	111.2	54.8	33.4
Romania	182 (1935)	116.7	74.6	49.4
USSR	181 (1926)	80.7	35.3	24.7
Yugoslavia	153 (1935)	118.4	87.7	55.5
AGRICULTURAL POPULATION *(active earners and dependents in agriculture as percent of total population)*				
Bulgaria	73.2% (1934)		45.2%	
Czechoslovakia	34.7% (1930)	24.9%	19.3%	13.2%
Hungary	51.9% (1930)	49.3%	34.8%	22.8%
Poland	60.0% (1931)	46.4%	37.8%	29.8%
Romania	72.3% (1930)			(45.1%)[b]
USSR	77.5% (1926)			22.8%
Yugoslavia	76.6% (1931)		49.6%	38.2%
URBANIZATION *(population in urban areas 20,000 and over as percent of total population)*				
Bulgaria	12.1% (1934)		(29.1%)[c]	39.7%
Czechoslovakia	16.6% (1930)	23.6%	25.3%	31.1%
Hungary	29.1% (1930)	34.3%	37.0%	
Poland	17.0% (1931)	25.6%	31.8%	37.3%
Romania	13.4% (1930)	17.1%	19.6%	28.4%
USSR	12.0% (1926)		35.6%	44.3%
Yugoslavia			18.8%	26.0%

[a] Average of 1956 and 1965 figures
[b] 1966 figure
[c] Average of 1956 and 1965 figures

Note. From *The East European and Soviet data handbook: Political, social, and developmental indicators, 1945-1975* (p. 382), by P. Shoup, 1981, New York: Columbia University Press.

copied from a printed source, put a source note under it that follows the appropriate style for your discipline. (The note for Table 5.1, p. 686, follows APA style.)

PRESENTING FIGURES

Put the caption for a figure—a graph or an illustration—just below the figure. The source note should follow the appropriate style. (The note for Figure 1 below follows APA style.)

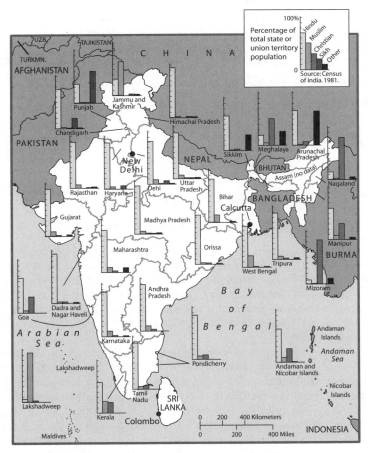

Figure 1. The Religions of India
Note. From *From voting to violence: Democratization and nationalist conflict* (p. 288), by J. Snyder, 2000, New York: Norton.

42.11 WRITING EXAMINATIONS, APPLICATIONS, AND LETTERS

WRITING EXAMINATION ESSAYS

The best way to start writing a good examination essay is to read the question carefully. On a final examination in a course on modern American history, for example, students were asked to "show how Lyndon Johnson's policies in Vietnam grew out of the policies pursued by his predecessors from 1941 on." The question was quite pointed. It asked not for general impressions of the Vietnam War but for a specific analysis of the succession of policies that led the United States into it.

After reading the question, one student made a single scratch outline inside the cover of his bluebook:

CONTAINMENT

1. FDR, Truman—Vietnam and Korea

2. Ike—1954, SEATO, South Vietnam

3. JFK—military buildup

Sum up Johnson's inheritance

With those few notes before him, the student then wrote the following essay:

American involvement in the Vietnam War did not begin with Johnson, or even with Kennedy. Rather, it began during World War II and was developed considerably during the years of containment of the Truman administration. As Stephen Ambrose puts it in his book, the U.S. was paying up on an insurance policy on containment that began with the Truman doctrine (1947), was extended to Korea (1950), and was applied finally to Vietnam (1954).

In 1941, Roosevelt supported the Vietnamese (specifically Ho Chi Minh), along with the French colonialists, against Japanese aggression. But after the Japanese were forced out, intense fighting broke out between the French and the Vietnamese, and in 1950 Truman signed a Mutual Defense Agreement with the French. From this point on, the U.S. had committed itself to support anyone against Ho Chi Minh and the communists of Hanoi. Truman was thus applying to Vietnam the containment policy he was also using in Korea. As in Korea, the U.S. aimed to halt the communism (in this case, of China) anywhere.

The next rung in the American ladder of involvement came in 1954. The Vietnamese defeat of the French at Dien Bien Phu signaled the end of

French involvement and the official beginning of American involvement. In September 1954 the Eisenhower administration formed the Southeast Asia Treaty Organization (SEATO) and committed the United States to the defense of South Vietnam as a bulwark against the expansion of Communist China.

Kennedy inherited much of Eisenhower's policy toward Vietnam and added some of his own thinking, leaving Johnson an even larger legacy of involvement. While Kennedy did not commit troops, his military actions were significant. First, he increased dramatically (to 16,000) the number of American advisers in Vietnam. Second, he gave American air support to South Vietnam and allowed American advisers to shoot back if shot at. Third, he began military preparations within the Pentagon. As a result of all these actions, the first death of an American soldier occurred during Kennedy's first year in office, and American casualties increased considerably from that point on.

When Kennedy was assassinated in 1963, Johnson inherited the Vietnam quagmire, and his inheritance was a rich one. From Roosevelt, he got the beginning of a U.S. role in Vietnam. From Truman, the policy of containment—the pledge to stop communist expansion at the hands of Ho Chi Minh. From Eisenhower he got an official commitment to the defense of South Vietnam. And from Kennedy, finally, he got the beginnings of a substantial U.S military involvement there.

So Johnson's decision to send troops to Vietnam in 1965 simply capitalized on the military preparations that Kennedy had made. Though Johnson imposed his own personality on Vietnam policy, he was strongly influenced by what Truman, Eisenhower, and Kennedy gave him: the need to succeed in Vietnam—militarily—along the lines of containment.

Like most examination essays, this one shows some signs of haste, such as the sentence fragment in the next-to-last paragraph. But no one taking a one- or two-hour exam has much time to worry about the finer points of diction and sentence structure. What we do find here are the three things essential to a good examination essay: (1) a response focused sharply and consistently on the question, (2) a substantial quantity of specific detail, and (3) strong organization. Throughout the essay, the author keeps his eye on the task of answering the question: of explaining what Johnson received from his predecessors and how that inheritance shaped his actions in Vietnam.

Now consider what another student did with a question on a sociology exam. Asked to "define 'economic-opportunity structure' and describe its relation to the traditional nuclear family," the student wrote this:

The "economic-opportunity structure" (EOS) refers to the "working world" and is most often associated with the practical aspect of marriage. Traditionally, males have had superior access to this structure and still do today.

In the traditional nuclear family, the male is the mediator between the family and the EOS. Such a position gives him considerable "power" within the family unit. If members of a family are totally dependent on the man for economic survival, they must concede all power and authority to him. He is the "king of the family." He brings home the fruits of the EOS, the production (usually monetary), and the family consumes these products, investing in various material possessions which in turn give them social status and prestige.

The man's degree of success in the EOS highly affects his relation to his wife and family. In the traditional family, if the man fulfills his "duty" as chief economic supporter, the wife "rewards" him with more attention to his needs and to her traditional duties—keeping a house and raising children. The husband then rewards her in various ways, with a car of her own, perhaps, or a fur coat, or a bigger house. It's an ongoing cycle. The higher-status wives are also more likely to concede that the husband should have the "upper hand" in the marriage.

This whole cycle works in reverse in lower-status families where the husband is unsuccessful as a breadwinner, causing resentment among the wives and unwillingness to submit to his authority.

If the wife in the traditional nuclear family decides to enter the EOS, her commitment to a career is usually far less than that of her husband. Her primary duty is still to her family and husband. The husband remains chief economic provider. But the woman gains more marital power because now she actually brings income into the house. Her occupation gives her self-esteem, and the marriage moves toward an egalitarian relation.

All of these cases show how economic power outside the family affects the balance of power within it. A successful breadwinner is rewarded with attention; an unsuccessful one has to put up with resentment; and the status of a wife within the family improves when she takes a job. Thus the power of any one member of a nuclear family seems to depend a lot on his or her performance in the "economic-opportunity structure"—the working world.

The question calls for a definition of a phrase and an explanation of a relationship. The answer provides both. It defines the phrase and explains the relationship of the "EOS" to the traditional nuclear family, showing how the husband's power to make money affects his power within the family and how the status of the wife is affected by her decision to take a job. This essay has no introduction because it needs none; in effect, it is introduced by the question. But it does have a conclusion.

To write a good examination essay, then, you should go directly to the point of the question. You should deal with the question as specifically as possible, and you should keep it continually in sight. Finally, you should end by summarizing your chief points and reaffirming the main point of the essay as a whole.

APPLYING FOR ADMISSION TO A SCHOOL OF BUSINESS, LAW, MEDICINE, OR GRADUATE STUDY: THE PERSONAL STATEMENT

Applying for admission to any kind of graduate program takes more than simply filling out an application form. Most schools ask you to write a personal statement in which you explain why you plan to go into business, medicine, law, or an academic field. Your chances of getting admitted will of course depend considerably on your college grades, your letters of recommendation, and your performance on examinations like the LSAT. But a personal statement often tells more about you than anything else can.

What kind of statement do admissions officers want? They want to know as specifically as possible what has led you to choose a particular career, what you hope to accomplish in it, and what you have already done to prepare yourself for it. The more specific you can be about your motivation, your experience, and your long-range plans, the more persuasive your statement will be. Consider this statement made by an applicant to medical school:

> A major turning point in my life occurred following my second year in college, when I was hired as a research assistant in pediatric hematology at the New England Medical Center. During the sixteen months I spent in Boston, I gained valuable insights into the practice of medicine and found that I had a special aptitude for research. I returned to college determined to become a doctor and quite motivated in my academic work.
>
> At the New England Medical Center I worked with very little supervision and was expected to be resourceful and creative in carrying out my lab responsibilities. I found that I had a talent for working out technical problems and the intellectual ability to design my own procedures. In addition to my laboratory work, I took the initiative to learn about the various diseases seen by the pediatric hematology department and about the treatment programs that were employed.
>
> I learned a great deal about terminal illness through my job, and also through the death, from leukemia, of the young son of close friends of mine. During the last months of this child's life, I spent a considerable amount of time with his family, helping them to cope with their impending loss. I found I was able to offer types of support other friends and family members could not. I matured and grew from this experience. I learned that I could be open and responsive when faced with difficult and painful situations. I also realized that a need existed for people who could assist the terminally ill and their families.
>
> In January 1993 I joined Hospice of Santa Cruz, where I was trained as a volunteer visitor and was assigned to the family of a man with stomach cancer. I feel that my involvement with the family is of benefit both to them and to me. I can support them by serving as a catalyst to get feelings expressed, and from them I am learning to be a compassionate listener. I

am convinced my experience with Hospice will help me, as a medical worker, to be understanding and open in dealing with death.

My academic work during the past two years has, for the most part, been of outstanding quality. I chose to complete a chemistry major, with emphasis in biochemistry, and will be graduating in December 1993. I have worked for the past year and a half on a senior research project in cryoenzymology. Laboratory work presents numerous technical and intellectual challenges, and I have become quite skilled and competent in approaching these problems. I have been attracted to research because it serves to ground the theory one learns in the classroom in practical day-to-day applications. Whereas I do not expect to pursue a career in research, my laboratory experience has given me a good perspective into the nature of scientific study, has helped me develop critical thinking skills, and has offered the pleasure and satisfaction that comes with the successful completion of a project.

This past academic year I have encountered for the first time the challenge of teaching. I have been a tutor in organic chemistry, introductory chemistry, and biochemistry. To be a good tutor one not only needs to have a solid command of the subject matter but must also look at the material from the student's perspective and seek creative methods to convey information in a way that can be grasped by the student. I have found that I can do this quite effectively, both at the very basic introductory level and at the more sophisticated level of biochemistry. Through tutoring I have discovered that I love teaching. I now realize that one of the compelling attractions that medicine offers me is the opportunity to be a teacher to all kinds of people, from patients to other physicians.

I am grateful to have had in these past five years a rich variety of experiences that have prepared me for the diversity I expect to encounter in a medical career. Research, teaching, the direct care of people who are sick, and encounters with death are all part of the practice of medicine. I have gained insights, limited though they may be, into all of these. As a result I am confident that I know what I will be facing as a doctor and that I have the skills and ability to be a creative and supportive physician.

This statement bristles with detail. It tells exactly how the writer discovered her interest in medicine and what she has already done to prepare herself for a career in it. By describing her experiences in laboratory research, college courses, teaching, and working with the families of the terminally ill, she shows that she has both the ability and the sensitivity to make a career in medicine.

Furthermore, this statement is well organized. Introduced with a paragraph on the particular experience that led the writer to a medical career, the statement concludes with a paragraph on the net effect of all her experiences. In between these two paragraphs, she tells in chronological order the story of her development, and each of her paragraphs develops a specific point about what she learned. Altogether, it is not hard to see why this writer was admitted to medical school.

To see what a difference good writing makes, compare her statement with one made by an applicant to a graduate school of business:

> Represented a Cable TV association in a twelve-million dollar public financing. Responsibilities included fostering a marketable image of our client and their objictives for the benifet of the underwriters and potential investors. This also involved making numerous decisions and analyses in regard to our interface with FCC requirements.
>
> The more significint factors impacting my long-range development from this experience include that I learned the coordination of financing needs and federal requirements. Throughly mastered quality control. Discovered how to identify areas of agreement and difference among the participants. Who eventually reached agreement through my involvement. Developed methods of meeting and turning around objections. And developed the ability to state my opinions in spite of intense pressure from various individules in a high demand environment situation.

The writer has obviously had a good deal of experience in business, but he has failed to describe it effectively. First of all, he has confused a personal statement with a résumé (see 43.1). A personal statement requires complete sentences. The lack of subjects in the first two sentences of the opening paragraph and the vagueness of *This* in the third sentence make the paragraph incoherent. Instead of an organized summary of the writer's experience, we get a string of disconnected remarks.

Second, the language is at once pretentious and sloppy. The writer uses pretentious jargon in phrases like *fostering a marketable image, in regard to our interface*, and *impacting my long-range development*. At the same time, he makes a number of spelling errors; *objictives* for *objectives*, *benifet* for *benefit*, *significint* for *significant*, and *individules* for *individuals*. In the second paragraph the writer claims to have *throughly mastered quality control*, but he has not yet mastered the spelling of *thoroughly*.

These two examples show what makes the difference between a bad statement and a good one, or—to put it bluntly—between rejection and acceptance. If you want to be rejected, put a lot of high-sounding words and phrases together without bothering to check your organization, sentence construction, or spelling, and without bothering to provide any clear and telling detail about what you have done. If you want to be accepted, write clearly, honestly, and specifically about your own experience and goals; take the time to see that your statement is well organized, that every sentence is complete and correct, and that every word is spelled right.

6

Writing in Nonacademic Contexts

Writing in the World of Work

43.1 APPLYING FOR A JOB: THE RÉSUMÉ AND THE COVER LETTER

The most important thing you need when applying for a job is a résumé—a list of your achievements and qualifications. The résumé should give all the essential facts about the position you seek, the date of your availability, your education, your work experience (with informative details), your extracurricular activities, and your special interests. You may include personal data, but you do not have to. The résumé should also list the names and addresses of your references—persons who can write to a prospective employer on your behalf; before listing their names, of course, you should get their permission to do so. The sample résumés in 12.3 show two formats we recommend.

The résumé alone, however, will seldom get you a job or even an interview. With the résumé you must send what a hiring officer expects to see first: a cover letter. Since the résumé will list all the essential facts about you, the cover letter may be brief. But it should nonetheless be carefully written. If the letter makes a bad first impression, you will have one strike against you even before your résumé is seen. You need to give yourself the best possible chance, and your cover letter can make a difference in the way your résumé is read.

What do hiring officers want in a cover letter? They look for a capsule summary of the résumé itself, and also for things that résumés don't often tell them: how much you know about the company you hope to work for, what kind of work you hope to do, where you want to work, and what special skills you may have that need to be emphasized. The résumé defines your past; the cover letter can define your future, indicating what you hope to do for the company if you are hired.

To see what a difference a cover letter can make, compare these two, both sent to the same company:

Dear Ms. ____:

In January 2000, you were interviewing at the ____ College campus. I was schedule to see you but I had just accepted a position with ____ Stores and canceled my interview.

At the present time I am working as an assistant buyer in Tulsa, Oklahoma. I have been commuting every two weeks to see my family in Chicago. I am seeking employment in the Chicago area.

Enclosed is my résumé for your consideration again. Thank you for your attention. I will look forward to hearing from you in the near future.

Sincerely,

Dear Ms. ____:

I am seeking a challenging position in marketing and consumer relations with a company in the Chicago area. I am particularly drawn to your firm because it is a utility, and utilities must maintain a proper balance between serving the public and protecting their own corporate interests. The challenge of maintaining this balance strongly appeals to me.

I have studied both marketing and consumer relations. At ____ College, from which I will shortly receive a B.A. in business administration, I took courses in such subjects as consumer attitudes, marketing strategies, and principles of retail management.

Along with my education, I have had job experience that has given me frequent contact with the public. Working in a small business for two summers, I learned firsthand how to deal with consumers, and in the second summer I was promoted from salesclerk to acting assistant manager.

I hope you will review the attached résumé. Although a position in my field of interest may not be open, I would appreciate your consideration for future management or marketing opportunities.

Yours truly,

These two letters make quite different impressions. The first writer opens by misspelling *scheduled* and by recalling that he once canceled an interview with the woman to whom he is now writing for a job; the second writer opens with a clear statement of her ambition. The first writer tells little about his interest in the company; the second tells exactly what makes the company appealing. The first writer asks to be hired because he wants to see more of his family; the second asks to be hired because her studies in marketing and consumer relations and her experience in selling will enable her to help the company. Which of these two applicants do you think the hiring officer will want to see?

(For the format of a cover letter, which is a kind of business letter, see the next section.)

43.2 WRITING A BUSINESS LETTER: THE PROPER FORMAT

The cover letter that accompanies a résumé is just one example of a business letter—a letter designed to initiate or transact business. Such a letter should be concise and forthright. In relatively short paragraphs it should accurately state all the information that the writer needs to convey.

FORMAT OF A BUSINESS LETTER

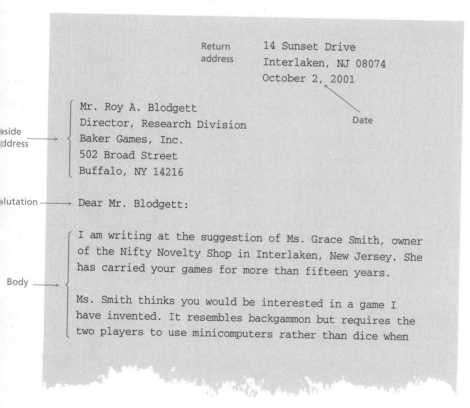

Return
address

14 Sunset Drive
Interlaken, NJ 08074
October 2, 2001

Date

Inside
address

Mr. Roy A. Blodgett
Director, Research Division
Baker Games, Inc.
502 Broad Street
Buffalo, NY 14216

Salutation

Dear Mr. Blodgett:

Body

I am writing at the suggestion of Ms. Grace Smith, owner of the Nifty Novelty Shop in Interlaken, New Jersey. She has carried your games for more than fifteen years.

Ms. Smith thinks you would be interested in a game I have invented. It resembles backgammon but requires the two players to use minicomputers rather than dice when

Body ——→ making a move. This step reduces the element of chance and rewards the players' skill. Friends tell me the game is more exciting than backgammon or chess.

If you would like to see the game. I would be glad to give a demonstration when you come to New York City for a meeting with your buyers in the area. I can be reached at the following number: (609) 555-2468.

Complimentary close ——→ Sincerely yours,

Signature ——→ *George A. Andrews*

Typed name ——→ George A. Andrews

FORMAT OF A BUSINESS ENVELOPE

George A. Andrews
14 Sunset Drive
Interlaken NJ 08074

Mr. Roy A. Blodgett
Director, Research Division
Baker Games, Inc.
502 Broad Street
Buffalo NY 14216

For a business letter you normally use medium-weight typing paper or white photocopy paper of standard size ($8\frac{1}{2}$ by 11 inches). Center the letter as well as you can, leaving side margins of at least $1\frac{1}{2}$ inches. Unless the body of the letter is extremely short, use single-spacing and block form; indentation is optional, but if you type the paragraphs without it, separate one from the next by a double space. Also leave a double space between the inside address and the salutation, between the salutation and the body, and between the body and the complimentary close. Leave at least four spaces for your signature between the complimentary close and the typed name.

Fold the completed letter in two places—a third of the way down from the top and up from the bottom—and insert it in a business envelope ($4\frac{1}{8}$ by $9\frac{1}{2}$ inches) addressed as shown on p. 700.

43.3 WRITING FOR YOUR RIGHTS

We live in a world of huge and increasingly impersonal corporations. Most of the bills and probably most of the letters you get come not from human beings but from machines. Bills are processed automatically; letters are clacked out by computers that know your address, your date of birth, and your Social Security number and have been taught to use your name in every other sentence, but nonetheless have not the faintest idea who you are or what your specific problems might be. How do you shout back at all this machinery? How do you make yourself heard?

In a word, write. If you think you have been overcharged or incorrectly billed or stuck with defective goods or shoddy service, don't keep silent. Write a letter to the company or the institution, and demand to have your letter answered by a live human being. If the facts are on your side and you state them plainly, you may win your case without ever going to court or spending one cent for legal advice.

A friend of ours was billed $86.00 for an emergency service that he thought his medical insurance should cover. When the insurance company denied the claim, he phoned the company, got the name of the president, and wrote this letter directly to him:

Dear Sir:

In connection with the enclosed bill for emergency-room service provided to my son Andrew on October 15, I write to ask for an explanation for your company's refusal to pay for this service.

Your company's statement for October indicates that the charge for emergency-room service is not covered because "use of emergency room is covered when in connection with accident or minor surgery." Does this mean that use of the emergency room is covered *only* when in connection with accident or minor injury? Andrew had neither of these, but his condition was a genuine emergency, and I don't see why you refuse to cover treatment for it.

Andrew has asthma. He has long been treated for it by Dr. ____, who is an allergy specialist, but from time to time he has severe respiratory attacks that require emergency treatment—or rather, that require adrenalin, which is available *only* at the emergency room of ____ Hospital. If Andrew could have received adrenalin anywhere else, I could understand your denial of our claim, but so long as the hospital dispenses adrenalin *only* to emergency-room patients, we have to take him there. If we hadn't taken him there on October 15, he might have stopped breathing.

I can fully understand why you stop short of reimbursing all visits to the emergency room, since that would be an open invitation for your subscribers to use the emergency room for any and all ailments. But I believe you must distinguish between genuine emergencies and routine problems. I therefore expect your company to pay this particular bill in full.

Yours truly,

This letter got fast results. The president of the company referred it to the vice-president in charge of claims, and within a week the vice-president wrote to say that an asthma attack was indeed a genuine emergency, so the company would pay the bill in full. Thus the letter writer saved himself $86.00—not bad pay for the half hour he took to write the letter.

What writing ability gives you is the power to express yourself on paper for any purpose you choose. The more you write, the more you will discover what writing can do for you. Very few things that college can give you will be more important to you afterward than the ability to put your thoughts and feelings into words.

Writing for Public Service **44**

44.1 WRITING TO SERVE AND INFLUENCE YOUR COMMUNITY

UNDERSTANDING NONPROFIT GROUPS

Nonprofit groups aim to educate and serve communities. Because they do not seek to make a profit, they are exempt from paying taxes. Some are sponsored by religious organizations; others are closely allied with political parties. Many operate independently.

One such group, Amnesty International, strives (on the global level) to free international political prisoners and (on the local level) to end the death penalty. Another group, Moms V.I.P., aims to help low-income pregnant women within its community get proper prenatal care.

PUBLIC SERVICE AS A FORM OF PARTNERSHIP

Community groups give you the chance to collaborate with others, to use what you have learned in college, and to understand how things work in the world beyond your campus. Public-service activities depend on partnerships and typically involve various types of expertise. You may have expert knowledge in your field of study, but people in the groups you work with have expert knowledge about your community as well as expert knowledge in getting things done.

44.2 BROCHURES AND MISSION STATEMENTS

A community group needs to get its message out—to define its purpose in order to gain support. *Brochures* and the *mission statements* they present can help a group do this.

KNOWING YOUR READERS AND YOUR PURPOSE

The first step in composing an effective brochure is defining its potential readers and purpose. For example, Kids First is a community group that tutors elementary and middle-school students in a poor rural community. In order to help these students, Kids First needs to inform parents and teachers about its services. So its brochure should speak to parents and teachers, not students.

COMPOSING A BROCHURE

An effective brochure does two things:

1. It explains the group and its purpose.

2. It explains how to contact the group. It provides addresses, phone numbers, hours, location, Web site and email addresses—even a map.

WRITING A MISSION STATEMENT

An effective mission statement answers questions about identity and goals:

▶ Who makes up the group? Who are its sponsors? Who is the director?

▶ What does the group do?

▶ Whom does the group aim to serve?

For example:

Kids First is an organization of parents, teachers, and student-teachers who provide free tutoring to Atkins County elementary and middle-school students. Sponsored by the Atkins County PTO and the Southeast State College Student Teachers Association, Kids First aims to help prepare our community's children for success in high school, college, and the world of work.

A brochure may also explain how the group got started. But answers to the questions listed above should be the most prominent part of the message.

THINKING ABOUT READERS IN COMMUNITIES

Give special thought to your readers' interests and concerns whenever your write for the public—especially when you write about difficult social problems.

Consider the task of writing about Kids First, which was organized in Atkins County after newspapers reported that the county's children scored last on the state's achievement tests. Many adults in the county were unable to read; and when two clothing manufacturers moved out of the area, many residents were driven into poverty. Writers of the Kids First brochure had to explain the purpose of the group without focusing on the children's low scores or the county's problems. To reach parents who couldn't read, they used pictures and graphic design extensively. (For more on designing brochures, see chapter 12.) To emphasize the children's future, they wrote that Kids First aimed to help students succeed in school and the working world.

44.3 WRITING PRESS RELEASES

Press releases tell the public about a community group's special events. Before sending a press release, call your local newspaper and broadcast stations to learn

- ▶ who should receive the announcement

- ▶ whether you should mail, email, or fax it

- ▶ how long before the event it should arrive

USING THE REPORTER'S QUESTIONS

Answer *the reporter's questions* in a press release:

1. Who? Begin by naming your group. If your group is well known in the community, you may not have to provide additional information. If you need to provide additional information, put it at the end of the press release.

2. What is the event?

3. When is the event?

4. Where is the event?

5. Why is the event taking place?

Though you might consult your media sources for samples of their preferred formats, press releases generally follow the format below:

- ▶ Heading: *Press Release* or *Media Advisory*

- ▶ Date sent to media

- ▶ Headline in capital letters

- ▶ Name of organization in capital letters

▶ Date information may be made public: either *For Immediate Release* or *For Release on* (provide date)

▶ Names and phone numbers of people to contact

▶ Place and date in parentheses

▶ Text

▶ End of release marked with these three symbols, centered: ###

PRESS RELEASE

March 5, 2001

Kids First Holds Pancake Breakfast

KIDS FIRST

For Immediate Release

Contacts:	Leana Baumlin	980-2223
	George Gold	966-0943

(Atkins County—March 4, 2000)

Kids First will hold its third annual Pancake Breakfast on Saturday, March 11, from 9 to 11:30 A.M. at the West Side YMCA, 2065 Mountain View Road. Volunteers will serve up pancakes, waffles, sausages, and juice. Prices are $4 for adults, $2 for children under 12. The Pancake Breakfast will benefit Kids First, an organization of parents, teachers, and student-teacher volunteers who are working to prepare Atkins County students for academic success.

###

TIPS FOR WRITING PRESS RELEASES

1. Use the group's letterhead.

2. Provide a headline.

3. Provide the name of the group.

4. Provide contact information.

5. Be concise.

6.   Carefully proofread your release. Check all names, addresses, and dates.

7.   Make sure you send your release to the appropriate person or department.

8.   Send your release well before the event.

9.   Indicate when the information should be made public. For example, you may want to wait until three or four weeks before the event.

44.4 HOLDING PRODUCTIVE MEETINGS

If you are involved in a community group, at some point you will probably be asked to organize and conduct a meeting. The following guidelines should make your job easier.

ORGANIZING A MEETING

1.   CONFIRM YOUR MEETING TIME AND PLACE BEFORE YOU SEND OUT A NOTICE. Make sure the meeting does not conflict with another meeting or event your members would be likely to attend. Make sure your meeting place is available.

2.   BE SURE YOUR MEETING TIME ACCOMMODATES AS MANY SCHEDULES AS POSSIBLE.   For example, teachers might be able to attend a meeting at 4 P.M., but working parents might not.

3.   BE SURE YOUR MEETING PLACE IS ACCESSIBLE TO ALL THOSE WHO WOULD LIKE TO ATTEND.

4.   GIVE PARTICIPANTS ADEQUATE NOTICE.   A month is best, but at least three weeks in advance. In addition, sending a reminder a day or two before the meeting can increase attendance.

5.   ARRIVE EARLY AT THE MEETING PLACE.   Arrange chairs and tables to encourage participation. If you have handouts, be ready to distribute them, so you don't waste valuable time shuffling papers.

CONDUCTING A MEETING

1. SET A CLEAR GOAL FOR THE MEETING. That goal may be long-term or short-term. For example, the long-term goal of a fund-raising committee might be to decide on four major fund-raising events over a two-year period. A short-term goal might be to finalize the details for a fund-raiser to be held in three months.

2. HAVE AN AGENDA. Know exactly what you want to accomplish in the meeting. For example, if your short-term goal is to finalize details for an upcoming event, make a list and check off items as they are dealt with.

3. STAY ON SUBJECT AND ON TASK. It is always tempting to use meeting times for socializing. However, those who want to socialize can always do so after the meeting; those who don't will not feel their time is being wasted.

4. CONCLUDE THE MEETING AT THE APPROPRIATE TIME. If your notice says the meeting will last from 7 to 8 P.M., conclude the meeting at 8. People will start avoiding meetings that habitually run overtime.

5. THANK PARTICIPANTS FOR ATTENDING.

6. KEEP A RECORD OF WHAT HAPPENED DURING THE MEETING. You should either have a secretary or ask a participant to perform that role, taking notes on business discussed and decisions made.

Grant Writing for Nonprofit Groups

45

45.1 WHAT ARE GRANTS?

Grants are monetary awards given to nonprofit groups that apply for them through written proposals. Grants are generally awarded by one of the following funding sources:

▶ a private foundation, usually set up by a wealthy donor

▶ a corporate foundation supported by a business

▶ an organization, such as the Rotary Club or the Lion's Club

▶ a county, state, or federal appropriation, money set aside by a government agency to support specific projects, such as drug prevention, prenatal care, and adult literacy

Groups can apply for grants for several different purposes:

▶ general operation support—a group's day-to-day operations, which involve such expenses as salaries, rent, utilities, postage, and equipment

▶ a capital request—for major purchases, such as a building or equipment

▶ a project—an activity or service, such as a summer program or conference, with specific beginning and end dates

▶ a program—an ongoing activity or service, such as a neighborhood group's after-school tutoring program

45.2 MATCHING FUNDING SOURCES WITH NONPROFIT GROUPS

The number and diversity of funding sources complicate the task of choosing the best one for your group. So unless you are simply reapplying for a grant that your group regularly receives, you may need help in your search. Try the Foundation Center (www.fdncenter.org), which offers databases for locating funding sources, online help in writing grants, and other resources. In over two hundred libraries around the country, you can find directories of funding sources published by the Center.

The right match between funding source and nonprofit group usually depends on

▶ SHARED MISSION OR SUBJECT AREA For example, some funding sources exist to help communities combat teen smoking or improve adult-literacy rates. Other funding sources simply define a specific subject area, such as the arts.

▶ GEOGRAPHICAL LOCATION Many funding sources aim to serve a specific region, state, or city. For example, Community Shares is a funding source in East Tennessee that supports nonprofit groups in Appalachia.

Before drafting a proposal to a particular funding source, be sure you understand its mission and special requirements. Don't waste your time seeking grants that don't fit your group.

45.3 THE GRANT WRITING PROCESS

WRITING A LETTER OF INQUIRY

Once you have found a funding source that is a good match for your group, write directly to the source. Succinctly identify your group, explain why and how your group meets the funding requirements of the source, and ask for its grant proposal guidelines.

STUDYING GRANT PROPOSAL GUIDELINES

Note each of the following items carefully:

▶ DEADLINES Though funding sources eagerly support worthy causes, many groups compete for these funds. Missing deadlines is the quickest way to disqualify your group for consideration.

▶ CONTENT Most funding sources want specific details on the project, program, or budget items for which you are requesting funds.

▶ ORGANIZATION Most funding sources want information placed in a certain order with specific headings.

▶ SUPPORTING DOCUMENTS These typically include official documents, such as an IRS letter that confirms the group's nonprofit status; a copy of the group's annual operating budget; and a list of the group's board of directors. Some funding sources also require letters of support from respected individuals, confirming the worthiness of your organization and the usefulness of the project for which you are requesting funding.

CONDUCTING RESEARCH

Before you can write an effective proposal, you must

1. INVESTIGATE THE FUNDING SOURCE. Besides reading carefully the guidelines furnished by the funding source, find out what kinds of projects it has funded in the past. Learn about the history of the source, its original purpose, and its key organizers. Try to get a copy of a proposal funded by the source.

2. INVESTIGATE THE PURPOSE OF YOUR GRANT. First, clearly define the goals for your request. Understand how your funding source would classify the purpose of your grant (45.1).

Second, understand all that is involved in your request. For example, if you are requesting funding for a conference, consider where and when the conference might be held and check a calendar of competing events in your area. If you are requesting funding for a new program, decide whether your group will need to hire more employees to carry out the program.

Third, calculate the costs of your request. For a project such as a conference, you need to determine a number of different expenses, including publicity, transportation for speakers, and building rental.

3. INVESTIGATE THE NEED FOR YOUR REQUEST. You must establish that your project meets a need or makes a creative contribution. Suppose you are helping a local environmental group educate the community about the need for regulating strip mining. You might be able to locate research or polls that provide statistics on the community's lack of knowledge about the problem.

You must also establish that the request you are making is the best way to meet that need. For example, your first instinct might be to organize a conference and bring in experts to educate the community about the consequences of strip mining. Your funding agency might agree that there is a need for education in the community. However, a conference might not be the best way to meet that need, especially if the community is in a rural area, where residents are unused to attending conferences. Your funding source might believe that a monthly newsletter better meets the community's educational needs.

4.   INVESTIGATE THE RELATIONSHIP OF YOUR REQUEST TO OTHER NONPROFITS. You may need to find out if another nonprofit in your area is already doing what you propose to do. Sources generally avoid funding two local projects with the same goal.

5.   DETERMINE HOW YOU WILL EVALUATE YOUR PROJECT OR PROGRAM. Nearly all funding sources want to know how you will measure the success of your project or program. For example, if you want funds to run a neighborhood tutoring program, you might keep a daily record of the number of students being tutored. You might interview students, parents, and teachers. You might also ask experts to help with the evaluation.

ORGANIZING THE PROPOSAL

Nearly every funding source has its own specific guidelines for organizing a proposal. Many proposals, however, require the following information:

1.   EXECUTIVE SUMMARY   A brief description that explains your objectives, why you need funding, and exactly how the requested funds will be used.

2.   PURPOSE OF THE GRANT   A detailed description of the need or problem your request addresses; the group of people who will be served, or target population (for example, if you are requesting funding for a neighborhood tutoring program, your target population is the students in that particular neighborhood); and the equipment, project, or program for which you are requesting funds.

3.   METHOD OF EVALUATING THE GRANT'S OUTCOME   A detailed description of your methods for evaluating the funded activity.

4.   BUDGET   A detailed and realistic estimate of all the expenses involved; this should include descriptions of the other sources that fund your organization.

5.   GROUP INFORMATION   A description of your group's purpose, history, record of accomplishment, present activities, and staff members.

6. ATTACHMENTS Supporting documents requested by your funding source, such as IRS documents, annual operating budget, and list of board of directors.

TIPS FOR GRANT WRITING

ASK FOR HELP. Writing a grant proposal is hard. Don't be timid about asking for help. Board members or the directors of other nonprofits may be willing to give advice and read drafts of your proposal. Often funding sources themselves have individuals whose job is to help groups write proposals. Organizations and colleges frequently offer free workshops in grant writing.

MAKE YOUR PROPOSAL AS ATTRACTIVE AS POSSIBLE. Your final proposal should be double-spaced, free of errors and corrections, and printed on high-quality paper.

MAKE SURE YOU HAVE FOLLOWED PROPOSAL GUIDELINES. Look for details such as the numbering and order of attachments, as well as the required number of copies requested by your funding source.

KEEP TRYING. Don't let a rejected proposal make you afraid to apply again. Often a funding source will explain why your request was not funded. Learn from your efforts.

Glossaries

Glossary of Usage

a, an   Use *a* before a word starting with a consonant, and *an* before a word starting with a vowel.

> *A* fool and his money are soon parted
> *An* empty bag cannot stand upright. —Ben Franklin

accept, except   *Accept* means "receive" or "agree to."

> Medical schools accept fewer than half the students who apply.

As a preposition, *except* means "other than."

> I can resist anything except temptation. —Oscar Wilde

As a verb, *except* means "exclude," "omit," "leave out."

> If you except that one math course, I received straight As.

A.D., B.C., C.E., B.C.E   (NOTE: MLA does not use periods in these abbreviations.) A.D. stands for *anno Domini*, "in the year of our Lord." It designates the period since the birth of Christ and precedes the year number.

> The emperor Claudius began the Roman conquest of England in A.D. 43.

B.C. designates the period before the birth of Christ and follows the year number. For this period, the lower the number, the more recent the year.

> Alexander the Great ruled Macedonia from 336 B.C. to his death in 323.

Instead of A.D., writers now often use C.E. (common era). In place of B.C., they use B.C.E. (before the common era).

> Julius Caesar died in 44 B.C.E.

advice, advise   *Advice* is a noun meaning "guidance."

> When a man is too old to give bad examples, he gives good advice.
> —La Rochefoucauld

717

Advise is a verb meaning "counsel," "give advice to," "recommend," or "notify."

> Shortly before the stock market crash of 1929, Bernard Baruch advised investors to buy bonds.

affect, effect   *Affect* is most often used as a verb meaning "change," "disturb," or "influence."

> The cost of healthcare affects the health of the economy.

It can also mean "feign" or "pretend to feel."

> Though she knew exactly what the package contained, she affected surprise when she opened it.

As a noun, it can mean only "feeling."

> Her face was blank, with no sign of affect.

Effect is most often used as a noun meaning "result" or "impact."

> His appeal for mercy had no effect on the judge.

It may also be used as a verb meaning "bring about," "accomplish," or "perform."

> With dazzling skill, the gymnast effected a triple somersault.

afraid   *See* frightened.

aggravate, irritate   *Aggravate* means "make worse."

> The recent bombing has aggravated racial hostilities.

Irritate means "annoy" or "bring discomfort to."

> His tuneless whistling irritated me.

all   *See* almost.

all ready, already   Use *all ready* when *all* refers to things or people.

> At noon the runners were all ready to start. [The meaning is that *all* the runners were *ready*.]

Use *already* to mean "by this time" or "by that time."

> I reached the halfway mark, but the frontrunners had already crossed the finish line.

all right, *alright   *All right* means "completely correct," "safe and sound," or "satisfactory."

My answers on the quiz were all right. [The meaning is that *all* the answers were *right*.]

The car was demolished, but aside from a muscle bruise in my shoulder and a few minor cuts, I was all right.

In formal writing, do not use *all right* to mean "satisfactorily" or "well."

*In spite of a bruised shoulder, Ashe played all right.

EDITED: In spite of a bruised shoulder, Ashe played well.

In formal writing, do not use *all right* to mean "very good" or "excellent."

*Her performance was all right.

EDITED: Her performance was excellent.

Do not use *alright anywhere; it is a misspelling of *all right*.

all together, altogether   Use *all together* when *all* refers to things or people.

The demonstrators stood all together at the gate of the nuclear power plant.

Use *altogether* to mean "entirely" or "wholly."

Never put off till tomorrow what you can avoid altogether. (Preston's Axiom)

allude, refer   *Allude* means "call attention indirectly."

When the speaker mentioned the "Watergate scandal," he alluded to a chain of events that led to the resignation of President Richard Nixon.

Refer means "call attention directly."

In the Declaration of Independence, Jefferson refers many times to England's mistreatment of the American colonies.

allusion, delusion, illusion   An *allusion* is an indirect reference.

Prufrock's vision of his own head "brought in upon a platter" is an allusion to John the Baptist, whose head was presented that way to Salome, Herod's daughter.

A *delusion* is a false opinion or belief, especially one that springs from self-deception or madness.

A megalomaniac suffers from the delusion that he or she is fabulously rich and powerful.

An *illusion* is a false impression, especially one that springs from false perception (an optical illusion, for example) or from wishful thinking.

The sight of palm trees on the horizon proved to be an illusion.

The so-called free gifts offered in advertisements feed the illusion that you can get something for nothing.

almost, most, mostly, all, *most all *Almost* means "nearly."

By the time we reached the gas station, the tank was almost empty.
Almost all the Republicans support the proposed amendment.

As an adjective or noun, *most* means "the greater part (of)" or "the majority (of)."

Most birds migrate in the fall and spring.
Most of the land has become a dust bowl.

As an adverb, *most* designates the superlative form of long adjectives and adverbs.

Truman thought MacArthur the most egotistical man he ever knew.

Mostly means "chiefly," "primarily."

Milk is mostly water.

All means "the whole amount," "the total number of," or "entirely."

All art is useless. —Oscar Wilde
The manufacturer has recalled all (of) the new models.
The new buildings are all finished.

In formal writing, do not use **most all.* Use *almost all* or *most.*

*Most all of the plants looked healthy, but two of the roses were dying.
EDITED: Almost all of the plants looked healthy, but two of the roses were dying.
*Most all of the refugees suffered from malnutrition.
EDITED: Most of the refugees suffered from malnutrition.

a lot, *alot *See* lots of.

already *See* all ready.

*alright *See* all right.

altogether *See* all together.

alumnus, alumni; alumna, alumnae Use *alumnus* for one male graduate of a school, college, or university, and *alumni* for two or more male graduates or for a predominantly male group of graduates.

Dartmouth alumni are extraordinarily loyal to their college.

Use *alumna* for one female graduate, and *alumnae* for two or more female graduates or for a predominantly female group of graduates.

> Vassar's alumnae include Mary McCarthy and Meryl Streep.

If you can't cope with all those Latin endings, use *graduate* for an individual of either sex, and just remember that *alumni* designates a male group, *alumnae* a female group. Do not refer to any one person of either sex as an *alumni*.

> *He is an alumni of Florida State.
> EDITED: He is an alumnus [*or* a graduate] of Florida State.

among, between   Use *among* with three or more persons, things, or groups.

> There is no honor among thieves.

In general, use *between* with two persons, two things, or two groups.

> Political freedom in America means the right to choose between a Democrat and a Republican.

amoral, immoral   *Amoral* means "without morals or a code of behavior," "beyond or outside the moral sphere."

> Rich, riotous, and totally amoral, he lived for nothing but excitement and pleasure.

Immoral means "wicked."

> The Roman emperor Nero was so immoral that he once kicked a pregnant woman to death.

amount, number   Use *amount* when discussing uncountable things.

> No one knows the amount of damage that a nuclear war would do.

Use *number* when discussing countable things or persons.

> The store offered a prize to anyone who could guess the number of marbles in a large glass jug.

anxious, eager   *Anxious* means "worried" or "fearfully desirous."

> The long silence on the other end of the line made her anxious.
> He took the long street at a dead run, anxious to reach home before the midnight curfew began.

Eager means "strongly desirous."

> After all I had heard about it, I was eager to see what remained of the famous prison on Alcatraz Island.

anyone, any one   *Anyone* is an indefinite pronoun (like *everyone, everybody*).

> Anyone who hates dogs and children can't be all bad.   —W. C. Fields

Any one means "any one of many."

> I felt wretched; I could not answer any one of the questions on the test.

apt   *See* likely.

as, as if, like   Use *as* or *as if* to introduce a subordinate clause.

> As I walked up the driveway, a huge dog suddenly leaped out at me.
> Susan looked as if she had just seen a ghost.

Use *like* as a preposition meaning "similar to."

> At first glance the organism looks like an amoeba.

Do not use *like* to mean "as if," "as," or "that."

> *Pat looked like he had just won the sweepstakes.
> EDITED: Pat looked as if he had just won the sweepstakes.
> *The hinge didn't work like the instructions said it would.
> EDITED: The hinge didn't work as the instructions said it would.
> *I felt like he resented me.
> EDITED: I felt that he resented me.

assure, ensure, insure   *Assure* means "state with confidence to one or more persons."

> The builders of the *Titanic* assured everyone that it could not sink.

Ensure and *insure* mean "make sure" or "guarantee."

> There is no way to ensure (*or* insure) that every provision of the treaty will be honored.

Insure also means "make a contract for payment in the event of specified loss, damage, injury, or death."

> I insured the package for fifty dollars.

avenge, revenge   *Avenge* is always a verb. It means "exact punishment on behalf of [someone] or in retaliation for [some wrong]."

> In slaying Claudius, Hamlet avenges his father.
> [or] In slaying Claudius, Hamlet avenges the murder of his father.

Revenge may be a verb or a noun. As a verb, it means "satisfy [oneself] by inflicting punishment on or upon [someone] who has injured [oneself]."

> In *Moby-Dick,* Ahab yearns to revenge himself upon the whale that has taken his leg.

As a noun, it means "retaliation."

> After Hindley beats him, Heathcliff grimly plans his revenge.

awfully *See* very.

bad, badly *Bad* is an adjective meaning "not good," "sick," or "sorry."

> We paid a lot for the meal, but it was bad.
> In spite of the medicine, I still felt bad.
> She felt bad about losing the ring.

Badly is an adverb meaning "not well."

> Anything that begins well ends badly. (Pudder's Law)

Used with *want* or *need*, *badly* means "very much."

> The fans badly wanted a victory.

Do not use *bad* as an adverb.

> *We played bad during the first half of the game.
> EDITED: We played badly during the first half of the game.

B.C., B.C.E. *See* A.D.

because, since, *being that Use *since* and *because* to introduce clauses. Do not use **being that*.

> Since fossil fuels are becoming scarce, scientists are working to develop synthetic forms of energy.
> The soldiers could not advance because they had run out of ammunition.

because of *See* due to.

*being that *See* because.

beside, besides *Beside* means "next to."

> A little restaurant stood beside the wharf.

As a preposition, *besides* means "in addition to."

> Besides working with the sun and the wind, engineers are seeking to harness the power of tides.

As a conjunctive adverb, *besides* means "moreover" or "also."

> When I visit New York City, I always stay at the same hotel. It's close to where my friends live; besides, it's not too expensive.

between *See* among.

can hardly, *can't hardly*   *Can hardly* means virtually the same thing as *cannot* or *can't*. Do not use **can't hardly*.

> *We can't hardly cut taxes without increasing the deficit.
> EDITED: We can hardly cut taxes without increasing the deficit.

capital, capitol   *Capital* means the seat of government of a country or state, the type of letter used at the beginning of a sentence, or a stock of accumulated wealth.

> Paris is the capital of France.
> This sentence begins with a capital *T*.
> What does capital consist of? It consists of money and commodities.
> —Karl Marx

Capitol means the building that houses the state or federal legislature. Remember that the *o* in *capitol* is like the *o* in the dome of a capitol.

> The governor delivered his first speech from the steps of the capitol.

C.E.   *See* A.D.

censor, censure   As a verb, *censor* means "expurgate."

> Television networks usually censor R-rated movies before broadcasting them.

As a noun, *censor* means "one who censors."

> Censors cut all the nudity out of the film.

As a verb, *censure* means "find fault with" or "reprimand."

> In the 1950s, Senator Joseph McCarthy was censured for publicly questioning the integrity of President Eisenhower.

As a noun, *censure* means "disapproval" or "blame."

> Ridicule often hurts more than censure.

childish, childlike   *Childish* means "disagreeably like a child."

> The childish whining of a chronic complainer soon becomes an unbearable bore.

Childlike means "agreeably like a child."

> Picasso's brilliant canvases express his childlike love of color.

cite   *See* sight.

compare, comparison, contrast   *Compare* means "bring together in order to note similarities and differences."

In *A Stillness at Appomattox,* Bruce Catton compares Lee and Grant not only to show the difference between a Virginia aristocrat and a rough-hewn frontiersman but also to show what these two men had in common.

Use *compare to* to stress similarities.

Lewis Thomas compares human societies to ant colonies, noting that individuals in each of these groups sometimes work together as if they were parts of a single organism.

Use *compare with* to stress differences.

Compared with Texas, Rhode Island is a postage stamp.

Comparison means "act of comparing."

Catton's comparison of Lee and Grant shows the difference between the South and the frontier.
In comparison with Texas, Rhode Island is a postage stamp.

As a transitive verb, *contrast* means "juxtapose to show one or more differences."

In *Huckleberry Finn,* Twain contrasts the peaceful, easy flow of life on the river with the tense and violent atmosphere of life on shore.

As an intransitive verb, *contrast* means "appear different in one or more ways."

In *Huckleberry Finn,* the peaceful flow of life on the river contrasts vividly with the violent atmosphere of life on shore.

As a noun, *contrast* means "striking difference."

To drive across America is to feel the contrast between the level plains of the Midwest and the towering peaks of the Rockies.

complement, compliment   As a verb, *complement* means "bring to perfect completion."

A red silk scarf complemented her white dress.

As a noun, *complement* means "something that makes a whole when combined with something else" or "the total number of persons needed in a group or team."

Experience is the complement of learning.
Without a full complement of volunteers, a small-town fire department cannot do its job.

As a verb, *compliment* means "praise."

The teacher complimented me on my handwriting but complained about everything else.

As a noun, *compliment* means "expression of praise."

> Cheryl's compliment made me tingle.

conscience, conscious   *Conscience* is a noun meaning "inner guide or voice in matters of right and wrong."

> A pacifist will not fight in any war because his or her conscience says that all killing is wrong.

Conscious is an adjective meaning "aware" or "able to perceive."

> Conscious of something on my leg, I looked down to see an ant crawling over my knee.
> I was conscious during the whole operation.

consul   *See* council.

continual, continuous   *Continual* means "going on with occasional slight interruptions."

> I grew up next to an airport. What I remember most from my childhood is the continual roaring of jet planes.

Continuous means "going on with no interruption."

> In some factories the assembly line never stops; production is continuous.

contrast   *See* compare.

could care less, couldn't care less   Don't use the first expression when you mean the second.

> *Carol likes hard rock and could care less about Beethoven and Brahms.
> EDITED: Carol likes hard rock and couldn't care less about Beethoven and Brahms.

council, counsel, consul   *Council* means "a group of persons who discuss and decide certain matters."

> The city council often disagrees with the mayor.

As a verb, *counsel* means "advise."

> President John F. Kennedy was badly counseled when he approved the American attack on Cuba at the Bay of Pigs.

As a noun, *counsel* means "advice" or "lawyer."

> Camp counselors tend to give orders more often than counsel.
> When the prosecution showed a picture of the victim's mangled corpse, the defense counsel vigorously objected.

A *consul* is a government official working in a foreign country to protect the interests of his or her country's citizens there.

> If you lose your passport in a foreign country, you will need to see the American consul there.

credible, credulous   *Credible* means "believable."

> A skillful liar can often sound highly credible.

Credulous means "overly ready to believe."

> Some people are credulous enough to believe anything they hear on television.

See also incredible, incredulous.

criterion, criteria   A *criterion* is a standard by which someone or something is judged.

> In art, the only criterion of lasting value is lasting recognition.

Criteria is the plural of *criterion*.

> What criteria influence voters in judging a presidential candidate?

data   *Data* is the plural of the Latin *datum*, meaning "something given"— a piece of information. *Data* should be treated as plural.

> The data transmitted by space satellites tell us much more about distant planets than we have ever known before.

delusion   *See* allusion.

different from, *different than   In formal writing do not use *than* after *different*. Use *from*.

> An adult's idea of a good time is often very different from a child's.

differ from, differ with   *Differ from* means "be unlike."

> The Metropolitan Museum of Art differs from the Guggenheim Museum not only in size but also in mission.

Differ with means "disagree with."

> Jung differed with Freud on the importance of the sex drive.

disinterested, uninterested   *Disinterested* means "impartial," "unbiased," "objective."

> Lawyers respect Judge Brown for his disinterested handling of controversial cases.

Uninterested means "indifferent," "not interested."

> Some people are so uninterested in politics that they do not even bother to vote.

due to, because of   *Due to* is adjectival and means "resulting from" or "the result of."

> Home-insurance policies sometimes fail to cover losses due to "acts of God," such as hurricanes and tornadoes.
> The senator's failure to win reelection was largely due to her lackluster campaigning.

Because of is adverbial and means "as a result of."

> Conflict persists in Northern Ireland because of animosities over three hundred years old.

Do not use *due to* to mean *because of*.

> *Due to a badly sprained ankle I had to drop out of the race.
> EDITED: Because of a badly sprained ankle I had to drop out of the race.

eager   *See* anxious.

effect   *See* affect.

emigrate   *See* immigrate.

eminent, imminent, immanent   *Eminent* means "distinguished," "prominent."

> An eminent biologist has recently redefined the concept of evolution.

Imminent means "about to happen."

> The leaden air and the black, heavy clouds told us that a thunderstorm was imminent.

Immanent means "inherent," "existing within."

> Pantheists believe that God is immanent in all things.

ensure   *See* assure.

envelop, envelope   *EnVELop* (second syllable accented) is a verb meaning "cover" or "enclose."

> Fog seemed to envelop the whole city.

ENvelope (first syllable accented) is a noun meaning "container used for mailing."

> The small white envelope contained a big check.

*etc., et al.   The abbreviation **etc.* stands for *et cetera,* "and other things." You should avoid it in formal writing. Instead, use *and so on,* or tell what the other things are.

> *Before setting out that morning, I put on my hat, mittens, etc.
> EDITED: Before setting out that morning, I put on my hat, mittens, scarf, and boots.

The abbreviation *et al.* stands for *et alia,* "and others." On using it when citing books by multiple authors, see 39.2 (MLA), 42.5 *(CMS),* and 42.7 (APA).

everyday, every day   *Everyday* means "ordinary" or "regular."

> The governor has a common touch; even in public speeches she likes to use everyday words.

Every day means "daily."

> While in training, Mary Thomas commonly runs at least ten miles every day.

except   *See* accept.

factor   *Factor* means "contributing element" or "partial cause." It can be used effectively, but far too often it simply clutters the sentence in which it appears. In general, you should avoid it.

> *One factor in the decay of the cities is the movement of middle-class families to the suburbs.
> EDITED: One reason for the decay of the cities is the movement of middle-class families to the surburbs.

farther, further   *Farther* means "a greater distance."

> The trail went farther into the bush than the hunter had expected.

As an adjective, *further* means "more."

> After high school, how many students really need further education?

As a conjunctive adverb, *further* means "besides."

> Lincoln disliked slavery; further, he abhorred secession.

As a transitive verb, *further* means "promote" or "advance."

> How much has the federal government done to further the development of solar energy?

fatal, fateful *Fatal* means "sure to cause death" or "resulting in death."

> Even a small dose of cyanide is fatal.
> In a fruitless and fatal attempt to save the manuscript she had spent ten years writing, the novelist rushed back into the burning house.

Fateful means "momentous in effect" and can be used whether the outcome is good or bad.

> In the end, Eisenhower made the fateful decision to land the Allies at Normandy.

few, little, less Use *few* or *fewer* with countable nouns.

> Few pianists even try to play the eerie music of George Crumb.

Use *little* (in the sense of "not much") or *less* with uncountable nouns.

> A little honey on your hands can be a big sticky nuisance.
> In spite of the grandiloquent title, the vice-president of the United States often has less power than a member of Congress.

flaunt, flout Use *flaunt* to mean "exhibit openly" or "show off."

> The new millionaire flaunted her wealth.

Use *flout* to mean "defy" or "disobey."

> Motorists who flout the law will be penalized.

former, formerly, formally As an adjective, *former* means "previous."

> When we moved in, the apartment was a mess. The former tenants had never even bothered to throw out the garbage.

As a noun, *former* refers to the first of two persons or things mentioned previously.

> Muhammad Ali first fought Leon Spinks in February 1978. At the time, the former was an international celebrity, while the latter was a twenty-four-year-old unknown.

Formerly means "at an earlier time."

> Most of the men in the tribe were formerly hunters, not farmers.

Formally means "in a formal or ceremonious manner."

> The president is elected in November, but he does not formally take office until the following January.

frightened, afraid   *Frightened* is followed by *at* or *by*.

> Many people are frightened at the thought of dying.
> As I walked down the deserted road, I was frightened by a snarling wolfhound.

Afraid is followed by *of.*

> Afraid of heights, Scott would not go near the edge of the cliff.

fun   Use *fun* as a noun, but not (in formal writing) as an adjective before a noun.

> As soon as Mark arrived, the fun began.
> *We spent a fun afternoon at the zoo.
> EDITED: We spent an enjoyable afternoon at the zoo.

further   *See* farther.

good, well   Use *good* as an adjective, but not as an adverb.

> The proposal to rebuild the chapel sounded good to many in the congregation.
> *She ran good for the first twenty miles, but then she collapsed.
> EDITED: She ran well for the first twenty miles, but then she collapsed.

Use *well* as an adverb when you mean "in an effective manner" or "ably."

> Fenneman did so well in practice that the coach decided to put him in the starting lineup for the opening game.

Use *well* as an adjective when you mean "in good health."

> My grandfather hasn't looked well since his operation.

*got to   *See* has to.

hanged, hung   *Hanged* means "killed by hanging."

> The prisoner was hanged at dawn.
> The distraught man hanged himself.

Hung means "suspended" or "held oneself up."

> I hung my coat on the back of the door and sat down.
> I hung on the side of the cliff, frantically seeking a foothold.

has to, have to, *got to   In formal writing, do not use **got to* to denote an obligation. Use *have to, has to,* or *must.*

> *Anyone who wants to win the nomination has got to run in the primaries.

EDITED: Anyone who wants to win the nomination has to run in the primaries. [or] Anyone who wants to win the nomination must run in the primaries.

hopefully   Use *hopefully* to modify a verb.

As the ice-cream truck approached, the children looked hopefully at their parents. [*Hopefully* modifies *looked,* telling how the children looked.]

Do not use *hopefully* when you mean "I hope that," "we hope that," or the like.

*Hopefully, the company will make a profit in the final quarter.
EDITED: The stockholders hope that the company will make a profit in the final quarter.

human, humane   *Human* means "pertaining to human beings."

To err is human.

Humane means "merciful," "kindhearted," or "considerate."

To forgive is both divine and humane.

illusion   *See* allusion.

immanent, imminent   *See* eminent.

immigrate, emigrate   *Immigrate* means "enter a country in order to live there permanently."

Professor Korowitz immigrated to the United States in 1955.

Emigrate means "leave one country in order to live in another."

My great-great-grandfather emigrated from Ireland in 1848.

immoral   *See* amoral.

imply, infer   *Imply* means "suggest" or "hint at something."

The manager implied that I could not be trusted with the job.

Infer means "reach a conclusion on the basis of evidence"; it is often used with *from.*

From the manager's letter I inferred that my chances were nil.

in, into, in to   Use *in* when referring to a direction, location, or position.

Everyone in the office tried the new low-carbohydrate diet.

Use *into* to mean movement toward the inside.

> Before she started drilling, the dentist shot Novocain into my gum.

Use *in to* when the two words have separate functions.

> The museum was open, so I walked in to look at the paintings.

In formal writing, do not use *into* to mean "occupied with" or "studying."

> Brenda has been into Tai Chi for the past year.
> EDITED: Brenda has been studying Tai Chi for the past year.

incredible, incredulous   *Incredible* means "not believable."

> Even though instrumental exploration of Mars has revealed some signs of life there, the idea that "Martians" could invade the Earth is still incredible.

In formal writing, do not use *incredible* to mean "amazingly bad," "compelling," "brilliant," or "extraordinary." In speech, you can indicate the meaning of *incredible* by the way you say it, but in writing, this word may be ambiguous and confusing.

> *Marian gave an incredible performance. [The reader has no way of knowing just how good it was.]
> EDITED: Marian gave a brilliant performance.

Incredulous means "unbelieving" or "skeptical."

> When Columbus argued that his ship would not fall off the edge of the Earth, many of his hearers were incredulous, for they believed the Earth was flat.

infer   *See* imply.

inferior to, *inferior than   Use *to* after *inferior,* not *than.*

> *American wines are no longer considered inferior than French or Italian wines.
> EDITED: American wines are no longer considered inferior to French or Italian wines.

insure   *See* assure.

***irregardless**   *See* regardless.

irritate   *See* aggravate.

its, it's   *Its* is the possessive form of *it.*

> We liked the house because of its appearance, its location, and its price.

It's means "it is."

> It's a pity that we seldom see ourselves as others see us.

kind of, sort of   In formal writing, do not use *kind of* or *sort of* to mean "somewhat" or "rather."

> *When I got off the roller coaster, I felt sort of sick.
> EDITED: When I got off the roller coaster, I felt rather sick.

later, latter   Use *later* when referring to time.

> Russia developed the atomic bomb later than the United States did.

Use *latter* when referring to the second of two persons or things mentioned previously.

> Muhammed Ali first fought Leon Spinks in February 1978. At the time, the former was an international celebrity, while the latter was a twenty-four-year-old unknown.

lay   *See* lie.

lead, led   *Lead* (rhymes with *seed*) is the present-tense and infinitive form of the verb meaning "cause," "guide," or "direct."

> Deficit spending leads to inflation.
> An effective president must be able to lead Congress without bullying it.

Led is the past-tense form and past participle of *lead*.

> During the Civil War, General Robert E. Lee led the Confederate forces.
> Some buyers are led astray by simpleminded slogans.

learn, teach   *Learn* means "gain knowledge, information, or skill."

Teach means "give lessons or instructions."

> If you want to know how well you have learned something, teach it to someone else.

leave, let   *Leave* as a verb means "go away from" or "put in a place."

> I had to leave the house at 6:00 A.M. to catch the bus.
> I had to leave my suitcase at the bus station.

Leave as a noun means "permission," including permission to go away.

> After an hour, I asked leave to speak.
> The sailors were granted a leave of twenty-four hours.

Let means "permit," "allow."

Some colleges let students take courses by mail.

led   *See* lead.

less   *See* few.

let   *See* leave.

let's, *let's us   Use *let's* before a verb. Do not follow *let's* with *us*; that would mean "let us us."

> *Let's us finish the job.
> EDITED: Let's finish the job.

liable   *See* likely.

lie, lay   *Lie (lie, lying, lay, lain)* is an intransitive verb meaning "rest," "recline," or "stay."

> I love to lie on the sand in the hot sun.
> Lying on the sand, I watched the clouds and listened to the surf.
> After she lay in the sun for three hours, she looked like a boiled lobster.
> On April 26, 1952, workers digging peat near Grueballe, Denmark, found a well-preserved body that had lain in the bog for fifteen hundred years.

Lay (lay, laying, laid) is a transitive verb meaning "put in a certain position."

> The rebels were told to lay down their weapons.
> A good education lays the foundation for a good life.
> The workers were laying bricks when an earthquake struck.
> He laid the book on the counter and walked out of the library.
> The earthquake struck after the foundation had been laid.

like   *See* as.

likely, apt, liable   *Likely* indicates future probability.

> As gas becomes scarcer and more expensive, battery-powered cars are likely to become popular.

Apt indicates a usual or habitual tendency.

> Most cars are apt to rust after two or three years.

Liable indicates a risk or adverse possibility.

> Cars left unlocked are liable to be stolen.

little   *See* few.

loose, lose   *Loose* (rhymes with *moose*) means "free" or "not securely tied or fastened."

> The center grabbed the loose ball and ran for a touchdown.
> From the rattling of the door, I could tell that the catch was loose.

Lose (sounds like *Lou's*) means "fail to keep" or "fail to win."

> In some cultures, to lose face is to lose everything.
> The truth about sports is that when somebody wins, somebody else loses.

lots of, a lot of, *alot of   *A lot of* and *lots of* are colloquial and wordy. In formal writing, use *much* for "a great amount" and *many* for "a great number." Do not use *alot* anywhere; it is a misspelling of *a lot*.

> Lots of students come to college with no clear notion of what they want to do.
> BETTER: Many students come to college with no clear notion of what they want to do.

many, much   Use *many* with countable nouns.

> Many hands make light work.

Use *much* with uncountable nouns.

> Much of the work has been done.

maybe, may be   *Maybe* means "perhaps."

> Maybe all cars will be electric by the year 2020.

May be is a verb phrase.

> By the year 2008, the president of the United States may be a woman.

might have, *might of   Use *might have*, not **might of*.

> *Oklahoma might of won the game if it had lasted just two minutes longer.
> EDITED: Oklahoma might have won the game if it had lasted just two minutes longer.

moral, morale   *MORal* (first syllable accented) is an adjective meaning "ethical" or "virtuous."

> To heed a cry for help is not a legal duty but a moral one.
> Piety and morality are two different things: a pious person can be immoral, and an impious person can be moral.

MoRALE (second syllable accented) is a noun meaning "spirit," "attitude."

> Eisenhower's habit of mixing with his troops before a battle kept up their morale.

most, mostly, *most all   *See* almost.

much   *See* many.

not very, none too, *not too   In formal writing, use *not very* or *none too* instead of **not too*.

> *Not too pleased with the dull and droning lecture, the students filled the air with spitballs and paper planes.
> EDITED: None too pleased with the dull and droning lecture, the students filled the air with spitballs and paper planes.

nowhere, *nowheres   Use *nowhere,* not **nowheres*.

> *The child was nowheres to be seen.
> EDITED: The child was nowhere to be seen.

number   *See* amount.

OK, O.K., okay   Avoid all three in formal writing. In business letters or informal writing, you can use *OK* as a noun meaning "endorsement" or "approval," or *okay* as a verb meaning "endorse," "approve."

> The stockholders have given their OK.
> Union negotiators have okayed the company's latest offer.

only   Place *only* carefully. Usually, it belongs just before the word, phrase, or clause it modifies.

> *At most colleges, students only get their diplomas if they have paid all their bills.
> EDITED: At most colleges, students get their diplomas only if they have paid all their bills.
> *Some busy executives only relax on Sundays.
> EDITED: Some busy executives relax only on Sundays.

For more on the placement of *only,* see 14.16.

ourselves, ourself   Use *ourselves* when the antecedent is plural.

> Nearly an hour after the frontrunners had come in, Sally and I dragged ourselves across the finish line.

Use *ourself* only on the rare occasion when the antecedent is a single person using the royal *we* in place of *I*.

> "Be as ourself in Denmark" (*Hamlet* 1.2.122).

passed, past   *Passed* means "went by" or "threw."

> The idiot passed me on the inside lane.
> Conversation ground to a painful halt, and minutes passed like hours.
> Seymour passed to Winowski, but the ball was intercepted.

As a noun, *past* means "a certain previous time" or "all previous time."

> Prehistoric monuments like Stonehenge speak to us of a past that we can only speculate about.

As an adjective, *past* means "connected with a certain previous time" or "connected with all previous time."

> Past experience never tells us everything we want to know about the future.

As a preposition, *past* means "beyond."

> The space probe *Pioneer 10* traveled past the limits of the solar system.

persecute, prosecute   *Persecute* means "pester," "harass," or "subject to cruel treatment."

> As Nero persecuted the Christians, Hitler persecuted the Jews.

Prosecute means "bring charges against someone in a formal, legal way."

> Al Capone ran his criminal empire so shrewdly that it was years before authorities were able to prosecute him.

personal, personnel   *PERsonal* (first syllable accented) is an adjective meaning "private" or "individual."

> In writing or speaking, you can sometimes use a personal experience to illustrate a general point.

PersonNEL (last syllable accented) is a noun meaning "persons in a firm or a military group."

> If you want a job with a big company, you normally have to see the director of personnel.

phenomenon, phenomena   *Phenomenon* means "something perceived by the senses" or "something extraordinary."

> A rainbow is a phenomenon caused by the separation of sunlight into various colors as it passes through raindrops.

Old Barney is a phenomenon. At eighty years of age he still swims five miles every day.

Phenomena is the plural of phenomenon.

The northern lights are among the most impressive phenomena in nature.

poor, poorly   Use *poor* as an adjective.

The poor man stood waiting in the rain.

Use *poorly* as an adverb.

Nearly half the applicants did poorly on the aptitude test.

Do not use *poor* as an adverb:

*The car starts poor in cold weather.
EDITED: The car starts poorly in cold weather.

Do not use *poorly* as an adjective.

*Heather looked poorly after the operation.
EDITED: Heather looked poor after the operation.

precede, proceed, proceeds, proceedings, procedure   To *precede* is "to come before or go before in place or time."

A dead calm often precedes a hurricane.

To *proceed* is "to move forward or go on."

With the bridge washed out, the bus could not proceed, so we had to get out and take a ferry across the river.

The bishop proceeded toward the cathedral.

After the judge silenced the uproar, she told the prosecutor to proceed with her questioning.

Proceeds are funds generated by a business deal or a money-raising event.

The proceeds of the auction went to buy new furniture for the Student Center.

Proceedings are formal actions, especially in an official meeting.

During a trial, a court stenographer takes down every word of the proceedings for the record.

A *procedure* is a standardized way of doing something.

Anyone who wants to run a meeting effectively should know the rules of parliamentary procedure.

principal, principle   As a noun, *principal* means "administrator" or "sum of money."

The school principal wanted all of us to think of him as a pal, but none of us did.

The interest on the principal came to $550 a year.

As an adjective, *principal* means "most important."

In most American households, television is the principal source of entertainment.

Principle means "rule of behavior," "basic truth," or "general law of nature." It serves only as a noun.

Whenever we officially recognize a government that abuses its own citizens, we are tacitly accepting the principle that might makes right.

proceed   *See* precede.

proceeds, proceedings, procedure   *See* precede.

prosecute   *See* persecute.

quote, quotation   *Quote* means "repeat the exact words of."

In his "Letter from Birmingham Jail," Martin Luther King Jr. quotes Lincoln: "This nation cannot survive half slave and half free."

Do not use *quote* to mean "refer to" or "paraphrase the view of." Use *cite*.

In defense of his stand against segregation, King cites more than a dozen authorities, and he quotes Lincoln: "This nation cannot survive half slave and half free."

Do not use *quote* as a noun to mean "something quoted." Use *quotation*.

*A sermon usually begins with a quote from Scripture.

EDITED: A sermon usually begins with a quotation from Scripture.

Quotation means "something quoted," as in the preceding example. But you should not normally use it to mean something *you* are quoting.

*In a quotation on the very first page of the book, Holden expresses his opinion of Hollywood. "If there's one thing I hate," he says, "it's the movies." [Holden is not quoting anybody. He is speaking for himself.]

EDITED: Holden states his opinion of Hollywood on the very first page of the book: "If there's one thing I hate," he says, "it's the movies."

raise, rise   *Raise (raise, raising, raised, raised)* is a transitive verb—one followed by an object.

The artist raised the curtain to display her new sculpture.

My grandmother has raised ten children.

Rise (rise, rising, rose, risen) is an intransitive verb—one that has no object.

> Puffs of smoke rose skyward.
> The farmhands rose at 5:00 A.M. Monday through Saturday.
> Have you ever risen early enough to see the sun rise?

rational, rationale, rationalize *Rational* means "able to reason," "sensible," or "logical."

> Can a rational person ever commit suicide?
> Is there such a thing as a rational argument for nuclear warfare?

Rationale means "justification," "explanation," or "underlying reason."

> The rationale for the new bypass is that it will reduce the flow of traffic through the center of town.

Rationalize means "justify with one or more fake reasons."

> He rationalized his extravagance by saying that he was only doing his part to keep money in circulation.

real, really *Real* means "actual."

> The unicorn is an imaginary beast, but it is made up of features taken from real ones.

Really means "actually."

> Petrified wood looks like ordinary wood, but it is really stone.

In formal writing, do not use *real* to modify an adjective.

> *In parts of the country, synthetic fuels have met real strong resistance.
> EDITED: In parts of the country, synthetic fuels have met really strong resistance.
> FURTHER REVISED: In parts of the country, synthetic fuels have met strong resistance. [This version eliminates *really*, which—like *very*—often weakens rather than strengthens the word it modifies.]

reason . . . is that, *reason . . . is because Use *reason* with *that*, not with *because,* or use *because* by itself.

> *The reason many college students have trouble with writing is because they did little or no writing in high school.
> EDITED: The reason many college students have trouble with writing is that they did little or no writing in high school. [or] Many college students have trouble with writing because they did little or no writing in high school.

refer *See* allude.

regardless, *irregardless   Use *regardless,* not *irregardless.*

> *Irregardless of what happens to school systems and public services, some cities and towns have voted to cut property taxes substantially.
>
> EDITED: Regardless of what happens to school systems and public services, some cities and towns have voted to cut property taxes substantially.

respectively, respectfully, respectably   *Respectively* means "in turn" or "in the order presented."

> The college presented honorary degrees to Harriet Brown and Emanuel Lee, who are, respectively, an Olympic medalist and a concert pianist.

Respectfully means "with respect."

> Parents who speak respectfully to their children are most likely to end up with children who speak respectfully to them.

Respectably means "presentably" or "in a manner deserving respect."

> She ran respectably but not quite successfully for the Senate.

revenge   *See* avenge.

rise   *See* raise.

set, sit   *Set (set, setting, set, set)* means "put" or "place."

> She set her trophy on the mantel.
> When daylight saving changes to standard time, I can never remember whether to set my watch forward or back.

Sit (sit, sitting, sat, sat) means "place oneself in a sitting position."

> On clear summer nights I love to sit outside, listen to crickets, and look at the stars.
> Grandfather sat in an easy chair and smoked his pipe.

sight, cite, site   As a verb, *sight* means "observe" or "perceive with the eyes."

> After twenty days on the open sea, the sailors sighted land.

As a noun, *sight* means "spectacle," "device for aiming," or "vision."

> Some travelers care only for the sights of a foreign country; they have no interest in its people.
> The deadliest weapon of all is a rifle with a telescopic sight.
> Most of us take the gift of sight for granted; only the blind know how much it is worth.

Cite means "refer to," "mention as an example or piece of evidence."

> Anyone opposed to nuclear power cites the case of Three Mile Island.

As a verb, *site* means "locate" or "place at a certain point."

> The architect sited the house on the side of a hill.

As a noun, *site* means "location" or "place," often the place where something has been or will be built.

> The site of the long-gone Globe Theatre, where Shakespeare himself once trod the boards, is now occupied by a reconstructed version of the Globe.

since   *See* because.

sit   *See* set.

site   *See* sight.

so   *See* very.

sometimes, sometime   *Sometimes* means "occasionally."

> Sometimes I lie awake at night and wonder what I will do with my life.

As an adverb, *sometime* means "at some point."

> Slot machine addicts invariably think they will sometime hit the jackpot.

somewhere, *somewheres   Use *somewhere,* not **somewheres.*

> *Somewheres in that pile of junk was a diamond necklace.
> EDITED: Somewhere in that pile of junk was a diamond necklace.

sort of   *See* kind of.

stationary, stationery   *Stationary* means "not moving."

> Before you can expect to hit a moving target, you need to practice with a stationary one.

Stationery means "writing paper," "writing materials."

> Since my parents sent me off to college with a big box of personalized stationery, I feel obliged to write to them occasionally.

statue, statute   *Statue* means "sculpted figure."

> The Statue of Liberty, in New York harbor, was given to America by France.

Statute means "law passed by a governing body."

Though the Supreme Court has ruled that abortion is legally permissible, some state legislatures have enacted statutes restricting the conditions under which it may be performed.

such a   Do not use *such a* as an intensifier unless you add a result clause beginning with *that*.

> WEAK: The commencement speech was such a bore.
> BETTER: The commencement speech was such a bore that I fell asleep after the first five minutes.

supposed to, *suppose to   Use *supposed to* when you mean "expected to" or "required to." Do not use **suppose to*.

> *Truman was suppose to lose when he ran against Dewey, but he surprised almost everyone by winning.
> EDITED: Truman was supposed to lose when he ran against Dewey, but he surprised almost everyone by winning.

teach   *See* learn.

than, then   Use *than* when writing comparisons.

> Many people spend money faster than they earn it.

Use *then* when referring to time.

> Lightning flashed, thunder cracked, and then the rain began.

that, which, who   Use *which* or *that* as the pronoun when the antecedent is a thing.

> There was nothing to drink but root beer, which I loathe.
> Any restaurant that doesn't serve grits ought to be closed.

Use *who* or *that* as the pronoun when the antecedent is a person or persons.

> I like people who can do things. —R. W. Emerson
> A team that cannot work together is likely to lose.

themselves, *theirselves, *theirself   Use *themselves*, not **theirselves* or **theirself*.

> *Fortunately, the children did not hurt theirselves when they fell out of the tree.
> EDITED: Fortunately, the children did not hurt themselves when they fell out of the tree.

then   *See* than.

there, their, they're Use *there* to mean "in that place" or "to that place," and in the expressions *there is* and *there are*.

> I have always wanted to see Las Vegas, but I have never been there.
> There is nothing we can do to change the past, but there are many things we can do to improve the future.

There is and *there are* should be used sparingly, since most sentences are tighter and better without them.

> We can do nothing to change the past, but many things to improve the future.

Use *their* as the possessive form of *they*.

> The immigrants had to leave most of their possessions behind.

Use *they're* when you mean "they are."

> I like cats because they're sleek, quiet, and sly.

thus, therefore, *thusly Use *thus* to mean "in that manner" or "by this means." In formal writing, do not use **thusly*.

> Carmichael bought a thousand shares of Microsoft when it was a brand-new company. Thus he became a millionaire.

Do not use *thus* to mean "therefore," "so," or "for this reason."

> A storm hit the mountain. *Thus the climbers had to take shelter.
> EDITED: A storm hit the mountain, so the climbers had to take shelter.

to, too Use *to* when writing about place, direction, or position, and with infinitives.

> We drove from Cleveland to Pittsburgh without stopping.
> Like many before him, Fenwick was determined to write the great American novel.

Use *too* when you mean "also" or "excessively."

> In spite of the cast on my foot, I too got up and danced.
> Some poems are too confusing to be enjoyable.

try to, *try and Use *try to*, not *try and*.

> * Whenever I feel depressed, I try and lose myself in science fiction.
> EDITED: Whenever I feel depressed, I try to lose myself in science fiction.

type Do not attach *-type* to the end of an adjective.

> *He had a psychosomatic-type illness.
> EDITED: He had a psychosomatic illness.

uninterested   *See* disinterested.

unique   *Unique* means "one of a kind."

> Among pop singers of the fifties, Elvis Presley was unique.

Do not use *unique* to mean "remarkable," "unusual," or "striking."

> *She wore a unique dress to the party.
> EDITED: She wore a striking dress to the party.

used to, *use to   Write *used to,* not **use to,* when you mean "did regularly" or "was accustomed to."

> *She use to practice the flute every morning.
> EDITED: She used to practice the flute every morning.

very, awfully, so   Use *very* sparingly, if at all. It can weaken the effect of potent modifiers.

> The very icy wind cut through us as we walked across the bridge.
> BETTER: The icy wind cut through us as we walked across the bridge.

Do not use *awfully* to mean "very."

> *We were awfully tired.
> EDITED: We were very tired.
> FURTHER REVISED: We were exhausted.

Do not use *so* as an intensifier unless you add a result clause beginning with *that.*

> *They were so tired.
> EDITED: They were so tired that they slept for ten hours.

wait for, wait on   To *wait for* means "to stay until someone arrives, something is provided, or something happens."

> The restaurant was so crowded that we had to wait half an hour for a table.

To *wait on* means "to serve."

> Sam waited on more than fifty people that night. When the restaurant closed, he could barely stand up.

way, ways   Use *way,* not *ways,* when writing about distance.

> *A short ways up the trail we found a dead rabbit.
> EDITED: A short way up the trail we found a dead rabbit.

well   *See* good.

were, we're   Use *were* as a verb or part of a verb phrase.

> The soldiers were a sorry sight.
> They were trudging across a wheat field.

Use *we're* when you mean "we are."

> We're trying to build a telescope for the observatory.
> Most Americans have lost the urge to roam. With television scanning the world for us, we're a nation of sitters.

which, who   *See* that.

whose, who's   *Whose,* meaning "of whom," is the possessive form of *who.*

> Whose property has been destroyed?

Who's means "who is."

> Who's deceived by such claims?

would have, *would of   Use *would have,* not **would of.*

> *Churchill said that he would of made a pact with the devil himself to defeat Hitler.
> EDITED: Churchill said that he would have made a pact with the devil himself to defeat Hitler.

Have, not *of,* is also customary after *may, might, must,* and *should.*

Glossary of Grammatical Terms

absolute phrase   A modifier usually made from a noun or noun phrase and a participle. It can modify a noun or pronoun or the whole of the base sentence to which it is attached.

> *Teeth chattering,* we waited for hours in the bitter cold.
> Who is the best person for the job, *all things considered?*

active voice   *See* voice.

adjective   A word that modifies a noun or pronoun, specifying such things as what kind, how many, and which one.

> For a *small* crime, he spent years in a *tiny* cell of the *old* prison.
> She is *intelligent.*

adjective phrase   A phrase that modifies a noun or pronoun.

> A *long, thin* scar was visible on his back.
> On the table was a vase *with red roses.*
> It was a *once-in-a-lifetime* opportunity.

adjective (relative) clause   A subordinate clause used as an adjective within a sentence. It normally begins with a relative pronoun—a word that relates the clause to a preceding word or phrase.

> Pablo Picasso, *who learned to paint by the age of twelve,* worked at his art for nearly eighty years.

adverb   A word that modifies a verb, an adjective, another adverb, or a clause. It tells such things as how, when, where, why, and for what purpose. It often ends in *-ly.*

[handwritten annotation: includes linking verbs.]

> He *seldom* spoke.
> The road was *extremely* bumpy.

[handwritten annotation: Three windows are in this room. adverbial adjunct.]

749

The cyclists were breathing *very heavily.*
Fortunately, no one was injured.

adverb clause   A subordinate clause used as an adverb within a sentence. It begins with a subordinator, a term like *because, if, when,* or *although.*

We canceled the deal *because the buyer could not get a loan.*
If the temperature falls below freezing, roads will become unsafe.
Excited *when his friends arrived,* he was miserable *when they left.*

adverb phrase   A phrase that modifies a verb, an adjective, another adverb, or a clause.

The fox hid *under the hedge.*
Wary *at first,* we approached *in silence.*
The children were eager *to see the clowns.*

agent   The source of the action in a passive-voice construction.

The preamble was written by *Alice Harvey.*
The launching of the space shuttle will be viewed by *millions.*

agreement of pronoun and antecedent   Correspondence in gender and number between a pronoun and its antecedent.

Nellie Bly, the American journalist, was noted for *her* daring. [*Her* is feminine and singular.]
Ms. Sterns handed Mr. Nichols *his* briefcase. [*His* is masculine and singular.]
You can't tell a book by *its* cover. [*Its* is neuter and singular.]
The Andrews Sisters sang some of *their* best-known songs during World War II. [*Their* is plural and used for all genders.]

agreement of subject and verb   Correspondence in number between the form of a verb and its subject. In most cases, the subject affects the form of the verb only in the present tense; when the subject is a singular noun or a third-person singular pronoun, the present tense is made by the addition of *-s* or *-es* to the bare form.

Jerry *paints* his houses.
He *fishes* every summer.

When the subject is not a singular noun or a third-person singular pronoun, the present tense is normally the same as the bare form.

I *paint* houses.
The men *fish* every summer.

The verb *be* has special forms in the present and the past, as shown in 21.3.

antecedent   The word or word group that a pronoun refers to.

> A   P
> *Oliver* said that he could eat a whole pizza.

> A   P
> *The police,* who have surrounded the building, expect to free the hostages
> tonight.

> A   P
> A *snake* sheds its skin several times a year.

appositive   A noun, noun phrase, or series of nouns used to identify another noun, noun phrase, or a pronoun.

> The blackjack player, *an expert at counting cards in play,* was barred from the
> casino.
> They were denied their favorite foods—*ice cream, pizza, and peanut butter.*
> He and she—*brother and sister*—opened a record store.

article   A short word (*a, an,* or *the*) commonly used before a noun or noun
equivalent.

> *The* bombing of *a* village provoked *an* outcry of protest.

See also determiner.

auxiliary (helping verb)   A verb used with a base verb to make a verb
phrase.

> I *have* seen the Kennedy Library.
> It *was* designed by I. M. Pei.
> People *do* find it impressive.

bare form   The verb form used in the present tense with every subject
except a singular noun and a third-person singular pronoun.

base (bare-bones) sentence   A sentence without modifiers.

> Prices rose.
> Orders dropped.
> Customers saved money.

base verb   The principal verb in a verb phrase made with an auxiliary.

> She has *earned* a promotion.
> She will be *supervising* all overseas operations.

case   The form that a noun or pronoun takes as determined by its role in a sentence. The **subject case** is used for a pronoun that is the subject of a verb.

> The dog was far from home, but *he* still wore a leather collar.

The **object case** is used for a pronoun that serves as an object (*see* object) or that immediately precedes an infinitive.

> I found *him* trailing a broken leash behind *him*.
> I wanted *him* to come home with *me*.

The **possessive case** of a noun or pronoun indicates ownership of something or close connection with it.

> The *dog's* hind feet were bleeding, and *his* coat was muddy.

The **reflexive/emphatic case** of a pronoun indicates a reflexive action—an action affecting the one who performs it. This case is also used for emphasis.

> The dog had hurt *himself;* as I tried to comfort him, the owner *herself* rushed up to me.

clause   A word group consisting of a subject and a predicate.

> S   P
> We / bought an old house. [one clause]
>   S   P   S   P
> After we / bought the house, we / found a crack in the foundation. [two clauses]
>   S   P   S   P
> Furthermore, the roof / leaked, the floors / sagged, and the
>   S   P
> furnace / was out of order. [three clauses]

collective noun   A noun naming a collection of people, animals, or things treated as an entity. Examples include *team, committee, herd, flock,* and *family.*

comma splice   The error of trying to link two independent clauses with nothing but a comma.

> *Sir Richard Burton failed to find the source of the Nile, John Hanning Speke discovered it in 1862.
> EDITED: Sir Richard Burton failed to find the source of the Nile; John Hanning Speke discovered it in 1862.

Separating the clauses with a period would give you two sentences.

common and progressive forms Forms of the verb. The common form indicates an action that is habitual, completed, or to be completed.

> They *take* excursions on weekends.
> He *opened* the door and *entered* the room.
> She *will finish* by dark.

The progressive form indicates a continuing action or one that was in progress when something else occurred.

> They *are taking* an excursion right now.
> He *was opening* the door when the cat scratched him.
> She *will be working* on the design throughout the day.

The progressive consists of some form of the auxiliary *be* followed by a present particle—a verb with *-ing* on the end.

comparative, positive, and superlative Forms of the adjective and adverb. The positive form describes a person or thing without drawing a comparison.

> This lemonade tastes *sour*.
> Ms. Berkle talks *loudly*.

The comparative is used to compare one person, thing, or group with another person, thing, or group.

> Los Angeles is *bigger* than Sacramento.
> Sarah was *more ambitious* than her classmates.
> Sheila argued *less persuasively* than Susan did.
> In general, women live *longer* than men.

The superlative is used to compare one person, thing, or group with all others in its class.

> Joan's quilt was the *most colorful* one on display.
> Whales are the *largest* of all mammals.
> Gold is the *most eagerly* sought mineral in the world.

complete subject *See* subject.

complex sentence A sentence consisting of one independent clause and at least one subordinate clause. The independent clause in a complex sentence is usually called the main clause.

> Although Frank pleaded with Ida [subordinate clause], she would not give him any money [main clause].

compound-complex sentence   A sentence consisting of two or more independent clauses and one or more subordinate clauses.

> When I moved to Chicago [subordinate clause], I first applied for a job [main clause], and then I looked for an apartment [main clause].

compound phrase   Words or phrases joined by a conjunction, a comma, or both.

> The plan was *simple but shrewd.*
> We saw an *enormous, old, rough-skinned* elephant.
> The kitten was *lively, friendly, and curious.*
> You must *either pay your dues on time or turn in your membership card.*

compound sentence   A sentence consisting of two or more independent clauses.

> Jill made the coffee, and Frank scrambled the eggs.
> He practiced many hours each day, but he never learned to play the piano well.

conditional sentence   A sentence normally consisting of an *if* clause, which states a condition, and a result clause, which states the result of that condition.

> If it rains on the Fourth of July, the fireworks will be canceled.
> If Social Security were abolished, millions of retirees would be destitute.

conjunction (coordinating conjunction)   A word used to show a relation between words, phrases, or clauses. The conjunctions are *and, yet, or, but, nor,* and—for joining clauses only—*for* and *so.*

> The tablecloth was red, white, *and* blue.
> Small *but* sturdy, the cabin had withstood many winters.
> Al *and* Joan walked to the meeting, *for* they liked exercise.

conjunctive adverb   A word or phrase used to show a relation between clauses or sentences. Conjunctive adverbs include *nevertheless, as a result, therefore, however,* and *likewise.*

> The ship was supposed to be unsinkable; *nevertheless,* it did not survive its collision with an iceberg.
> The lawyer spoke for an hour; the jury, *however,* was unimpressed.

coordinating conjunction   *See* conjunction.

coordination   An arrangement that makes two or more parts of a sentence equal in grammatical rank.

Martha *took the script* home and *read it* to her friend.
The fight ended, and *the crowd dispersed.*
A porcupine or *a raccoon* had raided the garbage can.

correlative   Words or phrases used in pairs to join words, phrases, or clauses. Correlatives include *both . . . and, not only . . . but also, either . . . or, neither . . . nor,* and *whether . . . or.*

The Web site is *both* fun *and* informative.
She *not only* got the part *but also* played it brilliantly.
Either they would visit us, *or* we would visit them.

dangling modifier   A modifier without a headword—a word or phrase that it can modify.

*Running angrily out the back door, a couple of flower pots were overturned.
EDITED: Running angrily out the back door, he overturned a couple of flower pots.

declarative sentence   A sentence that makes a statement and ends with a period.

The Earth orbits the sun.
Many Americans are overweight.

definite pronouns   *See* pronoun.

dependent clause   *See* subordinate clause.

determiner   A modifier that always precedes a noun or noun equivalent and marks it as such. Determiners include articles *(a, an, the),* demonstratives (such as *this*), indefinites (such as *some*), possessives (such as *her*), ordinal numbers (such as *ten*), and cardinal numbers (such as *third*). Unlike adjectives (A), determiners cannot follow the nouns they modify and have no comparative or superlative forms.

The first ten customers each got *a* box of popcorn.
    A   A
The manager, smiling and happy, greeted *every* customer.
                        A
His smiling made them happier.

direct object   *See* object.

direct and indirect reporting   Two ways of reporting spoken or written statements and questions. A direct report reproduces within quotation marks the words someone spoke or wrote.

755

"He that cannot obey, cannot command," writes Benjamin Franklin.

An indirect report turns the original statement into a subordinate clause usually starting with *that*.

> Franklin writes that anyone who cannot obey is unable to command.

double negative   The error of using two negative words to make one negative statement.

> *We *didn't* need *no* guide.
> EDITED: We *didn't* need a guide. [or] We needed *no* guide.

expletive   A word used before a linking verb when the subject follows it.

> *There* was no food in the house.
> *It* was exciting to see the bald eagles.

faulty comparison   The omission of one or more words needed to make a comparison clear.

> *The neighborhood is more violent than five years ago.
> EDITED: The neighborhood is more violent than it was five years ago.

faulty parallelism   A construction in which two or more elements are parallel in meaning but not in form.

> *He wants to write with clarity, power, and logically.
> EDITED: He wants to write *clearly, powerfully,* and *logically.*

faulty predication   Using words after a linking verb that are not compatible with the subject.

> *A necessary step in any campaign to lose weight is *eating habits.*
> EDITED: A necessary step in any campaign to lose weight is *to change one's eating habits.*

faulty shift in tense   An unjustified shift from one tense to another, or an inconsistency between the tense of a subordinate verb and the tense of the main verb.

> *I lit a candle, but the darkness *is* so thick I saw nothing.
> EDITED: I lit a candle, but the darkness was so thick I saw nothing.
> *Though the trumpeter *blows* as hard as she could, the drummer drowned her out.
> EDITED: Though the trumpeter blew as hard as she could, the drummer drowned her out.

fragment   *See* sentence fragment.

fused sentence *See* run-on sentence.

future perfect tense *See* tense.

future tense *See* tense.

gender The form of a pronoun as determined by the sex of its antecedent, which may be masculine, feminine, or neuter.

> Bill [antecedent] brought *his* guitar, and Sally [antecedent] brought *her* drums.
> The sun [antecedent] shed *its* rays over the lake.

gerund A verbal noun made from the present participle.

> *Gambling* takes nerve.
> Fawn hated *washing dishes.*

headword (H) A word or phrase modified (M) by another word, phrase, or clause.

>   M   H
> A black leather *wallet* was found in the men's room.
>   M   H
> Running for the elevator, *Pritchett* nearly knocked over Mr. Givens.
> M H   M
> The *breeze* that refreshes us comes from the ocean.

helping verb *See* auxiliary.

imperative *See* mood.

indefinite pronoun *See* pronoun.

independent clause A clause that can stand by itself as a simple sentence.

> The roof leaks.

It can be combined with one or more independent clauses in a compound sentence.

> The roof leaks, and the floor sags.

And it can serve as the main clause in a complex sentence.

> Whenever it rains, the roof leaks.

indicative mood   *See* mood.

indirect object   *See* object.

indirect report   *See* direct and indirect reporting.

infinitive   A form usually made by the placing of *to* before the bare form of a verb.

> Some say that politicians are born *to run*.
> The prisoners of war refused to *continue* their forced march.

After some verbs the *to* in the infinitive is omitted. Compare:

> Jack wanted the little boy *to feed* the ducks.
> Jack watched the little boy *feed* the ducks.

infinitive phrase   A phrase formed by an infinitive and its object, its modifiers, or both.

> She hates *to see horror movies*.
> It was beginning *to rain furiously*.
> I hoped *to have found a job by July 4*.

interrogative pronoun   A pronoun that begins a question.

> *What* is making that noise?

interrogative sentence   A sentence that asks a question and ends with a question mark.

> Do whales have lungs?

intransitive verb   *See* transitive and intransitive verbs.

irregular verb   *See* regular and irregular verbs.

linking verb   A verb followed by a word or word group that identifies or describes the subject.

> This machine *is* a drill press.
> I *feel* good today.
> That perfume *smells* sweet.

main clause   The independent clause in a complex sentence.

> Since the refrigerator was empty, *we went to a restaurant*.

main verb   The verb of the independent clause in a complex sentence.

I *cut* the grass before the storm came.
Since the store was closed, we *drove* away.

misplaced modifier   A modifier that does not clearly point to its headword
—the word or phrase it modifies.

*Sleeping in an empty shoebox, Michelle discovered the missing kitten.
EDITED: Michelle discovered the missing kitten sleeping in an empty
shoebox.

mixed construction   Any combination of words that do not fit together
grammatically or meaningfully.

*Fearful of punishment caused the boy to stutter.
EDITED: Fear of punishment caused the boy to stutter.
[or] Fearful of punishment, the boy stuttered.

modal auxiliary   A helping verb that indicates the subjunctive mood.

The children *should* be here on Father's Day this year.
I'm not so sure that the average citizen *can* fight City Hall.

Besides *should* and *can,* the modal auxiliaries include *would, could, may,*
might, must, and *ought.*

modifier   A word or word group that describes, limits, or qualifies another
word or word group in a sentence.

Pat smiled *winningly.*
I *rarely* travel *anymore.*
The big gray cat seized *the little* mouse *as it ran up the stairs.*
Polished to a high gloss, the mahogany table *immediately* drew *our* attention.

See also determiner.

mood   The form of a verb that indicates the writer's attitude toward a
particular statement as it is made. The indicative is the mood used in
statements of actuality or strong probability.

He always *lingers* over his second cup of coffee.
We *will* sleep well tonight.

The imperative is the mood of commands and requests made directly.

Be quiet!
Please *go* away.
Let us pray.
Stop!

The subjunctive is the mood used in statements of hypothetical conditions or of wishes, recommendations, requirements, demands, or suggestions. Normally the subjunctive requires either a modal auxiliary or a subjunctive verb form.

> I wish I *could go.* [modal auxiliary expressing a wish]
> I wish I *were* a rock star. [subjunctive verb form expressing a wish]
> Each member *must* pay her dues by December 1. [modal auxiliary expressing a requirement]
> The rules require that each member *pay* her dues by December 1. [subjunctive verb form expressing a requirement]

nonrestrictive modifier   *See* restrictive and nonrestrictive modifiers.

noun   A word that names a person, creature, place, thing, activity, condition, or idea.

noun clause   A subordinate clause that is used as a noun within a sentence. It serves as subject, object, predicate noun, or object of a preposition.

> *Whoever contributed to the office party* deserves many thanks.
> I said *that I was hungry.*
> You are *what you eat.*
> The station offered a prize to *whoever called first with the right answer.*

noun equivalent   A verbal noun or a noun clause.

noun marker   *See* determiner.

noun phrase   A phrase formed by a noun (N) and its modifiers (M).

>   M   N
> They swam contentedly in the warm, clear water.
>   M   N
> The *eighteenth-century building* was declared a landmark last week.

number   The form of a word as determined by the number of persons or things it refers to. Most nouns and many pronouns may be singular or plural.

> A *carpenter* [singular] works hard.
> *Carpenters* [plural] work hard.
> Jeff said that *he* [singular] would give the party.
> All *his* [singular] friends said that *they* [plural] would come.

object   A word or word group naming a person or thing affected by the action that a verb, a participle, an infinitive, or a gerund specifies.

I hit *the ball.*
Sighting *the bear,* he started to aim *his rifle.*
Splitting *wood* is hard work.

A direct object names the person or thing directly affected by the action specified.

The accountant prepared *my tax return.*

An indirect object names the person or thing indirectly affected by the action specified.

I gave *Joe* a bit of advice.
She bought *her father* a shirt.

The object of a preposition is any word or word group that immediately follows a preposition.

For *her,* the meeting was crucial.
I found the sponge under *the kitchen sink.*

object case   *See* case.

object complement   A word or word group that immediately follows a direct object and identifies or describes it.

I found the first chapter *fascinating.*
Many sportswriters used to consider Greg Louganis *the best diver in the world.*

parallel construction   The arrangement of two or more elements of a sentence in grammatically equivalent patterns: noun lined up with noun, verb with verb, phrase with phrase, and clause with clause.

Sink or swim, live or die, survive or perish, I give *my hand* and *my heart* to this vote. —Daniel Webster
We must *take the risk* or *lose our chance.*
I'll take either *the chocolate cake* or *the coconut pie.*

particle   A preposition used as an adverb. Particles always follow a verb and strongly affect its meaning.

I looked *up* the word in the dictionary.
The rich sometimes look *down on* the poor.

participle   A term usually made by the addition of *-ing, -d,* or *-ed,* to the bare form of a verb.

PRESENT PARTICIPLE:	calling	living	burning	lifting
PAST PARTICIPLE:	called	lived	burned	lifted

A **perfect participle** is made by the combination of *having* or *having been* with the past participle.

> having called   having been lifted

participle phrase   A phrase formed by a participle and its object, its modifiers, or both. Usually a participle phrase modifies a noun or pronoun.

> *Wearied after their long climb,* the hikers were glad to stop and make camp.
> She picked at the knot, *loosening it gradually.*

passive voice   *See* voice.

past participle   *See* participle.

past perfect tense   *See* tense.

past tense   *See* tense.

perfect infinitive   The form of the infinitive made with *have* and the past participle.

> I was glad *to have finished* the project by the deadline.

perfect participle   *See* participle.

person   In English grammar the term *person* designates the following system of classification.

	SINGULAR	PLURAL
FIRST PERSON	I, me, mine, my	we, us, ours, our
SECOND PERSON	you, yours, your	you, yours, your
THIRD PERSON	he, him, his	
	she, her, hers	they, them, theirs, their
	it, its	
	and singular nouns	*and* plural nouns

phrase   A sequence of two or more words that serves as a unit within or attached to a clause.

> *A bright red kimono* caught my eye.
> *Encouraged by her friends,* Helen bought the house.
> I hurried *to reach the post office.*

Helen, who was encouraged
by her friends, bought the house.

possessive case   *See* case.

predicate   A word or word group that normally follows the subject of a sentence and tells what it does, has, or is, or what is done to it.

> The pastry chef *makes doughnuts, napoleons, and éclairs.*
> Venice *is a golden city interlaced with canals.*

A **base predicate** (**simple predicate**) is a predicate without its modifiers.

> Simon and Garfunkel *sang* for a crowd of almost half a million.
> The children *threw snowballs* at passing cars.
> They *were* soon *punished.*

predeterminer   A word that precedes a determiner.

> *Half* the pie is yours.
> We met *both* the girls.

The main predeterminers are *all, both,* and *half.*

predicate adjective   An adjective or adjective phrase that follows a linking verb and describes the subject.

> Velvet feels *soft.*
> Henry seems *upset by the vote.*

predicate noun   A noun or noun phrase that follows a linking verb and identifies the subject.

> Time was our only *enemy.*
> J. D. Salinger is *a very reclusive writer.*

preposition   A word followed by its object—a noun, pronoun, or noun equivalent. A preposition shows the relation between its object and another word or word group in the sentence.

> The table was set *under* a tree.
> Hounded *by* his creditors, he finally declared himself bankrupt.

Besides *under* and *by,* prepositions include *with, at, of, in, from, over, after,* and *on.*

prepositional phrase   A phrase that starts with a preposition and ends with its object. Phrases of this type are regularly used as adjectives or adverbs.

> Helen admired women *with strong ambition.*
> Have you ridden *on the Ferris wheel?*
> I took the suitcase *from the woman / in the room / on the left.*

present participle   *See* participle.

present perfect tense   *See* tense.

present tense   *See* tense.

principal parts   The following parts of a verb:

PRESENT (BARE FORM)	PRESENT PARTICIPLE	PAST	PAST PARTICIPLE
see	seeing	saw	seen
work	working	worked	worked

progressive form   *See* common and progressive forms.

pronoun   A word that commonly takes the place of a noun or noun phrase. Pronouns may be definite or indefinite. A definite pronoun refers to an antecedent (A), a noun or noun phrase appearing before or shortly after the pronoun.

> A
> As soon as Grant saw the enemy, *he* ordered his men to fire.

> A
> Janis Joplin was only twenty-seven when *she* died.

> A
> Though *he* won the battle, Nelson did not live to savor the victory.

An indefinite pronoun refers to unspecified persons or things. It has no antecedent.

> *Everyone* likes Janet.
> Marvin will do *anything* to help a friend.

An interrogative pronoun introduces a question.

> *What* did the officer say?
> *Who* is pitching for the Blue Jays tomorrow?

pronoun-antecedent agreement   *See* agreement of pronoun and antecedent.

reflexive/emphatic case   *See* case.

regular and irregular verbs   A regular verb is one for which the past tense and past participle are formed by the addition of *-d* or *-ed* to the present.

PRESENT (BARE FORM)	PAST	PAST PARTICIPLE
work	worked	worked
tickle	tickled	tickled
walk	walked	walked

An irregular verb is one for which the past, the past participle, or both are formed in other ways.

sew	sewed	sewn
have	had	had
eat	ate	eaten

relative clause   *See* adjective clause.

relative pronoun   A pronoun that introduces an adjective clause.

College students *who* enjoy doing their laundry are hard to find.
Some companies now make furnaces *that* burn wood as well as oil.
I'm looking for someone *whose* degree is in economics.

The relative pronouns are *which, that, who, whom,* and *whose.*

restricter   An adverb that limits or restricts the meaning of the word immediately after it.

On the first day, we hiked *just* five miles.
Walking along the beach, she *almost* stepped on a crab.
I ate *nearly* all the turkey.

Restricters include *almost, hardly, just, only,* and *nearly.* When used at the end of a sentence, a restricter limits the meaning of the word just before it.

Tickets were sold to adults *only.*

restrictive and nonrestrictive modifiers   A restrictive modifier restricts or limits the meaning of its headword.

All taxpayers *who fail to file their returns by April 15* will be fined.

A restrictive modifier is essential to the meaning of a sentence. Without the modifier, the meaning of the sample sentence would be fundamentally different.

All taxpayers will be fined.

A nonrestrictive modifier does not restrict or limit the meaning of its headword.

Sam, *who loves football,* cheered louder than anyone else.

A nonrestrictive modifier is not essential to the meaning of a sentence. Without the modifier, the meaning of the sample sentence remains basically the same.

> Sam cheered louder than anyone else.

run-on sentence (fused sentence)   Two or more independent clauses run together with no punctuation or conjunction between them.

> *Mosquitoes arrived at dusk they whined about our ears as we huddled in our sleeping bags.
> EDITED: Mosquitoes arrived at dusk, and they whined about our ears as we huddled in our sleeping bags.

sentence   A word group consisting of at least one independent clause. A sentence begins with a capital letter and closes with a period, a question mark, or an exclamation point.

> The telephone was ringing.
> By the time I got out of the shower, the caller had hung up.
> I was furious!
> Was the call important?

sentence fragment   A part of a sentence punctuated as if it were a whole one.

> The plant drooped. *And died.*
> I could not get into the house. *Because I had forgotten my key.*

sequence of tenses   The relation between the tenses of the verbs in a sentence that contains more than one verb, or in a passage of several sentences.

> By the time I *arrived,* everyone else *had left.*
> When the parade *goes* through town, all the townspeople *come* to see it.

simple sentence   A sentence consisting of just one independent clause.

> The problem was complex.
> It challenged the skill of experts.
> For months there was no solution.
> Then a solution was found by two veterans in the decoding department.

simple subject   *See* subject.

split infinitive   An infinitive in which one or more words are wedged between *to* and the verb.

> The purchasing department is going *to carefully check* each new order.

BETTER: The purchasing department is going to check each new order carefully.

squinting modifier   A modifier placed so that it could plausibly modify either the word(s) before it or the word(s) after it.

> *Cutting classes frequently leads to low grades.
> EDITED: Frequent cutting of classes leads to low grades.
> [or] Frequently, cutting classes leads to low grades.
> [or] Cutting classes leads frequently to low grades.

subject   A word or word group that tells who or what performs or undergoes the action named by a verb, or that is described or identified in a linking verb construction.

> *Gossip* fascinates me.
> *Morgan* hit one of Johnson's best pitches.
> *Piccadilly Circus* is the Times Square of London.
> Does *your allergy* cause a rash?
> *Jan and I* were pelted by the rain.
> There was *a snake* under the chair.

A **simple subject** is a subject without its modifiers.

> The old dusty *volumes* fell to the floor.

A **complete subject** is a subject with its modifiers.

> *The old dusty volumes* fell to the floor.

subject case   *See* case.

subject complement   A word or word group that immediately follows a linking verb and identifies or describes the subject:

> Blue is *my favorite color.*
> The house was *enormous.*

subject-verb agreement   *See* agreement of subject and verb.

subjunctive mood   *See* mood.

subordinate (dependent) clause   A clause that normally begins with a subordinator or a relative pronoun. Such a clause cannot stand alone as a sentence. In formal writing it must be connected to or included in a main clause.

> *Because Mrs. Braithwait was writing her memoirs,* she reviewed all her old diaries and correspondence.

Has anyone ever seen the bullet *that killed John F. Kennedy?*
I didn't know *where she had left the key.*

subordinate verb   The verb of a subordinate clause in a complex sentence.

I cut the grass before the storm *came.*
Since the door *was* open, I walked in.

subordinating conjunction   *See* subordinator.

subordination   An arrangement that makes one or more parts of a sentence secondary to and dependent upon another part.

WITHOUT SUBORDINATION: The dog ate lunch, and then he took a nap.
WITH SUBORDINATION: *After the dog ate lunch,* he took a nap.

subordinator (subordinating conjunction)   A word or phrase regularly used to introduce a subordinate clause.

When we left, I locked all the doors.
They can do nothing *if* the drought continues.

superlative   *See* comparative, positive, and superlative.

tense   The form of a verb that helps to indicate the time of an action or condition.

PRESENT: I jump.
PAST: I jumped.
FUTURE: I will jump.
PRESENT PERFECT: I have jumped.
PAST PERFECT: I had jumped.
FUTURE PERFECT: I will have jumped.

transitive and intransitive verbs   A transitive verb names an action that directly affects a person or thing specified in the predicate.

He *struck* the gong.
Water *erodes* even granite.
Did you *mail* the letters?
We *elected* Sloan.

An intransitive verb names an action that has no direct impact on anyone or anything specified in the predicate.

Wilson *smiled* at the comedian's best efforts, but he did not *laugh.*

768

verb   A word or phrase naming an action done by or to a subject, a state of being experienced by a subject, or an occurrence.

> My uncle *was* asleep when the hurricane *destroyed* his house.

verbal noun   A word or phrase formed from a verb and used as a noun.

> *Hunting* was once the sport of kings.
> I want *to travel.*
> *Fixing bicycles* keeps me busy.
> *To sacrifice his rook* would have been Gilman's best move.

verb phrase   A phrase formed by two or more verbs—a base verb and at least one auxiliary.

> Richard *may complete* his experiment by July.
> Alison *would have come* earlier if you *had called* her.

voice   The aspect of a verb that indicates whether the subject acts or is acted upon. A verb is in the active voice when the subject performs the action named by the verb.

> The officer *told* me to leave.
> A famous surgeon *performed* the operation.

A verb is in the passive voice when the subject undergoes the action named by the verb.

> I *was told* to do it that way.
> The operation *will be performed* by a famous surgeon.

PERMISSIONS ACKNOWLEDGMENTS

TEXT

Bikini Kill: "Jet Ski," "No Backrub," "Finale," and "Distinct Complicity." Reprinted by permission of the band.

Gwendolyn Brooks: "Mrs. Small" by Gwendolyn Brooks © 1991, from her book *Blacks,* published by Third World Press, Chicago, 1991. Reprinted by permission of the author.

Christian Science Monitor: "Saving the Cultural Environment" from *The Christian Science Monitor.* This article first appeared in *The Christian Science Monitor* on June 6, 1992, and is reproduced with permission. Copyright © 1992 The Christian Science Publishing Society. All rights reserved.

Definition of *Cool:* Copyright © 1996 by Houghton Mifflin Company. Reproduced by permission from *The American Heritage Dictionary of the English Language,* Third Edition.

Loren Eiseley: "Man of the Future" from *The Immense Journey* by Loren Eiseley. Copyright © 1946, 1950, 1951, 1953, 1955, 1956, 1957 by Loren Eiseley. Reprinted by permission of Random House, Inc.

Lani Guinier: "Dangers of Majority Rule." Reprinted with the permission of The Free Press, a division of Simon & Schuster, Inc., from *The Tyranny of the Majority: Fundamental Fairness in Representative Democracy* by Lani Guinier. Copyright © 1994 by Lani Guinier.

Ayres Haxton (DJ Ayres): "DJ Riz—Live From Brooklyn" from *Loop Hole Magazine (<loopholemag.com>).* Reprinted by permission.

Janet Heller: "About Morris Heller" from *The New York Times,* May 7, 1976. Copyright © 1976 by the New York Times Company. Reprinted by permission.

X. J. Kennedy: "Who Killed King Kong?" from *Dissent.* Reprinted by permission of the author and *Dissent* magazine.

Huggy Bear: "Different Worlds, Different Struggles." Published by Famous Monsters of Filmland. Reprinted with permission.

Meridel Le Sueur: "The Girl" from *Salute to Spring and Other Stories.* Copyright © 1940 by Meridel Le Sueur. Reprinted by permission of International Publishers Company, Inc.

Jennifer Moses: "Small Is Beautiful; Washington, LA" from *The New York Times,* May 9, 1999. Copyright © 1999 by the New York Times Company. Reprinted by permission.

Rosa Parks: "The Montgomery Bus Boycott, 1955–56" from *Voices of Freedom* by Henry Hampton and Steve Fayer, copyright © 1990 by Blackside, Inc. Used by permission of Bantam Books, a division of Random House, Inc.

Victor Pelevin: "Russian Graffiti" from *The New York Times Magazine,* June 8, 1997. Reprinted by permission of Victor Pelevin and the Watkins/Loomis Agency.

Reynolds Price: "Permanent Errors." Reprinted with the permission of Harriet Wasserman Literary Agency, Inc., and by Scribner, a Division of Simon & Schuster, from *Permanent Errors* by Reynolds Price. Copyright © 1970 Reynolds Price.

Sleater-Kinney: "Burn, Don't Freeze." Reprinted by permission of the band and Kill Rock Stars.

Jon Spayde: "15 Ideas That Could Shake the World—The Bioneer Movement" from *Utne Reader.* Reprinted by permission of the author.

Brandon Scott Sweeten: "Conflict Stalemate and Conflict Resolutions: Implementing the Native American Graves and Repatriation Act." Reprinted by permission of Brandon Scott Sweeten.

Lewis Thomas: "Medical Lessons from History," "Notes on Punctuation." Copyright © 1979 by Lewis Thomas, from *The Medusa and the Snail* by Lewis Thomas, copyright © 1974, 1975, 1976, 1977, 1978, 1979 by Lewis Thomas. Used by permission of Viking Penguin, a division of Penguin Putnam, Inc.

Richard Traubner: "Review of Piazzolla: *Maria de Buenos Aires*" from *Opera News,* February 1999. Reprinted by permission of the author and *Opera News.*

Elizabeth Weise: "Money Slants Search Results; Microsoft 'Wins' Big Brother Award" from *USA Today,* April 12, 1999. Copyright © 1999 *USA Today.* Reprinted with permission.

Utne Reader: "Patently Absurd: Will Ideas Become the Next Hot Commodity?" from *Utne Reader,* May/June 1999. Reprinted by permission from *Utne Reader.*

Every effort has been made to contact the copyright holders of each of these selections. Rights holders of any selection not credited should contact W. W. Norton & Company, Inc., 500 Fifth Avenue, New York, NY 10110, in order for a correction to be made in the next reprinting of our work.

ILLUSTRATIONS

Alizé Red Passion: Reprinted by permission. Copyright © 1999 Kobrand Corporation.

BLADES Board and Skate: Reprinted by permission of Monkey Boy Advertising, BLADES Board and Skate, Bob Scott Photography.

Excite: Copyright © 2000 Excite, Inc. All rights reserved. Excite and the Excite Logo are registered service marks of Excite, Inc., in the United States and other countries. Reprinted by permission.

HotBot ® is a registered trademark and/or service mark of Wired Ventures, Inc., a Lycos Company. All rights reserved. Reprinted by permission.

PR*Bar reprinted by permission of PR Nutrition, Inc.

Religions of India: From *From Voting to Violence: Democratization and Nationalist Conflict* by Jack Snyder. Copyright © 2000 by W. W. Norton & Company. Used by permission of W. W. Norton & Company, Inc.

University of Tennessee: Web pages reprinted by permission.

Vaulted Interior of Modena Duomo, Italy: Copyright © John Heseltine/CORBIS. Reprinted by permission.

Yahoo!: Reproduced with permission of Yahoo! Inc. Copyright © 1999 by Yahoo! Inc. YAHOO! and the YAHOO! logo are trademarks of Yahoo! Inc.

Index

"G" preceding a page number refers to a glossary entry. Page numbers of exercises are followed by "(ex)." Page numbers of In Brief boxes are followed by "(box)."

article(s), G751
  academic English for nonnative speakers,
      417–26, 423(ex), 426–27(box), 428(ex)
  see also determiners
articles (periodical):
  APA style, *see* APA style, articles
  CMS system, *see* CMS *(Chicago Manual of Style)*
      system, books
  MLA parenthetical style, *see* MLA (Modern
      Language Association) parenthetical style,
      article or essay
  see also magazine articles; newspapers; periodi-
      cals; scholarly journals
Art Index, The, 537
Arts & Humanities Citation Index, 564
artwork, MLA parenthetical style for, 599
as, as if, like, G722
ASI (American Statistics Index), 538
assertion made with a number, 43
assure, ensure, insure, G722
atlases, 528
Atwood, Margaret, 141
Auden, W. H., 287
audience:
  planning text, considering when, 65–66,
      67(box), 67(ex)
  revising to suit your, 158–59, 159(ex)
Austen, Jane, 648–51
author, learning about the, to understand the
      context, 34–35
authorial primary sources, 564
authority, citing an, 186
auxiliaries, G751
  forming tenses with, 364
  modal auxiliaries and subjunctive mood,
      396–98, 398(ex), 429
avenge, revenge, G722–23
awfully, very, so, G746
Ayres, DJ, 127

bad, badly, G723
Balay, Robert, 525
Baldwin, James, 255
bar and column graphs, 218–19
bare form of a verb, G751
base (bare-bones) sentence, G751
base (or simple) predicate, G763
base verb, G751
Bates, Robert L., 682

B.C., C.E., B.C.E., A.D., G717
be:
  agreement with subjects, 351, 356
  in subjunctive mood, 399, 402(ex)
  using verbs of action instead of, 169, 412
because, since, "being that," G723
because of, due to, G728
begging the question (circular argument), 195
"being that," because, since, G723
Beloved (Morrison), 660–61
Bennett, Alice, 663
beside, besides, G723
between, among, G721
Bible, MLA parenthetical style for documenting,
      587
bibliographies, 565, 630
  CMS (Chicago Manual of Style) system, *see* CMS
      (Chicago Manual of Style) system
biographical guides, 528–29
biology, documentation style for, 682
Bird, Caroline, 75–76, 455
Black, Roger, 210, 243
Blake, William, 619, 621, 622
boldface, use of, 214–15
Bolter, Jay David, 210*n*
Bombeck, Erma, 304
books:
  APA style, *see* APA style, books
  with bibliographies, 565
  CMS system, *see* CMS *(Chicago Manual of Style)*
      system, books
  deriving context from titles of, 35
  locating, for research purposes, 529–36,
      538–40, 541(ex)
  MLA parenthetical style, *see* MLA (Modern
      Language Association) parenthetical style,
      books
  source card for, 562–63, 563(ex)
  subdivisions, abbreviation of, 512
  titles, italics or underlining for, 507
Boolean or word filter search, 546
Booth, Wayne, 485, 653, 656
Borland, Hal, 382
both, 425–26
boxes, In Brief, *see* In Brief boxes
brackets to mark changes in quotation, 480
Bradstreet, Anne, 481
brainstorming, 22
branching and looping, 22–24
branching diagram, 576

Index

Index

INSTRUCTOR'S MANUAL FOR

FIFTH EDITION

Writing

A COLLEGE HANDBOOK

James A. W. Heffernan

John E. Lincoln

Janet Atwill

Contents

Contents

Contents

PART 3 PUNCTUATION AND MECHANICS

Contents

PART 6   WRITING IN NONACADEMIC CONTEXTS

The Process of Writing

Building Rhetorical Power

CHAPTER OVERVIEW

This chapter explores the multiple contexts and purposes of writing. It examines both the relationship between reader and writer and the ways in which writing allows individuals to participate in communities. The four-step exercise at the end of the chapter encourages students to examine their own reading and writing experiences and to see themselves as part of a community of readers and writers. Here are some teaching tips for the exercise:

1. Suggest examples of both academic and nonacademic writing students might do in an average week. For an introductory writing assignment, have students compose short autobiographies of themselves as writers.

2. Students may cite journal writing, poetry, and fiction as examples of writing they do to record feelings and experiences. Have students describe the process they go through for this kind of writing. Contrast the process with the integrated reading and writing described in 1.1.

3. Many students will cite television as a strong influence in their voting decisions. Have them consider the role of writing in television programming and encourage them to name other sources of written information about campaigns.

NOTE ON NONNATIVE SPEAKERS

What is considered rhetorically necessary or appropriate in a successful piece of writing may vary from culture to culture. The role of reading and writing in expressing oneself or in building a community, the value placed on the written word versus speech, and the importance of electronic communication may be markedly different for international students. Scholars who study the values placed on writing in different cultures use the term *contrastive rhetoric* to describe the diverse rhetorical paradigms with which international students are acquainted. If you have international students in your class, you might want to familiarize yourself with the rhetorical conventions of their home cultures. Excellent resources on the topic include:

Corson, David, ed. *Encyclopedia of Language and Education,* Vol. 4. Dordrecht, Netherlands: Kluwer Academic Publishers, 1997.

Dong, Yu Ren. "From Writing in Their Native Language to Writing in English: What ESL Students Bring to Our Writing Classroom." *College ESL* 8.2 (Dec. 1998): 87–105.

Leki, Ilona. *Understanding ESL Writers: A Guide for Teachers.* Portsmouth, NH: Boynton/Cook, Heinemann, 1992.

1.1 WHAT IS RHETORICAL POWER?

This section illustrates how reading serves as a foundation for building rhetorical power in writing. In a class discussion, ask students to consider the stages of their own writing processes based on past experience. Referring to the model of Susan's experience described in the text, have students recount the stages they have gone through to prepare specific writing assignments. Encourage them to describe in as much detail as possible the role reading played in shaping their ideas and their writing. Have them enumerate the tasks, as in "First I considered several topics and made a list of pros and cons for doing research on each. Then I checked the Internet to see which has the most sources," and so on.

1.2 WHY READ AND WRITE?

This section makes explicit the difference between writing solely for self-expression and writing to reach a particular audience for a particular purpose. It also demonstrates how expressive writing can serve as a foundation for community-oriented writing.

Since this section briefly considers the relationship between literacy and social change, you might have students read documents such as the

Declaration of Independence, the Gettysburg Address, and Martin Luther King Jr.'s "Letter from a Birmingham Jail" or "I Have a Dream" speech and then discuss the role reading and writing have played in shaping change. You might also include memos from the workplace that discuss procedural changes, bylaws and policy statements for student organizations, email exchanges between group members trying to build consensus around particular issues, and so on.

In discussing the role of computers in reading and writing, you might ask students the following questions: What kind of reading and writing do you do on the Internet? If you belong to an Internet community, what kinds of reading and writing are involved?

Readings on literacy, education, and social change include:

Cushman, Ellen. *The Struggle and the Tools: Oral and Literate Strategies in an Inner City Community.* Albany, NY: SUNY UP, 1998.

hooks, bell. *Teaching to Transgress: Education as the Practice of Freedom.* New York and London: Routledge, 1994.

Shor, Ira. *Empowering Education: Critical Teaching for Social Change.* Chicago and London: U of Chicago P, 1992.

Shor, Ira, and Carolina Pari, eds. *Critical Literacy in Action.* Portsmouth, NY: Boynton/Cook, Heinemann, 1999.

Readings on literacy in cyberspace include:

Anson, Chris M. "Distant Voices: Teaching and Writing in a Culture of Technology." *College English* 61.3 (Jan. 1999): 261–80.

Holeton, Richard, ed. *Composing Cyberspace: Identity, Community, and Knowledge in the Electronic Age.* Boston: McGraw-Hill, 1998.

Preparing to Write 2

CHAPTER OVERVIEW

This chapter focuses on the beginning stages of the writing process. It discusses how the investigation of purpose and context shapes that process. The discussion and exercises encourage students to view writing as not simply the expression of fully formed ideas but also, in the early planning, a means to consider a variety of possibilities.

NOTE ON NONNATIVE SPEAKERS

International students may bring with them a wide range of experiences with and ideas about the writing process. Some students may never have taken a "writing class" per se, while others may have learned from native speakers of English well schooled in the most up-to-date teaching approaches. Additionally, how these students conceive purpose, context, and the writing process itself may be shaped by their home cultures. For example, depending on how a particular culture views authority, a student may be uncomfortable with the notion that a piece of persuasive writing can directly call into question the authority of an individual, a group, or a policy. Another student may not wish to share the work she does in the early stages of the writing process because she fears displeasing the teacher with imperfect writing. Yet another student may be eager to receive comments, perhaps to gain a sense of what will please the teacher.

To gain a sense of how international students think about the writing process, be sure to involve them in class discussions. Sometimes these students are reluctant to speak in front of a large group because they aren't fluent in English. However, having students work together in small, culturally and linguistically diverse groups can provide a good opportunity for classmates to compare their experiences with writing. In such settings, you might have students interview each other about their writing experiences and then have them report their findings to the rest of the class. You and the international students may also benefit from their composing a writer's autobiography (discussed above in the overview for chapter 1). Encourage these students to focus on academic writing experiences and ask what they recall about learning to write.

For background on diverse rhetorical strategies, see Leki's book cited in the "Note on Nonnative Speakers" for chapter 1. Another helpful source is Ramanathan, Vai, and Dwight Atkinson. "Individualism, Academic Writing, and ESL Writers." *Journal of Second Language Writing* 8.1 (1999): 45–75.

2.1 WHY USE PLANNING STRATEGIES?

To continue the analogy between planning a trip and planning to write, you might ask students what happens on a trip when something unexpected (either good or bad) occurs. Ask them to extend their description of that experience to the writing process, to demonstrate that sometimes old strategies need to be reinvented or new strategies created.

2.2 CRAFTING EXPLORATORY QUESTIONS

When asked to investigate the meaning of a term such as *sell out,* students often begin by turning to the authority of a dictionary. To help students move beyond the "dictionary approach," provide additional illustrations of the difference between a simple question of definition and an exploratory question. For example, have students compare the following questions and potential responses to each:

What is meant by the term *minimum wage?*

What is the purpose of a society setting a minimum wage?

Respondents to the first question may take the "dictionary approach" or cite a specific amount of money. In answering the second question, students will explore wider concerns regarding the value placed on work and compensation.

2.3 UNDERSTANDING RHETORICAL CONTEXTS

After discussing the various kinds of purpose, have students prepare an inventory of their experiences writing for each of the purposes in the past year. Have them discuss the purposes with which they are most familiar. Ask them what it would take to feel comfortable writing with another purpose. Then ask students to list the kinds of reading and writing they have done in the past one or two weeks. What genres were involved? What writer and reader roles? Finally, have students experiment with different writer and reader roles. For example, they might try explaining a campus issue, problem, or event—first, in the role of one student to another and, second, in the role of a student to someone outside campus, such as a parent, friend, relative, or younger sibling.

In discussing writer and reader roles, have students work in groups to create a biographical sketch of someone they imagine would read a given sample text. The piece of writing might be a selection from a college textbook, an article from a school or local newspaper, an electronic publication, or an explanation of a technical procedure. Assign different types of texts to different groups. Once students have created their sketches, ask them to note contextual factors that might influence this particular reader's understanding of the text.

2.4 WRITING IN RESPONSE TO CLASSROOM ASSIGNMENTS

Use sample student texts from other disciplines to help students understand the demands of writing assignments that require them to work in unfamiliar contexts. Referring to "In Brief: Writing in Unfamiliar Contexts," ask students to analyze the texts for purpose, writer and reader roles, and tone. Then ask them to write their own versions of the essay prompts or assignment descriptions to which the texts are responses. Follow this up by comparing the actual assignment descriptions with the student versions.

2.5 CYBERSPACE AS A RHETORICAL SITUATION

Ask students to describe the genres they encounter online. Also ask them to list their recent online interactions. What kinds of writer and reader roles are involved? How do online writer/reader relationships differ from other kinds of writer/reader relationships?

For background on constructing identity in cyberspace see Kornbluth, Jesse. "{you make me feel like} A Virtual Woman." *Composing in Cyberspace: Identity, Community, and Knowledge in the Electronic Age.* Ed. Richard Holeton. Boston: McGraw-Hill, 1998. 76–79. Also see Dale Spender's article "Gender Bending" in the same collection, 69–75.

3 Strategies for Active Writing and Reading

CHAPTER OVERVIEW

While students may be willing to acknowledge that what they read can influence what they think, it is no easy task to clarify *how* reading shapes one's own writing. Additionally, students often need to be made more aware of how writing can be used as a critical tool to better understand what they read.

Students face many challenges in this regard. The first and perhaps most fundamental is that they may perceive what has been written as fixed, indeed, as the final word on a topic. This perception affects students' thinking both in relation to their own writing and in their responses to reading. Because they see the written word as vested with authority, students may feel that once a thought takes written form it cannot be shaped or changed. They may be reluctant to see their own writing as a process of exploration, or they may hesitate to question texts they read. To help students break out of this confining model, this chapter provides a variety of approaches, first to writing, then to active reading and writing in response to a text.

Note: Students who lack confidence in their ability to detect the boundaries between their own ideas and those of outside sources may be reluctant to use these sources in writing, or they may not properly acknowledge the sources. For this reason you might want students to develop citation skills from the beginning of the term so that they aren't overwhelmed by the task when a major research paper comes due. In the course of this chapter, assign an informal paper in which students explore their subjective responses to a specific article. Tell the students you want the first draft to reflect their honest opinions about the ideas expressed in the article and to acknowledge the source informally in the introduction. Then, during the revision process, require students to summarize or quote a portion of the reading that relates to a point made in the rough draft. Demonstrate the use of lead-in verbs and phrases to introduce material from sources, and supply the formats for proper parenthetical citation and a Works Cited entry. Once you have established good citation habits, you can present assignments that build on these skills throughout the term.

3.1–3.4 WHY USE STRATEGIES . . .?, CHOOSING STRATEGIES . . ., WRITING ON A TOPIC, *AND* STRATEGIES FOR EXPLORING THROUGH WRITING

The strategies discussed here are brainstorming; branching and looping; triple-viewing; dramatizing the topic with questions; and questioning assumptions about gender, race, and class. If students already use some of these strategies, encourage them to try out new strategies for different situations. Exercise 1, for example, asks students to dramatize a topic by asking basic questions, and in this way they can discover how much they already know about a given topic and what else they would like to learn about it. In addition to having students ask questions about their own topics, you might present them with hypothetical topics. You might also hand out pieces of writing that offer good opportunities to consider assumptions about gender, race, and class.

3.5 EXPLORING THROUGH TALKING AND OBSERVING

Because the role discussion and observation play in shaping written text is often overlooked, this section discusses sharing ideas with others, doing field research, conducting an interview, and creating a survey. In doing the kinds of qualitative research presented here, students gather and analyze ideas from individuals or groups, most often in activities that incorporate reading and writing. In this way, rather than thinking of the text itself as the center of authority, students come to see the research participants, including themselves, as sources of authority. For more on the role of discussion and observation in the writing process, see Ratcliffe, Krista. "Rhetorical Listening: A Trope for Interpretive Invention and a 'Code of Cross Cultural Conduct.'" *College Composition and Communication* 5.2 (Dec. 1999): 195–224.

3.6 EXPLORING THROUGH READING: GUIDELINES FOR ACTIVE READING

Encourage students to try different active-reading strategies, to improve their understanding of the fundamentals. You might assign selected readings and have students complete the tasks outlined in "In Brief: Guidelines for Active Reading."

3.7 WRITING IN RESPONSE TO READING

This section moves students from subjective experience to analytical response. Components of the latter include finding the writer's main point, judging supporting points, summarizing, and paraphrasing.

Allowing students to respond subjectively to a piece of writing helps them validate their own experiences of texts in general. To foster their confidence, have students discuss their subjective responses in peer groups. Ask them to consider why group members might agree or disagree. What is it about each student's background, culture, values, and so on, that might affect his or her response to the text?

The traditional model of active analytical reading involves students' highlighting texts and scribbling notes in the margins of books they own in order to remember main points. In many cases, however, students need to learn how to recognize and interpret main points before they can highlight them or take effective notes. You might devote some time to the discussion of how to find a writer's main point before you assign exercise 3. In addition to having students locate the main points of the texts given (or others you provide), encourage students to summarize their understanding of those points and to offer subjective responses. This activity integrates several strategies presented in the chapter.

To help students understand the difference between fact and opinion in judging a text, you might have them apply the questions regarding supporting points to a recent newspaper editorial.

Be sure to emphasize that summarizing can be an analytical skill. Students are sometimes warned away from summarizing, especially in essays on literary texts, because teachers fear that summary—or more precisely, plot summary—will take the place of analysis. But a good summary is in fact the product of analysis; it is the concentrated statement of what the reader has absorbed. To write even a good sequential plot summary, the reader must be able to grasp the main events of a work and state them succinctly; and to write a comprehensive plot summary or a summary of an essay, the reader must be able to grasp and state the writer's main theme or point and its relation to subordinate themes or points. If you discuss in class the answers to exercise 5, students can learn just what is and is not essential in a summary. You may also wish to have students summarize other texts of your choosing or theirs.

Paraphrasing is closely related to summarizing, since both involve restatement of a text in the reader's words, and as the example from the essay on *Walden* shows, paraphrasing often entails some compression of the original. But whether or not it compresses the original, a paraphrase tests the reader's comprehension of a text and his or her capacity to assimilate it—to incorporate it in a new piece of writing. Practicing paraphrasing, therefore, is a good way to prepare for the writing of an analytical essay or even a research paper.

3.8–3.9 ANALYZING ADVERTISING *AND* ANALYZING CULTURAL CODES

College students are surrounded by consumer culture, and advertisements in all forms provide excellent opportunities to question claims and analyze cultural codes. Begin by having students work in peer groups to analyze ads. Reinforce the points made in 3.7 by encouraging them to begin with subjective responses and then move toward analytical concerns, such as the assumptions advertisers are making about their target audience.

You might ask the groups to annotate the elements of a print advertisement or to create a script for a satirical commercial similar to those presented on popular late-night programs such as *Saturday Night Live* and *Mad TV*. (The magazine *Adbusters* also offers thought-provoking ironic responses to advertisements.) In addition, encourage students to think about the role of advertising on the Internet. For instance, ask them to count and analyze the ads that appear when they call up a search engine, ask them to think about the relationship between Internet ads and the contents of a given Web site, and so on.

Readings on the topic of ad analysis include:

Foreman, Joel, and David R. Shumway. "Cultural Studies: Reading Visual Texts." *Cultural Studies in the English Classroom*. Ed. James A. Berlin and Michael J. Vivion. Portsmouth, NH: Boynton/Cook, Heinemann, 244–61.

Rank, Hugh. *The Pitch*. Counter-Propaganda Press, July 1991.

NOTE ON NONNATIVE SPEAKERS

Since international students may not be familiar with the cultural codes represented in U.S. ads, try to partner them with native speakers who can provide some background during the discussion. You might in turn ask international students to discuss the role of advertising in their home cultures. In addition, students may come from cultures with very different expectations regarding the acknowledgment of source material. (Plagiarism is discussed extensively in 37.8.) For more information on how international students incorporate reading into their writing processes, see Leki (cited in the notes for chapter 1), especially chapter 6, "Writing Behaviors." Also see

Campbell, C. "Writing with Others' Words: Using Background Reading Text in Academic Compositions." *Second Language Writing*. Ed. Barbara Kroll. New York: Cambridge, 1990.

Sengupta, Sima. "Rhetorical Consciousness Raising in the L2 Reading Classroom." *Journal of Second Language Writing* 8.3 (1999): 291–319.

Exploratory Drafting and Thesis Statements 4

CHAPTER OVERVIEW

Most student writers are quick to acknowledge that creating a good thesis around which to build an essay is no easy task. This may be because students feel they need to begin with a thesis before they can actually start to write, and this can seem a bit like pulling a main idea mysteriously out of the ether. Rather than insisting on a thesis as the starting point of the drafting process, chapter 4 presents an exploratory approach in which students can get to a thesis by writing in response to their own questions about a topic. In addition, placing priority on the *exploratory* nature of a draft encourages students to see the process as leading them to a discovery about their own ideas. Whereas the term *rough draft* can make a text seem as though it needs only a little *fixing up* in terms of grammar, spelling, or organization, the word *exploratory* suggests that the draft is really going somewhere and may change substantially in the process.

4.1 EXPLORATORY DRAFTING

You might need to provide some background on punk feminism to give students a perspective on the exploratory draft used as an example here, or you might find volunteers eager to share their knowledge. If possible, begin your discussion of the draft by playing some of the songs Carmen mentions or music by similar bands. Have students discuss their own tastes in music, and ask them to consider how these interests relate to their cultural values. Have them generate exploratory questions of their own on the topic.

4.2–4.3 USING AN EXPLORATORY DRAFT *AND* ANSWERING AN EXPLORATORY QUESTION WITH A THESIS STATEMENT

Many students have trouble distinguishing between a thesis and a topic. One way of helping them grasp this distinction is to invite any student to suggest a topic, which you then write on the board as a phrase. Next, ask the other students to suggest a declarative sentence *about* the topic.

Once they see the purely formal difference between a topic (a phrase) and a thesis (a sentence including the phrase), they can begin to learn the difference between a vague generalization (often no more than a topic sentence) and an effective thesis: the kind of statement that can generate—or encapsulate—an engaging essay. With the help of the examples given here, they should be able to recognize the difference, since it is really the difference between a dull statement and a stimulating or provocative one.

Seeing the difference between a vague generalization and an effective thesis is of course not the same as actually *constructing* the latter. Even after producing an exploratory draft, students may have trouble recognizing their own best ideas, or deciding what is most important about their topics. One way to guide them here is to circulate copies of an exploratory draft written by a student and invite the class to identify all of its points or details as you *list* them on the blackboard. Then you can ask the class to suggest ways of organizing the list by subordinating some points to others. In the process of thus organizing the items in the list, students can be led to see which item can be used to *connect* all the others: which item, that is, can be used to formulate a thesis.

Alternatively, you and the class can consider the exploratory draft along with the results of exercise 1. Then you can see how well each student has identified the potential strength of his or her own material and expressed it in a thesis.

Either way, the crucial thing for students to learn is how to read their own drafts purposefully, how to mine them as quarries of ideas.

For more on teaching students how to connect a general idea to illustrative details, see Shaughnessy, Mina. *Errors and Expectations: A Guide for the Teachers of Basic Writing*. New York: Oxford UP, 1977. 251–74. For an extended discussion of what makes a thesis interesting, see Gage, John. *The Shape of Reason: Argumentative Writing in College,* 2nd ed. New York: Macmillan, 1991.

NOTE ON NONNATIVE SPEAKERS

International students may find the notion of a thesis statement hard to grasp because in many of their cultures the reader is expected to see what the writer is driving at without being explicitly told. Though this chapter notes that the thesis of an essay is sometimes merely implied, U.S. students are customarily taught to formulate a thesis for their own guidance at least (as we suggest here). International students will need special help in achieving the kind of specificity that a good thesis statement embodies.

For more on this point, see Hinds, J. "Reader Versus Writer Responsibility: A New Typology." *Writing Across Languages: Analysis of L2 Text*. Ed. U. Connor and R. Kaplan. Reading: Addison, 1986. 141–52.

Planning and Organizing Your Text 5

CHAPTER OVERVIEW

Now that the first four chapters have explained how to generate material in the early stages of the writing process, this one shows how to use that material. At this stage, students will begin shaping their texts with a particular audience in mind. They will also learn to experiment with the arrangement of their ideas to see how the pieces best fit together for a specific rhetorical situation. Like exploratory drafting (discussed in the preceding chapter), planning and organizing require writers to remain flexible, to allow new ideas to emerge in the process, and to reshape existing material.

5.2 PLANNING WITH YOUR READERS IN MIND

Most students would probably say that shaping begins with an outline. But even before making an outline, students need to consider the question of whom they are writing *for,* of what their readers will expect. The sooner they can move beyond the notion that writing is just something done for the teacher, for the person who gives a grade, the sooner they will begin to learn what writing can do in the world beyond the classroom.

In one sense, they will of course be writing for you. You give the assignments and the grades. But since your students will eventually write for a variety of readers both in college and out of it, they must learn to consider how one kind of reader differs from another. Together with this section, exercise 1 should help them see what writers can do to reach a particular group of readers. Selected responses to both parts of exercise 1 could stimulate an informative class discussion, especially if students of differing views or differing interests are asked to say just how effectively a particular student writer addresses them.

You can lay the groundwork for this discussion by pairing off students and asking them to read each other's work—not just for this exercise but for any other writing they do in your course. The more they read each other's work and the more they hear from readers they can see around them, the better they will learn to anticipate the reactions of readers they don't see.

NOTE ON NONNATIVE SPEAKERS

Some international students may not understand the assumptions we make about a student writer's responsibilities. In order to better help them learn what is expected of the writer, you might familiarize yourself with the rhetorical paradigms of other cultures, which may be quite different from that taught in the U.S. For example, because they place such value on indirectness and subtlety, Japanese writers often assume that readers will understand the point through nuances rather than direct claims supported by the weight of evidence. In fact, the Japanese might consider it rude to be overly explicit because this would imply readers' lack of intelligence. Some scholars use the terms *reader-responsible* and *writer-responsible* to denote the different expectations regarding writer and reader roles. In the U.S., student writing is generally writer-responsible.

5.3 PLANNING THE ORGANIZATION OF MAJOR POINTS

Most students need guidance in learning how to arrange their points. With practice, they may be able to take the material they developed in an exploratory draft—a topic, a set of questions, a basic question—and go directly to an outline (see 5.4) However, some students may feel restricted by having to arrange an entire essay in advance. Encourage them to first simply underline the major ideas in an exploratory draft. With their ideas in mind, these students will be prepared to consider the various arrangements presented in 5.3 and then choose the one best suited to the material.

Of the arrangements presented in 5.3, students often have the most trouble with cause and effect order. To supplement the examples here, you might discuss single effects that result from groups of causes, or single causes that have many effects. Consider, for example, the many effects of the Internet, or the multiple causes of tropical-rainforest destruction. Also link causes in a chain: a videotape of Los Angeles police officers beating a man led to a trial of the police involved; in turn, the acquittal of the officers provoked riots.

NOTE ON NONNATIVE SPEAKERS

Some international students, especially native Arabic speakers, may introduce so many causes or effects that they confuse the reader. Latin American and Japanese writers prefer to construct a chain of causes, often in "if . . . then" patterns. See

Burtoff, M. "The Logical Organization of Written Expository Discourse in English: A Comparative Study of Japanese, Arabic, and Native Speaker Strategies." *Dissertation Abstracts International* 45.9 (1983): 2857A.

Henry, Alexandra. "Strategies of Elaboration." *Second Language Rhetorics in Process: A Comparison of Arabic, Chinese, and Spanish.* New York: Lang, 1993. 89–96.

5.4 PLANNING WITH AN OUTLINE

This section presents two ways of outlining points: the vertical list and the tree diagram.

The vertical outline is traditional, perhaps because it looks so tidy. It helps students arrange what they have generated. But the superficial order of the vertical outline often masks illogic and lack of significant connection between one point and another. Also, it is hard to use the vertical outline as a tool for *thinking* about a text because it looks like the *result* of thought—the record of plans already made. For this reason, your students will probably find the tree diagram easier to produce—especially since it resembles the branching diagram that they may already have drawn. One great advantage of the tree diagram is that it allows for growth and discovery in the process of planning a text.

For a good discussion of outlining, see Murray, Donald. *Write to Learn.* New York: Holt, 1987. 143–54.

NOTE ON NONNATIVE SPEAKERS

International students may need extra work with the vertical outline precisely *because* its arrangement is so tidy and because it represents so clearly the subordination of one point to another. Academic writing in the U.S. puts a high value on subordination (in the essay as a whole as well as in the individual sentence) and typically requires that three to five major points be made to dominate lesser points. (On the high value of subordination in Western culture, see Corbett, E. P. J. *Classical Rhetoric for the Modern Student.* New York: Oxford UP, 1965. 410–11.) But other cultures have different ideas about subordination. Native Arabic speakers, for instance, will find the American concept of rhetorical subordination difficult to grasp because it runs counter to Arabic syntax and rhetoric.

5.5 INTRODUCING AN ESSAY

This section treats the title and introduction to an essay as the writer's first chance to draw the reader into the subject. (For good advice about using titles to focus ideas, see Donald Murray's *Write to Learn,* cited above.) Students are sometimes told that an introduction should consist of a single paragraph that starts with a broad generalization and tapers down to a specific statement of the thesis. Yet that is just one kind of introduction. Instead of trying to formulate rules about the structure of all introductions, this section illustrates various ways of forecasting what is to come. Students should be stimulated to learn that writers can introduce their essays in many different ways, that an introduction sometimes takes two paragraphs instead of one, that it may end with a provocative question instead of a statement.

In item 2, the question Andrew poses is the purely practical one of how he and his friend could escape. In the course of the essay, this practical question gives way to the more reflective question of what he learned from the experience of escaping. So even though it doesn't announce the most important question of the essay, the introduction does lead the reader *to* that question.

In item 4, Mead starts with a generalization about American families. She then writes two sentences about her own family's attitude toward college, and ends with a sentence about her personal expectations. She thus introduces an essay that will explain how her first year of college actually disappointed her. You might ask your students to say whether or not she could have improved this introduction by mentioning her disappointment.

In item 6, Caroline Bird's paragraphs will help students see that an introduction can be more than one paragraph, taking the form of a one-two punch. You might ask students to imitate Bird's opening with a couple of paragraphs about any issue on which they have strong feelings. See how fairly they can state the case for the other side in the first paragraph before stating their own case in the second.

To supplement these examples, you might ask students to find—in print or online sources—examples of introductions they like, to bring these examples to class, and to say why they like them.

NOTE ON NONNATIVE SPEAKERS

International students are accustomed to writing for readers whose expectations differ from those of U.S. readers. For this reason, you might want to stress that they can effectively introduce their essays by any one of the various means illustrated here. Item 7—establishing the historical context for a topic—is not a common American strategy but is often used by international students. It may help them to see that their own strategy is just one of many that can work with American readers. You might also ask them to explain to their classmates how and why they use this strategy. It is helpful for all students to realize that virtually any topic can be presented—and very briefly—in a historical frame.

See Scarcella, R. "How Writers Orient Their Readers in Expository Essays: A Comparative Study of Native and Nonnative English Writers." *TESOL Quarterly* 18 (1984): 671–88.

5.6 SHAPING THE MIDDLE PARAGRAPHS

Students who have trouble organizing a paragraph will need the advice given in chapter 7. For now, remind them of what Carmen did almost instinctively in her exploratory draft in chapter 4: starting a new paragraph because she was taking a new tack. You might also ask them why Carmen made the changes she did as she shaped the material from her exploratory draft into the text that appears here.

5.7 CONCLUDING AN ESSAY

Like the treatment of introductions in 5.5, the discussion of endings surveys various methods rather than prescribing a single formula. As you emphasize that effective endings can take many different forms, encourage students to find other examples and to share them with the class.

NOTE ON NONNATIVE SPEAKERS

Alexandra Henry has found that some international students—specifically the Japanese—generally avoid summarizing their essays at the end. In "Strategies of Conclusion," *Second Language Rhetorics* (cited above) 96–102, she also explains that international students as a whole generally end an essay in one of the following ways:

OBJECTIVE STRATEGIES

1. presenting the thesis for the first time

2. summarizing the main points

3. stating a truism or maxim

SUBJECTIVE STRATEGIES

1. stating a personal opinion

2. giving a personal recommendation

3. making a wish, promise, or prediction about the future

LINGUISTIC STRATEGIES

1. using one of the above strategies in a defined linguistic form, such as a rhetorical question or a conditional sentence ("If . . . then")

2. giving a purely linguistic signal of ending: "in short," "in sum," "to conclude," "finally," and even "that's all" or "thank you"

6   *Developing Your Text*

CHAPTER OVERVIEW

Teachers of English often put writing into categories of description, narration, exposition, and persuasion. But good writing seldom fits into just one of these categories by itself because good writers commonly use description and narration to explain or persuade. So this section treats both description and narration as methods of development, and it shows how they can be used—along with other methods such as comparison and contrast—to serve the writer's general aim.

NOTE ON NONNATIVE SPEAKERS

International students generally benefit from practicing different methods of development. Though not all of the methods presented here are equally valued in their cultures, some rhetorical traditions—Arabic, for instance—favor using a variety of methods in one text.

6.1 USING DESCRIPTION

External description commonly focuses on the shape and color of objects and their arrangement in space. But you might point out that a good external description of any living creature will normally refer to the way it moves, as in the following description of baby turtles:

> Baby turtles in a turtle bowl are a puzzle in geometrics. They're as decorative as pansy petals, but they are also self-directed building blocks, propping themselves on one another in different arrangements, before upending the tower. The timid individuals turn fearless, or vice versa. If one gets a bit arrogant he will push the others off the rock and afterwards climb down into the water and cling to the back of one of those he has bullied, tickling him with his hind feet until he bucks like a bronco.
> —Edward Hoagland, "The Courage of Turtles"

Hoagland uses several images to help us visualize the turtles in motion. He uses "pansy petals" for their varieties of color, "building blocks" for the shapes they make in climbing on each other, and "bucks like a bronco" for the way one turtle throws another off its back. By revealing the energy and determination of baby turtles, this description serves the larger aim of the essay, which is to explain the courage of turtles.

Since exercise 2 calls for analytical or technical description, you might want to assign it as an alternative to exercise 1 for students with specialized knowledge: for budding architects, let us say, who might analytically describe a keystone arch, or premed students, who might analytically describe the human foot.

You might ask students to discuss just what makes the passage by Alice Walker so evocative. How does the language appeal to the senses? Rather than assigning exercise 3 as homework, you might then propose it as a topic for in-class discussion. With a little prompting, students should see that the writer of the first version gets between us and the town, telling about his feelings instead of showing what specific details provoked them. By contrast, Jordan makes no reference to himself or his feelings. Instead, he tells us what he saw, heard, and smelled. After considering Walker's description and the examples in exercise 3, have students work on exercise 4. Encourage them to begin by listing memories of sensory impressions, which they can then incorporate into a kind of sensory snapshot of the place.

As a supplement to exercises 3 and 4, you can ask all students to describe the same thing: a person they all know, the local pizza parlor, a bowling alley, a particular building, a piece of sculpture, or even the classroom where they meet. The advantage of such an assignment is twofold:

students can base their descriptions on fresh observation or "field research," and in class discussion they can compare their descriptions, learning from each other how to observe; how to catch vivid, specific details; and how to organize those details to convey a general effect.

6.2 USING NARRATION

This section shows students how to give a coherent and meaningful account of actions in time. The examples here illustrate that narration is more than the mere recording of events strung together by a succession of *and then*s. In the passage about feminism, Castells uses narration not just to record events but to illustrate thematic connections between feminism and civil rights.

You can supplement the exercises on narration by asking all students—or groups, at least—to write short narratives of an event they saw or participated in together: a game, a race, a road trip, a backpacking trip, a party, a meeting, a brawl, the demolition of an old building, or the opening of a new one. As with description, when two or more students narrate the same event and compare their narratives in class discussion, each student can learn from the other.

6.3 COMBINING DESCRIPTION AND NARRATION

To underscore how description enriches Rosa Parks's narration, you might remove all the descriptive material from this passage and then ask students to compare the stripped-down version with the original.

6.4 USING EXAMPLES

Beginning with this section, the rest of this chapter treats what are commonly regarded as methods of exposition. But since any one of these methods may be used to persuade as well as to explain, they are presented simply as methods of development. The point to stress is that they are all *methods*.

6.5–6.6 USING ANALOGY *AND* USING COMPARISON AND CONTRAST

The fact that a method is the means to an end is what students too often forget. Asked to compare two things, for instance, many students will enumerate their similarities and differences without any real sense of what the enumeration shows. Sections 6.5 and 6.6 can help them realize that analogy and comparison and contrast are each a means to an end and that the end should be made clear. In using analogy, for instance, the writer forges a link between two very different things in order to help us understand one of them. You might therefore ask students to say just what passage 3 in 6.5 helps to explain about superconduction. Then you might ask if any of your scientifically minded students can think of an analogy to explain another scientific process, such as catalysis.

You may want to say something about the slipperiness of the word *comparison,* which is variously used to mean "a noting of similarities" and "a noting of similarities and differences." Here *comparison* means the latter. You might also point out that comparing is not the same as likening. Likening means noting similarities alone, which is what analogy does; comparing usually means juxtaposing two similar things in order to note where they match and where they don't.

Exercises 15–17 are cumulative, building up to the writing of a whole essay. Exercise 17 asks students to answer a "why" question in their essays so that they will be forced to think of comparison and contrast not as an end in itself but as the means to an end.

6.7 USING DEFINITIONS

This section will help students see that quoting the dictionary is only one way to define a word. To get them beyond the dictionary and prepare them for exercise 18, give them a short list of words or phrases they are likely to know (such as *rock 'n' roll, middle class, flirt, pornographic,* and *party*) and ask them to bring to class the dictionary definitions of these words. Then invite the class to say what the dictionary definition of each word lacks and to expand the definition by any of the methods listed here. Ask students to say how they would explain these terms to a nonnative speaker of English. And if you have any such speakers in the class, invite them to respond.

To underscore the point, you might explain that writers sometimes formulate special or restricted definitions for special purposes. For instance, *Webster's New Collegiate Dictionary* defines *diagram* as "a line drawing made for mathematical or scientific purposes." But Kenneth Clark defines *diagram* somewhat differently—in order to explain how it functions in art:

> By "diagram" I mean a rational statement in a visible form, involving measurements, and usually done with an ulterior motive. The theorem of Pythagoras is proved by a diagram. Leonardo's drawings of light striking a sphere are diagrams; but the works of Mondrian, although made up of straight lines, are not diagrams, because they are not done in order to prove or measure some experience, but to please the eye.
>
> —"The Blot and the Diagram"

Strikingly enough, Clark defines *diagram* not as a drawing but as a "statement in a visible form," a way of proving or showing something. Then he gives examples of what a diagram is and what it is not. More than an incidental piece of clarification, this definition is an essential part of Clark's essay.

Class discussion of exercise 18 can help students understand why writers take the time to define certain words and how a particular definition can serve the writer's aim. After your students have written out their definitions, invite them to consider the circumstances under which these definitions might be used. For what sort of readership, for instance, would a writer feel obliged to define *cyberspace?* And if words like *racism* and *poverty* and *feminist* are widely known, why define them at all? By pursuing these questions, students may come to see that definitions can serve various purposes—from explaining an uncommon word to developing a major point. Consider, for instance, the rhetorical difference between defining a *feminist* as (1) a woman who thinks all men oppress women, and (2) a person who believes that women deserve the same political and economic rights as are granted to men. Words often used are just as often misunderstood. Defining such words can play a crucial role in sharpening the key terms of an explanation or argument.

6.8 EXPLAINING BY ANALYZING: CLASSIFICATION AND DIVISION

This section will give students one way of understanding what it means to "analyze" something—as they are so often asked to do in papers and exams. To prepare them for exercise 19, you might ask the class to analyze itself. First, invite students to name the various general categories by which they might be classified, such as region of origin, gender, race, career goals, and extracurricular interests. Then ask the class to *apply* one or more of the categories to themselves as a group, one category at a time. Finally, ask the class to say what the process of classification reveals about them.

6.9 EXPLAINING A PROCESS

This section concerns the kind of writing that lends itself most readily to practical evaluation. If a student writes a teaching explanation of how to do something that can be done in the classroom (loading a camera, for instance, or performing a card trick), another student can test the practicability of the explanation by performing the specified steps, and the whole class—looking on—can learn something about the complex relation between words and actions.

You probably won't be able to test the reporting explanations of exercise 21 in this way, but you can try to pair students with similar interests—so that one student's explanation of rock climbing, for instance, is read and critiqued by another student who has written an explanation of the same thing.

6.10 EXPLAINING CAUSE AND EFFECT

This section will help students see how a single action or situation can lead the writer backward to its cause, forward to its effect, or in both directions, a point that exercise 22 reinforces. To prepare students for this exercise, you might ask them to discuss their views on the causes and effects of a recent situation or event, such as the growing popularity of the Internet, lawsuits targeting the tobacco and gun industries, or the dominant item in local, national, or world news.

6.11 COMBINING METHODS OF DEVELOPMENT

This section ends the chapter by inviting students to see how one method of exposition can reinforce the effect of another. As a follow-up to exercise 23, you might ask each student to read another student's essay, identify the methods of exposition used, and say in writing or in class discussion how effectively they are used.

7 *Writing Paragraphs*

CHAPTER OVERVIEW

The chapter starts by discussing why a text is normally broken up into paragraphs. Instead of defining abstractly what a paragraph is, it invites students to see why and how good writers use paragraphing to mark the divisions in their thought.

7.1 WHY USE PARAGRAPHS?

By comparing one group of sentences with another, and by working with paragraph divisions in exercises 1 and 2, students should see the principles of connection that link sentences within a set and that distinguish one set from another.

7.2 COMMUNICATING YOUR MAIN POINT

The traditional way to teach paragraphing is to say that every paragraph should start with a topic sentence. But there are two problems with this old rule.

First, a topic sentence is—strictly speaking—a sentence that simply states the *topic* of the paragraph ("Consider the problem of adult illiteracy in the United States"). But the phrase is commonly used to mean a sentence that states the *main point* of the paragraph ("Several American corporations are now teaching their employees how to read").

Second, as the examples here show, a topic sentence—whether or not it states the main point—is just one of several good ways to start a paragraph. Over twenty years ago, in fact, Richard Braddock demonstrated that contemporary professional writers do *not* regularly begin each paragraph with a topic sentence (see "The Frequency and Placement of Topic Sentences in Expository Prose." *Research in the Teaching of English* 8 [1974]: 287–302). So this section replaces the old rule with a new one designed to help students write the sort of paragraphs that will satisfy their readers.

Since what readers want as they work their way through a paragraph is a continuing sense of direction, almost everything this chapter says to students about paragraphing can be summed up in just eight words: *forecast your main point and signal your turns.*

In the first batch or at least in one of the earlier batches of your students' papers, try to find some good examples of effective forecasting in the opening sentence of a paragraph and of clear signaling within the paragraph. It's always valuable for students to know that at least some of them are already using the techniques they need to be good writers. With these positive examples you might include a few negative ones—poor forecasting and/or missing transitions.

Emphasis is a somewhat abstract notion, but this section makes it concrete by giving specific advice about repetition and arrangement. Since many students have been taught to avoid repetition, you might spend some class time discussing how repetition can be used for emphasis in a paragraph.

7.3 PARAGRAPH DEVELOPMENT

After working through 7.2, students should have a good grasp of how to communicate the main point in a paragraph, but they may still need guidance in how to develop that point. To help students develop a main point in a coherent fashion, 7.3 explains two basic types of paragraph structure: list and chain.

While too much emphasis on list structure can lead to mechanical paragraphing and monotonous parallelism, list structure is relatively easy for students to grasp and to start using at once, as exercise 4 invites them to do.

Chain structure allows more freedom than list structure, but you may want to point out that chain-structure freedom stops short of free association. In Bronowski's paragraph, a perfect example of chain structure, the key word *learning* appears in sentence D as an echo of *learning* in the lead sentence. Bronowski gives himself room to roam, but he doesn't forget where he started from.

Note, by the way, that Bronowski sometimes achieves coherence by linking the end of a sentence to the beginning of the one following it, as in "They are inquisitive and they experiment. An experiment is . . ." This way of achieving coherence illustrates one of the basic tenets of the Prague School of Linguists, which is that readers process information more easily when a new sentence starts with something old or already given and then leads on to new information at the end. Joseph Williams has made a similar point: "Put at the end of a sentence the information that you intend to develop in the next sentence" (*Style: Ten Lessons in Clarity and Grace.* Glenview: Scott, 1981. 121). But this is only one way of achieving coherence, and using it throughout a paragraph would lead to some awkwardness: "Essential to our lives is the process of learning. It is deliberately sought by all higher animals. They are inquisitive. . . ." So while the end-beginning link is a good one for students to know about and practice, they should also realize that there are other ways of linking one sentence to another.

W. Ross Winterowd identifies and illustrates seven ways of relating sentences to form paragraphs, as well as relating paragraphs to each other ("The Grammar of Coherence." *Contemporary Rhetoric: A Conceptual Background with Readings.* New York: Harcourt, 1975. 225–33). A number of these relationships are signaled by the transitional words and phrases we have listed in 7.4.

Note that to do exercise 6, "Using List and Chain Structure Together," students may need to visit the library or selected Web sites. In doing so, they can begin to learn something about the research process, which is covered extensively in Part 4.

7.4 TRANSITIONS WITHIN PARAGRAPHS

To help students learn how to signal turns within a paragraph, you might duplicate for them a well-written passage of one or more paragraphs in which all transitional words and phrases have been replaced by blanks. Then go through the passage in class, inviting students to say how each blank might be filled. This process should prepare them for exercise 7, which not only requires the insertion of transitional signals but also (since it has no blanks) asks students to figure out where they are needed.

"Paragraphing in Action" presents the sort of "paragraph" that often turns up in students' essays—a jumbled heap of sentences that resolutely resists and rejects any quick fix. The writer's situation is a little unusual for a first-year college student (she's a wife and mother), but if anything, the special nature of her situation is more likely to stimulate class discussion than to stifle it. In any case, there's nothing rare about the incoherence of her passage. It typifies what students of every age, race, class, and gender have to struggle with as they shape their writing, as they turn their exploratory drafts into finished texts.

Though this essay receives a lot of attention, it isn't fully revised here. Many changes are suggested, and exercise 8 asks students to make a particular one.

For exercise 9, here is a teaching tip (from Kistler, Suzanne. "Scrambling the Unscramblable: Coherence in the Classroom." *College Composition and Communication* 29 [1978]: 198–200). First, after your students have individually rearranged the sentences in the exercise, invite one or more students to write their arrangements on the blackboard (they can refer to each sentence by number), and discuss with the class the principles of coherence exemplified by the new order. Invite students to see, for instance, why sentence 5, which ends with the word *zoetrope,* should be followed by sentence 2, which defines the word. Then scramble one or more paragraphs drawn from the writing of your students, duplicate the scrambled versions, and ask your students—working alone or in small groups—to unscramble them.

Unscrambling student paragraphs is harder than doing exercise 9 because the individual sentences of such paragraphs may be fragmentary or confusing, and because the paragraphs may contain gaps in coherence. But the struggle to find the original order of a student paragraph should be illuminating. As your students learn to recognize both missed connections and made connections between one sentence and another, they will also learn to grasp and apply principles of coherence in their own writing.

The final step is for each student to rewrite a paragraph of his or her own, striving to make it as clear and coherent as possible.

NOTE ON NONNATIVE SPEAKERS

Since methods of ensuring coherence vary from one culture to another, international students may find the list of transitional words and phrases particularly helpful. You might point out to them—and to other students as well—that many of these transitional signals can be used to link one paragraph to another as well as one sentence to another.

7.5 TRANSITIONS BETWEEN PARAGRAPHS

This section reminds students that a paragraph is normally part of an essay, not a self-contained unit standing on its own. If students have practiced using transitional words to link sentences within a paragraph, they can be readily introduced to the various methods of linking paragraphs within an essay. Exercise 10 will test their capacity to forge such links, first with a single word or phrase, and then—more challengingly—with a whole sentence.

Of course, linking each new paragraph to the one before it is not the only way of *unifying* a succession of paragraphs. They can also be unified if each new paragraph is clearly linked to the thesis of the essay as a whole. But even when the essay is thus unified, a transitional signal linking each new paragraph to the one before it helps to steer the reader along as the writer moves from one point to the next.

For a brief analysis of how three well-known writers (Thoreau, Emerson, and Carlyle) use a combination of connective words and repetition to link paragraphs together, see Ross, Donald Jr. "Composition as a Stylistic Feature." *Style* 4 (1970): 1–8.

8   *Style: Using a Community's Language*

CHAPTER OVERVIEW

This chapter should get students thinking and talking about the effect of a single word on a piece of writing. Classroom discussion about gender-inclusive language or which word to choose for the passage about Mars (8.4) will probably draw them at once into the topics addressed here: language and identity, levels of diction, denotation and connotation, and so on.

8.1   LANGUAGE AND GROUP IDENTITY

To supplement exercise 1, you might have students list specialized terms related to the Internet, such as *browser, hacker, dotcom, download,* and *search engine.* Ask students how often and in what contexts they use these terms, how recently the terms became part of their own and our cultural vocabularies, and if they know or know of people who aren't familiar with this language. What effects might that lack of knowledge have? This should serve as an illustration of how communities use language and how access to specialized terms can become a mark of privilege for particular groups.

8.3 RESPECTING OTHERS

Discussing racist, sexist, or homophobic language might make you and your students uncomfortable, but such dialogue is important. If some students object to what they see as the ideological tyranny of "political correctness," you will need to steer the discussion toward the ways in which language generates as well as registers social change, especially change in how we think about ourselves among the diverse races and cultures of the world. You might point out that words now readily recognized as racist were once used widely—before the civil rights movement, for example, *colored* was considered acceptable. Only through frank conversation and active consciousness-raising are such words and the thinking they represent called into question and subject to change. See Nowlan, Robert Andrew. "Teaching Against Racism in the Radical College Composition Classroom: A Reply to a Student." *Left Margins: Cultural Studies and Composition Pedagogy.* Ed. Karen Fitts and Alan W. France. Albany: State U of New York P, 1995.

8.4 MAKING LANGUAGE CHOICES

To supplement this discussion, you can duplicate any passage from which you have blanked out one word, make a list of synonyms including that word (a dictionary or thesaurus can help you with this), and ask students to say which word they would use to fill the blank. If you want to make this a homework assignment, you could give them several passages containing blanks and ask them to explain each of their choices in writing. They might need the help of a dictionary to explain the choice of one synonym over another (see 8.14).

8.5–8.6 CHOOSING WORDS FOR THEIR DENOTATION *AND* CHOOSING WORDS FOR THEIR CONNOTATION

The treatments here should prompt students to recall and continue their debate about the Mars passage (8.4). To stimulate further discussion, you might duplicate from their recent work one or more sentences in which a word needs to be replaced with one of more exact meaning. Then blank out the word, furnish a short list of alternatives, and invite each student (including the author) to choose a word for the blank *and* briefly explain the choice.

8.7 CHOOSING GENERAL AND SPECIFIC WORDS

To stimulate discussion, you might do exercises 9–11 in class, writing on the board the words students suggest.

8.8–8.9 USING WORDS FIGURATIVELY: SIMILE AND METAPHOR *AND* AVOIDING MIXED METAPHOR

Though figurative language generally gets plenty of attention in the teaching of poetry, it typically is neglected in the teaching of writing. This is an opportunity lost, because metaphor and simile can be vital sources of rhetorical power. Far more than ornamentation for the "literal" expression of thought, they are ways of *thinking:* "Greatest of all attempts to say one thing in terms of another," according to Robert Frost, "is the philosophical attempt to say matter in terms of spirit, or spirit in terms of matter. . . . [I]t is the height of poetry, the height of all thinking, the height of all poetic thinking." While perhaps not reaching quite that high, the examples cited here, some of them by college students, should give your students an idea of what they can do with figurative language.

To encourage their explorations, you might do exercise 12 in class, asking students to give you as many different figures of speech as they can think of for each italicized word or phrase. Then ask each student to pick a sentence from a recent essay and enliven it with a figure of speech.

Readings on figurative language include:

Kittay, Eva Feder. *Metaphor: Its Cognitive and Linguistic Structure.* Oxford: Clarendon, 1987.

Sacks, Sheldon, ed. *On Metaphor.* Chicago: U of Chicago P, 1978.

8.10 CONTROLLING CLICHÉS

Invite students to talk about why people use clichés so often, why they say (or write) "chew the fat" instead of "talked," or "could not see eye to eye" instead of "could not agree." In talking about examples such as these, students may come to see that we tend to use clichés because most clichés are ready-made figures of speech, and thus gratify—however inadequately—the desire that all of us have for the stimulus that figurative language provides. To avoid clichés, therefore, students must learn to resist their tacky allure even before they learn to respect the simple virtue of plain words like "talked" and the value of coining their own figures of speech: something that takes real work by the imagination but is well worth the effort.

8.11 USING IDIOMS

NOTE ON NONNATIVE SPEAKERS

Nonnative speakers have special difficulty with idioms because no clear rules govern their use. The idioms and their use must simply be memorized. See chapter 28 for examples of phrasal verbs and other highly idiomatic expressions that give nonnative speakers difficulty. Web sites such as *Dave's ESL Cafe* (<www.pacificnet.net/~sperling/eslcafe.html>) offer helpful lists of idioms and links to other resources.

8.12 AVOIDING JARGON, PRETENTIOUS WORDS, AND EUPHEMISMS

Jargon, pretentious words, and euphemisms can be just as hard to resist as clichés, though for a different reason: they invest writing with a fake grandeur or with a spuriously official tone. The most effective weapon against these would-be glamorizing terms is ridicule. If you can get students to laugh at things like "lucrative financial rewards," you've already begun to drive such language out of their writing.

The quotation given under "Euphemisms" comes from George Orwell's classic essay "Politics and the English Language," which cogently dissects not only jargon and euphemisms but also clichés—more precisely exhausted metaphors—along with various other kinds of enfeebled and enfeebling diction.

For good measure, here is Orwell's recasting of a passage from the Book of Ecclesiastes in bureaucratese:

Ecclesiastes: I returned and saw under the sun, that the race is not to the swift, nor the battle to the strong, neither yet bread to the wise, nor yet riches to men of understanding, nor yet favor to men of skill; but time and chance happeneth to them all.

Orwell: Objective consideration of contemporary phenomena compels the conclusion that success or failure in competitive activities exhibits no tendency to be commensurate with innate capacity, but that a considerable element of the unpredictable must invariably be taken into account.

To supplement exercise 6, you might ask students to find examples of jargon and pretentious words in print or online sources. The speech of politicians and bureaucrats is a particularly rich source. For example, when H. R. Haldeman, Richard Nixon's chief of staff, was asked if he had investigated a certain matter, he reportedly said, "There was an attempt made to reduce the area of the nonknowledge." You can also find excruciating euphemisms each year in the NCTE announcement of the Orwell Award.

8.13 AVOIDING WORDINESS

Wordiness is a common failing of student writing. While they should feel free to be wordy when generating raw material or writing a first draft, students must learn to recognize and eliminate unnecessary words when producing finished essays. To help them see the reason for doing so, ask them to compare the long and short versions of the sentences provided here. Ask them which version is easier on the reader, and get them to say why. Perhaps provide additional examples of wordiness and ask the class to edit them. You might also have students do peer work in which they edit essay drafts for wordiness.

8.14 USING THE DICTIONARY

Students increasingly rely on online dictionaries, some of which have quite thorough entries. However, students most often use dictionaries, both electronic and print, simply to check spelling or learn the most common definition of a word. They often do not notice or know how to use the rest of the information presented. Encourage your students to read entries more carefully and to pay particular attention to lists of synonyms, which may help them see the shades of difference among words closely related in meaning.

Revising Your Text 9

CHAPTER OVERVIEW

This chapter treats revising as a task of making big changes rather than small ones, an essentially creative process of rethinking and restructuring a draft. If you are accustomed—as many teachers are—to marking all the errors in any piece of writing a student submits, you may find it hard to overlook such things as misspelled words, faulty sentence constructions, and punctuation errors. However, your marking all these local errors in early drafts may discourage students from looking at larger issues of development; students may have the impression that all they need do to improve their writing is "correct" the errors marked by the teacher. You may want to point out one or two of the more persistent repeated errors (such as comma errors) and direct students to the chapter(s) and exercises addressing the problem. But in general, revision at the early stages will be more productive if you encourage students to concentrate on content and organization.

9.2 MAKING AND RECEIVING COMMENTS ON A DRAFT

Students come to college with a range of experience with and views regarding peer work. In order to get a sense of students' ideas, you might devote some class time to discussing potential benefits and drawbacks of peer review. Ask students who have participated in it to share their experiences. Ask the class to consider the purposes of peer review and to suggest how the process can be used to their best advantage. If students who are accustomed to a teacher-centered classroom seem reluctant to accept and respect the comments of other students, or even see peer review as a waste of time, you may need to make the benefits explicit.

Readings on the topic include:

Herrington, Anne J., and Deborah Cadman. "Peer Review and Revising in an Anthropology Course: Lessons for Learning." *College Composition and Communication* 42 (1991): 184–99.

Spigelman, Candace. "Habits of Mind: Historical Configurations of Textual Ownership in Peer Writing Groups." *CCC* 49.2 (May 1998): 234–55.

9.3 CLARIFYING YOUR PURPOSE

Some students may feel that reconsidering the general aim of a text after writing out a full draft is going back to square one. But rethinking one's basic approach seldom requires throwing out all of what one has written. More often it requires adjustments in emphasis so that the material appears in a new light. For example, rather than revising an entire draft to fit a thesis carved in stone, a student might revise the thesis to more accurately reflect the contents of the draft.

9.5 REVISING FOR STRUCTURE

Some of the questions given here are also in the peer review questionnaire, but since this set of questions focuses exclusively on structure, it should help your students to see what sorts of reconstruction their essays may need. For at least the first few weeks of your course, the best way to ensure that students actually think about these questions while revising is to require that they submit their answers in writing—besides making their revisions. After they've learned how to use the questions as guides to revision, they can skip writing answers and just *act* on the questions.

9.6 STRENGTHENING TEXTURE

Typically, first drafts offer too many generalizations and not enough specific details to substantiate them. The opposite problem—too many details without a controlling generalization—is less common but no less important to reckon with. Here, after having reconsidered the aim, tone, and structure of their essays, students are asked to think about connecting the general and the specific, the abstract and the concrete. The Hanson and Heath passage in exercise 3 nicely illustrates the combination of the two, and in effect, exercises 4 and 5 invite students to imitate the technique. You may find that they need some help in spotting their own overuse of generalizations (exercise 6) or underuse of them (exercise 7). So you may want to mark the relevant passages in their drafts for them to work on after they have done these exercises. Then you might photocopy some before-and-after versions of these passages for class discussion.

9.7 SAMPLE STUDENT PAPER

The draft and unedited revision presented here invite comparison. They may also provide a good opportunity to demonstrate the relationship between generalizations and specific details since, in discussing the two versions, you can begin by asking students to make general statements about each text and then to find specific examples from each to support the points they make through generalizations. You might structure class discussion a bit by posing questions about specific areas of concern, such as organization, use of transitions, use of support, and so on.

Editing and Proofreading 10

CHAPTER OVERVIEW

This chapter focuses on points of grammar, rhetoric, punctuation, and spelling within the context of editing a whole text. The explanations and exercises should help students spot and correct errors that interfere with the clear expression of ideas. As they learn the techniques outlined here, students will likely pay more attention to editing and proofreading in the drafting process.

To supplement the exercises, you might select from your own students' essays a few sentences that illustrate the problems discussed here. With the authors' permission, share the sentences with the class, but don't label the errors. Instead, have your students work collaboratively to identify and correct errors. Chances are, the groups will provide a number of suggestions for solving the problems. Discuss with the whole class the merits and weaknesses of various solutions offered.

Since this chapter presents a large amount of information about a number of rhetorical and grammatical points, you might have students focus on one or two sections at a time for each essay they write. For instance, for their first essay you might have them pay more attention to 10.2 and 10.3, and for the second essay you might have them focus on 10.4. By encouraging students to return to this chapter, you will reinforce the message that editing and proofreading are ongoing processes.

10.2 MAKING YOUR SENTENCES RHETORICALLY POWERFUL

NOTE ON NONNATIVE SPEAKERS

Syntactic subordination is more highly valued in the U.S. and Western Europe generally than in some other countries. But with the help of chapter 17, international students should be able to understand the purpose of subordination as well as the various ways of achieving it.

10.3 CHECKING YOUR CHOICE OF WORDS

Here you might remind your students of the material covered in chapter 8. Discuss the ways in which different communities' language expectations might affect students' writing.

NOTE ON NONNATIVE SPEAKERS

Nonnative speakers of any language sometimes have difficulty moving smoothly between formal and informal diction and using such registers appropriately. You might ask nonnative speakers to talk about levels of formality in their own languages (such as the use of honorifics with elders and persons of authority), and then have the class discuss such distinctions as they exist in English. Working in peer groups with native speakers might help nonnative speakers avoid overly formal or overly informal phrases.

10.5 CHECKING YOUR PUNCTUATION

NOTE ON NONNATIVE SPEAKERS

Punctuation varies from one culture to another. Even British rules of punctuation differ somewhat from U.S. rules. So as soon as possible, international students should be guided to Part 3 of this book, where U.S. rules of punctuation are explained in detail. International students may find the semicolon especially strange.

10.6 CHECK YOUR SPELLING, CAPITALIZATION, AND APOSTROPHES

NOTE ON NONNATIVE SPEAKERS

International students often use British spellings because they were taught by speakers of British English. You shouldn't consider such spellings "errors" on the students' part, but do point out that alternative American spellings exist for a number of words and encourage the students to invest in a good college-level American-English dictionary.

In addition, not all international students are familiar with categories for proper and common nouns. Refer them to Part 3 for help with capitalization.

10.7 PROOFREADING YOUR TEXT

NOTE ON NONNATIVE SPEAKERS

Before you pair nonnative speakers with native speakers for proofreading exercises, try to get a sense of the individual students' abilities. While some nonnative speakers will not be ready to respond at the same level as native speakers, others will have deliberately learned rules of English grammar and will be able to articulate them better than native speakers who learned the rules unconsciously. In addition, while native speakers may notice errors in nonnative speakers' writing, they might not be able to explain the problems and will be tempted to simply correct the errors rather than helping the nonnative speakers avoid them in the future. In such a situation, you might ask native speakers to mark errors but not correct them. You can then isolate the nonnative speakers' error patterns and refer them to the appropriate chapters for help.

Persuasion and Argument

CHAPTER OVERVIEW

To introduce the concept of persuasion, you might want to spend a little time discussing what could loosely be called the psychology of persuasion. Referring back to the material covered in 3.8–3.9, you could talk about various kinds of persuasion, about selling and advertising as well as argument. If you haven't already, you might ask students to bring in advertisements that they find effective or ineffective, and if some of your students have had experience in selling, you might ask them to talk about their experiences. How did they sell their products? What objections did they meet? How did they overcome those objections? What kinds of appeal did they make? Questions like these can help the whole class see just what the art of persuasion requires.

Salespersons know very well, of course, that to sell a product or service, they must first sell themselves. They must come across as likable and trustworthy, which is exactly how the insurance ad described here is trying to sound. This component of an argument—the character of the person making it—is what classical rhetoricians called *ethos*. According to them, it's the combination of *ethos* with *logos* and *pathos*—logical argument and emotional appeal—that persuades an audience.

11.1 WHAT IS PERSUASION?

Most of the persuading done by advertisements in this country—whether commercial or political—is done by pictures. Think, for instance, of the glowing scenes that show families reunited when they "reach out and touch someone" through long-distance phone calls. So you might ask students what it means to persuade with—or to be persuaded by—the written word alone. How does this kind of persuasion differ from illustrated ads in magazines and newspapers and on the Internet, or TV commercials, or the *spoken* word of radio advertising?

One answer is that the written word can persuade only those able to read it, which excludes the roughly fifty million American adults who are functionally illiterate. Even among those who can read, many more don't read much. So students need to realize that when they try to persuade with the written word alone, they are writing for the rather restricted audience of those who not only *can* read but regularly do so.

This does not mean an audience of intellectuals. It does mean a readership generally more thoughtful than the rest of the population, more likely to be struck by the force of ideas. But no reader can be stirred much by rational means alone. So learning the art of persuasion means learning how to make rational argument and emotional appeal work together.

We all know from experience that the personality of a speaker—the personal impression that he or she makes on us—strongly affects the persuasiveness of what is said. But how does a piece of writing express the personality or character of the writer? The insurance ad described here gives one example; several others can be found in the discussion of tone in 2.3, for tone is the very sound of a writer's character, or of the character the writer wants to assume. But the best way to get students talking about the "character issue" in persuasive writing is to give them one or more persuasive essays and ask them to do three things: (1) describe the character expressed by the essay; (2) identify the specific elements that create this character for the reader; (3) say how their impression of the character affects the persuasiveness of the essay.

11.2 WHAT IS AN ARGUMENT?

The passages on bear hunting in this section illustrate the difference between rational argument and emotional appeal as well as the difference between exposition and argument. Like nuclear power, which comes up in examples later in this chapter, hunting is a controversial topic. To help students feel as well as see what can be done with such a topic, we have given arguments on both sides of this one. Some of your students may feel that all hunters are bloodthirsty, but even these students should be struck by the contrast between the violently emotional tone of the first antihunting paragraph (#2) and the reasonable tone of the prohunting paragraph that follows it as well as of the second antihunting paragraph (#4). That contrast should help students see that effective persuasion requires a good deal more than expression of the writer's feelings.

Note that "In Brief: Basic Elements of an Argument" presents a simplified analysis of argumentation that comes, with some modifications, from Toulmin, Stephen. *The Uses of Argument.* Cambridge: Cambridge UP, 1958. Where Toulmin uses *ground* we use *evidence,* and where he uses *warrant* we use *assumption.*

NOTE ON NONNATIVE SPEAKERS

Like everything else in language, techniques of persuasion and argumentation are culture-specific. What persuades people in the United States is sometimes quite different from what persuades people in other countries. You should point out to international students that this chapter explains how to write persuasively for U.S. readers.

11.3 SUPPORTING CLAIMS WITH EVIDENCE

This section recalls 9.6, "Strengthening Texture." You might remind students of the earlier section and emphasize again that the combining of generalizations and specifics is the basic strategy that underlies all formal strategies of development. The student paragraphs on male and female athletes should help to show how this basic strategy can be used in argument and how an argument can be buttressed by specific facts.

To stimulate discussion about "Citing Sources and Authorities," you might have each student select and copy from any print or online source a passage in which the writer uses statistics to make an argument. Then ask each student to submit a written commentary that (1) explains how well the statistics serve the writer's argument; (2) says what source, if any, the writer cites for the statistics; (3) says what questions about the statistics could be raised by someone opposed to the writer's argument.

NOTE ON NONNATIVE SPEAKERS

While U.S. readers are typically persuaded by facts, figures, examples, and statistics, authority carries more weight in other cultures, and international students sometimes use mythical or religious authorities to support their points. For this reason, they may need special guidance in learning to cite authorities for U.S. readers.

11.4 DEDUCTION AND INDUCTION

Throughout this section, we repeatedly try to help students answer the question "What do I have to do to persuade a skeptical reader?" Part of the answer to this question is: Formulate one or more credible assumptions. So you might ask students to discuss the problem of formulating assumptions about nuclear power plants, taking as an example the assumption about the reliability of the Rasmussen study (in "Making Deductive Arguments Persuasive"). Some of your students will undoubtedly question that assumption, and some will express opposition to nuclear power plants. You could therefore invite one or more students to formulate one or more assumptions on which a no-nuke argument could be based, and then ask the rest of the class to judge the credibility of those assumptions. Students may be surprised to find how hard it is to formulate an assumption that can be believed by anyone who is not already on their side.

"Deduction and Validity" describes only the simplest type of deductive argument. Not all deductive arguments follow this three-part form, and not all premises consist of an assumption and a statement of fact. Strictly speaking, the major premise is what contains the predicate term of the conclusion (in this case "help bears") while the minor premise contains the subject term (in this case "Bear hunters"). For a detailed account of deduction, see Kelley, David. *The Art of Reasoning*. Norton, 1988.

Once students understand what an assumption is, they need to learn about validity. The traditional way to teach this concept is to explain the difference between validity and invalidity, usually by means of syllogisms and Venn diagrams:

All men are mortal.
John is a man.
Therefore John is mortal. [valid conclusion]

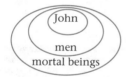

All men are mortal.
Ants are mortal.
Therefore men are ants. [invalid conclusion]

mortal beings

You might use these syllogisms and diagrams. In particular, they can help you explain the fallacy of arguing by association (treated in 11.5), since the second diagram clearly shows that two things connected to a third are not necessarily connected to each other. While a valid argument leads to a necessary conclusion, an invalid argument does not.

To help students grasp the concept of validity, you might compare the reaching of a conclusion to the scoring of a touchdown in a football game. To score a touchdown, the runner has to keep the ball within bounds. Likewise, to reach a valid conclusion, the maker of an argument has to stay within the bounds laid down by the premises—by the assumptions and facts. If the ball goes out of bounds, there is no touchdown; if the writer steps out of bounds, the conclusion is invalid.

You could then apply this concept of validity to an argument for the abolition of a nuclear power plant. Suppose the writer begins by assuming that any power plant that has had a fatal accident should be shut down. This reasonably credible assumption could be followed by the statement that Plant X has had a nearly fatal accident. But if the writer concluded that Plant X should be shut down, that conclusion would be invalid. In reaching such a conclusion, the writer would be stepping over the boundary between "fatal" and "nearly fatal."

In "Combining Induction and Deduction," the example is a passage from Martin Luther King Jr.'s "Letter from Birmingham Jail," written on April 16, 1963, in response to a statement published by eight Alabama clergymen urging King to desist from his "unwise and untimely" efforts to end segregation by acts of civil disobedience. Here the contrast between the syllogism and the passage by King shows the powerful difference between pure deduction and deduction reinforced by induction—as well as by emotional appeal. Ask your students to say what specific words, phrases, and sentences in this passage excite the reader's feelings.

11.5 AVOIDING FALLACIES

To supplement this discussion of fallacies, you might ask your students to bring to class examples of fallacious argument in editorials, TV commercials, print ads, and online sources. Political advertising of all kinds (TV, radio, and print) is an especially rich source of fallacies.

Technically, arguing by association is the fallacy of the undistributed middle term. The middle term is the term common to both premises, the predicate of each; in the example here, the middle term is essentially "support the voucher system." In a valid syllogism, the middle term must be distributed in one of the premises, which means that one of the premises must refer to *all* members of the class designated by the middle term. If, for instance, we could assume that *all* supporters of the voucher system are conservatives, then Senator Blank's support of the voucher system would prove her to be one. But if neither premise distributes the middle term, as here and in the syllogism about men and ants given above, the conclusion is invalid. The senator's support of the voucher system no more proves her to be conservative than the mortality of men proves them to be ants.

To show how analogy can be misused to make an argument, you might discuss with your class the sinister analogy that has occasionally been drawn between a particular group of people and a set of germs that must be eradicated from the body. All too easily, this analogy can lead to the sort of ethnic "cleansing" suffered by the Jewish people of Nazi Germany and the Muslims of present-day Bosnia. The following passage develops this point:

> Few people exhibit much compunction about attacking the microorganisms that invade their bodies. We use antibiotics to slaughter bacteria and we try to enhance our natural defenses to resist viruses. In our century, we have withstood similarly ruthless attempts to suppress what are viewed as infections of the body politic. Thinking of members of particular groups—most prominently Jews—as vectors of social disease, "forward-minded" political thinkers have sought to cleanse society by eliminating what they view as human pathologies. As in the case of germs, nothing less than a final solution will do.
>
> Such programs of social hygiene depend on two repugnant assumptions. One is a system of values that styles the members of offending groups as loathsome, evil and threatening. The other is the dehumanization of those members by likening them to microorganisms, culminating in a view of their attributes as inherent to their nature as members of the pertinent groups. So, for example, the Jew is held to be bound as a member of that ethnic group (or race), to exhibit the offensive attributes. There is no hope of modifying the traits, of integrating the offenders into healthy society. Society either suffers the infection or eradicates the sources of disease.
>
> —Philip Kitcher, Review of *Final Solutions* by Richard M. Lerner,
> *New York Times Book Review,* August 2, 1992

11.6 TREATING THE OPPOSITION WITH RESPECT

In learning to make concessions, students may also begin to move beyond the common assumption that persuasion is an essentially competitive sport, a game in which one side must win and the other lose. Catherine Lamb mounted a feminist critique of this win-lose model of persuasion, arguing that negotiation and mediation are more suited to contemporary needs and feminine sensibilities (see "Beyond Argument in Feminist Composition." *College Composition and Communication* 42 [1991]: 11–24). But all writers—male and female—can learn something by considering this win-win model of persuasion, which seeks not so much to conquer the other side as to establish common ground and common advantage.

"Defining the Position You will Oppose" reinforces and develops some of the points made in 5.2, "Planning with Your Readers in Mind." Together with the examples in "Making Concessions," the contrast between Roth's treatment of gun defenders and Thomas's treatment of Nader's Raiders should help students to see why they should reckon fairly with the opposition when they seek to persuade. Exercises 6 and 7 will of course test their ability to do so. For class discussion, you might photocopy some of the responses to exercise 7 and invite students to say whether or not the author of a particular response supports or opposes the position defined.

11.7 APPEALING TO THE EMOTIONS

Along with the passage from King's "Letter" in 11.4, this section should help to show students how to use emotional appeal both responsibly and effectively. For yet another example of how emotional appeal can be used to punctuate an essentially rational argument, here's the concluding paragraph to Tom Regan's rigorously analytical "Case for Animal Rights":

> Finally, I am reminded of my thoughtful critic, the one I mentioned earlier, who chastised me for being too cerebral. Well, cerebral I have been: indirect duty views, utilitarianism, contractarianism—hardly the stuff deep passions are made of. I am also reminded, however, of the image another friend once set before me—the image of the ballerina as expressive of disciplined passion. Long hours of sweat and toil, of loneliness and practice, of doubt and fatigue: those are the discipline of her craft. But the passion is there too, the fierce drive to excel, to speak through her body, to do it right, to pierce our minds. That is the image of philosophy I would leave with you, not "too cerebral" but *disciplined passion*. Of the discipline enough has been seen. As for the passion; there are times and these not infrequent, when tears come to my eyes when I see, or read, or hear of the wretched plight of animals in the hands of humans. Their pain, their suffering, their loneliness, their innocence, their death. Anger. Rage. Pity. Sorrow. Disgust. The whole creation groans under the weight of the evil we humans visit upon these mute, powerless creatures. It *is* our hearts, not just our heads, that call for an end to it all, that demand of us that we overcome, for them, the habits and forces behind their systematic oppression. All great movements, it is written, go through three stages; ridicule, discussion, adoption. It is the realization of this third stage, adoption, that

requires both our passion and our discipline, our hearts and our heads. The fate of animals is in our hands. God grant we are equal to the task.

To supplement these passages, you might have students find and bring to class writings in which an emotional appeal is made either effectively or ineffectively. They can look for emotional appeals in editorials, in letters to the editor, and in unsolicited mail from political organizations. Discussion of these examples should prepare them for exercise 8.

11.9 CONSTRUCTING AN ARGUMENTATIVE ESSAY

This section builds on the previous ones by showing how various argumentative techniques can work together in an argumentative essay. To supplement the items provided for exercise 10, you might ask each student to bring in a recent news item on the issue of gun control. You could then circulate a list of these items and ask students to use them along with the items listed in the text. But even without extra items, this exercise should certainly challenge students to reckon fairly with the opposition on a highly controversial issue, and comparison of the results—especially if you photocopy essays taking opposite sides—should generate a lively discussion.

Document Design 12

CHAPTER OVERVIEW

Throughout their academic and professional careers, students will need to produce specific documents ranging from research papers in MLA style to résumés, memos, brochures, and Web pages. To help them create effective visual presentations, this chapter outlines basic design concepts. For the purposes of the composition classroom, you might focus on 12.3, "Academic Documents." However, it will be worthwhile to spend some class time discussing the design ideas given here and how they can be used as tools to aid in both document production and document analysis. In fact, after they read this chapter, you might have students reconsider their answers to exercise 9 in chapter 3, which asked them to evaluate two print ads. Exercise 1 in 12.4 will be a good follow-up activity.

Readings on document design include:

Bernhardt, Stephen. "Seeing the Text." *College Composition and Communication* 37.1 (1986): 66–78.

Kalmbach, James. *The Computer and the Page: Publishing, Technology, and the Classroom.* Norwood, NJ: Ablex, 1997.

Kostelnick, Charles, and David D. Roberts. *Designing Visual Language: Strategies for Professional Communicators.* Boston: Allyn & Bacon, 1998.

Kress, Gunther. "English at the Crossroads: Rethinking Curricula of Communication in the Context of the Turn to the Visual." *Passions, Pedagogies, and 21st Century Technologies.* Ed. Gail Hawisher and Cynthia Self. Logan: Utah State UP, 1998.

Stephens, Mitchell. *The Rise of the Image and the Fall of the Word.* New York: Oxford UP, 1998.

---. "Desktop Publishing: A Powerful Tool for Advanced Composition Courses." *College Composition and Communication* 39.3 (Oct. 1988): 433–47.

Sullivan, Patricia. "Taking Control of the Page: Electronic Writing and Word Publishing." *Evolving Perspectives on Computers and Composition Studies: Questions for the 1990s.* Ed. Gail Hawisher and Cynthia Selfe. Urbana, IL: National Council of Teachers of English; Houghton, MI: Computers and Composition, Michigan Technological U, 1991.

Tufte, Edward. *The Visual Display of Quantitative Information* (1983), *Envisioning Information* (1990), and *Visual Explanations: Images and Quantities, Evidence and Narrative* (1997). All published by Graphics Press in Cheshire, CT.

Wysocki, Anne Frances. "Monitoring Order: Visual Desire, the Organization of Web Pages and Teaching the Rules of Design." *Kairos: A Journal for Teachers of Writing in Webbed Environments.* 16 Nov. 1998. 17 May 1999
<http://english.ttu.edu/kairos/3.2/features/wysocki/bridge.html>.

PART 2

Crafting Sentences

PART OVERVIEW

Part 2 addresses both grammatical and stylistic concerns. Since students will likely come to your course with varied skills and backgrounds in this regard, you might wait to assign specific chapters or sections until you've received one or two batches of papers. Then, if many students seem to need work in a specific area, say in building complex or compound sentences (chapters 15–18), you might assign certain chapters or exercises to the entire class. You can also assign chapters on an as-needed basis to individual students who should work on specific problem areas.

The Simple Sentence   13

CHAPTER OVERVIEW

This chapter has two purposes: (1) to explain the essential elements of sentence structure as a basis for the chapters that follow, and (2) to give students a preliminary "feel" for the elasticity of sentence structure, for the variety of things that can be done with it.

In the words of Mina P. Shaughnessy, the ability "not only to recognize sentences but to account for their constituent parts is probably the most essential of all grammatical skills." You can help your students develop both skills in several ways. (1) Ask them to imitate examples in the text and identify the constituent parts. (2) Write a bare-bones simple sentence on the board and ask your students to expand it. (3) Write a simple but heavily modified sentence on the board, and ask your students to identify the bare-bones parts. (4) Ask whether they could move any of the parts to a new position.

(there are)
Different strategies
of learning how
to write a
good sentence.

To the degree students learn to add, delete, and move words about within a simple sentence, they will understand what is meant by "structure."

13.3 TYPES OF VERBS

NOTE ON NONNATIVE SPEAKERS

Nonnative speakers often have problems with verbs. Some make linking constructions without linking verbs: "He not ready," "The book hard," "They not here now." Some have difficulty with the formation and uses of gerunds and infinitives. And some, when using a transitive verb, misplace an adverb: "I watch often television."

For help with these matters and other uses of verbs, refer students to chapter 28. Try to have students focus on one or two grammar problems at a time to eliminate repeated errors. In marking drafts, you should indicate the location and type of error and refer the student to the appropriate chapter so that in the future, the student will be able to correct errors on his or her own. In addition, if your college or university has a writing center, you may want to encourage your students to seek extra grammar help from tutors.

13.7 USING MODIFIERS

If your students have trouble distinguishing between gerunds and participles, you can speak of participles simply as modifiers for the time being, and then ask them to compare two sentences such as these:

> The rattling carburetor worried me.
> The rattling of the carburetor worried me.

In the second example, the signal that *rattling* is not a modifier but a verbal noun is the word *of* after it. Other signals of the difference between a modifier and a gerund can be illustrated by examples like the following:

MODIFIER
Boring movies make me sleepy. [Movies that are boring . . .]

GERUND
Making movies takes money. [The making of movies . . .]

MODIFIER
The conductor, *tapping a baton,* called the orchestra to attention.

GERUND
The conductor's *tapping of a baton* called the orchestra to attention.

Modifiers 14

CHAPTER OVERVIEW

If your students have completed chapter 13, they have already done some preliminary work with modifiers. Chapter 14 builds on that work with two main objectives: first, to show how modifying words and phrases can enrich and reinforce the impact of a sentence, and second, to show how modifiers can be clearly connected to their headwords—the words they are supposed to modify. To let your students know about misplaced, squinting, and dangling modifiers, you may want to move at once to our discussion of those errors in 14.15–14.17. But if you first want students to see what modifiers can do *for* a sentence, you can follow the order of the sections in the chapter.

NOTE ON NONNATIVE SPEAKERS

Some nonnative speakers will need special help with the articles *(a, an, the).* See 28.1.

14.2–14.5 USING ADJECTIVES AND ADJECTIVE PHRASES, OVERUSING NOUNS AS ADJECTIVES, USING ADVERBS AND ADVERB PHRASES, *AND* MISUSING ADJECTIVES AS ADVERBS

Although students may find adjectives and adverbs easy to identify, usage of these modifiers can be somewhat confusing. Don't be surprised to find students using adverbs in place of adjectives and vice versa. While you should encourage them to use modifiers to add color to their writing, you may want to caution against excessive use, pointing out that too many unnecessary adverbs or adjectives can clutter a sentence and actually obscure its meaning. Be sure to provide sample paragraphs to edit, both for incorrect usage and for overuse.

14.8 DOUBLE NEGATIVES

The traditional way of explaining what is wrong with the double negative is to say that two negatives make a positive: if you DON'T want NO pills, you must want SOME pills. But language is not algebra. In algebra, the minus of a minus number is always a plus, so that minus −2 is the same as +2. Verbal negatives work differently. When a French speaker says, "Je ne sais pas," he or she doesn't mean "I don't not know" or "I'm not ignorant" but simply "I don't know." In French, as in various other languages, one negative (such as *pas*) reinforces another *(ne)* rather than negating it. England's prime minister Harold Macmillan used the double negative this way when he declared at a London press conference in 1955, "There ain't gonna be no war."

Macmillan's "ain't" and "gonna," however, plainly signal that he was linguistically slumming, slipping down into the sort of old slang that makes the double negative essential for such things as the proclamation of one's innocence ("I wuddn' doin' nuttin' ") or the confession of one's loneliness ("I ain't got nobody"). Standard English reserves the double negative for a different use: expressing something *between* a positive and a negative. To say that you are not unhappy doesn't mean that you are happy; it means that your feelings fall somewhere between happiness and unhappiness—the intermediate state where most of us (let's face it) live for much of the time. If you initiate a class discussion on the meaning of phrases such as "not unhappy," you may help students learn what can be said with the double negative when it is correctly used.

14.10 USING PARTICIPLES AND PARTICIPLE PHRASES

Once students know how to identify and use participles, you might want to share with them the following quotation from James Joyce's *Ulysses:* "Grossbooted draymen rolled barrels dullthudding out of

Prince's stores and bumped them up on the brewery float. On the brewery float bumped dullthudding barrel rolled by grossbooted draymen out of Prince's stores." These lines demonstrate how word endings and placement within sentences can tell us something about their meaning and relationship to the words they modify, even if the vocabulary is unfamiliar. For native speakers, such a sense of what is "grammatical" is often innate.

14.11 MISFORMING THE PAST PARTICIPLE

Since exercise 1 is a sentence-combining exercise that asks for more than one combination of each set, you can get students to compare different ways of combining the same set of materials and (in class discussion) to talk about placing modifiers even before they have heard about misplacing them.

NOTE ON NONNATIVE SPEAKERS

Some nonnative speakers may be unfamiliar with infinitives and infinitive phrases. Refer them to 28.3 for more information.

Sentence-expanding exercises can be used to generate class discussion or to measure the progress of individual students. If you call on students to read aloud their answers to exercise 2, the whole class can see what different modifiers do to the same base sentence and thus observe the different effects that modifiers can have. In addition, if you assign the exercise more than once, you can watch your students' command of modifiers grow. That is, you can start by asking them to add just adjectives, then adjectives and adverbs, then adjectives and adverbs and participles, and so on, up to participle phrases, infinitive phrases of purpose, appositive phrases, and especially absolute phrases. As your students discover how, where, and when to use these, they will gain confidence. At the same time, you may want to warn them against overloading a sentence with modifiers, and you will want to stress the importance of placing them carefully. The key to placing modifiers well is knowing that the words of almost any sentence can be arranged in more than one way. For this reason, students using computers should be urged to experiment with all possible arrangements on the screen, to take full advantage of the flexibility that working online allows them.

14.15 PLACING MODIFIERS

Francis Christensen has usefully emphasized the value of urging students to write the cumulative sentence—the sentence in which the main point comes first and the modifiers follow. As 14.15 explains, this method allows the student to shape the sentence in the act of writing it instead of having to plan it all out beforehand. And this method also—not incidentally—has its own way of cutting down on dangling modifiers. Most dangling modifiers result from the writer's effort to *begin* with a modifier and then find some hook to hang it on later in the sentence. When the sentence begins with its main point, the hook is already in place. There is something to be modified, and the student can simply use modifiers to make the sentence grow.

Counting the modifiers in a sentence will help students learn to keep them under control. Ask them to choose one of their longest sentences, extricate the base sentence (the bare bones without modifiers), and write it down with extra spaces between the words. Then ask them to list, in a vertical column below each word, all of its modifiers. The image formed by this arrangement will help them see how modifiers can flesh out the skeletal structure of a base sentence.

14.16 EDITING MISPLACED MODIFIERS

Since squinting modifiers and the misplacement of what we call "restricters" (words such as *only*) can cause genuine confusion (not just amusement), they receive special attention here. To supplement the examples of misplacement in 14.15–14.17, you can ask your students to compose and label their own examples of each type of misplacement and then submit the set for class discussion.

14.17 EDITING DANGLING MODIFIERS

To treat dangling modifiers, distribute a sheet of paper on which you have typed a number of sentences beginning with participle phrases. Some of the phrases should be danglers. Ask a student to read one of the sentences aloud twice. During the second reading, have the student pause after reading the introductory phrase and say "Who?" or "What?" If the grammatical subject doesn't identify the Who or What, the phrase is probably a dangler.

Coordination: Compound Sentences 15

CHAPTER OVERVIEW

This chapter explains the various ways in which the parts of a sentence can be coordinated. Since many students produce a comma splice or a run-on sentence when they try to use coordination, you may wish to go directly to 15.6 and 15.7, which treat these errors. But by taking the sections of the chapter in order, you can first show your students how to use coordination effectively.

You can introduce the compound sentence by comparing it with the compound phrase, already treated in 13.8. The compound phrase compresses the statements it joins (*I played football* and *I played hockey* become *I played football and hockey*); the compound sentence leaves the statements intact. For this reason, the compound sentence can more effectively stress the distinction between two statements, as in *She stumbled at the halfway mark, but she still won the race.*

Coordination of simple sentences is one good way of learning *coherence* in writing, since a compound sentence can reveal various relationships between the clauses it joins. At the same time, practice in the coordinating of clauses can lead to the greater coherence attainable in complex sentences (chapter 17).

15.3 OVERUSING *AND*

Ask students who overuse *and* to circle the word in their paragraphs and to circle twice any *and* that joins independent clauses. Ask them to rewrite any sentence containing a twice-circled *and* and then to say which version they prefer.

When rewriting sentences with *and*, some students will use subordination. For this reason, you may want to postpone this exercise until you treat chapter 17.

NOTE ON NONNATIVE SPEAKERS

Some native Arabic speakers may overuse *and* in English because the Arabic equivalent serves more purposes than the English *and*. Also, Arabic allows more independent clauses within one sentence than English does, stressing the value of parallel constructions.

15.5 COMPOUNDING WITH CONJUNCTIVE ADVERBS

To help students grasp the variety of relations that can be shown in a compound sentence, exercise 1 asks them to state the relationship indicated by each combination formed. This exercise can also help them compare the effect of a conjunction with that of a conjunctive adverb. Since different students will join the sentences in different ways, and since more than one combination may be possible, you can get them to explain and defend their choices, to say whether a particular combination works better with *but* or *nevertheless*, with *so* or *therefore*, with *and* or *furthermore*. And if students read their combinations aloud, they can focus on the meaning and effect of conjunctive terms rather than on punctuation errors, which you may choose to deal with later.

15.6–15.7 EDITING COMMA SPLICES *AND* EDITING RUN-ON (FUSED) SENTENCES

Correcting the comma splice and the run-on sentence requires some command of grammar. Students must be able to see where one independent clause ends and another begins. A conjunctive adverb often signals the dividing point, but conjunctive adverbs may be used within as well as between clauses, and some clauses may be joined with a semicolon alone. What students must learn to recognize, therefore, is the end of a clause.

Two things can help them do so. One is learning to identify subjects and predicates, as explained in chapter 13. The other is reading aloud some of the sentences in exercises 2 and 3. If they can begin to hear the points at which their own voices pause or drop, they may also begin to hear the end of one clause and the beginning of another.

NOTE ON NONNATIVE SPEAKERS

In some foreign languages, the use of a comma between independent clauses is customary.

Parallel Construction 16

CHAPTER OVERVIEW

Most of the time, parallel construction is the frosting on the cake of coordination. It can appear in sentences with subordinate structure *(When she talks, I listen)*, but more often it serves to enhance coordination, for with parallel construction, sentence elements that are equal in rank become correspondingly equivalent in form.

The large number of examples given here should help your students see and feel the effect that parallel structure can have. You might ask students to find examples of their own to read aloud in class; and to supplement the exercises, you might ask them to imitate one or two of the examples. Here, for instance, is how one might imitate the sentence from Ecclesiastes in 16.2.

A *true* enemy is better than a *false* friend.

As this example shows, there is often more than one way of making the elements of a sentence parallel. So you can invite students to read aloud and compare their answers to exercises 2 and 3.

16.3 USING CORRELATIVES WITH PARALLELISM

Placing correlatives correctly is difficult for many, with *not only . . . but also* the chief demon. Students often write sentences like this: "The car cost not only ten thousand dollars, but I was also stuck with high repair bills." So you might begin with pairs of single words, move to short phrases, and end with two independent clauses: "The portable radio is not only *powerful* but also *sturdy.*" "The manufacturer has made improvements not only *in design* but also *in performance.*" "Not only *does the radio receive signals clearly,* but also *it transmits them over hundreds of miles.*" The inversion at the start of this last example requires extra attention.

16.4 EDITING FAULTY PARALLELISM

To supplement the examples and exercises given here, you could explain why *that* must sometimes be repeated to mark a succession of noun clauses following verbs like *think, believe, argue,* and *state:* "Environmentalists argue that wetlands nurture many kinds of wildlife and that humans also benefit greatly from wetland conservation." To skip the second *that* would be to leave an unanswered question: Who is making the remark about humans—environmentalists or the writer of the sentence?

17 *Subordination: Complex Sentences*

CHAPTER OVERVIEW

Subordination is probably the most complicated thing about sentence structure that students have to learn. Students who need to work on subordination—as almost all students do—fall roughly into two categories: those who simply run facts one after another like beads on a string, and those who tangle the string in their effort to make the beads form a pattern. A student of the first type uses *and* chronically, with an occasional *so* or *but,* keeping all statements on the same level.

> We were tired, and it was late, and we wanted something to eat, so we went out to buy pizzas, but the place was closed.

A student of the second type wants to use words like *because* and *although* and *which* and *when* but has no very clear idea of what to do with them.

> We were tired because it was late although we wanted something to eat, so we went out to buy pizzas which unfortunately when we got there the place was closed.

Initially, the problem of the first student looks easier to solve than that of the second. The first student is plodding but nevertheless clear; the second has produced a syntactical skein that will take some doing to untangle. The second student, in fact, will probably have to go back to writing simple sentences in order to relearn the art of arranging them clearly. (On this point, see 18.2, "Untangling Sentences.") Yet the second student does have one advantage over the first: an impulse to subordinate one thought to another. It is the impulse to subordinate—to arrange the parts of a sentence according to their relative importance—that this chapter tries to elicit and encourage.

17.1 WHAT SUBORDINATION DOES

The series of sentences about the dog should help students see how subordination throws various parts of a sentence into relief. You might want to describe subordination as a way of stacking—that is, of arranging the parts of a sentence so that what is most important comes out (so to speak) on top, what is least important falls to the bottom, and what is moderately important settles in between. Thus subordination lets the writer control the emphasis of the sentence.

One way to demonstrate the logic behind subordination is to have students arrange sentence parts in outline form with the most important point first and supporting details listed below. Then work the exercise in reverse, giving students an outline from which they construct a sentence using subordination.

17.3 USING ADJECTIVE (RELATIVE) CLAUSES

The adjective clause is treated here because it is really an extension of the adjective, the most basic of all modifiers. But you may want to leave adjective clauses until later because of the special handling required by relative pronouns.

For this reason, you could start your teaching of subordination with adverb clauses (17.8–17.12). Students can experiment with placement as they learn the meaning of subordinators. Then you can have them use noun clauses (17.13) after verbs of knowing and stating, followed by more difficult experiments using noun clauses as subjects and predicate nouns.

This section presents adjective clauses as substitutes for adjectives and tries to show the effect of such substitutions. Using the explanations here as a point of departure, you might invite your students to turn adjectives into clauses. Once they see how *fatal disease* can become *disease that takes thousands of lives every year,* they can use an adjective clause to develop a sentence like this:

Noisy drivers make me nervous.

SAMPLE DEVELOPMENT: Drivers *who honk at every traffic light* make me nervous.

As you demonstrate this kind of sentence development, be sure to point out how adjective clauses make descriptive language more precise. Expanding sentences by including adjective clauses may tempt some students into wordiness, so be sure to stress that such clauses should be used only when they make a sentence more exact in meaning.

17.4 CHOOSING RELATIVE PRONOUNS

Previous users of this book have asked us to explain how to choose between *who* and *that* and between *which* and *that*. Though this section treats all of these pronouns, it may not make as many distinctions as you would like.

Some teachers believe that nonrestrictive clauses which follow an antecedent denoting a thing should start with *which,* and restrictive clauses with *that*. If that is your own rule, we hope nothing we say here will keep you from expressing and enforcing it. But we stop short of doing so for two reasons:

1. You must make an exception for any restrictive clause introduced with a preposition, such as "for which our ancestors fought."

2. By forbidding a writer to switch from *that* to *which*, the rule mandates inelegant repetition. Ask yourself which of the following is more readable:

Some teachers firmly believe that restrictive clauses that follow an antecedent denoting a thing should start with *that*.

Some teachers firmly believe that restrictive clauses which follow an antecedent denoting a thing should start with *that*.

17.5–17.6 PLACING THE ADJECTIVE CLAUSE *AND* PUNCTUATING ADJECTIVE CLAUSES

You may want to point out that the relative pronoun can be skipped when it is the object of the verb in the relative clause:

Newhouse made a proposal [that] nobody else liked.

The next person [whom] we elect should have a good record of community service.

17.7 OVERUSING ADJECTIVE CLAUSES

A great advantage of sentence-combining exercises is that you can present them as exercises in problem solving. As the student examines each set of sentences, he or she should be asking questions: Which sentence out of the set do I want to emphasize, and why? If I turn a sentence into an adjective clause, where shall I put the clause, and why do I choose one position over another? Students should also ask these questions about the work of their classmates; they should compare and discuss the various ways in which a set of sentences can be combined, and the differences in emphasis that result. The more students realize that writing is a process of deliberate arrangement, of composition in the literal sense, the better they will learn the art of subordination.

You can supplement the sentence-combining exercises in this chapter (exercises 2, 3, 4, and 7) by making up short sentences to be developed, or better still, you can ask students to make them up for each other, or to supply them to each other from their own essays. They can then discover, compare, and discuss the various ways in which subordinate clauses can be used to enrich and develop a sentence.

17.10–17.11 PLACING ADVERB CLAUSES *AND* PUNCTUATING ADVERB CLAUSES

To help students understand the importance of adverb clauses, try furnishing a context that calls for them. For example, to encourage the use of subordinators denoting causality, ask students to say in one sentence why they like or dislike any recent movie. To encourage the use of subordinators denoting concession, ask students to say in one sentence—starting with *although*—what offsets the defects of the movie.

17.13 USING NOUN CLAUSES

Just as adjective clauses take the place of adjectives and adverb clauses take the place of adverbs, noun clauses take the place of nouns. For this reason a noun clause is sometimes called a "substitute clause." To help students grasp this idea and to supplement exercise 6, you can make up a few sentences with italicized nouns and a parenthesized word as a starter. Then ask students to substitute a noun clause for the italicized noun:

I could not understand *the mystery.* (how)

SAMPLE DEVELOPMENT: I could not understand *how the burglar entered the house.*

After signaling me to stop, the policeman asked me *a question.* (why)

SAMPLE DEVELOPMENT: After signaling me to stop, the policeman asked *why I was driving on the left side of the road.*

Exercise 7 tests the student's understanding of the chapter as a whole. As a follow-up to this exercise, you could ask students to pick any set of three or more simple sentences from one of their recent essays and to use subordination in combining these sentences. Also, besides assigning sentence-combining exercises like #7, you could dictate short paragraphs containing subordinate clauses. Then ask students to identify the subordinate clauses and to explain why the material in them has been subordinated.

18 *Coordination and Subordination*

CHAPTER OVERVIEW

As students begin to build complexity into their writing at the sentence level, they will likely continue to struggle with sentence clarity. The task of untangling complex ideas can be overwhelming, and if you simply mark "unclear" next to the faulty constructions of complex sentences, students will be tempted to write only simple sentences in order to ensure clarity. And if they do so, students will miss the chance to express the sophisticated relationships between ideas that subordination and coordination offer. Thus in showing them how to create complex sentences through co-ordination and subordination, this chapter helps students to make and strengthen connections between their ideas.

18.1 USING COORDINATION AND SUBORDINATION TOGETHER

You can stimulate students to use coordination and subordination to-gether by suggesting a context for it. Ask them, for instance, to explain what would happen to someone or something under certain conditions. You might start them off with a dependent clause: "If all electric power in [your town or city] suddenly failed . . ."; "If gas-powered cars were en-tirely replaced by electric cars . . ."; "Though we have not yet found evi-dence of intelligent life in outer space . . ."

18.2 UNTANGLING SENTENCES

NOTE ON NONNATIVE SPEAKERS

While some nonnative speakers may be able to generate compound-complex sentences, others will lose control. Such students may need extra time to master the structure of simple, compound, and complex sentences. They can also learn by taking dictation of passages you prepare with an eye to clarity and structure. The act of hearing the passage, writing it down accu-rately, and seeing it afterward in print can help them to grasp the com-plexities of sentence structure.

Sentence Fragments 19

CHAPTER OVERVIEW

As Karen Elizabeth Gordon has put it, sentence fragments are generally "grammatical blunder[s] of the most atrocious order." In certain contexts, however, they are acceptable and even preferable forms of communication. The college essay is not typically one of those contexts, though student writers in good control of their language might use fragments for rhetorical effect. This chapter will help students identify and correct fragments, but you may want to discuss issues of context. Since your students will most likely come across fragments in advertisements and headlines every day, they may wonder why fragments are discouraged in college writing. You will need to point out that academic writing demands a different level of formality and that the articulation of complex ideas requires complete sentences.

19.1 USING AND MISUSING SENTENCE FRAGMENTS

You might collect examples of fragments from print and online sources, or ask your students to collect them with you and bring them in for class discussion of their stylistic effects. Here, for instance, is the opening paragraph of Dickens's *Bleak House*—a paragraph made entirely with "grammatical blunder[s] of the most atrocious order":

> London. Michaelmas Term lately over, and Lord Chancellor sitting in Lincoln's Inn Hall. Implacable November weather. As much mud in the streets, as if the waters had but newly retired from the face of the earth, and it would not be wonderful to meet a Megalosaurus forty feet long or so, waddling like an elephantine lizard up Holborn Hill. Smoke lowering down from chimney-pots, making a soft black drizzle, with flakes of soot in it as big as full-grown snow-flakes—gone into mourning, one might imagine, for the death of the sun. Dogs, undistinguishable in mire. Horses, scarcely better; splashed to their very blinkers. Foot passengers, jostling one another's umbrellas, in a general infection of ill-temper, and losing their foot-hold at street-corners, where tens of thousands of other foot passengers have been slipping and sliding since the day broke (if this day ever broke), adding new deposits to the crust upon crust of mud, sticking at those points tenaciously to the pavement, and accumulating at compound interest.

19.2 SPOTTING AND EDITING SENTENCE FRAGMENTS

Students with little formal knowledge of grammatical structure can sometimes learn to distinguish fragments by writing down passages that are carefully dictated. After dictating several passages that consist wholly of sentences, tell them that the next passage will contain one or two fragments, which they are expected to mark with asterisks.

Students can also learn to spot fragments in their own writing by starting with the end of each paragraph and reading its sentences in reverse order. Reading each sentence in this way, they are less likely to be misled by the previous sentence.

NOTE ON NONNATIVE SPEAKERS

Typically, nonnative speakers produce more run-on sentences than sentence fragments. Nonetheless, distinguishing between sentences and sentence fragments is difficult for students whose native languages do not use linking verbs.

Using Pronouns 20

CHAPTER OVERVIEW

Since a pronoun must agree with its antecedent in number and gender wherever possible and must also be written in the appropriate case, students often have trouble managing all aspects of correct usage. Personal pronouns call for particular attention.

20.1 USING PRONOUNS WITH ANTECEDENTS

To help students identify antecedents, distribute a double-spaced passage containing many pronouns and antecedents. (Include a few adjective clauses.) Have your students circle the pronouns and draw arrows to the antecedents. After students have completed this exercise, have them complete the same task with passages from their own or their classmates' writing.

20.2 USING PRONOUNS WITHOUT ANTECEDENTS

NOTE ON NONNATIVE SPEAKERS

Rules and customs of pronoun use vary from one language to another. Pronouns occur more often in many other languages than in English, especially formal academic English, which requires frequent use of nouns—especially key words or synonyms for them. One reason for this difference may be the greater homogeneity of some other cultures: a greater body of shared understanding between writer and audience permits more frequent use of pronouns because the audience more readily understands the antecedent of each one. Whatever the reason for the difference, nonnative speakers may need special help in learning to use pronouns less often than they do in their native languages, as well as in learning to connect them clearly and correctly with their antecedents.

20.8, 20.10, 20.12 AVOIDING FAULTY SHIFTS IN PRONOUN REFERENCE, USING PRONOUN CASE, *AND* MISUSING PRONOUN CASE FORMS

Since faulty shifts in pronoun reference and the misuse of pronoun case forms (20.12) are both common problems, you may want to discuss exercises 3–5 in class, and you could supplement the exercises by culling examples of misused pronouns from student essays.

21 Subject-Verb Agreement

CHAPTER OVERVIEW

Essentially, this chapter has two purposes. Sections 21.1–21.4 are meant to help students who speak an ethnic or regional dialect and who need special help in learning academic English rules of agreement. The other sections are meant to combat errors of a more complicated kind. So you may find yourself referring a good many of your students to this chapter, even if you do not discuss it in class.

21.2 MAKING VERBS AGREE WITH SUBJECTS

The following comes from Mina P. Shaughnessy:

> To decide whether a subject "agrees" with a verb, a student must:
>
> 1. Understand what is meant by the term *agreement*.
>
> 2. Identify the base words of the subject and predicate.
>
> 3. Determine whether the subject should be counted as one or more than one according to the conventions of formal English.
>
> 4. Know the appropriate form for indicating the number of a particular noun.
>
> 5. Know the appropriate form for indicating the number of a particular verb.
>
> Thus an error that appears on the surface of a sentence as a detail of usage may in fact be so interlocked with other grammatical concepts that the teacher is like someone who, seeing only the tip of the elephant's tail, finds upon grasping it that he has the whole bulk of an animal (in this case a language) in tow.

NOTE ON NONNATIVE SPEAKERS

Nonnative speakers often have trouble with agreement because, first of all, what marks the plural form of many nouns (dogs, messes) marks the third-person singular of most simple present-tense verbs (walks, witnesses). Furthermore, some nonnative speakers find it hard to hear and pronounce the final -s.

In addition, they may find it difficult to manage all the forms of *be* and the two forms of *have* and to recognize the grammatical number of singular nouns ending in -s, of nouns pluralized without -s, and of collective nouns. Using *be* in questions and after *there* also troubles some of them. Finally, some have special difficulties because their native language does not mark number in both the subject and the verb.

These students often *know* the rules of agreement, or at least that subjects and verbs need to agree in number in English, but they are not always able to apply the rules consistently. To some extent, the exercises in this chapter will help remind them how to apply the rules. If students have consistent problems with agreement, ask them to select one of their own drafts and to underline each subject in it. Then ask them to mark each subject as singular or plural. Next have students locate the main verb, connect it to the subject, and correct any disagreement the labeling exposes. This exercise is time-consuming and thus impractical to do with each essay, but attempting it a few times on selected drafts will help nonnative students sharpen the particular editing skills.

21.4 AVOIDING DIALECTAL MISTAKES IN AGREEMENT

Since exercise 1 is really a test of basic competence in managing agreement, you can use it diagnostically. If you have assigned the *Workbook*, ask the students who have trouble with this exercise to do those in chapter 9 of the *Workbook*, then let them proceed to the rest of the exercises in this chapter. Students must know the basic rules of agreement before they can be expected to apply those rules to sentences in which the subject may be difficult to identify or difficult to classify as singular or plural.

22 *Verbs: Tense*

CHAPTER OVERVIEW

This chapter is meant largely for reference. It has two aims: to explain the forms of the tenses and to show students how to use them.

Students who get a tense form wrong (as in *I walk there yesterday*) can use exercise 2 (or any similar exercise; see 22.10 below) as a diagnostic tool on tense forms. Those who have trouble with this exercise should be asked to read 22.1–22.2 and to do exercise 1. If you are also using the *Workbook*, refer them to the exercises in chapter 10 there.

22.2 FORMING THE TENSES

NOTE ON NONNATIVE SPEAKERS

Nonnative speakers with little exposure to English often rely on one tense (usually the simple present) when speaking and writing about events in the past, present, and future. They may or may not signal time with markers like "last month" and "tomorrow." More advanced nonnative speakers can manage the simple past and the future, but sometimes stumble when using the simple present with verbs expressing perception, knowledge, belief, ownership, volition, or affection: "I am liking my English class." Also, many use a present-tense verb when they need the present perfect ("I am living in San Diego for two years") or the present participle when they need the perfect one ("Buying a new overcoat last week, I am warm now").

Some nonnative speakers use *going to* instead of *will* to indicate action in the future. While this is perfectly all right in speech, *will* is more concise ("The sun will rise" versus "The sun is going to rise") as well as more suitable in formal writing.

For more on such problems with progressive forms, see 28.3.

22.10 MANAGING TENSE AND TIME WITH PARTICIPLES AND INFINITIVES

To supplement exercise 2, you can readily make up similar exercises with any passage of your choice, replacing each verb with a blank and giving the base form in parentheses.

22.11 FORMING THE PRINCIPLE PARTS OF COMMONLY USED IRREGULAR VERBS

Teaching the forms of irregular verbs may require a different approach from that needed to teach the correct forms of regular verbs. You might ask students who incorrectly write one of the verb forms listed here to simply memorize each form of the problem verb, but the student will need to reinforce this memorization by using the verb in a sentence. Having students write sentences using the different forms will help them see usage patterns in specific contexts. Having them mark uses of irregular verbs in essay drafts will broaden the contexts.

To demonstrate the use of irregular verbs, you might share some of the following quotations with your students:

> Like other parties of the kind, it was first silent, then talky, then argumentative, then disputatious, then unintelligible, then altogethery, then inarticulate, and then drunk. —Byron

> Fashion can be bought. Style one must possess.   —Edna Woolman Chase

The first time Adam had a chance, he laid the blame on women.

—Nancy Astor

The officer and the office, the doer and the thing done, seldom fit so exactly that we can say they were almost made for each other.

—Sydney Smith

For frequent tears have run
The colours from my life.

—Elizabeth Barrett Browning

They never sought in vain that sought the Lord aright.   —Robert Burns

My tongue swore, but my mind's unsworn.
   —Hippolytus lamenting his breaking of an oath in Euripides' *Hippolytus*

That stony effigy in frozen music, horned and terrible, of the human form divine, that eternal symbol of wisdom and prophecy which, if aught that the imagination or the hand of sculptor has wrought in marble of soultransfigured or soultransfiguring deserves to live, deserves to live.

—J. J. O'Molloy quoting Seymour Bushe on
Michelangelo's Moses in James Joyce's *Ulysses*

23 *Verbs: Sequence of Tenses*

CHAPTER OVERVIEW

This chapter presupposes a knowledge of the material presented in chapter 22. You should ask students who have trouble forming tenses or using them in a one-verb sentence to read chapter 22 and complete the exercises in it before tackling this chapter.

   Managing the sequence of tenses is something that students often find difficult. This chapter explains the basic rules that govern the sequence of tenses and furnishes exercises on the topic, but to supplement this material, you might ask your students to identify the tense of each verb in a passage of assigned reading and then consider when and why the writer shifts from one tense to another.

23.3 SEQUENCES IN COMPLEX SENTENCES

You might ask students to read the examples aloud so that they hear as well as see the verbs again and again. Next the students could alter some of the content but not the tenses in the examples: "Most children learn to talk after they have learned to walk"; "Most children learn to run after they have learned to walk." Then you might ask them to compose sentences of their own in which the sequences of tenses follow those in the examples.

23.6 CORRECTING FAULTY TENSE SHIFTS IN PARAGRAPHS

Since the ear often catches what the eye misses, you might ask students who have particular trouble with faulty tense shifts to read their work aloud, and ask other students to raise their hands whenever they hear a faulty tense shift.

To supplement exercise 3, you might make up others from any passage of your choice by simply changing some of its verb tenses and then asking students to correct the faulty shifts. Alternatively, you can change every verb to its base form and ask students to choose the appropriate tense.

Item 1 is a passage about the movie *King Kong*. Since many students mistakenly use the past tense in writing about movies, plays, and literary works, you could supplement this exercise by asking each student to (1) choose a passage from a recent review of any movie, play, or novel; (2) underline each verb and identify its tense; (3) explain the tense of any verb that is not in the present.

After they do this exercise, you might ask students to summarize the plot of any movie, play, novel, or TV episode they choose.

NOTE ON NONNATIVE SPEAKERS

Nonnative speakers, like native speakers, will benefit from seeing, hearing, and writing short summaries. Dictations are especially helpful because students hear the sentences, write them down, and then see the tenses. After they take dictation and do exercise 3, nonnative speakers should be ready to do the activities described above.

24 Verbs: Active and Passive Voice

CHAPTER OVERVIEW

Good writers must be able to move back and forth between the active and the passive voice. This chapter illustrates the difference between the two and explains how to use each in appropriate contexts. While exercises 1 and 2 emphasize active voice, exercise 3 shows how the passive and the active can be used effectively together.

24.2 FORMING THE ACTIVE AND THE PASSIVE VOICE

Many students will need to have grammatical voice defined and illustrated. Check their understanding of voice by giving them a passage and asking them to change the voice of each transitive verb. When reviewing the results, note their handling of tense as well as voice. (You may want to exhibit your own revisions with an overhead projector or on the blackboard so that the still-puzzled can see and hear how you manage the transformations.)

NOTE ON NONNATIVE SPEAKERS

Many nonnative speakers will have trouble with active-passive transformations, which require them to know the forms of *to be* as well as of irregular verbs. Some will find the movement of agent and subject puzzling and control of word order elusive. For more practice in active-passive transformations, they can do the exercises in chapter 12 of the *Workbook* if you're using it with them.

24.4 CHOOSING THE PASSIVE VOICE

The hard thing about teaching voice is that while nearly all students must learn to use the active voice more often, they *also* need to understand when and how to use the passive voice for rhetorical effect. In the Phyllis McGinley passage given here, for instance, repeated use of the passive voice not only keeps the focus on women, who are repeatedly acted on; it also helps to ensure coherence.

Item 2 in this section implicitly raises a question about the ethics of using the passive: should students be encouraged to use a construction that can represent an action without an agent—that is, without indicating who or what is responsible for it? We all know that the passive voice is an instrument of evasion, especially bureaucratic evasion. Where is the CEO who would dare to write, "I have decided to lay off five hundred workers" rather than "Regrettably, a decision to lay off five hundred workers has been made"? But the simple truth is that we do not always know who or what is responsible for the actions we want to write about. Even when we do know the agents, they aren't always important to the point we want to make. Does it really matter, for instance, who found the traces of the oil in Newfoundland?

To help your students understand when a writer may legitimately use the passive without an agent, invite them to (1) note the passives in the following passage; (2) say whether or not any missing agents should be supplied; and (3) if the answer to question 2 is no, justify the absence of agents.

> Although similar in many ways, Seattle and Vancouver differ markedly in their approaches to the regulation of firearms. . . . In Seattle, handguns may be purchased legally for self-defense in the street or at home. After a 30-day waiting period, a permit can be obtained to carry a handgun as a concealed weapon. The recreational use of handguns is minimally restricted.
>
> In Vancouver, self-defense is not considered a valid or legal reason to purchase a handgun. Concealed weapons are not permitted. Recreational uses of handguns (such as target shooting and collecting) are regulated by the province, and the purchase of a handgun requires a restricted-weapons permit. A permit to carry a weapon must also be obtained in order to transport a handgun, and these weapons can be discharged only at a licensed shooting club. Handguns can be transported by car, but only if they are stored in the trunk in a locked box.
>
> —John Henry Sloan et al., "Handgun Regulations, Crime, Assaults, and Homicide"

To follow up the discussion of these issues and this passage, you might consider the regular use of the passive in professional articles on subjects such as biology and sociology (see chapter 42), and ask students what they think of this practice.

24.5 MISUSING THE PASSIVE

Exercise 3 is meant to be challenging. Since the sentence-combining aspect will require a certain amount of coordination and subordination, you may want your students to review chapter 18 before doing it.

The exercise itself should help students see that a shift in voice is sometimes an essential part of sentence combining. To stress this point, and also to get them started, you might want to do the opening sentences with them in class. You could begin by asking how the first two sentences might be combined. With a little prodding ("Can you somehow subordinate the second sentence to the first?"), they should be able to come up with something like this:

> The political structure of modern China was largely created by Mao Zedong, who led the Chinese Communist revolution.

You might want to note the advantages of leaving the first sentence in the passive voice, so that *Mao Zedong* can be immediately followed by the *who* clause. Then you could ask whether sentences 3 and 4 could be combined with the new sentence. With a little more prodding ("Is there any way of connecting sentences 3 and 4 with the *who* clause?"), students should see that in order to do that, they must make the verbs in sentences 3 and 4 active. Then they can produce this:

> The political structure of modern China was largely created by Mao Zedong, who led the Chinese Communist revolution, formulated the theory behind it, and virtually ruled China from 1949 to his death in 1976.

To supplement exercise 3, you might select a passage from any writer you like, make all the active verbs passive, and then ask students to restore the active voice except where they find the passive voice justified. You could also select from their own essays passages weakened by misuse of the passive and invite the class to transform the verbs.

25   *Verbs: Mood*

CHAPTER OVERVIEW

> Verbs may be tense and moody, but don't assume you can shift their tenses and moods whenever the whim seizes you.
>
> —Karen Elizabeth Gordon

Mood is hard to define—much more elusive than voice, which can be explained and illustrated fairly easily. Most students know how to use modal auxiliaries (not many write sentences like *He might could win the race*), but subjunctive verb forms can be tricky. Unlike the change from active to passive voice, the change from one mood to another often leaves the form of the verb unchanged:

> INDICATIVE: They *win* every game.
> SUBJUNCTIVE: The coach insists that they *win* every game.
> IMPERATIVE: *Win* this one for the Gipper!

Subjunctive verb forms in conditional sentences are especially hard to manage, and since many writers now get by (more or less) without them, you may decide that they are more trouble to teach and learn than they are worth. The use of *was* instead of *were* for contrary-to-fact conditions ("If I was president, I would veto the bill") is becoming increasingly common and may eventually become standard, along with the use of the simple past (rather than the past perfect) for conditions contrary to past fact.

Still, you may want to say something about mood to students who write sentences like these:

1. I wish I have a part-time job.

2. The director insists that everyone comes to every rehearsal.

3. If the moon was inhabited, we would probably be fighting the inhabitants right now.

4. If I stayed for the party after the game, I would have missed the last bus home.

But when you find sentences like these in a student paper that has many other kinds of errors, you have to ask yourself whether you really want to pounce on the student's ignorance of subjunctive verb forms. Partly because many writers get along with very few of them, and partly because mood is a relatively sophisticated concept, you may want to postpone assigning this chapter to any student who has serious problems with other aspects of sentence structure—especially with tense or subject-verb agreement.

25.4 USING THE SUBJUNCTIVE: MODAL AUXILIARIES

NOTE ON NONNATIVE SPEAKERS

Many nonnative speakers will need help with the modal auxiliaries—with both their meanings and their role in the structure of verb phrases. Consider, for example, the knowledge required to write "I might have been injured if the bus had not stopped." To supplement the exercises in this chapter, students can do the exercises in chapter 13 of the *Workbook* if you're using it.

25.5   USING THE SUBJUNCTIVE: SPECIAL VERB FORMS

To help students learn how to use the present subjunctive after verbs of demanding, try a substitution drill—one in which students change only one item as they go from one sentence to the next ("The manager insisted that John work"; "The manager insisted that John speak"; "The manager insisted that John pay"). Point out that the subjunctive form does not change with a change in the tense of the main verb ("The manager insists that John work"; "The manager will insist that John work").

26   *Direct and Indirect Reporting of Discourse*

CHAPTER OVERVIEW

This is another of the chapters that you may want to use for reference only. But if you do ask all your students to read the chapter and complete the exercises, you might then get them to discuss in class whether particular statements in exercise 1 should be reported directly or indirectly. Because each way of reporting has its own advantages, effective writing often combines the two.

26.2   INDIRECT REPORTING OF STATEMENTS

NOTE ON NONNATIVE SPEAKERS

Nonnative speakers often struggle with indirect and direct discourse, especially when it comes to deciding whether to use the words *say* or *tell*. For instance, it is not unusual for a nonnative speaker to use the preposition *to* after the word *tell*, as in *She **told to** me that she was leaving.* Point out that in reporting statements, the verb *tell* is always followed by an indirect object and a noun clause (*Jake told **me** that he had gotten a new job*), and that when it is used with imperatives, it is followed by an indirect object plus an infinitive (*He told **me** to move **my car***). *Say* is followed by a noun clause, though *to* plus an indirect object would also be acceptable, as in *She said (to me) that she was working late.*

26.3 DIRECT REPORTING OF QUESTIONS

NOTE ON NONNATIVE SPEAKERS

Some nonnative speakers will need guidance in managing every aspect of direct and indirect discourse. To supplement the exercises given here, students can do the exercises in chapter 14 of the *Workbook* if you are using it. You can also use dictation to help them learn how to punctuate quotations.

Since nonnative speakers are likely to overuse *say* as a tag, you might give them a list of alternatives. Besides *write* and *observe* (both illustrated in 26.1), such a list would include *declare, announce,* and *state.*

26.6 FITTING QUOTATIONS INTO YOUR OWN PROSE

Point out to your students that the art of introducing quotations and embedding them within a sentence is essential to the writing of a research paper. Managing quotations is discussed in chapters 39, 41, and 42.

Invigorating Your Style 27

CHAPTER OVERVIEW

Each section of this chapter treats a specific way of invigorating style. Section 27.1, for example, shows students some effects they can achieve by varying the length of their sentences. You may want to teach this section along with selections from chapters 15–18. Sections 27.3 and 27.5 are essentially cross-references to the treatments of voice (chapter 24) and wordiness (8.13), so you may want to assign these discussions together with the earlier ones.

That students have trouble recognizing stylistic weaknesses in their own writing or that of their peers may be due, in part, to lack of experience with reading and writing academic prose. It is difficult to identify stylistic problems without first recognizing the marks of superior style. So you might begin by accentuating the positive, choosing from students' work sentences or passages that struck you or a peer editor as particularly lively, concise, or unique in voice or style. With students' permission (and anonymously, if they prefer), duplicate these models and discuss with the class what makes them effective. Once students have gained a sense of good style, you may want to share some weaker sentences, again with students' permission, and ask the class to work in groups and revise them. Alternatively, you can present for discussion a mixture of strong and weak sentences, ask students to sort them into the two categories, and discuss their decisions.

The exercise at the end of the chapter asks for a good deal of sentence combining by means of coordination and subordination, but its real purpose is to help students see what they can do to make a sequence of sentences come alive. For class discussion, you could photocopy several responses and ask students to say which one is liveliest—and why. You could also ask students to use techniques of invigoration on a set of their own sentences. And to supplement the exercise, you could have students do with a set of their own sentences what they have done with the sentences in the exercise.

Finally, you might share a few of the following quotations with your students. Ask them why American academic culture encourages a "clean" prose style.

> Both speech and reasoning are lively in proportion as they make us seize a new idea promptly. —Aristotle

> Clutter is the disease of American writing. We are a society strangling in unnecessary words, circular constructions, pompous frills and meaningless jargon. [Yet] fighting clutter is like fighting weeds—the writer is always slightly behind. —William Zinsser

> Good, clean writing should be like a taut rope pulling the meaning tight. There should be no unnecessary slack, no loops or wrinkles that are doing no work of pulling. . . . If a word adds nothing to your meaning, it should go. —Alan Warner

NOTE ON NONNATIVE SPEAKERS

Nonnative speakers often have trouble negotiating levels of formality (register) in written English. Differences in register may seem less strongly marked in written American English than in a student's own language, or formality may seem synonymous with dullness and rigidity. As students learn more about formal and informal English discourse, you might stress that liveliness is perfectly compatible with the level of formality normally expected in American academic writing. For more on this point, refer students to chapter 8.

Academic English for Nonnative Speakers

28

Please see the opening paragraph of this chapter for an overview. Readings on the topic include Leki's book cited in the "Note on Nonnative Speakers" for chapter 1 and:

Byrd, Patricia, and Joy M. Reid. *Grammar in the Composition Classroom: Essays on Teaching ESL for College-Bound Students.* Boston, MA: Heinle and Heinle, 1998.

Gebhard, Jerry. *Teaching English as a Foreign Language: A Self-Development and Methodology Guide.* Ann Arbor: U of Michigan P, 1996.

Jordan, R. R. *English for Academic Purposes: A Guide and Resource Book for Teachers.* Cambridge, England: Cambridge UP, 1997.

28.1 ARTICLES AND OTHER DETERMINERS

The term *determiner,* used throughout the chapter, may be unfamiliar to you, but it's a useful name for a type of modifier that works differently from adjectives and other adjectival modifiers. (Note that grammarians have not yet agreed on a definition of *determiner* or on precisely which words belong in each subgroup of determiners.) Though native speakers normally have no trouble using words such as *a, an, the, same,* and *first,* nonnative speakers do. So they need to understand the special characteristics of such words, which may also be called "noun markers"—that is, words that tell the reader a noun is on the way. The following sentences show how determiners (D) mark as nouns (N) the words that follow them:

> D N   D N
> Going out the door, she met a man who looked tough.

> D N   D N
> When the going gets tough, the tough get going.

Besides marking nouns as such, determiners differ in two ways from adjectives, as shown in this section.

28.6 TIPS ON SENTENCE STRUCTURE AND STYLE

NOTE ON NONNATIVE SPEAKERS

Because nonnative speakers are often afraid of making mistakes in writing, they may avoid composing longer complex or compound sentences in favor of the more familiar simple subject-verb-object (SVO) pattern. Encourage these students to strive for a variety of sentence patterns and refer them to selected exercises in chapters 15–18.

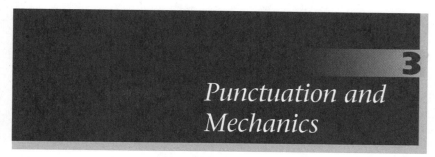

Punctuation and Mechanics

3

PART OVERVIEW

Part 3 is intended for reference rather than classroom study. But you might want to take a little class time to discuss the whys of punctuation and the purpose of punctuation marks. One way to get students talking is to have one of them read aloud a passage that has little or no punctuation, such as the exercise at the end of chapter 31. Ask the reader to talk about the experience of reading without punctuation, and have other students discuss how punctuation marks guide a reader. As a creative exercise, ask students to compare specific marks of punctuation to road signs (the period = the stop sign, the comma = yield, and so on). As with part 2, assign chapters and exercises here on an as-needed basis.

The Comma

29

CHAPTER OVERVIEW

The commas are the most useful and usable of all the stops. It is highly important to put them in place as you go along. If you try to come back after doing a paragraph and stick them in the various spots that tempt you you will discover that they tend to swarm like minnows into all sorts of crevices whose existence you hadn't realized and before you know it the whole long sentence becomes immobilized and lashed up squirming in commas. Better to use them sparingly, and with affection, precisely when the need for each one arises, nicely, by itself.

—Lewis Thomas, "Notes on Punctuation"

Students, especially beginning college writers, often have trouble deciding where to use commas. It is not unusual for students to claim to be mystified by this particular point, as if the comma were the one mark of punctuation that behaves according to an arcane and complex set of rules for which no logical explanation can ever be offered. Actually, this confusion sometimes stems from students' difficulties in understanding the basic components of a sentence, that is, what qualifies as a dependent or an independent clause, a restrictive or nonrestrictive clause, and so on. In teaching use of the comma, you may find your students will need to review earlier presentations on sentence structure, especially chapters 15–19, in order for them to grasp more clearly the explanations offered here. If students understand how sentence components determine placement of the comma, the decisions they make about comma use will be better informed and more logical.

Encourage students to *listen* for the pauses in their sentences. To illustrate how the placement of pauses changes the meaning of a sentence, share with them the following examples:

> Have you met Antonio?
> Have you met, Antonio?

> A woman without her man is nothing.
> A woman: without her, man is nothing.

30 The Semicolon and the Colon

30.1 USING THE SEMICOLON

The semicolon is a hybrid, something between a period and a comma. In the first four uses illustrated here, it works like a period; in the last, it becomes a supercomma. Consider the following quotation:

> Special attention must be called to [the semicolon] because so many students seem to suffer from semicolonitis; semicolons break out like measles all over the face of their compositions. Apparently this is caused by the widespread belief that a semicolon is a kind of dignified comma. It is not.
> —Lucile Vaughan Payne

30.3 USING THE COLON

Regarding the colon, consider the following:

> Colons are a lot less attractive [than semicolons], for several reasons: firstly, they give you the feeling of being rather ordered around, or at least having your nose pointed in a direction you might not be inclined to take if left to yourself, and, secondly, you suspect you're in for one of those sentences that will be labeling the points to be made: firstly, secondly and so forth, with the implication that you haven't sense enough to keep track of a sequence of notions without having them numbered. Also, many writers use this system loosely and incompletely, starting out with number one and number two as though counting off on their fingers but then going on and on without the succession of labels you've been led to expect, leaving you floundering about searching for the ninethly or seventeenthly that ought to be there but isn't.
>
> —Lewis Thomas, "Notes on Punctuation"

End Marks   31

This chapter is intended as a refresher. You might want to direct your students' attention to the coverage of abbreviations (in 31.1), which are a common source of errors.

Quotation Marks and Quoting   32

CHAPTER OVERVIEW

Many of the mechanical points presented here are likely to come up again for students writing research papers. Refer students back to this chapter when you cover Parts 4 (Research and Writing) and 5 (Writing in Academic Contexts).

NOTE ON NONNATIVE SPEAKERS

Since some of your students may have learned British punctuation, you should explain that it differs from American punctuation in its placement of periods and commas with quotation marks. One big difference is that the British use *single* quotation marks for ordinary quotations ('Go,' he said) and *double* quotation marks for quotations *within* quotations ('What does that "Go" mean?' she asked).

33 The Dash, Parentheses, the Slash

In teaching uses of the dash and parentheses, consider the following observation:

> When explanatory matter, comments, or asides not intended to be part of the main thought are dropped into a sentence, they may be set off either by dashes or by parentheses. . . . Parentheses have one slight advantage over dashes in this kind of interpolation: they signal clearly that an interpolation is coming; indeed, when you see the first mark you know for sure that a second lies somewhere down the line. The dash, on the other hand, is used for other purposes . . . and the signal may not be quite so clear, especially if the interpolated matter is long.
>
> —Theodore M. Bernstein

34 Spelling, Hyphen, Apostrophe

CHAPTER OVERVIEW

"I have no respect," said Thomas Jefferson, "for a man who can think of only one way to spell a word." Not many of us would ever have lost Jefferson's respect on this account. Some of the best writers have been notoriously bad spellers. They have struggled with a language in which the sound of a word frequently diverges from the way it is spelled, a language in which the same set of letters may be sounded several different ways in several different words. The letters *ough,* for instance, are sounded four different ways in the words *rough, through, bough,* and *thorough.* No wonder George Bernard Shaw could demonstrate the irrationality of English by spelling fish "ghoti." As Shaw noted, the *f* sound of *gh* in *rough,* the *i* sound of *o* in *women,* and the *sh* sound of *ti* in *diction* will together make a fish— or, he might have said, a very fishy word.

Yet in spite of all these difficulties, careful writers learn to spell their words correctly. They do so because they know that misspelled words can confuse as well as annoy the reader. The difference between *principle* and *principal,* for instance, is a difference in meaning as well as in spelling.

How can your students learn to spell all of their words correctly? The simplest answer is a good dictionary, supplemented by one or more of the methods explained in this chapter.

NOTE ON NONNATIVE SPEAKERS

Some nonnative speakers, particularly those who come from former British colonies, may have received English-language instruction under a British system, and these students will likely use spellings such as *colour, favour, gaol,* and so on. You shouldn't penalize students for such spellings, but do make them aware, if they are not already, of the American spellings.

34.2 LISTING YOUR SPELLING DEMONS

As an in-class exercise, ask your students to list their spelling demons off the tops of their heads. Perhaps have them share these demons in small groups and check each others' spellings against a dictionary. Encourage willing students to share their demons with the class, and share a few of your own as well. Also share with them the example of Shaw's spelling of *fish* as "ghoti" (noted above). This sort of discussion may help decrease some of the anxiety students have about being "bad spellers" and encourage them to look up words more often and more carefully.

You may be surprised to see that we don't include here the old rhyme about *i* before *e:*

Put *i* before *e*
Except after *c*
Or when pronounced *a*
As in *neighbor* and *weigh*

The large number of exceptions *to the exception* make the rule far too confusing to be of any real use. Here's a partial list of words with an *ei* combination that neither follows *c* nor is pronounced *a: either, neither, leisure, seize, weird, atheist,* and *sheik.*

35 *Mechanics*

> Anything that reduces the fussiness of typography makes for easier reading.
> —*The Chicago Manual of Style*

This chapter is an overview of mechanical problems that do not fit neatly into broader categories but about which many students still have questions. Refer your students to this section for guidance on using capital letters, italics or underlining, titles, abbreviations, and numbers.

Research and Writing

4

PART OVERVIEW

The thought of writing a research-based documented essay fills many students with dread. The whole process seems to bristle with complication and mystery. They have to get into the library; learn to use databases and online catalogs; find, read, and evaluate sources; take and organize notes; synthesize their own ideas with those from sources; and learn to document sources properly. In the process they are likely to encounter many unexpected glitches and dead ends. It is no wonder that some students are tempted to buy research papers rather than write them. Indeed, with the growth of the Internet and the increasing number of research papers available for purchase online, plagiarism is a growing concern. Even students who do not intentionally plagiarize often write papers so overburdened with source material that the final product represents little of the students' own thinking.

To keep students from becoming overwhelmed by the scope of a research project, you will need to demystify the process, make it less intimidating. One way to accomplish this is by dividing the process of producing a research paper into a sequence of discrete tasks, with each one building on previously acquired skills. By having students work on the paper in stages, and by giving them feedback at each stage, you will be able to monitor their progress, offer support along the way, and, let's hope, keep them from plagiarizing. The exercises in the following chapters are designed to offer students just such a sequence of assignments. In taking your students through these exercises, you may want to draw parallels between the process of research writing presented here and related topics in Part 1, "The Process of Writing." For instance, chapters 1, 2, and 4 provide a foundation for 36.1 and 36.2. Similarly, the strategies presented in chapter 3 become increasingly important as students acquire and evaluate sources (discussed in 36.3–36.7, 37.3). Chapters 5 and 6 present organizational basics that students will use again in chapter 38, while chapter 10 addresses editorial and proofreading techniques also pertinent to final research-paper preparations discussed in chapter 40. The more students see writing the research paper as a specific application of writing principles they have already learned, the more likely they will be to succeed.

36   *The Research Process*

CHAPTER OVERVIEW

Research-paper assignments vary from course to course, but in most cases, even when specific topics are assigned, students have some leeway in focusing research-based essays. While much of the information here applies to the types of papers most often assigned in composition courses, the skills this chapter aims to build will be useful for students doing research in a range of disciplines (on different disciplines, see chapter 42).

36.1–36.3   WHY DO RESEARCH?, UNDERSTANDING A RESEARCH ASSIGNMENT . . . , *AND* DEVELOPING A RESEARCH STRATEGY

These early sections will help students understand the parameters of research assignments in general and will sharpen their focus on topics. Before students embark on research projects, they often select hot-button topics about which they are sure they will find many books and articles. Some even browse online databases and catalogs before choosing a topic, just to be sure sources are easily available. These sections, however, encourage students to examine their own interests first, with the expectation that they will be more interested in writing research papers about topics in which they are already invested. Once they have chosen suitable topics, students should be more motivated in undertaking the actual research process outlined in the rest of the chapter.

In choosing their topics, students should be encouraged to take risks, to move beyond the comfortable. Here is Toni-Lee Caposella in the February 1991 issue of *College Composition and Communication*:

> The technical complexity of the form [research papers], in addition to the daunting job of finding one's way around a college library in short order,

encourages risk-reduction on all other fronts: students are likely to choose a safe topic, to structure the paper along extremely simple lines, and to espouse a water-tight opinion—unless, of course, it's possible to avoid opinion completely and write a purely "knowledge-telling" paper. Ambrose Bierce refers to this kind of drudge work as "moving tombstones from one graveyard to another," and readers as well as writers are dragged down by the lifeless enterprise that his metaphor so accurately reflects. (75)

To supplement the list of topics generated in exercise 1, you might do a little brainstorming with your class to find out what interests them. What do they really want to know more about? Is it child abuse, China, space travel, AIDS, contraception, battery-powered cars? As students consider possible topics, let them begin to see that writing a research paper is a chance to explore enticing subjects that may not be covered in traditional college courses.

Questions are essential to the process of research, for without them it will very soon lose its momentum. But the questions must be thoughtfully framed. "In ethics," writes George Moore, "as in all other philosophical studies, the difficulties and disagreements, of which history is full, are mainly due to a very simple cause: namely to the attempt to answer questions, without first discovering precisely what question it is you wish to answer."

Students beginning to focus their research on a question or particular questions would do well to ask themselves periodically "who cares?" In *What Makes Writing Good,* Larry Levy quotes Senator William Proxmire: "Many officials, when faced with a request for a research grant, fail to ask themselves the simple question, 'who really cares what the answer to this investigation is?' Sometimes the answer obviously is 'No one.'" If a student cannot honestly say who will care about the results of his or her research on a particular topic, that's a good sign that the topic itself should be radically reconsidered.

NOTE ON NONNATIVE SPEAKERS

Since perceptions of authority and research-topic legitimacy vary from culture to culture, some international students may have trouble understanding what is considered a suitable topic for research or what constitutes a legitimate source according to U.S. academic standards. Furthermore, since the critical thinking required by the research process may call certain authoritative assumptions into question, the very nature of a college research essay may go against some international students' previous academic training, which might have encouraged wide and respectful (that is, unquestioning) acceptance of authority. For these reasons, nonnative speakers may require some extra guidance in topic selection and source evaluation.

36.4–36.5 STARTING WITH GENERAL AND SPECIALIZED REFERENCE WORKS *AND* LOCATING BOOKS AND PERIODICALS

Once students have settled into their topics, they will need to get comfortable in the library. It is important that students become as self-sufficient as possible in using online catalogs and databases. They also need to understand library floor plans and call-numbering systems. For first-term students especially, it may be helpful for you to give a library tour and to set aside class time for general library instruction. Some universities provide formal library instruction or computerized tutorials as a patron service. Reference librarians are wonderful resources as well, and you should introduce them to your students. However, you should also encourage students to work as independently as possible at first and to seek out librarians for specific questions that arise in the research process rather than for general assistance in locating source materials.

Exercise 2 requires students to go to the library and look at specific types of sources. To supplement the exercise, you may want to have a few students report their findings to the class. You could also have students work in teams on related topics, with some team members evaluating a general-encyclopedia article and others evaluating a specialized-encyclopedia article on the same topic. Have team members compare results in the next class period.

Efficient online-catalog and database search skills are essential to the research process. Catalog systems vary from institution to institution, but general search principles always apply. As a supplement to exercises 4 and 5, you may want to have your students brainstorm for additional Library of Congress headings and search terms associated with their topics. This will help them to frame their search from different perspectives and give them a wider range of alternatives to help navigate around dead ends.

36.6 USING THE INTERNET AS A RESEARCH RESOURCE

In addition to library sources, students have come to rely increasingly on the World Wide Web for information. However, it is often difficult to assess the credibility of Web sources. Section 36.6 demonstrates techniques for effective Web searches and provides advice on evaluating sources. If possible, you may want to conduct a class in a computer lab to complete exercises

6–9. Once students have looked at a number of sites, they should be able to come up with some source-evaluation criteria of their own. In discussing exercise 9, you may want to create a list of student-generated evaluation criteria to supplement the questions given under "Evaluating Web Sites."

Notetaking

CHAPTER OVERVIEW

Before students begin taking notes on sources, they need to understand two concepts: source evaluation and plagiarism. To waste time taking notes on what may turn out to be a useless source can be frustrating for any researcher, but this is especially so for beginning college writers. Thus this chapter treats notetaking and source evaluation as related concepts. In addition, since a clear understanding of what constitutes plagiarism will also help students sharpen their notetaking skills, this chapter stresses the importance of correct source acknowledgment and encourages students to include such acknowledgments in the notetaking process.

37.1–37.4 KEEPING TRACK OF YOUR SOURCES, CHOOSING WHICH SOURCES TO CONSULT, EXAMINING AND EVALUATING . . . , *AND* TAKING NOTES

Keeping track of sources is vital to successful research. While filling out note cards on specific books and articles is one means of doing this (37.1 and 37.4), researchers also compile files of photocopies (37.4) and database printouts. Instead of filling out cards for these sources, students may prefer to jot down all the vital information directly on the photocopies and printouts.

As an exercise in source evaluation, you might give your students a checklist developed from criteria presented in 37.2. To gauge their evaluation abilities, have your students complete checklists for two sources and hand them in along with the texts. You might ask them to write a few sentences justifying their choice of sources.

37.6 CONDUCTING AN INTERVIEW

Interviews are valuable but often overlooked research tools. You can do several things to help students plan and conduct interviews. First, circulate to the entire class a list of the topics on which the students are working. Second, invite the students to offer suggestions about possible interviewees. Third, ask the class to draw up a list of questions that could be put to one or more such interviewees for each topic. Finally, if you can, arrange for one of the interviews to take place in front of the class.

37.8 AVOIDING PLAGIARISM

The notetaking stage is the point at which students sometimes confuse their own words with the words of the source from which they are taking notes. When that happens, they can all too easily end up with a paper that fails to acknowledge all of its sources clearly—or in other words, that contains plagiarized material. So it's crucial for them to learn to cite the source of every single note they take, using the author's last name, title word, and page for positive identification of each. If they get into the habit of recording these three bits of information with every note, they will know exactly where each note came from when they write their papers. In teaching 37.8, you might refer students back to the examples of source citation in 37.1 and 37.4. Encourage them to make such acknowledgments a regular part of the notetaking process.

Since plagiarism is perhaps the single biggest spectre threatening the whole project of writing a research paper, you will doubtless want to spend some class time discussing it. You might begin by inviting students to talk candidly about their attitudes toward it. Aside from the danger of being caught, you might ask, is there any reason to avoid plagiarism? You might even admit that a case can be made for the answer *no*. If I take from your desk drawer the novel on which you have been slaving for ten years and sell it as my own for a million dollar advance, that is quite obviously stealing. But if I claim some of your published words in an essay that will be read only by my teacher, what harm have I done to you?

In this case, the answer has to focus not on the relation between the student and the author being plagiarized, but on the relation between the student and the teacher, and the mutual trust it presupposes. Just as students trust their teachers to grade them fairly for the work they do, teachers must be able to trust their students to *do* the work they claim as their own. Plagiarism sabotages that trust and thus poisons the relation between student and teacher.

Having established that point as well as you can, you can reinforce it by explaining the penalties for plagiarism at your institution. You might also invite questions about the examples of plagiarism given here. Then you could assign exercise 3 to be done in class, with discussion immediately following. Some biographical information might be helpful to you during the discussion: Carl Gustav Jung (1875–1961) was a Swiss psychiatrist whose work on the human subconscious first supported and then broke dramatically from the theories of Sigmund Freud. After a close friendship of eight years, Jung and Freud eventually separated bitterly as Jung moved away from Freud's emphasis on repression and early childhood experience. Jung formulated his own vision of psychological wholeness—a vision that sees no clear distinction between psychology and spirituality.

To supplement the exercise, you might ask students to submit the following items from their work in progress: (1) a passage including one or more quoted sentences, (2) a passage including quoted phrases, (3) a passage including a paraphrase of source material, (4) a passage including a summary of source material. Each passage should be accompanied by a photocopy of the page or pages from which material has been quoted, summarized, or paraphrased; the material thus used should be underlined or highlighted on the photocopy; and all source material used in any way should be underlined in the student's passage. A selection of your students' responses to this exercise would make very good material for class discussion of how to avoid plagiarism.

NOTE ON NONNATIVE SPEAKERS

Some international students have great trouble understanding why they must acknowledge source material that they have summarized or paraphrased. Because words seem to them inseparable from what the words express, they believe that if you change the words of a source, you change its ideas; and if the words are yours, so are the ideas. It is very hard to get such students to realize that this concept of what constitutes legitimate appropriation is culture-specific rather than universal. But you might ask such students whether they believe that *translators* have the right to claim as their own whatever *they* put into their own words. However they may answer that question, international students sometimes use source material verbatim without acknowledgment because, in effect, they have been trained to do so.

In many cases, they have been taught in their home countries to memorize well-phrased sentences and use them in their writing. They believe that using another's words in this way—even without acknowledging the source—is a form of homage. They may also have been taught to use English sentences in their writing to improve their English. Some Eastern Europeans, for example, have said—in no uncertain terms—that their teachers told them to plagiarize, to appropriate English sentences so as to make their writing internationally accessible and absolutely clear.

Obviously, students taught in this way will find it difficult to unlearn their ideas about plagiarism. But they must be made to realize what the rules against plagiarism are in the United States and in English-speaking countries generally—not just in college.

38 Writing the Research Paper

CHAPTER OVERVIEW

Writing a research paper offers students a chance to apply the composing techniques discussed in Part 1 to a more formal academic discourse. Much of the material presented here on thesis formulation, branching, and outlining will be familiar to your students. In presenting the research paper assignment, you might want to remind your students that the basic composing skills they are striving to master are the foundation for even the longest and most heavily documented academic essays.

38.1 FORMULATING YOUR THESIS

If you are supervising the progress of your students as they work on their research papers, you will probably ask each student to submit a working statement of thesis and an outline. This is also an ideal time to schedule individual conferences, since now is the stage at which the student's notes must be organized and arranged to make a coherent argument.

The first thing to discuss is the student's thesis. It will usually tell you a great deal about how well the student understands the topic and how well focused the argument of the paper is likely to be.

Compare, for instance, these two statements about the Native American Graves Protection and Repatriation Act:

> The Repatriation Act causes a lot of problems for scientific researchers.

> The Native American Graves Protection and Repatriation Act has produced conflict stalemate when parties have insisted on furthering only their own interests and conflict resolution when each party has been willing to respect the interests of the others.

The first sentence, really no more than a statement of topic, is the sort of thing students often produce when asked for a thesis. The second, the product of considerable thought and some revision, makes the kind of contention that can spearhead an argument. The question, then, is how to help a student move from one kind of statement to another.

There are two ways of doing so—by class discussion or individual conference. If you choose class discussion, you could invite students to talk about one or two of the theses submitted, and you might even duplicate for distribution beforehand the notes that each author has compiled. Students could then be invited to consider each proposed thesis in light of the material that will be used to support it.

Since you will probably not have time for class discussion of every thesis submitted, you may find individual conferences a more effective way to sharpen each thesis. If students bring to the conference all of their notes as well as the thesis itself, you can help them draw from their notes what they need to make the thesis effective. Also, you might encourage them to look back at chapters 4 and 7, which talk in some detail about developing a strong thesis and about the importance of such a thesis to any argument.

Along with a working statement of thesis, you will probably wish to see an outline. Three different kinds are illustrated here, ranging from least formal (the branching diagram) to most formal (the sentence outline). You can require just one kind, or let students choose which kind, or ask them to do more than one, as shown here, with revisions made in each successive version. In any case, if a student brings to the individual conference an outline of any kind along with a set of notes and a statement of thesis, you can quickly see how well the student has planned the paper and what further guidance he or she may need.

39 *Documenting the Research Paper*

CHAPTER OVERVIEW

This chapter focuses on the MLA parenthetical style, which is widely used in many of the general elective humanities courses most colleges and universities require. Parenthetical citing has real advantages. It spares both you and your students the trouble of turning back and forth from text to documentary notes, and it simplifies the process of documentation by requiring full citation of each source just once—in the Works Cited list at the end of the paper.

While MLA style is quite widely used, students need to be aware that different disciplines use different documentation styles. For this reason, chapter 42 presents material on the styles of the American Psychological Association (APA), the Council of Biology (now Council of Science) Editors (CBE), and *The Chicago Manual of Style (CMS)*.

39.1 THE MLA PARENTHETICAL STYLE: BASIC PROCEDURES

When presenting MLA style, be sure to remind students that parenthetical references alone do not complete the job of documenting sources. On occasion, a student may have the misguided impression that a Works Cited page is optional so long as source use is indicated within the text of the paper. To avoid this circumstance, you may want to give your students a check-off list for documentation tasks and include criteria for both parenthetical citations and a Works Cited page. Additionally, require Works Cited pages to be submitted along with any exploratory drafts or outlines.

It is worth stressing to your students that all authors of a book or article must be listed on the Works Cited page. "Et al." is both practical and appropriate for parenthetical citing within the text, but professional courtesy dictates that the name of every author appear in the full citation at the end of the paper.

Preparing the Final Copy of the Research Paper 40

40.1 BASIC PROCEDURES

While computers and word-processing programs have greatly simplified the task of typing a paper according to the proper format, students often need instruction on how to set software specifications. In giving paper assignments, you should be specific about your expectations regarding such things as font size and style, line spacing, margins, page numbering, running heads, and the like. You may also want to spend a portion of a class period in a computer lab to demonstrate how to change software settings.

40.2 SAMPLE RESEARCH PAPER WITH MLA PARENTHETICAL STYLE

The sample paper included in this chapter should provide some key points for discussion of final drafts. In addition to meeting basic specifications with regard to appearance, "Conflict Stalemate and Conflict Resolutions: Implementing the Native American Graves and Repatriation Act" demonstrates the writer's commitment to a thoughtful analysis of a complex issue. As you discuss the paper with your students, be sure to point out that the thesis doesn't appear until page three. Students who are accustomed to putting the thesis at the beginning of the opening paragraph may be surprised by this. Ask your students to consider why the writer made this choice. You may need to prompt them to think about the likeliness of a typical reader's familiarity with the topic and the writer's need to provide background before taking a stance on the issue.

As your students continue their analysis of the paper, ask them to recount the writer's points in particular paragraphs and to locate supporting evidence for those points. To further engage them, you might have your students summarize the positions of the parties involved and state where their sympathies lie and why. Then ask them to consider how their own position on the subject compares to the writer's.

5 Writing in Academic Contexts

41 Writing about Literature

CHAPTER OVERVIEW

You will quickly perceive that the approach to the interpretation of literature in this chapter is largely based on what is known as "New Criticism." The study of literary form is a good way to *begin* the study of literature on a college level, but the opening paragraph here notes various other methods of analyzing literary works, and 41.12 briefly shows how literature can be linked to biography and history.

For a brief and highly readable—but also highly polemical—survey of critical approaches to literature, see Eagleton, Terry. *Literary Theory: An Introduction,* 2nd ed. Minneapolis: U of Minnesota P, 1996. Outspokenly Marxist, Eagleton disparages New Criticism and any other critical approach that privileges "the work itself" over the socioeconomic conditions that surrounded—and inevitably influenced—its production.

41.1 THE LITERARY WORK AS A CREATED WORLD

Literature was not born the day when a boy crying "wolf, wolf" came running out of the neanderthal valley with a big gray wolf at his heels: literature was born on the day when a boy came crying "wolf, wolf" and there was no wolf behind him. —Vladimir Nabokov

In linguistics, the nature of the signified has given rise to discussions which have centered chiefly on its degree of "reality"; all agree, however, on emphasizing the fact that the signified is not "a thing" but a mental representation of the "thing." —Roland Barthes

William Blake (1757–1827) was an English Romantic poet and artist whose work was little known in his own time but has since been recognized as both original and extraordinary. "Infant Sorrow" is one of the *Songs of Experience,* a set of illuminated (engraved and hand-colored) poems that Blake first issued in 1794. As Blake issued it, the poem is a work of composite art that integrates text and design. Ideally, therefore, the text of the poem should be read and studied in relation to its design as well as in relation to the other *Songs of Experience* and the *Songs of Innocence* (1789), especially "Infant Joy." If you have access to a facsimile of either of these volumes, or even a reproduction of an illuminated page from one of them, you might give your students a glimpse of Blake's composite art and invite them to talk about it. Among other things, you might ask them to consider why the study of literature—and the acquisition of literacy itself—is typically divorced from the experience of pictures.

For an additional example of Walt Whitman's explicit involvement of his reader in the fabric of his poems, see lines 33–37 of "Song of Myself":

> Stop this day and night with me and you shall possess the origin of all poems,
> You shall possess the good of the earth and sun, (there are millions of suns left,)
> You shall no longer take things at second or third hand, nor look through the eyes of the dead, nor feed on the spectres in books,
> You shall not look through my eyes either, nor take things from me,
> You shall listen to all sides and filter them from your self.

NOTE ON NONNATIVE SPEAKERS

International students generally have great trouble writing in English about British and American literature because they don't know enough about its cultural background and because literary language is semantically denser than most nonfiction prose. Of course you may well respond that the same could be said of American students, who are all too often woefully ignorant of the cultural context surrounding a literary work and ill-equipped to catch the complexities of its meaning. But these familiar difficulties are compounded for international students.

Before you discuss literary interpretation with the class as a whole, therefore, you might talk individually with your international students to see what literature they have read in their own languages, what they are accustomed to look for in a literary work, and what they have written about literature.

41.2 LITERARY GENRE: POETRY, FICTION, DRAMA

I could no more define poetry than a terrier can define a rat.
—A. E. Houseman

Poetry is the spontaneous overflow of powerful feeling; it takes its origin from emotion recollected in tranquillity.   —William Wordsworth

Eloquence is heard; poetry is overheard.   —John Stuart Mill

From our quarrel with others we make rhetoric; we make poetry from our quarrel with ourselves.   —W. B. Yeats

I hear ghostly Academics in Limbo screeching about form.
—Allen Ginsberg

Among the many helpful academic screechings about form are Fussel, Paul. *Poetic Meter and Poetic Form* (1965) and Hollander, John. *Rhyme's Reason* (1981; enl. 1989). Both focus usefully on the *rationale* of rhyme, verse, and meter: on what they contribute to the total meaning and effect of a poem.

In teaching the fiction section here, you might find it helpful to have some biographical information on William Faulkner. Faulkner (1897–1962), who was born and spent much of his life in Mississippi, focused his fiction on the anguish and deterioration of the South after the Civil War. In short stories and in novels such as *The Sound and the Fury* (1929), he used the imaginary Yoknapatawpha County as a microcosm of southern life. In 1949 he was awarded the Nobel Prize for literature.

41.3 NOTING SIGNIFICANT DETAIL

In teaching 41.3, you may want to provide your students with some biographical information on Meridel Le Sueur. Born in Iowa in 1900, Le Sueur was strongly influenced by her socialist parents, prairie populists, and Marxists such as Emma Goldman. During the Great Depression, the stories and articles she wrote for largely left-wing periodicals dramatized the quietly heroic lives of midwestern women and the struggles of working people. After a collection of her writings appeared in 1940 under the title *Salute to Spring*, her reputation languished, but it was revived—especially among feminist critics—with the 1978 publication of her novel *The Girl* (written in 1939, and quite distinct from "The Girl"). Le Sueur died in 1996. For a good selection of her work, together with a detailed and informative discussion of it, see *Ripening: Selected Work, 1927–1980,* ed. Elaine Hedges (1982).

41.4 RECORDING YOUR PERSONAL REACTIONS

Teachers of literature courses often ask students to select a brief passage from the text assigned for a particular day and to write one to two pages of informal commentary on it. Generally they don't grade the commentaries; they simply read and make comments on them, focusing on what students have to say rather than on niceties of form. On average it takes about five minutes to read and comment on each one, so these comments aren't nearly as time-consuming as an ordinary stack of papers. Other advantages: (1) they ensure that *every* student in the class will have something to say about the assigned text; (2) assigned regularly, they continually prompt students to articulate their *experience* of literature; (3) they sometimes prompt students to find truly significant detail; (4) they show what students are discovering on their own, before classroom discussion of a text; (5) they enable each student to build up a reservoir of personal insights for use in preparing a paper.

41.5 CHOOSING AND REFINING YOUR TOPIC

Choosing a practicable topic on a work of literature is something many students find hard—so hard that they often want you to do it for them. ("I can't think what to write about" is an all too familiar refrain.) A good topic combines specificity, density of suggestion, and relevance to the general theme or major issues of the work in question. If your students are regularly writing commentaries on the works assigned, urge them to look again at the passages they originally selected for analysis. Why, you might ask them occasionally, did you choose this particular passage? What made it provocative? Why did the passage become—if only for the time being—your personal handle on the text? Questions like these can lead the students to discover and formulate topics for themselves, which is often better than receiving them ready-made from the teacher.

One way to go to work is to read your author once or twice over having an eye out for anything that occurs to you as you read whether appreciative contradictory corroborative or *parallel* (can't spell). There should be more or less of a jumble in your head or on your note paper after the first time and even after the second. Much that you will think of in connection will come to nothing and be wasted. But some of it ought to go together under one idea. . . . One idea and a few subordinate ideas—it's to have those happen to you as you read and catch them—not let them escape you in your direct interest in your author. The sidelong glance is what you depend on. You look at your author but you keep the tail of your eye on what is happening over and above your author in your own mind and nature.

—Robert Frost, from a letter of 1919 to his daughter Lesley,
then a sophomore at Barnard College

41.6 CONSULTING SECONDARY SOURCES

For various reasons, you may prefer not to require any secondary sources on a short critical paper: you don't want to burden students yet with the complications of research, you want to let them develop their own ideas unencumbered by the weight of established critical authority, and so on. But a provocative critical essay can be a real stimulus for students—especially if you take the time to discuss it with them in class.

After first discussing the work it concerns, you might assign a critical essay and ask students to select a passage from it for a page or two of informal commentary. In writing such commentaries, they would inevitably begin to develop the habit of thinking critically about literature. At the same time, they would be preparing themselves for what should be a highly productive class discussion.

41.7 FORMULATING A THESIS

Along with choosing a practicable topic, formulating an effective thesis about a work of literature is something many students find particularly tough. You might take some class time to discuss the difference between stating a fact, a topic, and a thesis, and then have your students write out—in class—an example of each that is based on any literary work you have been reading. When read aloud, the results of this in-class assignment could become a springboard for further discussion.

41.8 SUMMARIZING AND INTERPRETING: KNOWING THE DIFFERENCE

You can reinforce the point of this section by inviting students to talk about the significant details (41.3) they have discovered in their reading. If you have them write informal commentaries on passages they select, they should already have some significant details on paper. But in any case, to show them how to gather evidence for a critical hypothesis, you can do as follows: (1) starting with a significant detail, ask what makes it significant—that is, what generalization about major issues of the work can be drawn from it; (2) ask the class to furnish other details from the work that could be used to support this generalization; (3) write the generalization and list the details on the board; (4) as an in-class assignment, have each student write a paragraph that links the generalization to the supporting details.

41.9 DEVELOPING YOUR INTERPRETATION: QUOTING AND CITING SOURCES

This very brief guide to the management of literary and critical sources is based on the MLA method of parenthetical citation. More detailed guidance can be found in chapter 39. If you really want to simplify citation for your students, just tell them to give the author's last name and the page number in parentheses for *every* reference to a prose work. A little redundancy in the mentioning of authors' names may be a small price to pay for a system of citation that is both easy to learn and unequivocally clear.

On Meridel Le Sueur, see 41.3 above and in the book itself. The story raises questions that the essay in 41.10 doesn't consider: Why, for instance, should the woman feel that she's rejecting life itself just because she rejects the sexual advances of a hitchhiker? Why must the woman be a "girl" caught in perpetual immaturity? Why is she trapped in the stereotypical role of the timid, dry, schoolteaching spinster? Why is she allowed no escape from this role while the sensuous male oaf—another stereotype—momentarily escapes his oafishness when he generously offers her the melon?

Some answers to these questions appear in 41.12, which briefly considers how the story can be read in its biographical context. But you may well opt to pursue these questions with your class if you decide to teach the story itself.

41.10 SAMPLE ESSAY ON A SHORT STORY: NO SECONDARY SOURCES

The introductory paragraph leads up to the thesis by summarizing the story. You might point out that this technique is especially useful in introducing an essay on a literary work that is not widely known, such as "The Girl." But even when writing on works that *are* widely known, students need to learn that they should establish a *context* for their interpretations, that they should situate the reader in the story before explaining just what line of questioning or interpretation they plan to pursue.

Note the *But* marking the shift from the summary to the statement of thesis in the final sentence. Invite students to say what else distinguishes the final sentence from those that have come before it.

Ask students to talk about the opening sentence of each paragraph after the first. What sort of expectations, for instance, does the first sentence of paragraph 2 generate? Does the paragraph satisfy those expectations? If so, how? You can also ask students to talk about how each opening sentence makes a *transition* from one paragraph to another. Note, for instance, the repeated use of the key term *order*, which is picked up from the thesis and used to open both paragraphs 2 and 3. Why is this term repeated? How is it developed? Discussion of these questions can help students to grasp some basic principles of organization.

Arturo identifies two things in this story as symbolic: the sun-baked land, which is said to symbolize the sexual appeal of the human body (pars. 5 and 6), and the melon, which is said to symbolize the pleasure that the woman has refused (par. 7). Invite your students to talk about how the student demonstrates that the story itself generates these symbolic meanings. How do we know, for instance, that the sun-baked land symbolizes sexuality? How do we know what the melon means? To pursue these questions fully, you would of course need to discuss with your students the story itself, but even without the story, you can use this paper to help them see how the words of a story—or any literary text—*guide* the reader to see what a particular image symbolizes or "means."

You might take a little time to discuss the style of Arturo's sentences. In the third sentence of paragraph 5, for instance, he uses a compound active verb *(repel and arouse)* to explain the complex effect of the landscape on the woman, and in the next sentence he uses parallel structure *(At first appalled . . . gradually entranced)* to develop his point about this complex effect. Sentences like these help to develop his argument about the inner conflicts that the woman feels.

This paper offers just one block quotation. The other quotations are all short enough to fit within the student's own text, and many consist of no more than a word or phrase. Invite students to talk about this method of quoting. If it's more effective than a parade of block quotations, ask them to say why. More precisely, why is it better to quote just one or two words (such as *glad* and *messy* in the student's third paragraph) rather than a passage of several sentences? This discussion may help to make two points about the value of keeping quotations short: (1) short quotations highlight significant details in a text, and (2) they allow plenty of room for the student critic's own commentary. If you have access to a copy of "The Girl," you might let your students see the story itself—so that they can see more clearly just how and why Arturo has chosen his quotations.

Finally, you might find it helpful to have some background information on repression:

> Strictly speaking, [repression] is an operation whereby the subject attempts to repel, or confine to the unconscious, representations (thoughts, images, memories) which are bound to an instinct. Repression occurs when to satisfy an instinct—though likely to be pleasurable in itself—would incur the risk of provoking displeasure because of other requirements.
> —J. LaPlanche and J.-B. Pontalis, *The Language of Psycho-Analysis* (New York: Norton, 1973) 390

As "the cornerstone on which the whole structure of psycho-analysis rests" (Freud, qtd. LaPlanche and Pontalis, p. 392), the concept of repression has generated a good deal of rather complicated technical discussion. But the general idea of repression—the idea that we try not to think about instincts and urges that threaten our self-control or "public" respectability—is not difficult to grasp. The student author of this paper learned a little about it from his English teacher, but he could have acquired a working knowledge of it by simply looking up the word in a good dictionary. Here, for instance, is how *The American Heritage Dictionary* defines it: "The unconscious exclusion of painful impulses, desires, or fears from the conscious mind."

41.11 SAMPLE ESSAY ON A POEM: SECONDARY SOURCES USED

Like the essay on "The Girl" (41.10), this one can be used to show what the first sentence of a paragraph can do to mark a transition, forecast a new argumentative point, or both. Note especially how the opening sentence of each paragraph after the first picks up a key term or key idea from the end of the paragraph before. Also note the three-step method of the introductory paragraph: (1) brief summary of what happens in the poem; (2) statement of topic—the conflict between male and female business; (3) statement of thesis in the final sentence.

Ask students to say how this paper treats the *form* of the poem—more precisely its rhyme scheme. With a little help, they should be able to see that in both the second paragraph and the last one, Cirri considers what the rhymes of this poem contribute to its meaning and effect. If they see how she explains the function of the rhymes, they can begin to see how to integrate the analysis of formal features in a poem with the analysis of its meaning.

You might ask your students to discuss Cirri's method of quoting, with just two indented quotations and all the others short enough to fit within the student's own text. This time they can compare the essay *on* the poem with the poem itself to see just how Cirri has made her selections—and why. Note in particular the focus on key words such as *pocketbook* and *pot* in paragraph 2. And note how paragraph 9 reaffirms Cirri's thesis and clinches it by quoting again the crucial words about "business."

You can also ask them to say just where and how Cirri has used her secondary sources. In paragraph 4, for instance, she uses a point made by Don Lee to buttress her own point. But in the first paragraph, she uses her secondary source differently. With a little discussion, your students may see that Cirri's thesis doesn't just hang from the point made by Maria Mootry. On the contrary, using a *But* to signal a change in direction, Cirri turns the critic's point around to state her *own* main point. Some discussion of her strategy here may help students realize that they can and should feel free to diverge from the critics they cite, to develop their own interpretation.

Finally, you might find it helpful to have some biographical information on Gwendolyn Brooks. Born in Topeka, Kansas, in 1917, Brooks grew up in Chicago, where she has lived all her life. In addition to *Maud Martha* (1953), a novella, she has published many books of poetry, including *A Street in Bronzeville* (1945), *Annie Allen* (1949), *The Bean Eaters* (1960), which includes "Mrs. Small," and *In the Mecca* (1968). In 1949 she became the first black woman ever to win a Pulitzer Prize for poetry.

41.12 LINKING LITERATURE TO HISTORY

It takes a great deal of history to produce a little literature.

—Henry James

This section offers a brief glimpse at an important alternative to the New Critical concentration on the formal properties of a literary text. Whereas the exponents of New Criticism declared their independence of biography and history, later generations of critics reasserted the historical significance of literature in terms of its capacity to reflect, support, or challenge the dominant culture and political power of its time. For some examples of this critical approach, see the collection of essays titled *The New Historicism,* ed. H. Aram Veeser (1989).

Though "The Girl" seems to depart from Meridel Le Sueur's populist writing of the 1930s, it delivers the kind of political message conveyed by much of her other work. "Like the schoolteacher here," says Elaine Hedges, "Le Sueur's sexually repressed women are usually middle-class; and 'intellectual' for Le Sueur is invariably a pejorative term. Working-class women, on the other hand, exhibit healthy sexual appetites. Despite such over-simplification, however, 'The Girl' effectively conveys Le Sueur's sense of the importance of living within the body and, for women especially, of accepting their own sexual feelings without the guilt or denial that American middle-class culture has traditionally imposed on them" (13).

Writing and Research in Different Disciplines

42

CHAPTER OVERVIEW

Before taking up with your students the various examples of writing in specified disciplines, you may want to discuss with them the very notion of what constitutes a discipline as such. Traditionally, academic disciplines have been regarded as fields defined by their *subject matter:* botany deals with plants, zoology with animals, astronomy with stars, psychology with the mind, and so on. But the work of critics such as Michel Foucault has shifted the focus to *language.* Foucault defines the various sciences as kinds of discourse resulting from what he calls "discursive formation." Every branch of scientific knowledge, he argues, is the product of a historically definable process, beginning with "the moment at which a single system for the formation of statements is put into operation" and "culminating in formalization, when a particular scientific discourse can define the axioms it needs, the elements it uses, and the propositional structures it recognizes as legitimate" *(The Archaeology of Knowledge* [1972] 186—87). In other words, every discipline—right across the spectrum of arts and sciences—can be regarded as the specialized *language* of a discourse community, a particular way of talking and writing adopted by those who share certain beliefs, assumptions, and practices.

42.1 THREE DISCIPLINES ILLUSTRATED: SPECIALISTS WRITING FOR SPECIALISTS

Some students believe that writing is something required only in English courses, and to support this belief, they may be able to cite professors in other disciplines who do not assign papers. But these students should know two things: (1) anyone who hopes to become an established specialist in a particular field must know how to write in that field, and (2) writing about a particular field is one of the best ways to learn about it and test one's understanding of it.

Wayne Booth's approach to fiction is explicitly and emphatically rhetorical. He argues that a work of fiction persuades us to accept the judgment of what he calls its "implied author." Section 42.2 touches on the historicist approach to fiction, which is treated more fully in 41.12.

Lawrence L. Shornack's essay appeared in the Autumn 1987 *International Social Science Review,* and its account of the "conjugal family" of "today" seems quite dated. Does Shornack's theory of *the* family explain the structure of the single-parent family, an increasingly common phenomenon of our time? You might also invite students to consider whether writing in the sciences or social sciences ages faster than writing in the humanities. Does Booth's passage, for instance, seem as dated now as Shornack's does?

To help your students to see how and why writing in the social and natural sciences differs from writing in the humanities, you could ask one of your colleagues in the sciences to visit the class and explain—preferably with the aid of some examples—what he or she regards as a good lab report or research paper on a scientific subject.

42.2 ASKING THE QUESTION THAT FITS YOUR DISCIPLINE

After arriving at an interpretation of a problem in *Wuthering Heights,* we do not discard the novel or cease to reinterpret it in the classroom and in professional articles; it cannot be reduced to a theory in the way that psychologist's data can be. So one cause of the difference between problem solving in literary interpretation and science lies in the value we place upon our initial data—literature itself.

If scientific (and social science) research problems are defined in ways that are publically discernible, finite in number, communally worked upon, and generalizable, as I have claimed, it should be clear that literary problems are not distinguished by any of those traits.

—Susan Peck MacDonald

Though the problems addressed in humanistic writing are—as MacDonald suggests above—fundamentally different from those addressed in articles by scientists and social scientists, an effective essay in the humanities is always generated by some sort of problem or question. And the more incisively the question is framed, the better the essay is likely to be. You can help your students by urging them to formulate and refine the questions they hope to answer in the course of their research.

You may want to point out that a fully contextualized approach to literature does more than consider how a particular literary work reflects the influence of the author's life, of historical events, or of intellectual developments in the author's time. Moving beyond this traditional way of connecting literature to history, new historicist critics situate the literary work within a whole network of cultural forces, where it is seen to play a vital part in *shaping* the ideology of a period, not just reflecting it. Harriet Beecher Stowe's *Uncle Tom's Cabin* (1852), for instance, fueled the fires of abolitionism in the years just before the Civil War.

42.5, 42.7, 42.9 DOCUMENTING SOURCES IN THE HUMANITIES, IN THE SOCIAL SCIENCES, *AND* IN THE SCIENCES

MLA documentation style is discussed at length in chapter 39. This chapter discusses systems established by the *Chicago Manual of Style (CMS)* in 42.5, the American Psychological Association (APA) in 42.7, and the Council of Biology Editors (now Science Editors, though the system is still called CBE) in 42.9. Though you may not have time to teach the intricacies of each documentation system, make your students aware that even though MLA style is suitable for many types of papers, other professors, particularly in upper-division specialty courses, will likely require familiarity with a discipline-specific style. As an exercise, you may want to have students consult a professional journal in another discipline to see what style is used. Or you may want to bring a selection of journals to class and have students work in groups to figure out which styles are preferred in particular disciplines.

6

Writing in Nonacademic Contexts

43 Writing in the World of Work

Chances are very good that some of your students will have immediate need for the skills explained and illustrated here, especially résumé writing and business correspondence. In teaching this chapter, remind your students that rhetorical concerns addressed in Part 1 need to be considered in nonacademic writing as well. For instance, cover letters offer good opportunities to discuss diction, tone, and the expectations of the reader.

As an imaginative exercise, you might have your students submit résumés and cover letters reflecting what they anticipate their credentials, experience, and goals will be upon graduation from college. (Students who have actual résumés in progress can submit those instead.) With the students' permission, share selected résumés and cover letters with the class. Have students work in "recruiting teams" to select the best résumés and require them to justify their choices.

44 Writing for Public Service

Many students are active members of nonprofit and community groups, service organizations, sororities, fraternities, alumni groups, parent organizations, sports clubs, and so on. This chapter aims to get students thinking about the communicative needs of such groups and how they as writers can help fulfill those needs.

As a means of illustrating the sort of writing done by and for members of community groups, you might ask students who belong to such groups (campus-based or otherwise) to bring in sample brochures, mission statements, bylaws, rules of play, and the like to share with the class. You might also share materials from one of your own community groups. Spend some time analyzing the content of, design of, and audience for selected items. As an alternative to an essay assignment, you might encourage your students to prepare written materials for a community group. Refer students back to chapter 12, on document design, and chapter 8, on style.

Grant Writing for Nonprofit Groups 45

Many people, including students, don't realize how they benefit, either directly or indirectly, from the resources of nonprofit groups. To increase awareness in the classroom, you might invite a member of a local nonprofit group to speak to the class about the group's work and funding sources. You also might show the class a sample grant application and discuss strategies a writer could use to complete specific sections. Ask students if they have applied for individual grants to fund their studies; then compare the demands of grant writing for individual projects and grant writing for community groups. As a research exercise, you might have students work in teams as they select a nonprofit group or an individual project, investigate funding sources, and prepare a short report about funding prospects.

Answers to the Exercises

Following are answers to all exercises with entries that have just one correct answer or a limited set of correct answers. Open-ended exercises, such as those in composing, are generally marked "No sample answers." The label "Sample Answers" means that other answers may also be acceptable.

PART 1   THE PROCESS OF WRITING

1.   BUILDING RHETORICAL POWER

EXERCISE: No sample answers.

2.   PREPARING TO WRITE

EXERCISES 1–2: No sample answers.

3.   STRATEGIES FOR ACTIVE WRITING AND READING

EXERCISES 1–2: No sample answers.

Exercise 3, Sample Answers

1. The history of Florida is measured in freezes.

2. A centenarian born in 1879 has seen, in the years of his own life, scientific and technological advances more sweeping and radical than those that took place in all the accumulated past.

Exercise 4, Sample Answers

1. The main point (stated in sentences 1 and 2) is that the exploration of North America was largely prompted by the desire to make money from selling beaver fur.

2. The supporting points appear in sentences 3–7.

3. Strictly speaking, the point made in sentence 7 is not relevant to the main point, since this sentence makes no connection between exploration and the killing of beavers in the 1840s. (Sentence 5 makes no reference to exploration either, but the following sentence links exploration to the facts stated in sentence 5.)

4. Sentences 4, 5, and 7 are clearly statements of fact. Sentence 3 might be taken as opinion, since resolving the question of just what was "the effective government of most of Canada" during a certain period requires some exercise of judgment. Also, sentence 6 implies an opinion. With the words "It's no wonder . . . ," it implies that the profitability of beaver trapping (specified in sentence 5) is what prompted the exploration of watersheds in the 1820s.

EXERCISE 5: No sample answers.

Exercise 6, Sample Answers

1. Most people who care about the English language would say that it's in trouble, but that we can't do anything to improve it.

2. A good urban neighborhood allows its people to have the privacy they need and yet also gives them the contact, the enjoyment, and the help they want from other people.

EXERCISES 7–9: No sample answers.

4. EXPLORATORY DRAFTING AND THESIS STATEMENTS

EXERCISES 1–3: No sample answers.

5. PLANNING AND ORGANIZING YOUR TEXT

EXERCISES 1–9: No sample answers.

6. DEVELOPING YOUR TEXT

EXERCISES 1–10: No sample answers.

Exercise 11, Sample Answers

1. Everything that happens in hockey happens fast.

2. All-or-none descriptions do not apply to things that fall in between categories, such as a half-eaten apple or the color gray.

EXERCISES 12–23: No sample answers.

7. WRITING PARAGRAPHS

Exercise 1, Sample Answer

The first paragraph can be ended after *repulsions* (line 8); its main point is that the study of human beings in time can be exhausting. The second paragraph can be ended after *planet* (line 15); its main point is that the writer is fascinated by a particular skull. The main point of the third paragraph is that the ancient skull anticipates the humans of the future.

Exercise 2, Sample Answer

The weekend rolls around, and most of us want to spend time with those dear to us. Our wallets tell us that we have ten bucks for an outing with the family. No problem—we can pack a lunch and head for the Smoky Mountain National Park. The ten dollars goes in the gas tank, and away we go for hiking, fishing, biking, or just sightseeing.

Unfortunately, this type of family recreation may become a fond but distant memory as our government considers passing a bill requiring entrance fees for admittance to the park. If this bill is passed, one of our greatest natural resources will be in danger. Families who frequent the park may no longer be able to afford it, while those who can pay to enter may decide that they want more for their money.

This, in turn, could cause more commercial development of the land inside the park. How long will it be before we can't tell the difference between a national park and an amusement park?

Exercise 3, Sample Answer

College made me my own parent.

EXERCISES 4–6: No sample answers.

Exercise 7, Sample Answers

1. Begin sentence 2 with *But.*

2. Begin sentence 4 with *As a result.*

3. Begin sentence 3 with *Likewise.*

4. Begin sentence 2 with *Today.*

Exercise 8, Sample Answer

My mother was a good mother who guided me in a very practical way. First of all, she made sure I learned how to cook, sew, and take care of a house. She also taught me how to handle money. Thanks to her, I learned to save and keep my debts under control. Finally, because she believed in the value of a good education, she helped me decide to work for a college degree.

Exercise 9, Sample Answer

Motion pictures originated from the discovery of the principle known as the persistence of vision. According to this principle, which was announced in 1824 by a British scholar named Peter Mark Roget, the human eye retains an image for a fraction of a second longer than the image is present. The announcement of this principle led scientists in the United States and Great Britain to test and prove it by various devices. One of these was a toy known as a zoetrope, a cylinder covered with images that merged into a single picture when the cylinder was spun. Another device was a small book of drawings that seemed to move when flipped by the thumb. These simple applications of Roget's principle eventually led to the development of the motion picture, which is actually a rapid succession of still pictures put together by the persistence of vision in the eye.

Exercise 10, Sample Answers

1. Janet Heller uses "But" to open the first sentence of the second paragraph.

2. In Price's book the second paragraph begins, "Far off as it was, still we dreaded each waking hour that the war might arrive on us." The third paragraph begins, "But of course we were safe. Our elders said that daily."

8.   STYLE: USING A COMMUNITY'S LANGUAGE

EXERCISE 1–2: No sample answers.

Exercise 3, Sample Answer

Since coming down from the trees, humans have faced the problem of survival, not as individuals but as members of social groups. Humankind's continued existence is testimony to the fact that people have succeeded in solving the problem; but the continued existence of want and misery, even in the richest of nations, is evidence that the solution has been, at best, a partial one.

EXERCISE 4: No sample answers.

Answers to the Exercises

Exercise 5, Sample Answers

In line 2 change *inhabited a house* to *lived*.
In line 5 change tresses to hair.
In line 7 change *more beneficial* to *better*.
In line 9 change *It is my considered opinion* to *I think*.
In line 12 change *mitts* to *hands*.
In line 13 change *present a request* to *ask*.
In lines 19–20 change *effrontery* to *gall, cheek,* or *nerve* and change *submit a bill for a monetary sum in excess of* to *charge more than*.

Exercise 6, Answers

1. harass

2. flout

3. toady

4. disinterested

5. denounce

Exercise 7, Answers

1. thrifty, frugal, stingy

2. scent, odor, stench

3. call, yell, scream

4. firmly, sternly, harshly

5. partial, prejudiced, bigoted

6. slender, skinny, emaciated

7. depart, retreat, flee

8. error, mistake, blunder

9. unintelligent, dull, stupid

10. ask, question, interrogate

Exercise 8, Sample Answers

1. daring

2. cautious

3. teases

4. unusual

5. casually

Exercise 9, Answers

1. property, furniture, sofa
2. animal, dog, poodle
3. creature, mammal, whale
4. shelter, dwelling, cottage
5. athlete, ballplayer, pitcher
6. vehicle, automobile, Chevrolet
7. move, run, sprint
8. food, meat, pork
9. literature, book, novel
10. problem, pain, toothache
11. plant, tree, maple

Exercise 10, Sample Answers

1. anger
2. exhaustion
3. amazement
4. wealth
5. celebration

Exercise 11, Sample Answers

1. crashes, collisions
2. potholes, ruts, cracks
3. rain, fog, sleet
4. skidded; struck a tree (hydrant, rock, signpost)
5. slid; ditch, trench
6. spun; suffered a blowout
7. broken leg, fractured skull

Exercise 12, Sample Answers

1. Travel books are telescopes that let us see far-off places.

2. Entering a roomful of strange people is like diving into a pool of murky water.

3. The first week of college is a kaleidoscope of new impressions.

4. The fat man lumbered across the street like an elephant.

5. The child accepted the story as a fish swallows a worm.

Exercise 13, Sample Answers

1. The Dean's recent report shocked the entire college.

2. It revealed that only half the students were doing their assignments regularly.

3. The rest were just enjoying themselves in town every night.

4. The president of the college said that all these students should start working consistently.

5. But she and the faculty couldn't agree on how to make them do so.

EXERCISE 14: No sample answers.

Exercise 15, Sample Answers

1. with, of, into

2. in, of

3. with

4. in, about

5. for, to, of *or* from

Exercise 16, Sample Answers

1. Young children need praise from their parents and teachers.

2. Criticism can hurt their development.

3. When talking with them, therefore, grownups should use encouraging words as much as possible.

4. Also, children should be urged to express their feelings, especially when they are sad.

5. A child whose mother or father has died, for instance, needs a sympathetic listener.

Exercise 17, Sample Answers

1. Nineteenth-century photographers faced many hardships and perils.

2. In their quest for perfect pictures, some fell off mountains or buildings.

3. While photographing wildlife, they were attacked by elephants, rhinoceroses, lions, tigers, and wild dogs.

4. But they were just as likely to die in the darkroom as in a jungle.

5. Darkrooms were dangerous because the chemicals required for film processing in the nineteenth century were highly poisonous.

6. Photographers had to breathe for several hours each day an atmosphere filled with noxious fumes.

7. In 1852 one photographer nearly died from inhaling mercury fumes.

8. Furthermore, some poisonous substances penetrated the skin.

9. Worst of all were the hazards of drinking anything in the darkroom.

10. In 1891 a well-known Baltimore photographer mistook a solution of pyrogallic acid for a glass of whiskey and water.

11. As a result, he died in three days.

12. For all these reasons, photography in the nineteenth century was considered an unhealthy occupation.

Exercise 18, Sample Answer

Black Boy is Richard Wright's story of his childhood. It tells how he struggled from birth against intimidating odds until he headed north to Chicago and how his strong sense of justice allowed him to succeed.

Richard would not submit to a punishment he felt was undeserved. When he was living with his grandmother and an aunt named Addie, the aunt was his teacher at a church school. To prove to the other students that she didn't favor him, Addie constantly punished Richard for things he had not done. She even tried to punish him at home for what she said he had done at school. When Richard denied her accusations, she became furious and threatened to beat him. Then he grabbed a kitchen knife to defend himself, telling her that he was innocent and that he would not let her abuse him just because she wanted to prove something to the other kids at school.

When Aunt Addie saw the knife, she became even angrier and told Richard that he was crazy. But from then on, she stopped accusing Richard and started ignoring him altogether, saying he was a lost cause. This reaction pleased Richard. He was glad that he had defied his aunt by rejecting what he felt was an unjust, undeserved punishment.

EXERCISE 19: No sample answers.

9.   REVISING YOUR TEXT

EXERCISE 1: No sample answers.

Exercise 2, Sample Answer

The author's tone is not consistent. In the last third of the passage, where he speaks of honesty as merely "refreshing," the mood of passionate conviction shifts to one of personal whim.

REVISION: [From the middle of the passage, "I have a dream."] King spoke straight from the heart. He touched his listeners because he passionately revealed his vision of how black and white people could live and work together in the United States. Unlike many political candidates, who often hide their feelings on sensitive issues so as to give no offense, King set an inspiring example of true sincerity.

Exercise 3, Sample Answers

General to specific: from Greek influence on cultural lives (line 1) to an adaptation of the *Odyssey* and to Romans' studying Homer (lines 3–4).

General to specific: from Rome challenging its dependence (lines 4–5) to Romans calling the Greeks unreliable, crooked, and so on (lines 5–7).

General to specific: from Romans raising their voices (line 7) to Juvenal and Marshall (lines 8–9).

Specific to general: from a good Roman (line 10) to the attitude of the English toward the French (lines 12–13).

EXERCISE 4: No sample answers.

Exercise 5, Sample Answer

The army offers specialized training and opportunities for advancement.

EXERCISES 6–8: No sample answers.

10.   EDITING AND PROOFREADING

Exercise 1, Answers

line 1: lying; otherwise (or "lying. Otherwise")

line 4: permanently

line 5: lie, the result (or "lie—the result")

line 7: putting

line 8: maintain

Exercise 2, Answers

line 3: layer

line 4: so thick that

line 5: couldn't

line 7: out, but they

line 10: relatively

line 12: precipice

11. PERSUASION AND ARGUMENT

Exercise 1, Sample Answers

1. The writer assumes the patent system's protection of intellectual property rights alone will create greater economic, social, and political inequality. This assumption ignores other factors that may contribute to such problems.

2. The writer assumes that only scientifically established cause-and-effect relationships are valid in making cautionary claims about activities that may pose threats to the environment or human health. This assumption ignores the possibility that science may not establish clear cause-and-effect relationships between certain activities and environmental or health problems until after the damage has been done.

EXERCISES 2–4: No sample answers.

Exercise 5, Sample Answers

1. FALLACY: Arguing by association.
   EXPLANATION: The fact that racist organizations and the Supreme Court both oppose restrictions on any particular kind of speech does not mean that the Court has anything else in common with such organizations. This kind of argument cannot be fixed by revision; it must simply be scrapped.

2. FALLACY: False analogy.

EXPLANATION: Divorce is fundamentally different from radioactive fallout. While radiation can injure everyone living in a given region, divorce cannot break up any couple that wishes to stay together. Also, what is legal for any family is hardly inevitable—merely *possible*. Once again, this argument cannot be saved by revision.

3. FALLACY: False cause.
   EXPLANATION: The fact that the Japanese bombed Pearl Harbor shortly after discussing peace with the United States does not prove that the peace discussions caused the bombing. A much more limited inference is needed here to make the argument valid.
   REVISION: On December 7, 1941, shortly after the U.S. government received Japanese envoys who had come to discuss peace, the Japanese bombed the U.S. naval base in Pearl Harbor. That event shows that discussions of peace do not necessarily prevent acts of war.

4. FALLACY: Irrelevant conclusion.
   EXPLANATION: Waste in government spending has nothing to do with whether or not the tax law is fair—that is, whether or not it requires all taxpayers to pay their fair share of what the government wants to collect. To make the conclusion relevant to the argument, the writer can either change the conclusion or revise the argument.
   REVISION: The only way to make the tax law truly fair is to cancel all deductions and exemptions. Under the present law, a combination of deductions and exemptions often enables wealthy persons to pay little or no tax at all.

5. FALLACY: Hasty generalization.
   EXPLANATION: How dangerous is "dangerous"? The writer leaps from some cases to the "health of the nation" with no reference to the percentage of smokers who have actually died from smoking or suffered serious illness because of it. To make the argument effective, the writer would need to supply this information.

EXERCISES 6–10: No sample answers.

12. DOCUMENT DESIGN

EXERCISES 1–2: No sample answers.

PART 2   CRAFTING SENTENCES

13. THE SIMPLE SENTENCE

Exercise 1, Answers

1. [As a television news correspondent, I] (am a watchdog for the images of black people.)

2. It (occurred to me) [that we had not been listening much to children in these recent years of "summit conferences" on education, of severe reports and ominous prescriptions.]

3. [Outside literature, the main motive for writing] (is to describe the world.)

4. [White Americans] (find it as difficult as white people elsewhere do to divest themselves of the notion that they are in possession of some intrinsic value that black people need, or want.)

5. [Reading James Baldwin's early essays in the fifties] (had stirred me with a sense that apparently "given" situations like racism could be analyzed and described and that this could lead to action, to change.)

6. At once [a black fin] (slit the pink cloud on the water, shearing it in two.)

7. [A work of art] (expresses a conception of life, emotion, inward reality.)

8. [Who] (will compute the lonely nights made less lonely by your songs, or the empty pots made less tragic by your tales?)

Exercise 2, Sample Answers

1. The painting was savage, sensuous, and brilliant.

2. It cost the artist hundreds of hours, demanded all of her skill, and left her exhausted but elated.

3. She had feared the demands on her strength, but could not spare herself.

4. She devoted the summer to sketching, the fall to painting, and the winter to repainting.

5. An artist must use her powers or lose them.

Exercise 3, Sample Answers

1. Climbing with sneakers in subzero weather nearly froze my toes. [or] By climbing with sneakers in subzero weather, I nearly froze my toes.

2. The numbing cold often made me stumble. [or] Numb with the cold, I often stumbled.

3. But on reaching a heated cabin before sundown, I restored circulation to my feet. [or] But reaching a heated cabin before sundown restored circulation to my feet.

4. A borrowed pair of insulated boots helped me get safely back down the mountain the next day. [or] Loaned a pair of insulated boots, I got safely back down the mountain the next day.

5. Out of all the trips in my experience, this one challenged me most.

Exercise 4, Sample Answers

1. A successful campaign is one in which the candidate attracts a wide range of voters.

2. The main fault of Claghorn's speeches was the offense they gave to voters over sixty.

3. Claghorn's worst mistake was recommending large cuts in Social Security payments.

4. The reason for the proposal was that he wanted to balance the federal budget. [or] He made the proposal because he wanted to balance the federal budget.

5. Correct.

Exercise 5, Answers

1. Davy Crockett's defending of the Alamo is one of the great heroic feats of American history.

2. Correct.

3. There was no chance of Davy's emerging from the battle alive.

4. Correct.

5. Since that fateful day in 1836, Americans faced with overwhelming odds have been inspired to hold firm by someone's shouting, "Remember the Alamo!"

14. MODIFIERS

Exercise 1, Sample Answers

1. COMBINATION 1: Wally sang, soulful, swaying, sensuous, dressed in a glittering white satin skinsuit, stroking his blue electric guitar with long, pink, nimble fingers.
COMBINATION 2: Soulful, swaying, sensuous, and dressed in a glittering white satin skinsuit, Wally sang, stroking his blue electric guitar with long, pink, nimble fingers.

2. COMBINATION 1: The dim spotlight faintly illuminated his slender form, drawing him out of the clammy darkness like an apparition.
COMBINATION 2: Drawing him out of the clammy darkness like an apparition, the dim spotlight faintly illuminated his slender form.

3. COMBINATION 1: He sang about a red-haired young woman dressed in a shiny black vinyl raincoat and standing on a crowded New York street corner, waiting for a bus.

   COMBINATION 2: He sang about a red-haired young woman standing on a crowded street corner in New York, dressed in a shiny black vinyl raincoat, and waiting for a bus.

4. COMBINATION 1: Clutching a big white suitcase covered with stickers marked "Broadway or Bust," she waited restlessly.

   COMBINATION 2: She waited restlessly, clutching a big white suitcase covered with stickers marked "Broadway or Bust."

5. COMBINATION 1: She had just arrived from a little town in eastern Oregon, filled with ambition and dreaming of a great career in the theater.

   COMBINATION 2: Filled with ambition and dreaming of a great career in the theater, she had just arrived from a little town in eastern Oregon.

EXERCISE 2: No sample answers.

Exercise 3, Sample Answers

1. to explore; to venture into new realms

2. to seek new lands beyond the horizon

3. to probe mysteries of the deep

4. to travel through space

5. to conduct research on a global scale

6. to re-create a human being

Exercise 4, Sample Answers

1. The nurse took a deep breath before starting to remove the bandage gently from the child's stomach.

2. The child, in turn, began to resist her with strong determination.

3. He exercised all of his cunning to distract her attention quickly from the task.

4. Then, after running out of distractions, he decided to grab her hands and bite them at the last moment.

5. Acceptable.

Exercise 5, Sample Answers

1. Janet rode the big wave, shoulders hunched, toes curled over the edge of the board, hair streaming in the wind.

2. The board sped forward, its slender frame propelled by surging water.

3. Her heart pounding and her eyes sparkling with excitement, Janet yelled with delight.

4. Meanwhile the lifeguard gripped the arms of his chair, knuckles white, hair standing on end, stomach heaving.

Exercise 6, Sample Answers

1. In a recently published essay, Alvin Toffler states that young Americans are becoming consumers of disposable goods.

2. After keeping an item for just a few months, children want to throw it out and get something new.

3. From conversations with my grandparents, I have learned that this practice marks a change.

4. In their childhood, a girl played with only one doll for years.

5. Then she would put it away, wrapped in tissue paper, against the day when she would present it with fond memories to a daughter or a niece.

6. Likewise a boy would keep his electric train carefully boxed so that he could give it to his children one day.

7. According to Toffler, there are several reasons why children no longer keep toys this way.

8. Correct.

9. Most toys were made by craftspeople who, until the late 1800s, devoted years just to mastering their trade and hours to shaping each product carefully by hand.

10. As a result, toys were expensive and hard to get; but each was a treasure, a unique creation.

11. Correct.

12. Most of these mass-produced toys captivate children for only a short time and then wind up in the trash.

13. Another reason why modern toys soon lose their appeal is that they are commonly made of plastic.

14. Plastic costs almost nothing to make; and when painted in bright, vivid colors, it can seem shiny and desirable.

15. Correct.

16. Finally, children are pressured by advertising to be habitual consumers.

17. Correct.

Exercise 7, Sample Answers

1. Correct.

2. Crawling from my bed, I put on my black wool cycling shorts along with my green-and-black shirt.

3. Correct.

4. Correct.

5. While I am hastily pulling on my shoes and tightening my helmet strap, my hands seem to need no help from my brain.

6. My legs begin to wake up as I wheel the bicycle out of the garage.

7. Once I am pedaling along the road, my circulation quickens, and I no longer feel the cold.

8. Turning left at Bank Street and beginning the rapid descent to River Road, I feel the air rushing through my helmet and my eyes watering uncontrollably.

9. Correct.

10. Exhilarated, I push my bike forward, eager to outrace the sun.

11. Correct.

12. Reaching the top of a long rise, I take a short break before turning back and heading home.

13. The morning sun has won the race, just as it always does when I pedal to the point of exhaustion.

Exercise 8, Sample Answer

The *New York Times Magazine* often publishes striking advertisements. One example from a recent issue of the magazine is an ad for Movado watches, which are made in Switzerland. The ad shows a cat with pitch-black fur standing in the center of a large, ten-by-fifteen-inch page and focusing its bright golden eyes on a fishbowl filled with sand, water, and coral. But the fishbowl contains no fish. It contains only two Movado watches resting among the pieces of coral. Below the fishbowl are a brief description of the watches and the words "Movado, a century of Swiss Watchcraft" printed in large white letters.

The ad designer has created an eerie effect by covering almost half the page in black, hiding the body of the cat in darkness, and showing only its head in a dim glow of light. Looking down at the fishbowl, the cat eyes the watches as if they were fish. But the watches also look like the cat. One has a black face set in a gold case, while the other has a gold face set in a black case. Thus both watches match the color of the cat's eyes and fur.

The ad succeeds because it catches the reader's attention. Leafing through the magazine, the average reader is struck by the mysterious-looking cat and carefully examines the watches. The combination of gold and black under water makes them look like treasures discovered at the bottom of the sea.

15. COORDINATION: COMPOUND SENTENCES

Exercise 1, Sample Answers

1. In sixteenth-century England women with literary talent undoubtedly wrote, but none was encouraged to publish her work. (contrast)

2. In the nineteenth century, Jane Austen earned little acclaim for her novels; today they are considered masterpieces. (time)

3. Some writers gain fame with their first major work; others win fame later or possibly never. (contrast)

4. Harriet Beecher Stowe became widely known with the publication of *Uncle Tom's Cabin* in 1852; Emily Dickinson, however, remained unacclaimed until fifty years after her death. (contrast)

5. James Joyce was a painstaking writer; in fact, he once spent half a day on the composition of a single sentence. (reinforcement)

6. Ernest Hemingway would have sympathized with Joyce, for Hemingway rewrote the last page of *A Farewell to Arms* thirty-nine times. (logical consequence)

7. In his later years John O'Hara is said to have disregarded revision altogether; he typed his pages and mailed them untouched to his publisher. (specification)

8. Fictions become reality for some writers; Balzac's characters, for example, walked about on his desk, speaking, striving, suffering. (reinforcement)

9. Georges Simenon used to impersonate his main characters before writing about them; as a result, his wife had to cope with a series of strangers. (cause and effect)

10. Joseph Conrad's native language was Polish, yet he wrote his novels and short stories in English. (contrast)

Exercise 2, Sample Answers

1. The sculpture represents Don Quixote and his horse Rocinante. The Don is the most famous knight in Spanish literature.

2. The knight looks ready for adventure; perhaps he has spotted giants disguised as windmills.

3. His left hand is grasping a shield, and his right hand holds a sturdy lance.

4. The appeal of the small work lies in its materials, for they could have been the contents of a mechanic's trash can. [or] ". . . materials, which could . . ." (This version entails subordination, treated in chapter 15.)

5. The sculptor has used bolts, screws, washers, and scraps of sheet metal; and they are all painted a flat black.

6. Correct.

7. Welded to the body are four legs; they are made from socket head cap screws.

8. Correct.

9. The Don's body is a threaded carriage bolt; one end is welded to the back of Rocinante.

10. Correct.

11. The Don's arms are made from two allen wrenches; in fact, they curve around his back to create the image of shoulders.

12. Two more allen wrenches form legs. Bent at the knees, they end in small globs of welding rods. The rods are molded to resemble boots with tiny spurs.

13. The knight's shield is a thin metal plate, and its rough edges and solder marks give it a battle-scarred look.

14. The lance is not particularly long; nonetheless, it looks like a potent weapon.

15. Correct.

Exercise 3, Sample Answers

1. On the coast of Maine is the small town of Pirates Cove. It resembles the old New England seaports depicted in paintings hanging in country inns and seafood restaurants.

2. The narrow streets are paved with irregularly shaped bricks, and these make walking an adventure.

3. Most of the buildings have a weathered look, for the shingles are gray and the blue of the shutters is faded from exposure to the salt air.

4. Correct.

5. Completing the scene is a welcome touch of wildness; large white gulls swoop over the boats and various clam shells lie on the sand.

6. Walking on the beach, I collect the shells; they slide and rattle in my bucket as I step over rocks.

16. PARALLEL CONSTRUCTION

Exercise 1, Answers

1. great concerns, little irritations

2. lies, excuses, plea

3. to live, to front

4. I open, I see; flapping gills, flattened eyes

5. is written, is read; without effort, without pleasure

Exercise 2, Sample Answers

1. Ancient Greek myths often describe the exploits of heroes confronting threats from violent men, evil monsters, and menacing gods.

2. The heroes seek undying fame, not wealth or comfort.

3. They generally display their remarkable prowess at an early age both by performing difficult tasks and by showing bravery in the face of danger.

4. The infant Hercules, for example, not only strangles two venomous serpents in his crib but laughs at the menace to show how little he fears it.

5. Young Theseus enters the dreaded labyrinth on Crete determined either to slay the Minotaur or to die in the attempt.

6. Correct.

7. A companion travels with the hero, and sometimes the companion is not a mortal but a god. [Note the *a* before *mortal*.] [or] ". . . not mortal but divine."

8. Athene, in perhaps the most famous story of all, not only guides young Telemachos during a voyage from Ithaca to Pylos, the home of Nestor, but also helps him to win the regard of kings.

9. Even for heroes, meeting a challenge can be as dangerous as playing Russian roulette.

10. In a major test of strength and courage, Jason has to yoke a pair of fire-breathing bulls, seed a field with dragon's teeth, and win a climactic battle against armed men sprouting from the seeds.

Exercise 3, Sample Answers

1. Most tarantulas live in the tropics, but some species inhabit the temperate zone, and a few species commonly occur in the southern United States.

2. With their large bodies and powerful fangs, some tarantulas can bite hard and wound deeply, but they don't attack human beings; their bite harms only certain small creatures, including insects and mice.

3. Tarantulas come out of their burrows at dusk and return to them at dawn; at night the mature males look for females and sometimes intrude in people's homes.

4. A fertilized female tarantula lays several hundred eggs at one time and then weaves a cocoon of silk to enclose them, but she does nothing more for her young.

5. When hatched, the young walk away and live alone; unlike ants and bees they do not live in colonies.

17. SUBORDINATION: COMPLEX SENTENCES

Exercise 1, Sample Answers

1. In Cedar Park workers are busy cleaning a statue that was designed by Phidias Gold in 1953.

2. The statue, which represents the American farmer, has been discolored by pollutants emitted by motor vehicles and nearby cement factories.

3. To honor Gold, whose works have earned him a reputation for bold designs, city officials are planning a parade and a banquet on Labor Day.

4. In an interview with reporters, the sculptor recently described a memorial that will honor the astronauts killed in the explosion of the space shuttle *Challenger.*

5. The *Challenger,* whose crew included the first schoolteacher ever sent into space, blew up within minutes of its launching on January 28, 1986.

Answers to the Exercises

Exercise 2, Sample Answers

1. On Interstate 70 in Colorado, a stretch *that extends from Idaho Springs to Glenwood Springs* offers tourists many attractive sights. (restrictive)

2. At Idaho Springs the countryside is dotted with the entrances to old silver mines *that were making people rich one hundred years ago.* (nonrestrictive)

3. Farther along, the highway enters Vail, *which draws thousands of skiers to its beautiful trails every winter.* (nonrestrictive)

4. Another rewarding place is Glenwood Canyon, *whose colorful walls rise steeply above a winding river.* (nonrestrictive)

5. Here, in the spring, men and women *who relish adventure and spectacular scenery* ride the rapids in rubber rafts. (restrictive)

Exercise 3, Sample Answers

1. Women owe their voting rights to early feminists like Susan B. Anthony, who was arrested in 1872 on the day when she led a group of women to the polls in Rochester, New York.

2. Feminism in the nineteenth century was also strongly promoted by Elizabeth Cady Stanton, who organized the first U.S. women's rights convention in 1848 and who presided over the National American Woman Suffrage Association from 1890 to 1892.

3. In the early twentieth century, the fight for women's rights was led by Carrie Chapman Catt, who became president of the National American Woman Suffrage Association in 1900.

4. She achieved her goal in 1920, when Congress passed the Nineteenth Amendment, which gave women the right to vote.

5. Since the 1960s, the spirit of feminism has been revived by the National Organization for Women, which has demanded for women the rights and opportunities that once were granted only to men.

Exercise 4, Sample Answers

1. If commercial airlines offer regular flights to the moon by the year 2050, the moon may become the new playground of the superrich. (condition)

2. Although this prospect is unlikely, scientists may eventually establish some kind of observatory on the moon. (concession and contrast)

3. Because the moon has no atmosphere it affords a perfectly clear view of the stars. (causality)

4. Even without a lunar observatory, we may be able to put a telescope in a permanently orbiting space station so that we will get an equally clear view. (result)

5. When we can study the stars without the least interference from the atmospheric disturbance, our understanding of them will dramatically increase. (time)

Exercise 5, Sample Answers

1. The old house on the bay at St. Anthony's Island looks just as good as it did twenty years ago.

2. Correct.

3. Also, the water in the bay was clearer than that of any other bay in the islands.

4. Correct.

5. And fishermen are not catching nearly as many cod and haddock as they did twenty years ago.

Exercise 6, Sample Answers

1. Whoever tries to resolve a conflict soon learns that nothing pleases everybody.
   Whoever buys an old car soon finds that maintaining it takes money.

2. What solves one problem often causes another.
   What pleases some people can infuriate others.

3. No one knows for sure whether the gains will be greater than the losses.
   We cannot tell yet whether the new method will be more effective than the old ones.

4. It soon becomes evident that progress is elusive.
   It finally seems clear that certain pesticides are harmful to humans.

5. Who can explain why negotiations sometimes take months?
   Is anyone investigating why the trees provide fewer apples?

Exercise 7, Sample Answers

1. Soon after the Sioux Indians settled down near the Black Hills in 1867, the hills were invaded by white men who were searching for gold.

2. Although a U.S. treaty forbade white men to enter the Black Hills, army cavalrymen entered them in 1874 under General George Custer, who had led the slaughter of the Southern Cheyenne in 1868.

3. Red Cloud, who led the Sioux, denounced Custer's invasion because it violated the treaty.

4. The violation led to disaster in 1876 at Little Bighorn River, where the Sioux attacked Custer so ferociously that he and all his men were killed.

5. Though Custer's extraordinary exploits in the Civil War made him the youngest general in the Union Army, most people know only that he was the central figure in "Custer's last stand."

18. COORDINATION AND SUBORDINATION

Exercise 1, Sample Answers

1. COMBINATION 1: According to some, the source of evil lies in society's institutions, which are said to nurture evil in otherwise good people; according to others, evil springs directly from human nature, which is said to be inherently corrupt.

   COMBINATION 2: Though some claim that society's institutions nurture evil in otherwise good people, others insist that evil springs directly from human nature, which they consider inherently corrupt.

2. COMBINATION 1: In his novel *Lord of the Flies,* William Golding nowhere states his opinion directly, but the setting, plot, and characters reveal it clearly.

   COMBINATION 2: Although William Golding never states his view directly in *Lord of the Flies,* the setting, plot, and characters of the novel clearly reveal it.

3. COMBINATION 1: The action is set on a beautiful South Pacific island that has a bountiful supply of fruit trees, springs of fresh water, and wild pigs that run freely through the thick vegetation.

   COMBINATION 2: The beautiful South Pacific island where the action is set has a bountiful supply of fruit trees, springs of fresh water, and pigs that run freely through the thick vegetation.

4. COMBINATION 1: The only human inhabitants are a group of British schoolchildren who survived the crash of a plane that was shot down during World War II.

   COMBINATION 2: The only human inhabitants, a group of British schoolchildren, survived the crash of a plane that was shot down during World War II.

5. COMBINATION 1: Ralph, the leader of the boys, summons them to meetings by using a large shell that makes a loud noise when he blows into it; the boys respond to the sound because the shell symbolizes both authority and order.

   COMBINATION 2: Ralph, the leader of the boys, summons them to meetings using a large shell that makes a loud noise when he blows into it; since the shell symbolizes order and authority to the boys, they respond to the sound.

6. COMBINATION 1: At first the older boys, who follow Ralph's lead, agree to build shelters, care for the youngest, and keep a fire burning on a hilltop so that it can serve as an SOS signal for passing ships.

   COMBINATION 2: At first the older boys follow Ralph's lead and agree to build shelters, care for the youngest, and keep a fire burning on a hilltop so that it can serve as an SOS signal for passing ships.

7. COMBINATION 1: But trouble develops shortly, for Ralph's leadership is challenged by Jack, who has been a leader of choirboys and wants to be chief again so that he can give orders, not take them.

   COMBINATION 2: But trouble develops shortly when Jack, who has been a leader of choirboys, challenges Ralph's leadership; in effect, Jack wants to be the chief again, to give orders rather than take them.

8. COMBINATION 1: Jack forms his own band of followers, who walk out on Ralph because they want to stop working on the signal fire and hunt wild pigs; for they like the excitement of the chase and the kill, when they stab the squealing pig with a wooden spear.

   COMBINATION 2: When Jack forms his own band of followers, they walk out on Ralph because they want to stop working on the signal fire; instead, they want to hunt wild pigs and enjoy the excitement of the chase and the kill, when they stab the squealing pig with a wooden spear.

9. COMBINATION 1: Jack's followers attack Ralph's group one night and take Piggy's glasses so that they can use the lenses to concentrate the sun's rays on firewood and make a fire that will cook the pig meat.

   COMBINATION 2: One night Jack's followers attack Ralph's group and take Piggy's glasses; they want to use the lenses to concentrate the sun's rays on firewood and make a fire that will cook the pig meat.

10. COMBINATION 1: In the end, the boys are discovered by a strong naval officer who scolds them because they look like savages and have been fighting among themselves; yet he too has been fighting, for he has come ashore from a warship that seeks to sink enemy warships and their crews.

    COMBINATION 2: In the end, a strong naval officer who discovers the boys scolds them because they look like savages and have been fighting among themselves; yet since he himself has come ashore from a warship whose mission is to sink enemy warships and their crews, he too has been fighting.

Exercise 2, Sample Answers

1. Since the average person does not worry that others are secretly plotting to seize and imprison him, anyone who really has that worry would probably be considered a paranoid schizophrenic.

2. Middle-class American women who want to experience the pleasures of motherhood must accept all the limitations of life in the suburbs.

3. Though products were once scarce and hard to get, the industrial revolution has begotten the clutter of modern life.

4. Imagination, which is the specifically human ability to make images and arrange them inside one's head, nurtures both science and literature.

5. To lie habitually is to lose contact with the unconscious, which speaks only truth.

Exercise 3, Sample Answers

1. STEP 1: Thoreau spent much of his time outdoors in nature.
He loved nature.
So he had no reason to keep it out of his cabin.
He thought something.
A doormat symbolized a mistake.
The mistake was avoiding natural things like dirt and leaves.
His neighbors made that mistake.
STEP 2: Since Thoreau spent much of his time outdoors in nature, which he loved, he saw no reason to keep it out of his cabin, and he thought that a doormat symbolized the mistake of avoiding natural things like dirt and leaves, as his neighbors did.

2. STEP 1: The bean field made him self-sufficient.
He believed something.
Human beings should be self-sufficient.
He could also see the bean field as an extension of himself.
Through the bean field, he was extending himself into nature.
He was returning to a natural state.
STEP 2: The bean field made him self-sufficient, which is what he believed human beings should be; he could also see that through the bean field, he was extending himself into nature and thus returning to a natural state.

3. STEP 1: The author of "The Cold Equations" is saying, in effect, something.
There is a difference between life on the frontier and life in settled communities.
The lives of people on the frontier are ruled by laws of nature.
They aren't ruled by laws of another kind.
People make those laws.
STEP 2: According to the author of "The Cold Equations," the difference between life on the frontier and life in settled communities is that the

lives of frontier people are ruled by laws of nature rather than by rules that people make.

4. STEP 1: For fifty years the people prospered under his rule.
Then he felt a personal responsibility for the welfare of his subjects and their safety.
The old king fought another monster.
The monster severely injured him.
He soon died.

STEP 2: For fifty years the people prospered under his rule; then, feeling a personal responsibility for the welfare of his subjects and their safety, the old king fought another monster that severely injured him, and he soon died.

19. SENTENCE FRAGMENTS

Exercise, Sample Answers

1.
line 2: assumption that
line 3: develop self-confidence if they
line 7: clues to the handicapped that they
lines 7–8: Because . . . gyms, they feel incompetent.
lines 10–13: Wanting to foster confidence, Special Olympics demands it of the contestants, who are already sure they are going to lose out because they lack a vital prerequisite for any competition—confidence.
line 15: morning practices, for which
line 20: Saturday practices for the free, supervised care.
line 21: handicapped, so that their competing
lines 22–23: loads the dice with unfortunate consequences for all.
line 24: feeling of superiority based on a false
line 25: shunned again, this time in
line 27: for others that the program's

2.
line 2: subgroups: the regulars
line 4: others, regulars
line 5: matters while
lines 6–7: carefully, placing . . . mouths and sipping
line 8: opportunity to relax
line 9: birthday under
lines 10–11: mother who . . . table while . . . meals for
lines 11–12: straws as they wait, blowing
line 14: what even
line 15: loudly despite
line 16: adults who

20. USING PRONOUNS

Exercise 1, Sample Answers

1. DIAGNOSIS: The reference of *it* is broad. The pronoun could refer to the whole preceding statement or to parts of it.
   CURE: The discovery made him leap out of the water with excitement.

2. DIAGNOSIS: The reference of *They* is muffled; the pronoun refers to something merely implied by what precedes it.
   CURE: The Syracusans [or] His fellow citizens must have been amazed to see him—or at least amused.

3. DIAGNOSIS: The reference of *He* is ambiguous; the pronoun has more than one possible antecedent.
   CURE: The king would surely be pleased.

4. DIAGNOSIS: The reference of *it* is ambiguous; the pronoun has more than one possible antecedent.
   CURE: The king wanted to know if the crown was pure gold.

5. DIAGNOSIS: The reference of *which* is broad; the pronoun refers to a whole statement containing one or more possible antecedents.
   CURE: The king was pleased to know that the weight of the crown exactly matched the weight of the original ingot.

6. Correct.

7. DIAGNOSIS: The reference of *you* is indefinite since the pronoun does not refer to the reader.
   CURE: Since the resulting alloy would look just like pure gold and weigh as much as the original ingot, no one could tell by appearance or weight what the goldsmith had done.

8. Correct.

9. DIAGNOSIS: The reference of *they* is muffled or free floating.
   CURE: To learn whether or not the crown was pure gold, then, the king and his consultants had to see whether its volume matched the volume of a pure gold ingot that weighed the same.

10. DIAGNOSIS: The reference of *it* is considered free floating or muffled. There is no clear antecedent.
    CURE: But the crown was so intricately shaped that no way of measuring known in Archimedes' time could establish its volume.

11. Correct.

12. DIAGNOSIS: The reference of *they* is ambiguous.
    CURE: By measuring the water displaced by the crown, and then measuring the water displaced by the ingot, he could easily tell whether or

not the two amounts of water matched in volume, and thus whether or not the crown was pure gold.

Exercise 2, Sample Answers

1. Sentence *b* is correct because the plural pronoun *their* matches the plural antecedent *members*.

2. Sentence *a* is correct because the plural pronoun *their* matches the plural *dogs*, the nearer of two antecedents linked by *or*.

3. Sentence *b* is correct because the singular pronoun *its* matches the singular antecedent *Everyone*.

4. Sentence *b* is correct because the plural pronoun *their* matches the plural antecedent *those stoical types*.

5. Sentence *a* is correct because the singular pronoun *his* matches the singular antecedent *he*.

6. Sentence *b* is correct because the singular pronouns *his or her* match the singular antecedent *Everyone*.

7. Sentence *a* is correct because the singular pronoun *its* matches the singular antecedent *every animal*.

8. Sentence *a* is correct because the singular pronoun *its* matches the singular antecedent *neither*.

Exercise 3, Sample Answers

1. The job of being a counselor in a girls' summer camp is not an easy one. A counselor has to meet her responsibilities twenty-four hours a day, and they may include such things as making sure her girls attend all the camp meetings, overseeing the cleaning of her cabin, and giving her campers archery lessons. Because of the demands on her, she sometimes becomes tired and even cross. At those times she wants a break—a chance to go someplace else and relax. In a well-run camp she can do this; the director gives every counselor a day off each week. After that she resumes her duties with a positive, cheerful attitude.

2. Our body language often expresses our emotions. Through gestures, posture, facial expressions, and other visible signs, we indicate our feelings. If we are elated, for example, we tend to speak with more tonal fluctuations and with more arm movement than we use when depressed. In a good mood, our eyes sparkle, our posture is erect, and we smile a lot. When we are angry, our body language tells the tale. Our faces scowl, our jaws are clenched, our gestures look aggressive, and sparks flash from our eyes. When we are sad, the feeling shows in our downcast eyes, limp shoulders, and shuffling walk.

Answers to the Exercises

Exercise 4, Sample Answers

1. *My* and *his* (the possessive case) are correct because they indicate a close relationship to *brother* and *wife* respectively.
   Their (the possessive case) indicates a close connection to *pastime.*

2. *Mine,* the possessive pronoun, can stand alone. *My* must be followed by a noun.

3. *I* (subject case) is one part of the compound subject of *argue.*

4. *I* (subject case) is one part of the compound subject of *agree.*
   Us (object case) comes immediately before the infinitive *to settle.*

5. *Himself* (reflexive/emphatic case) stresses the word before it.
   His (possessive case) comes before the gerund *arguing.*
   Me (object case) is the direct object of the verb phrase *will convince.*
   Us (object case) is the object of the preposition *between.*

6. *They* (subject case) is the subject of the verb phrase *are missing.*

7. *Their* (possessive case) indicates a close relationship to *steadiness.*

8. *My* (possessive case) precedes the gerund *saying.*

9. *Them* (object case) is the object of the preposition *to.*

10. *Ourselves* (reflexive/emphatic case) is the direct object of the verb phrase *would talk* and refers to the subject *we.*
    Me (object case) comes immediately before the infinitive *to stop.*

Exercise 5, Sample Answers

1. Every spring my Aunt Mary and I go fishing in the mountains.

2. We put two sets of camping gear in the truck—mine and hers.

3. Correct.

4. The rangers themselves have never fished with us; they just want to help us get our quota.

5. Once my cousin Roger asked if he could go fishing with Aunt Mary and me.

6. Aunt Mary had to decide whom to take—him or me.

7. There wasn't room for us two in the truck, and neither he nor I had a car.

8. That spring she and Roger caught the biggest trout she had ever seen.

9. I heard all about it when Roger arrived home; nobody talks more than he (does).

10. He can hardly wait until Aunt Mary and he go fishing again.

21. SUBJECT-VERB AGREEMENT

Exercise 1, Answers

1. is

2. drives, spends, does

3. do, find

4. die

5. is, likes

6. does, has

7. is, gets, devotes

8. is

9. makes, does, chases, speak, invites

10. is, are

Exercise 2, Answers

1. *Is* should be *are* because the subject is *Members,* a plural noun

2. *Has* should be *have* because the subject is *complaints,* a plural noun.

3. *Are* should be *is* because the subject is *attorney,* a singular noun.

4. *Have* should be *has* because the subject is *Each,* a third-person singular pronoun.

5. *Is* should be *are* because the complete subject is the plural phrase *A number of shoppers.*

6. *Are* should be *is* because the subject is *She,* a third-person singular pronoun. The singleness of the subject here is not affected by anything in the phrase that modifies it ("along with . . .").

7. *Is* should be *are* because the complete subject is *Three-quarters of the gripes,* which is plural because it refers to elements of a unit.

8. *Are* should be *is* because the complete subject is *Fifteen minutes,* which is singular because it refers to a unit.

9. *Wants* is correct because the subject is *No one,* a third-person singular pronoun.

10. *Need* should be *needs* because the subject is *means,* which is singular because the article *A* is used before it.

Answers to the Exercises

Exercise 3, Answers

> lines 3–4: efficiency and level . . . are usually measured
>
> line 5: tests which require
>
> line 8: which provide (*Which* is plural because its antecedent, *new techniques,* is plural.)
>
> lines 11–12: sex differences . . . have not been demonstrated.
>
> lines 13–14: Measurements . . . do not differ
>
> line 15: as is the consistency
>
> lines 17–18: each of whom was tested
>
> lines 20–21: One of the behaviors . . . was vocalization (The long modifier between the subject and the verb does not affect the number of the verb. The subject of *were observed* [line 22] is *patterns,* so that verb is correct.)

22. VERBS: TENSE

Exercise 1, Answers

1. fly, flying, flew, flown

2. give, giving, gave, given

3. sleep, sleeping, slept, slept

4. witness, witnessing, witnessed, witnessed, forget, forgetting, forgot, forgotten

5. lay, laying, laid, laid

6. break, breaking, broken, broken

Exercise 2, Sample Answer

In 1901, when Houdini *took* on the Imperial Police, he *was* not *whistling* in the dark. By the time he *left* America at the end of the nineteenth century he *had dissected* every kind of lock he *could* find in the New World, and whatever he *could* import from the old one. Arriving in London, Houdini *could* write that there *were* only a few kinds of British handcuffs, "seven or eight at the utmost," and these *were* some of the simplest he *had* ever seen. He *searched* the markets, antique shops, and locksmiths, buying up all the European locks he *could* find so he *could* dismantle and study them.

23. VERBS: SEQUENCE OF TENSES

Exercise 1, Answers

1. On April 9, 1865, when Lee's Army of Northern Virginia *had* already *been defeated,* Ulysses S. Grant *met* Robert E. Lee at Appomattox Court House, Virginia.

2. Historians *believe* that this meeting *ended* the Civil War.

3. The Confederate government *struggled* to survive for a short time even after Lee *(had)* formally *surrendered* to Grant.

4. But Grant and Lee both *knew* that the war *was* over.

5. They *realized* that the time for peace *had come.*

Exercise 2, Answers

1. Filters are being installed in water systems that *have been threatened* (or *are threatened*) by pollutants from industrial wastes.

2. The pollutants were first discovered last July when inspectors from the city's water department *checked* the systems.

3. At that time, inspectors found that pollutants *had* already *made* the water unsafe to drink.

4. The water will be drinkable again after the filters *have been installed.*

5. But until the installation *is complete,* residents will drink bottled water.

Exercise 3, Answers

1.
line 3: manfully thrashes
line 4: is turned
line 6: He fondles her, then turns
line 8: are utterly without hope
line 12: enters his dull brain
lines 13–14: to pluck Fay
line 15: is impossible

2.
line 4: She had to talk
lines 5–6: which turned out
line 6: Susan went
line 11: she became
line 12: she had had (or *has had*)

24. VERBS: ACTIVE AND PASSIVE VOICE

Exercise 1, Sample Answers

1. William Carlos Williams's short story "The Use of Force" dramatizes a terrible conflict between a doctor and a child.

2. At the start of the story, the doctor enters the house of a blue-collar family knowing that he has to obtain a throat culture from a frightened girl.

3. No one in the family, however, gives him the cooperation that he needs.

4. The girl thwarts his initial efforts to examine her when she knocks his glasses to the floor.

5. Acceptable.

6. In addition, the father displays ambivalence over the examination when he first tightens and then loosens his hold on his daughter's arms.

7. With no support from the family, the doctor wonders whether he should end his visit.

8. Acceptable.

9. He rejects the idea of leaving, however, as his increasing anger and wounded pride overrule his better judgment.

10. He must defeat the child; he must overcome her resistance.

11. He launches an attack with the aid of a metal spoon that he jams between her teeth and presses down hard like a lever.

Exercise 2, Sample Answer

At the sound of a bell, I entered a huge red building along with hundreds of others. Just inside the entrance, a mean-looking old lady was yelling instructions at us. I clutched my lunchbox and followed [or] Clutching my lunchbox, I followed a crowd of six-year-olds down a long hallway, up some steps, and down another corridor. We were looking for Mrs. Nearing's room. I knew we had reached our destination when I was greeted loudly by a tall, black-haired woman. She asked me my name. Then she printed my name on a sticky tag and pressed it to my chest. Inside the room I could see other six-year-olds. Some looked big. Finally, Mrs. Nearing closed the classroom door and made [or . . . door, making] a loud bang in the process. The small pane of glass near the top was kept from shattering by a network of wires. To my imagination, the wires looked like the bars in a prison. I was back in school.

Exercise 3, Sample Answer

The political structure of modern China was largely created by Mao Zedong, who led the Chinese Communist revolution, <u>formulated</u> the theory behind it, and virtually <u>ruled</u> the country from 1949 to his death in 1976. Mao worked for revolution throughout much of his early life. In 1911, when he was eighteen, he <u>joined</u> the Nationalist armed forces of Hunan Province in their revolt against the Manchu dynasty. In 1921 he helped to found the Chinese Communist party, and in the spring of 1928, he and a fellow revolutionary named Zhu De <u>organized</u> the Fourth Chinese Red Army. In 1934–35, he and Zhu De led a six-thousand-mile march of Chinese Communist forces to northwest China, where the two leaders <u>established</u> a new base of operations against the Kuomintang, the Nationalist political organization headed by Generalissimo Chiang Kai-shek. Mao and Chiang joined forces during World War II in order to fight their common enemy, the Japanese. But in the summer of 1946, Mao <u>resumed</u> full-scale civil war against the Nationalists, and Mao's forces won the war in three years. On September 21, 1949, Mao <u>proclaimed</u> the establishment of the People's Republic of China. He then <u>assumed</u> a succession of increasingly powerful posts: chairmanship of the Government Council, chairmanship of the Republic, and most important, chairmanship of the Chinese Communist party. In effect, Mao <u>ruled</u> China for nearly thirty years. For better or worse, he <u>made</u> a lasting change in that country, and he <u>will</u> be long <u>remembered</u> as one of the most important revolutionaries of the twentieth century.

25. VERBS: MOOD

Exercise 1, Answers

1. may (or *can*) (permission)

2. must (absolute obligation)

3. should (advice)

4. can (or *may*) (capability or permission)

5. might (or *may*) (remote or mild possibility); should (expectation)

Exercise 2, Answers

1. served

2. had bought

3. goes up

4. had conquered

5. had lost

Exercise 3, Answers

line 1: were

line 2: ended

line 5: begin

line 6: began

line 9: were

26. DIRECT AND INDIRECT REPORTING OF DISCOURSE

Exercise 1, Sample Answers

1. DIRECT: "You will have to earn your own spending money," my father said to me.
   INDIRECT: My father told me that I would have to earn my own *spending money.*

   The content is more important than the exact words.

2. DIRECT: "I do not mind lying, but I hate inaccuracy," wrote Samuel Butler.
   INDIRECT: Samuel Butler wrote that he did not mind lying, but that he hated inaccuracy.

   The exact words are needed to preserve the flavor of Butler's wit.

3. DIRECT: "I will pay you $3.50 an hour," the manager said to me.
   INDIRECT: The manager told me that he would pay me $3.50 an hour.

   The content is more important than the exact words.

4. DIRECT: "You have been baptized in fire and blood and have come out steel," General Patton told the battle survivors.
   INDIRECT: General Patton told the battle survivors that they had been baptized in fire and blood and had come out steel.

   The exact words are needed to preserve the direct appeal of the general's statement.

5. DIRECT: "Nothing in education," writes Henry Adams, "is so astonishing as the amount of ignorance it accumulates in the form of inert facts."
   INDIRECT: Henry Adams writes that nothing in education is so astonishing as the amount of ignorance it accumulates in the form of inert facts.

Though in this case both versions preserve Adams's exact words, the direct report is preferable because the quotation marks assure the reader that they are indeed his words.

6. DIRECT: "Fanaticism," writes George Santayana, "consists in redoubling your efforts when you have forgotten your aim."
INDIRECT: George Santayana writes that fanaticism consists in redoubling your efforts when you have forgotten your aim.

Once again, though both versions preserve the writer's exact words, the quotation marks assure the reader that they are indeed his words.

27. INVIGORATING YOUR STYLE

Exercise, Sample Answers

1.   According to the French, no other culture approximates theirs in value or quality. To maintain its excellence, they strive hard to protect it from contamination, especially the taint of American English. The defenders of French culture insist that French men and women violate the purity of their language when they use American words. One of the many electronic machines made by Americans since 1945 is the computer, and Americans widely use the word *computer* along with many other related words. But do the French use these words? They do not. Instead they have created their own terms, calling a computer an *ordinateur,* software *le logiciel,* and data processing *l'informatatique.* The guardians of French culture believe that the French must speak and write French-sounding words.

2.   Critics of detective stories make three complaints. First, they find too much senseless violence, with many characters killed and others badly beaten. But even in books such as John D. MacDonald's *The Lonely Silver Rain,* where more than twenty people are killed, the violence and deaths make sense because they furnish clues to the detective. Secondly, critics fault the use of old, lifeless plots. The plots are old, but the writing usually rejuvenates them by dramatizing both places and characters. Rex Stout, for example, vividly describes interiors, and Ed McBain makes his characters sound like real people. Ignoring this vitality, critics make a third complaint. They say that the detectives are cardboard cutouts and the other characters are wooden statues. But is this charge fair? Actually, fictional detectives resemble real human beings with real problems. Agatha Christie's Hercule Poirot must cope with old age just as Ross MacDonald's Lew Archer has to confront the haunting memories of a failed marriage. Given these and other examples, I ask one question: Have the critics ever read the stories they criticize?

3. The modern city endangers decent people because it continually exposes them to crime. But I believe that we can solve this problem. While my solution may sound crazy, new ideas often sound this way. I propose that criminals and law-abiding citizens switch places—literally. Released from prison into the perilous freedom of our cities, criminals will be victimized by their own robberies, muggings, and killings until they destroy themselves. Meanwhile prisons will be remodeled for all decent citizens. Single persons will each have a cell, and multicell units will house families. Those who want to live alone may apply for solitary confinement on a first-come, first-served basis. What will inmates get? They will have food, medical services, and educational TV on the large screens in every cell. They will be entertained at block parties, with games for children and dances for adults. At the end of each party, inmates will watch a movie about the bad old days to remind themselves of the dangers before the big switch.

5. In "The American Scholar" Emerson explains the wise and unwise use of books. Readers, Emerson says, use a book unwisely whenever they take its contents as final truth. They fail to see that the truth of one period does not necessarily survive in another, and also that authors make mistakes, so that what a book says may be false to begin with. In addition, some readers become bookworms. They enter the paper and binding of a book but do not penetrate its contents. How do wise readers act? According to Emerson, they study books to learn history, to absorb scientific facts, and to gain illumination. Wisely used, books can serve readers well.

28. ACADEMIC ENGLISH FOR NONNATIVE SPEAKERS

Exercise 1, Sample Answer

Three summers ago I became interested in plants and gardening. I began to plan a garden. It would include three flower beds, a small sundial, and a stone wall. In the center of the garden, I wanted to put a lily pool. By the end of the summer, I had constructed the pool and laid a stone wall around it. Beyond the wall were three flower beds, each of which was shaped like an arc circling one part of the pool. My sundial rested on top of a large rock between two of the flower beds. Because of a drought, the soil was the driest it had been in ten years, so only a few of the plants grew well.

During the following winter, I had many new ideas. I taught myself about gardening in general and water gardening in particular by reading lots of books. In the spring I redid the lily pool and the three flower beds, adding a waterfall, water lilies, and many other aquatic plants, as well as stocking the pool with goldfish. I enlarged the flower beds and fertilized the soil with compost, peat, and manure, working the material into the soil with my hands and a small trowel. During the summer, which was wetter than the one before, every single plant quadrupled in size and stayed healthy.

Exercise 2, Sample Answer

In the evening of April 18, 1775, British troops occupying Boston prepared to make a surprise attack on the American colonists who lived in nearby villages. As soon as night fell, many small boats began to ferry the British soldiers across the Charles River from Boston to Cambridge. The British believed that they were acting in secret. In reality, however, many agents of the American patriots were watching every move of the redcoats. On discovering the enemy's plan, the agents dispatched several messengers, who hoped to warn the villagers of the threat to their safety.

At ten o'clock one of the messengers, Paul Revere by name, left his home and hastened to Christ Church in Boston. From there he hurried to the Charles River, which he crossed in a small rowboat using muffled oars. Then he reported to another agent, who gave him a horse and wished him Godspeed. Although Paul Revere was almost captured many times by British patrols, he managed to elude his pursuers and to reach Lexington shortly after midnight. Shouting with much excitement, he warned the townspeople about the British soldiers and then rode to Concord, where he repeated his message.

Revere's work was well done. As a result of his now-famous ride in the dark, the American colonists living in Lexington were ready to defend themselves when the British soldiers reached the village.

Exercise 3, Answers

1. My basketball coach does not look like a typical coach.

2. Correct.

3. During practice he sometimes does not bring a ball, and he does not have a whistle.

4. What do we players think?

5. We do not think that he is a good coach.

6. But we play hard for him, no matter what he does during practice.

Exercise 4, Answers

1. Some corporations want their employees to get along with each other.

2. Friendly employees help one another keep on working efficiently.

3. They even look for ways to reduce waste and increase production.

4. As a result, the corporations can keep up with their competitors.

5. No worker can be fully effective if he or she is made to put up with troublesome coworkers.

6. For this reason good managers regularly look into complaints whenever they are made to a supervisor.

7. Some companies devise training programs to break down hostility between workers.

8. Every month a few trainees drop out of the programs.

9. The dropouts cannot put up with the demands being placed upon them.

10. But most trainees learn to keep up with those demands.

Exercise 5, Answers

1. Juanita usually exercises before having supper.

2. She dislikes going without a workout at the end of a day.

3. On weekends she often has an urge to take a long hike.

4. After working at the office all week, she enjoys roaming.

5. She sometimes walks for hours without stopping.

6. She likes to look (or, looking) for elk and deer.

7. The thrill of seeing wild birds and animals delights her.

8. Juanita's friends never grow tired of hearing her stories of life in the wilds.

9. We are always ready to hear a new tale.

10. It is a pleasure to know her.

Exercise 6, Answers

1. Children were wading in the cold water of a brook.

2. The water was swirling about in a small pool shaped by boulders from the ice age.

3. As the glacier covering the region was receding (or . . . the region receded), it left behind a trail marked by boulders, sand beds, and narrow gorges.

4. The children, of course, were not thinking of such things as they frolicked in water that only moments earlier had been tumbling down the
mountainside.

5. They were wiggling their toes against moss-covered rocks and splashing friends with handfuls of sparkling water.

6. Squeals of laughter echoed in the clear air as busy hands scooping beneath the surface sent yet another shower cascading into the sunlight.

7. Earlier that day the children had been hiking up a trail covered with
roots, loose stones, and pine needles.

8. At first, they had been pleased with the adventure and delighted to be
carrying backpacks like the grownups.

9. But as the minutes passed and the sun's rays grew hotter, they grew
weary of the ever-rising trail.

10. The pool of cold water had appeared just in time to restore their flag-
ging spirits and their pleasure in the day.

Exercise 7, Answers

1. Phillipa wants to find a new apartment that overlooks the city park.

2. Her present apartment, which she has rented for two years, has too
many drawbacks.

3. For one thing, the plumbing keeps breaking down; for another thing,
the landlords keep raising the rent.

4. The rent that she now has to pay comes to more than half of what she
earns at work.

5. With any luck, the new place will cost her less money than she has to
spend on the old one, and the facilities will function without a hitch.

Exercise 8, Sample Answer

Electricity is very important in our lives. Yet we rarely think about it. We
take it for granted until something is wrong. When there is nothing we can
do, we realize we are helpless without its power. In the summer of 1959,
everyone in New York City was (*or* became) unhappy when the city's
power plant broke down for many hours. Electric fans and air conditioners
stopped working. Apartments and offices were soon (*or* soon became) hot.
Elevators were motionless, and subways stopped on their tracks. That
night, streets were dark and gloomy. People were scared. In the emergency,
there was little the police could do. They were helpless too. Then there was
a sudden change. Lights shone again, trains began moving, and fans

stirred the air in hot, stuffy rooms. All of the people were glad. They were safe. They had their precious electricity again.

PART 3   PUNCTUATION AND MECHANICS

29. THE COMMA

Exercise 1, Sample Answers

1. Ithaca, but he

2. Poseidon, so he

3. Polyphemos, and he
   herds of sheep and goats

4. one day, for he

5. Correct.

6. doomed, but Odysseus blinds the giant and escapes

7. rams, for the giant

8. giant, so the giant

Exercise 2, Sample Answers

1. cave, they sail

2. Correct [or] Aeolus, Odysseus

3. days, Odysseus
   Ithaca; nevertheless, they

4. Correct [or] result, they

5. Correct [or] Aiaia, they

6. see her, she

7. fate, Odysseus

8. Correct [or] in fact, they

9. Fortunately, he

10. Correct.

Exercise 3, Sample Answers

1. DECISION: nonrestrictive
   car, a 1979 Ford Fiesta, looks like

2. DECISION: nonrestrictive
   interior, which . . . cleaned, is

3. DECISION: nonrestrictive
   ashtray, which

4. DECISION: restrictive
   Correct.

5. DECISION: restrictive
   for anyone with normal vision to read

6. DECISION: nonrestrictive
   driver's seat, which . . . vinyl, smells

7. DECISION: nonrestrictive
   exterior, with its layers of grime, rust spots, and dents, looks

8. DECISION: nonrestrictive
   rear window, lacking . . . wiper, looks
   DECISION: restrictive
   boards that collect

9. DECISION: nonrestrictive
   windshield, on the other hand, has
   DECISION: restrictive
   clear spot made by

10. DECISION: restrictive
    car dealer who

11. DECISION: restrictive
    a car that stands

Exercise 4, Sample Answers

1. Last summer my brother, my father, *and I* visited a *busy logging* camp in a rugged, picturesque, largely uninhabited part of Maine.

2. From dawn to dusk, *hardy, skilled* lumberjacks felled trees, cut them into logs, and cleared the thick, green underbrush.

3. Our guide was a *slow-moving, infirm* old man with dark brown eyes; but he could still repair *broken or sputtering* chain saws.

4. Dressed in his *bright red flannel jacket,* he had a *sturdy workbench* in a pleasant, shaded area next to the *large equipment* shed.

5. Inside the shed were various things, including coils of *thick, heavy rope,* stacks of *wooden axe* handles, and *bright yellow slickers* for rainy days.

6. Our guide's *worn carpenter's chest* contained pliers, screwdrivers with *hard rubber* handles, a set of *galvanized steel* wrenches, two copper oil cans, and bolts of many different sizes.

7. *Carefully, expertly,* and patiently he worked on *each broken chain saw* until its motor coughed, wheezed, and sputtered into life.

8. Then, with a *deft and* clever adjustment of the carburetor, he would soon have the motor purring like a cat stretched out before a *warm, cozy* fire.

9. My father, *my brother, and* I wondered how many kinds of discarded appliances might be thus *revived and saved* from the trash *can and* the dump.

Exercise 5, Sample Answer

Many early American homes were decorated with block-printed wallpapers. Imported from England and France, the papers made the arrival of ships from abroad an exciting event for Colonial homemakers. Merchants looking for sales advertised that papering was cheaper than whitewashing, and they urged would-be customers to examine the endless variety of brightly colored patterns. Indeed, by today's standards the colors in many Colonial papers seem vibrant, intense, and even gaudy. One wonders whether the citizens of Boston, Massachusetts, and Providence, Rhode Island, yearned for bright reds, greens, and blues because of the grey New England winters.

The process of reproducing historic wallpapers requires the finesse of a craftsman. To establish a particular paper's full pattern, the expert may have to fit together the fragments of surviving samples that he finds in museums, in the attics of old houses, and even under layers of other papers. He determines the original hue of the colors in various ways: he runs chemical tests, or he matches a fragment to a fresh original in some museum. Even then he must be careful before proceeding to the next step, printing the design. As a final precaution, therefore, he makes a blacklight examination, knowing it may reveal the otherwise indistinguishable elements of the pattern.

One of the leading experts in America is Dorothy Waterhouse, co-founder of Waterhouse Hangings. She first became interested in historic wallpapers in 1932, when she was restoring an old house on Cape Cod, Massachusetts. While stripping the walls in one room, she got down to the eighth and bottom layer of paper. She became very excited. She knew it had to be over 140 years old. That discovery was the first of many. Today she has a collection of some three hundred historic wallpapers, all carefully stored in her Boston home.

30. THE SEMICOLON AND THE COLON

Exercise 1, Sample Answers

1. opportunity; in particular, it
   America's pioneers, who ventured

2. north, lusty

3. gateway; it was

4. would be; on the contrary, they

5. hog; they

Exercise 2, Sample Answers

line 1: 10:00

line 2: service: [or] service;

line 3: ceases;

line 5: close;

line 7: task:

lines 7–8: 11:00 to 1:00

line 9: fare:

line 13: present:

line 14: sadness;

line 16: 9:00

lines 17–18: order: first comes a band playing a funeral march;

line 19: Cross;

line 20: soldiers;

line 22: meaning; [or keep the period]

31. END MARKS

Exercise, Sample Answer

How do historians rate the contributions of General Gordon to his country? Their opinions differ. Some consider him a military genius, one of the greatest soldiers in British history. Others criticize him severely. In their opinion, General C. G. Gordon, or "Chinese" Gordon as he was popularly known, acted impulsively. He was rash. He was dangerous. He was not fit to hold a command. Did he seek death on January 26, 1885? Historians give conflicting answers.

32. QUOTATION MARKS AND QUOTING

Exercise, Sample Answers

1. What writer asked, "Who has deceived thee so oft as thyself?"

2. Did Ambrose Bierce define a bore as "a person who talks when you wish him to listen"?

3. Alexander Pope wrote, "True wit is nature to advantage dressed. / What oft was thought, but ne'er so well expressed."

4. "The history of the earth," says Rachel Carson, "has been a history of interaction between living things and their surroundings."

5. *Continual* means "going on with occasional slight interruptions." *Continuous* means "going on with no interruption."

6. Perhaps the poet John Donne was right when he wrote: "One short sleep past, we wake eternally / And Death shall be no more."

7. My roommate torments me by repeating trite sayings like "better safe than sorry."

8. "This song, which was composed by Bailey in 1928 [1930], reflects the influence of his five years in New Orleans."

9. "The most popular recording of the song featured Bix Dandy on the trumpit [trumpet]."

10. "Each of these passages has faults of its own, but . . . two qualities are common to all of them."

11. "Now it is clear that the decline of a language must ultimately have political and economic causes. . . . But an effect can become a cause, reinforcing the original cause and producing the same effect in an intensified form, and so on indefinitely."

33. THE DASH, PARENTHESES, THE SLASH

Exercise, Sample Answers

1. Somalia—officially the Somali Democratic Republic—is a country of over nine million (9,000,000) people located on the east coast of Africa just south of the Arabian Peninsula.

2. The country is made up of dry but varying terrain, with coastal low-lands rising to an inland plateau that is generally about 3,000 feet/910 meters high and reaches to the highlands in the north and west.

3. Herding of animals—they include camel, sheep, goats, and cattle—is the chief occupation.

4. Somalia chiefly exports live animals, hides, skins, and clarified butter (it is known as ghee).

5. Somali—they constitute more than 80 percent of the population—are Sunni Muslims, and Islam is the state religion.

6. In the nineteenth century, the region now known as Somalia was colonized by Italy and Britain, which conquered Italian Somaliland in World War II; renamed Somalia, the former colony gained full independence in 1960 (it had already gained internal autonomy in 1956).

7. In 1969, an army coup engineered by Major General Muhammad Siyad Barre led to a socialist government that was supported by the Soviet Union until 1977, when the Soviet advisors—six thousand in all—were expelled.

8. In the late 1970s, the Somali army invaded the Ogaden region of Ethiopia (it borders Somalia on the west) but was driven back by Ethiopian forces.

34. SPELLING, HYPHEN, APOSTROPHE

Exercise 1, Answers

line 1: successful

line 2: skillful; herd

line 3: consisting

line 5: their; operation

line 6: systems

line 8: altogether; scene

line 10: morning

line 11: arrive; getting

lines 11–12: hay; preparing

line 13: literally

line 14: possible; asks

Answers to the Exercises

line 15: moving

line 15: Usually

line 17: someone

line 18: unbelievable; endurance

line 19: Fortunately

line 20: benefit

Exercise 2, Answers

1. The long-distance runners looked buoyant as they passed the fifteen-mile mark.

2. Organized by a well-known sponsor, the race had attracted a number of world-renowned athletes to compete before an all-European audience.

3. Correct.

4. Many had come from medium-sized towns with populations ranging from twenty-one thousand to over fifty-five thousand.

5. The front-runners moved so fast that even spectators on ten-speed bicycles had trouble keeping up with them.

6. After the race the winner told reporters of his long-term plans for acquiring more trophies.

Exercise 3, Answer

Everyone's talking about Frank Smith's novel. Its plot seems to be based on something that happened to him during his freshman year. It's weird to read about characters you've seen in class or in the student's lounge. I don't think there are many of his classmates who won't be annoyed when they discover they've been depicted as thugs and morons. It's as if Frank thought that his experiences were the same as everyone's—Juanita's, Murray's, and Mike's. That kind of thinking can be overlooked in someone who's in his early teens, but it isn't all right for someone in his twenties.

35. MECHANICS

Exercise 1, Answers

1. The Grand Canyon extends over 270 miles from east to west, measures 18 miles from rim to rim at its widest point, and reaches a depth of approximately 1 mile.

2. The canyon has been formed over billions of years by a combination of forces, including wind, erosion, and, in particular, the action of the mighty Colorado River.

3. Some of the canyon's most spectacular sights are to be found within Grand Canyon National Park, which lies in northwestern Arizona.

4. To protect the canyon from commercial development, President Theodore Roosevelt declared it a national monument in 1908; then in 1919 the Congress of the United States proclaimed it a national park.

5. Today the park attracts visitors from all of the fifty states as well as from countries far and near, including Japan, South Korea, France, and Canada; the tourists prefer to arrive in July and August.

6. All who view the canyon marvel at the extraordinary rock formations, many of which have impressive names like Thor Temple, Dragon Head, and Cheops Pyramid.

7. According to one report, the canyon received its present name from Major John Wesley Powell, who in 1869 was the first to travel through the canyon by boat. A brave man, he had lost part of an arm in the Civil War.

8. He began the journey in Wyoming with nine companions and four boats; he ended the journey three months later at the Virgin River near Lake Mead with only three boats and six men.

9. Modern tourists have an easier time, hiking along well-marked trails or riding in automobiles to scenic spots like Powell Memorial and Hopi Point.

10. Like the other national parks in the United States, Grand Canyon National Park is maintained by the National Park Service of the U.S. Department of the Interior.

Exercise 2, Answers

1. motorboat; <u>The Calex</u>

2. <u>Paradise;</u> <u>s</u> or a <u>c</u>

3. drink; <u>frappé;</u> <u>frost</u>

4. yoga; karate; pizza; <u>harassment</u>

5. <u>mother;</u> <u>moder;</u> <u>mater</u>

6. first edition; <u>All Quiet on the Western Front</u>

Answers to the Exercises

Exercise 3, Answers

1. <u>Carmen</u>

2. "Politics and Leadership"

3. "My Old Kentucky Home"

4. <u>Washington Post</u>

5. "What Freud Forgot"

6. <u>60 Minutes</u>

7. <u>The Will of Zeus</u>

8. <u>John Brown's Body</u>

9. "The Mismatch between School and Children"

10. <u>Natural History</u>

11. Solutions to the Energy Problem

12. The Role of Fate in Shakespeare's <u>Romeo and Juliet</u>

13. Imagery in "The Battle Hymn of the Republic"

14. <u>Barefoot in the Park</u>

15. <u>The Age of Innocence</u>

Exercise 4, Answers

1. Mississippi River; Cascade Mountains

2. First; twenty-five hundred

3. Reverend; 7:15

4. three-quarters; Association

5. $700.72

6. 65 mph

7. St. Louis; Friday, August 9

PART 4   RESEARCH AND WRITING

36. THE RESEARCH PROCESS

EXERCISES 1–10: No sample answers

37. NOTETAKING

Exercises 1–2: No sample answers.

Exercise 3, Answer

The following terms should be in quotation marks: "plain foolishness," "dream symbol," "fighting with useless weapons," "running hard yet getting nowhere," "considered in the context of . . . dream itself."

38. WRITING THE RESEARCH PAPER

No exercises.

39. DOCUMENTING THE RESEARCH PAPER

Exercise, Answers

1. *Parenthetical Citation*
   (121–23)
   In Works Cited
   Showalter, Elaine. *A Literature of Their Own: British Women Novelists from Brontë to Lessing.* Princeton: Princeton UP, 1977.

2. *Parenthetical Citation*
   (vi)
   In Works Cited
   Moser, Thomas C. Preface. *Lord Jim.* By Joseph Conrad. New York: Norton, 1968.

3. *Parenthetical Citation*
   (Thiong'o 86)
   In Works Cited
   Thiong'o, Ngũgĩ wa. *Decolonizing the Mind: The Politics of Language in African Literature.* London: Heinemann, 1986.

4. *Parenthetical Citation*
   (156)
   In Works Cited
   Levine, Stewart. "Emerson and Modern Social Concepts." *Emerson: Prospect and Retrospect.* Ed. Joel Porte. Cambridge, MA: Harvard UP, 1982. 155–78.

5. *Parenthetical Citation*
   (Kennan, "America's Unstable Soviet Policy" 79)
   In Works Cited
   Kennan, George F. "America's Unstable Soviet Policy." *The Atlantic Monthly* Nov. 1982: 71–80.

6. *Parenthetical Citation*
(2: 210–14)
In Works Cited
Hugo, Victor. *Les Miserables* Trans. Norman Denny. 2 vols. 1976. Harmondsworth, Eng.: Penguin, 1980.

7. *Parenthetical Citation*
("Polling Power" 15)
In Works Cited
"Polling Power." Editorial. *Christian Science Monitor* 9 Nov. 1984: 15.

8. *Parenthetical Citation*
(none necessary)
In Works Cited
Eliot, T. S. "The Love Song of J. Alfred Prufrock." *T. S. Eliot Reading Poems and Choruses.* Caedmon, TC 1045, 1955.

40. PREPARING THE FINAL COPY OF THE RESEARCH PAPER

No exercises.

There are no exercises in Parts 5 and 6, "Writing in Academic Contexts" and "Writing in Nonacademic Contexts."

COMMON REVISION SYMBOLS

cap	Problem with capitalization	**10.6**
cs	Comma splice	**15.6, 29.3**
d	Inappropriate diction	**8.4**
dg	Dangling modifier	**14.17**
frag	Sentence fragment	**chapter 19**
fal	Fallacy or unsound argument	**11.5**
mm	Misplaced modifier	**13.7, chapter 14**
pass	Misuse of passive voice	**24.5**
pr agr / n	Error in pronoun-number agreement	**20.6–20.7**
pr ca	Error in pronoun case	**20.9–20.12**
pr ref	Error in pronoun reference	**20.4**
pr shift	Error in pronoun reference shift	**20.8**
run-on	Run-on sentence	**15.7**
sv agr	Error in subject-verb agreement	**chapter 21**
sexist	Sexist language	**8.2**
tf	Incorrect tense form	**chapter 22**
trans bp	Transition needed between paragraphs	**7.5**
t shift	Faulty tense shift within sentence	**23.5**
wdy	Wordiness	**8.13**
¶	New paragraph needed	**7.1**
¶ coh	Paragraph lacks coherence or internal transition	**7.4**
(//)	Faulty parallelism	**16.4**
(" ")	Error with quotation marks	**chapter 32**
⊓⊔	Transpose these two elements	

TEN WAYS TO INVIGORATE YOUR STYLE

1. Combine general and abstract terms with concrete and specific words. **(8.7)**
2. Use words figuratively. **(8.8)**
3. Use modifiers. **(13.7)**
4. Use parallel construction. **(chapter 16)**
5. Use subordination to highlight your main point. **(chapter 17)**
6. Make the voice of your verbs emphasize your meaning. **(chapter 24, 27.3)**
7. Vary the length of your sentences. **(27.1)**
8. Use action verbs instead of *be*. **(27.2)**
9. Ask questions. **(27.4)**
10. Be concise. **(27.5)**